American Popular Music

A Multicultural History

Glenn Appell

Diablo Valley College

David Hemphill

San Francisco State University

SCHIRMER
CENGAGE Learning

Australia • Brazil • Japan • Korea • Mexico • Singapore • Spain • United Kingdom • United States

SCHIRMER
CENGAGE Learning

American Popular Music:
A Multicultural History
Glenn Appell and David Hemphill

Publisher: Clark Baxter

Associate Development Editor: Julie
Yardley

Editorial Assistant: Emily Perkins

Executive Technology Project Manager:
Matt Dorsey

Executive Marketing Manager:
Diane Wenckebach

Marketing Assistant: Marla Nasser

Marketing Communications Manager:
Patrick Rooney

Project Manager, Editorial Production:
Trudy Brown

Creative Director: Rob Hugel

Executive Art Director: Maria Epes

Print Buyer: Karen Hunt

Permissions Editor: Sarah Harkrader

Production Service:
Strawberry Field Publishing

Text Designer: Lisa Devenish

Photo Researcher: Sue Howard
and Glenn Appell

Copy Editor: Molly Roth

Cover Designer: Chris Cassler,
Lisa Devenish

Cover Image: Photo © Chris Strachwitz,
www. arhoolie.com

Compositor: Newgen

For product information and technology assistance, contact us at
Cengage Learning Customer & Sales Support, 1-800-354-9706

For permission to use material from this text or product,
submit all requests online **www.cengage.com/permissions**
Further permissions questions can be emailed to
permissionrequest@cengage.com

Library of Congress Control Number: 2005927069

ISBN-13: 978-0-15-506229-0

ISBN-10: 0-15-506229-8

Schirmer
20 Davis Drive
Belmont, CA 94002-3098
USA

Cengage Learning is a leading provider of customized learning solutions
with office locations around the globe, including Singapore, the United
Kingdom, Australia, Mexico, Brazil, and Japan. Locate your local office at
www.cengage.com/global

Cengage Learning products are represented in Canada by
Nelson Education, Ltd.

To learn more about Schirmer, visit **www.cengage.com/schirmer**

Purchase any of our products at your local college store or at our
preferred online store **www.cengagebrain.com**

This book is dedicated to the generations of musicians, many unrecognized, who have drawn upon their rich cultural heritages to create the vital, evolving textures of American popular music.

Printed in the United States of America
5 6 7 8 9   21 20 19 18 17

Brief Contents

Contents

Box List

CD Listening Exercise Boxes

American Popular Music: A Multicultural History is an undergraduate college text for general education courses in American popular music appreciation, in humanities, or in cultural studies. The text emphasizes an interdisciplinary approach that incorporates contemporary multicultural perspectives and critical social analysis into the appreciation of American popular music.

The seventeen-chapter book presents a history of American popular music in a way that differs from many other texts of its kind. Although we discuss what some might call the dominant twentieth-century story line of American popular music—the blues, R & B, jazz, and rock—we simultaneously give voice to a broader array of artists and styles than survey texts often do. The book investigates a 200-year history that is organized thematically into the following sections, each containing multiple chapters: (1) African American Roots, (2) European American Traditions and Influences, (3) Latin Musics in America, (4) Native American and Asian Influences, and (5) From Modern Jazz to Hip-Hop. Each chapter of the book proceeds chronologically. Along the way, the book covers such diverse genres as church music, opera, wind bands, parlor songs, minstrelsy, ragtime, blues, jazz, country, Tin Pan Alley, R & B, Broadway, mambo, bluegrass, rock, salsa, gospel, soul, funk, merengue, hip-hop, reggae, *banda, narcocorridos,* metal, electronica, turntablism, and alternative rock.

In recent years, the study of popular culture has gained prominence, with popular music providing a particularly powerful and visible dimension of popular culture. American popular music today has become one of the world's most pervasive forms of cultural expression. Music can also serve as one of the clearest identifying points of any culture. Consequently, in this text we offer the opportunity for students of diverse cultural backgrounds to reflect on their own musical and cultural heritages in a historical context. We also examine the "borderlands" between cultures, which are some of the most fertile grounds for the creation of new art and music. In doing so, we explore the process of cultural *hybridity*—the blending of diverse cultural features to create new forms of expression. The diversity of American popular music grows every day, and it is our hope that this text will enable the reader to gain a deeper understanding of the cultural and musical richness and significance of American popular music.

FEATURES

Two-CD Set of Listening Exercises

The two-CD set that accompanies the text includes important licensable musical selections corresponding to brief listening exercises located throughout the text. The songs included on the CDs represent a broad range of genres and cultural styles important to the development of American popular music. Some of the selections have been excerpted to allow for the inclusion of a greater number of selections.

Internet Listening Samples

Throughout the text, students will also find numerous recommended selections listed as Internet Listening Exercises. Because most commercial music websites now allow browsers to listen to 30-second and one-minute samples of songs, this creates the opportunity for students to access brief excerpts of virtually every style and artist covered in the text. Among the many sites with available samples are the following: iTunes.com, amazon.com, towerrecords.com, allmusic.com, music.msn.com, and sonymusic.com. We also encourage students to purchase music legally through these websites or other legal sources when they come across selections they wish to own.

Multicultural Notes

To amplify the interdisciplinary nature of popular music history, we have provided throughout the text a series of brief essays, observations, and questions that tie multicultural issues to the historical narrative.

Music Industry Notes

This series of text boxes highlights musical inventions and significant music industry issues that have played prominent roles in the evolution of popular styles.

Timelines

Chapters begin with chronological timelines that match chapter time frames and call out significant musical events within a larger historical context.

Study and Discussion Questions

Each chapter concludes with a series of study questions that can be used for classroom discussions or individual review.

Key Terms and Glossary

Each chapter also ends with a comprehensive list of key terms introduced in the chapter. All key terms are defined in an extensive glossary.

Primary Research Interviews

Although survey texts draw primarily on secondary research, we have also conducted a significant number of original interviews with prominent artists and music industry professionals.

Website

Students can access a website that contains many features to enhance learning:

- Complete bibliography
- Recommendations for further listening and viewing, including a chapter-by-chapter discography
- In-depth artist profiles
- Recommendations for follow-up activities

ACKNOWLEDGMENTS

We would like to express our gratitude to a great many individuals who supported the development of *American Popular Music: A Multicultural History*. We thank editor John Swanson, whose initial excitement about the project led to a contract first with Harcourt College Publishing and later with Schirmer, Cengage Learning. We also extend special appreciation to acquisitions editor Clark Baxter, who believed in the concept of a project he had inherited through a corporate merger, and to developmental editor Julie Yardley, who shepherded the text through to completion. We thank project manager Trudy Brown and art director Maria Epes for their wonderful design work, Chris Cassler for his arresting cover design, Melanie Field at Strawberry Field Publishing for production assistance, and Sue Howard for photo research. We also recognize the outstanding work of copy editor Molly Roth, who made our sometimes convoluted language accessible. In addition, we recognize Tom Laskey at Sony, who secured the necessary permissions to make our CD set an excellent companion to the text.

Numerous primary source interviews flavor the narrative of *American Popular Music: A Multicultural History*. We sincerely thank the many professional musicians who took the time to share their experiences with us, including DJ Amber, Danny Caron, Pete Escovedo, Chris Gonzales Clarke, Jon Jang, Robbie Kwock, Melecio Magdaluyo, Rebeca Mauleón, R. Carlos Nakai, Jacob Perea, John-Carlos Perea, Travis Rimando (DJ Pone), Russell Rodriguez, John Sampson, John Santos, David Stephens, the members of Ulali, Wayne Wallace, John Worley, and George Yoshida.

We also thank friends in the music industry and journalism who freely offered their insights, including Arhoolie Records founder and roots music expert Chris Strachwitz, *San Francisco Chronicle* Senior Pop Music Critic Joel Selvin, blues/R & B historian Lee Hildebrand, Indian radio expert Peggy Berryhill, and

Native American radio DJ/producer Gregg McVickar. Special thanks also to the musicians who played on the listening examples on the CD set: vocalist Clairdee, pianist Rebeca Mauleón, bassist Ron Belcher, drummer Paul Van Wageningen, and Coventry Studios producer/pianist Jon Herbst.

Thanks to our colleagues around the country who carefully reviewed our work offering numerous suggestions and commentary that helped improve the book in many ways, including T. Dennis Brown, University of Massachusetts, Amherst; Guy Cantwell, Cabrillo College; Annmarie George, Gannon University; Robert L. Glarner, Central Connecticut State University; Deborah Holland, California State University, Los Angeles; Mark Hosler, Clemson University; Forrest McGinley, Tri-County Community College; Robert Young McMahan, The College of New Jersey; Richard Montalto, Mississippi University for Women; Barry Salwen, University of North Carolina at Wilmington; Ellen Grolman Schlegel, Frostburg State University; Roberta Freund Schwartz, University of Kansas; Suzanne Thierry, Chambersburg Area School District; and Cathryn Wilkinson, Concordia University–River Forest.

Many personal friends and family members also helped move the project forward in numerous ways. David thanks his father, Robert F. Hemphill, Sr., for sharing his deep knowledge and love of jazz and swing, and his late mother, Elizabeth Anne Hemphill, for fostering a spirit of critical inquiry. Thanks also go to David's colleagues at San Francisco State University, including Dean Jacob Perea for his flexibility, mentorship, and understanding; Ewa Zachoszcz for her superb administrative support; and the P.O.E.T.S. (Providers of Educational Technology Services), Seanchan Owen and Kamil Walas, for superb technical assistance. Glenn thanks Dr. Jose Cuellar, who encouraged the project at an early point, as well as Brent Goff, Barbara Speed, Ellen Green Teninty, and Laurie Appell for editorial assistance. A big hug also goes to Glenn's mother, Dr. Clara Appell, for her tireless review of print media, and special gratitude to his late father, Dr. Morris L. Appell, for being an outstanding role model. Glenn also thanks Melina Corona, John Thomson, Rhonda Kinard, and the Michael Ochs Archives for photo research assistance; ethnomusicologist Bruce Cook for suggestions and insights; colleagues at Diablo Valley College for their support and understanding; and Mingus Murray for being in the right place at the right time for the book cover photo.

Most of all, we thank our loving families—Jennifer, Lydia, and Elizabeth Hemphill and Kate Squire and Amelia Appell—for supporting a seemingly unending project and encouraging us every step of the way.

Glenn Appell is a professional musician and educator who has been teaching at the college level for twenty years. He is currently the director of Jazz Studies at Diablo Valley College, teaching jazz and rock history, improvisation, jazz ensembles, and Latin jazz. He formerly directed the jazz program at Contra Costa College, and he taught at Solano College and Ohlone College. Glenn received his B.S. in Music Performance and Education from the City University of New York (CUNY) in 1980 and his interdisciplinary M.A. in Multicultural Music Education from San Francisco State University in 1998, where David Hemphill was his graduate advisor. Glenn has published on jazz education and music advocacy in urban schools.

Glenn has also maintained an active freelance career for over twenty-five years performing on trumpet, flugelhorn, harmonica, and Native American flute. He has toured and recorded with a variety of artists and performing groups including the San Francisco Mime Troupe, the Johnny Nocturne Band, Pete and Sheila Escovedo, Barbara Morrison, Clairdee, O. J. Ekemode, Charles Brown, Ruth Brown, John Santos, Junior Mance, David Bromberg, and Dr. Loco's Rockin' Jalapeño Band, as well as with songwriter Alex Call. In addition, Glenn has done extensive recording for documentary and feature films. He currently leads the Tutti Forza! Trumpet Quartet and the Just Say Jazz Sextet, whose primary focus is jazz education. This professional group has performed in over 150 schools, museums, and community centers in Northern California over the last fourteen years. Glenn also currently performs with the acclaimed ten-piece brass ensemble Brazzissimo.

David Hemphill is a university professor, multicultural researcher, university administrator, and musician. He is currently Associate Dean for Graduate Studies, Research, and Development in the College of Education at San Francisco State University, where he has been on the faculty for over twenty years. He also co-directs the Joint Doctoral Program on Leadership for Educational Equity with the University of California–Berkeley and two other California State University campuses, and he teaches graduate courses on critical and postmodern pedagogies; culture, cognition, and power issues in education; and education and globalization. Prior to coming to the university, David worked for ten years as a classroom teacher and program director in immigrant education programs in Oakland and San Francisco. He is the author of two language-teaching textbook series, an award-winning study of literacy and technology, and numerous articles and monographs. His most recent book, *Life at the Margins: Language, Literacy, and Technology in Everyday Life* (Columbia Teachers College Press), examines issues of language, literacy, culture, and technology. His textbook series include *English That Works* (Scott, Foresman) and *The Working Culture* (Prentice-Hall). He consults widely on issues of culture, language, and diversity in education.

David is also a trombonist and arranger. Since the 1970s, he has played professionally in funk, Latin, New Orleans jazz, swing, and R & B groups in the San Francisco Bay Area. He has shared the stage with R & B artists Jackie Wilson, Little Frankie Lee, and Jesse "Mister Soul" James; jazz artists Freddie Hubbard, George Duke, Gap Mangione, Barbara Morrison, Bill Bell, Clairdee, and Brenda Boykin; and Latin artists Sapo, Pete Escovedo, Karl Perazza, Ray Obiedo, and John Santos. He currently leads the horn section for East Bay Mudd, an eleven-piece R & B revival band.

For comments, questions, and suggestions, the authors can be reached at appell_hemphill@sbcglobal.net.

Chapter 1

A Multicultural Approach to Popular Music Appreciation

Over the past fifty years, American popular music has become a dominant force throughout the world. No corner of the globe has been left untouched by the scream of an electric guitar or the crunch of a funky backbeat. Popular music is also a primary embodiment of popular culture, a field that continues to grow in importance across multiple disciplines. This book broadens the traditional investigation of American popular music by including musics and cultures not previously addressed, and it uses resources from different academic fields—an interdisciplinary approach—to examine the broad implications of popular music and culture.

As we begin the study of American popular music history, we must also examine how we listen to music, and we must develop a common musical vocabulary. Over hundreds of years, Western musicians and musicologists have evolved a language to analyze and describe music. American popular musicians in turn have added to these concepts, generating their own unique contributions to a language of music.

IN THIS CHAPTER

- Culture and Music
- Music in a Multicultural Society
- Hearing versus Listening
- Exploring Musical Tastes
- Developing a Popular Music Vocabulary
- The Rhythm Section

CULTURE AND MUSIC

Culture is a powerful process that is integral to what makes us human. According to researcher Sonia Nieto,

> Culture can be understood as the ever-changing values, traditions, social and political relationships, and world view shared by a group of people bound together by a combination of factors that can include a common history, language, social class and/or religion.[1]

Culture includes tangible elements such as music, food, clothing, holidays, and forms of artistic expression, as well as more subtle factors such as attitudes, communication styles, and thinking patterns.

CD LISTENING EXERCISE

Listen to each of the following songs, which transmit differing cultural messages.

- Hank Williams: "Your Cheatin' Heart" (sadness and loss) **CD 1/23**
- Cypress Hill: "Insane in the Brain" (resistance and affirmation of identity) **CD 2/21**
- Louis Jordan: "Saturday Night Fish Fry" (humor and community) **CD 2/9**

© CORBIS

Members of the early gangsta rap group NWA in 1990 (left to right, DJ Yella, MC Ren, Eazy-E, and Dr. Dre) standing in front of an abandoned convenience store.

Culture is above all a system of meanings, which humans use to make sense of their lives, and it is constructed through symbol systems that are shared and transmitted over generations. One such system is language; another is music. American popular music is an especially powerful transmitter of cultural messages.

Culture constantly evolves in a fluid process. Further, there are no "pure" cultures; all cultures are blends, or hybrids. Music is a fascinating medium for understanding cultural **hybridity** and change, and jazz, rock, blues, salsa, reggae, hip hop, and country are all hybrids.

American popular music also often acts as a political medium, and it can influence our ideas or behaviors about right, wrong, who is powerful, and what is desirable. Music and other mass media often shape gender roles and cultural identities; alternatively, popular music and culture also serve to question the way things are. Throughout its history, popular music has functioned sometimes as a voice for change, sometimes as the voice of the status quo.

CD LISTENING EXERCISE

Listen to each of the following songs as examples of different kinds of hybrids.

- Jimmie Rodgers: "Waiting for a Train" (a song by the "father" of country, blending the blues and southern mountain music) **CD 1/21**
- Bill Haley: "Rock around the Clock" (early 1950s rock, blending R & B and western swing) **CD 2/10**
- Ritchie Valens: *"La Bamba"* (a Chicano rocker blending 1950s rock and Mexican folkloric music) **CD 1/32**

MUSIC IN A MULTICULTURAL SOCIETY

In a multicultural society like the United States, different cultural groups have access to different levels of power. A **dominant culture,** or one that is more powerful than other groups, stands at the center of society. Cultures that are less dominant are called **subordinate cultures** because they lack access to power and resources. The history of American popular music can help us see how subordinate cultures (African Americans, poor rural white southerners, or Mexican Americans, for example) have used music to create cultural strength, unity, and self-expression under conditions of domination. Although U.S. society has seen major social changes through the early twenty-first century, the dominant center of our culture still reflects white, upper-middle-class, heterosexual male perspectives sometimes called **Eurocentrism.**

CD LISTENING EXERCISE

Listen to "Blowin' in the Wind," recorded by Bob Dylan in the 1960s (CD 2/18). The song is a political commentary on war and civil rights. Next listen to *"Plástico"* by Willie Colón and Rubén Blades (CD 1/28). The song is a commentary on the shallowness of materialism and consumption.

For many years the terms *culture* and *cultured* implied the appreciation of fine arts as defined Eurocentrically. People were cultured if they attended museums, the ballet, or the symphony; they were considered "culturally deprived" if they did not. In recent years, scholars in the arts, humanities, and social sciences have developed new perspectives in order to move beyond Eurocentric conceptions of culture. They have also begun to see that **popular culture**—the mass cultural forms of everyday life—are as important as the high culture of symphonies and art museums.

Questioning the presumed superiority of Eurocentric cultural forms is not easy, but in doing so scholars and artists have reexamined the Western **canon**—the body of cultural knowledge that is said to be important for an educated or cultured person to know. This questioning has engendered many changes. New York City's Lincoln Center, for example, one of the world's leading centers of fine arts, granted its jazz program full status in 1996. Jazz at Lincoln Center, directed by trumpeter Wynton Marsalis, now has the same status as the New York Philharmonic Orchestra and the Metropolitan Opera. This was a significant step toward reshaping the boundaries of art and culture in the United States.

Many of us have multiple cultural identities, viewing ourselves as part of more than one cultural group, and we often use music to express those identities. In some aspects of our lives (at work, for example), we might be part of the culture of the dominant center, but in other parts of our lives we might be more outside the mainstream. Such circumstances make it particularly important to avoid stereotyping (overgeneralizing), which can have extremely destructive consequences. People can be stereotyped ("All white people from the rural South like country music"), and so can music ("All hip-hop is made by gangsters who disrespect women").

The challenge is to understand and respect our cultural diversity while avoiding narrow cultural definitions that create stereotypes, and it is a fine line to walk. For example, it would be absurd on the one hand to say that *Tejano*

CD LISTENING EXERCISE

Listen to the following examples of songs by artists reflecting on life in cultural borderlands.

- Lydia Mendoza: *"Mal Hombre"* (a Mexican American *canción*-style song about love and betrayal in the borderlands) **CD 1/30**

- T-Bone Walker: "Stormy Monday Blues" (an electric blues reflecting on a dead-end job and waiting for the weekend) **CD 1/10**

- Carter Family: "Keep on the Sunny Side" (early classic country mountain music about getting through rural poverty and the Depression with the virtues of faith and family) **CD 1/20**

Courtesy of Hispanic Communications

Publicity poster featuring one of the most popular Mexicano groups in the United States, Los Tigres Del Norte, as well as popular banda/hip-hop group AKWID.

conjunto music is not a fundamental part of Chicano music and culture on the grounds that not all Chicanos identify with it, or on the other hand to say that *conjunto* music is a stereotype. It is a vital Chicano musical form that some—not all—Chicanos prefer. Similarly, while few people question that jazz originated primarily from African American culture, not all African Americans like or listen to jazz. Each cultural group includes numerous subcultures and unique individuals with different beliefs, values, styles, and musical tastes.

The cultures in our society are distinct, yet interconnected and interactive, and their boundaries and contents are flexible and fluid. Many people also find themselves in the cultural or transitional spaces between cultures where people do not belong fully to one culture or another, or may identify with multiple cultures. New immigrants, for example, often exist between cultures. **Borderlands** often generate cultural innovation. For example, many musicians affected by living in cultural borderlands have dramatically affected the history of American popular music. The history of American popular music provides numerous examples of artistic creativity in the face of cultural displacement and adversity, and the use of music to cope with poverty or discrimination has motivated the development of the blues, jazz, country, *corridos* (Mexican ballads that provide historical narrative), folk music, and other styles.

The borderland experience has also fostered "crossing over" from one musical category to another, which in turn has ensured the commercial success of some songs. Musical **crossover** takes place when a song or musician associated with one style takes on the characteristics of another style and achieves popularity in two or more genres. Latin jazz percussionist and band leader Pete Escovedo reflected on the challenges and contradictions of crossing over to get radio airplay:

I had an eight or nine year layoff where I did not record, so I had to get on the radio again and in the record stores. It was a way to get on the smooth jazz stations, and you have to get on those if you want to sell records. That's why I went with the cover songs [versions of other artists' popular songs]. I had to pick and choose what I wanted to play and I didn't want to lose my fan base. But this new one I'm going to put together, I'm going straight-ahead Latin jazz.[2]

HEARING VERSUS LISTENING

The pervasiveness of music in everyday life sometimes causes us to take it for granted. Just a little over 100 years ago, music had to be heard live, because there was no sound recording. Today, people can hear recorded music virtually any time and anywhere in the world. Some of you probably have some music on as you read this book.

What is the difference between hearing and listening to music? *Hearing* music means that we are simply aware of its presence in our environment. When we enter a restaurant or store, recorded music is so pervasive that we often notice it only subliminally. On the other hand, most of us have also felt a familiar melody "jump out" at us from the soft haze of Muzak. Further reflection may reveal that this version lacks the vocals, drums, guitar, or other vibrant ingredients of the original. For a few moments our level of involvement has changed from hearing to listening.

Listening requires a greater level of attention than hearing does. To appreciate the range of musical styles presented in this book—to expand your awareness and understanding—you will need to develop the capacity to listen carefully. One often hears comments like "I hate country music!" or "I can't stand rap!" Everyone has certain preconceptions, but when we explore unfamiliar music, we must make a special effort to listen with an open mind. Although we are accustomed nowadays to channel surfing or jumping music tracks, we need to work against the tendency to turn off the unfamiliar. Listening with an open mind can lead us to appreciate unfamiliar styles.

CD LISTENING EXERCISE

Listen to the following examples of songs that were crossover hits in different genres.

- John Coltrane: "My Favorite Things" (a hit Broadway show tune, covered by a jazz innovator to produce his only pop crossover hit) **CD 2/7**
- Bob Wills: "New San Antonio Rose" (a western swing hit of the 1930s that crossed over to the pop mainstream after being covered by crooner Bing Crosby) **CD 1/22**
- Sugar Hill Gang: "Rapper's Delight" (the first rap hit record for a major label, which crossed over to R & B and the mainstream market in 1979 to initiate the rise of hip-hop) **CD 2/20**

Original caption: "Cowboy band leader Bob Wills and his vocalist and guitarist, Tommy Duncan, do a little impromptu cowboy jiving at Bob's home in Hollywood, August 12, 1944."

© Bettmann/CORBIS

EXPLORING MUSICAL TASTES

No one knows the true origins of music, but it has existed since the dawn of humanity and is deeply woven into the fabric of daily life in many cultures. Why do you listen to music—to relax, to worship, to party, to relive a memory, to dance, to express your identity, or just to feel good? Several factors affect our musical tastes. Our families' preferences affect us, and even though we may not embrace the music of our parents, we often have musical memories from childhood. Our cultures also affect our musical tastes, with music often serving as a fundamental source of identity and connection. Throughout history, music has played a central role in religion, so many people develop an affinity for music through spiritual practices. Where we live influences our musical preferences as well; despite globalization, significant musical differences remain among nations, cultures, and regions. Music often plays an important role in peer group interaction and identity—the music that our friends like can impact our tastes: Admitting that we listen to music that our friends do not like can be difficult. Finally, our education also plays a part in developing our musical tastes, affecting our exposure to different musical styles.

To understand more about how you listen, think about your listening habits. How often do you listen to music for "music's sake," not simply as background for some other activity? Where do you listen to music—at home, at work, in the car, at parties, in the shower, at live concerts or nightclubs, in church, or somewhere else? The difference between experiencing a live performance and listening to recorded music cannot be overstated. Advancements in sound reproduction, notably the introduction of digital technologies in the 1980s, vastly improved the fidelity of recorded music, but hearing live music is still worth the effort. Recorded music cannot yet duplicate the visceral experience of being in the same time and space with the musicians who are creating music.

CD LISTENING EXERCISE

Listen to James Brown's funk tune "Mother Popcorn" (1969). The tune focuses primarily on the beat (CD 2/15). Brown was one of the inventors of **funk,** a highly syncopated style of pop music, and he was sampled extensively by hip-hop artists to create new grooves. Next, listen to the driving polka rhythm of *"Muchachos Alegres"* (1946) by Narciso Martinez (CD 1/31), the "father" of *conjunto* music, an accordion-based hybrid style that emerged in Texas and northern Mexico in the 1930s. The *polka* is a European rhythm that became central to border music at the turn of the twentieth century. Finally, listen to "It's Mighty Dark to Travel" (1947) by bluegrass founder Bill Monroe (CD 1/24). The song was one of the first definitive recordings of bluegrass music. Compare the different types of rhythmic drive in these three tunes.

DEVELOPING A POPULAR MUSIC VOCABULARY

To discuss popular music, we need a common vocabulary. Here we introduce popular music terms that will be used throughout the book.

Rhythm

Rhythm refers to the arrangement of time in music. The term is derived from the Greek word meaning "to flow." Rhythm comprises four elements: **beat** (the underlying pulse of the rhythm), **tempo** (the speed of the beat), **measure** (a consistent grouping of beats in time), and **meter** (the way beats are grouped, or number of beats per measure). The beat has been a key feature of the rhythm of American popular music over the past 100 years. Whether we call it the groove, the feel, or the energy, it is the element that makes us feel the music and move to it.

Multicultural Note

Eurocentrism and Musical Descriptions

Most musicians trained in Western classical music—and most pop musicians—use Italian words such as *ritard, rubato, crescendo,* and *forte* to describe the details of musical performance. This tradition dates back to the seventeenth century, although other European languages have also been used to describe music since Beethoven's time. The fact that so many musicians still use these terms reflects the European influence on much of our musical language. Does the use of these concepts influence how we think about music and how we interpret non-Western musics?

Tempo describes the speed of the beat in a piece of music. The tempo tells musicians how quickly or slowly to play a piece of music, often dramatically affecting its mood. In popular music, songs generally use strict tempos, or tempos that remain at one speed from beginning to end. This is because popular music is often played for dancing. However, shifting tempos within a composition can be used to create changes in mood. A common use of tempo change is to slow down at the end of a song—to **ritard,** which is a word of Italian origin. Another tempo-related Italian musical term is the word **rubato,** which signals that music is to be played in a relaxed, less strict rhythm.

Meter describes how beats are grouped and emphasized, and beats are divided into units of time called *measures*. Each measure of music in a composition generally contains the same number of beats throughout. While it is possible for a composition to change meter midway through a tune (for example, to go from a waltz to a march), few contemporary popular styles do this. The **waltz** is a style written in groupings of three beats, or three beats per measure. The formal term for this is simple **triple meter,** which is also called "three/four" (3/4) time. Triple-meter waltzes were quite popular at the end of the nineteenth century.

Most popular music of the past fifty years has been written in groups of four beats. The pattern, formally known as simple **quadruple meter,** is more often called "four/four" (4/4) time. Try counting and clapping the following pattern of four beats with an emphasis on the first beat of each group:

1 2 3 4 **1** 2 3 4 **1** 2 3 4

The **backbeat** is one of the most powerful four-beat rhythms of American popular music. Created

CD LISTENING EXERCISE

CD 2/16

Listen to "(You Make Me Feel Like) A Natural Woman" (1967) performed by Aretha Franklin and written by Carole King. Can you hear the underlying three-beat pulse? Try counting and clapping this three-beat pattern, emphasizing the first beat of each three-beat group:

1 2 3 **1** 2 3 **1** 2 3

How common is triple meter in popular music today?

CD LISTENING EXERCISE

Listen to ragtime composer Scott Joplin's "Maple Leaf Rag," written in 1899 (CD 1/11). This classic song, which sold over a million copies as sheet music, is an example of 4/4 time—simple quadruple meter. Next listen to "I'm Your Hoochie Coochie Man" recorded in 1954 by blues legend Muddy Waters, the founder of the electric Chicago blues (CD 1/9). The tune, also written in 4/4 time, uses the backbeat.

CD LISTENING EXERCISE

Listen again to James Brown's "Mother Popcorn" (CD 2/15). The tune's funk groove is layered with syncopation created by the interplay of the rhythm section, and it is further accented by the vocals and the horn section. Next, listen again to the salsa tune *"Plástico"* (1978) by Rubén Blades and Willie Colón (CD 1/28). Latin music introduces a variety of syncopated elements into the basic groove, notably the clave—a syncopated two-measure rhythmic pattern that functions as the unifying rhythm of much Afro-Cuban music.

by emphasizing beats two and four, it is prevalent in almost every American style, from New Orleans jazz to rock. The backbeat is also one of numerous popular music practices with African cultural roots. Listen to the difference as you count and clap from one to four with accents on beats two and four.

1 **2** 3 **4** 1 **2** 3 **4** 1 **2** 3 **4**

Syncopation describes rhythms that place the accent off the expected beat. Before the 1950s, the backbeat itself could have served as one of the easiest examples of a basic syncopation, but as popular music evolved into R & B and rock, the use of the backbeat has become so ubiquitous that we now expect its use. The creation of a rhythmic accent that occurs off the "expected" beat thus depends on the musical traditions the listener knows. A simpler definition of syncopation would be the placement of rhythmic emphasis on the weaker part of a beat. In contemporary music, syncopation is readily found in funk and Afro-Caribbean music, where rhythms are intentionally subdivided and accented in unexpected ways.

Melody

Another central ingredient of popular music is melody; for many people, the melody is the key to remembering a song. **Melody** can be defined as a succession of musical notes or pitches that seem to have a relation to one another and that express a musical thought. A melody can also be thought of as a song or tune. Melodies range from simple children's tunes to complex musical constructions, and every style of music contains endless melodic possibilities. Simple melodies are the first musical elements that most children learn; for many listeners, melody is the element that distinguishes one song from another.

The musical strength of a good melody is key to what makes a song popular, but what makes a melody work? Although no universal answer exists, we can say that culture influences how we interpret melody, and that we respond more positively to a culturally familiar melody than to an unfamiliar one. Moreover, melody does not exist in isolation; an exciting rhythm, for example, can interact powerfully with a simple arrangement of pitches and thereby turn it into a memorable experience.

Another key to constructing a good melody is the way a composer uses melodic **intervals**—the distances in pitch between two notes.

One component that can make a song memorable is what songwriters call the **hook:** a catchy melody, rhythm, or lyric that we cannot forget, even when we try. Hooks are often found in the chorus of a song, although they may appear anywhere, and some songs have two or more hooks.

Lyrics

Words or vocal sounds in musical compositions are called **lyrics.** For some listeners, the lyrics are the most important part of a song. We often derive our emotional connection to a popular song from the words, and lyrics and melody often go hand in hand, becoming intertwined in our memory. Lyrics can also be more than words. Popular songs are full grunts, moans, nonsense words, and sacred sounds. Songs like "Tutti Frutti" by Little Richard use nonsense words as hooks, and the use of improvised nonsense syllables in vocal jazz improvisation is called **scat singing.** In Native American music, one often hears *vocables,* words with no definitive linguistic origin that are often considered sacred.

The art of lyric writing reflects the ability to use language rhythmically and poetically. Some songwriters compose both music and lyrics, but composers and lyricists working as a team have also produced much of our popular music. For example, songwriting teams such as Richard Rodgers and Oscar Hammerstein II, or George and Ira Gershwin, wrote many of Broadway's greatest shows. Similarly, the Motown era of the 1960s owed much to the songwriting team of

CD LISTENING EXERCISE

CD 1/18

The opening phrase of "Maria" (1957) from the cast recording of the Broadway musical *West Side Story* by Leonard Bernstein demonstrates the dramatic power of intervals in songwriting. Focus on the first three notes of the melody sung to the word *Maria.* The first interval is called a *tritone*—an interval of three whole steps. This dissonant interval creates tension that is resolved as the melody climbs one half-step more to create the familiar interval of a perfect fifth. The melodies in several songs from *West Side Story* provide some of the finest examples of melodic construction in American musical theater. Can you name other songs that make dramatic use of intervals to create excitement or tension?

CD LISTENING EXERCISE

Listen to the classic 1960s soul tune "My Girl," performed by the Temptations (CD 2/17). Many people recognize the tune before the first measure is even completed. Almost every section of the piece contains a powerful hook: in the lyrics, in the melody, or in the instrumental phrases. Next, listen to *"La Bamba"* (1958), a bilingual 1950s rock tune by Ritchie Valens (CD 1/32). Where is the hook? Does the use of the Spanish language alter the effect of a melodic hook? Finally, listen to the modal jazz tune "So What" (1959) by Miles Davis (CD 2/6). Identify the hook in this instrumental composition.

CD LISTENING EXERCISE

Listen to "Tutti Frutti" (1954), written and recorded by Little Richard (CD 2/11). Note how the rhythmic nonsense syllables—"a-wop-bop-a-loo-lop a-lop-bam-boo"—work as an attention-getting break used repeatedly throughout the song. Next, listen to Ella Fitzgerald scat singing on the jazz standard "How High the Moon" (1954, CD 1/15). Do the scat syllables make her voice sound like a horn? Jazz singers frequently imitate horn players and vice versa. Finally, listen to the Native American a cappella vocal group Ulali singing the song "Mother" (1994, CD 2/1). This is an example of the use of Native American vocables.

Lamont Dozier and Brian and Eddie Holland. Rock in the late 1960s saw a shift in popular songwriting to singer-songwriters like Bob Dylan, who wrote music and lyrics and also performed their own songs.

Rap and hip-hop have pushed the envelope of popular song styles, often dropping the use of melody altogether and emphasizing the rhythm of the spoken lyric instead. While the popularity of these spoken-word styles has only recently come to commercial music, its roots lie in the tradition of the West African *griot* or tribal storyteller. The early history of rural blues in America also contained many examples of story-songs performed in a half-sung, half-spoken style, and other echoes of the African spoken-word tradition occur in the work of R & B legend Louis Jordan from the 1940s.

CD LISTENING EXERCISE

Listen to *"Folk Story"* performed by a contemporary *griot* named Wolof Gewel (CD 1/3). Next, listen to the recording of "Saturday Night Fish Fry" (1947) by early R & B legend Louis Jordan (CD 2/9). Finally, listen to the gangsta rap hit "Insane in the Brain" (1993) by Cypress Hill (CD 2/21). What are the similarities and differences among the three songs?

The choice of whether to use English or another language can play a decisive role in a song's acceptance. Until recently, few songs in languages other than English had found commercial success. Because English is the language of the dominant culture in the United States, the choice by Latin music artists to perform in Spanish or in English, for example, has major commercial implications. Performing in English can lead to wider recognition and sales, but it can also alienate an artist's Spanish-speaking fan base. The work of the late Chicano superstar Selena was a case in point. Her first language was English, yet she chose to perform exclusively in Spanish. Only after she attained superstardom in the Chicano community did she choose to record in English, shortly before her tragic death. The early twenty-first century saw signs of increasing acceptance of bilingual songs in pop music, as popular Latino artists such as Jennifer Lopez, Marc Antony, Christina Aguilera, and Shakira recorded bilingual hits. The first annual Latin Grammy awards ceremony in 2000 also marked a significant step forward in the commercial viability of Spanish-language musics.

CD LISTENING EXERCISE

Listen to *"La Bamba"* (1958) by Ritchie Valens (CD 1/32). Based on a Mexican folk song, this was the first rock hit in Spanish. Next, listen to Carlos Santana's *"Oye Como Va"* (1970), which was a hit even though many listeners had no idea what the Spanish lyrics meant (CD 1/33). Finally, listen to legendary Mexican American vocalist Lydia Mendoza's *"Mal Hombre"* (1934, CD 1/30). The tune was a huge hit with Latinos in the Southwest, yet most non-Spanish speakers never heard of the song.

Harmony

Another important musical concept is **harmony.** This term has three meanings in music: (1) two or more musical notes produced or sounded at the same time, (2) the underlying chord structure of a song or piece of music, or (3) the study of the overall musical structure within a composition, genre, or style. For many of us, the first definition—two notes produced simultaneously—is the most familiar. Almost everyone can appreciate the beautiful sound of two well-matched human voices singing in simple, two-part harmony. Classical musicians use the terms **monophonic** to describe the sound of a single unaccompanied melody, and **homophonic** to describe the same melody performed with simple harmonic accompaniment. A **polyphonic** composition is one that contains a more complex harmonic structure than homophony, and in which different melodies and rhythms interlock. If you have ever sung a round like "Row, Row, Row Your Boat," you have sung polyphonic harmony. This is also known as **counterpoint.**

A second definition of *harmony* is the underlying chord structure of a song. A **chord** is a group of three or more notes sounded simultaneously or melodically. Almost all musics based on Western European music contain elements of harmony in this sense. There are of course exceptions; for example, some folk songs are monophonic—performed by solo voices or instruments with one melody and no harmony.

Although complex harmonic forms have developed in European classical music for over 500 years, American popular song styles have relied on somewhat simpler harmonies. The earliest influences on harmony in American popular music were English parlor songs, church hymns, and folk music from the early nineteenth century. The birth of jazz a century later generated a much larger range of harmonic possibilities. In fact, some contemporary jazz compositions have surpassed the harmonic complexity of European classical music. Not everyone, however, finds these more complex forms appealing; as such, simple harmonic structures still largely dominate popular music in the United States.

> ## CD LISTENING EXERCISE
>
> Listen again to "Mother" by the a cappella group Ulali (CD 2/1). This Cree "round dance" begins in a monophonic style with many voices in unison. After two verses, the performers shift to a contemporary homophonic style by adding three-part harmony. Next, listen again to "Keep on the Sunny Side" (1927) recorded by the Carter Family (CD 1/20). The song employs three-part harmony based on musical practices of the Anglo-American church in the rural South.

Tone and Texture

The **sonority** of a particular piece of music, or its overall tonal texture, greatly affects the music's impact on the listener. Sonority results largely from the tone of the various musical sounds the listener hears. **Tone** has four main components: **pitch** (how high or low a given note sounds, measured as vibrations per second, or frequency), **timbre** (the unique quality of the sound produced by a specific instrument or voice, sometimes called tone color), **duration** (how long a tone lasts), and **dynamics** (changes of volume within a piece). These components combine in complex ways to produce a variety of responses in listeners. New technologies continue to stretch the range of tonal possibilities through the production of electronic sounds that stretch our ideas of what is aesthetically acceptable. Cultural background also partly determines which tones and related timbres will appeal to the listener.

Texture is the overall timbre created by a variety of instruments or voices producing musical sounds in a performance. Texture is a direct result of **instrumentation**—the choice of instruments used in a performance. Musicians,

Multicultural Note

Whose Aesthetics?

Cultural influences strongly affect our sense of musical aesthetics, and the concept of what is appealing changes from one culture to another. For example, traditional African musical aesthetics value the alteration of the timbre of an instrument or voice, while European aesthetics value "purity" of sound. A profound development in American popular music was the broadening of its early European-derived musical aesthetics to encompass African and other aesthetics.

CD LISTENING EXERCISE

CD 1/5 and 6

Listen to the following two examples of the song "Amazing Grace" performed by Clairdee. The first example is performed in a traditional European style; the second, in a jazzy gospel style. Which style do you prefer? The second example contains pitch and timbre alterations with slides between notes and guttural growls that have strong African roots. Some European aesthetic elements are also heard in the second example—much of the singing is performed with a clear, pure tone.

for example, often say that they will "thicken" the texture of a composition by adding more instruments or voices. The resulting sonority and blending of any specific instrumentation can dramatically affect the listening experience.

Improvisation

Improvisation is the spontaneous creation of musical ideas—music that is composed "on the spot." Improvisation is found globally in many styles of music. It is a central component of American popular music, and most American styles of improvisation have African roots. Improvisation can occur in solo performance or in larger musical ensembles. When in an ensemble, it often takes the form of an improvised solo or melody spontaneously composed by a single musician based on the harmony implied by the chord structure of the song being played. Improvisation does not occur in a vacuum—it has to make sense in terms of the surrounding chord structure and musical style of the song being played. A complex blend of thought and emotion, improvisation serves as an important means of individual self-expression. It is the defining element of jazz but also occurs in many other styles, from rock and soul to gospel and country.

Form

Form refers to the organizational structure of a musical composition. The forms of American popular music are not complex, and songwriters have generally relied on a few basic song forms. American popular song forms are in fact fairly simple, compared with many European classical forms. American popular songs often employ a form called *verse/chorus,* with melodic sections that re-

CD LISTENING EXERCISE

Listen to the following examples by artists in differing styles displaying a range of musical textures:

- Robert Johnson: "Cross Road Blues" (a solo blues voice accompanied by acoustic slide guitar) **CD 1/8**
- Duke Ellington: "Harlem Airshaft" (a jazz ensemble playing a swing piece written to depict the sounds of life in an urban apartment building) **CD 1/13**
- *West Side Story* cast: "Maria" (a piece in the classical American musical theater tradition) **CD 1/18**
- DJ Q-Bert: "Razor Blade Alcohol Slide" (an example of turntablism and scratching, put together by a DJ to produce a variety of musical textures) **CD 2/3**

CD LISTENING EXERCISE

Listen to the following examples of improvisation drawn from a variety of styles.

- Louis Armstrong: "Potato Head Blues" (an early jazz classic from the 1920s that includes collective and individual improvisation) **CD 1/12**
- John Coltrane: "My Favorite Things" (a Rodgers and Hammerstein Broadway song from *The Sound of Music*, reworked in 1960 as a modal jazz tune) **CD 2/7**
- Santana: *"Oye Como Va"* (a Latin classic written by Tito Puente, reworked as a Latin rock tune in the late 1960s, featuring Carlos Santana's improvised electric guitar work) **CD 1/33**

peat throughout the song. A **verse** is usually a lyric statement that tells a story; each verse of a song presents new information to the listener while following a similar melodic structure. A **chorus** is a new lyric and melodic statement, following the verse, that is often repeated periodically throughout the song. This use of repetition often causes the chorus to become the hook of a song. The origins of the verse/chorus form are found in Anglo-Celtic folk music.

One prominent example of the verse/chorus form is the **32-bar form**, which dominated Broadway and Tin Pan Alley for the first half of the twentieth century. The form consists of an eight-measure verse (A) followed by a melodically identical eight-measure verse (A) containing new lyrics. An eight-measure chorus (B) occurs next, followed by a final eight-measure verse (A) that may contain new lyrics or a restatement of an earlier verse. This can also be described as an AABA structure. Note that the B structure here serves as what is called a **bridge** or release—a transitional passage that connects two musical passages of greater importance.

THE 32-BAR SONG FORM

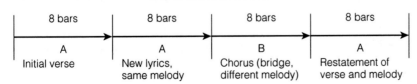

8 bars	8 bars	8 bars	8 bars
A	A	B	A
Initial verse	New lyrics, same melody	Chorus (bridge, different melody)	Restatement of verse and melody

THE 12-BAR BLUES FORM

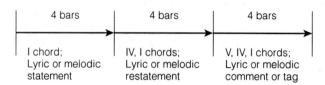

4 bars	4 bars	4 bars
I chord; Lyric or melodic statement	IV, I chords; Lyric or melodic restatement	V, IV, I chords; Lyric or melodic comment or tag

Other song forms are found in popular American music. Much African American–influenced music often relies less on the use of the chorus and more on repeated melodic and rhythmic themes. These repeated, open-ended structures—sometimes called a groove, a riff, or a vamp—are often used in R & B, funk, hip-hop, rock, and jazz to form **groove-based tunes.** The blues is another pervasive form in American popular music. With its strong African roots, the blues appears in almost every style and context. The traditional form of the blues blends the verse/chorus song form with the groove-based approach. The standard **12-bar blues** is written in three phrases of four measures each, and the form can be repeated many times without the use of a chorus.

CD LISTENING EXERCISE

CD 1/14

Listen to Count Basie's 1938 recording of "Jumpin' at the Woodside." The tune's 32-bar form has an AABA structure. The opening melody, based on a **riff** (short musical phrase), is eight measures long and is repeated two times. This is followed by eight measures of improvisation, and finally by a restatement of the opening theme. The rest of the arrangement maintains this 32-bar structure.

CD LISTENING EXERCISE

Listen to the following examples of groove-based tunes and blues songs.

- James Brown: "Mother Popcorn" (a 1968 early funk tune that exemplifies a groove-based approach) **CD 2/15**

- Sly and the Family Stone: "Thank You (Falettinme Be Mice Elf Agin)" (a 1968 funk tune providing another example of the groove-based form) **CD 2/19**

- Bessie Smith: "Empty Bed Blues" (a classic 12-bar blues recorded in 1928, filled with double meanings and accompanied by a raucous trombone) **CD 1/7**

- Chuck Berry: "Roll over Beethoven" (a 1950s rock classic based on a 12-bar blues) **CD 2/12**

THE RHYTHM SECTION

Over the past 75 years, American popular music has come to rely on what is now a standard **rhythm section**—drum set, acoustic or electric bass, guitar, and piano or keyboard—to serve as a rhythmic anchor. There are many possible variations to this instrumentation that reflect changing cultural influences. For example, the use of Latin percussion (timbales, conga drums, bongo, guiro, claves, and cow bell) is common in salsa and Latin jazz, and the accordion is a defining component of *Tejano* and *conjunto* music. Rock musicians commonly use two or more guitars and sometimes no keyboard. The development of the rhythm section had strong African American roots; although the instruments did not originate in Africa, the way they now function reflects African rhythmic aesthetics. The emergence of jazz in the early twentieth century, notably the swing era, played a central role in the rhythm section's development.

The Drum Set

The **trap drum set** (drum set, trap set) was a uniquely American invention that developed into a sophisticated set of interconnected percussion instruments. It originated around the turn of the twentieth century as drummers began to play more than one drum at a time. The drums used in assembling the trap set were originally part of the traditional marching band percussion section: bass drum, tom tom, snare drum, and cymbals. The use of a foot pedal connected to a mallet for the bass drum and the invention of the high hat (cymbal) enabled one drummer to play four instruments at once. The techniques used in trap set playing came initially from European classical percussion technique, and the music generally reflected **motor rhythm,** a constant beat played at a consistent tempo. Over time, African rhythmic influences became increasingly dominant in trap drumming.

The Piano

The piano has played a central role in popular American music since the early nineteenth century, when upright pianos were first widely sold. Long before the development of the rhythm section, the piano provided harmonic and rhythmic support for most popular music. The instrument's rhythmic pos-

MICHAEL OCHS ARCHIVES.COM

Considered by many to be the true "King of Swing," bandleader and drumming legend Chick Webb poses behind an early trap set in the 1930s.

Multicultural Note

Drumming and Cultural Hybridity

Drumming traditions in American popular music are cultural hybrids. Marching band music, initially a European style, developed into jazz in New Orleans in the early twentieth century by taking on African influences. The evolution of trap set playing from marching band percussion furthered the blending, as African musical aesthetics gradually reshaped the use of European instruments and practices.

CD LISTENING EXERCISE

CD 1/1

Listen to "Drum Set Samples" and identify the following parts of the trap set: bass drum, snare drum, tom tom, ride cymbal, crash cymbal, and high hat. Next, listen to the following rhythmic grooves played on the trap set: (1) a New Orleans–flavored "second line" drum beat, evoking the rhythms of a Mardi Gras parade band; (2) a swing rhythm, common to many jazz styles; and (3) a hip-hop rhythm which evolved out of funk.

sibilities emerged in the ragtime music that first developed at the end of the nineteenth century; *ragtime* was a highly rhythmic, percussive solo piano music that fed into the evolution of jazz and popular song. In the early twentieth century, the piano was used as the principal chord-making instrument in the early rhythm section, and piano styles in most popular genres evolved throughout the century. The invention of the electric piano and the keyboard synthesizer in the 1960s and 1970s further transformed the sound of the rhythm section. Ultimately, through electronic sampling technologies, the electronic keyboard developed the capacity to replicate the sound of almost any instrument.

The Guitar

The guitar is now the primary instrumental icon of American popular music, but this was not always the case. At the turn of the twentieth century, the instrument played only a minimal role in the rhythm section, although its prominence in folk musics was already established. With the invention of the electric guitar in the 1930s, stylistic innovations began to take off, and with the birth of rock in the 1950s, the instrument took center stage to transform the sound of

MICHAEL OCHS ARCHIVES.COM

A Capitol records publicity photo from 1952 showing a giant Gibson electric guitar provocatively saddled by electric guitar and sound recording innovator Les Paul and his wife, vocalist Mary Ford.

the rhythm section. Today the guitar is the dominant voice in solo improvisation in popular music, and many styles use both piano and guitar in the rhythm section. Both instruments can work as the lead or melody instrument, and they share the role of keeping time as rhythm instruments by playing coordinated riffs or chords.

The Bass

The bass anchors the rhythm section. Early jazz and traditional concert band music often used the tuba for bass parts because it was louder than the unamplified string bass. An early rudimentary string bass consisted of a piece of catgut or wire connected to a washtub and a long bendable pole. Improvements in amplification technology caused the bass to become much more important during the twentieth century. The acoustic string bass and the electric bass guitar are now the most prevalent bass instruments in American popular music. The role of the bass varies, depending on the style of music, but it often functions to emphasize the bass note or root of each chord, using these notes in a rhythmic way to build a groove. Many listeners feel the bass as much as hear it. The acoustic bass is the preferred instrument for acoustic styles such as straight-ahead jazz or folk music, while the electric bass guitar dominates rock, country, and R & B.

CD LISTENING EXERCISE

CD 1/2

Listen to "Bass Samples." (1) First you will hear an acoustic bass playing a *walking* bass line. Why is it called a walking bass line? This style of bass playing is commonly found in jazz and blues. (2) Next, listen to an electric bass playing a Motown-style bass part. How does this bass line differ from the walking bass in the previous example? (3) Following, listen to the same instrument playing a funky bass line using a popping technique that developed in the seventies. (4) Finally, listen to a synthesized bass part played on a keyboard. Listen for the difference between the "synth" bass and the earlier acoustic or electric bass examples.

Chapter Summary

- Culture can be defined as the changing pattern of human knowledge, belief, and behavior learned and transmitted through generations. A culture is a meaning system. There are no "pure cultures"—all cultures are blends or hybrids. Culture can also act as a political medium.

- Many scholars now question the Eurocentric view that the fine arts of Western cultures set the standards for creative expression. Respect has grown for the importance of popular culture, including forms of popular culture such as popular music.

- When we examine music from a multicultural perspective, we must avoid creating stereotypes. Within each large cultural group are numerous subcultures and individuals with different beliefs, values, styles, and musical tastes.

- The concept of cultural borderlands helps explain the development of American popular music. As we begin to understand the way cultures interact, we can see how hybrid styles and crossovers develop from those interactions.

- We all listen to music for different reasons. There is a difference between hearing and listening, in that listening requires focused attention. By practicing open-minded listening, we open ourselves to a range of new musical experiences.

- Attending a live performance is still the best way to experience music. The physical presence of musicians playing live creates an energy that cannot yet be duplicated via recorded means.

- Music functions in society to embody a broad array of human experiences. Whether one is listening while working, driving, praying, or dancing, music plays a special role in our everyday lives.

- We need a vocabulary for understanding and discussing music, and the language we now use is a hybrid, based on classical European as well as contemporary popular sources. These include rhythm, melody, lyrics, harmony, tone and texture, improvisation, and form (see the Vocabulary Review).

- The rhythm section is an important contribution of American popular music that serves as the instrumental backbone of much popular music throughout the world. It generally consists of a drum set, piano, guitar, and bass.

Vocabulary Review

- **Chord**—a combination of three or more notes sounded or played simultaneously.
- **Form**—the organizational structure of a musical composition.
- **Harmony**—two or more musical notes produced or sounded at the same time, or the underlying chord structure of a song or piece of music.
- **Hook**—a catchy melody, rhythm, or lyric that stays with the listener.
- **Improvisation**—the spontaneous creation of musical ideas; music that is composed on the spot.
- **Instrumentation**—the group of instruments used in a performance.
- **Lyrics**—the words or vocal sounds included in a musical composition.
- **Melody**—a song or tune; a succession of related musical notes or pitches that seem to have a relation to one another and that express a musical thought.
- **Rhythm**—the arrangement of time in music, consisting of beat (the underlying pulse of the rhythm), tempo (speed of the beat), measure (a consistent grouping of beats in time), and meter (the way the beats are grouped, or number of beats per measure).

- **Sonority**—the overall tonal texture of a musical composition or performance.

- **Syncopation**—accenting the weak or unexpected part of the beat.

- **Texture**—the overall timbre created by a variety of instruments or voices producing musical sounds in a performance.

- **Tone**—a quality of music that has four main components: pitch (how high or low a given note sounds), timbre (tone color or the quality of sound associated with a specific instrument or voice), duration (how long a note lasts), and dynamics (changes of volume within a piece).

Key Terms

backbeat

beat

borderland

bridge

canon

chord

chorus

counterpoint

crossover

culture

dominant culture

Eurocentrism

form

funk

groove-based tune

harmony

homophonic

hook

hybridity

improvisation

instrumentation

interval

lyrics

measure

melody

meter

monophonic

motor rhythm

polyphonic

popular culture

quadruple meter
  (4/4)

rhythm

rhythm section

riff

ritard

rubato

scat singing

sonority

subordinate culture

syncopation

tempo

texture

32-bar form

tone

trap drum set

triple meter (3/4)

12-bar blues

verse

waltz

Study and Discussion Questions

1. What is culture?

2. Are there any "pure" cultures? What is hybridity?

3. What is cultural domination? Give some examples from American popular music.

4. Why is it hard to describe particular cultures? What is the danger of stereotypes?

5. Why do we call the idea of "fine arts" a Eurocentric concept? Why are many scholars broadening this perspective to include popular culture?

6. What are cultural borderlands, and what does "crossing over" mean?

7. When, why, where, and how often do you listen to music?

8. How does cultural background influence listening experiences and musical preferences?

9. How have your experiences with live performances differed from your listening to recordings?

10. Why is rhythm an essential ingredient of popular music? What effect does the use of a backbeat produce in a song?

11. What are the musical components of melody?

12. How does a musical hook work? Name at least five songs with strong hooks.

13. What are the range of approaches to lyrics found in American popular music?

14. How do European and African aesthetics regarding musical tone differ?

15. What is improvisation, and what is its function in American popular music?

16. How are the following song forms defined: 32-bar song, 12-bar blues, groove-based tune?

Notes

1. Sonia Nieto, *Affirming Diversity: The Sociopolitical Context of Multicultural Education* (New York: Longman, 1992), 111.

2. Interview with the authors.

1600 - 1900

1600s Complex, communal musical forms thrive and develop in Africa's many cultures throughout the century ♪

1600s African slaves in the Americas draw on African roots and adapt available musical resources from European cultures ♪

1607 First British community in North America, Jamestown, settled

1619 First African slaves brought to America

1682 Philadelphia, largest colonial city, founded

1700s American colonies expand

1700s Instruments such as the banjo develop, demonstrating African retentions in a new hybrid form ♪

1700s Slave "musicianers" provide music for social functions, reflecting African *griot* traditions and setting the stage for itinerant bluesmen ♪

1700s African Americans perform in military bands and other groups, taking on European influences to blend with African retentions ♪

1707 Isaac Watts's first hymnal published, influencing African American religious and secular music ♪

1776 Declaration of Independence and beginning of Revolutionary War

1789 U.S. Constitution ratified

1794 African Methodist Episcopal (AME) church founded, establishing an important center of community activity ♪

1800s African slaves participate in camp meetings; begin to adapt European religious music, producing spirituals ♪

1800s African American work, social, and religious musics develop ♪

1801 AME church publishes *Richard Allen Hymnal,* first African American hymnal ♪

1803 Louisiana Purchase annexes vast western lands from France

1812 War with Britain

1821 Liberia founded in Africa

1821 African Grove Theater founded in New York, the nation's first black theater ♪

1830s Minstrelsy emerges, establishing a pattern that would influence the blues and American popular theater ♪

1831 Nat Turner slave revolt in Virginia

1849 California gold rush

1861–1865 Civil War

1863 Emancipation Proclamation

1865–1877 Reconstruction

1865 After emancipation, new styles develop: gospel, blues, and jazz ♪

1867 *Slave Songs of the United States,* the first collection of African American spirituals, is published ♪

1870–1900 African Americans migrate north

Chapter 2

African Roots

African and African American musics have contributed fundamentally to American popular music, profoundly impacting styles as diverse as the blues, jazz, rock, R & B, Latin, and country music. Given our country's history of slavery and racism, the influence of African musical retentions is particularly significant. Examining these African origins is challenging because they were **vernacular music,** which means they existed as folk or traditional music played in communities as a part of everyday life. As producer and historian Chris Strachwitz notes, "Vernacular traditions are on the one hand neglected or even discarded, while on the other exploited and devoured by the dominant mass culture."[1] Because fewer resources have been dedicated to the study of vernacular music than of European classical music, less concrete historical information on the former exists. Moreover, there was no sound recording before 1900. Finally, flawed presentations of African American culture by eighteenth- and nineteenth-century historians have compounded the problem. Nonetheless, the last five decades have seen dramatic growth in research on our rich African musical heritage.

A HOLISTIC APPROACH TO LIFE

The African approach to life was holistic, with few distinctions between religion and everyday life. Music played a major function in the daily lives of Africans, as historian Eileen Southern explains: "For almost every activity in the life of the individual or the community there was an appropriate music; it was an integral part of life from the hour of birth to beyond the grave."[2] Music embodied life events ranging from the mundane to the spiritual. It was used for ceremonial functions such as the installation of kings, agricultural rites, religious ceremonies, rites of passage, preparations for war, hunting expeditions, and recreation. The integration of African music into everyday life helps explains how it survived and evolved even under the oppressive conditions of slavery.

One European explorer, Thomas Edward Bowdich, described a West African festival in 1817:

> The king, his tributaries, and captains, were resplendent in the distance, surrounded by attendants of every description. . . . More than a hundred bands

© Lindsay Hebberd/CORBIS

African musician Vieux Diop plays the twenty-one-stringed *kora*, one of the traditional instruments of Aftican *griots*.

burst at once on our arrival, [all playing] the peculiar airs of the several chiefs; the horns flourished their defiances [fanfare melodies], with the beating of innumerable drums and metal instruments, and then yielded for a while to the soft breathings of their long flutes, which were truly harmonious; and a pleasing instrument like a bagpipe without a drone, was happily blended.[3]

The music of West Africa from the seventeenth through the nineteenth centuries was a highly evolved art form, according to musicologist and composer Gunther Schuller:

> It is a misconception that African musical forms are "primitive." African music is replete with highly "civilized" concepts. . . . Some observers have confused their very complexity with formlessness. . . . Nothing could be further from the truth.[4]

Held in high regard, West African musicians often served as honored members of a tribal king's household. Every village had master musicians, the most important of whom was the **griot**, serving as storyteller, tribal historian, and entertainer. Although of low social caste, *griots* were of paramount importance, admired as performers and valued as oral historians. The performance style of modern *griots* is a half-sung, half-spoken delivery, often accompanied by the *kora* (21-string lute) or a drum.

Multicultural Note

How Are African Languages and American Slang Related?

Several African terms from the Wolof language may have been the source of some popular-musician slang that found its way into American English. Linguist David Dalby argues that the following English slang terms may have been derived from the West African Wolof language:[5]

Wolof Terms	Related American English Terms
• *dega* (to understand)	• to *dig*
• *jev* (to talk disparagingly)	• *jive*
• *hipi* (to open one's eyes)	• to be *hip* to something
• *bania, banjer,* or *banshaw* (a stringed instrument of Senegal)	• *banjo*

AFRICAN MUSICAL AESTHETICS

The aesthetics of African music profoundly affected American popular music, from the passionate guttural exclamations of James Brown to the shrieking, wailing guitar of Jimi Hendrix. One important feature of African musical aesthetics is what African American composer Olly Wilson called a **heterogeneous** [consisting of many different, contrasting elements] **sound ideal:** "A mosaic created by the interaction between lead voice, chorus, rattle, metallic gong, hand clapping, various wind or string instruments, and drums, which exist in greater or lesser degrees of complexity in all African ensemble music."[6] A good example of this in American music is the collective improvisation of a traditional New Orleans jazz band, where each instrument has its own discrete musical voice, yet the ensemble plays together in a unified way.

Another important attribute of African music is **call and response**—a musical statement by a singer or instrumentalist followed by a response from other vocalists or instruments. Sometimes the response repeats the call; other times, the response completes the musical idea stated in the call. Although call and response is found in the music of many cultures, the African version of the technique flavors the blues, jazz, ragtime, gospel, and R & B.

African vocal performance styles also have several unique characteristics. One involves guttural effects such as screams, moans, and shouts. Another is lyric improvisation, by which vocalists change lyrics to achieve desired effects. Other vocal features include shifts between singing and speaking modes, falsetto singing, and vocal *rhythmization*—using vocal sounds for rhythmic purposes. Vocal rhythmization is used in jazz scat singing, gospel, rock, and soul. African American vocal styles also employ metaphors and figures of speech with hidden meanings. Such "musical codes" enabled African American music to serve as a means of communication during slavery. Finally, influential African

CD LISTENING EXERCISE

Listen to *"Folk Story"* (1986), recorded by *griot* Wolof Gewel (CD 1/3). This is an example of modern *griot* performing in the narrative song style. How do the music and rhythm of the instrument and the voice interact? Next, listen to the alternating phrases of Henry Ratcliff's blues lament entitled "Louisiana," juxtaposed with the work song of a Senegalese field worker (CD 1/4). What similarities do you hear between these two musicians?

 **Internet Listening Exercise**

The following samples demonstrate a range of African-influenced vocal aesthetics.

Salif Keita: *"Madan"*

Youssou N'Dour: *"Yo Le Le (Fulani Groove)"*

Northern Neck Chantey Singers: "Menhaden Chantey"

Ray Charles: "What'd I Say"

Louis Armstrong: "Mack the Knife"

Mahalia Jackson: "Move on up a Little Higher"

Robert Johnson: "Come on in My Kitchen"

Grandmaster Flash: "The Message"

 Multicultural Note

Music as Coded Resistance

African American music served as a means of communication during slavery, when hymns and songs were used to promote escape to the North. Music was also vital to the operations of the Underground Railroad, an organization that helped fugitive slaves escape to freedom. One of the best-known songs of the movement was "Follow the Drinkin' Gourd," which directed fugitives to travel north in the direction of the "drinkin' gourd" (the Big Dipper) in the sky.

vocal features include "bending" notes (microtonal inflections) and using **blue notes** (the flatted third, fifth, and seventh of a major scale).

African rhythmic features such as syncopation, rhythmic improvisation, the groove, and swing have also shaped American popular music. As we have seen, syncopation unexpectedly accents the weak rather than strong pulses in a measure, and rhythmic improvisation allows for spontaneous rhythmic variations. The **groove** is built by playing several highly rhythmic parts simultaneously, creating a momentary feeling of resolution when multiple parts arrive on the same beat. When the complex rhythmic parts of a rap, funk, jazz, hip-hop, or gospel tune "lock in," as James Brown would say, "the groove is here." **Swing** is another African-derived rhythmic feature of American popular music. Here, the term does not refer to the style of music popularized in the 1930s but to the triplet-based rhythmic feel often encountered in jazz, blues, and R & B. The rhythmic pulse of swing creates a lilting feeling of forward momentum; it is easy to feel but difficult to notate (write down).

CD LISTENING EXERCISE

Listen to James Brown's "Mother Popcorn" (CD 2/15). How does Brown's use of syncopation work to create a unified groove? How does this song exemplify the heterogeneous sound ideal? What other African retentions are evident? Next, listen to Count Basie's "Jumpin' at the Woodside" (CD 1/14), Ella Fitzgerald's "How High the Moon" (CD 1/15), and Miles Davis's "So What" (CD 2/6) for examples of swing rhythm. Then listen to "Rapper's Delight" by Sugar Hill Gang to identify other African rhythmic features (CD 2/20).

African melodic features also influenced American popular music through the use of the minor **pentatonic scale** (five-note scale) and the blues scale. While the minor pentatonic scale occurs in music around the globe, African versions of the scale were a primary source for American popular music. In the key of C, the notes of this scale would be C, E♭, F, G, B♭, and C. Much African American folk music prior to the twentieth century featured pentatonic melodies, and gospel, blues, rock, and R & B still do. The **blues scale** is an African American creation closely related to the minor pentatonic scale. It uses six notes, including the flatted third, fifth, and seventh, to reach an octave, and it is called a hexatonic (six-tone) scale. This, too, is used in gospel, blues, jazz, rock, and R & B. In the key of C, the blues scale would be C, E♭, F, G♭, G, B♭, and C.

African music also uses microtones in ambiguous modes. A **microtone** is a note that falls between two notes on the Western chromatic twelve-note scale. You can visualize this by imagining a note that falls between two adjacent keys on the piano. The flatted third of the blues is sometimes described as a microtone that actually falls between the major third and the flatted third of a major scale. **Ambiguous mode** means that one cannot tell if a tune is written in a major or a minor key. In most Western classical music, the distinction between major and minor modes is quite clear, but in African American music this is not always the case.

Summary of African-Influenced Musical Aesthetics

- **Heterogeneous Sound Ideal:** Complex interaction of contrasting musical elements

- **Call and Response:** Statement by singer or instrumentalist followed by response from others
- **Vocal Styles:** Guttural effects, lyric improvisation, vocal rhythmization, blue notes, falsetto, metaphors/codes
- **Rhythmic Features:** Syncopation, rhythmic improvisation, the groove, swing, body rhythm
- **Melodic Features:** Minor pentatonic and blues scale, microtones in ambiguous modes

AFRICAN INSTRUMENTS

Ethnomusicologists, scholars who study music in sociocultural contexts, classify traditional instruments of African music into four principal groups: membranophones (drums), idiophones (other percussion), aerophones (wind instruments), and chordophones (stringed instruments). **Membranophones,** which came in every shape and size, were made from animal skins stretched over hollowed logs and played with fingers, palms, or crooked sticks. The drum is a sacred instrument in many cultures, and it is probably the earliest musical instrument other than the human voice. African drums provided a powerful form of communication, often audible over great distances, and people used them to communicate with the spirit realm and to create trances. Slave owners in much of the South forbade drumming, fearing its political and religious effects.

Idiophones were instruments such as bells, gongs, shakers, rattles, thumb pianos, and xylophones that were made of materials that had their own unique sound, such as wood, ceramics, or metal. **Aerophones** appeared less in African music, though people played horns and trumpets made of elephant tusks and animal horns. Most numerous were small flutes, some of which were connected to progressively longer flutes to form panpipes. African Americans called panpipes "quills," because the instrument was sometimes made of porcupine quills in Africa. The flutelike instruments were made from reeds or other local materials in the rural South.

Chordophones included fiddles, harps, lyres, lutes, and zithers. Lutes and fiddles were made of gourds covered by animal skins cut open for the sound to resonate, with long sticks for the neck and wood or bone for the bridge. Strings were made of horse or cow hair, and instruments had varying numbers of strings. Fiddles were played by plucking the strings or using bows. European travelers in Africa compared the sound of harplike instruments they encountered to the banjo, which was an African American hybrid.

CD LISTENING EXERCISE

Listen to the 1928 recording of Bessie Smith singing "Empty Bed Blues" (CD 1/7). This recording includes most of the African musical aesthetics we have examined, including metaphors, call and response, blues inflections, blues scales, swing, syncopation, and improvisation. Smith also employs the classic form of the 12-bar blues. What role does the trombone play in relationship to the singing? What metaphors and indirect statements with hidden (or not so hidden) meanings do you hear in the song? Next, listen again to jazz vocalist Clairdee's two versions of "Amazing Grace" (CD 1/5 and 6). Contrast the first European-style version with the second gospel-flavored version. The latter version reflects most of the same African musical aesthetics as Bessie Smith's "Empty Bed Blues," with the addition of guttural effect and vocal rhythmization.

Internet Listening Exercise

Go to Rounder Records (http://www.rounder.com) and listen to the following samples of early twentieth-century African American folk music, which reflect African retentions:

Deep River of Song: Mississippi Saints and Sinners: "Emmaline Take Your Time," "Hog Hunt"

AFRICAN AMERICAN MUSIC DURING SLAVERY

Two key factors influenced the retention and development of African musical traditions in the Americas: the cultures of the slave owners and the cultures of the African slaves. Spanish, French, and Portuguese colonists who settled in New Orleans, the Caribbean, and Central or South America were relatively tolerant of African culture, allowing slaves to maintain their musical traditions. In New Orleans, for example, slaves and free Africans were allowed to gather every Sunday in Congo Square to drum and dance, and the practice continued until the late nineteenth century. Slaves in Cuba under Spanish rule were sometimes allowed to buy their own freedom, and music flourished in this environment, retaining many African elements. African musical influences also abounded in Brazil, which had the largest population of people of African descent in the Western Hemisphere.

Slaves in French, Spanish, and Portuguese Catholic colonies also continued to practice African religious traditions by embedding them in the rituals of Roman Catholicism. This process produced the hybrid religions of Santeria and *Abakuá* in Cuba, *Voudou* in Haiti, and *Candomblé* and *Macumba* in Brazil. Adherents of the religions used music and drumming as a central focus of their spiritual practice. In contrast, British and American slave owners in North America often believed it was their duty to convert slaves from their traditional belief systems to Protestant Christianity by eliminating vestiges of African culture. Further, when concern grew in the nineteenth century over slave rebellions, most plantation owners forbade drums, in order to prevent their use for communication or religion. Slaves were instead encouraged to perform church music, work songs, and European popular music to entertain slave owners. Although Christianity was not a choice at first for Africans, many embraced the religion and found solace. In doing so, they also transformed existing worship styles to create spirituals, gospel, and the blues.

The Historic New Orleans Collection, accession no. 1974.25.23.53

Congo Square in New Orleans was one of the few places in the United States where African music and dance traditions were permitted during much of the nineteenth century.

African American Musicians during Slavery

African slaves were resilient and creative within the confines of their captivity, and although families were intentionally broken up and those of similar language background separated, slavery could not eliminate the African integration of music and daily life. Drums may have been forbidden, but syncopated rhythms could still be stomped, tapped, and clapped; anything in the environment that could make a sound was turned into an instrument. The body became a rhythm instrument through clapping, foot tapping, and **patting juba** (body drumming—striking the knees, shoulders, or other body parts with the hands to produce a rhythmic sound). Later incarnated as hambone or hand jive, patting juba served as the source of rock and R & B rhythms generations later.

The two most commonly played slave instruments were the banjo and the fiddle. An African American invention, the banjo was based on African stringed instruments; banjolike instruments made of gourds with necks and various numbers of strings first appeared in the United States in the late seventeenth century. The European violin, similar to several African stringed instruments, was particularly popular among African Americans prior to the Civil War, and slaves who learned to fiddle were often highly respected. In later years, African American musicians contributed to the development of the string band and jug band, now more commonly associated with white musicians of Appalachia.

African slaves who played music professionally were called **musicianers.** They sometimes received special privileges and occasionally could buy their freedom, but for the most part they remained as valuable property used to entertain whites. Slaves also sometimes played in European-style marching bands or fife and drum corps, and such music became a part of southern black folk

Internet Listening Exercise

The following samples reflect music generated by Cuban and Brazilian hybrid religions.

John Santos and Machete: *"Eleguá Agó"*

Clara Nunes: *"A Deusa Dos Orixas"*

Conjunto Céspedes: *"Que Viva Chango"*

© CORBIS

Nineteenth-century drawing of freed slaves playing music for Union troops during the Civil War.

culture. The music also fed into the street parade styles of New Orleans in the late nineteenth century.

Not all African Americans were enslaved, and free blacks were often musically active in the North. New York City, for example, saw the founding of the African Grove Theater, the nation's first black theater, in 1821. It offered tragedies, operas, and musicals. Free African Americans also played in brass bands, dance bands, and orchestras. Historian Eileen Southern cites the example of Frank Johnson, a famous nineteenth-century African American cornetist and bandleader in Philadelphia:

> During his short career he accumulated an amazing number of "firsts" as a black musician: first to win wide acclaim in the nation and England; first to publish sheet music; first to develop a school of black musicians; first to give formal band concerts; first to tour widely in the nation; and first to appear in integrated concerts with white musicians.[7]

Musical Styles during Slavery

The absence of instruments encouraged singing among slaves in work as well as worship. **Field hollers** were an early example, usually sung or chanted by individual workers in rhythm with their work. Hollers subsequently evolved into group **work songs,** which often included call and response: A lead singer acting as foreman sang a lyric to direct the work, then workers answered and performed the required task. The rhythm of the singing helped coordinate loading barges, driving mules, or laying railroad ties. Field hollers and work songs contributed greatly to the development of African American music. In them one can hear African melodic inflection, microtones, and pentatonic melodies.

The development of spirituals resulted from an exchange of musical styles between the races in the eighteenth and nineteenth centuries when many African Americans converted to Christianity. **Spirituals** offered biblical stories as metaphors for liberation, offered hope for a better life, and helped preserve African cultural memory. For over two centuries, the hymns of English composer Issac Watts (1674–1748) were particularly popular among African Americans, and these hymns served as the improvisational basis for the development of spirituals. Because most people, white and black, could not read music or text, hymns were often learned through the Scottish custom called lining out. In **lining out,** leaders sang one line at a time to the congregation, who repeated the newly learned material in a call and response format. The African American church also developed its own liturgy and music with the establishment of the first African Methodist Episcopal (AME) church in Philadelphia in 1794. The church's minister, Richard Allen, subsequently published the first hymnal of the African American church in 1801.

Innovation in the development of early spirituals also took place at **camp meetings,** which stemmed from the Second Awakening, an evangelical movement of the early nineteenth century. The revivals were large, multiday, outdoor religious celebrations attended by both blacks and whites, where worship went on day and night. Blacks at the events spent hours singing, praying, and participating in the **ring shout**—a shuffling circular dance of chanting and

Internet Listening Exercise

Go to Rounder Records (http://www.rounder.com) and listen to the following field holler and work song samples:

Deep River of Song: Mississippi Saints and Sinners: "One Morning at the Break of Day," "Workin' on the Levee, Sleepin' on de Ground"

Late nineteenth-century camp meeting in Hattiesburg, Mississippi.

hand clapping that often transported participants into an ecstatic trance. Refrains from hymns provided the starting point for improvisation, and spontaneous songs were composed with frequent affirmations such as "Hallelujah" and "Amen." At the camp meetings, outside the confines and restrictions of the formal church setting, African musical practices blended with simple hymn melodies to generate new hybrids. The songs that developed were called camp-meeting hymns or spiritual songs, and the first collection of this music, *Slave Songs of the United States*, was published in 1867. One white listener described the sound of early camp-meeting spirituals:

> There is no singing in parts as we understand it and yet no two appear to be singing the same thing—the leading singer starts the words of each verse, often improvising, and the others who base him, as it is called, strike in with the refrain, or even join in the solo when the words are familiar.[8]

THE END OF SLAVERY AND THE BEGINNING OF A NEW AMERICAN MUSIC

With the end of the Civil War and the demise of slavery, the South was in turmoil. Although most newly freed slaves were as impoverished as before, the change in their level of personal freedom was revolutionary. They could now travel, seek work, and make personal choices. This newfound freedom contributed to advances in music, including the development of gospel music, the blues, and jazz. Gospel music expanded on spirituals to integrate popular influences and uptempo rhythms, the blues reflected new social realities in the black population by reflecting complex emotional needs, and jazz represented a new interpretation of the African tradition of collective improvisation. The new genres, all rooted in African music, also marked the beginning of a new African American

Internet Listening Exercise

Listen to samples of the following spirituals, all originally found in *Slave Songs of the United States*, performed by a variety of artists.

The Southernaires: "Roll Jordan Roll"

Bernice Johnson Reagon: "Jacob's Ladder"

Harry Belafonte: "Michael Row the Boat Ashore"

Swan Silvertones: "Rock My Soul"

Marian Anderson: "Nobody Knows the Trouble I've Seen"

Paul Robeson: "Deep River"

popular culture of performance that would have an enduring impact on American music.

Chapter Summary

- African music and culture of the seventeenth through the nineteenth centuries greatly influenced American popular American music, despite the oppressive conditions of slavery. The accuracy of our knowledge of African music prior to the age of sound recording is hampered by the lack of written records, but recent research and interest in vernacular music has improved our understanding.

- Music played a central role in African life and was incorporated into festivals, agricultural rites, religious ceremonies, preparations for war, hunting expeditions, recreation, and rites of passage.

- African culture held musicians in high regard. *Griots*, or tribal storytellers, served as historians and entertainers with the important task of maintaining and transmitting history through poetry and song.

- African music employs a complex system of aesthetics that differs from that of European classical music. Historically, many key African musical elements were retained and further developed in American popular music.

- There are four principal groups of instruments in West Africa: membranophones (drums), idiophones (percussion instruments), aerophones (wind instruments), and chordophones (stringed instruments).

- Several African instruments took on hybrid forms in the United States: the banjo, the flute, and the quills (panpipes made of reeds).

- European slave owners had different standards of conduct for slaves. The Spanish, French, and Portuguese permitted them to keep their drums, play African music, and maintain African religions; the British and Americans banished drums and most African traditions, although work songs and field hollers were allowed, and many slaves were required to attend church, leading to the development of spirituals, blues, and gospel.

- Free African Americans were active musically, particularly in northern cities such as Philadelphia and New York.

- The end of slavery in 1865 saw increased personal freedom for African Americans, resulting in new musical developments such as gospel, blues, and jazz.

Key Terms

aerophones	call and response	*griot*
ambiguous mode	camp meeting	groove
blues scale	chordophones	heterogeneous sound
blue notes	field holler	ideal

idiophones	musicianer	spiritual
lining out	patting juba	swing
membranophones	pentatonic scale	vernacular music
microtone	ring shout	work song

Study and Discussion Questions

1. Why did African musical retentions persist despite oppressive conditions of slavery?
2. What roles did music play in African cultures during the seventeenth through the nineteenth centuries?
3. What is the African heterogeneous sound ideal?
4. What are some features of African musical aesthetics?
5. What are the principal instrument groups in traditional African music?
6. What American musical instruments are of African origin?
7. How did African musical and religious traditions fare in Cuba and Brazil as opposed to mainland North America?
8. What was the function of musicianers and what instruments did they play?
9. What were camp meetings and how did they influence musical innovation?
10. Why did African American slaves embrace a religion in which they were at first forced to participate?
11. What effect did Emancipation have on African American music and culture?

Notes

1. Interview with the authors.
2. Eileen Southern, *The Music of Black Americans: A History,* 3rd ed. (New York: Norton, 1997), 5.
3. Ibid., 5–7.
4. Gunther Schuller, *Early Jazz: Its Roots and Musical Development* (New York: Oxford University Press, 1968), 26–27.
5. Robert Palmer, *Deep Blues* (New York: Viking Press, 1981), 31.
6. Olly Wilson, "The Heterogeneous Sound Ideal in African-American Music," in *New Perspectives on Music: Essays in Honor of Eileen Southern,* ed. R. Wright and S. Floyd (Warren, MI: Harmonie Peak Press, 1992), 330.
7. Southern, *Music of Black Americans,* 107.
8. Samuel Floyd, *The Power of Black Music: Interpreting Its History from Africa to the United States* (New York: Oxford University Press, 1995), 37.

1820 - 1980

1830s First white minstrel shows establish a genre that influences the blues and American musical theater ♪
1839–1860 Underground Railroad operates to help escaped slaves reach the North

1849 Stephen Foster, America's greatest 19th-century songwriter, publishes "Oh! Susanna," one of his biggest hits ♪

1861–1865 Civil War and Emancipation Proclamation
1870 Georgia Minstrels, a black minstrel group, tours Europe, demonstrating international appeal of African American performance styles ♪
1877 Thomas Edison invents first sound recording device ♪

1914–1918 World War I
1914 W. C. Handy's "St. Louis Blues" is published and becomes first blues hit ♪
1917 Large African American migration to North is under way
1919–1933 Prohibition

1920 Mamie Smith's "Crazy Blues," the first blues record ♪
1923 Bessie Smith's "Downhearted Blues" sells 750,000 copies, demonstrating a market for the blues ♪
Mid-1920s Harlem Renaissance ♪
1926 Blind Lemon Jefferson makes "Black Snake Moan," the first rural blues record ♪
1927 The great Mississippi River flood
1927 Charles Lindbergh flies across the Atlantic
1929–1930s Great Depression; New Deal begins
1930s Bluebird Records in Chicago promotes urban blues and creates first record studio "house sound" ♪
1930 First electric guitar marketed by Dobro company ♪
1933 Wurlitzer manufactures first jukeboxes ♪
1936 Gibson markets first Les Paul electric guitar ♪
1936 Robert Johnson records seminal "Cross Road Blues" ♪
1938 First "Spirituals to Swing" concert in New York, showing links among different African American musical genres ♪

Early 1940s African Americans migrate North
1941–1945 U.S. participates in World War II
1941 Muddy Waters, architect of electric blues, first recorded by Alan Lomax ♪
1944 Louis Jordan's "GI Jive" reaches top of pop charts ♪
1947 T-Bone Walker releases "Call it Stormy Monday" ♪
1948 *Billboard* magazine initiates R & B chart, ceases use of "race records" category; WDIA in Memphis, first all-black station, goes on the air ♪
1950s 12-bar blues becomes a standard form in early rock ♪
1952 B. B. King's first hit, "Three O'Clock Blues," released ♪
1954 School segregation outlawed; civil rights movement begins

1960s Blues has major impact on the British Invasion and acid rock ♪
1963 Civil rights march on Washington; John Kennedy assassinated
1964–1973 Vietnam War
1964 Newport Folk Festival "discovers" blues artists ♪
1968 Martin Luther King and Robert Kennedy assassinated
1969 B. B. King and Muddy Waters cross over to a mainstream audience and perform at Fillmore East ♪

1980 *Blues Brothers* movie released ♪
1983 Stevie Ray Vaughan releases *Texas Flood* ♪
1986 Robert Cray releases *Strong Persuader* ♪
1989 Bonnie Raitt wins Grammy for *Nick of Time* ♪

| 1820 | 1840 | 1860 | 1880 | 1900 | 1920 | 1940 | 1960 | 1980 |

Chapter 3

From Minstrelsy to the Blues

The blues is one of the core elements of American popular music. As historian Samuel Floyd observed, "The blues appears to be basic to most forms of black music, and it seems to be the most prominent factor in maintaining continuity between most of them."[1] This statement could be extended to many styles of American popular music, including rock, jazz, R & B, and country. Growing out of a blend of field hollers, minstrelsy, church music, and the songster tradition, the blues gradually took a consistent 12-bar form that came to flavor much of American popular music. The blues has existed for a century. To understand its origins, we examine the events and artists that shaped the genre from the nineteenth century through the present.

MINSTRELSY

The story of the blues is actually preceded by **minstrelsy,** which was the first indigenous American theatrical and popular music genre. This genre helped shape the blues as well as twentieth-century American musical theater. Minstrelsy emerged around 1820 and reached its height between 1850 and 1870 with variety show performances based on crude stereotypes of African Americans. For close to four decades, it was the country's most popular form of theatrical entertainment. In minstrelsy, white actors performed in **blackface,** a makeup style in which the face was darkened with burnt cork and exaggerated facial features such as large lips and big eyes were drawn. Black artists also performed in minstrelsy, and in the early twentieth century, black minstrel shows served to disseminate the first blues music. Minstrelsy was also one of the first examples of the appropriation and adaptation of African American music by whites, setting a pattern that would continue for over 150 years.

The Origins of Minstrelsy

As early as 1769, what were then called "Negro songs" were being presented in blackface in New York theatrical productions, sometimes between the acts of plays or operas. The "father" of American minstrelsy was Thomas "Daddy" Rice, an actor from New York. Rice created a character called **Jim Crow,** a disabled

IN THIS CHAPTER

- Minstrelsy
- Origins of the Blues
- Marketing the Blues and the Invention of Sound Recording
- Classic versus Rural Blues
- Urban Blues
- Influences of Technology and World War II
- The Electric Blues: Muddy Waters, T-Bone Walker, and B. B. King
- Blues Revivals
- The Power of the Blues

Multicultural Note

Cultural Appropriation

Cultural appropriation describes what happens when members of one cultural group take cultural elements from another cultural group, reshape them, and claim them as their own. The cultural elements taken (appropriated) in this way often change as they are interpreted in a new cultural context, but they are generally still recognizable. The history of American popular music presents many examples of cultural appropriation, from the earliest jazz recordings (by the Original Dixieland Jazz Band, a white New Orleans group appropriating the music of early African American jazz artists) to the white "boy bands" of the 1990s (Backstreet Boys and *Nsync, appropriating African American soul and hip-hop performance styles).

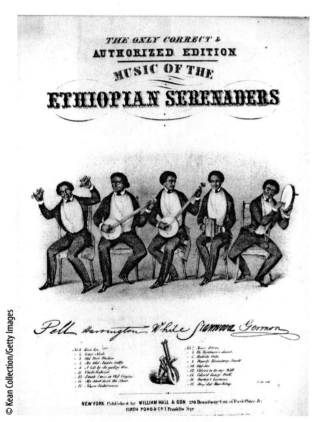

Sheet music cover for minstrel music of the Ethiopian Serenaders, dated 1847. Notice the format attire of the participants, the stereotyped images, and the classic minstrel show instrumentation of banjos, tambourines, and bone rattles.

black stable hand who moved with a shuffle. Although the songs sung by Rice belonged to folk traditions of Southern slaves, according to historian Eileen Southern, Rice changed the words in order to "disparage the black man and his life style."[2] During the same period, another minstrel character, **Zip Coon,** became popularized in a song whose melody resembled that of "Turkey in the Straw." Zip Coon was an African American "city slicker" who made imperfect attempts to imitate white city folk. These two contrasting characters—Jim Crow the country bumpkin and Zip Coon the city slicker—established the character foundations for the minstrel show, as well as stereotypes that lasted for over a century. Well into the 1950s, laws that enforced segregation in the South were still called "Jim Crow" laws, and the word *coon* persisted as a racist term.

Minstrel performances developed into full-length variety shows during the 1830s. The two most famous minstrel troupes, the Virginia Minstrels and the Christy Minstrels, began in the 1840s. The latter group performed on Broadway for ten years, formalizing the minstrel show genre. Cast members stood or sat in a semicircle around an "interlocutor" who dressed in formal attire and acted as MC. He bantered with two end men, "Mr. Bones," who rattled bones, and "Mr. Tambo," who played the tambourine. Shows opened with a chorus and grand processional, followed by jokes, dialogue, songs, sketches, and instrumental numbers. Because the performers spoke and sang in poor imitations of Black English dialect, they were called **Ethiopian delineators.** Instrumentation consisted of many of the same instruments associated with plantation life: banjos, fiddles, tambourines, and bone castanets. Later minstrel shows incorporated wind band instrumentation as well as guitars and mandolins.

Debate about the origins of minstrel songs persists. Composers often claimed that their music was based on slave songs heard on plantations, and some did visit the South. However, by the time the music reached the stage, original elements had been changed, and clear influences of English, Irish, and Scottish folk songs could often be heard. For many white Americans at the time, minstrel music was linked to a sense of patriotism, and its popularity reflected an attempt to fashion a new American musical identity that rejected the sentimentality of British parlor songs. As historian Ken Emerson has observed, "A shared feeling of superiority to blacks was one of the few things that unified a nation of immigrants, many of them more recent arrivals than the African Americans they mocked."[3] Minstrel music may also have served as a vehicle to express nostalgia for an imagined "simpler" rural life amid early industrialization or to discuss "forbidden" topics like race, class, sex, money, and violence. America's greatest popular songwriter of the nineteenth century, Stephen Foster, wrote extensively for minstrelsy, including the popular tunes "Old Folks at Home," "Oh! Susanna," and "Camptown Races." Minstrelsy pervaded American popular music well into the twentieth century: *The Jazz Singer* (1927), the first motion picture with sound, featured popular entertainer Al Jolson performing in blackface.

Black Minstrels

Minstrelsy provided a contradictory venue for early mass exposure of African American artists. Black minstrel troupes performed as early as the 1840s, and solo black performers of "Ethiopian music" were found even earlier. "Signor Cornmeali" (Mr. Cornmeal) performed as a street vendor in New Orleans, influencing "Daddy" Rice, who added a skit called "Cornmeal" to his routine. Dancer William Henry Lane ("Master Juba") was one of the first African Americans to tour and perform with white minstrel groups, and his work reflected traditional African American performance styles.

The end of slavery in 1865 broadened choices for African American performers, and many more black minstrel troupes formed. The Georgia Minstrels were the most famous of these; with a large cast and 13-piece brass band, they successfully toured Europe in 1870. The troupes served as a major source of employment for African American entertainers well into the twentieth century, and many great artists—including W. C. Handy, Bessie Smith, Ma Rainey, T-Bone Walker, Louis Jordan, and Rufus Thomas—started out in minstrelsy. According to bandleader/composer W. C. Handy, "The minstrel show at that time was one of the greatest outlets for talented musicians and artists. All of the best talent of that generation came down the same drain. . . . The minstrel show got them all."[4] James Bland was the most important African American composer of minstrel music, with such tunes as "Carry Me Back to Old Virginny," "In the Evening by the Moonlight," and "Dem Golden Slippers" to his credit.

Internet Listening Exercise

All of the following tunes, performed by a variety of artists, were part of the minstrelsy repertoire.

Emmett Miller: "Dusky Stevedore"

Al Jolson: "My Mammy"

Golden Gate Quartet/Josh White: "Old Dan Tucker"

Louis Armstrong/Mills Brothers: "Carry Me Back to Old Virginny"

Michelle Shocked: "Jump Jim Crow"

Multicultural Note

The Contradictions of Black Minstrelsy

Despite its opportunities, black minstrelsy presented a dilemma for African American performers. On the one hand, they could claim authenticity for their portrayals of African American life; on the other, they used caricatures previously developed by white performers. This "imitation of an imitation" unavoidably reinforced racist portrayals. The opportunity for social mobility provided by minstrelsy, however, subsequently enabled African American performers to shift to other performance styles.

ORIGINS OF THE BLUES

In his book, *Father of the Blues*, W. C. Handy related a legendary story about his "discovery" of the blues. In 1903, while stranded at a railroad station in northern Mississippi, Handy lay down uncomfortably to take a nap. Some time during the evening, an African American man in tattered clothes sat beside him and started to play the guitar. Handy awoke to the sound of the guitar being played with a knife pressed against the strings, creating a slurred, moaning sound. In Handy's words, "It was the weirdest music I ever heard." The man sang, "Goin' where the Southern Cross the Dog," repeating the line three times in a call and response style with the guitar. When Handy asked him what the words meant, the singer explained that south of the station the tracks of the Southern Railroad crossed those of the Yazoo and Mississippi Valley Railroad—also known as the "Yellow Dog." He was singing about his destination.[5] What Handy described was an early example of the blues. He had heard work songs and field hollers before, but never anything quite like this. The guitar playing was intricate, with complex rhythmic patterns and melodic responses to the singing. The experience made a lasting impression, and Handy went on to publish some of the earliest blues music.

For some, the blues is a specific musical style; for others, it is an emotion evoked by music with blueslike features; for still others, it is a form of social commentary:[6]

> The Blues always impressed me as being very sad, sadder than the Spirituals,
> because their sadness is not softened with tears, but hardened with laughter,
> the absurd, incongruous laughter of a sadness without even a god to appeal to.
> (Langston Hughes)

> I've got a disposition and a way of my own
> When my man starts kicking I let him find another home
> I get full of good liquor, walk the streets all night
> Go home and put my man out if he don't act right
> Wild women don't worry, Wild women don't have them blues. (Ida Cox)

The musical characteristics of what we now call the blues came together in consistent form around 1900.

Characteristics of the Blues

- Repeated 12-bar (measure) form.
- Blue notes—flatting the third, fifth, and seventh notes of a major scale.
- Bending pitches and sliding between notes.
- Call and response, often between accompanying instruments and a vocalist.
- AAB lyric pattern and rhyme scheme: One line of lyrics is sung, then repeated, then a new third line concludes the verse.

The African roots of the blues included the ring shout traditions of chants, vocal improvisation, and call and response, as well as the tradition of the *griot* (musical storyteller). There were strong similarities between the *griot* and the storytelling blues musician, as most *griots* accompanied themselves on stringed instruments and traveled from place to place, like early blues musicians. They differed, however, in the social function of their performances: The *griot* provided tribal history as well as entertainment, whereas the blues musician was primarily an entertainer. Early blues guitar techniques probably mirrored African stringed instrument styles, and slave owners may have unintentionally enhanced the retention of African stringed instrumental traditions by banning drums.

American musical roots of the blues lay in the music of itinerant black musicians called songsters, and in the field hollers and work songs of slaves. **Songsters** played instruments and sang an eclectic and multicultural repertoire with European and African sources that included comic songs, social songs, ballads, minstrel songs, and eventually the blues. In the late nineteenth century, the blueslike qualities associated with field hollers began to appear in the Delta region of Mississippi, although early blues star Ma Rainey also spoke of hearing music called the blues while traveling with a tent show in Missouri in 1902, and pianist/composer Jelly Roll Morton told of hearing songs called the blues in New Orleans in 1905. Similar stories placed the blues in regions throughout the South. Mississippi blues legend Son House also gave his take on the roots of the blues:

> People wonder a lot about where the blues come from. Well, when I was coming up, people did more singing in the fields than they did anywhere else. . . . They'd make it sound good, too. You could hear them half-a-mile off, they'd be singing so loud. . . . You'd hear them talking and one would say, "You know ol' so and so can really sing the blues!"[7]

In northwestern Mississippi, the Mississippi and Arkansas Rivers intersect to form a triangle called the Mississippi Delta. This was one of the poorest areas in the United States at the turn of the twentieth century. Land was farmed by poor African American sharecroppers who rented land, seed, and tools from white landowners and worked with little chance of coming out ahead. The region's hot climate, backbreaking work, and unending cycle of debt formed the context of the **Delta or rural blues.** Songsters in the region started to merge field hollers with simple guitar chords and lyrics describing hardships and hopes. The chords they used were probably influenced by the harmonic structure of church hymns, and earthy themes of love and lust also found a home in the music's AAB lyric structure. Many legendary blues performers were born or grew up in the Delta, including Charley Patton, Son House, Robert Johnson, Muddy Waters, John Lee Hooker, Howlin' Wolf, and B. B. King.

MARKETING THE BLUES AND THE INVENTION OF SOUND RECORDING

The earliest blues songs were transmitted orally by songsters performing throughout the South, but it was a handful of music promoters who saw the style's appeal and brought it to a wider audience. The most prominent blues entrepreneur was **W. C. Handy** (1873–1958), a formally-trained musician from a middle-class background who was working as trumpeter/bandleader for Mahara's Minstrels in the Delta. Because sound recording was still in its infancy, the main market for music lay in sheet music publishing. Handy published his first blues, the "Memphis Blues," in 1912, and he followed up with "St. Louis Blues," one of the most enduring songs of the twentieth century, in 1914. The song was not a pure 12-bar blues: Its first and second verses used the 12-bar form, while the third verse was a tango, a popular rhythm recently arrived from Argentina.

Just before 1900, the recording industry in the United States began, and it grew steadily during the first 20 years of the new century. Although early sound quality was poor, the novelty of the invention and continuing drops in price encouraged consumers to give recorded music a chance. White artists dominated the early recording industry, with opera and wind band music the most popular styles recorded. Nonetheless, the industry included a few African American artists. Some of inventor Thomas Edison's best-selling recordings of the late nineteenth century featured a former slave, George Washington Johnson, performing "The Laughing Song" and "The Whistling Coon." Bert Williams, one of the last great African American minstrel performers, also recorded a variety of vaudeville and minstrel songs between 1900 and 1920, and recordings of African American bandleader James Reese Europe's influential syncopated wind band music were released in 1914.

The first blues record, Mamie Smith's "Crazy Blues," did not appear until 1920. When the tune sold 75,000 copies in its first month, the era of recorded blues had begun, established as a new category called "race records." Most African American pop vocal recordings, regardless of style, were subsequently classed as race records until 1948 when the category was renamed "rhythm and

Internet Listening Exercise

Compare three different versions of W. C. Handy's "St. Louis Blues."

W. C. Handy: "St. Louis Blues"

Bessie Smith: "St. Louis Blues"

Herbie Hancock/Stevie Wonder: "St. Louis Blues"

Music Industry Note

The Invention of Sound Recording

In 1877 American inventor Thomas Edison created the **phonograph**—the first device capable of reproducing sound by recording onto a metal cylinder covered with foil. His first recording was a spoken-word version of "Mary Had a Little Lamb." Commercial **wax cylinder** recordings using Edison's invention became available in 1890. To record sounds effectively, they had to be loud; therefore, some of the most popular cylinders of the time were recordings of John Philip Sousa and the U.S. Marine Band. Poor sound quality and short, two-minute playback time discouraged the recording of much classical music, with the exception of opera aria selections. Edison's technology had other problems as well. There was no way to make multiple copies of cylinders, so each had to be a newly recorded performance. Prices were also exorbitant for the time—each phonograph cost $190. Nor did Edison have any interest in using his device for entertainment; he believed its main use was to help the visually and aurally impaired.

In 1887 Emile Berliner took another path and revolutionized sound recording with the invention of the **gramophone,** a device that recorded sounds on a heavy plate-glass disc etched by the vibrations of a stylus. Berliner worked quickly to improve sound quality and ease of reproduction, and by 1893 his early record players played shellac disks and cost as little as $12. The early players were cranked by hand, making constant pitch and speed difficult to maintain, but in 1896 a new motor-driven version arrived. The gramophone—later called the phonograph, playing vinyl disks —dominated the recording industry for the next 90 years.

Internet Listening Exercise

Listen to the following wax cylinder recording samples from *Phonographic Yearbook: The 1890s Vol. 1.*

George W. Johnson: "The Laughing Song"

Sousa's Band: "El Capitan"

Billy Golden: "Turkey in the Straw"

---

blues" by *Billboard* magazine. Black artists who followed up on Smith's recording success were primarily vaudeville (variety show) performers. Many of them toured throughout the country with shows produced by the white-owned Theater Owners Booking Association (**TOBA**—many performers swore it stood for "tough on black a——"). Early blues legends Ma Rainey, Bessie Smith, and others worked the TOBA circuit. Conditions for performers varied widely; headliners fared well, others did not. Touring schedules were nightmarish; artists faced low salaries, poor working conditions, and segregation; and they often traveled in fear of racial harassment. Nevertheless, according to historian Daphne Duval Harrison,

> Black communities across the country benefited economically and culturally when a train uncoupled the show car at the local railroad siding. The traditional parade that followed not only brought folks to the show, it brought business to the little shops, cafes, and "joints" as people crowded in to mingle with the show people. And high spirits remained for weeks after the train was gone.[8]

Internet Listening Exercise

Listen to a sample of the first blues recording, made in 1920.

Mamie Smith: "Crazy Blues"

CLASSIC VERSUS RURAL BLUES

By 1921, records were challenging sheet music in the marketplace. Race records had also unlocked a vast new African American market, so that record companies pushed to record anything with "blues" in the title. For the next few years female blues artists such as Ma Rainey, Bessie Smith, Ida Cox, Alberta Hunter, and Ethel Waters dominated the market with an early style now called **classic blues.** It had a sophisticated and distinctively urban flavor, with accompaniments by early jazz masters such as trumpeter Louis Armstrong and pianist Earl "Fatha" Hines.

Gertrude "Ma" Rainey (1886–1939) was often called the Mother of the Blues. The Georgia-born Rainey was a powerful and exciting singer, and although her vocal range was only one octave, the soulful qualities of her contralto voice made up for it. According to Thomas Dorsey, Rainey's musical director (and later a major gospel music innovator),

> She was a natural born artist . . . didn't need no school didn't go to no school; didn't take no music didn't need no music. . . . Ma had the real thing she just issued out there. It had everything in it needed, just like somebody issue a plate of food out say everything's on the plate . . . take it or leave it.[9]

With a gold lamé headband, sequins, plumes, and a necklace of $20 gold pieces, Rainey burst out of a giant cardboard gramophone in her stage show. Funny and charismatic, she performed songs of alienation, infidelity, revenge, and lost love. One of the biggest stars on the TOBA circuit, she became the first African

Photo by Frank Driggs Collection/ Getty Images

Ma Rainey with her Georgia Jazz Band, including blues and gospel innovator Thomas Dorsey at the piano. Notice the jazz band instrumentation and primitive drum set in the foreground.

American pop star, with numerous recordings. Rainey was also a successful businesswoman, like several other female blues stars of the period.

Bessie Smith (1894–1937), known as the "Empress of the Blues," began her career in a minstrel troupe and debuted with the hit "Down Hearted Blues" in 1923. She made 160 recordings and sold almost ten million records. Attracting black and white audiences, Smith was a superstar in the 1920s, and she appeared in one film, *The St. Louis Blues,* as well as a Broadway show. At the height of her career, she traveled in her own private railroad car, supporting an entourage of 40 musicians, dancers, singers, and comedians. Smith's repertoire was eclectic, encompassing show tunes and Tin Pan Alley songs such as Irving Berlin's "Alexander's Ragtime Band" as well as the blues. Her expressive style and phrasing influenced musicians of many styles, including jazz, gospel, and R & B. Smith's blues "emanated from the violence and complexities of the urban experience and its effects on black women."[10]

The end of the 1920s saw the decline of the classic blues. The Depression played a part in the shift, as did the development of sound films and the demise of vaudeville, tent shows, and TOBA performances. Female classic blues singers continued to perform, however, and artists such as Ethel Waters and Alberta Hunter influenced the development of an evolving jazz vocal style.

By 1925 the record industry began to pay attention to Delta or rural blues. The industry sought out new artists throughout the South and recorded them in makeshift studios set up in hotel rooms or store fronts. The trips yielded recordings of a range of rural blues artists, including Charley Patton, Son House, Huddie Ledbetter ("Leadbelly"), and Robert Johnson. Record producer Frank Walker described how he worked with rural blues performers:

> We recorded in a little hotel in Atlanta, and we used to put singers up and pay a dollar a day for food and a place to sleep in another little hotel. . . . You couldn't bring songs to them because they couldn't learn them. Their repertoire would consist of eight or ten things that they did well, and that was all they knew. So when you picked out the three or four that were best in a man's so-called repertoire you were through with that man as an artist. That was all. . . . They went back home. They had made a phonograph record and that was the next best thing to being the president of the United States in their mind.[11]

Unfortunately, the record industry's narrow commercial conception of the blues limited the recorded repertoires of many of the rural songsters. The record companies also created the myth of the solo itinerant blues singer singing his "lonesome, tragic tale." Many early rural blues performers actually performed in ensembles and played a variety of musical styles, but record companies re-

Internet Listening Exercise

Listen to Ma Rainey's interpretation of a classic blues later recorded by scores of blues and jazz artists.

Ma Rainey: "See See Rider Blues"

CD LISTENING EXERCISE

CD 1/7

Listen to Bessie Smith's recording of "Empty Bed Blues." Describe the quality of Smith's vocal work. Consider the earthy lyrical content and liberal use of double entendres. Describe the sound of the trombone, used in a call and response format with Smith's vocal. "Empty Bed Blues" exemplifies the standard 12-bar blues form as well as the traditional lyric form of three stanzas per chorus (one time through the 12-measure form), with the first two repeated. What made Smith such a popular vocalist?

Multicultural Note

The "Pure" Blues?

Is there a "pure" blues? Are there pure examples of any art form? Musicians seldom work in isolation from other musicians, musical styles are in a constant state of evolution, and all styles are in some sense hybrids. But blues scholars have argued for years about whether or not certain songs or artists represent the "real" blues, and some artists are criticized because their work does not meet an imposed standard of blues "purity." The 12-bar blues structure is often used as a benchmark, although legendary performers such as John Lee Hooker rarely followed the form. Many of the early legends of the blues actually sang a diverse repertoire of songs and styles, yet they were labeled blues artists. Why is music often categorized in such a rigid way?

© Hulton Archive/Getty Images

This "autographed" photo from the 1920s is the only known image of Blind Lemon Jefferson and originally appeared in a Paramount record catalog. Jefferson, the first commercially successful rural blues recording artist, died mysteriously on a Chicago doorstep in a snowstorm at the age of 33 in winter 1930.

corded them solo and playing only one style, because it simplified production and marketing.

Texas-born **Blind Lemon Jefferson** (1897–1930) made one of the first successful rural blues recordings, "Black Snake Moan," in 1926. He was a virtuoso guitarist and songster fluent in a range of styles. Jefferson's high-pitched singing had a direct urgency, and his skilled guitar work encompassed multiple influences. Jefferson spent much of his life as an itinerant musician in the South and the Midwest, and he made over 100 recordings that impacted rural blues styles.

Charley Patton (1887–1934) is often referred to as the "Father of the Delta Blues." Born of mixed African and Native American heritage, he grew up on Dockery's plantation in Mississippi, a location rich in blues mythology. The plantation played a central role during the early development of the blues, with numerous accounts of musicians traveling to Dockery's to learn the blues from Patton. Like many rural blues songsters, he knew a wide variety of styles in addition to the blues, and his intense singing was accompanied by slide guitar in a call and response. The slide guitar style, first developed in Hawaii, was incorporated into rural blues and country music in the late 1920s, and Patton was an early innovator of the technique. Also known as "bottle-

Music Industry Note

Juke Joints

The word *juke* is probably an African retention meaning "evil, disorderly, or wicked." In American English, *juke* has multiple meanings: to *juke* is to dance; a *juke box* is a mechanized record player found in a nightclub or restaurant; and a *juke joint* is a rudimentary nightclub or bar, usually located in an old building outside of town. **Juke joints** were generally open on weekends, providing entertainment for African Americans in the rural South. During Prohibition (1919–1933), jukes freely sold moonshine and provided a place for gambling, music, and dancing. Jukes were important performance venues for rural blues, and by the end of the twentieth century their ambiance was commodified by the "House of Blues" nightclub chain.

neck," the style was played with the guitar tuned to an open chord, which allowed the musician to change chords by sliding a hard object over the strings. Patton used the blunt edge of a knife or the neck of a glass bottle to slide across the strings, creating haunting instrumental responses to his voice. Patton performed at parties, social gatherings, and juke joints.

One of Charley Patton's best-known disciples was **Son House** (1902–1988), a pivotal figure in the evolution of rural blues. He learned the blues from Patton and went on to influence such greats as Robert Johnson and Muddy Waters, but he was conflicted about being a blues musician. As a part-time preacher, he personified the split between church music and secular music. Despite the common origins of the blues and gospel music, the two styles became separate genres, and many Christians, black and white, called the blues "the devil's music." Although the two styles shared many musical features, their lyrical content differed greatly. Son House played and sang with the rhythmic intensity of a rural preacher delivering a sermon, but an inner conflict between the blues and his religion made him shut down his blues career several times. He was rediscovered in 1941 by researcher Alan Lomax, who was recording rural blues artists for the Library of Congress.

Robert Johnson (1911–1938) was the most famous of the rural blues artists, with a rich lore surrounding his name. He was said to have sold his soul to the devil in exchange for his prodigious musical talents at a lonely crossroads somewhere in the Delta. With provocative song titles such as "Hellhound on My Trail," "Me and the Devil Blues," "Cross Road Blues," Johnson built the myth of the blues artist as a romantic and dangerous loner on the move. The Mississippi-born Johnson was influenced by Son House, performed in juke joints, and practiced an itinerant lifestyle that led to an early death by poisoning at 27. Only months after Johnson's death, producer John Hammond came south looking for him to perform in New York at Carnegie Hall in the legendary

Internet Listening Exercise

The following are all classic early rural blues recordings.

Blind Lemon Jefferson: "Black Snake Moan"

Charley Patton: "Screamin' and Hollerin' the Blues"

Son House: "Preachin' Blues"

Multicultural Note

Commodification and the Blues

Commodification takes place when a cultural phenomenon (a song, a story, a picture, even an artist) is turned into a commodity and marketed. When white record producers recorded Robert Johnson in a small hotel room in the early 1930s, he was in the initial stages of being commodified. He was paid a small fee and died shortly thereafter, but the process of commodifying him continues. Johnson's records have been issued and reissued, his image has been repeatedly invoked by white artists such as Eric Clapton, and the movie *Crossroads* was made to profit from the commodity called Robert Johnson.

"From Spirituals to Swing" concert, a program that traced the history of African American music.

As a singer and guitarist, Johnson added much to the vocabulary of the blues. The intensity of his acoustic guitar style foretold the amplified sound of Chicago blues and the impending emergence of the electric guitar as a major voice. Johnson's entire output consisted of twenty-nine songs recorded between 1936 and 1937, and only one of his tunes, "Terraplane Blues," became a minor hit, selling fewer than 4,000 copies. By contrast, the 1990 release of *Robert Johnson: The Complete Recordings* sold over 600,000 copies in six months. Johnson's songs were repeatedly covered by a wide variety of artists, including Eric Clapton and Cream, Johnny Winter, the Rolling Stones, the Allman Brothers, Bonnie Raitt, and the Red Hot Chili Peppers. In the words of guitarist Eric Clapton,

> Robert Johnson to me is the most important blues musician who ever lived. . . . I have never found anything more deeply soulful than Robert Johnson. His music remains the most powerful cry that I think you can find in the human voice.[12]

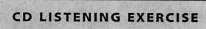

CD LISTENING EXERCISE

CD 1/8

Listen to Robert Johnson's recording of "Cross Road Blues." This song was covered by a variety of artists, notably Eric Clapton when performing with the 1960s rock trio Cream. "Cross Road" tells Johnson's legendary story of trading his soul to the devil. Does the timbre of his high-pitched, edgy, singing style add to the drama of the lyrics? Johnson's guitar style and extensive vocabulary of blues licks have influenced rock and blues musicians for over fifty years. Next, listen online to a sample of Clapton's version of the same song ("Crossroads") recorded with Cream, and compare the two performances.

URBAN BLUES

Lured by good-paying jobs, large numbers of African Americans migrated to the North in the first two decades of the twentieth century. By the 1930s, sizable black populations lived in many major Northern cities, and the newcomers demanded downhome music from entertainers. As African American culture became urbanized, the blues followed suit.

One of the first urban blues tunes, "How Long How Long Blues," was recorded in 1928 by pianist Leroy Carr. The song had an introspective flavor, with lyrics that pondered the distance traveled from the rural South to the urban North. It presaged the development of the urban blues of the 1930s. The **urban blues** was characterized by the coordinated use of guitar, piano, and sometimes a full rhythm section in an ensemble setting, playing a consistent, often up-tempo rhythm. Chicago played a central role in the development of the urban blues style, with artists such as Tampa Red, Memphis Minnie, and Big Bill Broonzy setting the tone in the 1930s. According to Francis Davis, "The blues scene in Chicago revolved around Tampa Red, whose apartment over a pawnshop was . . . a 'madhouse of old musicians.'"[13] Tampa Red's 1928 hit, "It's Tight Like That," had a lighter feel than either the classic or rural blues, anticipating much of the music recorded in Chicago for the next decade.

Bluebird Records was the best-known Chicago blues label in the 1930s. It was also the first label to develop a consistent "house sound"—the Bluebird beat—an approach later used by Chess Records, Blue Note, Motown, and others. Bluebird records were light and happy, with little of the soul-searching of the rural blues. They had a regular, danceable beat driven by a combination of guitar, piano, and bass, eliminating the unpredictable rhythmic variations and contrasting timbres characteristic of the rural blues. Leading Bluebird artists included Tampa Red, Big Bill Broonzy, and Memphis Minnie.

Prominent on the Chicago blues scene of the 1930s, vocalist/guitarist **Memphis Minnie** (1897–1973) was an early innovator on the electric guitar. Her career transcended and combined two blues stereotypes—the female classic blues singer and the male itinerant rural blues singer. The Louisiana-born artist made her recording debut in 1929 with "When the Levee Breaks," a song recalling the catastrophe of the great Mississippi River flood of 1927. This major disaster extended through much of the Midwest and left thousands of African Americans stranded. Minnie's powerful singing and guitar work embodied the transition from rural to urban blues. She was also a beautiful woman who modeled her stage presence on classic blues stars of the 1920s. Poet Langston Hughes sums up the urban blues experience in a description of a Memphis Minnie performance he attended in 1943:

> Memphis Minnie sits on top of the icebox at the 230 Club in Chicago and beats out blues on an electric guitar. . . . She grabs the microphone and yells, "Hey now!" . . . Then, through the smoke and racket of the noisy Chicago bar float Louisiana bayous, muddy old swamps, Mississippi dust and sun, cotton fields, lonesome roads, train whistles in the night.[14]

Internet Listening Exercise

The following tunes embody the urban blues sound of the 1930s.

Leroy Carr: "How Long How Long Blues"

Tampa Red: "It's Tight Like That"

Memphis Minnie: "Looking the World Over"

INFLUENCES OF TECHNOLOGY AND WORLD WAR II

The blues continued to evolve throughout the 1930s and 1940s, influencing jazz and other popular music styles. The emergence of radio and the electric guitar, as well as the onset of World War II, shaped this evolution. The invention of radio hastened the development of African American music by making it freely available on a wide basis for the first time. Although the first experimental sound radio broadcasts were made around 1906, several decades passed before commercial radio developed. By the 1930s, radio featured live performances, recordings, and a wide range of cultural programming. By the late 1940s, blues and gospel programs were being broadcast to wide audiences throughout the South. One of the most famous blues outlets was KFFA in Helena, Arkansas, which covered the Delta region. The station's most popular blues show was *King Biscuit Time*, sponsored by a local grocer. It was broadcast live daily at noon and made stars of the artists whose music it showcased. WDIA in Memphis, which called itself "America's only 50,000 watt Negro radio station," served a large African American market throughout the South with blues and gospel programming that made Memphis a magnet for people migrating north. Blues artist Howlin' Wolf also got his start broadcasting on the radio in Memphis in 1948 with an electric blues band, and a year later bluesman B. B. King started out as a Memphis DJ.

The development of the electric guitar was central to the evolution of the blues, R & B, and rock. Until the 1930s, the acoustic guitar was used in rural blues and country music as a rhythm instrument, although some rural blues artists developed it as a solo voice. In jazz, banjos rather than guitars were used in rhythm sections throughout much of the 1920s, but by the 1930s jazz bands were switching to guitar. Although it fit well into the sound of swing, the guitar was often too soft to be heard, so musicians and inventors began to experiment with amplification. The Dobro company commercially manufactured the first electric guitar in 1930, followed a year later by Rickenbacker. In 1936 Gibson contributed its own model, further legitimizing the new instrument.

The advent of World War II also influenced stylistic developments in the blues. Many African Americans moved from the South to other parts of the country to take jobs in defense industries; these jobs had become available be-

---

 Music Industry Note

The Guitar Pickup

A key element of electric guitar design was the **pickup,** a device made by wrapping a coil of wire around a magnet. The coil was placed under metal guitar strings, and their movement created an electric signal that was enhanced by an amplifier and heard through a speaker. With amplification, not only did volume increase, but guitarists could now sustain tones for long periods. This added to the possibilities of using the instrument as a solo voice, and as guitarists experimented further they found that they could manipulate the instrument's sound through distortion and feedback. The electric guitar ultimately became the signature icon of American popular music.

cause of an executive order issued by Franklin Roosevelt in 1941 in response to strong African American labor union pressure. Migrants took the most direct routes from their homes to the new jobs: People from the Southeast went to New York, those from the Deep South went to Chicago and Detroit, and those from the Midwest and Southwest often ended up on the West Coast. New regional blues styles developed as a result.

THE ELECTRIC BLUES: MUDDY WATERS, T-BONE WALKER, AND B. B. KING

A key architect of the electric blues was Chicago-based vocalist/guitarist **Muddy Waters** (1915–1983), and his work heavily influenced artists such as the Rolling Stones, Eric Clapton, Bonnie Raitt, and B. B. King. The **electric blues,** which began in the 1940s, used amplified, sometimes distorted instrumental sounds of the guitar and harmonica in an ensemble setting. Differing electric styles developed in Chicago, Memphis, and Texas. The Mississippi-born Waters grew up on a cotton plantation learning blues guitar and vocal styles from Delta blues masters Charley Patton, Son House, and Robert Johnson. When folklorist Alan Lomax came through town in 1941 looking for undiscovered blues artists to record, he helped Waters make his first recording. Waters headed for Chicago in 1943, where he found work in a paper factory and started playing music. He soon realized that there was a new style of amplified blues being played in the

town: "I started playing amplified guitar when I came to Chicago. Everybody else was playing them and I had to get something to go with that too."[15]

At first, Waters's down-home Delta blues sound was too raw for club owners, who were looking for the smoother, jazzier sound of popular artists such as Louis Jordan, Charles Brown, or Nat "King" Cole. Waters started to record for Chess Records in 1947, beginning a string of hits that included "I Can't Be Satisfied" and "I Feel Like Going Home." His greatest accomplishment was the development of an electric blues band sound. Working from the old Delta blues, the Waters band had a raucous and powerful sound flavored by the distortion of amplified instruments. Willie Dixon's fine songwriting ("Just Make Love to Me" and "I'm Your Hoochie Coochie Man"), the band's brawling amplified sound, and Waters's vocals combined to produce the classic Chicago-style electric blues. After Waters, the sound of electrical distortion and overloaded amplifiers became a staple of rock and blues, from Jimi Hendrix to heavy metal to grunge. In the words of B. B. King,

Muddy Waters, the architect of the Chicago blues.

© Terry Cryer/CORBIS

CD LISTENING EXERCISE

CD 1/9

Listen to "I'm Your Hoochie Coochie Man" recorded in 1954 by Muddy Waters. What is the overall feel of the song? What is the instrumentation of the band? How does the amplified harmonica blend with the electric guitar? What roles do the piano and bass play? How does the use of "stop time" breaks, when the entire band stops playing momentarily, and the slow tempo contrast with the intensity of the lyrics and vocal delivery? What might dancing to this tune in a dark club on a Saturday night with the band in the groove playing at high volume have felt like?

Muddy might have been the most magnificent of all the bluesmen to come out of Mississippi. . . . Muddy became a father figure to generations of musicians, black and white. . . . No one had Muddy's authority. He was the boss of Chicago and the reason some call Chicago the sure-enough home of the blues.[16]

Anyone who has enjoyed the music of B. B. King, Buddy Guy, Chuck Berry, Robert Cray, Eric Clapton, Stevie Ray Vaughan, Johnny Winter, or Albert King has heard echoes of guitarist/vocalist **T-Bone Walker** (1910–1975). As one of the first electric bluesmen, Walker forged the connection between the older acoustic blues and the new electric sound, successfully blending the Delta and Texas blues traditions. Raised in Dallas, Texas, as a boy Walker led bluesman Blind Lemon Jefferson around the streets of Dallas:

Blind Lemon I remember well. Though I was only a kid, he had me to lead him around. He kept the guitar strapped on his chest, a tin cup on the neck. . . . Lemon sang things he wrote himself about life—good times and bad. Mostly bad, I guess. Everybody knew what he was singing about. There's nothing new in the blues. It's everything that's going on.[17]

Walker soon performed with traveling shows, and his flashy stage moves—including doing the splits and picking up a table with his teeth—were perfected at an early age. As he developed on the guitar, he became friends with jazz guitar legend Charlie Christian, also a Texan. By 1934 Walker was fronting his own group, and in 1936 he moved to Los Angeles, where he was so popular by the end of the decade that he worked in the most fashionable white clubs on Sunset Strip. Walker mastered the new sound of the electric guitar in the early 1940s, and from 1945 through 1947 he recorded over 50 tunes, including such classics as "T-Bone Shuffle" and "Call It Stormy Monday." He toured frequently in package shows with other artists, but nobody wanted to follow Walker; his stage act was so spectacular that he always closed the shows.

Vocalist/guitarist **B. B. King** (1925–) has become the best-known bluesman in the world, with a simple melodic style that blended gospel, jazz, and Delta blues. He has influenced generations of blues and rock guitarists—including Buddy Guy, Eric Clapton, Mike Bloomfield, the Butterfield Blues

CD LISTENING EXERCISE

CD 1/10

Listen to "Stormy Monday Blues" recorded in 1947 by T-Bone Walker. This is one of the best-known blues songs ever recorded, with hundreds of versions by various artists. Notice the laid-back, introspective quality of the tune. How does it contrast with the feel of Muddy Waters's "Hoochie Coochie Man"? What is different about Walker's vocal style? Notice the different tones Walker gets from the guitar—from the low-register chords at the start to the fills and solos later in the song. How does he use *sustain*—the ability of the electric guitar to elongate a tone? Could Walker's melody lines have sounded as appropriate on a horn?

Guitarist/vocalist T-Bone Walker during the 1940s in a legendary performance pose. His stage style predated the later guitar heroics of such artists as Chuck Berry and Jimi Hendrix.

Band, Bonnie Raitt, Robert Cray, Keb' Mo', and Stevie Ray Vaughan. The Grammy-winning artist's career spanned more than four decades, over 50 albums, and numerous awards. As a performer, King patterned himself after vocalist/saxophonist Louis Jordan, while his guitar style used bends, vibrato, and jazzy runs influenced by T-Bone Walker. According to King,

> I've never really been accepted by the blues purists because they say I use too many clichés. I could never be a real jazz musician because I don't improvise well enough. . . . So I'm kind of in-between. I don't sing gospel well enough to be considered a gospel singer.[18]

King hailed from the Mississippi Delta, and his first musical influence was gospel. But he soon found that he could triple his day wages by playing the blues on street corners, and he headed for Memphis in 1946. King described his first impression of the city:

> It was like a fantasy come true. . . . Beale Street was famous, of course, because of W. C. Handy, Father of the Blues, and his composition "Beale Street Blues.". . . I knew Handy was black and that he stayed in Memphis and was known the world over. . . . His stature gave the blues pride. . . . Walking down Beale, I saw white people shopping the same street as blacks. That was new for me.[19]

The Selvin Collection

B. B. King publicity photo for BluesWay Records from the late 1960s.

Memphis was also developing as a recording center in the late 1940s. Sam Phillips started his Sun Records studio there in 1950, recorded numerous blues greats, and pressed Elvis Presley's first recordings. Other influential blues and R & B artists to record in Memphis included Howlin' Wolf, Ike Turner, Bobby "Blue" Bland, and Rufus Thomas. King was hired to play on blues radio shows and was soon promoted to DJ, calling himself "Beale Street Blues Boy," later shortened to "B. B." His first hit was "Three O'Clock Blues" in 1952, and though he toured the R & B circuit throughout the 1950s and early 1960s, he could not cross over to mainstream acceptance the way so many other R & B artists had in the fifties rock era. Around 1965 the final barriers to blues popularity began to fall when white America first heard the music of Son House and other Delta blues artists at the Newport Folk Festival. King capitalized on the new interest with the 1966 release of his signature hit, "The Thrill Is Gone," and he built on it to record and tour extensively before mainstream audiences. He ultimately became the face of the blues for mainstream America.

Internet Listening Exercise

Listen to two of B. B. King's signature tunes.

B. B. King: "The Thrill Is Gone," "Every Day I Have the Blues"

Internet Listening Exercise

These artists were popular in the blues revivals of the 1950s and 1960s.

Leadbelly: "Midnight Special"

Big Bill Broonzy: "All by Myself"

Paul Butterfield Blues Band: "Walkin' Blues"

BLUES REVIVALS

Every few years new generations rediscover the blues. One of the first blues revivals came in the late fifties and early sixties when folk music pervaded college campuses. In addition to white folk artists such as Pete Seeger and Peter, Paul, and Mary, some acoustic blues performers—for example, Leadbelly, Big Bill Broonzy, and Son House—were presented to white audiences as "folk blues" artists. Such presentations could unfortunately be demeaning, and sophisticated and urbane Chicago bluesman Big Bill Broonzy was sometimes reduced to wearing overalls and shabby clothes in concert appearances to project an expected down-home ambiance.

The mid-1960s saw an electric blues revival, fueled by British interest in all forms of the blues. The 1965 Newport Folk Festival finally broke electric blues to a U.S. mass audience with the rock-infused blues of white artists such as the Paul Butterfield Blues Band. Both the blues and R & B influenced British Invasion groups such as the Beatles, Rolling Stones, Animals, and Yardbirds; late-1960s rock artists such as Cream (featuring Eric Clapton), Janis Joplin, and Jimi Hendrix were even more deeply rooted in the blues. For a time, the pop music audience was exposed to B. B. King, Muddy Waters, T-Bone Walker, Howlin' Wolf, Albert King, Bobby "Blue" Bland, and others who had labored for decades in relative obscurity. Interest in the blues continued in the early 1970s with the popularity of southern white blues artists such as the Allman Brothers, Lynyrd Skynyrd, and Johnny and Edgar Winter.

The 1980s and 1990s saw another blues revival signaled by the release of two *Blues Brothers* films and an interest in "roots" music. White artists Stevie Ray Vaughan, Bonnie Raitt, Eric Clapton, and others spearheaded the new popularization, and a new generation of African American blues artists including Robert Cray and Keb' Mo' also appeared. Stevie Ray Vaughan, who drew equally from bluesmen such as Albert King and Muddy Waters and rockers such as Jimi Hendrix, released multiple gold albums with his band Double Trouble in the mid-1980s. Bonnie Raitt won a Grammy for her 1989 album, *Nick of Time,* and seasoned veterans such as singer/pianist Charles Brown and singer/guitarist John Lee Hooker were brought out of retirement to tour with her. In 1992 Clapton recorded a concert for *MTV Unplugged* that produced the biggest-selling record of his career. Performance venues for the blues expanded, and festivals promoted the style. As cities like Chicago and Memphis discovered the commercial potential of their blues heritage, "blues districts" were established. A thriving blues scene also developed in Austin, fostering performers such as the Fabulous Thunderbirds and Marcia Ball. Despite the

Blues and rock singer/slide guitarist Bonnie Raitt performing in 1978. Raitt redefines the role of women in contemporary blues.

revivals, the commercial recording scene for most black blues artists did not improve much. Although a few stars like B. B. King recorded on major labels, most were limited to smaller regional labels—Malaco, Alligator, Blind Pig, and a few others. Because renewed interest in the blues fueled research and educational efforts, blues archives were established in Chicago, Memphis, and Mississippi.

THE POWER OF THE BLUES

The blues greatly influenced many styles of American popular music—jazz, rock, R & B, gospel, zydeco, and country, among others. For example, trumpeter Wynton Marsalis once called the blues "the blood of jazz." [20] Many of trumpeter Louis Armstrong's earliest recordings were 12-bar blues, and jazz legends Duke Ellington and Count Basie created big band music deeply rooted in blues styles. Trumpeter Miles Davis's most popular album was entitled *Kind of Blue,* and even saxophonist John Coltrane's first recording as a leader was called *Blue Train.*

The roots of gospel, rock, and R & B are also steeped in the blues. One of the great early blues composers, Thomas Dorsey, subsequently became the founder

Internet Listening Exercise

These artists were popular in the blues revivals of the 1980s and 1990s.

Stevie Ray Vaughan: *Texas Flood*

Robert Cray: "Strong Persuader"

Bonnie Raitt: *Nick of Time*

Keb' Mo': "Henry"

of modern gospel music. The demise of the big bands in the late 1940s led to the small-band jump blues style, epitomized by Louis Jordan, which influenced early rock artists such as Bill Haley. Many classic rock tunes of the 1950s, including "Tutti Frutti," "Roll over Beethoven," and "Rock around the Clock," were all 12-bar blues. The blues formed the basis of most rock—in singing style, guitar riffs, chord progressions, and attitude. As we have seen, the bands of the 1960s British Invasion were also blues-influenced, as was the work of rock artists Jimi Hendrix, Janis Joplin, Led Zeppelin, and Creedence Clearwater Revival. James Brown, Otis Redding, and many other pioneers of soul were rooted in the blues as well.

Zydeco, an accordion-driven hybrid of rhythm and blues and Cajun music, is also steeped in the blues. Clifton Chenier was the originator of the style, which has grown in popularity since its birth in the early 1950s. Even country music retains close ties to blues traditions, as heard in the work of seminal country artists such as Jimmie Rodgers and Hank Williams. The blues is a lasting treasure of American popular music—it is African in its roots, but it is also a uniquely American music that shaped multiple genres.

Chapter Summary

- The blues is a core element of American popular music. Almost all styles of popular music, including jazz, gospel, rock, R & B, and country, reflect its influence.

- The evolution of African American and popular American musical traditions took place in a context of cultural appropriation and commodification. This began with minstrelsy and continues to the present.

- The first indigenous American theatrical and popular music genre, minstrelsy, shaped the blues as well as twentieth-century American musical theater. Based on racist stereotypes, minstrel shows were performed by white men in blackface from the 1830s into the twentieth century. After the Civil War, black minstrel troupes provided African Americans opportunities to work as mass popular entertainers.

- The blues includes many characteristics, including the 12-bar form, use of blue notes, call and response, bends and slides between notes, and an AAB lyric pattern. Much of American popular music retains some of these blueslike qualities.

- From its roots in Africa, the blues grew out of a blend of field hollers, minstrelsy, and church music.

- The first blues songs emerged around 1900 in the repertoire of itinerant black songsters. The Mississippi Delta is often cited as the birthplace of the blues, although the genre developed in other parts of the South as well.

- The first successful commercialization of the blues was W. C. Handy's publication of the "St Louis Blues" in 1914, and Mamie Smith's 1920 "Crazy Blues" was the first successful blues recording, leading to the development of race records.

- Two schools of blues recordings developed in the 1920s: classic blues, dominated by female artists such as Bessie Smith and Ma Rainey, and rural blues, dominated by men such as Blind Lemon Jefferson, Charlie Patton, Son House, and Robert Johnson. The record industry did much to shape the two styles.

- The Depression saw the demise of the classic blues and the beginnings of a new, band-oriented sound called the urban blues.

- The invention of the electric guitar and popularization of the radio in the 1930s and 1940s, along with northward African American migration, expanded the musical possibilities and fan base for blues. Artists such as Muddy Waters, T-Bone Walker, and B. B. King greatly contributed to the development of the genre. The popularity of the blues continues to rise and fall.

Key Terms

blackface	Ethiopian delineators	pickup
classic blues	gramophone	songster
commodification	Jim Crow	TOBA
cultural appropriation	juke joint	urban blues
Delta or rural blues	minstrelsy	wax cylinder
electric blues	phonograph	Zip Coon

Study and Discussion Questions

1. What role did minstrelsy play in the development of popular music and culture in America?

2. What are the African roots of the blues?

3. What are the musical qualities of the blues?

4. What were the two schools of early blues, and what led to their development?

5. How did the development of sound recording impact the evolution of the blues?

6. What role did technology and World War II play in the development of the blues?

7. Who were the early women of the blues, and what role did they play as musical and cultural role models?

8. How are the following artists important to the history of the blues: Ma Rainey, Bessie Smith, Robert Johnson, Muddy Waters, T-Bone Walker, and B. B. King?

9. What musical styles did the blues influence? Why did the blues affect so many popular music styles?

Notes

1. Samuel Floyd, *The Power of Black Music: Interpreting Its History from Africa to the United States* (New York: Oxford University Press, 1995), 79.

2. Eileen Southern, *The Music of Black Americans: A History,* 3rd ed. (New York: Norton, 1997), 91.

3. Ken Emerson, *Doo-Dah! Stephen Foster and the Rise of American Popular Music* (New York: Da Capo Press, 1998), 62.

4. Southern, *Music of Black Americans,* 237.

5. Cited in Robert Palmer, *Deep Blues* (New York: Viking Press, 1981), 45.

6. Blues definitions from Steven Tracy, *Write Me a Few of Your Lines: A Blues Reader* (Amherst: University of Massachusetts Press, 1999), 10–12.

7. David Evans, "Folk and Popular Blues," in Tracy, *Write Me a Few of Your Lines,* 120.

8. Daphne Duval Harrison, *Black Pearls: Blues Queens of the 1920s* (Piscataway, NJ: Rutgers University Press, 1988), 34.

9. Ibid., 36.

10. Ibid., 53.

11. Lawrence Cohn, ed., *Nothing but the Blues* (New York: Abbeville Press, 1993), 25.

12. Liner notes, *Robert Johnson: The Complete Recordings,* Sony Legacy 1C2K64916.

13. Francis Davis, *The History of the Blues* (New York: Hyperion, 1995), 138.

14. Paul and Beth Garon, *Woman with Guitar: Memphis Minnie's Blues* (New York: Da Capo Press, 1992), 124.

15. Steve Waksman, *Instruments of Desire: The Electric Guitar and the Shaping of Musical Experience* (Cambridge, MA: Harvard University Press, 2000), 122.

16. B. B. King with D. Ritz, *Blues All around Me: The Autobiography of B. B. King* (New York: Avon Books, 1996), 77.

17. Helen Dance, *The T-Bone Walker Story* (Baton Rouge: Louisiana State University Press, 1987), 13.

18. King, *Blues All around Me*, 234.

19. Ibid., 65.

20. "Gumbo," in *Jazz*, DVD, directed by Ken Burns (Washington, DC: Florentine Films, WETA, 2000).

1890 - 1940

1890–1910 Early jazz styles begin to emerge in New Orleans ♪

1897 First player pianos become commercially available ♪

1898 Spanish American War

1899 "Maple Leaf Rag" published by Scott Joplin, becoming the first sheet music to sell over a million copies ♪

1914 "St. Louis Blues" by W. C. Handy, the first blues hit ♪

1914 James P. Johnson, father of stride piano, releases "Carolina Shout," his biggest hit ♪

1914–1918 World War I

1914 Panama Canal opens

1917 Large African American migration to North is under way

1917 Original Dixieland Jazz Band, a white group, makes first jazz recording ♪

1918 Louis Armstrong goes to Chicago to join King Oliver, bringing New Orleans sound north ♪

1919–1933 Prohibition

1920 Nineteenth Amendment gives women right to vote

1920s Chicago becomes center of the jazz world ♪

1920 *Race records* established as music industry term for African American popular music recordings ♪

1923 Fletcher Henderson band premieres in New York, introducing the big band sound that would become swing ♪

1924 Paul Whiteman introduces Gershwin's *Rhapsody in Blue,* building the popularity of jazz and blending with classical music ♪

Mid-1920s Harlem Renaissance

1925 Louis Armstrong's first Hot Five recordings transform jazz by putting solo improvisation center stage ♪

1929–1930s Great Depression; New Deal begins

1930s New York becomes the center of the jazz world ♪

1935–1945 Swing era; jazz is America's most popular music ♪

1938 First "Spirituals to Swing" concert in New York recaps the history of African American popular music; Ella Fitzgerald records first hit, "A-Tisket, A-Tasket"; Benny Goodman's Carnegie Hall concert marks the arrival of swing ♪

1941–1945 U.S. participates in World War II

Early 1940s Major migration of African Americans from the South to the North and the West Coast

1943 Duke Ellington presents *Black, Brown, and Beige,* one of the first extended-length jazz compositions, at Carnegie Hall ♪

| 1890 | 1900 | 1910 | 1920 | 1930 | 1940 |

Chapter 4

Early Jazz: From Ragtime to Swing

Jazz is recognized worldwide as one of America's most significant musical and cultural contributions; some historians refer to it as America's "classical" music. Over its 100-year history, jazz has also influenced most styles of American popular music. It shares with the blues a strong African American influence, as well as the same date of birth—around 1900. In addition, it serves as a striking example of cultural hybridity, for it evolved through the blending of disparate elements of African, European, Latino, and other musics to create a uniquely American contribution to world culture. This chapter examines the first fifty years of jazz history.

WHAT IS JAZZ?

Jazz is a multifaceted musical genre that has evolved into many styles during its 100-year history. Since its inception in New Orleans, jazz has generated debates about its nature; these have intensified with the introduction of each new jazz style. Although jazz today encompasses a variety of sounds and approaches, it usually includes certain characteristic features such as improvisation, a swing rhythmic feel, and a historical lineage of innovators and associated styles.[1] A key component of jazz is improvisation—creating music on the spot. As we saw in Chapter 1, improvisation involves composing and performing at the same time, and no two improvised performances are exactly the same. Jazz can be improvised on any musical instrument, or by the human voice, and the practice is probably an outgrowth of the improvised nature of much African music. Most jazz combines improvisation with composed music, and jazz compositions often integrate formally written melodies, rhythms, and harmonies with sections devoted to improvisation.

Another defining element in most styles of jazz is *swing,* a rhythm that makes people want to move, dance, or snap their fingers. Swing is easy to feel but difficult to notate and define, and its rhythmic flavor has evolved over time. Swing rhythm can be approximated by taking a series of even beats, then lengthening the first and shortening the second beat to create a sequence of pairs of long and short notes. Duke Ellington offered this description of swing: "When the music feels like it's going faster, but it's not."[2]

Although the swing feel has been present throughout much of jazz history, it is not found in all jazz styles. For example, free jazz (avant-garde jazz with very few rules) and fusion (jazz blended with rock) do not usually swing. In recent years, the concept of swing has expanded to encompass any jazz that is played well and grooves.

We can also define jazz in terms of the historical contributions of the music's innovators and the styles they created. As jazz evolved, a distinct **jazz lineage** developed, and legends such as Louis Armstrong, Duke Ellington, Billie Holiday, Charlie Parker, Dizzy Gillespie, Miles Davis, Thelonious Monk, and John Coltrane established new musical directions that many other musicians followed and expanded on.

RAGTIME

The development of ragtime in the late nineteenth century significantly contributed to the evolution of jazz. Much of the music of the era that we would now call jazz was then known as ragtime, because the word *jazz* had not yet been coined and the two genres overlapped and influenced one another. **Ragtime** was a piano-based music in which musicians mixed complex syncopated rhythms with traditional European marches, parlor songs, and light classical music in a style called "ragging," for the ragged (syncopated) rhythms they created. Early ragtime may also have originated in the adaptation of a syncopated

Multicultural Note

Origins of the Word Jazz

The origins of the term *jazz* are clouded. It first appeared in print around 1915, spelled as *jass*, when a newspaper reporter used the word to mean "speed up" or "pep," claiming it was of Creole origin. Newspaper stories from the 1920s relate a version of the word's origins in which a musician named Jasbo, Jasper, Razz, or Chaz excited a crowd with his playing. The audience was said to have shouted, "Go Jass, go!"

Linguistic research has suggested a possible connection to the French verb *jaser*, meaning "to tattle or gossip," but the most commonly accepted theory of the original meaning of the word is that it was a slang reference to sexual intercourse.

style of banjo music to the piano. Another influence may have been the *habanera*, a Cuban dance rhythm popular in the United States in the early 1870s. The catchy beat of ragtime found its way into a variety of styles and ensembles, even Sousa marches. By the turn of the century, it was the most popular music in the country.

The Columbian Exposition, a world's fair held in Chicago in 1893, served as a gathering place for musicians, quickening the development of ragtime. **Scott Joplin** (1868–1917), ragtime's greatest innovator, was one of the many musicians whose attendance at the fair shaped their music. The Texas-born Joplin was a classically trained pianist and composer who subsequently settled in Sedalia, Missouri. In 1897 Joplin wrote his most famous composition, the "Maple Leaf Rag," which was the first piece of sheet music to sell over a million copies. Joplin's body of work eventually encompassed seventeen piano rags, a ballet, and two operas, the most famous of which was called *Treemonisha*. A Joplin rag called "The Entertainer" was later used in numerous film soundtracks, including the 1960s hit *The Sting*. Joplin's music and ragtime in general had a special place in embodying the culture of turn-of-the-century America, and composer Irving Berlin suggested that the essence of ragtime's popularity was its ability to capture the "speed and snap" of modern American life.

CD LISTENING EXERCISE

CD 1/11

Listen to the "Maple Leaf Rag." This is Scott Joplin's actual performance recorded on a player piano roll only a few months before his death in 1917. Listen for the syncopation in this familiar piano rag. Next, listen online to a sample of Jelly Roll Morton's later improvised version of "Maple Leaf Rag." What are the similarities and differences? Is the tempo the same? Has the "feel" of the rhythm changed? Jelly Roll added a swing feel that does not appear in Joplin's version. Improvised versions of ragtime melodies were an important ingredient of early jazz.

Music Industry Note

The Player Piano

The **player piano** (also called the pianola) was the first mechanism for recording and reproducing music with good fidelity. This turn-of-the-century invention "recorded" a piece of music by punching small holes onto a roll of paper. Each perforation corresponded to a different key on the piano. The piano roll, as it was called, then passed over a "tracker bar" with 88 air holes, one for each piano key. As each hole passed over the corresponding piano key hole, it let air through, triggering a pneumatic lifter to strike the appropriate key. The only job left for the performer was to push the pedals that worked the air bellows.

The player piano enabled people to enjoy piano music without having a musician play it live. The first player pianos became commercially available in 1897, the same year ragtime music was first published. By 1919, half of all pianos manufactured in the United States were player pianos.

NEW ORLEANS: THE BIRTHPLACE OF JAZZ

Several musical styles merged in the late nineteenth century to create the first jazz in New Orleans. Throughout its long history, the culture of New Orleans was shaped by a blend of European, African, and Latino influences. Located in a small crescent of land near the mouth of the Mississippi River, the city was founded by the French in 1718, ceded to Spain in 1764, and annexed by the United States in 1803 through the Louisiana Purchase. The cultural gumbo of New Orleans would nurture many great hybrid musical styles, including jazz, blues, Cajun, zydeco, and R & B.

Cultural Influences

The nineteenth-century social climate of New Orleans supported a more open approach to race relations than the rest of the South did. As pianist Jelly Roll Morton described it, "We had every different kind of person in New Orleans. We had French, we had Spanish, we had West Indian, we had American, and we all mixed on an equal basis."[3] As a result, **Congo Square** was established in 1817 as one of the few places in the United States where African dance and music were allowed to flourish. Slaves and free blacks gathered at the square every Sunday, where they performed an eclectic mix of African and African American music and dance. The ring shout was a common feature of the gatherings (see Chapter 2). Congo Square remained an active center of music and dance until the late nineteenth century, when new laws banned the performances.

In eighteenth- and nineteenth-century New Orleans, men of French and Spanish descent often had slave mistresses, and these liaisons produced a mixed-race social class called "Creoles of color." **Creoles** were often well-educated and financially successful, and Creole musicians generally received training in the European classical tradition. In 1894 a civil rights dispute involving a Creole of color ended with the U.S. Supreme Court establishing the doctrine of "separate but equal" and effectively legalizing segregation in America. From this time on, all people of mixed African descent were considered "Negro." Creole musicians then found themselves on the same social footing as musicians from the black underclass, and the musical skills of both groups merged. Some black musicians who had previously played by ear learned to read music, and their new Creole colleagues learned to play in a "hotter," improvised style.

Black fraternal organizations and social clubs, formed to replace traditional African forms of community destroyed by slavery, also played a significant role in the development of jazz. The groups hosted meetings, parties, weddings, and funerals; many also formed bands to provide music for their events. As Jelly Roll Morton recalled,

> New Orleans was very organization-minded. I have never seen such beautiful clubs as they had there—the Broadway Swells, the High Arts, the Orleans Aides, the Bulls and Bears, the Tramps, the Iroquois, the Allegros . . . and those clubs would parade at least once a week. They'd have a great big band.[4]

Finally, partying was an undeniable dimension of jazz origins, and New Orleans had a long history as a party town. The city's French and Spanish heritage probably contributed to its permissive climate, but the difficulties of everyday life likely also fed the escapist atmosphere. Life was especially difficult for poor African Americans, who experienced high infant mortality rates, chronic unemployment, and low life expectancy.

Musical Influences

Wind bands consisting of brass, woodwind, and percussion instruments were popular in New Orleans. Band instruments were fairly easy to obtain, and a local tradition of street parades (especially during Mardi Gras) added to the city's interest in band music. Bands frequently generated their own improvised versions of march music by ear. According to Duke Ellington, early New Orleans jazz was "an animated music with a strong African pulse beneath what often sounded like a caricature of a military band."[5] Another interesting influence on band styles in New Orleans was the visit of the Mexican Cavalry Band in 1885, which introduced a **Latin tinge** to the music by flavoring it with syncopated rhythms and melodies. One of the most common venues for New Orleans wind bands was the funeral procession. As Jelly Roll Morton recollected,

> You could hear the band come up the street taking the gentleman for his last ride, playing different dead marches. . . . When they would leave the graveyard the . . . boys in the band would just tear loose, while the second line swung down the street singing, "Didn't He Ramble."[6]

Mourners and celebrants who accompanied the bands were referred to as the **second line,** with young musician wannabes carrying the instrument cases of band members. The term *second line* is now also used by musicians to describe a syncopated beat of contemporary New Orleans jazz and R & B.

The blues also flavored early jazz, as a steady flow of African Americans from all parts of the South came to New Orleans looking for work. Blues singing changed the playing of early jazz cornetists such as Buddy Bolden and Freddie Keppard, who shifted from military band interpretations to the flowing, expressive sound of the blues. Blues inflections, growls, slides between notes, and the use of **vibrato** (slight and rapid variations in pitch) became characteristic features of early New Orleans jazz. Recall that trumpeter Wynton Marsalis called the blues "the blood of jazz," and filmmaker Ken Burns described the style as "the underground aquifer that would feed all streams of American music, including jazz."[7]

One of the first jazz legends of New Orleans was cornetist **Buddy Bolden** (1877–1931). He formed a band in the early 1890s that was well known for its syncopated, blues-influenced sounds. Although no recordings of Bolden's work exist, New Orleans musicians repeatedly cited him as one of the foremost jazz innovators. According to Jelly Roll Morton,

Buddy Bolden (was) the most powerful trumpet player I've ever heard. . . . We'd be hanging around some corner. . . . Then we'd hear old Buddy's trumpet coming in and we'd all start. . . . He'd turn his big trumpet around toward the city and blow his blues, "calling his children home," as he used to say.[8]

Other great cornetists of the era included Bunk Johnson, Freddie Keppard, King Oliver, and later, Louis Armstrong. Innovators on other instruments included reed player Sidney Bechet, trombonist Kid Ory, and pianist Jelly Roll Morton. In addition to black and Creole musicians, white and Latino musicians also developed early New Orleans jazz.

The experiments of the musicians led to a formalized set of musical practices: there was a **front line** of three or more horns—usually cornet or trumpet, trombone, and clarinet; there was also a rhythm section of drums, tuba or string bass, and banjo, guitar, or piano to provide chords. The music centered on three song forms: rags, marches, and the blues. New Orleans jazz also emphasized **collective improvisation,** a practice derived from African music, in which several musicians would simultaneously improvise. Loose rules emerged: the cornet or trumpet played the melody, the clarinet embellished it in the upper register, the trombone played a lower register countermelody, and the rhythm section kept time. This arrangement mirrored the organizational structure of wind band music. Although collectively improvised, New Orleans jazz was not a free-for-all—it had a set of rules. The style remains vital for fans worldwide who support jazz societies, festivals, and jubilees. In the 1990s, trumpeters Wynton Marsalis and Nicholas Payton paid respect to the complexity and vitality of the music.

The first jazz recordings were made in New York in 1917 by a group of white New Orleans jazz musicians called the Original Dixieland Jazz Band (ODJB). Led by Nick LaRocca, the group developed its sound in New Orleans under the influence of leading African American innovators. As one musician recalled, "The LaRocca boys of the Dixieland Jazz Band used to hang around and got a lot of ideas from King Oliver's band."[9] The ODJB repertoire was an eclectic mix of jazz, blues, rag, pop, and novelty songs. They were good musicians, but probably not major jazz innovators, and they copyrighted many tunes, in their own names, that were in wide circulation among other bands in New Orleans (see the Multicultural Note).

CD LISTENING EXERCISE

CD 1/12

Listen to "Potato Head Blues," recorded by Louis Armstrong and His Hot Seven in 1926. What roles do the trumpet, trombone, and clarinet play? How do the parts weave together? Do the different instruments play the same rhythms in harmony? Can you distinguish the sections of the piece that include collective improvisation?

JELLY ROLL MORTON: THE FIRST GREAT JAZZ COMPOSER

Jelly Roll Morton (1890–1941), the first jazz composer, pioneered the use of orchestration and arrangement for jazz band. His compositions were original works containing multiple themes, and many became **jazz standards**—the fundamental repertoire of many jazz musicians. Morton was also an influential

Multicultural Note

Impacts of the ODJB's Cultural Appropriation

The case of the Original Dixieland Jazz Band exemplifies cultural appropriation. The members of the group appropriated music developed by another cultural group, reshaped it, and claimed it as their own. Unfortunately, to the end of his life, bandleader Nick LaRocca was unwilling to admit the seminal contributions of African Americans to the jazz music he popularized.

Although derivative, the songs of the ODJB were influential because of their wide distribution. According to historian James Lincoln Collier, "Young musicians, especially but not exclusively white, studied the new music bar by bar, playing and replaying the records until they had learned by heart the parts for their own instruments." [10]

pianist who combined elements of ragtime, blues, and vaudeville into a highly original jazz style.

Born Ferdinand Joseph LaMothe, Morton grew up in the sophisticated Creole culture of New Orleans. He got his first gig in Storyville, the red light district of New Orleans. According to Louis Armstrong,

> The District never closed. . . . He played in the leading whore house called Lulu White. Jelly Roll with lighter skin than the average piano players, he got the job because they did not want a Black piano player for the job. He claimed he was from an Indian or Spanish race. . . . But no matter how much his diamond sparkled he still had to eat in the kitchen, the same as we Blacks. [11]

Morton was also a hustler, but music always came first. He began touring extensively in 1915, performing as a sideman and fronting his own bands, and wherever he traveled, he was noticed. Morton was a big spender, with an extensive wardrobe and a diamond in his tooth. According to one bandleader, "He couldn't stay in one band too long, because he was too eccentric and too temperamental, and he was a one-man band himself." [12]

In 1926 Morton put a group of fine New Orleans musicians together in Chicago to form the Red Hot Peppers, one of the first studio bands in popular mu-

Pianist Jelly Roll Morton, who styled himself as the "inventor" of jazz, was the first major jazz composer and arranger and influenced the early development of jazz piano styles.

© CORBIS

Internet Listening Exercise

Listen to samples from Jelly Roll Morton's classic Chicago "Red Hot Peppers" sessions, taking note of his use of collective improvisation and compositional structure.

Jelly Roll Morton: *Birth of the Hot*

sic history. He wrote and recorded sixteen carefully arranged compositions with the group, many of which are considered some of the finest New Orleans–style jazz on record. He moved on to New York in 1930, where he found adjusting to the new, big band style of swing difficult. Morton ended up in Washington, D.C., where he sat for a series of landmark musical interviews for the Library of Congress, recorded by ethnomusicologist Alan Lomax. In these sessions, Morton recounted in words and music his version of the origins of jazz. Although he did not "invent" jazz, as he claimed, Morton was probably the first to think about and articulate a theory of the new music, including the influences of Latin music on jazz, which he called "the Spanish tinge." As he put it, "If you can't manage to put tinges of Spanish in your tunes, you will never be able to get the right seasoning, I call it, for jazz."[13]

LOUIS ARMSTRONG: THE FIRST GREAT SOLOIST

According to Duke Ellington, **Louis Armstrong** (1901–1971) "was the epitome of jazz and always will be."[14] His playing, singing, and outlook on life and art shaped the direction of jazz as a unique expression of American culture. The New Orleans native first performed as part of a vocal group singing popular songs on the street; he soon learned to play the cornet as well. At age eleven, Armstrong went to jail for shooting off a gun in the air. While in a reform school called the Colored Waif's Home, he developed important performance skills as leader of the school band. After his release, Armstrong developed a name for himself among the city's musicians, including cornetists Bunk Johnson and Joe "King" Oliver and reedman Sidney Bechet. At age eighteen he took King Oliver's place in Kid Ory's band when Oliver left for Chicago.

In 1922 Armstrong joined King Oliver's Creole Jazz Band in Chicago. The members of the band at the time were all accomplished New Orleans musicians; he played second cornet, fashioning harmonies to King Oliver's lines. Armstrong's chance to display his virtuosity came in **cutting contests,** competitions in which rival musicians challenge one another's prowess. Armstrong moved on to New York in 1924 to play in Fletcher Henderson's Orchestra, where his soloing and rhythmic conception had a major impact on the band and the entire New York jazz scene. According to Duke Ellington, "So when Smack's [Henderson's] band hit town and Louis was with them, the guys had never heard anything just like it. There weren't the words coined for describing that kick."[15] During his time in New York, Armstrong also made recordings with blues singers, including one that produced Bessie Smith's classic version of "St. Louis Blues."

Armstrong moved back to Chicago in 1925 and formed two recording groups —the Hot Five and the Hot Seven. With Armstrong at the peak of his creative powers, their recordings became jazz classics. These recordings redefined jazz language by shifting the focus of the music to solo rather than collective improvisation. Armstrong's playing also expanded jazz rhythms and the range of the trumpet, and his singing introduced a new jazz vocal style.

By the early 1930s, Armstrong was a national star. He toured Europe and the United States with his own band as well as with the influential all-black show, *Hot Chocolates*. He also appeared in dozens of movies, including *Pennies from Heaven* (1936), *Cabin in the Sky* (1942), and *High Society* (1956). He was one of the most highly paid African American film actors of his time. Some argued that the roles he played reinforced racial stereotypes; others suggested that he transcended the negative images through his musical genius.

In 1947 Armstrong formed a small group called the Louis Armstrong All Stars, featuring such musicians as clarinetist Barney Bigard and trombonist Jack Teagarden. The group became perennially popular, touring extensively in Africa, Asia, Europe, and South America for the next two decades. He even scored a hit with his version of "Hello Dolly" in 1964, knocking the Beatles off the top of the charts. Although he had long ceased to be an innovator, Armstrong still retained the ability to stand at the forefront of American popular music.

CD LISTENING EXERCISE

CD 1/12

Listen to Armstrong's recording of "Potato Head Blues" again. Notice how the record begins with collective improvisation. What happens next? Which instruments perform individual solos? Describe Armstrong's syncopated solo over the stop-time rhythmic background. Recording technology of the time made the recording of drums extremely difficult. Armstrong's rhythmic intensity on this famous solo demonstrates his ability to internalize what the drums may have sounded like.

Courtesy of the Louis Armstrong House & Archives, Queens College

Trumpeter/vocalist Louis Armstrong, an icon of twentieth-century American popular music, here plays with neighborhood kids on the steps of his home in Queens, New York.

Louis Armstrong's Contributions

Instrumental Technique

His technical ability on the trumpet was unsurpassed; he played with better range, power, tone, and agility than any prior jazz trumpeter had.

Improvisation

He was the first great soloist in jazz history, making the improvised solo the centerpiece of jazz. Although trained in the New Orleans jazz tradition of collective improvisation, he established a new solo improvisational approach emulated by most jazz musicians. His solos were well structured and superbly paced, and he broke away from melodic paraphrasing to base his improvisations on chord structures.

Rhythm

He was one of the first jazz musicians to develop a swing approach to rhythm that abandoned the stiffness of ragtime, and he demonstrated ingenious phrasing and use of syncopation.

Singing

His vocal style reshaped American popular singing and influenced many singers, including Bing Crosby, Billie Holiday, and Ella Fitzgerald. He also popularized scat singing.

CHICAGO AND THE JAZZ AGE

Many New Orleans musicians migrated to Chicago in the 1920s, reflecting a general pattern of African American migration from the South, and by the late 1920s and early 1930s Chicago became a major center for jazz. According to one musician, "There were many of the New Orleans group in Chicago then—King Oliver, Freddie Keppard, Sidney Bechet, Preston Jackson, Jimmie Noone, Manuel Perez, et cetera—twenty or thirty of them." [16] The city's black population grew fivefold from 1910 to 1930, and it became a new center of African American cultural life. Further, a new generation of innovators such as pianist Earl Hines and saxophonist Coleman Hawkins began to adapt Louis Armstrong's trumpet style to other instruments. Finally, Prohibition (1919–1933), which made the production, sales, and consumption of alcohol illegal, also affected the jazz in the city. Illegal clubs called speakeasies, which sold alcohol, often provided work for jazz artists.

Although jazz initially grew out of African American cultural innovation, many young white players were listening carefully to the New Orleans sound and using it to develop their own musical ideas. Swing stars Benny Goodman, Glenn Miller, Jimmy and Tommy Dorsey, and Gene Krupa all got their start as part of a group of young white Chicago musicians called the Austin High School

Gang. Other early white jazz innovators included cornetist Bix Beiderbecke, saxophonist Frankie Trumbauer, and trombonist Jack Teagarden.

One of the most influential trumpeters of the 1920s, **Bix Beiderbecke** (1903–1931) was one of the first great white jazz innovators. The Iowa-born Beiderbecke moved to Chicago, where he was influenced by Armstrong and other New Orleans–style musicians. According to composer Hoagy Carmichael, "Bix's breaks were not as wild as Armstrong's . . . and he selected each note with musical care. He showed me that jazz could be musical and beautiful as well as hot." [17] Beiderbecke often strung together unusual note choices with modern harmonies, creating a sound still admired by many. Unlike many other early jazz cornetists, he did not bend notes and he rarely altered his tone with growls or effects. Some called him the first "cool" jazz player for his lyricism, clarity, and purity of sound.

Internet Listening Exercise

Listen for the artist's smooth, lyrical cornet style in the following sample.

Bix Beiderbecke: "Singin' the Blues"

NEW YORK AND THE EVOLUTION OF JAZZ PIANO STYLES

New York also served as a scene of major jazz innovation. Early jazz could already be heard throughout the city by the end of World War I, and by the mid-1930s the city had become the center of the jazz world. In addition, New York witnessed the Harlem Renaissance of the 1920s, a flowering of African American cultural and intellectual life.

The piano was central to jazz developments in New York, according to Duke Ellington:

> On the East Coast . . . more of the musicians there had had the benefit of formal schooling and even conservatory training. This was in contrast with the experience of most of the early New Orleans musicians, who played by ear. They tended to emphasize the instruments of the brass band, whereas on the East Coast the string instruments, and particularly pianos, had a more significant place. [18]

Stride piano, a style played in Harlem in the late 1920s and early 1930s, served as a bridge between ragtime and jazz. **James P. Johnson** (1894–1955) was the father of stride piano. Like Jelly Roll Morton, Johnson embodied the transition from ragtime to jazz, and his famous 1914 piece, "Carolina Shout," influenced many young artists such as Fats Waller and Duke Ellington. In the stride style, the pianist used fingers of the left hand to play a bass note on the first and third of every four beats and a basic chord on the second and fourth beats. The motion resembled the stride of a person walking. The right hand then played melodies. Stride pianists often took part in cutting contests in New York, as Duke Ellington recalled:

> Jazz was and is a highly competitive form of music. And many of the ideas that transformed it were first heard in what were called "cutting contests" or "jam sessions," where the musicians tried to learn from and outdo one another. [19]

**Internet
Listening Exercise**

Contrast the styles of these influential pianists, ranging from the
classic stride of James P. Johnson
to the flowery complexity of Art
Tatum.

James P. Johnson: "Carolina Shout"

Fats Waller: "Ain't Misbehavin'"

Earl Fatha Hines: "Rosetta"

Art Tatum: "Willow Weep for Me"

Pianist/vocalist **Fats Waller** (1904–1943) was one of the most popular jazz musicians of the 1920s and 1930s, as well as the composer of songs such as "Ain't Misbehavin'" and "Honeysuckle Rose." His prolific influential output produced more than 600 releases over a twenty-year period, and he was prominent in radio, film, and musical theater. Waller was both a master of stride and a gifted entertainer with a tremendous sense of fun who performed in a witty half-sung, half-spoken vocal style. The playing of Art Tatum, Count Basie, and Dave Brubeck reflects Waller's influence.

Earl Hines (1903–1983) was one of the most influential jazz pianists of the swing era and beyond. First known through his work with Louis Armstrong on the Hot Five and Hot Seven recordings, he went on to make well-regarded recordings with his own influential big band. Hines's playing was often described as "hornlike" or "trumpet-style," for it was punchy and loud in order to be heard in the days before amplification.

Art Tatum (1910–1956), who was blind, was one of the most technically gifted of jazz pianists, with a highly ornamented style. According to Fats Waller, "He had too much technique. When that man turns on the powerhouse, don't no one play him down. He sounds like a brass band."[20] Tatum employed dense chord structures as well as challenging harmonic and rhythmic variations mixed with flowery runs. Tatum easily blended African American and European classical traditions. He also developed an influential approach to jazz playing called **chord substitution**, which involves the adding and changing of chords in the performance of standard pop tunes.

An influential post-stride piano style called **boogie woogie** also flourished in the 1930s and 1940s. Boogie woogie originated in the honky-tonks of east Texas and southern Arkansas. In this style, the left hand plays bass-line patterns based on blues progressions, while the right hand plays rapid high-register chords or syncopated melody lines. The term first came into use in a 1928 tune by pianist Pine Top Smith called "Pine Top's Boogie Woogie." Trombonist/bandleader Tommy Dorsey later adapted the tune, renaming it "Boogie Woogie" to produce a swing hit in the late 1930s. The Andrews Sisters vocal trio also had a hit in 1941 with a tune called "Boogie Woogie Bugle Boy," later reprised in campy fashion by vocalist Bette Midler in the 1970s. Well-known boogie woogie pianists included Meade Lux Lewis, Albert Ammons, Mary Lou Williams, and Jimmy Yancey. Echoes of boogie woogie also appeared in the work of Fats Waller and Count Basie. Boogie woogie straddled the boundaries between blues and jazz. It also later served as a building block of R & B, rock, and country music, as in the R & B of Louis Jordan, the western swing of Bob Wills and the Texas Playboys, and the early rock of Little Richard, Jerry Lee Lewis, Bill Haley, and Elvis Presley.

**Internet
Listening Exercise**

Note the different uses and evolution of boogie woogie in the
following samples.

Pine Top Perkins: "Pine Top's Boogie
Woogie"

Meade Lux Lewis: "Honky Tonk
Train Blues"

Mary Lou Williams: "Roll 'Em"

Little Richard: "Long Tall Sally"

Jerry Lee Lewis: "Whole Lotta
Shakin' Goin' On"

DUKE ELLINGTON: TRUE JAZZ ROYALTY

Edward Kennedy "Duke" Ellington (1899–1974) was one of the greatest American composers of the twentieth century. He wrote over 2,000 compositions in his lifetime and served as composer, pianist, and leader of the longest-lived and most respected ensemble in jazz history. Born in Washington, D.C., Ellington had classical training as a child but was fascinated with ragtime and blues styles. He found success as a bandleader in the 1920s, first in Washington, D.C., then in New York City. Ellington had the ability to recruit fine musicians with unique musical voices. The first of these was trumpeter James "Bubber" Miley, whose plunger mute technique played a major role in developing Ellington's early trademark sound by creating a variety of talking, sliding, and growling sounds.

In 1927 Ellington landed a job at Harlem's Cotton Club, a whites-only establishment where blacks could perform but were denied admission as patrons. Because it was the site of a nationally broadcast radio program, the club provided a superb venue for national exposure. From 1927 to 1930, Ellington secured his place in jazz history by writing and performing some of his most distinctive compositions, including "Mood Indigo," "Rockin' in Rhythm," and "Creole Rhapsody." His band's style during the era, often called **jungle music,** featured a mix of growling muted brass, unusual blends of saxophone and clarinet lines, and driving rhythms. From 1930 to 1940, Ellington toured throughout Europe and the United States. He remained one of the few successful working bands during the Depression, adding "Sophisticated Lady," "In a Sentimental Mood," "It Don't Mean a Thing If It Ain't Got That Swing," and "In a Mellow Tone" to his repertoire.

Ellington began a lifelong collaboration with pianist and composer Billy Strayhorn in 1941. Strayhorn's first composition for Ellington was the hit "Take

Composer Duke Ellington (left) and his co-composer and arranger Billy Strayhorn discussing an arrangement. Ellington was one of the greatest composers of twentieth-century American popular music, and Strayhorn made major contributions to the Ellington repertoire, including the signature tune "Take the 'A' Train."

© Underwood and Underwood/CORBIS

CD LISTENING EXERCISE

CD 1/13

Listen to Duke Ellington's 1940 recording of "Harlem Airshaft." According to trumpeter Wynton Marsalis, Ellington wanted the song to be a pastiche of sounds that could be heard through the ventilation system of a Harlem apartment building. Notice how the first part of the song sounds like a collage of different songs across a radio dial. Once a consistent groove locks in, subtle quotations appear from Glenn Miller's "In the Mood," which was popular at the time. Notice also the use of African American musical elements, including call and response, breaks, shout chorus, diverse tonal textures, and the groove. Consider how Ellington's restless creativity incorporated such diverse sounds into one three-minute song.

the 'A' Train," which became the Ellington band's theme song. Strayhorn was Ellington's co-composer on a great number of pieces, often finishing work that Ellington started. He was also a major composer in his own right, authoring songs such as "Lush Life" and "Chelsea Bridge." For the most part, Strayhorn avoided the limelight, possibly because he was openly gay. Ellington valued Strayhorn as a friend and lifelong collaborator.

In the 1940s Ellington began composing extended works beyond the usual three-minute dance tune format dictated by the length of the 78 rpm records of the time. He broke new ground at Carnegie Hall in 1943 when he premiered his first extended work, *Black, Brown, and Beige*, a three-movement piece depicting African American history. Although critics at that time panned Ellington for trying to enter the world of "serious" art music, the work is now viewed as one of the most important extended compositions in jazz history. Ellington toured long after the swing era had ended, often financing the band with his own money, and he continued to compose, working on extended pieces and adding global influences to his compositions until the end of his life.

Duke Ellington's Contributions

Commitment

He led the most stable band in jazz history for 50 years, with many musicians working with him for 20 or 30 years. He also wrote over 2,000 compositions and numerous arrangements and rearrangements.

Variety

His repertoire covered a range of jazz styles, including big band jazz, small groups, solo piano, concertos for individual players, sacred concerts, romantic ballads, and the first extended jazz compositions.

Tone Colors and "Voicings Across" the Band

He made extensive use of brass mutes to create an array of moods, he integrated sounds from his environment such as trains and urban life, and he employed wordless vocals, a style of vocalization using the voice as a hornlike instrument. He was also one of the first jazz composers to "voice across" sections of the big band—writing passages that blended instruments from different sections.

Focus on Individual Musicians

He composed for the individual musical personalities, unique skills, and instrumental timbres of his virtuoso players.

THE SWING ERA

The Swing Era of the 1930s and 1940s represented the zenith of jazz popularity in America. As historian Ted Gioia puts it,

> For over a decade, swing music would remain the paradigm for popular music in America. If jazz ever enjoyed a golden age this would be it. And through especially fortuitous circumstances, this was equally the golden age of the American popular song. . . . Never again would popular music be so jazzy, or jazz music so popular.[21]

Swing bands barnstormed the country, performing in any venue with a dance floor. Radio broadcasting, the recording industry, the movies, and magazines all cashed in on the national phenomenon. The trend actually started in the late 1920s as jazz moved away from the small-group styles of New Orleans and Chicago toward larger ensembles known as big bands or swing bands. Shifting trends in popular music and dance contributed to the new direction, and as bands began to play in large dance halls and ballrooms, they had to grow bigger to produce a bigger sound. Duke Ellington explained,

> In those days, before electrical amplification, big bands were essential in big ballrooms, and singers had to use megaphones. Ballrooms were very important in the jazz story, and so was the inspiration we derived from the people who danced in them.[22]

The Big Band Sound Arrives

The music of New York–based, African American band leader **James Reese Europe** (1881–1919) was an important precursor to the big band. Prior to World War I, he led the Society Orchestra, a large ensemble that played in a heavily syncopated ragtime style and accompanied the dance team of Vernon and Irene Castle, who introduced America to the tango in 1914. During World War I, Europe formed a military band to accompany a successful African American regiment, known as the Hellfighters, to France. The band popularized African American music with overseas and American audiences during and after the war. Impressed by the reception for his music in France, Europe commented, on his return to the United States,

> I have come back from France more convinced than ever that Negroes should write Negro music. We won fame by playing music that was ours and not a pale imitation of others, and if we are to develop in America we must develop along our own lines.[23]

Library of Congress, John Hay Library, Brown University

"Good Night Angeline," 1919 sheet music for bandleader James Reese Europe. His syncopated wind band music was a vital link in the transition from ragtime to large-ensemble jazz.

Fletcher Henderson (1897–1952) also greatly influenced the development of the big band sound. He pioneered a revolutionary approach to arranging for large jazz ensemble that used the brass, reed, and rhythm sections in call and response fashion to craft the characteristic sound of big band swing. His band's new arrangements differed greatly from the New Orleans style of polyphonic, collective improvisation. The power of the brass section pitted against the reed section, followed by the entire band playing together in a "shout chorus," had never been heard before. Duke Ellington described the Henderson band's impact:

> Henderson's, more than any other, was the band that introduced what became known as the Swing Era. Fletcher was a big inspiration to me. His was the band I always wanted mine to sound like when I got ready to have a big band. Obviously a lot of other musicians wanted the same thing, and when Benny Goodman was ready for a big band, he sent for Fletcher Henderson to do his arrangements.[24]

Henderson's band emerged at the same time that the saxophone was replacing the clarinet as the dominant reed instrument in jazz. Featured tenor saxophonist Coleman Hawkins, sometimes referred to as the father of the jazz tenor saxophone, influenced many other players with his melodic approach and warm, deep tone while in the band. In 1924 Henderson secured his band's place in jazz history by hiring Louis Armstrong, whose original use of syncopation and endless flow of "hot" melodic ideas influenced Hawkins, Henderson's arranger Don Redman, and most other jazz musicians in New York.

By the early 1930s, the **big band** format was set: three or four trumpets, two to four trombones, and three to five saxophones with most saxophone players doubling on clarinet. The rhythm section also took the shape that remained consistent in American popular music for the next seventy-five years: piano as the central harmonic instrument, string bass (replacing the tuba), and guitar (replacing the banjo). The drum set developed into a complete one-person percussion section, including bass drum, snare drum, tom toms, high hat, and cymbals. Big band instrumentation also encouraged a new compositional style, in which written arrangements featured the ensemble more than they did individual improvisers. Syncopated, high-energy dance music played by a large ensemble also required a unified concept of phrasing with smoother articulation and rhythmic interpretation.

Bandleader Fletcher Henderson (center, back row) with his group in New York in 1924, including saxophonist Coleman Hawkins (second from left), Louis Armstrong (third from left), and Don Redman (extreme right).

Comparing the Instrumentation of Two Jazz Ensemble Styles

Traditional New Orleans Jazz Ensemble

Front Line
Trumpet/Cornet
Clarinet
Trombone

Rhythm Section
Piano
Tuba/Bass
Simple Drum Kit
Banjo/Guitar

Big Band Swing Ensemble

Trumpets
3–5 (4 became standard)
Reeds
3–5 (including alto, tenor, and baritone sax, frequent doubling on clarinet, sometimes flutes)
Trombones
2–5 (tenor trombones, bass trombone later)
Rhythm Section
Piano
Bass
Drums
Guitar

The Popularization of Swing

The popularity of the big band sound opened the doors for numerous variations. Although great black swing band leaders such as Fletcher Henderson, Chick Webb, and Jimmie Lunceford led the way, white bands were most popular. The Paul Whiteman Orchestra was the most popular white jazz ensemble of the late 1920s, playing a jazzy style of classically infused dance music. The group featured a six-piece string section and vocal group in addition to a big band horn lineup and rhythm section. **Paul Whiteman** (1890–1967) was an astute entrepreneur, dubbed the "King of Jazz," who purveyed a "sweet" style that was popular with the general public. The band had a string of hits, including singer Bing Crosby's first big seller, "After You've Gone." Segregation prevented Whiteman from hiring black musicians, but he recruited many of the best white jazz musicians of the day, including cornetist Bix Beiderbecke and saxophonist Frank Trumbauer. He also commissioned composers Ferde Grofé as well as George Gershwin, who wrote his classic *Rhapsody in Blue* for the Whiteman band.

The most popular performer of the swing era—and the person most often credited with bringing swing into the public eye—was clarinetist/bandleader **Benny Goodman** (1909–1986), sometimes known as the "King of Swing." An excellent jazz and classical clarinetist, Goodman was a perfectionist as a performer and bandleader. He also broke the "color barrier" to form the first nationally recognized band integrating white and black musicians. Some jazz historians, however, claim that Goodman's musical contributions to jazz mattered less than his contributions to popularizing the music, and an important key to his success was hiring Fletcher Henderson as one of his principal arrangers. Often, a composition included just the melody and chords and sometimes lyrics. As an **arranger,** Henderson would write individual parts for the instruments transforming often simple compositions into dramatic, swinging, ensemble statements. As Goodman explained, "Without Fletcher I probably would have had a pretty good band, but it would have been something quite different from what it eventually turned out to be. His ideas were far ahead of anybody else's at the time."[25]

Goodman was born in Chicago to Eastern European Jewish immigrant parents, who saw music as a way out of the urban ghetto for their son. Although he studied classical clarinet, he was drawn to jazz, like his other musically inclined friends in the Austin High Gang. By the beginning of the Depression, Goodman had established his career, working as a studio musician in New York. Paying close attention to the hotter-sounding African American bands of Fletcher Henderson, Duke Ellington, and Chick Webb, he soon formed his own big band with the help of producer John Hammond.

Historians often cite 1935 as the beginning of the swing era. Certainly, Goodman's national tour that summer put *swing* into the national vocabulary. His high-energy style, appropriated from the black bands of the period, found an enthusiastic mass audience. A major reason for his success stemmed from his talented musicians—black and white—including drummer Gene Krupa, trumpeter Harry James, pianist Teddy Wilson, vibraphonist Lionel Hampton, and the

Internet Listening Exercise

Contrast the differing styles of these three large early jazz ensembles.

James Reese Europe: "Memphis Blues"

Fletcher Henderson: "Wrapping It Up (The Lindy Glide)"

Paul Whiteman: "There Ain't No Sweet Man (Worth the Salt of My Tears)" first virtuoso of the electric guitar, Charlie Christian. Goodman reached his zenith in a legendary 1938 performance at Carnegie Hall. There Goodman, who had become the most popular bandleader in the country, broke two final barriers to the recognition of jazz: presenting a racially integrated band and performing at a nationally recognized center of fine arts.

From 1939 to 1942, trombonist **Glenn Miller** (1904–1944) led the most popular big band of the swing era. He developed the **sweet band** style: a smooth musical formula that featured catchy melodies and riffs with easily identifiable hooks and that downplayed improvisation in favor of a smooth, well-blended saxophone section that meshed with a warm brass sound. For many listeners, the sweet band sound was a more accessible style. Miller exemplified this style, as did trumpeter/bandleader Harry James and trombonist/bandleader Tommy Dorsey. Miller scored hits with "Pennsylvania 6-5000," "Tuxedo Junction," "String of Pearls," and one of the most popular tunes of the swing era, "In the Mood." Big band swing did not last long at the top of the charts after World War II, however, and by the 1950s, R & B and rock had moved to the forefront.

Internet Listening Exercise

Compare the hotter sound of Goodman's band with the sweeter styles of the other groups.

Benny Goodman: "Sing Sing Sing"

Tommy Dorsey: "Marie"

Glenn Miller: "In the Mood"

Harry James: "I've Heard That Song Before"

Kansas City Swing

While much jazz innovation took place in the New Orleans–Chicago–New York trajectory, important developments took place in other parts of the country as well. *Territory bands,* for example, were mostly black swing bands of the Midwest and West that enjoyed local prestige but received little national recognition. Kansas City was a beacon for such bands and became its own center of jazz innovation. A key to the Kansas City jazz style was the *riff,* a short melodic phrase stated in forceful terms, usually contained in the first few bars of a piece. Riff-based jazz tunes, often called **head arrangements,** could be played by a large ensemble without much sheet music, and they served as the musical structure for improvisation. The **jam session** was another signature element of

Multicultural Note

But Is It "Jazz"?

Glenn Miller's music is part of the standard repertoire of swing-style dance bands, and almost any function that features big band dance music today includes Miller's tunes. But is it jazz? Some critics have suggested that Miller's smooth sound and lack of focus on improvisation eliminates his music from the jazz repertoire. Many older listeners, however, argue that Miller's music is the only jazz they listen to—that it was the soundtrack of their youth. Who decides whether something should or should not be called jazz?

Kansas City jazz. When well-known musicians came through town, the word went out, and local musicians gathered after hours in clubs to match skills with the visiting big-name players. Later, Kansas City–bred musicians such as saxophonists Charlie Parker and Lester Young carried the spirit of the Kansas City jam session to New York, where it became a key element of bebop musical culture in the 1940s (see Chapter 12).

CD LISTENING EXERCISE

CD 1/14

Listen to Count Basie's 1938 recording of "Jumpin' at the Woodside." How are riffs used? What is the simple four-note riff that the composition is based on? The 32-bar form of the tune has an AABA structure: an eight-bar phrase repeated twice, followed by eight bars of new material (the bridge), ending with a reprise of the first eight bars. Listen to Basie's spare style of piano playing. How does he punctuate the rhythm? Listen to Lester Young's tenor playing. Notice the melodic lines. How does the rhythm section drive the band?

William "Count" Basie (1904–1984) was the musician most closely associated with the riff-based improvisational style of Kansas City jazz, and his group was one of the hardest-swinging bands of the era. Basie and bassist Walter Page anchored the band's rhythm section, together with guitarist Freddie Green and drummer Jo Jones. As a pianist, Basie displayed a unique touch, an impeccable sense of timing, and a superb choice of notes. The Basie rhythm section stood out in big band jazz for its sense of tempo and ability to swing consistently without a heavy-handed feeling. Basie also built reed and brass sections that rivaled those of Duke Ellington. Basie's most important early commercial success came in the "Spirituals to Swing" concert organized by Columbia Records producer John Hammond at Carnegie Hall in 1938. The concert featured a revue of the history of African American music, including blues shouters from Kansas City, boogie woogie pianists from Chicago, gospel singers from the South, country blues performers, stride pianists, New Orleans jazz players, and the Basie band in multiple configurations. Basie enjoyed a long career of touring and recording. Historian Gary Giddins describes Basie's band from the 1950s as "the most irreproachable virtuoso ensemble ever to work the dance band idiom."[26]

Count Basie's Contributions

Rhythm Section

He set a new standard for the rhythm section in the swing style. His rhythm section could convey a relaxed feel, swinging without being heavy handed. Basie's rhythm section became the model for the rhythm sections of Louis Jordan and other great early R & B groups of the 1940s and 1950s.

Piano Style

His distinctive minimalist piano style made superb use of space, and his choice of notes was flawless.

Use of Riffs

The band pioneered the use of riffs in jazz. Originally a Kansas City jazz style, the practice later became common in bebop and R & B.

Influential Big Band Arrangements

With arrangers such as Neal Hefti, Quincy Jones, Frank Foster, and Sammy Nestico, his band codified the big band style. Many Basie arrangements were published and widely distributed for high school, college, and professional big band ensembles.

Pianist/arranger **Mary Lou Williams** (1910–1981), long associated with the Kansas City jazz scene, was one of America's best known and most revered jazzwomen. As a sought-after pianist in Kansas City, she was often billed as "The Lady Who Swings the Band." Williams influenced the development of the Kansas City big band sound as an arranger and player, and by the late 1930s she was arranging for Duke Ellington, Louis Armstrong, Tommy Dorsey, and Benny Goodman. When she moved to New York in the 1940s, she easily made the transition to the new bebop style. She later led several all-female bands, wrote a variety of compositions for large and small ensembles, and founded the first female-owned recording company. In describing her experience as a woman in jazz before feminism, Williams said simply, "You've got to play, that's all."[27]

Lester Young's (1909–1959) elegant, floating tenor saxophone style and long, improvised melodic lines showed the way for an entire generation of tenor saxophonists. The Mississippi-born Young was Count Basie's best-known soloist of the 1930s and 1940s. He also found fame for his small-group work and musical association with vocalist Billie Holiday. Young's early influences included white saxophonist Frankie Trumbauer, known for his light sound and melodic style. When Young moved to Kansas City to join Count Basie's band in 1934, he established his sound as a new approach to jazz improvisation. His playing foreshadowed the coming of bebop, and later, cool jazz. As jazz historian Leonard Feather puts it, "Young symbolized the gradual evolution from hot jazz to 'cool' jazz."[28] By the mid-1940s, Young placed second only to Charlie Parker as the most influential saxophonist in jazz.

CD LISTENING EXERCISE

CD 1/14

Listen again to Count Basie's 1938 recording of "Jumpin' at the Woodside," focusing on Lester Young's solo. How does the solo begin? Notice how his melodic lines flow across choruses and bar lines. Can you feel the laid-back quality of Young's approach?

Multicultural Swing

Swing-era groups diversified in terms of gender and ethnicity to a degree not seen before in American popular music. Although the role of women in early swing bands was limited to vocalist, often called the "girl singer" or sometimes the "chirper," "torcher," "warbler," or "canary," according to historian Linda Dahl a more significant role for women performers evolved with the onset of World War II.[29] When the war broke out, many male musicians were drafted, and numerous female bands formed to fill the growing demand for swing. Several of these bands were integrated well before many all-male bands broke the

Ina Ray Hutton and Her Melodears were one of the first all-female bands in jazz. During World War II, several all-women bands made it into the national spotlight for the first time.

color barrier. One of the most famous of the "all-girl" bands was Ina Ray Hutton and the Melodears, a fifteen-piece band that traveled the nation, often featuring the attractive Hutton twirling a baton and tap dancing, with constant costume changes. Hutton was also a skilled entrepreneur who gained complete financial control of her band. Another well-known female swing band was the International Sweethearts of Rhythm. The sixteen-piece band, formed at a school for poor and orphaned black children in Mississippi, included African American, Latina, American Indian, Chinese American, and white members. Other all-female bands of the 1940s included Phil Spitalny's Hours of Charm, the Darlings of Rhythm, and the Sharon Rogers All-Girl Band.

Filipino and Japanese immigrant communities on the West Coast also liked swing. Nisei, or second generation Japanese American, youths formed many dance bands and continued to play even while incarcerated in internment camps. The swing era also saw the growth of connections between jazz and Latin music as musicians from Puerto Rico, Cuba, and Mexico became increasingly active. Particularly prominent were Puerto Rican–born valve trombonist Juan Tizol, who played with Duke Ellington, and Cuban trumpeter Mario Bauzá, who teamed up with Cuban percussionist Machito (Frank Grillo) in the 1940s to form Machito and the Afro-Cubans, the first Latin jazz big band. In turn, swing influenced Chicano music, as in the development of the *orquesta tejana* in Texas and the *pachuco* youth culture in Southern California.

THE DEVELOPMENT OF VOCAL JAZZ TRADITIONS

Internet Listening Exercise

Listen to Billie Holiday's poignant signature ballad on the subject of southern lynchings.

Billie Holiday: "Strange Fruit"

As we have seen, Louis Armstrong played a key role in vocal jazz. Many jazz historians consider Billie Holiday and Ella Fitzgerald—together with Armstrong—the most important figures in the initial development of vocal jazz traditions. The styles and emotions expressed by Holiday and Fitzgerald could not have been more different: As jazz historian Gary Giddins notes, "Ella Fitzgerald taught us something vital about joy. . . . Billie Holiday taught us something vital about pain." [30]

Billie Holiday's (1915–1959) life was tragic and complex. Many have called her singing style "pure emotion." Although her vocal range was modest and her voice was not powerful, Holiday was one of the most expressive singers in jazz. Louis Armstrong's capacity to sing behind the beat, as well as his use of rhythmic stress to add meaning to lyrics, profoundly influenced her vocal approach. Classic blues vocalists Bessie Smith and Ethel Waters also inspired her.

Holiday made a string of recordings in the 1930s and 1940s with some of the finest jazz musicians of the era, including the artist who was to become Holiday's musical soul mate, tenor saxophonist Lester Young. Holiday and Young shared a unique chemistry, and sessions they recorded together produced some of Holiday's finest moments in tunes such as "All of Me," "Mean to Me," and "He's Funny That Way." Young also gave Holiday her lifelong nickname, "Lady Day," and Holiday called Young "Pres." In 1939 Holiday recorded a controversial tune entitled "Strange Fruit," the wrenching story of a lynching, which became part of her persona for the rest of her career. The artist's impassioned performance of the tragic song reflected the pain of her personal problems with alcohol and drugs, which mounted when she became addicted to heroin and was imprisoned. When released, she found that she could no longer perform in New York City nightclubs because a city law prevented felons from obtaining a "cabaret card." Holiday still managed to perform and record, and in 1952 she made a recording comeback. Although her voice was scarred by years of abuse, some felt that her later recordings displayed a level of nuance and emotion that few singers ever achieve.

Ella Fitzgerald (1918–1996) was one of the greatest American singers of the twentieth century. Although her pure tone, three-octave range, superb pitch, and flawless phrasing alone would have established her as a notable figure, her talents as a jazz singer extended beyond technical excellence, and her interpretations of many of the classics of American popular song set the standard for how the pieces would be remembered. Fitzgerald was also the greatest scat singer in jazz history, able to imitate vocally almost any instrument and any style of jazz. The vocalist got her start, while still a teen in New York, in a band led by drummer Chick Webb, one of the major innovators of swing-era drumming. Fitzgerald had her first hit in 1938 with a children's novelty song called "A-Tisket, A-Tasket." From the 1940s through the early 1950s, she recorded a variety of material and collaborated with artists ranging

Courtesy Morgan Collection

Vocalist Ella Fitzgerald is featured in the foreground of this World War II–era sheet music for "Cow Cow Boogie," a song she performed in the film *Ride 'em Cow-boy*. Legendary drummer/bandleader Chick Webb sits in the upper right-hand corner.

CD LISTENING EXERCISE

CD 1/15

Listen to "How High the Moon," a signature tune recorded by Fitzgerald in 1947. The first verse is sung at a medium-swing tempo and then abruptly becomes faster. Musicians call this "double time." At this point Fitzgerald begins to swing hard, and then she begins scat singing. At one point she paraphrases a famous Charlie Parker melody (entitled "Ornithology") set to the same chords as "How High the Moon." Made only two years after the birth of bebop, this recording clearly demonstrates Fitzgerald's fluency in the bebop style. What type of instrument do you think she may be trying to imitate in her scat solo?

from trumpeter/vocalist Louis Armstrong to R & B legend Louis Jordan.

In the mid-1950s, Fitzgerald recorded the "Ella Fitzgerald Songbook Series." The albums explored the work of America's greatest popular song composers and contain songs now considered *jazz standards*—pieces that every jazz player is expected to know. The "Songbook" albums numbered among the earliest **concept albums**—recorded works with a unifying artistic theme—and the artist's interpretations of the songs cemented their status as jazz standards.

Chapter Summary

- Jazz is recognized throughout the world as one of America's most significant musical and cultural contributions. Only during the swing era of the 1930s and 1940s, however, was jazz the most popular music in America.

- A definition of jazz usually includes improvisation, swing rhythm, and the historical lineage of jazz musicians.

- Jazz was born in New Orleans at the turn of the twentieth century. The blues, ragtime, wind bands, and Latin music all contributed to its creation, with the unique cultural milieu of New Orleans also playing a role. African American culture was another dominant force in the creation of the style.

- Many New Orleans jazz musicians found their way to Chicago, which became a jazz center in the 1920s. African American innovators such as King Oliver, Louis Armstrong, and Jelly Roll Morton influenced a new generation of white musicians, including Bix Beiderbecke and Benny Goodman.

- In 1917 the Original Dixieland Jazz Band, a white group, made the first jazz recording. The most important figures in the development of early jazz traditions were trumpeter/vocalist Louis Armstrong and pianist/composer Jelly Roll Morton. Throughout his sixty-year career, Armstrong did more to influence the development of jazz than any other artist did. Morton was the first great jazz composer.

- James P. Johnson (the father of stride), Fats Waller, Earl "Fatha" Hines, and Art Tatum pioneered jazz piano styles in New York in the 1920s and 1930s.

- The swing era lasted from the 1930s through the 1940s. Duke Ellington was probably the most important composer in jazz history. Other important contributors to the swing era include bandleader Fletcher Henderson, clarinetist/bandleader Benny Goodman, bandleader Glenn Miller, and pianist/bandleader Count Basie.

- Kansas City served as an important center of jazz innovation for a time, producing such great musicians as Count Basie, Lester Young, and Charlie Parker. Kansas City's contributions to jazz style included jam sessions and the use of riffs.

- The popularity of jazz in the swing era crossed ethnic, racial, and gender barriers. The appearance of all-female bands, Asian swing bands, swing-influenced hybrids in Chicano communities, and new Latin jazz styles in New York all demonstrated the multicultural appeal of swing.

- The development of jazz vocal traditions was fundamentally shaped by two quite different singers—Billie Holiday and Ella Fitzgerald.

Key Terms

arranger	cutting contest	player piano
big band	front line	ragtime
boogie woogie	head arrangements	second line
chord substitution	jam session	stride piano
collective improvisation	jazz lineage	sweet band
concept albums	jazz standard	vibrato
Congo Square	jungle music	wind band
Creole	Latin tinge	

Study and Discussion Questions

1. What is jazz? What are some of its characteristic features?

2. What historical and musical events shaped the development of the style?

3. Why was Jelly Roll Morton important to early jazz?

4. Why was Louis Armstrong called the father of jazz improvisation? What other important contributions did he make to jazz?

5. How did musical styles change as jazz moved from New Orleans to Chicago and New York?

6. What roles did the following performers play in the evolution of jazz piano: Scott Joplin, James P. Johnson, Fats Waller, and Count Basie?

7. How did traditional New Orleans jazz and big band swing differ?

8. What was boogie woogie, and what later styles did it influence?

9. What were the roles and contributions of the following swing era bandleaders: Fletcher Henderson, Duke Ellington, Count Basie, Benny Goodman, and Glenn Miller?

10. What were the roles and importance of singers Ella Fitzgerald and Billie Holiday?

Notes

1. Conceptualization of the definitions of jazz and the early roots of jazz owes a great deal to the work of jazz historian Mark C. Gridley, found in his textbooks *Jazz Styles: History and Analysis*, 8th ed. (Upper Saddle River, NJ: Prentice-Hall, 2003) and *Concise Guide to Jazz*, 4th ed. (Upper Saddle River, NJ: Prentice-Hall, 2004).

2. Duke Ellington, *Music Is My Mistress* (New York: Da Capo Press, 1973), 419.

3. Alan Lomax, *Mister Jelly Roll: The Fortunes of Jelly Roll Morton, New Orleans Creole and "Inventor of Jazz"* (New York: Duell, Sloan, and Pierce, 1950), xv.

4. Ibid., 16.

5. Ellington, *Music Is My Mistress*, 415.

6. Lomax, *Mister Jelly Roll*, 12.

7. "Gumbo," in *Jazz*, DVD, directed by Ken Burns (Washington, DC: Florentine Films, WETA, 2000).

8. Lomax, *Mister Jelly Roll*, 60.

9. Nat Shapiro and Nat Hentoff, eds., *Hear Me Talkin' to Ya: The Story of Jazz as Told by the Men Who Made It* (New York: Dover, 1955), 124.

10. James Lincoln Collier, *The Making of Jazz: A Comprehensive History* (Boston: Houghton Mifflin Co., 1978), 87.

11. Louis Armstrong, *Louis Armstrong, in His Own Words: Selected Writings* (New York: Oxford University Press, 1999), 67.

12. Shapiro and Hentoff, *Hear Me Talkin' to Ya*, 95.

13. Lomax, *Mister Jelly Roll*, 62.

14. Ellington, *Music Is My Mistress*, 236.

15. Ibid., 49.

16. Shapiro and Hentoff, *Hear Me Talkin' to Ya*, 38.

17. Ibid., 127.

18. Ellington, *Music Is My Mistress*, 416.

19. Ibid., 420.

20. Shapiro and Hentoff, *Hear Me Talkin' to Ya*, 143.

21. Ted Gioia, *The History of Jazz* (New York: Oxford University Press, 1997), 145.

22. Ellington, *Music Is My Mistress*, 419.

23. Gioia, *History of Jazz*, 106.

24. Ellington, *Music Is My Mistress*, 419.

25. Shapiro and Hentoff, *Hear Me Talkin' to Ya*, 157.

26. Gary Giddins, *Visions of Jazz: The First Century* (New York: Oxford University Press, 1998), 183.

27. Linda Dahl, *Stormy Weather: The Music and Lives of a Century of Jazz Women* (New York: Pantheon Books, 1984), 183.

28. Shapiro and Hentoff, *Hear Me Talkin' to Ya,* 194.

29. Dahl, *Stormy Weather,* 72.

30. Giddins, *Visions of Jazz,* 196.

1600 - 1900

1607 First British community in North America, Jamestown, settled

1619 First African slaves brought to America

1620 Pilgrims arrive at Plymouth Rock

1640 *Bay Psalm Book* published, the first American collection of religious music ♪

1682 Philadelphia, largest colonial city, founded

1700s American colonies expand

1728 *The Beggars Opera,* an early ballad opera, performed for the first time ♪

1745 "Yankee Doodle," a broadside ballad that became a revolutionary and popular song, is written ♪

1754–1763 French and Indian War

1776 Declaration of Independence and beginning of Revolutionary War

1778 William Billings writes "Chester," originally a hymn, which also becomes a revolutionary song ♪

1790 First National Copyright Act passes, establishing early protection of intellectual property ♪

1803 Louisiana Purchase annexes vast western lands from France

1808 *Moore's Irish Melodies* published, an influential collection of some of the most popular songs of the century ♪

1812 War with Britain

1820s Birth of the American piano industry ♪

1823 Henry Bishop writes "Home, Sweet Home," one of the most popular parlor songs of the 19th century ♪

1825 First steam locomotive

1831 Nat Turner slave revolt in Virginia

1837 Henry Russell writes "Woodman Spare That Tree," a classic parlor song ♪

1848 End of Mexican War; Southwest annexed by U.S.

1848 Stephen Foster writes "Oh! Susanna," an early hit that would remain popular for over 150 years ♪

1849 California gold rush

1861–1865 Civil War

1863 Emancipation Proclamation

1865–1877 Reconstruction

1877 Thomas Edison invents the first sound recording device ♪

1893 Panic of 1893, a major economic recession

1897 The first player pianos become commercially available, broadening access to music reproduction ♪

1898 Spanish American War

1898 "March King" John Philip Sousa writes "Stars and Stripes Forever," one of his most memorable works ♪

1600   **1700**   **1800**

Chapter 5

From Hymns to Wind Bands

The first popular musical styles in the United States—other than Native American music—were of European origin. Influences of England, Ireland, Scotland, Italy, and other European cultures were gradually hybridized over three centuries with African, Latino, and other sources to form new American traditions. This chapter discusses popular music of the seventeenth, eighteenth, and nineteenth centuries, which ranged from church music to patriotic tunes to parlor songs to brass bands.

CHURCH MUSIC AND PATRIOTIC SONGS

Religious music was probably the earliest form of music that European settlers played in the New World. For example, colonists brought the Thanksgiving song "We Gather Together" from the Netherlands to New Amsterdam—now New York. By the mid-1600s, ministers in Massachusetts had published a collection of religious songs called the *Bay Psalm Book*. According to historian Wilfrid Mellers, "For worship in church the psalms were sung at rather fast tempi and in unison—so that God would have no difficulty in understanding the words."[1] People also sang psalms for entertainment at home, often in multipart harmony, following British musical practices.

William Billings (1746–1800) was America's first professional composer. He pioneered the concept of singing schools, founded some of America's earliest church choirs, and introduced dance rhythms into religious music. Billings's best-known works then included "By the Waters of Babylon" and "When Jesus Wept," both of which are still performed by gospel and reggae artists. The composer's most famous song, "Chester" (1790), was a hymn that later helped mobilize the revolutionary spirit of American colonists against England. During the American Revolution, relatively little new popular music was written, because the Continental Congress banned theatrical activities, declaring the following:

> Frequenting Play Houses and theatrical entertainment has a fatal tendency to divert the minds of people from a due attention to the means necessary for the defense of their country and preservation of their liberties.[2]

Multicultural Note

Popular and Religious Music—Sacred or Secular?

Many links have existed between **secular** (worldly) and **sacred** (religious) styles throughout American popular music history, although religious adherents frequently tried to maintain clear distinctions between religious music and "the devil's music." The crossovers have been numerous: Anglo-European church music influenced early popular and country music; African American church music influenced blues, jazz, and soul; and popular music repeatedly influenced church music. From a religious point of view, why would one want to keep sacred musical traditions distinct from popular music?

This sheet music cover for a parlor song by Charles Henry emphasizes a nostalgic view of home and family typical of this mid-nineteenth-century genre.

After the war ended in 1789, however, development began in earnest as active music publishers sprang up in all major American cities. With the passage of the first National Copyright Act in 1790, hundreds of new songs were published.

ENGLISH, IRISH, SCOTTISH, AND ITALIAN INFLUENCES

British composers wrote many of the most popular songs in America in the late eighteenth century. They often intended for these songs to be used in London's pleasure gardens or in ballad and comic operas. **Pleasure gardens** were private parks featuring arbors, fruit trees, mineral springs, tea gardens, fireworks, and music. As gardens based on the British model arose in North America, composers often wrote love songs filled with rustic images for them. These later became the basis for parlor songs, a style that lasted for almost a century in England and America.

Other influential British styles included broadside ballads and ballad operas. **Broadside ballads** were witty, often ribald, topical verses that used everyday vocabulary. Usually sung to popular folk melodies, they were printed quickly and sold cheaply—"Yankee Doodle" is one famous example. A *ballad* is usually a song that tells a story, and **ballad opera** was a form of musical theater that used spoken English dialogue and songs, in contrast to Italian opera. An early example of the new style, *The Beggar's Opera* (1728), featured a

Library of Congress

Multicultural Note

The Complex Tale of "Yankee Doodle"

Although debate continues over the origins of "Yankee Doodle," one scholar has traced the lyrics to the American colonies in 1745. The song undoubtedly enjoyed wide circulation in the colonies by the 1760s, and it appeared in 1767 in the first American ballad opera, Andrew Barton's *The Disappointment.* "Yankee Doodle" was also popularized by British troops, who sang it to mock colonists. The American revolutionaries soon reclaimed it, however, playing it at the British surrender in Yorktown in 1781.

stage packed with criminals and street life rather than the kings and princes of grand opera. Often written to lampoon society, ballad operas were one precursor of musical comedy.

British social dance also influenced early American popular music. Plantation owners in Virginia preserved the refinements of Old World living by throwing large balls where couples danced the minuet, the gavotte, the jig, and a dance later named the Virginia reel. English, Irish, Scottish, and Welsh ballads, many later collected by Francis Child as the *Child Ballads,* also figured prominently in the popular music of the time. Tunes such as "Barbara Allen" and "Lord Randal" were particularly well known. The latter was called a "riddling song" because it used a question-and-answer dialogue.

Spurred by economic hardship and British political repression, Irish immigrants came to North America in large numbers beginning in the first decades of the seventeenth century. As historian Charles Hamm notes, "The Irish came early and often to America."[3] By the early nineteenth century, hundreds of thousands of Irish had settled in all parts of the United States, bringing with them a rich oral musical tradition. An influential collection called *Moore's Irish Melodies* was first published by 1808, containing well-known pieces such as "'Tis the Last Rose of Summer" and "Believe Me, If All Those Endearing Young Charms." The vernacular nature of Irish music lent it directness and passion, and many of the songs were written in the first person, directly describing rich emotions from a personal point of view.

Scottish folk music also influenced popular music in the United States. Famed Scottish poet Robert Burns collaborated on the production of the *Scots Musical Museum,* a 1787 anthology of Scottish songs similar to *Moore's Irish Melodies.* The anthology included well-known works such as "Auld Lang Syne" and "Comin' Thro' the Rye," which later became popular as a gospel song. "The Blue Bell of Scotland," the most popular Scottish song of all time in America, was published in 1800.

The 1820s saw a growing American interest in Italian opera. Although viewed as art music today, the genre originally appealed to a wide audience. When **opera** initially emerged in Italy in the sixteenth century, it opened new

Internet Listening Exercise

Listen to these samples of early American popular songs performed by artists in a variety of styles.

Quincy Choral Society: "We Gather Together"

Discovery String Band: "Chester"

The Melodians: "Rivers of Babylon"

Pete Seeger: "Yankee Doodle"

Everly Brothers: "Barbara Allen"

Josh White: "Lord Randal"

Internet Listening Exercise

Listen to samples of classic Irish and Scottish songs performed by artists in a variety of styles.

John McCormack: "Believe Me, If All Those Endearing Young Charms"

Robert White: "'Tis the Last Rose of Summer"

Josh White: "Auld Lang Syne"

Stuff Smith/Dizzy Gillespie/Oscar Peterson: "Comin' Thro' the Rye"

possibilities for dramatizing words set to music through introduction of characters and plot. An Italian style of singing called ***bel canto*** ("beautiful singing") accompanied opera; this style emphasized a clear understanding of vocal technique to produce a beautiful sound that was equally effective in the parlor or on the grand operatic stage. In 1825 Rossini's *Il Barbiere di Siviglia* (*The Barber of Seville*) was the first Italian opera produced in New York. Although greeted initially with enthusiasm, the genre was not well accepted until the introduction of English translations. Once an English version of Rossini's *La Cenerentola* (*Cinderella*) was performed in New York in 1832, it made its way to other American cities in adapted versions, and sheet music for this and other popular operas —including Mozart's *Magic Flute* and *Don Giovanni* and Verdi's *Rigoletto*—was widely distributed. Opera's greatest influence ultimately came via this sheet music, and numerous tunes appeared with melodies adapted from operatic themes. This popularity coincided with the emergence of the American piano industry and parlor songs. Ultimately, however, opera became upper-class art music by the late nineteenth century.

Internet Listening Exercise

Listen to the following samples of famous opera arias.

Rossini: "Overture," *The Barber of Seville* (*Il Barbiere di Siviglia*)

Mozart: "Serenade" (*Don Giovanni*)

Verdi: "La Donna e Mobile" (*Rigoletto*)

PARLOR SONGS

Sentimental ballads called **parlor songs,** which spoke of life, home, hearth, and family, prevailed in nineteenth-century American popular music. "Home, Sweet Home" (1823), one of the most popular songs of the time, exemplified the style with its familiar lyrics: "Be it ever so humble, there's no place like home." The sentimental appeal of the style was summarized by historian Denes Agay:

> These audiences it seems loved pathos, and craved tear-drenched sentimentality. They were deeply moved by "Lilly Dale," "Rosalie," "The Prairie Flower" and the entire sorority of young maidens who shared a curiously similar fate; they died young, and were resting in a flowery vale, in a "Fadeless Bow'r" under the mournful branches of the weeping willow or amidst other heart breaking or picturesque scenery.[4]

The demand for parlor songs grew apace with the American piano industry, as the piano increasingly became an essential component of middle-class homes in the nineteenth century. Because recording technology was still only a fantasy, and live performance was the only music available, parlor song sheet music fit the bill for performance on piano in the home.

Henry Russell (1812–1900) was the first major American composer of parlor songs, as well as the country's foremost popular songwriter prior to Stephen Foster. Historian Charles Hamm describes Russell as "an English-born Jew who studied music in Italy, moved to Canada and then the United States, and composed music in an Italian style with nostalgic, Irish-influenced lyrics."[5] Russell's best-known songs were "Woodman Spare That Tree" (1837) and "The Old Arm Chair" (1840). The simple and accessible melodies accompanied lyrics that covered common parlor song themes: home, parents, lost innocence, old friends, and nostalgia for youth.

STEPHEN FOSTER: AMERICA'S FIRST GREAT SONGWRITER

Internet Listening Exercise

Listen to examples of parlor songs performed by Douglas Jimerson on *Robert E. Lee Remembered.*

Henry Russell: "Woodman Spare That Tree"

Anonymous: "Green Grow the Lilacs"

In songs such as "Oh! Susanna," "Old Folks at Home" ("Way Down upon the Swanee River"), and "Camptown Races," composer **Stephen Foster** (1826–1864) developed a uniquely American style of songwriting that established a new tradition in popular song. The most important American popular songwriter of the nineteenth century, he composed over 200 songs in his lifetime, and his work retained sufficient appeal into the twenty-first century to win a 2005 Grammy for a traditional folk album. Minstrelsy, *bel canto,* Irish folk songs, and the musics of other immigrant communities all influenced Foster's songwriting style. Many of the composer's best songs included memorable hooks, and his position as America's greatest songwriter remained unchallenged until the birth of Tin Pan Alley in the late nineteenth century.

Foster's earliest successes came with rhythmic minstrel songs. He wrote twenty such tunes, most with lyrics that are offensive by contemporary standards. As his career progressed, Foster became concerned at the crude, racist nature of the songs. He had his name deleted from some and revised others to portray African Americans in a more sympathetic and humanistic light, which he then called **plantation songs.** He also eventually dropped the use of **Ethiopian dialect**—a stereotyped imitation of African American speech. Foster's first hit, "Oh! Susanna," was published in 1848, and over the next fifteen years he composed prolifically. Famous parlor songs he wrote included "Jeanie with the Light Brown Hair" and "Beautiful Dreamer." A lasting quality of Foster's music was his ability to humanize the characters in his songs, as African American abolitionist Frederick Douglas commented:

Stephen Foster, the most popular U.S. songwriter of the nineteenth century, was also the first American composer to make a living as a composer of popular song.

> They are heart songs, and the finest feelings of human nature are expressed in them. "Lucy Neal," "Old Kentucky Home," and "Uncle Ned" can make the heart sad as well as merry and can call forth a tear as well as a smile. They awaken sympathies for the slave, in which anti-slavery principles take root, grow and flourish.[6]

Multicultural Note

Situating Stephen Foster

Most people today would find listening to Foster's sentimentalization of slavery difficult. Many of his best-known songs such as "Old Folks at Home" and even "Oh! Susanna" are seldom performed, in part for this reason. Some argue, however, that Foster did try to represent African Americans as real and capable of a wide range of emotions—including hope, sorrow, fear, love, and pain. African American abolitionist Frederick Douglass also described the composer in a positive light. How should we remember Stephen Foster?

CD LISTENING EXERCISE

CD 1/16

Listen to "Oh! Susanna" performed by twentieth-century folk musician Pete Seeger with banjo accompaniment. Seeger's folk version demonstrates the rhythmic appeal of Foster's song which has remained popular for more than 150 years. Next, go online and listen to samples from the 2005 Grammy-winning album *Beautiful Dreamer: The Songs of Stephen Foster* featuring contemporary renditions of Foster's music by a variety of artists. What is appealing about Foster's songs?

NINETEENTH-CENTURY CHURCH MUSIC

Many poor and nonliterate Anglo-European immigrants and their descendants were drawn to Baptist and other populist Christian denominations that sprang up in the eighteenth and nineteenth centuries, particularly in the South, and new musical developments that influenced popular music emerged in these settings. The Scottish vocal technique called lining out—originally developed in the seventeenth century—was common in many of these churches, and African American worshipers adopted it as well. Another musical practice, called **shape note** singing, developed in the late eighteenth century in New England and spread to the South and West through singing schools and songbooks. The system gave each note in the scale a different shape—triangles, squares, circles, or diamonds—enabling nonliterate congregations to perform complex multipart choral arrangements. As singing schools and songbooks developed, they took on local flavor, influenced by vernacular songs, fiddle and banjo music, and other southern styles. A particularly influential songbook of the time was *The Southern Harmony,* which contained hymns, anthems, and Anglo-Irish folk-influenced pieces such as "New Britain"—later retitled "Amazing Grace."

New vernacular traditions in southern church music also developed at the outdoor camp meeting revivals of the Second Awakening evangelical movement. The music played was accessible, written in popular styles of the day, and easily learned. By the mid-nineteenth century, the camp meeting tradition produced a flood of evangelists, many of whom teamed up with song leaders. A particularly influential evangelist, Dwight L. Moody, collaborated with musician Ira David Sankey in the 1870s. In the words of one convert, the pair's revivals "reduced the population of hell by a million souls." [7] The gospel songs that

This shape note version of "New Britain" ("Amazing Grace") was published as part of William Walker's 1854 edition of *Southern Harmony.* (Source: *The Southern Harmony and Musical Companion,* Author: William Walker, Editor: Glenn C. Wilcox, copyright 1993, The University of Kentucky Press.)

The original caption from this 1882 engraving by artist Charles Upham was "A Sunday Service in St. Louis—A Revivalist Preaching on the Levee."

grew out of the meetings embodied the religious and musical experiences of black and white working-class people and influenced subsequent developments in country and modern gospel music.

CIVIL WAR MUSIC AND WIND BANDS

One of the most dramatic events in U.S. history, the Civil War (1861–1865) aroused depths of feeling among Americans that remained long after its conclusion. The war also left a rich musical heritage, and as late as 1909 the bulk of an anthology of American songs called *Heartsongs* still centered on Civil War songs. "John Brown's Body," "When Johnny Comes Marching Home," and "Battle Hymn of the Republic" came from the North; "Dixie" and "Bonnie Blue Flag" from the South. Music played a key role in the war itself; as one Virginia soldier wrote, "We are on one side of the Rappahannock, the enemy on the other. Our boys will sing a Southern song, the Yankees will reply by singing the same tune to Yankee words." [8] On another night before the Battle of Murfreesboro, a Northern band played "Yankee Doodle," a Southern band responded with a Southern tune, and then both bands played "Home, Sweet Home" together. The next day thousands were slaughtered in battle.

The famous Southern patriotic song "Dixie" was originally written for New York minstrel shows by Dan D. Emmett in 1859, but it soon became a Southern anthem. Another Southern song that stood the test of time was "Aura Lee."

Internet Listening Exercise

Listen to a range of interpretations of the following selections from *The Southern Harmony.*

The Statler Brothers: "Amazing Grace"

Shirley Caesar: "Rock of Ages"

Tennessee Ernie Ford: "What a Friend We Have in Jesus"

Elvis Presley: "How Great Thou Art"

© Bettmann/CORBIS

An 1865 photograph of a Union Army brass band.

**Internet
Listening Exercise**

Listen to samples of Civil War songs performed by artists in a variety of styles.

Pete Seeger: "John Brown's Body"

Wilbur De Paris: "Battle Hymn of the Republic"

Dinah Shore: "Dixie"

The Cumberland Three: "Aura Lee"

Elvis Presley: "Love Me Tender"

Written in 1861, it remained popular for over a century in several versions: first in its original form, then adapted as "Army Blue" (a traditional West Point song), and popularized again in 1956 with new words as "Love Me Tender" by Elvis Presley.

From the Civil War through the early twentieth century, wind band music was one of the most popular musical styles in America. Although wind ensembles existed in the European classical tradition as "harmony bands," they were usually made up of small ensembles of oboes, clarinets, horns, and bassoons. A new instrument called the **keyed bugle,** which was developed in 1810, was a technical breakthrough that fostered the formation of all-brass ensembles—a new kind of wind band, the **brass band,** that could play outdoors or in other settings inhospitable to chamber music. The invention of the valve cornet in 1825 was another step in the development of brass instruments that were durable, reliable, and easy to play, and the wind band movement was soon launched.

An early wind band innovator was African American composer/cornetist Frank Johnson. As early as 1812 he was leading an integrated band and playing outdoor concerts in Philadelphia, and he subsequently performed throughout the Northeast, composing over 300 pieces in his lifetime. One of the first nationally recognized wind bands, the Boston Brass Band, formed in 1835 and became a model for community ensembles around the country. The onset of the Civil War in 1861 provided further impetus, and by 1900 almost every community had a band that played for weddings, funerals, picnics, and parties—

Multicultural Note

The Multicultural Roots and Impacts of Wind Bands

Wind bands symbolized Western military might in the nineteenth century, but they originated in the *janissary* army bands of the Turkish Ottoman empire in the fourteenth century. The Turks were the first to integrate metal and woodwind instruments with loud percussion—cymbals, massive bass drums, bells, triangles, and whistles—into large, imposing ensembles; Turkish families still dominate cymbal manufacturing today. Performance techniques now widely used in U.S. marching bands—juggling drumsticks, twirling elaborate drum major's batons, marching in menacing, close formations, and so forth—were also part of the original Turkish *janissary* band spectacle.

During wars with the Ottoman empire, the imposing *janissary* bands impressed European armies. A range of Turkish instruments—including large bass drums—quickly found a place in the regimental music of European armies, as well as major orchestras. Well-known European composers such as Beethoven, Mozart, and Haydn also began to compose *alla turca* (in a Turkish style).

As European nations colonized the world, military and missionary wind bands played a part. Local musicians soon blended wind band and indigenous styles, resulting in resilient hybrids, including Mexican *banda*, West African high life, and Indian/Nepalese wedding bands. New Orleans jazz was another example of such hybridization.

providing entertainment in an era before records, movies, or TV. At the peak of the band movement in 1910, the United States had more than 40,000 bands, with over a million members. In the days before electronic amplification, the visceral impact of a large wind band was powerful, as composer/bandleader John Philip Sousa noted:

> We were marching down Pennsylvania Avenue. On the reviewing stand were President Harrison and an immense number of guests. I had so timed the playing of our march that the trumpet theme would be heard for the first time, just as we got to the front of the reviewing stand. Suddenly ten extra trumpets were shot in the air, and the theme was pealed out in unison. Nothing like it had ever been heard there before.[9]

Composer/bandleader **John Philip Sousa** (1854–1932), the "March King," composed some of America's most popular wind band music. Sousa became conductor of the U.S. Marine Corps Band in 1880 at age twenty-five and left a decade later to form the Sousa Band, which toured internationally for almost forty years, giving over 10,000 concerts. When Sousa's band came to town, it was a big event: Banks and schools shut down to see the band arrive in its own

**Internet
Listening Exercise**

Listen to samples of marches by John Philip Sousa.

John Philip Sousa: *The March King*

© CORBIS

John Philip Sousa, the "March King," dressed in his finest attire as director of the U.S. Marine Band, sometime in the 1880s.

private train, and the "March King" gave as many as three concerts a day until the band left town. Throughout his career, Sousa composed hundreds of marches, operettas, and other pieces, including "The Stars and Stripes Forever," "Washington Post March," and "Semper Fideles." He was also a successful businessman, earning close to half a million dollars from sheet music sales of "The Stars and Stripes Forever" alone, and he was a recording industry pioneer whose performances were consistent top sellers.

The arrangement and instrumentation of Sousa marches also influenced the early development of jazz. The trumpets often introduced the melodies, with the woodwinds playing accompanying arpeggios and the trombones and low brass providing bass lines and countermelodies. The same division of musical responsibility appeared in early New Orleans jazz bands.

The wind band tradition continues in the United States and throughout the world. Many schools and communities have active band programs, and the sound of a marching band remains an American icon. Wind bands also remain integral to the military services, and youth drum and bugle corps units are also found in many parts of the country. The contemporary wind band repertoire is now composed of everything from traditional Sousa marches to Broadway, Hollywood, pop, jazz, classical, and world music styles. Historically black colleges such as Florida A&M have also developed complex choreography and rhythms that push the envelope for marching field shows, and Mexican American communities have incorporated Mexican *banda* into contemporary wind and marching bands. New Orleans also saw a rebirth of traditional wind bands with a contemporary R & B beat in groups such as the Dirty Dozen Brass Band and the Rebirth Jazz Band.

Chapter Summary

- Religious music was probably the earliest style played in the Americas by European settlers. Early seventeenth-century colonists in New England brought with them the psalm-singing traditions of European Protestant churches. Popular styles in the eighteenth century included British pleasure-garden songs, broadside ballads, and ballad operas.

- English, Irish, and Scottish music flavored early nineteenth-century American popular music. Italian opera also enjoyed brief popularity, introducing Americans to the beauty of the *bel canto* vocal tradition.

- The parlor song was developed by composers such as Henry Russell, one of the first popular composers to express a distinctly American style. Stephen Foster was the most important composer of American popular song in the nineteenth century, crafting classics such as "Oh! Susanna" and "Camptown Races."

- Many poor Anglo-European immigrants were drawn to the Baptist church and other populist denominations in the eighteenth and nineteenth centuries, particularly in the South. The techniques of lining out and shape note singing, as well as singing schools and camp meetings, spread church music, which subsequently influenced country and modern gospel music.

- The Civil War greatly influenced American popular song, with hundreds of memorable songs written during this tragic period of internal strife.

- The development of wind bands in the latter half of the nineteenth century led to national popularity, and by 1910 there were over 40,000 bands throughout the United States. The most popular bandleader and composer of the era was John Philip Sousa, whose marches are still widely performed.

Key Terms

ballad opera
bel canto
brass band
broadside ballad
Ethiopian dialect
keyed bugle
opera

parlor songs
plantation songs
pleasure gardens
sacred
secular
shape note

Study and Discussion Questions

1. What role did church music play in the development of early popular music in America? How did it influence later styles of American popular music?

2. How did British pleasure-garden music influence American popular music?

3. What were the dominant themes of broadside ballads and ballad operas?

4. Why did Irish music appeal to American popular songwriters and audiences? What connections were there between Irish music and parlor songs?

5. What are the origins and significance of the *bel canto* style of popular singing?

6. What were the dominant social themes of parlor songs? What role did Henry Russell play in the development of this style?

7. What is Stephen Foster's place in American popular music?

8. How did the camp meetings and evangelism of the nineteenth century affect popular music developments?

9. What were lining out and shape note singing, and what were their origins?

10. Why were wind bands popular in the late nineteenth and early twentieth centuries?

Notes

1. Wilfrid Mellers, *Music in a New Found Land: Themes and Developments in the History of American Music* (New York: Alfred A. Knopf, 1967), 6.

2. Charles Hamm, *Yesterdays: Popular Song in America* (New York: Norton, 1979), 2.

3. Hamm, *Yesterdays,* 42.

4. Denes Agay, *Best Loved Songs of the American People* (New York: Doubleday, 1975), 51.

5. Hamm, *Yesterdays,* 176–78.

6. David S. Reynolds, *Walt Whitman's America: A Cultural Biography* (New York: Knopf, 1995), 148.

7. Charles Hamm, *Music in the New World* (New York: Norton, 1983), 276.

8. Hamm, *Yesterdays,* 231.

9. David Ewen, *All the Years of American Popular Music* (Englewood Cliffs, NJ: Prentice-Hall, 1977), 143.

1890 - 2000

1881 Tony Pastor, an early vaudeville entrepreneur, opens his most famous New York vaudeville theater ♪

1890s New York City becomes the center of the music publishing industry, soon known as Tin Pan Alley ♪

1892 Charles K. Harris publishes one of the first Tin Pan Alley hits, "After the Ball" ♪

1898 Spanish American War

1899 Scott Joplin's biggest ragtime hit, "The Maple Leaf Rag," is published and sells over a million copies ♪

1904 George M. Cohan's first show, *Little Johnny Jones,* opens, signaling a new era of the Broadway musical ♪

1911 Irving Berlin's "Alexander's Ragtime Band" published ♪

1914–1918 World War I

1914 ASCAP formed to insure royalty payments to musicians and publishers ♪

1919–1933 Prohibition

1924 George Gershwin's classical/popular hybrid *Rhapsody in Blue* premieres ♪

1927 *The Jazz Singer,* the first sound film, is released ♪

1927 Jerome Kern's socially conscious *Showboat* opens ♪

1929–1930s Great Depression; New Deal begins

1935 George Gershwin's folk opera *Porgy and Bess* opens ♪

1941–1945 U.S. participates in World War II

1942 Frank Sinatra releases first hit, "I'll Never Smile Again" ♪

1943 Richard Rodgers's *Oklahoma!* opens with first full integration of plot, music, and choreography ♪

1948 Introduction of the 33⅓ rpm LP recording ♪

1950–1953 Korean War

1950s Frank Sinatra pioneers the concept album ♪

1954 School segregation outlawed; civil rights movement begins

1957 Leonard Bernstein's multicultural musical *West Side Story* opens ♪

1963 Civil rights march on Washington; John Kennedy assassinated

1964–1973 Vietnam War

1964 *Fiddler on the Roof,* the last of the fully developed musicals, opens ♪

1967 *Hair,* the first successful rock musical, opens ♪

1968 Martin Luther King and Robert Kennedy assassinated

1970 Steven Sondheim introduces the concept musical ♪

1975 *A Chorus Line,* Broadway's longest running show, opens ♪

1981 AIDS epidemic first recognized

1988 Andrew Lloyd Webber's *The Phantom of the Opera* opens ♪

1990s American economic high-tech "bubble"

1996 Rent, a rock-flavored portrait of contemporary urban life, opens ♪

1998 *The Lion King,* adapted from an animated Disney film, opens ♪

2000 Mel Brooks's *The Producers* breaks Tony award record ♪

2001 9/11 terrorist attacks

| 1880 | 1900 | 1920 | 1940 | 1960 | 1980 | 2000 |

Chapter 6

The Golden Age of American Popular Song

The late nineteenth through the mid-twentieth centuries, often called the "golden age" of American songwriting, saw the development of New York's Tin Pan Alley as the country's center of songwriting and music publishing. The period also witnessed the birth of Broadway and subsequent developments over the next hundred years of American musical theater. Many of the era's greatest songwriters were recent European immigrants or children of immigrants whose music voiced their newfound "American-ness" as well as reflecting their cultural roots. Some of their songs were utopian flights of fantasy, others were gritty reality checks. These composers gave us one of the world's richest traditions of popular song.

IN THIS CHAPTER

- Tin Pan Alley and Turn-of-the-Century Popular Styles

- Vaudeville, Early Musical Theater, and Operetta

- The Evolution of Twentieth-Century American Musical Theater

- Multicultural Broadway

- Great Performers of American Popular Song

- The Rise and Fall of the Tin Pan Alley Standard

TIN PAN ALLEY AND TURN-OF-THE-CENTURY POPULAR STYLES

The music publishing industry operated in several major metropolitan areas of the United States for most of the nineteenth century, but by the 1880s it had consolidated in New York under a new approach that emphasized mass production and efficiency. According to historian Craig Roell,

> The entire music industry, from sheet music publishing and piano manufacturing to teaching, competed with not only new commodities but a new ideology, shifting recreation away from the home and redefining social distinction, leisure time, and personal identity in terms of consumption.[1]

At first, the industry primarily sold sheet music. **Tin Pan Alley,** located at 28th and Broadway in New York City, soon became the center of the industry. The name was coined by a journalist visiting songwriter Harry Von Tilzer, whose out-of-tune, upright piano was said to sound like a "tin pan." Music firms lined the streets, their offices packed with songwriters hoping for a hit. For seventy-five years Tin Pan Alley was synonymous with the music publishing industry.

Songwriter/publisher **Charles K. Harris** (1864–1930) was an early success story. Realizing that publishing would be the profit center of the industry, he started his own publishing company and composed and published "After the Ball," a waltz with a popular hook, in 1892. Two million copies were sold, and

www **Internet Listening Exercise**

Listen to these samples of classic triple-meter songs from the 1890s.

Joan Morris: "After the Ball"

Joanie Pallatto: "Daisy Bell (On a Bicycle Built for Two)"

Mel Torme: "Sidewalks of New York"

Leake County Revelers: "In the Good Old Summer Time"

Guy Lombardo: "The Band Played On"

myriad other publishing firms sprang up in the wake of Harris's success. Scores of popular songs of the 1890s followed in the wake of "After the Ball" using triple meter (3/4) waltz time, including "Daisy Bell (On a Bicycle Built for Two)," "Sidewalks of New York," "In the Good Old Summer Time," "Meet Me in St. Louis, Louis," and "The Band Played On." Most were composed in the verse-chorus form with a new use of the chorus as the song's hook, a songwriting practice still in wide use.

The economic boom in the sheet music industry benefited primarily publishing company owners, with most songwriters paid only a small fee per song with no further compensation. **Song pluggers** were also hired to put sheet music into the hands of successful vaudeville performers. They would stand outside the publishing houses, grabbing at the arms of performers looking for new songs. According to Harris,

> The real start at popularizing a song is to sell it to the performer. . . . The bigger the reputation and ability of the performer . . . the more chances of catching the public's favor. . . . A new song must be sung, played, hummed and drummed into the ears of the public, not in one city alone, but in every city, town and village, before it ever becomes popular.[2]

Publishers controlled the choice and style of songs published, and most believed that the public wanted familiar songs. Consequently, Tin Pan Alley song styles remained consistent for about five decades.

Two new technologies in particular—the player piano and the motion picture—fostered song promotion. Recall that the player piano was one of the first methods of recording music. In 1898 the invention of a coin-operated version expanded the possibilities for marketing new songs. A forerunner of the jukebox, it was installed wherever people gathered. Companies such as Wurlitzer and Seeburg, which produced the coin-operated pianos, were also early industry leaders in the jukebox industry that developed in the mid-1920s. The birth of the film industry in the late 1890s offered another venue for song promotion. Because most films for the first thirty years of the industry were silent, either live musicians or a version of the player piano called a photoplayer accompanied them. Song pluggers also vied to perform the latest Tin Pan Alley releases during intermissions.

The **coon song** was a popular style in the late nineteenth century, featuring strong rhythms, syncopation, and quick tempos that demanded a robust delivery. An outgrowth of minstrelsy, many of the songs denigrated African Americans, and sheet music covers frequently featured images people today would find offensive. Coon songs were so popular that even successful African American composers such as Ben Harney and Ernest Hogan wrote them. Female performers of the style were called "coon shouters," such as the famous Sophie Tucker and May Irwin.

In the early 1900s, ragtime songs superseded coon songs; the market soon flooded with songs that had "rag" in the title. A typical ragtime song had a simple syncopated rhythmic pattern of short-long-short notes, as in the popular "Hello! My Baby," composed by Joseph Howard in 1899. Ragtime's greatest composer,

Scott Joplin, published his famous "The Maple Leaf Rag" the same year. Other popular ragtime releases included "You're in the Right Church, but in the Wrong Pew" and "Let It Alone," sung by African American vaudeville performer Bert Williams, and "That Lovin' Rag" and "Carrie," performed by Sophie Tucker. By the time Irving Berlin wrote "Alexander's Ragtime Band" in 1911, the country was in the throes of a ragtime craze. Although the major share of profits from ragtime went to the white publishers, performers, and composers, Scott Joplin and a handful of other black ragtime composers realized a modest profit. Ragtime did have its detractors; many in the art music world detested the style, and critics were often hostile: "This cheap, trashy stuff could not elevate even the most degraded minds, nor could it possibly urge any one to greater effort in the acquisition of culture in any phase." [3] European art music composers Antonin Dvořák, Igor Stravinsky, and Erik Satie, however, were reported to be impressed with ragtime and other African American styles, and Stravinsky and Satie both incorporated rags into their compositions.

Singer Al Jolson starred in *The Jazz Singer*, the first "talkie" or motion picture with sound, in 1927.

Irving Berlin's (1888–1989) career as composer, publisher, and theater owner was unparalleled in American popular music. He epitomized Tin Pan Alley: For sixty years he was one of America's most prolific composers of popular song. A product of the multicultural milieu of New York City at the turn of the century, Berlin came to the United States as a child from Eastern Europe fleeing anti-Semitism. He got a job as a song plugger on Tin Pan Alley at age sixteen, published his first tune in 1907, and had his first success in 1910 with ethnic novelty songs (see the Multicultural Note). Performed by stars such as Sophie Tucker and Bessie Smith, Berlin's 1911 hit "Alexander's Ragtime Band"

 **Internet Listening Exercise**

Listen to these samples of coon songs and ragtime songs performed by a variety of artists.

May Irwin: "The Bully"

Bert Williams: "Let It Alone"

Phish: "Hello! My Baby"

Al Jolson: "Waiting for the Robert E. Lee"

 Multicultural Note

···

Race and Generational Bias against New Music

Ragtime was one of the first popular musical styles to appeal primarily to young people. It was also the first of many subsequent styles to be viewed with disfavor by an older generation. People later expressed similar views about jazz, R & B, rock, and hip-hop. A common link among all these styles was their African American roots. How did generational and racial bias interact?

Music Industry Note

ASCAP—The American Society of Composers, Authors, and Publishers

In 1914 a group of composers, including John Philip Sousa, Victor Herbert, Irving Berlin, and Jerome Kern, created **ASCAP**—the American Society of Composers, Authors, and Publishers. Established to enforce royalty payments to the copyright owner of any piece of music, it served as a new source of copyright, and therefore revenue, protection. In 1917 the Supreme Court ruled that all places of live public performance of music must purchase a performance license from ASCAP, and eventually the law would include radio and sound film.

By the mid-1930s, ASCAP was collecting millions in annual fees, but the increased use of recorded music prompted it to try to double the fees it charged the National Association of Broadcasters (NAB). This led to a major legal battle, which saw the banning of all ASCAP material from the radio. Eventually NAB formed its own licensing organization, Broadcast Music Incorporated (BMI). ASCAP and BMI are now the two primary music licensing organizations in the world.

vaulted him to success as the "Ragtime King." By the 1920s, Berlin was writing songs for Broadway, and he became adept at the slow ballad style of the era with tunes such as "Blue Skies" and "How Deep Is the Ocean." He subsequently worked on Broadway and Hollywood film musicals during the 1930s, yielding tunes such as "Easter Parade" and "Cheek to Cheek." In 1938, following a trip to Europe that exposed him to the growth of fascism, Berlin wrote the best-selling patriotic song, "God Bless America," which reemerged in 2001 as an anthem in

Internet Listening Exercise

Listen to the following samples of ethnic novelty songs.

Nora Bayes: "How Can They Tell That Oi'm Irish?"

Al Jolson: "The Spaniard That Blighted My Life"

Irving Berlin: "Oh How That German Could Love"

Irving Berlin: "Marie from Sunny Italy"

Multicultural Note

Ethnic Novelty Songs in Vaudeville

From the early days of vaudeville through about 1920, **ethnic novelty songs,** which portrayed members of ethnic groups in humorous but demeaning ways, were common. The songs contained stereotypes and were usually sung in accented ethnic dialect. Irving Berlin was particularly prolific in the genre, writing songs about Italians ("Sweet Marie, Make-a Rag-a Time Dance wid Me"), Jews ("Yiddle, on Your Fiddle, Play Some Ragtime"), Germans ("Oh How That German Could Love"), Arabs ("In My Harem"), and rural Americans or "rubes" ("Down on Uncle Jerry's Farm"). The most popular ethnic novelty songs of all were coon songs, and Berlin composed several dozen of them. Why did composers, who were sometimes members of the same ethnic groups themselves, write these songs?

response to the 9/11 terror attacks. He also wrote his all-time classic, "White Christmas," in the late 1930s. After World War II, Berlin achieved his greatest Broadway success with *Annie Get Your Gun* (1946).

Berlin had almost no musical training, and he played piano by ear in only one key. Despite this, his great ear and shrewd business sense made him the most successful popular music composer in U.S. history. He shaped the Tin Pan Alley song style, maintaining it for many years with his continuing creativity, and dominated our music as a gifted composer and lyricist for over sixty years. As Jerome Kern put it, "Irving Berlin has no place in American music. He is American music."[4]

Songwriter Irving Berlin accompanies singer/dancer Fred Astaire, shown here with his dance partner, Ginger Rogers.

© Bettmann/CORBIS

VAUDEVILLE, EARLY MUSICAL THEATER, AND OPERETTA

Vaudeville, a variety show featuring songs, dances, and comedy sketches with minimal plots, was an outgrowth of minstrelsy that coincided with the rise of Tin Pan Alley. Compared with minstrelsy, vaudeville had less racist lampooning and a wider range of performance styles, as singers, dancers, comedians, acrobats, magicians, animal acts, and jugglers took the stage one act at a time. A symbiotic relationship also grew up between vaudeville and the music industry: Entertainers needed music, Tin Pan Alley supplied it, and vaudeville exposed new songs to potential sheet-music buyers.

Tony Pastor (1837–1908) was a leading figure in early vaudeville in New York. He opened his first popular venue in 1865, following up in 1881 with his famous Tony Pastor's New Fourteenth Street Theater. He aimed at providing entertainment suitable for women and children; to achieve it, he banned swearing, smoking, and drinking and offered door prizes of groceries, dress patterns, and kitchenware. Many of the most famous names in vaudeville and early Broadway theater appeared at Pastor's: the Irish comedy and song team of Edward Harrigan and Tony Hart, soprano Lillian Russell, and early Broadway star George M. Cohan.

The late nineteenth century saw another theater style related to vaudeville that went by such names as "burlesque," "spectacle," or "extravaganza"—sometimes a combination of all three. **Burlesque** extravaganzas contained a unifying thematic element, comedy with sexual themes, and female dancers. A precursor to burlesque was a five-hour melodrama called *The Black Crook* (1866), which featured provocative sexual content and over a hundred dancers. Burlesque remained popular through the 1920s, but over time the style devolved into a seedy sideshow. Another popular Broadway offering called **revue** appeared in the early 1900s. While borrowing provocative elements of burlesque, revues were aimed at women as well as men. The most famous example was *Ziegfeld's Follies,* presented by impresario Florenz Ziegfeld, who perfected a blend

🌐 Internet Listening Exercise

Listen to these samples of songs by Irving Berlin performed by artists in a variety of styles.

Willie Nelson: "Blue Skies"

Diana Krall: "How Deep Is the Ocean"

Judy Garland: "Easter Parade"

Ella Fitzgerald/Louis Armstrong: "Cheek to Cheek"

Bing Crosby: "White Christmas"

Irving Berlin: "God Bless America"

Library of Congress

Publicity poster for *The Black Crook*, a four-act, five-and-a-half-hour theatrical melodrama and precursor to the Broadway musical.

Internet Listening Exercise

Listen to the following samples of songs from early musical theater.

John Steel: "A Pretty Girl Is Like a Melody" *(Ziegfeld Follies of 1919)*

Fanny Brice: "My Man" *(Ziegfeld Follies of 1921)*

Gilbert and Sullivan: "A Rollicking Band of Pirates We" *(Pirates of Penzance)*

Gilbert and Sullivan: "I Am the Captain of the *Pinafore*" *(H.M.S. Pinafore)*

Victor Herbert: "March of the Toys" *(Babes in Toyland)*

of music, comedy, dance, simple plots, and female dancers. *Ziegfeld's Follies* remained popular on stage and in film for over twenty-five years.

During the 1870s and 1880s, a European style of musical theater called **operetta,** which blended plot, music, lyrics, dance, and an integrated story line, gained popularity in the United States. Based on European art music, the style was an important precursor to American musical comedy. The first operettas, called *operas bouffes* (comic operas), were written in the 1850s by German composer Jacques Offenbach. British composers William Gilbert and Arthur Sullivan followed over the next two decades with a light and humorous style of operetta that became popular on both sides of the Atlantic and that works such as *H.M.S. Pinafore, The Pirates of Penzance*, and *The Mikado* exemplified. The first successful American composer of operetta was Irish immigrant **Victor Herbert** (1859–1924). He composed over forty operettas, blending the wit and syncopation of American popular song with European operetta to produce such works as *Babes in Toyland*. American and European operettas remained popular until the start of World War I, when a wave of patriotic fervor caused a backlash against works seen as "foreign."

THE EVOLUTION OF TWENTIETH-CENTURY AMERICAN MUSICAL THEATER

The first half of the twentieth century was a golden era for American musical theater. The work of many great composers, producers, and performers combined to give shape to Broadway musicals that today stand as landmarks of American popular music. During the period, the Broadway musical developed into a sophisticated theatrical form, culminating in a full integration of plot, music, and choreography.

George M. Cohan: The Irish "Yankee Doodle Dandy"

Irish American performer **George M. Cohan** (1878–1942) gave American musical theater a unique flavor and vitality in the early twentieth century. He wrote, produced, directed, and starred in a long list of shows that yielded famous tunes such as "You're a Grand Old Flag," "Yankee Doodle Dandy," and "Give My Regards to Broadway." His career embraced every aspect of musical theater. Cohan's trademarks—self-confidence and patriotism—helped his work convey a strong American personality; he also filled his musicals with characters from everyday settings who spoke in slang and sang simple, sentimental songs with mass appeal.

Cohan began his career in vaudeville, and his first Broadway hit, *Little Johnny Jones,* came in 1904. Between 1910 and 1917, he saw eleven of his shows mounted on Broadway. Periodic revivals and tributes to his work, including a film of his life and a Broadway musical, followed. According to critic Clive Barnes, Cohan's songs "by now have burned their way into the heart and into immortality." [5]

 Internet Listening Exercise

Listen to these samples of music by George M. Cohan.

James Cagney: "You're a Grand Old Flag"

George M Cast: "Yankee Doodle Dandy"

Judy Garland: "Give My Regards to Broadway"

Showboat and the Music of Jerome Kern

The opening of *Showboat* in 1927 marked a new development in Broadway musical style. Based on a novel by Edna Ferber, the work was written by composer Jerome Kern and playwright/lyricist Oscar Hammerstein II. *Showboat* was

---

🎼 **Music Industry Note**
....

Song Interpolation in Musical Comedy

Early Broadway shows were often used as vehicles to promote the latest hit songs through the practice of **interpolation**—the addition of a new, unrelated song to an existing show. Although it seems odd today to add an unrelated song to a show, the practice had been common since the 1890s, when Charles K. Harris's biggest hit, "After the Ball," was interpolated into a show called *A Trip to Chinatown.* In the early twentieth century, Tin Pan Alley composers were producing so many new songs that they saw interpolation as necessary for ensuring wide exposure.

Paul Robeson in his role as Joe from the film version of *Showboat*.

![www] **Internet Listening Exercise**

Listen to samples of the following songs by Jerome Kern.

Paul Robeson: "Ol' Man River"

Frances Langford: "Why Do I Love You"

Barbra Streisand: "All the Things You Are"

The Platters: "Smoke Gets in Your Eyes"

the first musical to deal with serious social issues such as racism and social class. Further, because it presented a well-developed story line with fully realized characters, beautiful sets, and costumes, it was the first musical to present credible drama. The score includes the classics "Why Do I Love You," "Can't Help Lovin' Dat Man," "Bill," and "Ol' Man River." *Showboat* ran for 572 performances, was twice made into a film, and was repeatedly revived on Broadway.

Showboat's composer, **Jerome Kern** (1885–1945), was one of the most successful popular music composers of his day, known for his ability to create memorable melodies. With an extensive musical education, he wrote almost exclusively for operetta and musical comedy. Kern's music ultimately appeared in over 120 Broadway shows and Hollywood films. Along with Irving Berlin, he influenced the writing styles of the next generation of songwriters with great songs such as "All the Things You Are," "Smoke Gets in Your Eyes," and "Yesterdays."

Porgy and Bess and the Music of George Gershwin

One of the greatest American composers of the twentieth century, **George Gershwin** (1898–1937), enjoyed the rare distinction of succeeding in both classical and popular idioms. Gershwin's folk opera *Porgy and Bess*, the story of a love affair between a disabled man and a prostitute set in the African American community of Charleston, South Carolina, was a milestone in the history of the Broadway musical. As in opera, Gershwin set all dialogue in the work to music, so that any words that were not part of a major song were delivered as *recitative*—text set to music. Nonetheless, when Gershwin insisted on using an African American cast for *Porgy and Bess*, the Metropolitan Opera rejected it. The work was then successfully produced on Broadway in 1935. In a perplexing conflict of reviews, classical music critics objected to songs such as "Summertime" and "I Got Plenty o' Nuttin'" as too much like popular music to be called opera, while theater critics objected to the work's extensive use of recitative. Many songs from the work became standards in jazz, blues, rock, and country; "Summertime," for example, has been one of the most widely performed songs in American popular music.

As a young composer, Gershwin was influenced by Tin Pan Alley composer Irving Berlin and classical composers including Franz Liszt, Claude Debussy, and Maurice Ravel. He composed his first Broadway show score in 1919 and he had his first hit with the song "Swanee," which was recorded in 1920 by Al Jolson and sold over a million copies. The composer soon began to work with his brother, lyricist Ira Gershwin, in a collaboration that lasted all their lives. Together they wrote a string of successful musicals in the late 1920s and early 1930s that yielded such hits as "Fascinating Rhythm," "Someone to Watch over Me," and "I Got Rhythm." In 1924, with the encouragement of bandleader Paul Whiteman, Gershwin composed *Rhapsody in Blue*, the first of a small number of classical orchestral works. Developed with the assistance of orchestrator and composer Ferde Grofé, the piece successfully straddled the classical-popular divide to become one of the most popular orchestral works of the twentieth century. Also fascinated with blues and jazz, Gershwin was one of the earliest white composers to develop relationships with African American innovators such as James Reese Europe and James P. Johnson. He incorporated blues, syncopation, and jazz into his work in a way that appealed to both white and black audiences. According to historian Charles Hamm,

> There was something in the music of black Americans that struck a responsive chord somewhere deep in Gershwin. . . . In turn, this same indefinable quality found its way into many of his songs, to which black Americans responded in a similarly instinctive way. . . . Almost any listing of repertoires of black jazz musicians in the 1920s, '30s, and even '40s will include songs by Gershwin.[6]

CD LISTENING EXERCISE

CD 1/17

Listen to "Summertime," composed by George Gershwin as it was performed in *Porgy and Bess*. The operatic style of the original version surprises many listeners who have only heard the work performed in more popular styles. The song is set in a 16-measure blues form.

Go online and listen to an instrumental version of "Summertime" by Miles Davis from the album *Miles Davis–Porgy and Bess* (1955). How are the texture and mood of the work changed? Does this instrumental version convey the mood of the original?

Finally, listen to Janis Joplin's 1968 recording of "Summertime" from the album *Cheap Thrills*. Today you can find hundreds of recorded versions of this remarkably simple song. Why does it remain so popular?

Internet Listening Exercise

Listen to samples of these Gershwin tunes done by artists in a variety of styles.

Al Jolson: "Swanee"

Ethel Merman: "I Got Rhythm"

Chet Baker: "Someone to Watch over Me"

Rod Stewart: "Embraceable You"

Sarah Vaughn: "Nice Work If You Can Get It"

Ella Fitzgerald: "They Can't Take That away from Me"

Cole Porter: "Just One of Those Things"

Although not a major innovator in the evolution of the Broadway musical, composer/lyricist **Cole Porter** (1891–1964) crafted a unique style of urbane, witty lyrics and smooth, sophisticated melodies to become a celebrated com-

Internet Listening Exercise

Listen to samples of these Cole Porter classics.

Louis Armstrong: "Let's Do It"

Frank Sinatra: "Night and Day"

Peggy Lee: "What Is This Thing Called Love"

Dinah Washington: "I've Got You under My Skin"

Lena Horne: "Just One of Those Things"

poser for stage and film. Unlike many of the other songwriters of his era who were children of immigrants, Porter was a child of privilege. Though he was gay, Porter married a rich widow in 1919 and settled in Paris to live a life of sophisticated luxury that he soon wrote about in his songs. His first hit, "Let's Do It," came in 1928, and he followed up with a steady series of show and film scores for the next fifteen years. Hit shows and songs included *Wake up and Dream* ("What Is This Thing Called Love"), *The Gay Divorcee* ("Night and Day"), *Anything Goes* ("I Get a Kick out of You"), and *Jubilee* ("Begin the Beguine," "Just One of Those Things"). Hits from films included "I've Got You under My Skin" and "You'd Be So Nice to Come Home To." Although a serious riding accident in 1937 made Porter a recluse, he continued to write and found his biggest Broadway success in 1948 with *Kiss Me, Kate,* a musical version of Shakespeare's *The Taming of the Shrew.* He wrote other successful Broadway scores such as *Can-Can* and *Silk Stockings* in the early 1950s. Critic Alec Wilder appraises Porter's body of work: "No one can deny that Porter added a certain theatrical elegance, as well as interest and sophistication, wit, and musical complexity to the popular song form. And for this we are deeply indebted."[7]

Oklahoma! and the Music of Rodgers and Hammerstein

Oklahoma! represented a new phase in the evolution of the Broadway musical. Many see the work's stylistic innovations as the culmination of the possibilities of traditional musical theater, influencing much work that followed. With music by **Richard Rodgers** (1902–1979) and lyrics by **Oscar Hammerstein II** (1895–1960), the musical opened in 1943 and broke all records over a continuous five-year run. *Oklahoma!* was the first collaboration between the famed writing team.

Prior to his work with Hammerstein, Rodgers had teamed up with another of Broadway's finest lyricists, **Lorenz Hart** (1895–1943), to produce such hits as "My Heart Stood Still" and "With a Song in My Heart." Lorenz Hart brought wit, rhyme, and irony to his lyrics. Rodgers's music came out of the jazz age of the 1920s and appeared mainly in musical theater and film. The team wrote music for a string of hit shows from the 1920s through the 1940s, including *A Connecticut Yankee* and *Pal Joey.*

When Hart died in 1943, Rodgers teamed up with Hammerstein to work on *Oklahoma!* Hits from the work included "People Will Say We're in Love," "Oh, What a Beautiful Morning," and "The Surrey with the Fringe on Top." Rodgers and Hammerstein followed up with a string of classic Broadway hit musicals, including *Carousel, South Pacific, The King and I,* and *The Sound of Music.* All were made into lavish Hollywood films, and *South Pacific* and *Oklahoma!* both received Pulitzer prizes. Further, *Oklahoma!* was successfully reprised on Broadway in the early 2000s.

The Contributions of Oklahoma!

Integration of Components

Complete integration of all theatrical components, including plot, songs, lyrics, instrumental music, and for the first time dance as part of the story line.

No Extraneous Elements

Removal of extraneous digressions of song and dance, previously common in Broadway shows. With no opening chorus line and no interpolated hit songs, audiences enjoyed a leaner musical that focused on story line and character development.

First Complete Cast Recording

The first complete, original cast recording of a Broadway musical. Such recordings became staples of all Broadway shows to follow.

Innovative Setting

The show's western setting opened new geographic possibilities for Broadway, which influenced settings for other shows including *The King and I* (Thailand) and *South Pacific* (a Pacific island).

Internet Listening Exercise

Listen to samples of the following songs composed by Richard Rodgers.

Gordon MacRae: "Oh, What a Beautiful Morning (*Oklahoma!*)

Ezio Pinza: "Some Enchanted Evening" (*South Pacific*)

Ella Fitzgerald: "The Lady Is a Tramp" (*Pal Joey*)

King and I Cast: "Shall We Dance" (*The King and I*)

Mary Martin: "My Favorite Things" (*The Sound of Music*)

West Side Story and the Music of Leonard Bernstein

Leonard Bernstein (1918–1990), one of the most important classical musicians of the twentieth century, contributed substantially to American musical theater with the musicals *Candide* and *West Side Story*. He derived both works from literary classics: *Candide* from Voltaire's eighteenth-century novel, and *West Side Story* from Shakespeare's *Romeo and Juliet*. Both also examined social issues: *Candide* the McCarthy hearings of the 1950s; *West Side Story* issues of interracial, urban violence, set as a love story between members of two rival New York street gangs. Working with director/choreographer Jerome Robbins, playwright Arthur Laurents, and lyricist Stephen Sondheim, Bernstein built on the musical theater elements pioneered by *Oklahoma!* By blending classical orchestral music with jazz and Afro-Cuban rhythms, the composer created a score that was multicultural and harmonically sophisticated, yet accessible. Bernstein's melodies in songs such as "Maria," "Somewhere," and "Tonight" contained some of the finest melodic writing in American popular song. Further, many of the show's pieces break from the traditional Tin Pan Alley 32-bar song form. In addition to his accomplishments as a com-

CD LISTENING EXERCISE

CD 1/18

Listen to "Maria" from *West Side Story*. Bernstein begins this melody with a dramatic interval called a *tritone*, which consists of two notes with three whole steps between them. The tension created by this dissonant interval is then resolved by moving the melody up one half-step on the word *Ma-ri-a*, thus creating a memorable melodic hook.

poser and conductor, Bernstein was also a fine concert pianist and music educator remembered for his well-regarded series of educational concerts for children. He was also one of the first celebrities of the fine arts world to embrace jazz as an important American art form.

Fiddler on the Roof and the End of an Era

American musical theater continued to produce important works into the early 1960s. The popular Alan Jay Lerner and Frederick Loewe musical *My Fair Lady* broke records in 1956 for consecutive performances, and soundtrack recordings of Broadway shows continued to top the charts. Successful musicals of the era included *Hello Dolly, Mame, The Music Man,* and *Bye Bye, Birdie*. The golden age of the Broadway musical saw one last major innovation in 1964—*Fiddler on the Roof*. Based on a series of short stories by Yiddish writer Sholem Aleichem, the work centered on a Jewish family living in a small village in Russia at the turn of the twentieth century. *Fiddler on the Roof* was an ethnic musical (see the Multicultural Note). Drawing on universal themes, it produced tunes such as "Tradition," "Sunrise Sunset," and "If I Were a Rich Man," which became modern-day Jewish folk songs. The musical also marked the end of an era as the last successful major work in the fully developed contemporary musical theater tradition. By the mid-1960s, the cost of such productions became prohibitive.

Multicultural Note

The Ethnic Musical

Some of the most highly-praised musicals from Broadway's golden age were **ethnic musicals,** or ones that took place in cultural settings exotic to the U.S. cultural mainstream. These included *South Pacific, The King and I, Flower Drum Song,* and *Porgy and Bess,* which some criticized for containing cultural stereotypes. Although *Fiddler on the Roof* initially avoided this criticism, a revival in the early 2000s was panned for its simplistic analysis of the oppression of Eastern European Jews. When questioned about ethnic musicals and cultural authenticity, composer Richard Rodgers replied,

> If my melodies [in *Oklahoma!*] were going to be authentic, they'd have to be authentic on my own terms. . . . It was true of my "Siamese" music for *The King and I*. Had I attempted to duplicate the real thing it would never have sounded genuine. . . . All a composer—any composer—can do is make an audience believe it is hearing an authentic sound without losing his own musical identity.[8]

How should a composer approach writing ethnically flavored music? How successful were Gershwin's versions of African American music?

Rock, Concept Musicals, and Other Trends

The Broadway musical declined in the mid-1960s as New York's Times Square theater district became run down and sales of Broadway show albums slumped against the rock onslaught. Popular tastes in music had turned, and Broadway scrambled to adapt. The first rock musical, *Hair*, opened in a small **off-Broadway** theater—a venue for the production of experimental works—in 1967. Originally billed as an "American tribal love-rock musical," *Hair* was at first considered too offensive for Broadway patrons, with its antiwar message, draft card burning, nudity, drug use, free love, and fundamental statement of 1960s youth rebellion—long hair. Despite its radical origins, *Hair* finally came to Broadway and subsequently became a movie. Other rock musicals followed in the early 1970s with Andrew Lloyd Webber's *Jesus Christ Superstar* and Stephen Schwartz's *Godspell*.

Stephen Sondheim (1930–) was a leading composer in American musical theater in the last three decades of the twentieth century. Following an early collaboration with Leonard Bernstein as lyricist for *West Side Story*, Sondheim pioneered an approach called the **concept musical** that focused on a single theme, often without a linear narrative or definitive resolution, and used small casts with minimal sets. Early works in the style included *Company* (1970), *Follies* (1971), and *A Little Night Music* (1973). Intrigued also by the challenge of writing music to represent a specific style or historical time period, Sondheim became known for his deft handling of a variety of styles. Relatively few of his songs functioned well outside of the shows as hits, with the exception of "Send in the Clowns" from *A Little Night Music*. Sondheim took a big gamble in 1976 with a play called *Pacific Overtures*, which used an Asian cast as well as traditional Asian instruments and theatrical styles. The show's multicultural approach was innovative, but it was not well received. Although Sondheim was a descendant of Broadway's golden age, he strove in his work to push the Broadway musical in new directions.

Broadway experienced a difficult period from the 1970s through the end of the century. The toll of the AIDS epidemic hit the theater community especially hard, devastating a generation and disrupting the continuity of artistic traditions. High costs also discouraged producers from mounting untested new musicals in New York. As a result, a theatrical "British Invasion" came about as lower-cost, London-originated musicals came to Broadway. British composer Andrew Lloyd Webber, director Trevor Nunn, and producer Cameron Mackintosh served as standard-bearers with works such as *Cats, Les Miserables, Phantom of the Opera*, and *Miss Saigon*. **Andrew Lloyd Webber** (1948–) was the most successful composer in musical theater at the turn of the twenty-first century. His musicals employed spectacular visual effects, "over-the-top" sets, lights, costumes, and multimedia displays. In Webber's *The Phantom of the Opera*, audiences were as likely to remember the chandelier that swooped over their heads as any specific song. Webber hits included "Memory" from *Cats*, "Don't Cry for Me Argentina" from *Evita*, and "I Don't Know How to Love Him," from *Jesus Christ Superstar*.

Internet Listening Exercise

Listen to samples of these tunes from early rock musicals.

Hair Cast: "Aquarius"

Hair Cast: "Hair"

Jesus Christ Superstar Cast: "Superstar"

Internet Listening Exercise

Listen to samples of these songs by Andrew Lloyd Webber.

Cats Cast: "Memory"

Evita Cast: "Don't Cry for Me Argentina"

Jesus Christ Superstar Cast: "I Don't Know How to Love Him"

A growth area for Broadway at the turn of the twenty-first century turned out to be revivals, both in New York and on tour, including *Showboat, Fiddler on the Roof, West Side Story, Oklahoma!* and *South Pacific*. The rock musical also gained new life from Jonathan Larson's *Rent* in 1996. Based on the plot of Puccini's opera *La Boheme, Rent* was the *Hair* of the 1990s, achieving cultlike status among young adults for its presentation of contemporary urban realities that focused on an interracial group of friends including gays, lesbians, and HIV-positive characters. Adaptations of animated Disney Films became another source of Broadway material with the 1998 production of *The Lion King,* and satirist Mel Brooks broke records with his stage version of his film *The Producers* in 2000. The tradition of dance-centered musicals that began in 1975 with *A Chorus Line* continued in 1998 with tap dancer Savion Glover's *Bring in 'da Noise, Bring in 'da Funk*. Another trend involved musicals about rock stars, and several productions examined the lives of Jimi Hendrix, Janis Joplin, and Jim Morrison. Beyond the lights of Broadway, schools, colleges, and community theaters continued to present musical theater productions that spanned the history of the genre.

MULTICULTURAL BROADWAY

A diverse set of cultural influences shaped the development of Tin Pan Alley and Broadway, including the contributions of Jewish American, African American, Latino, and female composers, lyricists, performers, and entrepreneurs.

Jewish American Influences

Jewish American contributions spanned the fields of publishing, composition, performance, production, and film. Because of the rise of violent **anti-Semitism** in Eastern Europe, the Jewish population of the United States grew exponentially at the turn of the twentieth century. For example, **pogroms** (genocide campaigns) against Jews had grown in intensity in the 1880s, and prohibitions against their living in the "Pale of Settlement"—an area previously designated for Jews in what are now Poland, Belarus, and the Ukraine—had radically tightened. Nearly two million Jews had left Russia and Eastern Europe by 1906, and many came to the United States, comprising over a quarter of New York City's population by 1910. The majority of the new arrivals were poorly educated and subject to discrimination. As other immigrant groups did, they clustered in certain businesses—in this case, garments, food, real estate, and entertainment. Because performing arts was a growing and accessible field, many entertainers, playwrights, artists, actors, and musicians developed in the Jewish immigrant community.

Jewish Americans had actually contributed to American popular song at a much earlier point. Henry Russell, the most important songwriter in America before Stephen Foster, was Jewish, as were Tin Pan Alley publishers and composers Charles K. Harris, Harry Von Tilzer, and Edward B. Marks. Vaudeville, too, was enriched by the talents of such Jewish Americans as Sophie Tucker, Al Jolson, Jack Benny, George Burns, and Milton Berle. Many vaudeville theater owners were of Jewish origin, and Jewish American "moguls" such as Louis B. Mayer, Samuel Goldwyn, William Fox, the Warner brothers, and the Selznicks built the movie industry. Moreover, great Jewish American composers and lyricists such as George and Ira Gershwin, Jerome Kern, Richard Rodgers, Oscar Hammerstein II, Harold Arlen, E. Y. "Yip" Harberg, and Irving Caesar dominated American popular song for the first half of the twentieth century.

Black Broadway

Numerous African American composers also made lasting contributions to American popular song, including Clarence Williams, Spencer Williams, Maceo Pinkard, James P. Johnson, Henry Creamer, J. Turner Layton, and Shelton Brooks. Most were members of ASCAP as well as the Clef Club, a professional organization for African American musicians in New York. Following the lead of many other Tin Pan Alley writers, Clarence Williams also started his own music publishing house and virtually monopolized early blues and jazz publishing in the 1920s. Beginning at the turn of the century, black composers and performers developed shows that periodically emerged on Broadway. Early works included *A Trip to Coontown,* which ran from 1898 to 1901, and Will Marion Cook's revue called *Clorindy; or, The Origin of the Cakewalk.* The shows enabled African Americans to break out of the minstrel show format for the first time. Two great African American vaudeville performers in particular, George Walker and Bert Williams, revolutionized black musical theater. Acclaimed for their dancing and singing ability, they produced several all-black Broadway shows, including the famous *Walker and Williams in Dahomey.* The show toured Europe and popularized the cakewalk, which was already a dance craze in America. Williams later crossed over to star in white-produced musicals such as *Ziegfeld's Follies.*

Black musical theater reemerged on Broadway in the 1920s with shows such as *Shuffle Along,* written by Eubie Blake and Noble Sissle. The work drew on African American folk roots with few concessions to white taste or Broadway clichés, and performers from the show, such as Josephine Baker and Paul Robeson, went on to stardom. Other popular black Broadway musicals included *Chocolate Dandies* (Eubie Blake and Spencer Williams), *Blackbirds of 1928* (Lew Leslie, Dorothy Fields, and Jimmy McHugh), *Hot Chocolates* (Fats Waller and Harry Brooks), and *Jump for Joy* (Duke Ellington). They shared a similar format of dancing, singing, solo, and chorus numbers with strong jazz content, as well as African American dance styles such as the buck and wing, soft shoe, tap dancing, and the Charleston. A prominent African American presence did not appear again on Broadway until the 1960s, when shows such as *Tambourines to Glory* and *Don't Bother Me, I Can't Cope* successfully blended jazz, blues, and gospel influences. The 1970s saw a black version of *The Wizard of Oz* called *The Wiz,* which yielded a film version starring Diana Ross and Michael Jackson. Another trend for black Broadway shows in the 1970s focused on nostalgia for the

Internet Listening Exercise

Listen to samples of these songs from different eras of black Broadway.

Bert Williams/George Walker: "Pretty Desdemone"

Eubie Blake: "I'm Just Wild about Harry"

Herb Jeffries/Duke Ellington: "Jump for Joy"

Fats Waller: "Ain't Misbehavin'"

Diana Ross/Michael Jackson: "Ease on Down the Road"

music of jazz masters of the 1920s and 1930s. Shows in this vein included *Bubbling Brown Sugar* (Eubie Blake and Fats Waller), *Ain't Misbehavin'* (Fats Waller), and *Sophisticated Ladies* (Duke Ellington). Several other shows such as *Hello Dolly, Guys and Dolls,* and *Dream Girls* were also produced with black casts.

A Broadway Latin Tinge

Music from Cuba, Mexico, Brazil, and Argentina periodically influenced Tin Pan Alley and Broadway, although, according to historian John Storm Roberts, "Tin Pan Alley and Broadway's way with Latin styles was always eclectic, and usually trivial. It was, nevertheless, part of the process by which the U.S. idioms absorbed Latin ingredients."[9] American composers experimented with Latin influences as early as 1896, in John Philip Sousa's operetta *El Capitan* and Victor Herbert's *The Idol's Eye.* Latin music also influenced African American composers, and the Cuban habanera dance rhythm had connections to ragtime and early jazz. Blues composer W. C. Handy was also fascinated with Cuban and Argentine music: He featured the Argentine tango rhythm in the bridge of his most famous work, the "St. Louis Blues." The tango, introduced to the United States in 1913 by the dance team of Irene and Vernon Castle, was the first authentic Latin style to become popular on Tin Pan Alley and Broadway.

The approval of U.S. citizenship for Puerto Ricans in 1917 and increased immigration expanded the Latin tinge in Tin Pan Alley, and by the mid-1920s many musicals had at least one song with a Latin theme. Mexican-influenced songs also appeared in the Tin Pan Alley repertoire of the 1920s, including "Mi Viejo Amor" by Mexican composer Alfonso Esparza Oteo and "The Rose of the Rio Grande" by Harry Warren. Cuban bandleader Don Azpiazu introduced U.S. audiences of the early 1930s to traditional Cuban percussion with his hit song "*El Manicero*—The Peanut Vendor" in 1931. Spanish bandleader Xavier Cugat also rose to prominence during the decade with an Americanized style of Latin music. During the same era, Brazilian singer and dancer Carmen Miranda became a major star of Broadway and film. In the 1950s, Leonard Bernstein explored Afro-Cuban rhythms in the score of *West Side Story.*

Internet Listening Exercise

Listen to samples of the following Latin-flavored tunes of Broadway and Tin Pan Alley.

Sousa's Band: "El Capitan"

Perez Prado: "Havana"

Duke Ellington/Ivie Anderson: "The Rose of the Rio Grande"

Xavier Cugat: "Perfidia"

Don Azpiazu: "*El Manicero — The Peanut Vendor*"

West Side Story Cast: "America"

The Women of Tin Pan Alley

Although men dominated the music business, a small number of female composers and lyricists made major contributions to American popular song. The most successful female songwriter of the era was lyricist **Dorothy Fields** (1905–1974). For six decades, longer than any other composer or lyricist of the American songbook, Fields composed the lyrics to over 400 songs, including such classics as "On the Sunny Side of the Street," "I'm in the Mood for Love," "A Fine Romance," and "Big Spender." Fields brought a refreshing woman's perspective to her collaborations with great composers such as Jerome Kern, Jimmy McHugh, Harold Arlen, and Harry Warren. Her first big hit, "I Can't Give You Anything but Love," was composed in collaboration with songwriter

Jimmy McHugh for the African American musical revue, *Blackbirds of 1928.* "On the Sunny Side of the Street," composed in 1930 at the height of the Depression, carried an upbeat message that made it one of the best-known songs of the twentieth century. Fields was also the first woman to win an Academy Award for best song—"The Way You Look Tonight," written with Jerome Kern. According to biographer Deborah Grace Winer,

> She was the only one to achieve an equal stature among the top echelon male writers who drove pop and show music, to be "one of the club," both in magnitude and consistency of hits, and in producing a body of significant, mainstream work spanning many decades.[10]

Julliard-trained composer Kay Swift (1905–1993) was well versed in both classical and popular styles, and her jazz-infused work was recognized for its melodic and original sound. Such hits as "Can This Be Love" and "Can't We Be Friends" were recorded repeatedly by performers such as Louis Armstrong, Ella Fitzgerald, Bing Crosby, Frank Sinatra, and Charlie Parker. Ann Ronell (1908–) composed one of the great jazz standards of all time, "Willow Weep for Me," as well as the popular children's song, "Who's Afraid of the Big Bad Wolf." She was also one of the most successful female film score composers in Hollywood. Gifted composer Dana Suesse (1911–1987) understood the complexities of blending classical composition with popular styles. She collaborated with many New York lyricists, who prized her jazz-inflected style and sophisticated harmony. Successes included "Whistling in the Dark" and "You Ought to Be in Pictures." Bandleader Paul Whiteman commissioned her in 1933 to write *Jazz Concerto in Three Rhythms,* which premiered at Carnegie Hall, and Suesse later wrote music for the 1950 film *Young Man with a Horn.*

Internet Listening Exercise

Listen to samples of the following tunes by female Tin Pan Alley composers.

Tony Bennett: "The Way You Look Tonight" (Dorothy Fields)

Louis Armstrong: "On the Sunny Side of the Street" (Dorothy Fields)

Ella Fitzgerald: "Can't We Be Friends?" (Kay Swift)

Frank Sinatra: "Willow Weep for Me" (Ann Ronell)

Doris Day: "You Ought to Be in Pictures" (Dana Suesse)

GREAT PERFORMERS OF AMERICAN POPULAR SONG

Many vocal artists gave life to the music of the golden age of popular song. Here we profile several of the most prominent singers.

With her big voice and infectious magnetism, **Sophie Tucker** (1888–1966) was a star during the early years of American popular song. With a career that spanned sixty-two years, she turned numerous songs into hits. She started out in vaudeville, where she was advised to blacken her face and concentrate on coon songs because she was large and not conventionally attractive. She did so for a time, but then stopped using blackface when she found she could hold an audience without it. One of Tucker's biggest hits was "Some of These Days" in 1910, written by African American composer Shelton Brooks, who also wrote the popular "Darktown Strutters Ball" in 1917. Billed as "the last of the red hot mamas," Tucker borrowed liberally from African American performance styles, performing continuously throughout her long life in vaudeville, musical theater, film, nightclubs, and even television—including the *Ed Sullivan Show.*

www **Internet Listening Exercise**

Listen to samples of the following songs popularized by Sophie Tucker and Al Jolson.

Sophie Tucker: "Some of These Days"

Sophie Tucker: "Darktown Strutters Ball"

Al Jolson: "My Mammy"

Al Jolson: "Toot, Toot, Tootsie"

Al Jolson (1886–1950) was a popular singer and blackface comedian in musical theater and motion pictures from 1910 to 1940. Known for his unique nasal singing style and charisma, Jolson influenced many other singers, including Bing Crosby. The son of a synagogue cantor, Jolson first performed in vaudeville and joined a minstrel troupe, where he started to wear blackface. His trademark number was Gershwin's "Swanee," and he also popularized other tunes, including "My Mammy," "Toot, Toot, Tootsie," and "California, Here I Come." Jolson was known for his "mammy bow," in which he went down on one knee and threw out his arms as if to embrace the audience. In 1927 the artist starred in *The Jazz Singer,* the first feature film to include speech, music, and sound effects. The film revolutionized the motion picture industry and marked the end of the silent-film era. Jolson was the last big star to perform frequently in blackface, and his continuation of the practice well past the prime of minstrelsy was widely criticized.

In the words of one jazz critic, **Bing Crosby** (1903–1977) "was the world's first multi-media superstar." [11] Over a fifty-year career, Crosby sold hundreds of millions of records and had thirty-eight number-one hits—more than the Beatles or Elvis Presley. Crosby's smooth, swinging vocal style and eclectic choice of songs—from jazz to cowboy songs to Hawaiian ballads—made his music accessible to a mass audience. Crosby was one of the first singers to develop the

© Bettmann/CORBIS

Bing Crosby appears in two photos commemorating thirty years as a radio performer, 1931–1960. Evolving microphone technology helped Crosby develop crooning.

smooth personal vocal style called **crooning.** According to Tony Bennett, "Bing dominated music because he created the art of intimate singing."[12] The microphone suited Crosby's voice and style. Prior to the advent of the microphone, popular songs had to be delivered at a high volume in a style called "belting" or "shouting," characteristic of singers such as Bessie Smith, Sophie Tucker, and Al Jolson. Technological improvements in the 1920s and 1930s enabled singers to perform with more subtlety, emphasizing the meaning of lyrics in a natural, almost conversational way.

Crosby had his first hits with the Paul Whiteman Orchestra, and in the mid-1930s he broadened his audience by hosting a radio show and starting his film career. By the 1940s, Crosby was one of Hollywood's biggest stars; in the hit film *Holiday Inn,* he introduced Irving Berlin's "White Christmas," which became one of the most popular songs ever recorded. Crosby was also one of the first major white singers to pay serious attention to African American musical innovations and styles, and the singing of Louis Armstrong was one of his biggest influences. Tony Bennett summed up Crosby's popularity: "If you took the Rolling Stones, Madonna, and Britney Spears and put them together, they wouldn't be as big as Bing Crosby was."[13]

Fred Astaire (1899–1987) was a great popular dancer, with movements characterized by coordination, lightness, and elegance; as a vocalist, he brought the elegance and simplicity of his dance to his singing. The Nebraska-born performer started in vaudeville, starred on Broadway in the 1920s, and teamed up with dancer Ginger Rogers in the 1930s to make a series of memorable films, including *Flying Down to Rio, The Gay Divorcee,* and *The Story of Vernon and Irene Castle.* The dancing in the Astaire-Rogers films revolutionized motion picture musical comedy.

As a vocalist, Astaire was well suited for the intimacy of the microphone, and his understatement, taste, subtlety, and lack of affectation made him the artist of choice for many composers to introduce their songs. Tunes associated with Astaire included "Fascinating Rhythm" (George and Ira Gershwin), "Night and Day" (Cole Porter), "Cheek to Cheek" (Irving Berlin), and "A Fine Romance" (Jerome Kern and Dorothy Fields).

African American singer/actor **Paul Robeson** (1898–1976) attained prominence as both a performer and political activist. A football star and Columbia University Law School graduate, Robeson turned to the performing arts in the 1920s because of discrimination in the legal profession. He appeared on Broadway in *Shuffle Along,* one of the most important African American musicals of the 1920s. He subsequently starred in Eugene O'Neill's 1924 play, *The Emperor Jones,* and in 1925 he showcased his baritone voice in a recital of African American spirituals, which became a central part of his repertoire. Robeson performed his most famous Broadway stage roles in Jerome Kern's *Showboat* and Shakespeare's *Othello,* and his performance of "Ol' Man River" in *Showboat* became his signature piece. Although the song's lyrics painted a submissive portrait, Robeson—who spoke twenty foreign languages—transformed it into a statement of struggle and resistance. The artist's focus on human rights gradu-

www Internet Listening Exercise

Listen to samples of the following tunes associated with Bing Crosby.

Bing Crosby: "White Christmas"

Bing Crosby: "Dear Hearts and Gentle People"

Bing Crosby: "Swingin' on a Star"

Bing Crosby: "Pennies from Heaven"

www Internet Listening Exercise

Listen to samples of the following tunes associated with Fred Astaire.

Fred Astaire: "Fascinating Rhythm"

Fred Astaire: "Cheek to Cheek"

Music Industry Note

The 33⅓ LP Record

The Columbia Broadcasting System (CBS) introduced the first long-playing (LP) recording in 1948. It played at the relatively slow speed of 33⅓ revolutions per minute (rpm), instead of 78 rpm, which had been the standard record speed up to that point. A simple, inexpensive turntable was also marketed to play the new records, which soon replaced the 78s. On the 78s, recorded performances had to be less than 3 minutes per side, so that companies had to record symphonies and other longer works on multiple disks and package them in bulky album sets. The new 33⅓ disks offered much greater flexibility, permitting up to 46 minutes of music to be recorded on a single, 12-inch vinyl disk. This enabled symphonies, extended jazz compositions, and Broadway musicals to be recorded on single disks, and it permitted pop musicians to record eight to ten songs on the two sides of an LP record.

ally became the central theme of his life, and he was increasingly targeted by the government for his outspoken socialist political views. The attacks ultimately damaged his health and overshadowed his artistic talents.

One of the greatest popular vocalists of the twentieth century, **Frank Sinatra** (1915–1998), was recognized for his smooth phrasing and ability to communicate personally to an audience. The New Jersey–born artist, who was

© 1979 William P. Gottlieb www.jazzphotos.com

Frank Sinatra and the Rat Pack in front of the Sands Hotel. Left to right: Peter Lawford, Sammy Davis, Jr., Frank Sinatra, Joey Bishop, and Dean Martin.

influenced by Bing Crosby, sang with the Tommy Dorsey band in the early 1940s and developed a vocal style that emulated trombonist Dorsey's instrumental phrasing. After his first hit, "I'll Never Smile Again," Sinatra became top male vocalist in 1942 in *Down Beat* magazine's poll, replacing Crosby, and he soon became the first pop star to attract hysterical teen female audiences. Although his career declined in the early 1950s, Sinatra made a comeback in 1954 in the movie *From Here to Eternity,* and he continued to work in music and film for the rest of his career. Sinatra also recorded a series of acclaimed "concept" albums for Capitol Records in the mid-1950s using the new 33⅓ LP format and offering classic treatments of popular standards backed by lush, swinging orchestrations. He was often in the public eye during the 1960s with a group of friends called the Rat Pack, which included entertainers Dean Martin, Sammy Davis, Jr., and Peter Lawford. At this time, he established a performance style featuring music from the golden age of American popular song and backed by big bands—a style that entertainers in the show rooms of Las Vegas and other resorts still maintain. Sinatra ultimately became a cultural icon whose sense of masculine style was periodically rediscovered.

Judy Garland (1922–1969) was a popular singer, actress, and cult figure whose compelling combination of talent and personal vulnerability made her a star of musical theater, film, recording, and live performance. She achieved early fame in the 1930s as a child actress performing Harold Arlen and E. Y. "Yip" Harberg's "Over the Rainbow" in her Oscar-winning role in *The Wizard of Oz*. Over time, Garland's career grew turbulent, characterized by swings between self-imposed isolation and wild popularity. In the late 1940s, she began to experience personal and health problems, but she continued to make concert appearances through the late 1950s and early 1960s. Garland's personal de-

CD LISTENING EXERCISE

CD 1/19

Listen to "All of Me," recorded by Frank Sinatra in 1944. During World War II, many musicians volunteered their time to record special "V-Discs" for overseas troops on the front lines. A concurrent musician's union strike and ban on recording meant that V-Discs were the only records being made for the most part. The greeting at the beginning of the song was a personal hello to the troops.

Like many jazz standards composed originally for Broadway stage or film, "All of Me" was composed by Seymour Simons for the film *Careless Lady* (1933). Sinatra's swinging performance accompanied by big band instrumentation became his signature style. His early recordings are reminiscent of 1940s superstar Bing Crosby.

© Joel Springer Collection/CORBIS

Judy Garland poses for a classic Hollywood publicity photo dated 1941.

Internet Listening Exercise

Listen to samples of these songs associated with Judy Garland.

Judy Garland: "Over the Rainbow"

Judy Garland: "The Man That Got Away"

Judy Garland: "Come Rain or Come Shine"

Judy Garland: "Chicago"

mons continued to plague her, however, and she passed away in 1969 of a drug overdose.

THE RISE AND FALL OF THE TIN PAN ALLEY STANDARD

The successful Tin Pan Alley song style changed little for over half a century. Close to 300,000 popular songs were copyrighted from 1900 to 1950, and New York City served as the industry center for the standard form of American popular song throughout the era. The Tin Pan Alley style combined elements of previous generations of American song, fresh ideas from European classical music, and innovations from African American and Latin music to produce some of the finest songs in the history of American popular music. By the 1950s, however, the mood of American popular music had changed, and Tin Pan Alley started to lose its creative edge. Through formulaic repetition of proven patterns, the industry gradually lost the attention of the pop audience. Approaches to song composition also changed in the post–World War II years as singer/songwriters began to write their own material, and new musical styles—R & B, rock, and country—took center stage.

Chapter Summary

- From the late nineteenth through the mid-twentieth centuries, Tin Pan Alley was the nation's center of songwriting and publishing. Beginning in the 1880s, the music industry consolidated in New York, giving birth to a new mass production approach to songwriting. The result was a consistent song style that remained almost unchanged for fifty years.

- Music publishers reaped the biggest financial rewards of the new industry, often at the expense of songwriters and lyricists. Songwriters such as Charles K. Harris and Irving Berlin saw the pattern and formed their own profitable publishing firms. Early Tin Pan Alley styles included waltzes, coon songs, and ragtime songs.

- A variety of new theatrical styles, including vaudeville, operetta, burlesque, and the musical revue, served as the foundation of American musical theater and the Broadway musical.

- George M. Cohan, a transitional figure who gave early American musical theater unique flavor and vitality, wrote, produced, and starred in a long list of shows.

- A series of important works exemplified the evolution of the Broadway show:

    1. Jerome Kern's *Showboat* (1927), the first musical to deal with serious social issues such as racism and social class

2. Gershwin's *Porgy and Bess* (1935), a further milestone that used an all-black cast in an operatic context

3. Rodgers and Hammerstein's *Oklahoma!* (1943), fully integrating all theatrical elements for the first time, removing extraneous elements, producing the first cast recording, and employing a novel, exotic setting

4. Leonard Bernstein's *West Side Story* (1957), blending an urban social message and classical orchestral music with jazz and Afro-Cuban rhythms, creating a popular multicultural score of operatic complexity

5. *Fiddler on the Roof* (1964), an ethnic musical about Russian Jewish village life with universal themes, and one of the last musicals in the fully-developed musical theater tradition

- From the 1960s through the end of the twentieth century, Broadway styles waxed and waned because of changing economic conditions, musical tastes, and shifting social contexts: There were rock musicals, concept musicals, British imports, adaptations of animated Disney films, and revivals.

- Diverse influences shaped Tin Pan Alley and Broadway, including the contributions of Jewish Americans, African Americans, Latinos, and women.

- The five decades between 1900 and 1950 saw many great songwriters and lyricists, including Cole Porter, Harold Arlen, E. Y. Harberg, Johnny Mercer, Hoagy Carmichael, Jimmy McHugh, James Van Heusen, and Harry Warren.

- Great performers of the era included Sophie Tucker, Al Jolson, Fred Astaire, Bing Crosby, Paul Robeson, Frank Sinatra, and Judy Garland.

Key Terms

anti-Semitism
ASCAP
burlesque
concept musical
coon song
crooning
ethnic musical
ethnic novelty song

interpolation
off-Broadway
operetta
pogrom
revue
song plugger
Tin Pan Alley
vaudeville

Study and Discussion Questions

1. What was Tin Pan Alley, what were the origins of its name, and how did it evolve?

2. How did new technologies affect the music industry at the turn of the twentieth century?

3. What popular song styles emerged between 1890 and 1920?

4. What role did Irving Berlin play in the development of American popular song?

5. What roles did vaudeville and operetta play in the development of musical theater? Who were the major innovators in these genres?

6. How has the Broadway musical developed from 1920 to the present? What shows served as benchmarks and why?

7. How did the evolution of musical styles in America interact with the evolution of musical theater?

8. What contributions did Jewish Americans, African Americans, Latinos, and women make to Broadway and the golden age of American popular song?

9. Why were Sophie Tucker, Al Jolson, Bing Crosby, Fred Astaire, Paul Robeson, Frank Sinatra, and Judy Garland important to popular song?

10. What social and musical developments contributed to the decline in the popularity of Tin Pan Alley styles?

Notes

1. Craig H. Roell, "The Development of Tin Pan Alley," in *America's Musical Pulse: Popular Music in Twentieth Century Society,* edited by Kenneth Bindas (New York: Greenwood, 1992), 114.

2. Charles Hamm, *Yesterdays: Popular Song in America* (New York: Norton, 1979), 288.

3. David Joyner, "The Ragtime Controversy," in *America's Musical Pulse: Popular Music in Twentieth Century Society,* edited by Kenneth Bindas (New York: Greenwood, 1992), 242.

4. David Ewen, *Great Men of American Popular Song* (Englewood Cliffs, NJ: Prentice-Hall, 1972), 171.

5. Ibid., 67.

6. Hamm, *Yesterdays,* 352.

7. Alec Wilder, *American Popular Song: The Great Innovators, 1900–1950* (New York: Oxford University Press, 1972), 252.

8. Joseph P. Swain, *The Broadway Musical: A Critical Musical Survey* (New York: Oxford University Press, 1990), 249.

9. John Storm Roberts, *The Latin Tinge: The Impact of Latin American Music on the United States* (Tivoli, NY: Original Music, 1985), 34.

10. Deborah Grace Winer, *On the Sunny Side of the Street: The Life and Times of Dorothy Fields* (New York: Schirmer, 1997), 42.

11. Jesse Hamlin, "Swing along with Bing," *San Francisco Chronicle Datebook,* January 21, 2001, p. 32.

12. Ibid.

13. Ibid.

1900 - 2001

1914–1918 World War I
1919–1933 Prohibition

1922 First country artists recorded by Victor in New York; first country music broadcast on WSB in Atlanta ♪
1925 *Grand Ole Opry* first broadcast on WSM in Nashville ♪
1927 Ralph Peer, country music's first record producer, records Jimmie Rodgers and Carter Family, establishing two dominant strands of country ♪
1929–1930s Great Depression; New Deal begins
1930 "Border" radio stations begin broadcasting, and country music is heard throughout the U.S. ♪
1933 Tennessee Valley Authority established; electric power brought to rural areas of South
1933 Honky-tonks begin to flourish with Prohibition repeal, establishing a new country sound ♪
1935 Bob Wills makes first records, establishing western swing ♪
1939 *Grand Ole Opry* carried nationwide over NBC for first time ♪

1941–1945 U.S. participates in World War II
1941 Bing Crosby has crossover pop hit with Bob Wills's "New San Antonio Rose" ♪
1944 Beginning of regular commercial recording in Nashville ♪
1945 Flatt and Scruggs join Bill Monroe, bluegrass emerges ♪
1946 Major Nashville publisher Acuff-Rose signs Hank Williams ♪
1947 Honky-tonker Ernest Tubb headlines at Carnegie Hall ♪
1950–1953 Korean War
1950 Pop vocalist Patti Page has crossover hit with "Tennessee Waltz" ♪
1952 Kitty Wells becomes first major female solo artist with hit "It Wasn't God Who Made Honky-Tonk Angels" ♪
1954 School segregation outlawed; civil rights movement begins
1954 Elvis Presley signals birth of rockabilly and rock with first recordings for Sam Phillips's Sun Records in Memphis ♪
1956 *Billboard* magazine adopts the term country and western ♪
1958 Country Music Association (CMA) founded ♪

1962 Ray Charles's country album hits number one on pop charts ♪
1963 Civil rights march on Washington; John Kennedy assassinated
1963 Patsy Cline dies in plane crash ♪
1964–1973 Vietnam War
1968 Country crossover hits "Harper Valley PTA," "Honey," and "Wichita Lineman" hit number one on pop charts ♪
1969 ABC debuts *Hee Haw* country TV show; Johnny Cash at San Quentin hits number one on pop album charts ♪
1970 Rock artists flock to record in Nashville ♪
1973 Loretta Lynn featured on cover of *Newsweek* ♪
1976 *Wanted: The Outlaws* becomes first platinum country LP ♪

1981 MTV debuts; Loretta Lynn film biography *Coal Miner's Daughter* released ♪
1983 County Music Television (CMT) and The Nashville Network (TNN) launched ♪
1990s American economic high-tech "bubble"
1990s Garth Brooks breaks sales records, introducing a new generation of young country artists ♪

2000 The film *O Brother, Where Art Thou?* is released ♪
2001 9/11 terrorist attacks

| 1900 | 1920 | 1940 | 1960 | 1980 | 2000 |

Chapter 7

Country Music

Country music is a unique and eclectic American hybrid shaped by folk music, church music, minstrelsy, the blues, jazz, Tin Pan Alley, rock, and the historical and cultural context of the South. The genre is instantly recognizable for its regional accents; high, close harmonies; wailing steel guitars; fiddles; banjos; and straightforward rhythms. It also has numerous variants and substyles. Country music was originally a working-class music, and many artists experienced grinding rural poverty firsthand. It also reflected two contradictory cultural strands: God, country, mother, and home versus drinking, partying, and sex—both often permeated with a sense of sadness and loss. With a national and global audience, country music now accounts for 10 to 15 percent of the recorded music purchased in the United States and may well be the most popular contemporary American musical genre.

FOLK ORIGINS AND EARLY INFLUENCES

The early roots of country originate in the music of Britain, Ireland, Wales, and Scotland. Folk music, dances, fiddle music, broadsides, ballads, and parlor songs from these cultures began to arrive in the southeastern mountains of the United States before the Declaration of Independence in 1776. An important feature of country music is that it often tells a story, and Anglo-Celtic ballads contributed much to southern musical storytelling. The recurring themes of British and American parlor songs—home, hearth, mother, family, and God—also found a comfortable fit in the rural South. The prevalence of rural lifestyles in a rugged terrain contributed to a sense of isolation that flavored country's development, and the challenges of daily life also played a part, according to historian Bill Malone:

> The average rural dweller needed few reminders from the Bible or any other source to know that life was indeed tragic—a brief period filled with unrewarded labor, sadness and disappointment and ending in death.[1]

A unique folk culture and musical style began to take shape in the South, a region some scholars have called the "fertile crescent" of country music.[2]

Because many southerners learned to sing in church, Protestant religious music greatly affected southern singing styles. In particular, church music influenced the development of vocal harmony in country music through the dissemination of the shape note system. The Great Revival of the nineteenth century also influenced southern music; the resulting southern church music came to employ hymns, folk music from European American and African American sources, as well as early forms of gospel music. Songs were often tinged with what Bill Malone called "folk fatalism," portraying Christians as pilgrims in an unfriendly world.[3] The Holiness-Pentecostal movement of the early twentieth century introduced flexible worship formats that reinforced the folk qualities of southern religious music, and it integrated popular styles, such as blues and jazz, that many Christians had previously condemned as "the devil's music." Pentecostal singing styles were rhythmic, passionate, and uninhibited, building a new style of southern singing free from earlier restraint.

Despite slavery and subsequent segregation, many southerners experienced frequent black–white cultural interaction as a part of daily life. Cross-racial musical exchanges went back as far as the seventeenth century, and the performance styles and repertoires of many late-nineteenth- and early-twentieth-century songsters—black and white—were probably similar. African American elements that made their way into country music included blueslike singing styles, the banjo and various banjo techniques, innovative guitar and fiddling styles, ragtime, and jazz. Black music and musicians influenced many country music legends, including A. P. Carter, Bill Monroe, Jimmie Rodgers, Bob Wills, and Hank Williams. African American music also significantly influenced white gospel styles, and white and black gospel styles developed in parallel. Many hymns popular in white communities were composed by such African Americans as Thomas Dorsey, though white southerners were not always aware of this.

Interactions between white and Mexican American musicians in the Southwest were also common, because much of the region was part of Mexico prior to 1848. The use of Anglo-Celtic ballads and *corridos* (Mexican ballads) was similar in the two cultures, and numerous country songs employed the ballad tradition. While heavily shaped by jazz, western swing was also influenced by mariachi music. In turn, western swing then influenced the Chicano *orquesta tejana* style. Further, the close vocal harmonies used by such groups as the Sons of the Pioneers resembled the traditional *dueto* and trio style of Mexican *ranchera* singing, and the polka rhythm, whose roots were European, entered country music via Mexico.

While life in the rural South may have been isolated, nineteenth- and early twentieth-century traveling shows exposed southern audiences to a range of musical styles that included parlor songs, Swiss yodelers, brass bands, Hawaiian string bands, and much more. Minstrel shows often featured the banjo and fiddle as principal instruments, and they introduced songs such as "Turkey in the Straw" (originally known as "Zip Coon") that became southern standards. Vaudeville brought Tin Pan Alley tunes to the South, and many of the songs then went through multiple countrified adaptations. The development of the railroad also impacted southern culture and music, making it possible for rural southerners to respond to the lure of city life. As historian Bill Malone describes,

> No one can document the number of people who have lain awake in quiet and darkened farmhouses listening to the lonesome wail of a distant freight engine or have seen it belching smoke as it thundered down the mountainside and longed for the exciting world that the iron monster seemed to symbolize.[4]

WHAT MAKES IT "COUNTRY"?

Musical elements that define country include songs, language, and instrumentation. Because few rural musicians could read music, early country versions of folk tunes, ballads, or parlor songs were often simplified so they could be learned by ear. Oral transmission contributed to this evolution, often creating completely new tunes from older ones. "Barbara Allen" was one such example: Originally a Scottish ballad, it dispersed throughout Appalachia, ending up in widely differing versions. The classic twang of southern speech is another distinguishing feature of country music. As contemporary country incorporated more rock and pop elements, southern accents sometimes became the primary distinguishing element of the genre.

The defining instrumentation of country music includes stringed instruments such as the fiddle, banjo, guitar, pedal steel guitar, Dobro, mandolin, dulcimer, string bass, and autoharp. Harmonica, jaw harp, washboard, and simple percussion have also been used, and in recent years the drum set, electric bass, and piano have become commonplace.

Historically, the fiddle was probably the most popular instrument in rural North America, arriving with the first colonists. The first reference to country music in America occurred in the announcement of a fiddling contest in a 1736 issue of the *Virginia Gazette*. Throughout the nineteenth century, the instrument appeared at most social functions and served as the centerpiece of rural house parties. The flavor of country fiddling evolved out of British and Irish folk music, jigs, reels, American folk songs, and minstrelsy. Because the fiddle was one of the most common instruments that slaves were allowed to play, African American fiddlers contributed much to the evolution of southern fiddle styles. In addition, string bands, minstrel shows, and early jazz and blues ensembles all used fiddles and influenced the fiddle repertoire.

The banjo is an American hybrid with African roots that has seen many changes during its 200-year North American history. Unfortunately, the rich tradition of African American banjo music has been largely lost. As far back as 1754, it was described in the *Maryland Gazette* as the "banjer."[5] Early versions of the instrument had four strings with no frets. The addition of a fifth ("drone") string in the 1830s, and frets in the 1880s, made the instrument easier to play, and the drone sound of the fifth string became a signature country sound.

The **steel guitar,** originally from Hawaii, became popular on the U.S. mainland in the early twentieth century. The sliding sound of the instrument influenced African American Delta blues guitarists and also found its way into country music. In its acoustic form, now called the **Dobro,** and in its electric pedal steel versions, the steel guitar provides another signature sound of country music. Acoustic guitars did not come into wide use among rural musicians until the late nineteenth century, but by the twentieth century the instrument was widely available via mail-order catalog, and it was soon second only to the fiddle in country string band instrumentation. The adoption of the electric guitar in country music came about with the rise of honky-tonk in the 1940s.

The **mandolin,** which was brought to the United States by European immigrants in the early twentieth century, is another instrument commonly used in country. The instrument has four paired strings that are tuned like a violin, which makes it easy for fiddlers to learn as a second instrument. The **dulcimer** also found a home in country music, with a gentle melodic sound that was perfect for accompanying solo love songs and ballads. In addition, the piano and harmonica commonly appear in country music.

EARLY COMMERCIALIZATION

The commercial development of country music paralleled and frequently overlapped with that of the blues and jazz. At first the commercial music industry did not know what to do with the rural southern musical genre that took shape in the 1920s. There was a vague sense that the music was old (or old-fashioned) and that it reflected southern rural culture: Brunswick Records called it "songs from Dixie," Columbia called it "old familiar tunes," and producer Ralph Peer coined the term *hillbilly* in 1925. Finally, *Billboard* magazine adopted the term *country and western* in 1949.

Radio

The invention of radio played a major role in the dissemination of country music. The earliest country music broadcast was heard in 1922 on Atlanta's WSB, with a lineup featuring a mountain quartet, gospel singers, and an old-time

---

Multicultural Note

Is it Country or Hillbilly?

In the early days of country music, the term **hillbilly** was often used by musicians, their fans, and their detractors. According to historian Bill Malone, "Artists ... have always reacted ambivalently to the term, sometimes resenting it as a presumed denigration of their music and the way of life it supposedly represents, but often proclaiming it proudly."[6] The contradictory meanings of *hillbilly* reflect a view that both sentimentalizes and rejects the rural roots of southern culture. What other cultural or ethnic designations produce conflicting sets of interpretations?

musician named Fiddlin' John Carson. Radio was ideally suited to rural America and the vast audience far outside city limits, for it could penetrate into isolated areas that lacked roads or rail access. As one Georgia farmer wrote to WSB in Atlanta, "I walked four miles and forded two streams just to hear your seven o'clock program."[7] Local or regional businesses owned many of these stations. For example, Sears Roebuck owned WLS in Chicago, and an insurance company owned WSM in Nashville, whose call letters stood for "We Shield Millions." Most country radio shows were commercially sponsored, many by the makers of patent medicines, which maintained a link between country and old-time touring medicine shows. Some of the more colorful medicinal sponsors were "Crazy Water Crystals," "Retonga Medicine," "Man-O-Ree," "Black Draught," and "Pe-Ru-Na." Other more prosaic underwriters included flour, coffee, farm machinery, snuff, and beverage companies.

The *barn dance* first appeared in 1923 as an early country radio format, and in 1925 WSM in Nashville started its own version—what became the legendary **Grand Ole Opry.** The early *Opry* featured string bands, traditional singers, gospel quartets, and banjo players, supported by colorful announcers, comedians, and ad-libbing costumed musicians. Early *Opry* stars included banjoist "Uncle" Dave Macon; Deford Bailey ("The Harmonica Wizard"); the Delmore Brothers, a vocal blues-gospel duo; and the Pickard Family, a traditional vocal trio. By the 1930s, the *Opry* and other barn dance shows were well established, and in 1944 *Billboard* magazine estimated that there were 600 country radio shows in the United States playing to an audience of forty million people. Powerful radio stations also sprang up in northern Mexico along the U.S. border, sending country music out to much of the United States.

Radio greatly influenced country performance styles. For example, the personality of the singer grew increasingly important as new microphone technologies permitted subtlety and dynamics. Humor also emerged as a significant element, and performers developed a closeness to their audiences that became a hallmark. Listeners often wrote letters to their favorite stars, and requests and dedications were answered on the air. Singer Bradley Kincaid sent this message out to his listeners,

> When I sing for you on the air, I always visualize you, a family group, sitting around the radio. . . . If I did not feel your presence, though you be a thousand miles away, the radio would be cold and unresponsive to me, and I in turn would sound the same way to you.[8]

By the 1950s, with the advent of television and rock, country radio started to take a battering. In response, the Country Music Association (CMA) formed in 1958. It successfully buttressed the industry, raising the number of country stations from 81 in 1961 to over 600 by 1969. It also ushered in an era of DJs, playlists, promoters, and tightly controlled formats that changed periodically with names such as "modern country," "countrypolitan," "real country," "contemporary country," and "young country." As of the early 2000s, about 19 percent of the 11,000 U.S. radio stations played country music, and almost all had strict playlists. Contemporary country radio rarely includes classic country or bluegrass artists, however. Even when the old-time and bluegrass music sound track to the film *O Brother, Where Art Thou?* won a Grammy in 2000, it received scant airplay. According to Luke Wood, president of the soundtrack's label,

> We operate in country within a box and you can run up in the corners of the box, but if you get outside of it the gatekeepers don't like it. A few radio programmers said to the record labels after the Grammys: "Don't get any ideas: we are not going to start playing Allison Krauss and Nickel Creek because of this."[9]

Country music radio today thrives as a commercial vehicle, but according to critic Edward Morris,

> Country radio has become very good at giving fans steady and reliably pleasant background music. But that is a shamefully tepid legacy for a vehicle that once provided the rough edged excitement of barn dances, the polyglot programming of bluegrass, country, and gospel.[10]

The Early Country Recording Industry

Internet Listening Exercise

Listen to samples of these early country recordings.

Fiddlin' John Carson: "The Little Log Cabin by the Stream"

Charlie Pool and the North Carolina Ramblers: "White House Blues"

Gid Tanner and His Skillet Lickers: "Soldier's Joy"

Vernon Dalhart: "The Prisoner's Song"

Early country recording was a byproduct of the successful movement to record African American talent, which started with Mamie Smith's "Crazy Blues" in 1920. The first commercial "hillbilly" recording was made of Eck Robertson, a Texas fiddler, in 1922. From the start, the record industry encouraged segregation by dividing southern vernacular music along racial lines: African American recordings were "race records"; white recordings were "hillbilly music." Ralph Peer (1892–1960), who had worked on the Mamie Smith recording session, pioneered country music recording. His earliest country recordings, made in 1923, included Fiddlin' John Carson, Gid Tanner and His Skillet Lickers, and Charlie Poole and the North Carolina Ramblers. A year later a classically trained vocalist named Vernon Dalhart scored some of the first country hits with "The Prisoner's Song" and "Wreck of the Old 97," two parlor songs with a simple guitar and fiddle accompaniment.

Having detected a large market for vernacular music, Peer quickly capitalized on it by setting up a legendary recording trip in 1927:

> I made a survey of various Southern cities. . . . In Bristol I appealed to the editor of a local newspaper and he ran a half column on his front page. This worked like dynamite. . . . Groups of singers who had not visited Bristol during their entire lifetime arrived by bus, horse and buggy, trains, or on foot.[11]

Among the artists he recorded in Bristol, Virginia, that year were the Carter Family, a traditional folk trio from southwestern Virginia, and Jimmie Rodgers, a bluesy singer/songwriter from Mississippi. As historian Nolan Porterfield has observed, "Bristol, August 1927 has come to signal the Big Bang of country music evolution, the genesis of every shape and species of Pickin'-and-Singin' down through the years."[12] The Carters and Rodgers shaped two seminal strands of country music. The Carters symbolized home, church, family, and tradition, while Rodgers personified rambling, drinking, partying, and the blues.

*Artists Influenced
by the Carter Family*

Roy Acuff
Delmore Brothers
Iris DeMent
Flatt and Scruggs
Woody Guthrie
Alison Krauss
Louvin Brothers
Bill Monroe
Ricky Skaggs
Stanley Brothers
Doc Watson
Gillian Welch

*Artists Influenced
by Jimmie Rodgers*

Gene Autry
Johnny Cash
Lefty Frizzell
Merle Haggard
Ray Price
George Strait
Floyd Tillman
Ernest Tubb
Hank Williams
Bob Wills
Dwight Yoakam

The Carter Family—A. P. Carter (1891–1960); his wife, Sara (1899–1979); and their sister-in-law Maybelle (1909–1978)—came from the mountains of southwestern Virginia. By the time they began recording in 1927, they had amassed a repertoire of traditional songs from Anglo-Celtic, religious, and sentimental sources. Their music featured two-part close vocal harmony led by Sara Carter, and the influential thumb-picked "Carter Scratch" guitar playing of Maybelle Carter. Sara and Maybelle Carter were the first female stars of country music in a time when women's roles were limited. It was only because A. P. Carter fronted the group that the women were able to perform at all, and advertising posters for their concerts assured people that "The Program Is Morally Good."[13] The Carters' repertoire of Anglo-American folk music (now simply called "Carter songs") was laboriously gathered across Appalachia by A. P. Carter, who was often assisted by Leslie Riddle, an African American blues singer and guitarist. Carter songs such as "Wildwood Flower," "Wabash Cannonball," "Can the Circle Be Unbroken," "Worried Man Blues," and "Keep on the Sunny Side" became standards.

Jimmie Rodgers (1897–1933), the "father" of country music, was a twentieth-century popular music original. He blended the blues, jazzy dance-band arrangements, a catchy vocal style, railroad images, yodeling, and steel guitar to shape an entire genre. The son of an itinerant railroad worker in Mississippi, he learned African American work songs and early blues styles, and he worked in medicine shows and minstrelsy. According to critic Nick Tosches, "Jimmie Rodgers made black music accessible to white audiences."[14] When Ralph Peer

CD LISTENING EXERCISE

CD 1/20

Listen to "Keep on the Sunny Side," recorded by the Carter Family in 1927. What is the overall feel of the song? What is its message? Notice how the lyrical content contrasts with the overall feel of the tune. What is the arrangement? Listen to Maybelle Carter's guitar playing. Does it sound familiar? How would you describe Sara Carter's lead vocal style? What is the nature of the harmonies?

© Eric Schaal/Time Life Pictures/Getty Images

The Carter Family, America's first family of country music, evoked traditional values with their folk-rooted acoustic music. In a 1941 photo, patriarch A. P. Carter (right) is flanked by group members, his sister-in-law Maybelle (on guitar), and his wife, Sara Carter (third from right). Daughter June Carter (second from left) later married singer Johnny Cash.

Multicultural Note

Yodeling and Hybridity in Country Music

How the yodel became a staple of country music provides an example of cultural hybridity. The word *yodel* is of German origin. In the early nineteenth century, south German vocalists performed the style on European stages. The yodel became part of American minstrelsy in the mid-nineteenth century and was included on the earliest Edison cylinder recordings of the 1890s. Yodeling records were popular through 1920.

The first country record to include yodeling was made in 1924, and in 1927 Jimmie Rodgers released his first recording with his **blue yodel** style. A *yodel* is a wordless vocal sound created in the back of the throat that rapidly alternates between two pitches, which Rodgers blended with blue notes to create the blue yodel. Several African American blues and jazz singers adopted the blue yodel, including Tampa Red, Bessie Smith, and Joe Williams. Gene Autry and Hank Williams also used the blue yodel style, consciously emulating Rodgers and making it a signature country sound.

auditioned Rodgers in 1927, he declared, "I was elated. . . . He had his own personal and peculiar style, and I thought that his yodel alone might spell success."[15] Rodgers recalled the same encounter: "They want these old-fashioned things. Love songs and plantation melodies and the old river ballads. Well, I'm ready with 'em."[16] Rodgers headed for New York after the Bristol sessions, and from that time until his death in 1933 he played traveling shows, broadcast throughout the South and Southwest, made a short film, and did multiple recording sessions each year. Rodgers was also one of the first major white artists to record with racially mixed bands. The story of the artist's final 1933 recording session in New York is a sad one. Sick with tuberculosis, he rested between takes on a cot in a rehearsal hall. Two days after the session, he was dead. Rodgers was the first artist inducted into the Country Music Hall of Fame when the award was established in 1961.

© Frank Driggs Collection/Getty Images

Vocalist/songwriter Jimmie Rodgers pioneered a blues-drenched style that shaped country music for decades to follow. Sometimes called "The Singing Brakeman" for his youth on the railroads, here Carter projects a sophisticated look that belies hillbilly stereotypes.

THE "WEST" JOINS COUNTRY

A "Western tinge" permeated country music in the 1930s and 1940s. Cowboy clothing and Western themes took country in a new direction, shaped by an oil boom in Texas and the westward economic migrations of the Depression and World War II.

Singing Cowboys

Jimmie Rodgers pioneered the concept of the **singing cowboy** and Western images in country music, and subsequent Texas performers—including Ernest Tubb, Lefty Frizzell, Floyd Tillman, and Bob Wills—often credited Rodgers as their inspiration. **Gene Autry** (1907–1998), the first full-blown singing cowboy, starred on the Chicago-based WLS *Barn Dance* radio show from 1931 to 1934 with a Rodgers-influenced style that included yodeling. Autry's hits included "Silver-Haired Daddy of Mine" and "South of the Border (Down Mexico Way)." Autry moved to Hollywood in 1934 to begin a long career as a singing cowboy, ultimately making over ninety movies.

With the popularity of the Hollywood image of the West, the term *Western music* was indiscriminately applied to all styles of southern rural music. The Western look—gaudy tailored suits, hats, and boots—prevailed, and many

CD LISTENING EXERCISE

CD 1/21

Listen to "Waiting for a Train," recorded by Jimmie Rodgers in 1928. Notice how the song blends complex sounds in an appealing way: steel guitar, yodeling, jazzy horns, and bluesy vocals, reflecting the life of a rambling railroad man. Why does this hybrid mix work so well? Notice the train sound at the beginning of the song. Listen to the New Orleans jazz break in the middle of the song.

Internet Listening Exercise

Listen to these samples of early Western tunes of the 1930s.

Gene Autry: "That Silver-Haired Daddy of Mine"

Tex Ritter: "Rye Whiskey"

Sons of the Pioneers: "Tumbling Tumbleweeds"

Herb Jeffries: "I'm a Happy Cowboy"

Patsy Montana: "I Want to Be a Cowboy's Sweetheart"

artists adopted Western-sounding names—the Light Crust Doughboys, the Sons of the Pioneers, Tex Ritter, and Roy Rogers among them. The Sons of the Pioneers were one of the most famous western groups of the era, known for their smooth, inventive harmonies and finely crafted songs. First organized in California in the 1930s by Roy Rogers, the trio sang every type of country song—even borrowing from Tin Pan Alley. Western hits for the group included "Cool Water" and "Tumbling Tumbleweeds."

Another successful cowboy artist, Tex Ritter (1905–1974), was a college-educated vocalist and performer from Texas. While trying to get work on Broadway, his thick Texas accent and storehouse of cowboy lore became his ticket to success. Cowboy music also spawned successful female artists and at least one artist of color. Among them were Patsy Montana (1908–1996), who released "I Want to Be a Cowboy's Sweetheart" in 1939. The song, which included yodeling and a polka rhythm, was the first hit for a female country singer. Herb Jeffries (1911–), an African American vocalist, starred in several movie westerns in the late 1930s as "The Bronze Buckaroo," a black singing cowboy, and also worked with Duke Ellington.

Honky-Tonk

Soon after the repeal of Prohibition in 1933, a brisk business arose in the honky-tonks of Texas and other parts of the West. Similar to juke joints, **honky-tonks** were usually built on the outskirts of town, with large dance floors, jukeboxes, and live music. Their development was fueled in Texas by an oil boom, and in California by migrant farm workers in the 1930s and defense industry workers in the 1940s. Throughout the West, displaced rural people living on the fringes of urban areas wanted to dance, drink, and forget their problems on a Saturday night. According to critic Nick Tosches, "In country music, honky-tonk came to be associated with the loud, small-group sound that developed in the redneck bars of east Texas and oil-boom towns: amplified guitars and lyrics of sex and whiskey."[17] Honky-tonks catered to a rough crowd, as vocalist Ray Price recalled:

> Some of them would be just one square building. No paint on the outside. And you'd go in and it would have a wooden dance floor, a long bar, tables, and a small bandstand. They fought an awful lot in those days. You'd sweep up earlobes and eyeballs every morning.[18]

In the honky-tonks, country music evolved lyrically and stylistically, recasting the nature of the genre. Motherhood and pastoral themes gave way to the problems of people in a changing social environment, and the music became louder to be heard over rowdy crowds. The honky-tonk *sock rhythm* developed, with a strong electric bass pulse on beats one and three and heavy rhythm guitar on beats two and four. Piano, drums, electric guitar, electric bass, and pedal steel guitar joined the classic fiddle and acoustic guitar lineup. Honky-tonk singers were unashamedly emotional, using vocal breaks, hiccups, yodels, and cries; they slurred phrases, bent notes, and shed tears. Classics of the era included Ernest Tubbs's "Walking the Floor over You," Al Dexter's "Pistol Packin' Mama," and Hank Williams's "Your Cheatin' Heart." Ernest Tubb (1914–1984), a disciple of Jimmie Rodgers, was the quintessential honky-tonk artist and became a country music institution over his long career. Tubbs built on a deep baritone voice and years in Texas honky-tonks to fashion his relaxed, widely admired style. Joining the *Grand Ole Opry* in 1943, he was the first to bring honky-tonk to Nashville. Other great honky-tonkers included Floyd Tillman, Lefty Frizzell, Hank Thompson, Hank Williams, and Ray Price.

Internet Listening Exercise

Listen to samples of these honky-tonk classics.

Ernest Tubb: "Walking the Floor over You"

Al Dexter: "Pistol Packin' Mama"

Lefty Frizzell: "If You've Got the Money, I've Got the Time"

Western Swing

By the end of the 1930s, Americans were turning to a new style called **western swing,** a hybrid of southern string bands, swing, Tin Pan Alley, and the African American, Cajun, Tex-Mex, German, Bohemian, and cowboy cultures of the Southwest. Major innovators included Bob Wills, Milton Brown, and Spade Cooley. **Bob Wills** (1905–1975) did the most to develop and popularize western swing. Originally a fiddler, he honed his performing skills in medicine shows, in fiddle bands, and with the Light Crust Doughboys, combining the fiddle music of his rural roots with blues and jazz. He also used a violin section, a practice probably borrowed from Mexican mariachi music. Wills formed his band, the Texas Playboys, in 1933 and began to broadcast and record regularly. The group featured fiddles, drums, steel and electric guitars, brass, and reeds— with up to eighteen members. Wills's best-known hits included "Steel Guitar Rag" and "New San Antonio Rose," which became a pop crossover hit for Bing Crosby in 1941. After World War II, Wills changed instrumentation and spotlighted the electric pedal steel guitar in country music for the first time. According to one description of Wills,

> His irresistible personality dominated every performance . . . as he strutted across the stage, dressed in the attire of a rancher, chomping on a cigar, and pointing toward musicians as they took their instrumental breaks. . . . His shouts and hollers . . . punctuated the performance of virtually every song: "Ahh haa," "Take it away, Leon," "Aw, come in, Tommy," and on and on.[19]

Wills provided an important link between jazz, blues, multiple country styles, and the rockabilly of the 1950s, influencing rock pioneer Bill Haley, who originally named his band "Bill Haley and the Four Aces of Western Swing."

Hank Williams

Singer/songwriter Hank Williams (1923–1953) was a country music icon who permanently bridged the gulf between country and pop, influencing generations of artists with a simple, earthy style. Williams's life encompassed a swift rise and sudden, tragic fall, awash in alcohol and drugs. The Alabaman started

CD LISTENING EXERCISE

CD 1/22

Listen to "New San Antonio Rose," recorded by Bob Wills and the Texas Playboys in 1940. Notice how the song starts with a horn-based swing introduction. How does Wills use vocal interjections to encourage the musicians? How does the entrance of the vocalist establish a country and western flavor? After the vocal part ends, notice the Mexican mariachi flavor of the first horn break followed by a schmaltzy woodwind swing passage. How many genres are blended in one song? How does "New San Antonio Rose" reflect cultural hybridity?

playing guitar at an early age and was tutored by an African American street singer named Tee-Tot (Rufus Payne). Roy Acuff and Ernest Tubb also influenced Williams's vocal style. Though rejected in his first try to get on the *Grand Ole Opry,* Williams returned to Nashville and was signed by a major publishing firm, recording "Move It on Over," "Honky Tonkin'," and several other early hits. He finally debuted on the *Grand Ole Opry* in 1949, where pandemonium erupted and he was brought back for six encores. Williams's hits included "I'm So Lonesome I Could Cry," "Your Cheatin' Heart," and "Hey Good Lookin'," along with crossover hits by others including Tony Bennett's "Cold Cold Heart" and Jo Stafford's "Jambalaya." Williams was a riveting performer. According to a fellow musician, "He had a voice that went through you like electricity, sent shivers up your spine, and made the hair rise on the back of your neck with the thrill. With a voice like that he could make you laugh or cry." Williams also pioneered a rocking, lightly gyrating posture that Elvis Presley expanded on a few years later. As comedienne Minnie Pearl put it, "He had a real animal magnetism. He destroyed the women in the audience." [20] Williams reflected on his own appeal:

> It can be explained in just one word: sincerity. When a hillbilly sings a crazy song, he feels crazy. When he sings "I Laid My Mother Away," he sees her a-laying right there in the coffin. He sings more sincere than most entertainers because the hillbilly was raised rougher than most entertainers. . . . You got to have smelt a lot of mule manure before you can sing like a hillbilly. [21]

Williams's short life ended sadly. An addiction to alcohol and pills adversely affected his career, and just as he was making a comeback in 1953, he died of a

Vocalist/songwriter Hank Williams, backed by his band, the Drifting Cowboys, was one of country music's greatest songwriters and a superstar of the early 1950s.

heart attack on the way to a gig. His funeral drew over 25,000 people, including all the greatest stars of country.

BLUEGRASS AND OLD-TIME MUSIC

Bluegrass developed as a new style in the 1940s, although it gave the impression of being an older style because it employed **old-time music,** or early Appalachian folk music. The style took its name from the Blue Grass Boys, a band led by mandolin player Bill Monroe, who is often called the father of bluegrass. Bluegrass instrumentation combines fiddle, banjo, mandolin, guitar, Dobro, and acoustic bass. Singing is often done in the **high lonesome style,** which originated in the clear, dry, high-pitched tone of Bill Monroe's singing voice. Bluegrass vocal harmonies contain two, three, or four parts rooted in the gospel quartet styles of southern church music, and many bluegrass song lyrics are religious.

Bluegrass was shaped by the performance styles of two of its founding artists, Bill Monroe and Earl Scruggs. Monroe's aggressive single-note mandolin solo style and backbeat rhythm accompaniment, together with Earl Scruggs's three-finger picking on the five-string banjo, set the tone for the genre. Bluegrass is performed faster than other country styles; musicologist Alan Lomax once called it "folk music in overdrive." It integrates driving, syncopated banjo picking with a steady four-beat feel; guitar and bass emphasize beats one and three while the mandolin and banjo answer on the backbeat. Bluegrass is also sometimes referred to as "country jazz," because of its frequent focus on improvised solos.

Kentuckian **Bill Monroe** (1911–1996) took up the mandolin as part of a family band. Arnold Schultz, an African American guitarist and fiddler, taught him blues licks and syncopated styles. According to Monroe, "People can tell my music is from Kentucky. . . . You see, there's feeling for Kentucky in it, the Methodists and Baptists, the old blues, the old fiddle and guitar." [22] Monroe appeared at barn dances and on the radio, first performing on the *Grand Ole Opry* in 1939. When his band's upbeat, syncopated sound started to coalesce around 1945, other musicians began to take note. **Lester Flatt** (1914–1979) and **Earl Scruggs** (1924–), two of the most innovative members of Monroe's band, left to form their own group called the Foggy Mountain Boys in 1948. Early compositions included "Foggy Mountain Breakdown," later made famous

---

CD LISTENING EXERCISE

CD 1/23

Listen to "Your Cheatin' Heart," recorded by Hank Williams in 1948. Focus on the lyrics. Notice their simplicity, straightforwardness, and honesty. What is the emotional feel of the song? What is the instrumentation? How does the simplicity of the arrangement "stay out of the way" of the lyrics? How would you describe the quality of Williams's voice? Why did Williams connect so powerfully to so many people?

CD LISTENING EXERCISE

CD 1/24

Listen to "It's Mighty Dark to Travel," recorded by Bill Monroe and the Blue Grass Boys in 1947. The musicians include Earl Scruggs on banjo, Lester Flatt on guitar and vocals, Chubby Wise on fiddle, and Howard Watts on string bass. Monroe's distinctive chop-chord mandolin style and Scruggs's syncopated three-finger banjo picking, as well as improvised solos, rhythmic drive, and "high lonesome" duet singing, exemplify the fundamentals of bluegrass style. This classic recording provided a model for succeeding generations of artists.

© Frank Driggs Collection

Singer/mandolinist Bill Monroe, the "father of bluegrass," toured with his band, the Blue Grass Boys, and appeared on the *Grand Ole Opry* beginning in the 1940s.

in the movie *Bonnie and Clyde,* and "Roll in My Sweet Baby's Arms." Flatt and Scruggs were known for flawless performance choreography and virtuoso playing, which maintained their long-term popularity. A third seminal bluegrass act, the **Stanley Brothers,** began in the late 1940s. Co-led by Ralph (1927–) and Carter Stanley (1925–1966), the group drew on traditional old-time mountain music. Ralph Stanley emerged as an elder statesman of bluegrass in the early 2000s, after his performance on the soundtrack of the film *O Brother, Where Art Thou?*

By the early 1950s, bluegrass was firmly established in the country music marketplace. However, even though side "B" of Presley's first single was a super-

Multicultural Note

When Does an Innovation Become a Recognized Style?

Rarely do individual musicians generate an entire style as Bill Monroe did. Historians often date the origin of the term *bluegrass* to the emergence of the Stanley Brothers, who clearly emulated Monroe's style. Although the term first appeared in the 1940s, writers and critics did not commonly use it for another ten years, and even then many musicians avoided it.

What bluegrass is depends on whom you ask. Although a classic repertoire exists, many artists venture far from the traditional Monroe model by including waltzes, old-time styles, Tin Pan Alley songs, rock, and pop tunes. Does labeling a style clarify or blur our understanding of music?

charged version of Bill Monroe's "Blue Moon of Kentucky," for example, the rock revolution presented a new challenge. The country music industry responded by shifting to the smoother Nashville studio sound, and bluegrass fell on hard times. The urban folk revival movement of the late 1950s and early 1960s, though, gave the style new life. Spurred by the popularity of such artists as Woody Guthrie, the Weavers, and Pete Seeger, the revival focused on acoustic music and traditional styles, rejecting mainstream pop and rock. Bluegrass was soon heard in urban areas and on college campuses, and bluegrass scenes developed in several northern cities. Earl Scruggs and the Stanley brothers performed at the first Newport Folk Festival in 1959.

Bluegrass periodically resurfaced in the public eye in succeeding decades. In the early 1960s, the Osborne Brothers had a crossover hit with "Rocky Top," and Flatt and Scruggs succeeded with "The Ballad of Jed Clampett," the theme from *The Beverly Hillbillies*. The soundtrack to the 1967 film *Bonnie and Clyde* also featured a Flatt and Scruggs bluegrass tune, and the 1972 film *Deliverance* showcased "Dueling Banjos." Further, in the 1960s a progressive bluegrass movement developed that maintained acoustic instrumentation while adding rock to the repertoire. Bluegrass also found new support in outdoor festivals, and today over 500 such events take place around the country every year.

In the 1980s and 1990s, mandolinist David Grisman became known for his progressive fusion of bluegrass and jazz, and he collaborated with a variety of artists on a series of popular recordings. Banjoist Béla Fleck went in a novel direction in the 1990s, playing a popular amalgam called "spacegrass" or "supergrass"—blending jazz, pop, and world music. Legendary guitarist Doc Watson kept traditional styles alive, and eclectic fiddler Mark O'Connor experimented with new bluegrass hybrids. Bluegrass and old-time music received another lease on life in the early 2000s with the success of the soundtrack from the film *O Brother, Where Art Thou?* Performers on the album included bluegrass legend Ralph Stanley, as well as contemporary artists Gillian Welch and Alison Krauss. Producer T-Bone Burnett reflected on the record's success: "We have machines today that can crank out perfect music all day long. This was real people playing and singing around real microphones."[23]

Fiddler, bandleader, and vocalist Alison Krauss (1971–) was already well known in bluegrass prior to *O Brother*. The Grammy-winning artist played on the *Grand Ole Opry* beginning in 1993 and toured widely with her band Union Station; she was also a respected studio musician and producer. Krauss and Gillian Welch were part of a community of contemporary female artists who broke through male-dominated traditions in bluegrass and old-time music. Rounder Records supported this trend with the 2001 release of *O Sister! The Women's Bluegrass Collection*.

THE RISE OF NASHVILLE

By the 1940s, Nashville had become the acknowledged center of country music. Country's commercial appeal exploded during World War II as southern soldiers came in contact with troops from other regions, leading country singer

Roy Acuff to top crooner Frank Sinatra in one poll of GIs. The demand continued after the war: According to *Newsweek,* "Hillbilly music is now such a vogue that it is just about pushing popular tunes, jazz, swing, bebop and everything else right out of the picture. . . . The demand for it has multiplied fivefold since the war."[24]

The *Grand Ole Opry*

The growth of radio station WSM's *Grand Ole Opry* had much to do with the rise of Nashville. Prominent artists such as Roy Acuff, Bill Monroe, and Minnie Pearl joined the show just before the onset of World War II, and after the war the *Opry* began an aggressive talent drive that netted Ernest Tubb, Eddy Arnold, Hank Snow, and Hank Williams. When NBC picked up the *Opry* for weekly national broadcast in 1943, Nashville had truly arrived. The RCA and Decca labels also began recording in Nashville in the 1940s, and other labels followed suit, benefiting from the presence of great studio musicians such as guitarist Chet Atkins. Most major labels still maintain a presence in Nashville.

Roy Acuff (1903–1992), a traditional mountain singer and fiddler from east Tennessee, shaped the performance style and content of the *Opry.* His singing shifted the largely instrumental *Opry* to feature more vocal performances, with a repertoire emphasizing sacred and traditional songs that he delivered emotionally, sometimes weeping openly. Acuff's hits included "The Great Speckled Bird" and "The Wabash Cannonball." He also cofounded Acuff-Rose, the most successful Nashville music publishing house, in 1942. Established in part because of the fight between ASCAP and the nation's broadcasters over music licensing rights (see Chapter 6), Acuff-Rose affiliated with the new BMI and supplied new country songs to the broadcast and recording industries. Other prominent Nashville-based music publishers included Peer-Southern (co-owned by Ralph Peer), Tree, and Cedarwood.

Internet Listening Exercise

Listen to samples of these signature tunes by Roy Acuff.

Roy Acuff: "The Great Speckled Bird," "Wabash Cannonball"

Tin Pan Alley, Nashville-Style

The growth of the music industry in Nashville attracted songwriters, recreating the climate of Tin Pan Alley with a country twang. Great songwriters such as Willie Nelson, Harlan Howard, Roger Miller, and Tom T. Hall often hung out at a bar near the *Opry,* hoping to catch the ear of stars. As one of their number recalled, "We would sit around at the old Tootsie's Orchid Lounge, and pick each other's brains about songs. There were dozens of hit songs that I heard for the first time in there."[25] The rise of Nashville paralleled the rise of legendary producers who crafted the signature Nashville sound. Most Nashville producers initially took their stylistic cues from the *Grand Ole Opry:* Fiddle and steel guitar were prominent; drums, mistrusted. The producers generally preferred the city's pool of studio musicians for recording, but the resulting sound, though consistent and professional, could be formulaic.

Elvis Presley's rockabilly explosion in 1954 presented a new challenge to Nashville. **Rockabilly** was a blend of country and black music that first emerged in the early 1950s. Developed at Sam Phillips's Sun Records Studios in Memphis by artists such as Elvis Presley, Carl Perkins, and Jerry Lee Lewis, the style took off quickly around 1954 and grew in popularity with contributions from the East (Everly Brothers, Gene Vincent), the Southwest (Buddy Holly, Wanda Jackson), and the West (Eddie Cochran). Nashville responded by playing an active role in the development of rockabilly and early rock. RCA opened a Nashville operation after signing Elvis Presley, where he recorded "Heartbreak Hotel" in 1956. The song was unlike any previous country record, and its worldwide success led to a redefinition of what could be done in Nashville. During the next few years, Gene Vincent, the Everly Brothers, Patsy Cline, Brenda Lee, Marty Robbins, and Johnny Cash were among the many singers who made records in Nashville that crossed over to mainstream pop. Among the other country artists popular in the late 1950s and early 1960s were George Jones, Don Gibson, Jim Reeves, Floyd Cramer, and Ray Charles.

Producers **Chet Atkins** (1924–2001) and **Owen Bradley** (1915–1998) are often credited with developing the **Nashville sound** that beat back the rockabilly challenge. Atkins was a respected guitarist and songwriter who headed RCA's office in Nashville for over two decades. He introduced electric instruments and polished arrangements, targeting an adult audience to broaden country's appeal. The Nashville sound also employed strings, horns, choral backgrounds, smooth tempos, reverb (echo), and innovative microphone techniques. When asked to describe the Nashville sound, Atkins jingled some coins in his pocket:

> People were in it to make a living. The Nashville Sound is just a sales tag. If there is a Nashville Sound, it's the Southern accent. You speak with it, maybe you play with it, too. . . . We took the twang out of it, Owen Bradley and I. What we did was try to make hit records. We wanted to keep our job.[26]

In addition to a skilled producer, Atkins was a sought-after session guitarist with a signature finger-picking style. He made more than a hundred recordings in his own name and hundreds more as a studio player, winning multiple Grammys. Although he belonged to the Nashville establishment, Atkins supported maverick artists later in his career, including Dolly Parton, Waylon Jennings, and Charley Pride.

Nashville in the 1960s and 1970s

Throughout the 1960s and 1970s, the success of country music paralleled the growth of country radio. Country artists popular in the 1960s included Ray Price, Roger Miller, Kenny Rogers, Glenn Campbell, Johnny Cash, Dolly Parton, and George Jones. The 1970s also saw the expansion of Nashville's record labels, with such stars as Loretta Lynn, Tammy Wynette, Charlie Daniels, Buck Owens, Charley Pride, Merle Haggard, Freddie Fender, and Crystal Gayle. Crossover hits also produced unprecedented sales, including "King of the Road" by Roger Miller, "A Boy Named Sue" by Johnny Cash, "Harper Valley P.T.A." by Jeannie C. Riley, and "Help Me Make It through the Night" and "Me and Bobby

Internet Listening Exercise

Listen to samples of a variety of tunes produced with the Nashville sound of the 1950s and 1960s.

Elvis Presley: "Heartbreak Hotel"

Everly Brothers: "Bye Bye Love"

Don Gibson: "Oh Lonesome Me"

Charlie Rich: "Who Will the Next Fool Be?"

Brenda Lee: "I'm Sorry"

Patsy Cline: "I Fall to Pieces"

Chet Atkins: "Mr. Sandman"

Floyd Cramer: "Last Date"

**Internet
Listening Exercise**

Listen to samples of these classic country tunes of the late 1960s and early 1970s.

Johnny Cash: "Folsom Prison Blues"

George Jones: "The Window up Above"

Kris Kristofferson: "Help Me Make It through the Night"

Roger Miller: "King of the Road"

McGee" by Kris Kristofferson. Well-publicized Nashville recording sessions by Bob Dylan and Joan Baez further enhanced country's appeal.

Johnny Cash (1932–2003) was an international country celebrity who became an American icon. "The Man in Black" emerged as a star in the mid-1950s with a distinctive bass-baritone voice and an insistent rhythm guitar sound. The Arkansan got his first break in Memphis and caught the ear of Sam Phillips at Sun Records to produce such early hits as "Folsom Prison Blues" and "I Walk the Line." Cash next joined the *Grand Ole Opry* and scored more hits while touring extensively throughout the 1960s. Although touring and drug use took their toll, Cash made a comeback in the late 1960s with his classic *Live At Folsom Prison* album, a television show, and an appearance on Bob Dylan's *Nashville Skyline* album. During the 1980s he collaborated with many other classic country and rock artists, and in the 1990s he signed with an independent record label to release Grammy-winning work with *American Recordings* and *Unchained*. Cash reflected on his obsessive love of the road:

> Home life's nice and quiet. But I love the road because I get to do that show every night. I like my bus. A daily fleeting anonymous existence. I go into a city. I see the city out the hotel window. I stay in the nicest hotel they've got. Then I'm gone.[27]

THE BAKERSFIELD SOUND

Bakersfield, California, emerged as a new center of country music in the 1950s and 1960s. This came about as a result of the great "Okie" migration of the late 1930s, in which hundreds of thousands of poor rural workers and families from Oklahoma, Texas, and Arkansas migrated to California in search of a better life, spurred by the lingering effects of the Depression and a multiyear drought that had turned their farmland into a "dust bowl." Many of the migrants brought with them their love of country music, so that by the 1950s Bakersfield stood at the heart of a burgeoning country scene. Surrounded by oil wells and agriculture, honky-tonks provided entertainment with a fresh Bakersfield style that launched the careers of Buck Owens and Merle Haggard.

Guitarist/songwriter Buck Owens (1929–) originated the Bakersfield sound, which was a blend of blues, rock, and country. Owens launched his recording career in the late 1950s with his band, the Buckaroos, and achieved nineteen number-one hits by the end of the 1960s. Owens's style featured his passionate tenor voice, high harmony singing, rockabilly guitar, and pedal steel guitar. Hits included "Excuse Me (I Think I've Got a Heartache)" and "Act Naturally," the latter of which the Beatles covered.

For over forty years, Merle Haggard (1937–) had one of the most influential careers in country music, with a rich baritone voice steeped in the influences of Jimmie Rodgers, Bob Wills, Lefty Frizzell, and dust-bowl ballads. Haggard recorded almost forty number-one songs, and artists as diverse as Elvis Costello, the Grateful Dead, Dean Martin, Dolly Parton, and Dwight Yoakam performed his compositions. Haggard's family participated in the great migration of the 1930s, and an early life of petty crime landed him in San Quentin

**Internet
Listening Exercise**

Listen to these samples of the characteristic styles of Buck Owens and Merle Haggard.

Buck Owens: "Excuse Me (I Think I've Got a Heartache)," "Act Naturally"

Merle Haggard: "Mama Tried," "Okie from Muskogee"

prison. After his release, he embarked on a music career, eventually scoring hits with "Mama Tried," "Branded Man," and "Hungry Eyes." During the late 1960s, Haggard became a superstar and target of controversy with songs that had conservative blue-collar themes, such as "Okie from Muskogee" and "The Fightin' Side of Me." He scored again in the 1970s with "Movin' On," and he stayed active into the 2000s, recording tribute albums for Jimmie Rodgers and Bob Wills.

THE AUSTIN SCENE AND THE OUTLAWS

In the late 1960s and early 1970s, a new musical counterculture began in Austin, Texas. The college town already hosted a thriving folk scene when a large nightclub called the Armadillo World Headquarters became the center of a new Austin scene, with a program of country and rock that bound cowboys and hippies together in a Texas mystique of beer, longhorns, and armadillos. The scene grew, and by the early 2000s Austin hosted *South by Southwest,* an influential annual national showcase for new rock acts.

In the 1970s, a group of country artists including Willie Nelson, Waylon Jennings, Kris Kristofferson, Johnny Cash, Jessi Colter, and Tompall Glaser grew tired of the formulaic Nashville sound and formed a loose network called the Outlaws. They wanted to control their own work, record with their own bands rather than studio musicians, and choose their own material, performance styles, and wardrobes. The term **Outlaw** originated with Waylon Jennings's 1972 album, *Ladies Love Outlaws,* and by the time RCA issued *Wanted! The Outlaws,* a compilation of reissues by Nelson, Jennings, Colter, and Glaser, the Outlaws had taken center stage in country music. The record was the first country album to sell over one million copies. Musically the Outlaws represented a return to the "hillbilly" roots of the music, as they termed it. Arrangements were relaxed and simple, to counter the production-heavy flavor of the Nashville sound, and many of the performers favored a tough, dressed-down appearance. By the end of the 1970s, the Outlaws were the new mainstream, and Nelson and Jennings had become superstars.

One of Nashville's finest songwriters of the 1960s, country music icon **Willie Nelson** (1933–) wrote hits such as Patsy Cline's "Crazy" and Ray Price's "Night Life." He had a modest early performing career but never fit into the Nashville scene. Originally a Texan, Nelson relocated to Austin in 1972 when the new scene there was in full swing. He grew a beard and long hair, sported a headband and earring, and sponsored large outdoor festivals that placed him at the center of the new Texas counterculture. According to Bill Malone,

> The swirling dust, unrelenting heat, boogieing fans, uninhibited youth in scanty or no clothing, marijuana fumes, and the proliferation of non-country performers such as Leon Russell combined to give these events the aura of country Woodstocks.[28]

The late 1970s were successful years for Nelson that included a duet album with Waylon Jennings and the release of the hit song "Mamas, Don't Let Your Babies

MICHAEL OCHS ARCHIVES.COM

Waylon Jennings and Willie Nelson at the peak of their "Outlaw" period in 1977.

www **Internet Listening Exercise**

Listen to examples of the Outlaw country style and Willie Nelson's ballad style.

Willie Nelson and Waylon Jennings: "Mamas, Don't Let Your Babies Grow up to Be Cowboys"

Waylon Jennings: "Luchenbach, Texas"

Willie Nelson: "Georgia on My Mind"

Grow up to Be Cowboys." Nelson followed up with the multiplatinum "Stardust," which featured sparse, country-jazz interpretations of Tin Pan Alley standards such as Irving Berlin's "Blue Skies" and Hoagy Carmichael's "Georgia on My Mind" and "Stardust." Nelson's vocal timbre and relaxed rhythmic phrasing made him one of country's most identifiable voices, and his sparse band arrangements and acoustic guitar gave his music an appealing intimacy.

Texas-born **Waylon Jennings** (1937–2002) was the definitive Outlaw. With one of the most resonant voices in country music, he performed with a distinctive blend of honky-tonk, rockabilly, rock, and blues. In his view, "Blues, rock 'n' roll and country are just about a beat apart." [29] Jennings started his career in the late 1950s as a rocker and bassist for Buddy Holly. He moved to Nashville in the 1960s but eventually grew frustrated with the town's formulaic sound. He began to insist on producing his own recordings and using his road band to record, moves that placed him at the vanguard of the Outlaws. Jennings made his first independent recording without strings, background vocals, or "studio sweetening"; grew long hair and a beard; and took on a tough "good ole boy" persona in the early 1970s. In 1976 he released *Wanted: The Outlaws* with Willie Nelson and won a Grammy for "Mamas, Don't Let Your Babies Grow up to Be Cowboys." Jennings summed up his country music experience in a song: "Come to Nashville, write some good songs, cut some hit records, make money, take all the drugs you can and drink all you can, become a wild man and all of a sudden you die." [30]

COUNTRY ROCK

By the late 1960s and early 1970s, rock groups had begun to experiment with country instrumentation and harmonies, producing a hybrid called **country rock.** Acts such as the Byrds, the Band, Poco, the Nitty Gritty Dirt Band, and Buffalo Springfield all incorporated country elements; established rock acts such as Bob Dylan, Neil Young, and Linda Ronstadt also released country-flavored efforts. In addition, a new genre called southern rock was being developed by the Allman Brothers, Lynyrd Skynyrd, the Charlie Daniels Band, and the Marshall Tucker Band (see Chapter 17).

Gram Parsons (1946–1973) was one of the first to bridge the boundary between rock and country with the albums he made in California in the late 1960s. As historian Patrick Carr put it,

> In some ways Parsons was another Jimmie Rodgers—a new creative bridge between urban-rural and folk-pop musical forms, an edge dweller. . . . But in the crucial area of image he had none of Rodgers's skills or resources. He had long hair, and he wore marijuana leaves emblazoned on his suit.[31]

Parsons's fusion of country music and rock began with his work on the Byrds' *Sweetheart of the Rodeo* album in 1968. He subsequently formed the prototype country-rock band, the Flying Burrito Brothers, to produce such tunes as "Sin City" and "Wheels." Parsons's pioneering sound was picked up in the 1970s by Los Angeles–based bands such as the Eagles, whose "Hotel California" was one of the best-selling rock records of all time. A final musical contribution Parsons made to country rock was his discovery of singer **Emmylou Harris** (1947–), who was a young folk artist when he introduced her to country. Harris succeeded where others failed in uniting country and rock fans, and she invigorated country music by exploring its roots, providing exposure for new songwriters and introducing new artists. Harris was a touchstone for a generation of subsequent female artists, and she supported the rise of the neotraditionalist movement of the 1980s as well as the alt-country movement of the 1990s.

Another milestone of country rock in the 1970s was the release of *Will the Circle Be Unbroken*, a classic album that bridged a generation gap and preserved in a respectful way the work of traditional country artists such as Mother Maybelle Carter, Earl Scruggs, and Roy Acuff. Organized by the members of the Nitty Gritty Dirt Band, a country rock act emphasizing roots music, the album also stunned the country music industry by selling a million copies, chiefly to young rock fans.

Internet Listening Exercise

Listen to these samples of early country rock.

The Flying Burrito Brothers: "Sin City"

The Byrds: "You Ain't Going Nowhere"

The Eagles: "Take It Easy"

Emmylou Harris: "Together Again"

FEMALE LEGENDS OF COUNTRY

Although country originated as a male-dominated genre, groundbreaking female artists periodically emerged to make significant contributions to the music. After Sara Carter retired in the 1940s, country music saw almost no women recording artists for close to ten years. Loretta Lynn recalled that when she was growing up in Kentucky in the 1940s, "You didn't hear any women. I never thought anything about it. Men came first. Men dominated."[32] This changed in 1952 with **Kitty Wells's** (1918–) release of "It Wasn't God Who Made Honky-Tonk Angels." The song, which voiced a woman's perspective on everyday life for the first time, was intended as a response to Hank Thompson's hit, "The Wild Side of Life." According to Wells,

> I sang "It Wasn't God Who Made Honky-Tonk Angels," but it had nothing to do with my life at all. I was looking for a hit just like everybody else. I think one of the reasons it was a hit was that it was telling the menfolk [off].[33]

Internet Listening Exercise

Listen to samples of Hank Thompson's song, then to Kitty Wells's musical response.

Hank Thompson: "The Wild Side of Life (I Didn't Know God Made Honky-Tonk Angels)"

Kitty Wells: "It Wasn't God Who Made Honky-Tonk Angels"

© Frank Driggs Collection/Getty Images

Vocalist Patsy Cline was known in the early 1950s for her passionate, earthy vocal work, which exemplified the Nashville sound. One author called her the first "down-home torch singer."

CD LISTENING EXERCISE

CD 1/25

Listen to Patsy Cline singing Willie Nelson's "Crazy," recorded in 1961. The song exemplifies the Nashville sound, with the instrumental sweetening of strings and background vocals. How does Cline's clear yet sultry voice mesh with the studio arrangement? Why was the song a major hit for Cline?

Wells became the first major female star of commercial country music, and throughout the 1950s and early 1960s her songs constantly appeared in the top ten on the country charts. In 1991, she became the first woman in country music history to receive a Lifetime Achievement Grammy Award.

Patsy Cline (1932–1963) was the first "bad-girl" superstar of country music. Cline's performing skills, however, belied her tough exterior. She was a consummate performer who, in the words of historian Nicholas Dawidoff, "brought a mannered sophistication to country music. Patsy Cline was the first down-home torch singer." [34] She skillfully embellished her full-voiced vocal tone with bent notes, sighs, and sensual growls that enabled her to cross over from country to pop, though she was ambivalent about doing so. Cline recorded her first major crossover hit, "I Fall to Pieces," in 1960, followed by Willie Nelson's "Crazy." Before Cline died in a plane crash in 1963, she had pushed country beyond its traditional borders to attract a new audience and build an enduring mystique.

Loretta Lynn (1935–) was a protégé and close friend of Patsy Cline, and her rise filled the void left by Cline's death. Lynn's prolific forty-year career, chronicled in her 1980 film autobiography, *Coal Miner's Daughter,* offered a compelling story. Born into abject poverty in the Kentucky coal country and married at age thirteen, she recorded her first single, "Honky Tonk Girl," for a small label in 1960 and then barnstormed the country with her husband to promote the record. Lynn signed with Decca in 1961 and recorded a string of hits throughout the 1960s. Like Kitty Wells and Patsy Cline, she offered a female perspective on issues of everyday life with songs during the late 1960s such as "Don't Come Home Drinkin' (With Lovin' on Your Mind)," "Coal Miner's Daughter," and "The Pill." Though she had long ceased to make the charts by the end of the century, her career rebounded in 2005 with the Grammy-winning album *Van Lear Rose,* a collaboration with rocker Jack White of the White Stripes.

Like Loretta Lynn, **Dolly Parton** (1946–) overcame a background of rural poverty to establish a successful career as a singer, songwriter, and star of film and television. Over a forty-year career, Parton enjoyed both country and pop hits and wrote over 3,000 compositions. Parton's first country hit, "Dumb

Blonde" (1967), punctured stereotypes and made her a regular on the *Porter Wagoner Show*. Her success continued in the 1970s and 1980s with hits including "Coat of Many Colors" and the title song from the film *9 to 5*, as well as collaborations with artists such as Kenny Rogers, Linda Ronstadt, Emmylou Harris, Tammy Wynette, and Loretta Lynn. Parton's writing talents were showcased by her song, "I Will Always Love You," which Whitney Houston covered in the 1990s. In the early 2000s, as Parton found herself left out of the mix by the youth-oriented climate of the country record industry, she returned to her Appalachian roots and released respected new work featuring all-acoustic old-time and bluegrass music.

MULTICULTURAL COUNTRY

You can find country music just about anywhere in the United States—especially in rural areas—and a diverse audience to go with it. One study from the early 1990s reported that 25 percent of the adult African American radio audience favored country music. Although white performers have dominated the genre, influential African American and Mexican American country artists have also contributed to it.

Vocalist/songwriter Dolly Parton, who was a superstar in the 1970s and 1980s, returned to her mountain music roots in the early 2000s. Here she plays the five-string banjo at Lincoln Center in 1987.

During country's formative years, integrated string bands played in rural communities throughout the South; black and white fiddlers and songsters commonly performed side by side at country dances, serving up ragtime, blues, and traditional string band music. **Deford Bailey** (1899–1982) was the first black star of country music and one of country music's seminal harmonica stylists. He first starred on the *Grand Ole Opry* in 1928, remaining a regular on the show until 1941. Bailey's famous "Pan American Blues," a musical portrait of a train leaving a station, was an *Opry* theme song for many years. Other African American artists such as singer/guitarist Lead Belly (Huddie Ledbetter), popular during the folk revival of the 1930s, also bridged the gap between hillbilly and race music.

Because radio broadcasts of black music in the South were rare prior to the 1940s, many black musicians spent their formative years listening to country music. Traces of country appeared in the work of early R & B artists such as Fats Domino, Wynonie Harris, Ivory Joe Hunter, Ester Phillips, and Etta James. According to James, "I want to show that gospel, country, blues, rhythm and blues, jazz, and rock and roll are really the same thing. Those are the American Music and that is the American Culture."[35] The most famous R & B–country

 **Internet Listening Exercise**

Listen to samples of songs by Dolly Parton and Loretta Lynn.

Dolly Parton: "Coat of Many Colors," "Blues Pastures"

Loretta Lynn: "Coal Miner's Daughter," "Don't Come Home Drinkin' (with Lovin' on Your Mind)"

Internet Listening Exercise

Listen to samples of the following country classics performed by black artists.

Deford Bailey: "Pan American Blues"

Ray Charles: "I Can't Stop Loving You"

Charley Pride: "Just between You and Me"

crossover recordings came from the great Ray Charles. A lifelong fan of country music, Charles released a two-record set called *Modern Sounds in Country and Western Music* in 1960, and two years later he released the country crossover hit, "I Can't Stop Loving You."

Country music's only African American superstar was the Grammy-winning **Charley Pride** (1938–). With his warm baritone voice and relaxed style, Pride scored twenty-nine number-one singles and multiple Grammys between 1966 and 1986. The Mississippi-born Pride listened to the *Grand Ole Opry* as a child and was influenced by Ernest Tubb, Hank Williams, and Roy Acuff. His musical talents blossomed in the early 1960s when he moved to Nashville and was signed by Chet Atkins at RCA. Billed as "Country Charley Pride," he saw his first single released in 1966 without a picture of him on the record jacket, to downplay his race. In performances, Pride often opened with an ice-breaker: "Ladies and gentlemen, I realize it's a little unique for me coming out here on a country show wearing this permanent tan." [36] Pride's rise coincided with the civil rights movement of the mid-1960s, and he found himself caught between an emerging black identity and the white country music world. As his popularity grew, Pride stopped apologizing for his "tan" and built a successful career.

Although Mexican and Chicano musical styles have had a symbiotic relationship with country music, only a few Chicano performers made it into the mainstream of country. One such performer, **Freddie Fender** (Baldemar G. Huerta, 1937–), began his career in the late 1950s playing rock in Spanish, but in 1960 he changed his name to Freddie Fender and began recording in English. Fender had his first big country hit in 1974, the bilingual "Before the Next Teardrop Falls." According to the artist,

Multicultural Note

Is Music Colorblind?

When Charley Pride first recorded, many listeners had no idea that he was black; similarly, when Elvis Presley first came on the radio, many people could not tell if he was white or black. According to producer Sam Phillips, the fact that Presley was "a white artist who sounded black" played a major role in his success. Jazz musicians, too, often comment that players sound white or black, and some Latin jazz players insist that they can tell if musicians grew up in Cuba or Puerto Rico by the way they play. Fans sometimes say that Ray Charles's country music sounded black because he made use of soulful vocal inflections, but Charley Pride's singing, in the words of Bill Malone, "was so country that no one suspected he was black until they saw his photograph or saw him in concert." [37] How much do race and ethnicity contribute to an artist's sound?

My roots are in Chicano music, mariachi music, black music, and a lot of that old rock & roll. But I had the good fortune of recording a country song and all of a sudden I'm a country entertainer.[38]

Fender continued a string of hits into the late 1970s, performing bilingual songs in a variety of styles including country, rock, and Tex-Mex. In the 1990s, he teamed up with Flaco Jimenez, Doug Sahm, and Augie Meyer to form the Texas Tornados, an eclectic group playing everything from *conjunto* to country. Johnny Rodriguez (1951–) was a Mexican-Irish Texan who had a string of country hits in the 1970s. More of a straight country singer than Fender, Rodriguez's performance style combined influences of Merle Haggard with Tex-Mex styles. His first hit, "Pass Me By," was followed by eleven number-one tunes, many of which were bilingual.

CONTEMPORARY COUNTRY

Throughout its history, country music has followed a recurring cycle of booms and busts. For example, the late 1970s and early 1980s saw an unprecedented boom with the popularity of the film *Urban Cowboy*, and country music, cowboy dress, pickup trucks, and mechanical bulls briefly permeated urban society, propelling classic artists such as Loretta Lynn, Dolly Parton, and Willie Nelson back into the limelight. But by 1985 the boom was over, country music's market share had fallen, and veteran artists were being cut loose by major labels.

The 1980s: Country Rock and Neotraditionalist Influences

The retrenchment of the mid-1980s led to the rise of a new generation of stars who had grown up on rock and were easier to package for new media outlets—especially video. The development of MTV, TNN (the Nashville Network), and CMT (Country Music Television) accelerated the pace of promoting artists, and country, like other styles, became as much a visual as an auditory medium. Popular female acts during the lean years of the 1980s included Barbara Mandrell, Tanya Tucker, Crystal Gayle, the Judds, and Reba McEntire. Male acts included Alabama, the Oak Ridge Boys, Ricky Skaggs, George Strait, and Dwight Yoakam. Country also took on a strong seventies rock flavor as its "twang" faded a bit. When the group Alabama pioneered the use of a rock band format, previously rare in country, they brought many young listeners reared on rock over to country. The group marketed an easy blend of pop and country influenced by artists like the Eagles, the Allman Brothers, and Charlie Daniels. Alabama parlayed flawless vocal harmonies, AOR (album-oriented rock), and showmanship into twenty-one consecutive number-one records, including "Mountain Music" and "Tennessee River."

Another new strand of country artists of the mid-1980s were the neotraditionalists, whose music represented a return to the various roots of country music—bluegrass, honky-tonk, classic country, and rockabilly. Vocalist and multi-

instrumentalist Ricky Skaggs (1954–) combined a country purist aesthetic, born-again religious convictions, and a contemporary bluegrass sensibility. Skaggs first appeared with Bill Monroe at nine and later began a decade-long run on the charts in the 1980s with tunes such as "Don't Get above Your Raising" and Bill Monroe's "Crying My Heart out over You." The Judds—Naomi Judd (1946–) and her daughter Wynonna (1964–)—combined a hard-rocking edge with traditional roots. Wynonna's soulful vocals and Naomi's harmonies brought a new youth audience to country music by producing hits such as "Mama He's Crazy" and "Grandpa (Tell Me 'bout the Good Old Days)." Reba McEntire's (1954–) work chronicled the lives of contemporary women and raised issues such as spousal abuse and the need for personal fulfillment. Major albums included *My Kind of Country* and the Grammy-winning *Whoever's in New England,* and she worked in films, Broadway, and television. George Strait (1952–) was a low-key Texan from a straight-ahead honky-tonk and western swing background. His minimalist sound and clean-cut look of pressed shirts, jeans, and crisp Stetson influenced an entire new generation of young male artists with hits such as "Does Fort Worth Ever Cross Your Mind" and "All My Ex's Live in Texas." Kentucky-born Dwight Yoakam (1956–) brought an edgy and ironic California honky-tonk attitude to hits such as "Guitars, Cadillacs," "Honky-Tonk Man," and "Ain't That Lonely Yet." Among his influences were Buck Owens, with whom he performed and recorded a tribute record; he also enjoyed a successful film career.

The 1990s and Early 2000s: Hat Acts, Steamy Videos, and Alt-Country

Country music experienced an upswing in the 1990s and early 2000s with a new generation of good-looking men in cowboy hats and tight jeans—sometimes called "hat acts"—and women with fashion-model looks. Nashville record sales soared, and artists' profits from touring and endorsements dwarfed prior country efforts. One reason for the music's increased success came in 1991 when *Billboard* magazine changed the way it tallied weekly record sales. Instead of relying on phone calls from record store retailers, it moved to a computer-based reporting system called Soundscan. Accurate record keeping revealed that the country music market was larger than previously reported, and the commercial scale of country music took a quantum leap. Popular male acts included Garth Brooks, Tim McGraw, Alan Jackson, Brooks and Dunn, Clint Black, Toby Keith, and Kenny Chesney. Female acts included Shania Twain, Faith Hill, Trisha Yearwood, the Dixie Chicks, LeAnn Rimes, Martina McBride, and LeeAnn Womack.

Garth Brooks (1962–), one of the biggest country acts of the 1990s, built a huge new mass audience for country by blending the honky-tonk flavor of George Strait, the arena-rock sounds of 1970s rock artists like the Eagles and Journey, and sentimental elements of singer/songwriters like James Taylor and Billy Joel. As a marketing graduate, he understood how image and publicity translated into album sales. In performance he played guitar, wore a cowboy hat and jeans, and conveyed small-town humility. But he was also a charismatic performer whose concerts were packed with stadium rock effects such as light shows and complex stage sets; for example, he would fly from the rafters on cables with a headset mike strapped across his face. Brooks's hits ranged from the barroom honky-tonk of "Friends in Low Places," to the seventies rock of "The Thunder Rolls," to sentimental ballads such as "The River" and "The Dance."

Shania Twain (1965–) was a Canadian-born vocalist who sang high-energy, hook-laden, rock-flavored country music that projected a glamorous image. Twain started her career in country but crossed over by giving a pop-rock edge to her country sound and showcasing her talent in provocative videos. Twain was the first woman to have two back-to-back albums sell over ten million: *The Woman in Me* and *Come on Over*. Her 2002 album, *Up!,* was released with two rhythm tracks—pop/electric and country/acoustic—to ensure the widest market appeal.

Faith Hill (1967–) and **Tim McGraw** (1967–) were "Mr. and Mrs. Country Music" of the late 1990s. Hill's two biggest-selling albums, *Faith* and *Breathe,* established her as one of the new Nashville divas of the 1990s by exploiting a pop-rock sound and her fashion-model looks. McGraw emerged in the mid-1990s to challenge the dominance of Garth Brooks. Although his voice was not particularly strong, his appeal lay in his everyman earthiness; he conveyed a directness and emotion—sometimes anger—that had commercial potential. His first hit was "Indian Outlaw," a dance-oriented novelty filled with offensive stereotypes.

The **Dixie Chicks,** a successful female trio that blended traditional bluegrass sounds with a post-punk visual look, represented a new direction for young country. Although the group's roots lay in the alt-country movement (discussed next), they broke out as mainstream stars with major albums in the late 1990s and early 2000s. The group appealed to a young audience while reflecting traditional roots. The group reflected some of the flavor of the earlier generation of Outlaws by playing their own instruments on recordings instead of relying on session musicians, controlling the production of their recordings, and challenging Nashville record companies over economic issues.

Another trend of the 1990s and early 2000s involved the crystallization of an alternative country movement known as **alt-country,** "Americana," "No Depression," or "roots revival," which developed in reaction to mainstream country's pursuit of pop styles and the youth market. The artists associated with the movement represented an eclectic mix of traditional country and post-punk that fell well outside Nashville parameters. Among them were country legends too old for contemporary country radio, established cult-figure singer/songwriters, bluegrass and old-time artists, and new alt-country artists. Performers associated with the movement included Lyle Lovett, Jimmie Dale Gilmore, Steve Earle, k.d. lang, Lucinda Williams, The Mavericks, Gillian Welch, Iris DeMent, Uncle Tupelo, Son Volt, Wilco, and Nickel Creek. As one record label executive put it,

> Alternative country is more of a rootsy kind of country. And artistically speaking, it's a better kind of country music. . . . And it's the kind of country that if we could ever get it on the radio, the people would absolutely love.[39]

Internet Listening Exercise

Listen to samples of these tunes by two contemporary country superstars.

Garth Brooks: "Friends in Low Places"

Shania Twain: "Man I Feel Like a Woman"

Internet Listening Exercise

Listen to samples of Faith Hill, Tim McGraw, and the Dixie Chicks.

Faith Hill: "Breathe"

Tim McGraw: "The Cowboy in Me"

Hill and McGraw: "It's Your Love"

Dixie Chicks: "Landslide"

Multicultural Note

Is Country Music Political?

The lyrics of country music traditionally focus on personal issues. Some country songs, though, have talked about politics. Sexual politics were addressed in Kitty Wells's "God Didn't Make Honky-Tonk Angels," and Loretta Lynn, Dolly Parton, and Reba McEntire have all explored female perspectives on personal relationships.

The most evident form of political expression in country lyrics has centered on conservatism, insularity, and patriotism. During the Vietnam War in the late 1960s, some country artists expressed their opposition to war protest: Merle Haggard in "The Fighting Side of Me" and "Okie from Muskogee" and Barry Sadler in "Ballad of the Green Berets." Hank Williams, Jr., later expressed anger and insularity in "A Country Boy Can Survive," and Tim McGraw used racial stereotypes in his 1994 hit, "Indian Outlaw."

The events of 9/11 generated contradictory political effects in country. Toby Keith produced the best-selling "Courtesy of the Red White and Blue (The Angry American)," whose video contained images of combat assault helicopters and confrontational lyrics; on the other hand, many country stations blacklisted the Dixie Chicks for openly stating their opposition to the U.S. invasion of Iraq. What other examples of politics can you identify in country music or other genres?

The Future of Country: Commerce versus Tradition

Country music is a flexible music built of complex cultural hybrids. Unfortunately, broadcast radio and video have forced the style into a single-format category. Whereas rock and R & B make use of multiple formats—classic rock, modern rock, alternative rock, classic soul, hip hop, and smooth jazz/R & B—country and its multiple strands do not have such a range available. This places classic and alternative country artists at a disadvantage, as the mainstream country music industry pursues multiplatinum sales. One of the most difficult issues country music faces is the contradiction between profit and connection to roots and classic artists, as Chet Atkins, the architect of the Nashville sound, put it:

> We almost do lose our identity sometimes. We get so pop that fans turn away. . . .
> To young folks right now, country music just means some guy with a tight ass
> and a white hat. . . . Right now we're in a curve with everything sounding alike,
> but somebody'll come along and get us back where we need to be.[40]

Chapter Summary

- Country music has a complex history. Although the stars of country have generally been of European descent, the style's roots originate in European folk traditions, church music, African American music, and Mexican American music.

- The development of radio and of the recording industry played major roles in the evolution of country music, and their influence continues.

- Multiple stylistic innovations over seventy-five years served as benchmarks in the evolution of country music:

1. Jimmie Rodgers and the Carter Family were seminal country acts, representing two strands of the genre: rambling, drinking, partying, and sex versus God, country, mother, and home.

2. The appearance of the singing cowboy in the 1930s completed the fusion of country with Western themes.

3. The blending of jazz elements with string band styles in the 1930s by artists such as Bob Wills led to the development of western swing.

4. Honky-tonk became the dominant sound of country in the 1940s and reached its zenith in the work of country legend Hank Williams in the early 1950s.

5. Bill Monroe's aggressive mandolin style combined with Earl Scruggs's finger-picking banjo technique to create the bluegrass style in the 1940s.

6. The establishment of Nashville as the center of the country music industry was followed by the emergence of the smooth Nashville sound of the 1950s and 1960s.

7. Beginning in the 1950s, the music of Kitty Wells, Patsy Cline, Loretta Lynn, and Dolly Parton surfaced women's perspectives in country music.

8. A West Coast honky-tonk tradition led by Merle Haggard and Buck Owens developed in Bakersfield in the 1950s and 1960s.

9. The Outlaws, led by Willie Nelson and Waylon Jennings, emerged out of Austin in the 1970s in response to the formulaic Nashville sound.

10. Music television and corporate control of country radio shaped a new breed of young, visually appealing country performers at the end of the twentieth century.

11. An unresolved tension between commerce and tradition continued into the 2000s with the appeal of alt-country, old-time music, and bluegrass.

Key Terms

alt-country	*Grand Ole Opry*	Outlaw
bluegrass	high lonesome style	rockabilly
blue yodel	hillbilly	singing cowboy
country rock	honky-tonk	steel guitar
Dobro	Nashville Sound	western swing
dulcimer	old-time music	

Study and Discussion Questions

1. What social and cultural factors coalesced in the South during the early twentieth century to contribute to the development of country music?

2. What roles did Jimmie Rodgers and the Carter Family play in the development of country music? Discuss the two aesthetic perspectives associated with these artists.

3. How did the evolution of radio and recording technology impact the development of country?

4. How did the emergence of the singing cowboy and the West affect country music?

5. What was western swing and what were its connections to other styles?

6. What was honky-tonk? Discuss important contributors to its development.

7. What distinguished bluegrass from other styles of country music? Who contributed to its development?

8. How did the emergence of the Nashville scene change country music? Who was Chet Atkins? What role does Nashville play today in the country music industry?

9. What was the significance of Kitty Wells, Patsy Cline, Loretta Lynn, and Dolly Parton to country music?

10. Who were the Outlaws and how did they affect the evolution of country music in the 1970s?

11. How did the development of music television impact country? What new trends have developed at the end of the twentieth century?

Notes

1. Bill C. Malone, *Country Music, U.S.A.*, rev. ed. (Austin: University of Texas Press, 1985), 15.

2. Ibid., 2.

3. Ibid., 13.

4. Ibid., 8.

5. Cecelia Conway, *African Banjo Echoes in Appalachia: A Study of Folk Traditions* (Knoxville: University of Tennessee Press, 1995), 304–5.

6. Country Music Foundation (CMF), *Country: The Music and the Musicians, Pickers, Slickers, Cheatin' Hearts, and Superstars* (New York: Abbeville Press, 1988), 57.

7. Ibid., 66.

8. Ibid., 87.

9. Neil Strauss, "The Country Music Country Radio Ignores," *New York Times*, March 24, 2002, Section 2, p. 12.

10. Country Music Foundation, *Country*, 107.

11. Ralph Peer, "Discovery of the First Hillbilly Great," *Billboard* 65 (No. 20, May 16, 1953): 20–21.

12. Country Music Foundation, *Country,* 17.

13. Nicholas Dawidoff, *In the Country of Country: People and Places in American Music* (New York: Pantheon Books, 1997), 60.

14. Nick Tosches, *Country: Living Legends and Dying Metaphors in America's Biggest Music* (New York: Scribner, 1985), 178.

15. Peer, "Discovery of the First Hillbilly Great," 20–21.

16. David Vinopal, Alabama Music Hall of Fame website, http://www.alamhof .org/rodgersj.htm.

17. Tosches, *Country: Living Legends,* 27.

18. Robert K. Oermann, *A Century of Country: An Illustrated History of Country Music* (New York: TV Books, 1999), 98.

19. Malone, *Country Music,* 174.

20. Bill C. Malone and Judith McCulloh, eds., *Stars of Country Music: Uncle Dave Macon to Johnny Rodriguez* (Urbana: University of Illinois Press, 1975), 245, 246.

21. Oermann, *Century of Country,* 104.

22. Dawidoff, *In the Country of Country,* 108.

23. *O Brother, Where Art Thou?* website, http://www.obrothermusic.com/ soundtrack.html.

24. Oermann, *Century of Country,* 96.

25. Ibid., 176.

26. Dawidoff, *In the Country of Country,* 50.

27. Ibid., 178.

28. Malone, *Country Music,* 397.

29. Jon Pareles, "Waylon Jennings, Singer, Songwriter and Outlaw of Country Music, Dies at 64," *New York Times,* February 14, 2002, p. C17.

30. Ibid.

31. Country Music Foundation, *Country,* 509–11.

32. Dawidoff, *In the Country of Country,* 63.

33. Ibid., 66.

34. Ibid., 70–71.

35. Liner notes for *From Where I Stand: The Black Experience in Country Music,* p. 44, Warner Brothers Records, 9-46428-2, 1998.

36. Ibid.

37. Ibid.

38. Liner notes for *The Best of Freddie Fender,* MCA CD 0881701902, 1996.

39. Oermann,*Century of Country,* 311.

40. Dawidoff, *In the Country of Country,* 50.

1830s The habanera, one of the first Cuban rhythms, emerges and is adapted by European composers ♪
1838 Britain emancipates African slaves in Jamaica

1850s American composer Louis Moreau Gottschalk visits Cuba and incorporates Cuban rhythms into his music ♪

1861–1865 U.S. Civil War
1870s African slaves continue to arrive in the Caribbean, bringing fresh African musical influences ♪

1880s African-influenced rumba emerges in Cuba and becomes one of the foundations of Afro-Cuban music ♪
1898 Spanish-American War ends and Puerto Rico becomes a U.S. colony

1910s Afro-Brazilian samba style develops in Brazil ♪
1910s Puerto Rican immigration to New York begins, bringing Afro-Caribbean music to the U.S. ♪
1912 Trío Matamoros plays early *son,* the stylistic root of *conjunto,* mambo, and later salsa ♪
1914–1918 World War I
1914 Panama Canal opens
1919–1933 Prohibition

1920s *Danzón* is the national dance of Cuba; *son* migrates from rural to urban areas of Cuba ♪
1929–1930s Great Depression; New Deal begins
1930s First steel drum prototypes appear in Trinidad ♪
1930 Don Azpiazu records "*El Manicero,*" the first traditional Afro-Cuban recording in the U.S. using a Cuban rhythm section ♪
1938 First mambo, the precursor to salsa, appears in Havana ♪

1940s Cuban *son* expands into *conjunto,* adding horns and piano ♪
1940s The birth of Latin jazz in New York, spearheaded by Machito and the Afro-Cubans ♪
1941–1945 U.S. participates in World War II
1947 Dizzy Gillespie records "Manteca" with Chano Pozo ♪
1950s Mambo craze starts in New York, setting the stage for the emergence of salsa ♪
1951 Puerto Ricans vote to become a commonwealth of the U.S.
1959 Cuban Revolution; ensuing American embargo leads to scarcity of new Cuban music in the U.S.

1960s Brazilian bossa nova craze reaches the U.S. and lasts until arrival of the Beatles ♪
1960s The rise of Latin soul, boogaloo, and early salsa ♪
1960s Ska develops in Jamaica ♪
1962 Jamaica becomes an independent nation
1964–1973 Vietnam War
1964 Fania Records enters market to become the voice of salsa ♪
1966 Palladium Ballroom, New York's home to the mambo for close to 20 years, closes ♪
1968 Martin Luther King and Robert Kennedy assassinated
1972 Reggae film *The Harder They Come* spreads the style around the world ♪
1975 Bob Marley records *Natty Dread,* one of his major hit albums ♪
1978 Willie Colón and Rubén Blades record their seminal salsa album, *Siembra* ♪

1985 Latin pop arrives with Gloria Estéfan's "Conga" ♪
1987 Merengue, a rhythm from the Dominican Republic, sweeps the Latin dance world ♪
1992 *The Mambo Kings* film creates international interest in classic Latin music ♪
1999 First Latin Grammy Awards ceremony ♪

2001 9/11 terrorist attacks

| 1820 | 1840 | 1860 | 1880 | 1900 | 1920 | 1940 | 1960 | 1980 | 2000 |

Chapter 8

America's Afro-Caribbean and Latin Musical Heritage

Afro-Caribbean and Latin musics have fundamentally influenced the development of many styles of American popular music. The evolution of jazz, Tin Pan Alley, Broadway, rock, and R & B owes a great debt to Latin rhythm and melodic conceptions. For example, jazz pioneer Jelly Roll Morton argued that a "Latin tinge" was essential to jazz, and Latin and Caribbean influences have repeatedly surfaced at the forefront of American popular music while simultaneously maintaining vibrant traditions among Caribbean and Latino communities in the United States and the Western Hemisphere. In this chapter we investigate the diverse musical cultures of Cuba, Puerto Rico, Brazil, the Dominican Republic, Jamaica, and Trinidad, focusing on their interactions with American popular music.

ROOTS AND TRADITIONS

Afro-Caribbean and Latin musical styles have resulted from the movement of peoples and cultures among Europe, Africa, and the Americas over several centuries, starting with the European conquests and followed by the African slave trade. Over the past century, consistent patterns of migration also took place from the Caribbean and parts of Latin America to the United States—as well as back again, through repeated U.S. military and economic interventions in the region. An array of diverse popular music styles offer highly visible evidence of diaspora in the Americas, including habanera, jazz, tango, *rumba,* calypso, R & B, ska, bolero, samba, Latin jazz, mambo, rock, reggae, bossa nova, salsa, funk, and dancehall.

Although the range of musical styles produced by Afro-Caribbean and Latin cultures is extensive, all were shaped by colonialism and slavery, all saw indigenous peoples displaced and annihilated, and all provided for the generation of new cultural hybrids from European, African, and Amerindian cultural sources. Specific local features varied because of the different languages, religions, economic practices, and social customs of the colonizing powers. In particular, differences in language continue to signify major distinctions among the musics of Spanish-, English-, French-, and Portuguese-speaking areas.

IN THIS CHAPTER

- Roots and Traditions
- Latin Music Instrumentation
- Cuban Popular Music Traditions
- Early Twentieth-Century Latin Music in the United States
- Latin Jazz and Mambo
- Transitions in the 1960s
- The 1970s and 1980s: Salsa!
- Multiple Directions in the 2000s
- Jamaican Influences: Ska, Reggae, Dub, and Dancehall
- Trinidad: Calypso, Soca, and Steel Bands

Multicultural Note

What Is a Diaspora?

A **diaspora** involves the scattering of people far from their homeland. When people migrate from one country to another, however, their relationship to their country of origin does not end. Because they remain connected to their homeland, sometimes even returning to it, they transmit cultural and economic resources back and forth. The Americas have seen numerous diasporas: Africans were forcibly brought to the New World as slaves, Europeans from diverse cultures came first as colonists and later as immigrants, and the twentieth century saw extensive migration from the Caribbean and Latin America to the United States. Resulting diasporic cultural forms such as music, dance, and language flow among the Americas, constantly reinterpreted and reinvented.

Internet Listening Exercise

Listen to samples that characterize the breadth of Afro-Caribbean and Latin styles from these albums.

Willie Colón: *Collección de Oro* (Nuyorican salsa)

Maria Bethanîa: *Anos Dourados* (Brazilian samba)

Los Van Van: *30 Years of Cuba's Greatest Dance Band* (Cuban *songo*)

Bob Marley: *Legend* (Jamaican reggae)

Mighty Sparrow: *16 Carnival Hits* (Trinidadian calypso)

African Influences and Retentions

Retention of African elements among Caribbean and Latin cultures varied, as slaves from specific African cultures were sometimes concentrated in one place and other times mixed with those from other cultures. Many Yorubans from West Africa were brought to Cuba and Brazil, where their musical practices became dominant, although influences of Congo, Dahomey, and Abakuá (Southern Nigeria) were also evident. By contrast, slaves taken to Jamaica by British slave owners in earlier years were from the Akan (Gold Coast) and Congolese (Central African) cultures. Because slavery continued longer in Spanish, Portuguese, and French colonies than in British-controlled areas, the former received fresh infusions of African culture for a longer time.

The policies of colonial powers toward African cultural practices also affected their retention. Some have argued that slavery in the Spanish, Portuguese, and French colonies allowed more cultural autonomy for Africans than it did in British colonies. For example, Spanish, Portuguese, and French slaves could buy their freedom and could form socioreligious clubs (*cabildos* in Cuba) which maintained cultural independence and traditional musical practices. In Brazil, slaves still on plantations *(fazendas)* organized themselves into brotherhoods *(irmandades)* under the patronage of the Catholic church and were allowed to save money to buy their freedom. Another influence on African cultural retention was the economic structure of different colonies. For instance, Jamaica was a plantation colony where slaves made up almost 90 percent of the population, experienced rigid controls, and exerted little cultural influence on whites. Cuba, on the other hand, was a settler colony with more ethnic interaction.

A final factor strongly affecting African cultural retention in Cuba and Brazil was the survival of African religions through transformation into religious hybrids—*Santería, Abakuá,* and *Palo* in Cuba; *Voudou* in Haiti; and *Candomblé* and *Macumba* in Brazil. African slaves took elements of Roman Catholicism —including the saints—and blended them with Yoruban or Congolese deities.

Catholic and African religious ritual styles overlapped enough to enable the African slaves to invoke their deities while performing Catholic rituals. Music served as an essential element of these religions. Summoned through drumming of specific rhythms and chants, spirits (*orishas* in *Santería*, *lua* in *Voudou*, *orixás* in *Candomblé*) arrived through mediums who took on the individual spirits. Music was used to create states of trance through *ostinatos*—repeated, highly rhythmic extended sections of music. Although people in Cuba practiced *Santería* secretly until the early part of the twentieth century, some of the island's greatest percussionists and singers emerged from Afro-Cuban religious traditions. Although rhythms became simplified as religious styles began to flavor popular music, one can still hear Yoruban elements in Cuban and Brazilian popular music.

The hallmark of Afro-Brazilian music, the **samba,** emerged prior to 1920 in Rio de Janeiro as a part of Carnival processions. **Carnival** was (and still is) a yearly celebration with outdoor celebrations and parades lasting for days. Groups of working-class residents from African-influenced regions such as Bahia came together to plan processions, drawing on music, rhythms, and dances from Afro-Brazilian religions to create the samba. In the 1930s, samba became an icon of a new Brazilian national identity that embraced African cultural elements. Today famous samba artists such as Maria Bethanîa and Gal Costa continue to integrate Afro-Brazilian religious elements in their performances.

Internet Listening Exercise

Listen to samples of the following music based on Cuban and Brazilian hybrid religions.

John Santos and Machete: *"Eleguá Agó"* (reflecting Cuban *Santería*)

Conjunto Céspedes: *"Que Viva Chango"* (reflecting Cuban *Abakuá*)

Clara Nunes: *"A Deusa Dos Orixas"* (reflecting Brazilian *Candomblé*)

European Influences

The music of the Iberian peninsula (Spain and Portugal) played a central role in the evolution of Latin music. Originally, people from North Africa and Europe populated the region, and Arabs ruled large parts of Spain for seven centuries (711–1492). Spanish and Portuguese music resulted from centuries of hybridization of North African, European, Judaic, Celtic, and Gypsy influences. Many of the Spanish *conquistadores* came from the poor Spanish regions of Andalucía and Extremadura, bringing folk music such as the Andalucían flamenco to many parts of Latin America. In addition, Spanish and Portuguese colonizers carried one of the richest European traditions of folk ballads and dances, as well as symphonic, military, and church musics. Among the dances contributed by the Iberian colonizers were *malagueñas, tanguillos,* minuets, *contradanzas,* and mazurkas. Spanish and Portuguese folk ballads influenced rural musics—now known as *música campesina* or *trova*— in Cuba, Puerto Rico, Brazil, and other Latin American countries. The lyrics of these and other Latin songs, including Cuban *son,* often take the traditional Spanish ten-line verse form called *décima.*

LATIN MUSIC INSTRUMENTATION

The textures of Afro-Caribbean and Latin music are flavored by African instruments, Afro-European hybrids, and a small number of indigenous Amerindian instruments. See the box for detailed descriptions.

African-Derived Instruments in Cuba

Yoruba (Lucumí) *Instruments*

Batá **drums:** Sacred two-headed drums traditionally played in sets of three drums; still used today as part of *Santería* ceremonies and by folkloric ensembles.
Agbe **or** *chékere:* A bead-covered gourd often played in sets of three or more.
Bembé **drums:** Drums made from palm tree logs with skins tuned by heat.

Dahomey (Arará) *Instruments*

Tumbas francesas **and** *Arará* **drums:** A set of four large log drums tuned with leather strapping.
Shakers and small hand percussion

Congo (Bantú)

Makuta **or** *ngoma* **drum:** A large barrel-shaped drum, precursor to the conga.
Marímbula: A large hollow wooden box with a thumb piano; used as a bass instrument in early Cuban *son* and other styles.

The European colonial presence influenced the formation of symphony orchestras and wind bands in the nineteenth century, making strings, brass, woodwinds, and European percussion central to many Afro-Caribbean and Latin musical styles. Instruments of the guitar family, including the *vihuela* and the *bandurria,* also came from Spain as early as the late fifteenth century. Early Spanish guitars had four, five, six, or seven strings, as well as pairs of strings, and stringed instruments such as the Cuban *tres* (guitar with three paired strings) and the Puerto Rican *cuatro* (guitar with five double strings) reflected these influences. Percussion instruments of the standard Latin rhythm section—**conga drums, bongo drums, timbales, claves,** cowbell, and **guiro,** along with the steel drums of Trinidad, were all hybrids developed in the Caribbean. Surviving indigenous instruments included maracas, log drums, and other percussion.

Legends of Latin Jazz (left to right): Graciela, Machito's sister (clave), "El Colorado" (congas), Rene Hernandez (piano), Jose Manguel, Sr. (bongos), Ubaldo Nieto (timbales), and Machito (maracas).

Afro-Caribbean Hybrid Instruments

Timbales

Adapted from the European tympani, *timbales* were a turn-of-the-century creation eliminating the kettle portion of the tympani, resulting in a pair of metal drums similar to the modern snare drum, but without the snare. Timbales were first used in traditional flute and string bands called *charangas.*

Conga drum (tumbadora)

A barrel-shaped drum that is made from strips of hardwood or fiberglass and played with hands and fingers. Conga drums have now crossed over into a wide variety of styles, including jazz and rock.

Bongo drums

Two small hand drums attached together with a piece of wood, one drum usually slightly larger than the other and pitched lower, played with the fingers and hands.

Guiro

A serrated cylinder made of gourds, metal, wood, or fiberglass that is scraped and struck with a stick in a variety of rhythmic patterns.

Tres

A small six-string guitar with three pairs of identically tuned strings, providing greater volume and resonance than single strings.

Cajones

Drums made of simple wooden boxes first developed by African slaves from shipping crates and played with bare hands or *palitos* (sticks). The earliest *rumbas* were performed on *cajones,* and they found their way back to Spain, becoming integral to modern flamenco.

Cencerro

Cowbell with the clapper removed, played with a wooden stick.

Claves

A pair of wooden sticks played by resting one stick on the fingertips of a cupped hand that acts as a resonator, while tapping with the other stick.

One instrument deserves special mention. *Clave* has two meanings in Latin music: It is a musical instrument as well as a rhythm. The instrumental claves are a pair of hardwood sticks. **Clave** also refers to a group of rhythmic patterns that connect the polyrhythms of Afro-Cuban music. The origins of *clave* were African, probably based on a 12/8 bell pattern that came to be simplified in Cuba. The two most common *clave* patterns are known as "three-two" and "two-three."

Three-Two CLAVE

Two-Three CLAVE

Once a *clave* pattern is established in a composition, all of the other rhythms generally "lock in" with it. In *rumba* and *son*, the *clave* rhythm is usually heard clearly, but in other Afro-Cuban styles the rhythmic patterns of other instruments may simply imply it. *Clave* also migrated into numerous non-Latin styles.

CUBAN POPULAR MUSIC TRADITIONS

Cuban music played a dominant role in the interaction of Caribbean and U.S. musics for almost 200 years, affecting the development of jazz, ragtime, Tin Pan Alley, and more recent pop styles.

The *contradanza habanera* (Havana-style contradance) was the first Cuban style to develop after European colonization. Derived from the formal Spanish **contradanza,** it was a group dance similar to the Virginia reel, using a caller to direct participants. The Cuban style added a syncopated beat and became known simply as **habanera.** The rhythm was popular in European classical music of the 1830s and appeared in works such as George Bizet's opera *Carmen.* New Orleans pianist/composer Louis Moreau Gottschalk (1829–1869) was one of the first U.S. composers to incorporate Cuban and other Latin music styles into his work after frequent visits to Cuba and Latin America during the 1850s and 1860s. He blended habanera rhythms with New Orleans styles such as the cakewalk, a precursor to ragtime. Jelly Roll Morton also incorporated the habanera into his compositions.

Rumba, the oldest African-derived secular style in Cuba, developed as a blend of Congolese traditions and Spanish flamenco in the late nineteenth century. *Rumba* was performed by dancers accompanied by Afro-Cuban percussion, lead singer, and a chorus. The absence of a chord-making instrument gave *rumba* a distinctively African sound that differed greatly from the U.S. "rhumba" of the 1930s, which was a simplified, generic Latin style.

In the 1880s, Cuban composer Miguel Faílde introduced another influential rhythm called *danzón,* which became the national dance of Cuba until the 1930s. **Danzón** was based on a repeated rhythmic pattern (ostinato), and was originally performed by *orquesta típica* ensembles—small groups similar to early New Orleans jazz bands. By the 1920s, the instrumentation had evolved into the **charanga** ensemble, which included wooden flute, violins, piano, string bass, guiro, and timbales. The ensembles generated a level of syncopated drive not normally expected from the flute-violin instrumentation.

Danzón Ostinato

Música campesina, the country music of Cuba, comprised a variety of styles that subsequently became popular worldwide. One was *guajira,* a folk song style with gentle melodies and rural lyrical themes accompanied by guitar or *tres* and simple percussion. One well-known example, "Guantanamera," was composed by Joseito Fernández and popularized in the United States in the 1960s by folk singer Pete Seeger. Another style of *música campesina, trova,* developed in the mid-nineteenth century. Like the Mexican *corrido, trova* often blended current political issues with narratives of everyday life. In recent years, the term *nueva canción* (new song) described contemporary music performed in the *trova* style. Cuban leaders of the genre included Pablo Milanés, Sara Gonzales, and Silvio Rodríguez.

Bolero first became popular in Cuba and throughout Latin America in the 1920s. This hybrid style combined European *bel canto* singing with slow romantic lyrics and music. Bolero migrated to Mexico, which became the center of the style by the mid-1940s.

Son was the most influential popular musical style emerging from Cuba. According to pianist/author Rebeca Mauleón, "*Son* is the grandfather of salsa."[1] The style developed in rural Cuba in the late nineteenth century from a blend of European and Afro-Cuban elements, and instrumentation of the earliest versions included the guitar or *tres,* claves, and maracas. Trío Matamoros, a vocal group founded in 1912, established a style that set the standard for similar groups throughout Latin America. *Son* moved to Havana in the 1920s, where bongos, *marímbula,* guiro, and trumpet were added. In the early 1940s, vocalist/bandleader Arsenio Rodríguez added an additional trumpet, a piano, and conga drums to form an enlarged *son* ensemble called **conjunto.** In the late 1940s, the addition of the piano contributed the syncopated, repeated piano vamp called **montuno.**

Internet Listening Exercise

Listen to samples of the songs listed below from the album *Master Sessions Volume I* by legendary bassist Israel "Cachao" López. This 1995 Grammy-winning CD presents a history of Cuban styles.

Cachao: "*Al Fin Te Vi/*Finally I Saw You" *(contradanza habanera)*

Cachao: "*Lindo Yambú/*Beautiful Yambú" *(rumba)*

Cachao: "*Isora Club*" *(danzón)*

Cachao: "*Mi Guajira/*My Country Girl" *(guajira/música campesina)*

Internet Listening Exercise

Listen to samples of the following boleros.

Trío Matamoros: "*Lágrimas Negras*" (an early bolero hit by a classic Cuban vocal trio of the 1930s and 1940s)

Pedro Infante: "*Historia de un Amor*" (a 1940s bolero sung by a beloved Mexican movie star/vocalist)

What Is Son?

- *Clave* **rhythm:** The underlying rhythm of the three-two or two-three *clave* is generally maintained throughout—played on the claves or rhythm instruments, sometimes implied by other instruments.

- *Tumbao* **bass line:** Establishes a rhythmic pattern anticipating the downbeat of each measure by playing on beat four of the previous measure rather than on beat one—origins attributed to Cuban bassist Israel "Cachao" López.

- *Martillo:* Guitar or bongo part accompanying the *clave* and *tumbao.*

- **Lyric structure:** Based on the Spanish *décima* folk song/poetic form.

- *Montuno:* Syncopated rhythmic pattern played by the piano, *tres,* or guitar that "locks" with the *tumbao* and *clave.*

- **Song structure:** Generally includes an introduction, verse, chorus, and refrain; modern salsa sometimes adds a mambo section with new melodies, as well as another refrain section called *sobre montuno*.
- **Refrain:** A repeated ostinato or vamp section, sometimes called the *coro* or *montuno*, where improvisation takes place and the groove builds.

CD LISTENING EXERCISE

CD 1/26

Listen to *clave, tumbao,* and *montuno* patterns on the CD set included with this book. Listen first to the two-three clave played on clave sticks. Next, listen to an example of the traditional *tumbao* bass pattern. In most U.S. popular dance music and in many styles of jazz, the bass plays on the downbeat (the first beat of each measure), but the *tumbao* does not do this. In common meter or 4/4 time, the *tumbao* plays on the upbeat of beat two (halfway through beat two) and on beat four. How does the syncopated *tumbao* bass line affect the feel of the rhythm? Next, listen to a simple *montuno* piano vamp accompanied by a two-three *clave* pattern. Listen for the rhythmic interlocking between the *clave* and the piano. Now listen to the same *montuno* with addition of the *tumbao* bass. These three interlocking parts form the heart of the contemporary *son* style.

Go online and listen to a sample of *"Meta y Guaguancó"* recorded by Arsenio Rodríguez in 1953, and you will hear the *clave, tumbao,* and other *son* elements played by a traditional *son* septet. Then listen to a sample of *"El Hijo de Obatala,"* an up-tempo salsa dance classic recorded by Ray Barretto. This piece is an example of these rhythms in a contemporary tune.

EARLY TWENTIETH-CENTURY LATIN MUSIC IN THE UNITED STATES

In the first half of the twentieth century, Latin music experienced periodic waves of popularity in the United States. New York and Hollywood served as centers of development, and the increase in Puerto Rican and Cuban immigration also had a major impact. The first wave of Latin influences came to New York in the form of an Argentine tango "craze" introduced in 1913 by dancers Irene and Vernon Castle. Latin themes also remained popular throughout the 1920s on Broadway and Tin Pan Alley, and many shows contained at least one Latin production number. Most such early uses of Latin and Afro-Caribbean flavors were superficial, exploiting the exotic.

Latin music reached Hollywood in the 1930s, and **Xavier Cugat** (1900–1990) was one of the first well-known Latin bandleaders. The Spanish-born violinist from Havana found his way to Hollywood with a tango band that became one of the first Latin acts to appear in Hollywood films. Cugat also popularized the "rhumba," a pasteurized blend of American, Afro-Caribbean, and Brazilian styles loosely based on Cuban *son*. As Cugat noted, "Americans know nothing about Latin music. They neither understand nor feel it. So they have to be given music more for the eyes than the ears." [2]

The arrival of thousands of Puerto Ricans and Cubans in New York in the early twentieth century furthered the growth of Afro-Caribbean styles as Puerto Rican neighborhoods developed throughout the city, including Spanish Harlem on the upper east side. Puerto Rican musical styles such as *bomba* and *plena* were soon heard on street corners along with Cuban *son* and *bolero*. Many Latin musicians arrived in New York with a high level of musical training, and they played a significant role in the jazzy ragtime sound of James Reese Europe's band, as well as the African American Broadway shows of the 1920s and 1930s.

In 1930 Cuban band leader **Don Azpiazu** (1893–1943) revolutionized Afro-Cuban music in New York when his band appeared with a complete Cuban rhythm section for the first time. His recording of *"El Manicero* (The Peanut Vendor)," based on the cries of street vendors in Havana, became a U.S. hit, establishing the commercial potential of Afro-Cuban music. By the late 1930s, two distinct Latin music scenes existed in New York: Americanized Latin styles played downtown for Anglo audiences, and traditional versions of the same tunes performed uptown for Latinos. The success of *"El Manicero"* led to a wave of Cuban-inspired compositions from American composers such as George Gershwin and Richard Rodgers, though most still reduced Latin music to a generic "rhumba." Latin themes also found their way into film, as in the first pairing of dancers Fred Astaire and Ginger Rogers in the 1933 film *Flying down to Rio*. It featured "Carioca," the earliest Brazilian samba-based tune to become popular in the United States. In 1939 Brazilian star Carmen Miranda (1909–1955) danced and sang in her first Broadway show, arrayed in exotic headgear piled high with fruit. Already prominent in Rio de Janeiro, Miranda became one of Broadway and Hollywood's biggest Latina stars. According to musicologist Walter Aaron Clark, "Miranda, more than any other person, helped create an all-purpose, homogeneous image of Latin Americans, their culture, and especially their music."[3] Swing-era big bands of the 1930s and 1940s also incorporated Latin themes into their repertoires.

LATIN JAZZ AND MAMBO

The blending of Afro-Caribbean Latin styles and jazz achieved a new level in the late 1930s and early 1940s by innovators such as Mario Bauzá, Machito, and Dizzy Gillespie, who worked to develop Latin jazz. It was followed in the 1950s by mambo, a new Latin music and dance craze with Cuban origins.

The Birth of Latin Jazz

Mario Bauzá (1911–1993) played a central role in the early development of Latin jazz. Originally a bass clarinetist with the Havana Philharmonic, Bauzá arrived in New York with Don Azpiazu's band, played saxophone with Noble Sissle's Orchestra in the 1930s, and played lead trumpet and worked as musical director for Chick Webb's influential swing band. Bauzá also worked briefly with Don Redman and Fletcher Henderson before joining Cab Calloway, where he first met trumpeter Dizzy Gillespie. Gillespie and Bauzá often discussed the possibilities of combining jazz with Cuban music. According to Bauzá,

> One day somebody in the Cab Calloway band made a remark that our sounds, Cuban music, were like hillbilly music. . . . That's because the bands that played here were a little of this, a little of that. . . . So I told him: "One day you are going to hear my music sound in a band better than Cab Calloway's."[4]

Internet Listening Exercise

Listen to samples of the following Latin music of the 1920s and 1930s.

Carlos Gardel: *"El Choclo"* (a classic Argentine tango sung by one of Argentina's most beloved vocalists)

Xavier Cugat: *"Perfidia"* (one of the biggest hits for the bandleader with the generic Latin sound)

Don Azpiazu: *"El Manicero"* (the first U.S. hit by an authentic Cuban ensemble)

Fred Astaire: *"The Carioca"* (Latin-flavored film hit tune)

Duke Ellington: *"Caravan"* (an Ellington standard written by Puerto Rican trombonist Juan Tizol)

Cab Calloway: *"The Conga-Conga"* (a Latin novelty tune by the jive-talking swing band leader)

**Internet
Listening Exercise**

Listen to a sample of an early Latin jazz classic.

Machito and the Afro-Cubans: "Tanga"

In 1940 Bauzá left the Calloway band, turned down offers from Duke Ellington and Count Basie, and teamed up with his brother-in-law, **Machito (Frank Grillo**, 1912–1984), to develop a deliberate hybrid of big band jazz and Cuban rhythms. They aimed at bringing Latin music up to the same standard as the best swing bands. Early instrumentation included three saxes, two trumpets, piano, bass, bongos, and timbales. Bauzá was the musical director, Machito the *sonero* (lead vocalist). They called the group "Machito and the Afro-Cubans," to the dismay of booking agents, who preferred to leave out references to Africa. The group had a hit in 1943 with Bauzá's composition, "Tanga," and it set new standards for Latin jazz by attracting guest jazz stars such as Charlie Parker, Thelonious Monk, Dizzy Gillespie, and Cannonball Adderley.

Although deeply involved in developing the new bebop style of jazz in the early 1940s, trumpeter Dizzy Gillespie was also fascinated with Afro-Cuban music. One of his most famous compositions was the Latin-tinged "A Night in Tunisia." In 1946, with bebop in full swing, Gillespie met Afro-Cuban composer, conga player, and dancer **Chano Pozo** (1915–1948), who joined Gillespie's big band. A respected artist in Cuba, Pozo had grown up immersed in Afro-Cuban culture and learned to sing and drum traditional Yoruba and *Abakuá* songs and chants. His joining forces with Gillespie marked a milestone in the evolution of Latin jazz. The two musicians collaborated on tunes such as "Manteca" and "Cubano Be, Cubano Bop," creating a new blend of Latin rhythms, *Abakuá* chants, swing, and bebop called **cubop.** Big band leader/arranger Stan Kenton also tried his hand at incorporating Latin styles into jazz in the early 1940s in a way some called "Latin-lite." Nonetheless, Kenton respected Cuban music:

> Rhythmically, the Cubans play the most exciting stuff. We won't copy them exactly but we will copy some of their devices and apply them to what we are trying to do. And we will keep moving toward the Cubans rhythmically, they're moving toward us melodically. We both have a lot to learn.[5]

Kenton's Latin-tinged compositions such as "Cuban Fire," "Cuban Carnival," and his own arrangement of "The Peanut Vendor" (*"El Manicero"*) encouraged further Latin jazz experimentation.

**Internet
Listening Exercise**

Listen to these early Latin jazz pieces.

Dizzy Gillespie: "Manteca," "Night in Tunisia"

Stan Kenton: "Cuban Carnival"

Mambo

In the 1950s, **mambo,** a music and dance craze with Cuban origins, dominated the Latin music scene in the United States. The style began with the 1938 song "Mambo" by Antonio Arcano's *danzón* orchestra. The piece was composed by the band's pianist Orestes López, who was accompanied by brothers Jesús López on cello and Israel "Cachao" López on bass. Mambo centered on a highly syncopated bass pattern played by Cachao, the father of Latin bass, and the syncopated piano playing of Orestes. At first, Cuban radio banned the mambo rhythm for sounding "too African," but eventually it found its way to New York where big band instrumentation was added. *"El Rey del Mambo,"* a song recorded by José Curbelo in 1946, was probably the first U.S. mambo recording. Curbelo's band included singer Tito Rodríguez and *timbalero*-vibist Tito Puente, who, along with Machito and Pérez Prado, were soon called the "Mambo Kings."

Music Industry Note

The Palladium Ballroom

In the late 1940s, Machito and the Afro-Cubans, along with the bands of Tito Puente and Tito Rodríguez, were leading acts at the Palladium Ballroom, a downtown night-club that was the center of New York's Latin music scene and mambo for twenty years. According to Tito Puente,

> The Palladium was a phenomenon.... The place was a big melting pot—Jews, Irish, Italians, Blacks, Puerto Ricans, Cubans, you name it. Everyone was equal under the roof of the Palladium because everyone was there to dig the music and to dance.[6]

Celebrities and Hollywood stars also frequented the club, and according to journalist Max Salazar, "Music, dance and the art of it all seemed to captivate the soul, exorcising the physical and cultural restrictions of a historically segregated society."[7]

Tito Puente (1923–2000), *"El Rey"* (The King), was one of the most important figures in the history of Latin music in the United States. During his six-decade career, Puente recorded over a hundred albums and performed with most major stars of Latin, jazz, and popular music, although he became best known to younger fans for composing *"Oye Como Va,"* popularized by guitarist

© AP/Wide World Photos

Tito Puente, "El Rey," performing on the timbales, his principal instrument.

Carlos Santana. Puente's importance in the world of Latin music paralleled Duke Ellington's status in jazz.

Puente was a **Nuyorican** (person of Puerto Rican descent born in New York) who dropped out of school to become a full-time musician, soon finding himself in the company of Cuban pianist José Curbelo and Puerto Rican singer Tito Rodríguez. These artists, along with Machito, shaped Puente's early musical direction. After serving in the U.S. Navy in World War II, Puente attended Juilliard School of Music, led his first band at the Palladium, and combined the bass drum and cymbals with *timbales* to create a Latin drum set that enabled him to drive his band like big band drummers. Puente, Machito, and Rodríguez served as the chief architects of the New York mambo sound of the 1950s, and Puente subsequently unfolded a fifty-year recording career that encompassed forays into multiple styles. Late-1950s albums with titles such as *Puente Goes Jazz, Cuban Carnival,* and *Dance Mania,* all quite different in style, became classics. Puente also hired young Latin musicians who later became stars, including pianist Charlie Palmieri, *conguero* Mongo Santamaría, and vocalists Celia Cruz and La Lupe. When the Palladium closed in 1966 and the new sounds of salsa beckoned, Puente continued to follow his own path:

> Salsa means sauce, literally; it's just a commercial term for Afro-Cuban dance music which was used to promote the music. My problem is that we don't play sauce, we play music, and Latin music has different styles; cha-cha, mambo, guaguancó, and son. Salsa doesn't address the complexities and the rich history of the music that we play. But it's become accepted now and it helped to get the music promoted.[8]

Puente recorded his 100th album in 1991, and until his death in 2000 he remained the most highly respected member of the Latin music community in America.

Tito Puente's main competitor for the title of "Mambo King" during the 1950s was Cuban-born pianist/band leader **Pérez Prado** (1916–1989). Prado first developed his distinctive mambo style while working in Havana in the early 1940s. Because his mix of big band jazz and Latin rhythms was not well received in Cuba, he left for Mexico City in 1948 and recorded there with Cuban vocalist Beny Moré, seen by many as the father of salsa singing styles. Prado recorded the hits "Mambo No. 5" and "Que Rico el Mambo" in 1949. (Later, Latin hip-hop artist Lou Bega adapted "Mambo No. 5" to score a major dance hit in the early 2000s.) Prado's style incorporated simple and accessible melodies played by a large brass section and dynamic Latin percussion. In the United States, 1954 was the "year of the mambo," and in the following year Prado scored his biggest hit, "Cherry Pink and Apple Blossom White," introducing the cha-cha dance style. Although boogaloo, *pachanga,*

CD LISTENING EXERCISE

CD 1/27

Listen to *"Mambo Gozón"* by Tito Puente. This riff-based mambo was originally released at the height of the mambo craze in the 1950s and is one of Puente's most popular compositions. Notice the way the different melodies are layered to create a dense, polyphonic texture. The implied two-three *clave* ties all the rhythms together to create a syncopated, danceable groove. Can you hear the *tumbao* bass line which begins after the introduction?

and salsa supplanted Prado's music in the 1960s in the United States, he remained popular throughout Latin America.

Another stage in the evolution of Latin jazz—West Coast Latin jazz—developed in the band of vibraphonist **Cal Tjader** (1925–1982) beginning in the late 1950s. Tjader pursued a contemporary jazz style that was rooted in Afro-Cuban traditions and that focused on listening rather than dancing. He surrounded himself with great players such as percussionist Armando Peraza (who later played with Carlos Santana), pianist Eddie Palmieri, and percussionists Willie Bobo, Mongo Santamaría, Poncho Sanchez, and Tito Puente. Tjader did much to broaden mass interest in Latin jazz, and after Tjader's death in 1982, Poncho Sanchez formed a group modeled on the Tjader band that continued as a high-profile Latin jazz act into the early 2000s.

TRANSITIONS IN THE 1960s

By the end of the 1950s, the popularity of the mambo and cha-cha had waned. The Latin big bands went into decline, and the closing of the Palladium Ballroom in 1966 marked the end of an era. With the Cuban revolution and the emergence of the Castro government in 1959, musicians in the United States lost direct access to Cuba as the source of musical innovation. In this absence, fresh hybrids developed as U.S.-born musicians of Puerto Rican heritage took Latin music in new directions. According to pianist/bandleader Charlie Palmieri:

> The end of the mambo, the closing of the Palladium, the Cuban crisis, changed everything. After that, the musicians stopped coming in, there was no more sheet music from Cuba, so the young musicians had to learn to write their own, and the musical arrangements changed.[9]

In place of big bands, a smaller type of ensemble developed featuring two or three horns—generally trumpets or trombones. The rise of rock and soul also led to experimentation with crossover styles such as boogaloo and Latin soul, and the lyrical content of Latin music took on an increasingly urban flavor as New York–born Latin musicians began to comment on life in the urban **barrios,** or Spanish-speaking neighborhoods. Early elements of salsa also developed in the 1960s, as did new record labels that later dominated the genre.

Charanga, Pachanga, and Latin Soul

The first new sound to emerge in the 1960s was *pachanga*, a hybridized form developed out of *charanga* in 1959 in which two horns often replaced the flute and violins of *charanga*. Cuban bandleader/flutist Gilberto Valdés first brought *charanga* to New York in the late 1950s, featuring Cuban conga player Mongo Santamaría and Dominican musician Johnny Pacheco. Pacheco soon split off to form the first New York–based *charanga* band, and visiting Puerto Rican singer/trombonist Mon Rivera forged a critical link by developing a brassy, two-trombone *charanga* ensemble that strongly influenced Eddie Palmieri, Willie

Internet
Listening Exercise

Listen to samples of the following mambo recordings, old and new.

Pérez Prado: "Cherry Pink and Apple Blossom White," "Mambo No. 5" (Prado's cha-cha and mambo hits)

Benny Moré: *Bonito y Sabroso* (a mambo by one of Cuba's greatest popular vocalists)

Lou Bega: "Mambo No. 5" (a modern hip-hop rendition of a Pérez Prado classic)

Internet Listening Exercise

Listen to samples of *pachanga* from the following CD from the 1960s.

Ray Barretto: *Carnaval (Latino!/Pachanga with Barretto)*

Internet Listening Exercise

Listen to samples of the following Latin soul tunes.

Mongo Santamaría: "Watermelon Man"

Willie Bobo: "Roots"

Cal Tjader: "Soul Sauce"

Joe Cuba: "Bang Bang"

Pucho and the Latin Soul Brothers: "Heat!"

Colón, and other subsequent salsa pioneers. All the major Latin bands of New York were soon playing *pachanga* with a punchy, horn-led sound that became central to salsa.

Other new styles included Latin soul and boogaloo. **Latin soul** integrated soul, rock, and English lyrics into Latin music, and **boogaloo** was a rhythmic style of Latin soul. African Americans and Puerto Ricans in New York had been interacting musically for many years, and the boogaloo and Latin soul repertoire soon ranged along a continuum from Latin sounds and rhythms with a touch of R & B, to R & B, funk, and soul with a touch of Latin. According to one Latin music producer, boogaloo was "the first Nuyorican music," and a young Latin bandleader called it "a kind of bridge, a way for the young, R & B–reared Latino musicians and fans to link back with their musical heritage."[10] Latin soul and boogaloo innovations included blended Spanish and English lyrics with urban themes, integration of trap drums with Latin percussion, introduction of electric guitar and bass, simplified Latin rhythms, and improvisation with a soul/R & B feel. Influential Latin soul artists included Joe Cuba, who had a major hit with "Bang Bang" (1966), Willie Bobo, and Pucho and the Latin Soul Brothers. Established artists Mongo Santamaría and Cal Tjader contributed to Latin soul with Tjader's hit album *Soul Sauce*, which included Santamaría's Latin jazz standard "Afro-Blue." Santamaría's biggest success in the Latin soul vein was his version of pianist Herbie Hancock's "Watermelon Man."

Although short-lived, the Latin soul and boogaloo explosion left its mark. For the first time, African American pop styles successfully blended with Latin music. Further, the use of rock elements and the electric guitar led to the West Coast Latin rock of Santana, El Chicano, and Malo.

Early Salsa

A new generation of Puerto Rican bands and bandleaders came on the scene in New York in the 1960s with the horn-led *pachanga* lineup. Prominent among them were Eddie and Charlie Palmieri and Ray Barretto.

Eddie Palmieri (1936–), one of the most influential musicians in Latin music, enjoyed a career spanning over forty years, more than thirty albums, and numerous awards. The New York–born piano prodigy organized a fiery *charanga* in the early 1960s called *La Perfecta*, which galvanized young Latinos. Palmieri's horn section featured two trombones, producing the powerful and influential sound heard in such hits as *"Echando pa' Lante"* ("Movin' Ahead") and *"Azúcar pa' Tí"* ("Sugar for You"). Palmieri's brother Charlie described *La Perfecta* as a *trombanga* (trombone + *charanga*): "It is a charanga in which the trombones have replaced the violins."[11] Palmieri went on to produce successful albums in the Latin and Latin jazz genres over the succeeding decades, and he remains popular worldwide. He never strayed far from his original influences of jazz and, above all, Cuban music: "Cuban music provides the fundamental from which I never move. Whatever has to be built must be built from there. It's that cross-cultural effect that makes magnificent music."[12]

Internet Listening Exercise

Listen to samples from the following CDs.

Eddie Palmieri: *The Best of Eddie Palmieri; Sun of Latin Music; Palmas; La Perfecta II*

For nearly fifty years, conga player and bandleader **Ray Barretto** (1929–) was one of the leading forces in Latin music and Latin jazz. The Brooklyn-born Barretto was the first U.S.-born percussionist to integrate the conga drum into jazz, and he was an early Latin jazz crossover artist. Barretto first came on the scene in the early 1950s when he joined Tito Puente's orchestra at the Palladium to fill in for Mongo Santamaría. He also became active as a studio musician and in 1962 formed his first ensemble, *Charanga La Moderna,* generating the boogaloo-flavored hit, "El Watusi." Barretto also began a long relationship with New York–based Latin record label Fania, becoming a member and eventually the music director of the famed Fania All Stars. After growing frustrated with the limitations of salsa, the artist in 1992 formed a jazz-oriented group called New World Spirit to explore new musical directions.

Brazilian Influences

In the late 1950s and early 1960s, American popular music discovered a new musical style from Brazil called **bossa nova.** Sometimes described as a slowed-down, ultracool samba, bossa nova had its own texture, which was established by the sound of the acoustic nylon string guitar playing simple, hypnotic rhythms to accompany songs of unexpected harmonic complexity. Bossa nova was developed in the mid-1950s by Brazilian musicians such as Joao Gilberto, Vinicius de Moraes, Luiz Bonfá, and Antonio Carlos Jobim. The style first received international exposure with the success of the 1959 Brazilian film *Black Orpheus,* which inspired many U.S. jazz musicians to visit Brazil. A 1962 album called *Jazz Samba* by Charlie Byrd and Stan Getz signaled the beginning of an American infatuation with the bossa nova, featuring tunes such as Antonio Carlos Jobim's "Desafinado."

The most famous bossa nova recording was "The Girl from Ipanema" (1964) from the album *Getz/Gilberto.* The record was a collaboration between American saxophonist Stan Getz, Brazilian singer/songwriter Joao Gilberto, vocalist Astrud Gilberto, and songwriter/pianist Antonio Carlos Jobim. Astrud Gilberto's cool, sensuous, style made the song a hit, winning a Grammy and establishing a permanent place for bossa nova in American music. Bossa nova was the last jazz-based style to reach the top ten in U.S. pop music: In 1964 the British Invasion displaced it.

Subsequent Brazilian influences on American music, while never reaching the level of popularity of bossa nova, continued in the mid- and late 1960s. *Música Popular Brazileira* (Brazilian Popular Music), or MPB, was a new Brazilian song style that blended American rock and folk music with Brazilian folk music, protest songs, bossa nova, and samba. Having emerged during a period of political repression in Brazil, the style produced songs admired for their distinctive melodies and harmonies, poetic and socially relevant lyrics, and complex rhythms. Only a few MPB artists, such as Caetano Veloso, Ivan Lins, Marisa Monte, Milton Nascimento, and Gilberto Gil, became known outside Brazil, although Sergio Mendes and his band Brazil '66 made inroads into the U.S. market in the late 1960s with a simplified version of the MPB style.

Internet Listening Exercise

Listen to samples from the following albums.

Ray Barretto: *The Best of Ray Barretto; Homage to Art Blakey and the Messengers*

Internet Listening Exercise

Listen to samples of the following songs that exemplify Brazilian influences on U.S. pop and jazz of the 1960s and 1970s.

Joao Gilberto: "The Girl from Ipanema"

Caetano Veloso: "Tropicalia"

Sergio Mendes and Brazil '66: *"Mais Que Nada"*

Milton Nascimento: *"Cravo e Canela"*

Deodato: "Also Sprach Zarathustra (2001)"

Chick Corea: "Light as a Feather"

Multicultural Note

Bossa Nova Hybridization

Many musical influences were at play in bossa nova's evolution. Composer Antonio Carlos Jobim cited the music of twentieth-century Brazilian classical composer Heitor Villa-Lobos as a major influence, and other bossa nova composers were influenced by West Coast cool jazz, a laid-back U.S. style of the 1950s. Bossa nova soon influenced jazz in turn. When many U.S. jazz artists adopted the style as an expressive vehicle for composition and performance, it found its way into the permanent jazz repertoire. Bossa nova also remains popular as the regional style of Rio de Janeiro.

The emergence of jazz-rock fusion—the blending of jazz with electric instruments that began in the late 1960s—served as another pathway for Brazilian influence on American styles. The work of singer Flora Purim; her husband, percussionist Airto Moreira; and keyboardist/arranger Eumir Deodato impacted the development of Latin/jazz/funk styles. The Brazilian fusion sound combined funky, soul jazz and post-cubop Latin jazz, and Purim's unique vocal style fit well into the sound of keyboardist/composer Chick Corea's fusion group, Return to Forever. Airto became one of the most popular jazz percussionists of the late 1960s and early 1970s, contributing to recording projects by pianist Herbie Hancock, saxophonist Wayne Shorter, and trumpeter Miles Davis. Deodato had a disco/funk hit in the early 1970s with a Brazilian-infused dance version of the theme from the film *2001: A Space Odyssey*.

Latin Record Labels

Three important Latin record labels—Alegre, Tico, and Fania—developed in New York in the 1960s. Fania Records ultimately dwarfed and absorbed the other two labels, but all three greatly contributed to the development of salsa and Latin popular music. Formed in 1964, Fania became the most influential label in Latin music history, and its name became synonymous with salsa. Hit records poured out of the "Latin Motown" studio and onto the charts throughout Latin America and U.S. barrios. Much like Motown and other U.S. record labels with a "house sound," Fania had its sound crafted by a group of musicians and composers. In 1971 Fania formed a supergroup of its major recording artists called the Fania All Stars, whose performances were recorded and filmed on multiple occasions. At the height of their popularity, the group performed in Yankee Stadium for 20,000 people and released *Salsa*, a 1974 film of the event. The artists on the date included bandleader Johnny Pacheco, vocalist Celia Cruz,

El Gran Combo, percussionist Ray Barretto, and percussionist Mongo Santa-maría. Fania's bands toured throughout Latin America and greatly influenced the development of salsa in the region. Fania dominated salsa and Latin music throughout the 1970s, but it faded in the 1980s as Latin music expanded into the commercial mainstream. By the early 2000s, RMM had supplanted Fania the main Latin record label.

THE 1970s AND 1980s: SALSA!

At the end of the 1960s, many Nuyoricans were developing a new cultural self-awareness. Musicians began to look to their Puerto Rican roots for ideas and to blend these with Cuban sounds as well as the harmonies and brass sonorities of New York jazz. The new Latin musical mindset produced **salsa,** a style built on the older Cuban *son*, but with an urban barrio punch. The term *salsa* suggested a spicy blend of exciting flavors—Caribbean rhythms, jazz harmonies, barrio life, and complex dances. With roots in the Cuban and Puerto Rican diasporas in New York City, salsa's hybrid style reflected strong interethnic participation. As Venezuelan percussionist Cheo Navarro put it,

> This music comes from the displacement of all those people that were brought as slaves and stayed. Then this genre takes off from Cuba with the son, danzón, and then the ensembles. . . . But the ones to give this music this other sound were the Nuyoricans and the Puerto Ricans. . . . I learned with the Nuyoricans. . . . (They) came up with new arrangements and a new musical sound and they are the ones who created the salsa sound.[13]

Many historians identify Eddie Palmieri as a pivotal figure in the change from the old Latin sound to salsa. Other Puerto Rican musicians, particularly Rafael Cortijo and Ismael Rivera, integrated the Afro–Puerto Rican genres of *plena* and *bomba* into the new salsa format, and the use of the Puerto Rican ten-string *cuatro* by Willie Colón and the Fania All Stars underscored salsa's Puerto Rican affiliations.

Internet Listening Exercise

Listen to samples from the following albums.

Fania All Stars: *Live at Yankee Stadium, Vols. I and II*

The Key Features of Salsa

- **"Locking" the Rhythm**
  Puerto Rican musicians speak of "locking" the rhythm—called *afinque* or *afinca'o*. In salsa, the Latin percussion section consisting of timbales, conga, bongo, guiro, and cowbell plays established rhythms that create a complex, interlocking groove with the bass and piano.

- *Clave*
  The application of the three-two or two-three *clave* throughout a piece is characteristic of salsa. With few exceptions, a specific form of *clave* is necessary, and those who do not apply the *clave* properly are said to have "crossed" *(cruzado)* the clave.

- *Fuerza*

  Fuerza (strength) connotes that musicians are playing in sync, with power and confidence.

- **Improvisation**

  Instrumental and vocal improvisation are central to salsa and reflect the music's African heritage. Salsa singers *(soneros)* are admired for the ability to improvise *(sonear)* lyrics between choruses *(coros)*.

- **Phrasing** *(Fraseo)*

  The ability to phrase artfully is also much admired in salsa singers and musicians.

- **Breaks**

  Dramatic interruptions of the musical groove create a heightened sense of excitement for dancers and listeners. Most breaks involve short, syncopated accents followed by a return to the groove.

- **Dance**

  Dance links all aspects of salsa, and it is through dance that people experience it most powerfully.

Note: Adapted from Marisol Berríos-Miranda, "Is Salsa a Musical Genre?" in Lise Waxer, *Situating Salsa* (New York: Routledge, 2002), 29–45, and an interview with Rebeca Mauleón.

Historians often credit **Willie Colón** (1950–), along with pianist Eddie Palmieri, with defining the sound of modern salsa. The Bronx-born trombonist/bandleader brought an urban feel to the Afro-Cuban sound, and many critics credit Colón with giving salsa an "attitude" by injecting social commentary without losing the groove. Colón released his seminal album *El Malo* ("The Bad Guy") in 1967 at age seventeen, with tunes in Spanish and English in a range of hybrid styles: mambo-jazz, boogaloo, *guaguancó, bomba,* and *son montuno.* In subsequent albums, Colón incorporated R & B and rock influences such as the funk-inspired slap-bass style without compromising his Latin identity. Colón began a legendary collaboration with vocalist/composer Rubén Blades in the late 1970s, and their partnership made salsa a vehicle for expressing politically progressive themes in New York, Puerto Rico, and Latin America. The collaboration reached its peak in 1978 with the release of the album *Siembra,* which remained salsa's best-selling album for nearly two decades. Its most powerful songs focused on barrio life ("Pedro Navaja") and rejections of consumerism and corporate domination ("Plástico").

The many talents of Panamanian-born **Rubén Blades** (1948–), another giant of salsa, ranged from music to film to politics. Originally trained as a law-

Salsa artists Rubén Blades and Willie Colón in a record publicity photo from the late 1970s.

yer, Blades immigrated to New York in 1974 and found a job in the Fania Records mailroom. He was soon signed with the label as a member of the Fania All Stars, and Blades's first solo Fania record —produced by Willie Colón—established an alliance between the two artists. When the Blades-Colón partnership ended in 1982, Blades formed a synthesizer-flavored group called *Seis del Solar* ("Six from the Tenements") and released the crossover album *Buscando América* ("Looking for America"), which featured doo-wop, reggae, Cuban jazz, and hip-hop. He subsequently collaborated with artists as diverse as Joe Jackson and Linda Ronstadt. In 1988 Blades released an album in English called *Nothing but the Truth,* and in 1996 he won a Grammy for *La Rosa de Los Vientos* ("Rose of the Winds"). Blades's stress on social and political issues in his lyrics reflected the Latin American *nueva canción* (new song) movement, which blended poetry and politics.

CD LISTENING EXERCISE

CD 1/28

Listen to excerpts from *"Plástico"* from the *Siembra* album recorded in 1978 by Willie Colón and Rubén Blades. Notice the slap-bass introduction and the transition into the Latin-style body of the song. What is the instrumentation? Can you feel the underlying rhythm of the clave? Analyze the lyrics reproduced and translated in the accompanying box. What is the feel at the end of the song, when Blades sings, *"Oye Latino, oye mano, oye mi amigo …"*? What is the significance of the "roll call" that Blades does at the end of the tune, calling out the names of different Latin American countries? How do you think this song was received in different parts of the world?

Plástico

(Ruben Blades, 1977, Vaya Publishing)

Ella era una chica plástica,	She was a plastic woman
de esas que veo por ahí,	One of those that I see from here,
de esas que cuando se agitan,	One of those, that when they get nervous
sudan Chanel number three.	sweats Chanel Number Three.
Que sueñan casarse con un doctor,	That dreams of marrying a doctor,
pues el puede mantenerlas mejor,	You see, he can keep her best taken care of
no le hablan a nadie si no es su igual,	She doesn't speak to just anyone
a menos que sea fulano de tal.	They must be Mr. or Ms. So-and-so
Bonitas, delgadas de buen vestir,	She's pretty, slender, well dressed
de mirada esquiva y falso reir.	With an avoiding look and a fake laugh.

Male artists dominated the world of salsa. Despite a strong historical tradition of Latin female singers and interpreters of romantic ballads, few major female salsa artists appeared. In more recent years, many more women have become involved with Latin music, including pianist/composer Rebeca Mauleón, who gained international recognition for writing some of the first method books for Afro-Cuban music ever published.

Celia Cruz, the undisputed "Queen of Salsa," performed only in her native Spanish and was considered one of the finest vocalists in Latin music.

Celia Cruz (1925–2003), universally recognized as the "Queen of Salsa," stood out with a career that spanned almost six decades. Cruz's vast repertoire of songs contained a history of the genre—from her first Afro-Cuban *son* band, to Tito Puente, to the Fania All Stars, to solo tributes to the Afro-Cuban deities of *Santería*. Cruz began her career in Cuba in the 1950s singing with the popular group *La Sonora Matancera*, then left Cuba in 1959 after the revolution and headed for New York where she witnessed the final days of the Palladium Ballroom. Signing with newly formed Tico Records, she began a decade-long association with bandleader Tito Puente. After she left Tico for Fania, her next album, *Celia y Johnny*, became one of the biggest-selling salsa records of all time. According to Cruz, "It was the term 'salsa' that made this music take off in popularity. It made it more accessible to people who didn't know what a guaracha, guaguancó, and the other rhythms were."[14] Powerful performances during the salsa boom of the 1970s solidified her reputation as the "Queen," and her appearance in the 1992 movie *The Mambo Kings* broadened her mainstream exposure. Cruz remained one of the most celebrated stars of Latino show business until her death in 2003.

Internet Listening Exercise

Listen to selected samples from the following albums by the leading women of salsa.

Celia Cruz: *100% Azúcar: The Best of Celia Cruz and La Sonora Matancera; La Negra Tiene Tumbao*

La India: *Llegó la India via Eddie Palmieri; Dicen Que Soy*

A Nuyorican singer from the Bronx, **La India** (Linda Caballero, 1970–) started out singing house music and hip-hop in the 1980s, then shifted her focus to salsa. After one album of English-language dance music, La India decided to explore her cultural roots and came to the attention of Eddie Palmieri. Palmieri produced India's first salsa album, *Llegó la India*, in 1992. Her robust, hard-edged style reminded many of Celia Cruz, and critics praised the album as one of the year's best. La India's audience included a large proportion of women, and she noted that her songs expressed women's perspectives: "Women see me as a figure they can respect. . . . They know I've been through a lot. I'm not going to let no man put me under."[15] La India kept control of her creative process by composing, arranging, and working closely with producers, and she consciously varied her musical style.

MULTIPLE DIRECTIONS IN THE 2000s

The commercial success of Latin music continued to grow at the end of the twentieth century, fueled in part by new genres like *salsa romántica* and Latin pop, as well as the growing popularity of merengue. New styles from Cuba and the birth of the Latin Grammys added further vitality to the music.

Salsa Romántica and Merengue

Salsa romántica developed in the mid-1980s as a blend of romantic ballads and bolero-style vocals backed by salsa dance rhythms. Critics compared the style's slick, commercial sound with Frank Sinatra's crooning over a hard-swinging big band. The best-selling album *Noche Caliente* ("Hot Night"), recorded by Fania producer/vibist Louie Ramírez and vocalists Ray de la Paz and José "El Canario" Alberto in 1982, signaled the genesis of the style. The clean, well-produced, but predictable flavor of *salsa romántica* soon became the dominant salsa sound.

The explosion of merengue into the Latin dance world soon followed. When the Dominican Republic went into a period of economic decline in the late 1980s, over half a million Dominicans moved to New York and brought with them their passion for **merengue,** their national music and dance. Although it was not a new style, with roots extending back over 150 years, a high-energy version of the merengue swept through the New York salsa scene, with some clubs switching to "all merengue all the time." Salsa gave way to merengue in the same way that boogaloo pushed mambo aside in the 1960s. Not all musicians favored the new style; according to trombonist Wayne Wallace, "Merengue represented a Dominican invasion of New York. It destroyed the salsa scene in New York and put the musicians out of work. With merengue, salsa became too stylized."[16] Merengue provided a hypnotic, up-tempo, two-beat feel that dancers loved. The fast tempos and set rhythms could limit musical options, however, and some Latin musicians felt boxed in by the style.

The musician usually credited with moving merengue into the mainstream of Latin dance music was Johnny Ventura (1940–). Beginning in 1956, Ventura revolutionized the style by speeding up the tempo, adding conga drums, and featuring the traditional *tambora* drum. He was a flashy dancer whose provocative stage moves made him a superstar throughout Latin America for over thirty years. Another merengue star, trumpeter Wilfrido Vargas (1949–), broadened the appeal of the style to the salsa world while touring with the Fania All Stars. Vargas put on lavish stage shows, and his 1970s hit song *"La Chica de los Ojos Cafés"* ("The Girl with the Coffee Eyes") blended Jamaican dancehall reggae with merengue. Beginning in the 1990s, Juan Luis Guerra (1957–) became one of the Dominican Republic's biggest stars, with recordings that represented a romantic, softer, and more poetic version of Dominican music. His 1991 Grammy-winning album *Bachata Rosa* ("Pink Bachata") featured both merengue and romantic versions of *bachata*, a Dominican folk style. As of the early 2000s, merengue was still a major factor in the international Latin dance world.

Fresh Sounds from Havana

The late 1980s also saw a Cuban resurgence in the Latin music world. After twenty-five years of relative isolation, the end of Cuba's economic dependence on the Soviet Union produced a gradual opening of commerce and cultural exchange with the United States. Cuba's role as a center of Latin music innovation

Internet Listening Exercise

Go online and listen to samples of the following *salsa romántica* and merengue albums.

Various Artists: *Noche Caliente*

Johnny Ventura: *The Best*

Juan Luis Guerra: *Bacheta Rosa*

Various Artists: *Merengue Hits 2000*

Internet Listening Exercise

Listen to samples from the following CDs or others by the same artist.

Los Van Van: *Legendary Los Van Van: Thirty Years of Cuba's Greatest Band; Lo Ultimo en Vivo (Live)*

was reestablished by the progressive salsa styles of artists such as Los Van Van, N.G. La Banda (New Generation Band), Son 14, Cubanismo, and Issac Delgado, as well as the contemporary Cuban jazz and funk sounds of Irakere and Afro-Cuba. Los Van Van's leader and bass player, Juan Formell (1942–), pioneered a new Cuban style called *songo* (literally, *son* + go go) that blended syncopated funk, rock, and Latin rhythms. Latin musicians who wanted to look beyond existing salsa forms embraced *songo* and a subsequent related style called *timba*, which incorporated elements of rap and hip-hop. According to pianist/composer Rebeca Mauleón,

> *Songo* started as *charanga* with trombones. . . . Juan Formell's songwriting had modulations and different harmonies not used before in *son*. He was at first influenced by the Beatles, then Blood, Sweat, and Tears and Earth, Wind, and Fire—then more James Brown influences.[17]

Latin Pop

The early 2000s saw the further expansion of a worldwide explosion in the popularity of Latin musical styles. Salsa had become a global dance club phenomenon, and the success of the 1992 film *The Mambo Kings* had renewed popular interest in classic Latin dance music. The influences of Latin music on jazz grew unabated, and the fastest-growing commercial market in Latin music was Latin pop, a movement throughout the Spanish-speaking world.

Some trace the emergence of Latin pop as a genre to the music of Spanish superstar **Julio Iglesias** (1943–), a smooth, romantic crooner who sold over 100 million albums worldwide in the 1970s and 1980s. **Gloria Estéfan** (1958–) also played a key role in the development of the genre. The Cuban-born Estéfan grew up in the anticommunist Cuban community of Miami. In 1975 she became lead singer of a band called the Miami Latin Boys led by future husband Emilio Estéfan. Within a year, the band changed its name to the Miami Sound Machine, recorded its first album in Spanish, and enjoyed a string of hits in Central and South America. Major U.S. recognition came with the release of

Multicultural Note

Language, Lyrics, and the Marketplace

In recent years, the U.S. pop music audience has become more accustomed to Spanish and bilingual lyrics, although few such songs existed in the English-dominated U.S. market prior to the 1990s. Contemporary artists now often record songs in both English and Spanish for distribution to different markets. What led to this change? How many older rock and pop songs can you name that are bilingual?

"Conga" (1985), a funky Latin disco tune. The song was a crossover hit, as well as the first single to crack *Billboard*'s pop, dance, black, and Latin charts at the same time. Estéfan and the band followed up with a string of hits in the 1980s and 1990s in both English and Spanish, and Estéfan became one of Latin music's biggest superstars, winning eight Grammys.

The crossover success of "Conga" opened the door for the Latin pop movement of the 1990s, spawning the careers of Marc Anthony, Shakira, Ricky Martin, Christina Aguilera, Enrique Iglesias, and Jennifer Lopez. All made significant use of bilingual lyrics and successfully blended a variety of African American and Latin styles to push Latin pop toward the center of the U.S. pop music mainstream. **Marc Anthony** (1968–) was one of the biggest Latin pop stars of the early 2000s. The Puerto Rican–born musician moved to New York and began his career on the New York dance club scene performing house music. In 1992, after Tito Puente invited Anthony to open for his revue at Madison Square Garden, Anthony began recording and performing in Spanish, and his popularity skyrocketed. He achieved status as an international Latin pop star with the 1999 release of *Marc Anthony* and a hit done in English and Spanish versions, "I Need to Know/*Dímelo.*"

The growing popularity of Latin pop in the early 1990s encouraged the National Academy of Recording Arts and Sciences (NARAS, the organizers of the Grammy Awards) to establish the Latin Academy of Recording Arts and Sciences in 1997. The inaugural Latin Grammy Awards ceremony in 1999 marked the first prime-time, primarily Spanish- and Portuguese-language telecast on American television and the most high-profile celebration of Latin culture ever presented on the U.S. domestic airwaves.

 **Internet Listening Exercise**

Listen to samples of Latin pop and the Buena Vista Social Club.

Gloria Estéfan: "Conga"

Marc Anthony: "I Need to Know/ *Dímelo*"

Buena Vista Social Club: "El Cuarto De Tula"

Buena Vista Social Club

In 1996 the eclectic American slide guitarist and world music aficionado Ry Cooder went to Cuba to record an album that would blend traditional Cuban styles with his own rootsy guitar. With the help of Cuban guitarist Juan de Marcos González, Cooder located several semiretired Cuban musicians. The resulting recording, *Buena Vista Social Club*, was a Grammy-winning hit that spawned

 Multicultural Note

Rediscovery or Romanticized Invention?

Not all critics glowed about Cooder's project, and some questioned the use of his power as an influential Los Angeles studio musician and producer to "recreate" the Buena Vista Social Club. To some, the *Buena Vista* music was a romanticized, nostalgic construction by Ry Cooder that appealed primarily to upper-middle-class white audiences. Few would have forecast that a group of semiretired Cuban octogenarians would become international celebrities.

a feature-length film. Although the club that gave the album its name no longer existed, Cooder's version of the music that had thrived there in the 1940s and 1950s acquired a new lease and allowed listeners to rediscover some of Cuba's forgotten musical voices. One of the most colorful members of the group, guitarist Compay Segundo, restarted his career at the age of eighty-nine, and in spring 2003 vocalist Ibrahim Ferrer, a former backup singer for Benny Moré, toured internationally with an eighteen-piece big band.

JAMAICAN INFLUENCES: SKA, REGGAE, DUB, AND DANCEHALL

No Caribbean culture besides Cuba has influenced American and world music as much as Jamaica. Through a series of innovative styles—from ska to reggae to dancehall—Jamaican popular music became the island's most influential export.

Musical Roots

The first documented African musical expression in Jamaica (1725) took place in an adaptation of the West African harvest festival of *Jonkanoo* featuring masked dancers and drumming. Numerous African-derived instruments—drums, rattles, flutes, and banjo—also came into use. By the mid-1700s, African slaves had begun to adopt European musical forms such as reels, quadrilles, and polkas, and fiddling had become popular. As late as 1965, ska tunes still referenced the quadrille.

Like Cuba, Jamaica gave birth to new religious hybrids: Revivalism, which practiced speaking in tongues; Kumina, a combination of Christianity and Bantu religion; and Pocomania, another Afro-Christian hybrid. Music was an essential part of the worship; hand clapping, foot stomping, and percussion produced a sound similar to early African American Baptist gospel music. The work of Toots and the Maytals, Bob Marley, and Jimmy Cliff later echoed this music at times.

In the late nineteenth and early twentieth centuries, large numbers of Jamaicans migrated to other parts of the Caribbean and Central America. Many kept ties with Jamaica, bringing back influences that produced a new style called **mento**, with *rumba*, tango, and samba layered over the African music of the *Jonkanoo* celebrations. A typical mento band lineup consisted of banjo, hand drums, guitar, and *marímbula*—sometimes augmented by a bamboo saxophone, penny whistle, or steel drum. In the 1970s, traces of mento still appeared in the work of roots reggae artists such as Peter Tosh. The style waned by the end of World War II as the sounds of U.S. big band swing predominated, producing artists such as ska pioneer trombonist Don Drummond. By the 1950s, bebop and the R & B of Louis Jordan, T-Bone Walker, and B. B. King had supplanted the big band in Jamaica.

Internet Listening Exercise

Listen to samples from the following CD of early Jamaican music.

Boogu Yagga Gal: Jamaican Mento 50s

Sound Systems, Ska, and Rock Steady

Most working-class Jamaicans did not own their own radios or record players, so the only way to hear the latest R & B was through a unique Jamaican invention: the **sound system.** The systems were like portable discos, consisting of up to thirty speakers, a turntable, and a DJ. Sporadically narrated by DJs, popular music thudded out of the speakers at earsplitting volume. The DJ's spoken words, called *toasting,* later influenced the development of rap. Sound system dances took over Jamaican popular music, and the sound system tradition is still popular in Jamaica today.

The Jamaican recording industry began in the late 1950s, when a young DJ and sound system helper named Prince Buster (Cecil Campbell) brought together some of the island's best musicians to develop a new mixture of American and Caribbean music called **ska.** One of Prince Buster's first pressings was "Oh Carolina" by the Folkes Brothers, later sampled by dancehall artist Shaggy in a 1993 hit. Another sound system operator, Clement Coxsone Dodd, created a consistent, house sound for his label and pushed ska away from American R & B by adding an unexpected emphasis on the off beat that lent a galloping, forward-leaning feel. The most influential early ska band, the Skatalites, formed in 1964 and played jazzy, horn-based instrumentals with improvised solos. The group was short-lived but prolific, recording hundreds of records in its fourteen months of existence and scoring hits with "The Guns of Navarone" and the theme from the movie *Exodus.* Ska also grew popular in Britain in the early 1960s, championed by members of the English mod movement.

Ska experienced three waves of popularity. The first wave saw the style's initial popularity in the 1960s in Jamaica and the United Kingdom. The second wave surfaced in the late 1970s in Britain with acts such as the Specials, Madness, the Beat, Selector, and even the Clash. The groups dominated the British pop charts and made some inroads into the U.S. new wave rock sound of the 1980s. Many second-wave ska groups were multiracial, promoting multiculturalism through the "2-tone" movement that brought together Jamaican "rude boys" and English working-class youth. A third wave of ska appeared on the U.S. rock scene in the 1990s, amalgamating the 2-tone ska sound of the 1980s with 1990s pop-punk sounds and traditional first-wave ska. Artists such as No Doubt, the Mighty Mighty Boss Tones, Sublime, Reel Big Fish, and 311 emerged in this wave.

In the mid-1960s, ska gave way to **rock steady,** a more laid-back style, which some fans still see as the pinnacle of Jamaican music. A transitional style, rock steady incorporated traces of ska while pointing the way to reggae, and numerous dancehall tunes of the early 2000s also referenced the style. In contrast with ska, rock steady slowed the beat down and emphasized vocals. The bass—now electric—also became more dominant, and the electric guitar played a steady off-beat rhythm that led to the signature sound of reggae. Artists such as the Wailers and Desmond Dekker gained early popularity with songs about the ghetto life, and groups such as the Paragons, Techniques, and Heptones took their cues from American soul and doo-wop. Rock steady hits in

Internet Listening Exercise

Listen to samples from the three waves of ska.

Various Artists: *Intensified! Original Ska, 1962–66* (a first-wave ska compendium)

The Specials: *The Specials* (second-wave, 2-tone ska)

Sublime: *Sublime* (third-wave, punk-ska)

the United States in the 1960s included Millie Jackson's "My Boy Lollipop" and Desmond Dekker's "The Israelites." This style also influenced important U.S. rock acts of the 1990s and early 2000s such as No Doubt and 311; in fact, No Doubt's 2001 hit album was entitled *Rock Steady*.

Reggae

Jamaican music changed its shape again in the late 1960s with the new sound of **reggae.** Musicians searching for a new beat hit on the idea of incorporating the old-time shuffle feel of mento, the beat of rock steady, and a heavy bass underpinning. One of the earliest reggae releases was "Do the Reggay" by Toots and the Maytals (1968). Politics and religion were important themes in the new style. Mistrust of the Jamaican political system's ability to provide for growing numbers of poor people flavored the music, as did the Rastafarian religion's blend of mysticism, radical protest, and divine sanction of *ganja* (marijuana). Rastafarians viewed Ethiopian emperor Haile Selassie as a holy figure, and by the mid-1970s many Jamaican musicians sported dreadlocks and sang about socially related subject matter while images of Haile Selassie and the red, gold, and green-colored Ethiopian flag abounded.

Toots and the Maytals, a seminal reggae group, began performing in the early 1960s, blending gospel harmonies with ska. Lead singer **Toots Hibbert** (1946–), whose vocal style was reminiscent of Otis Redding, made a series of records that introduced reggae to a mainstream pop audience, including "54-46 That's My Number," "Pressure Drop," and even John Denver's "Country Roads." *The Harder They Come* (1972), Jamaica's first internationally successful film, starred vocalist **Jimmy Cliff** (1948–) and exposed the international audience to reggae for the first time. The film's sound track featured selections by Jimmy Cliff ("Many Rivers to Cross") and the Melodians ("The Rivers of Babylon") and caused *Rolling Stone* to select it as movie of the year.

Reggae superstar **Bob Marley** (1945–1981) was the product of an upbringing in the Trenchtown ghetto of Kingston, but rural mento songs and his mother's gospel music influenced him as well. He joined the Wailers, originally a ska vocal group in the 1960s, and had a hit with "Simmer Down" (1964), a reaction to street gang violence. When the group signed with Island Records in 1972, their fortunes took off, and a series of albums, including *Catch A Fire, Burnin', Natty Dread,* and *Rastaman Vibration,* chronicled Marley's rise to global iconic status. A cover of Marley's "I Shot the Sheriff" by rocker Eric Clapton topped the U.S. charts in 1974 to fuel broader U.S. interest in reggae. Marley's message of strength and social criticism made a potent impact during the mid-1970s, when rock had lost its sense of rebellion. In 1978 Marley made a famous concert appearance at a time when Jamaica appeared

Reggae legend Bob Marley performing in the late 1970s.

headed for civil war, symbolically linking the arms of the nation's two opposing political leaders while singing his hit "One Love." Marley's popularity in Africa was also legendary, and a 1980 concert in Zimbabwe highlighted the celebration of the country's independence. Just over a year after the Zimbabwe concert, Marley died of cancer at age thirty-seven. He was probably the most influential of all world music artists, and when reggae is played in Africa, Asia, Europe, or the Americas, Marley serves as the role model, with his influential message of struggle and pride.

Many great reggae artists emerged in the 1970s and 1980s, including Burning Spear, Third World, Sly and Robbie, Inner Circle, and Black Uhuru. The sound of classic 1970s reggae became known over time as *roots reggae,* and it migrated to new homes around the globe. In Africa, Ivory Coast's Alpha Blondy and South Africa's Lucky Dube played roots reggae, and the style also flourished in the United Kingdom with the work of Guyanese immigrant Eddy Grant ("Electric Avenue," 1983), Aswad ("Don't Turn Around," 1988), and poet/singer Linton Kwesi Johnston. Reggae also influenced the Clash and the Police in the 1980s. Finally, the style was hybridized by artists such as the United Kingdom's Apache Indian, who blended it with South Asian pop influences ("Boom Shakalak," 1993), the U.S. Native American reggae band Native Roots, and many Hawaiian artists who incorporated reggae into their "Jawaiian" sound.

CD LISTENING EXERCISE

CD 1/29

Listen to "Get Up, Stand Up" recorded by Peter Tosh, an original member of the Wailers. Describe the sound of the song. What theme do the lyrics present? Listen to the classic reggae rhythm guitar, which emphasizes beats two and four. Compare it to similar off-beat rhythms from ska and rock steady. Listen to the bass and notice how it seldom lands on beat one and often plays melodic patterns. Listen also to the drums and note which beats are emphasized and how fills are used. How different is the sound of this classic roots reggae song from the R & B of the early 1970s?

Next, go online and listen to samples of the following classic reggae albums.

• Toots and the Maytals: *Funky Kingston*
• Various Artists: *The Harder They Come*
• Bob Marley: *Legend*

Dub, Dancehall, and Ragga

While reggae was going global, the focus of Jamaican music shifted back to the toasting of sound system DJs. At this time, the term **dub** came into use to describe mixed-down versions of tunes stripped to their instrumental basics to allow DJs to toast over them in dancehall settings. Dub evolved into an entire genre of instrumental remixes of existing recordings that radically reshaped them through use of sound effects. Early dub was also the prelude to many later dance and pop styles including hip-hop, turntablism, and electronica. In the late 1960s artists such as King Tubby, U-Roy, I-Roy, and Big Youth pioneered dub in Jamaica. King Tubby (Osbourne Ruddock) was the first to turn the mixing board into an instrument, with the DJ assuming the role of performer, using unique echo and reverb effects. The artist's landmark dub album was *Blackboard Jungle* (1973), and other producers followed suit by putting out instrumental/rhythm versions on B-sides of singles to give birth to the dub genre.

**Internet Listening Exercise**

Listen to samples of early dub.

King Tubby Meets Rockers Uptown

www **Internet Listening Exercise**

Listen to samples from the following dancehall albums.

Shabba Ranks: *Shabba Ranks Greatest Hits*

Shaggy: *The Best of Shaggy Part One*

Buju Banton: *Til Shiloh*

Jamaican music continued to evolve in the directions established by dub, shaped by the shift to digital sound production and recording technologies of the mid-1980s and early 1990s. In 1980, when more Jamaican records were being released by DJs than singers, the term **dancehall** came into use to describe music that featured digital beats and worldly, often raw lyrics reflecting an attitude of "slackness": guns, drugs, women's body parts, and men's sexual prowess. The term **ragga** (short for *raggamuffin*) was also used to describe digitized dancehall music. Shabba Ranks (1966–) was a quintessential dancehall artist whose 1989 hit "Wicked in Bed" exemplified slackness. There was also a moral back-and-forth over the lyrical content of dancehall and ragga—shifting between the worldliness of slackness and a spiritually and politically oriented style called *conscious*. Buju Banton (1973–) exemplified the latter attitude in his hit "Til Shiloh" in 1995, although he received accusations of homophobia for some of his lyrics in the early 2000s. Other artists associated with dancehall and ragga were Shaggy, Barrington Levy, and Beenie Man. Dancehall and ragga influenced—and were influenced by—hip-hop, electronica, and other globalized dance pop genres.

TRINIDAD: CALYPSO, SOCA, AND STEEL BANDS

The multicultural history of the island of Trinidad produced two important musical genres: calypso and steel bands. Although neither style consistently ventured far into the American popular music mainstream, they did surface periodically in film scores, jazz, and pop songs.

Calypso and Soca

The origins of **calypso** go back over 200 years, stemming from creole songs, neo-African styles, British ballads, and a song style called *calinda*, the musical accompaniment to a nineteenth-century stick-fighting ritual. Fighters and onlookers were egged on by a **chantwell,** who sang songs that praised one fighter while suggestively insulting the other. By the mid-nineteenth century, the multiday Carnival tradition was a mainstay in Trinidad; however, in the early 1880s, the British banned all drumming at Carnival or other public gatherings. Calypso emerged as a result. By 1900 two styles of calypso had emerged—one based on the masquerade processions during Carnival in which revelers sang rowdy call and response chants, the other a more text-oriented style performed in large tents where audiences focused on wordplay and banter.

In the 1930s, Trinidadian artists began making calypso recordings in New York. The Andrews Sisters, a U.S. vocal trio, sold five million copies with their cover of a calypso tune called "Rum and Coca Cola" in the 1940s, and Jamaican American vocalist Harry Belafonte popularized the style in the United States in the 1950s with his hit "Jamaican Farewell." Calypso rhythms appeared frequently in jazz, notably in saxophonist Sonny Rollins's jazz standard

"St. Thomas." In addition, calypso was popular in film and television sound tracks, including the Disney film *The Little Mermaid*.

Contemporary Trinidadian calypso centers on rhythmic topical commentary performed to a syncopated rhythm with a two-beat feel and lyrical content peppered with sexual innuendo and humor. **Soca** emerged in the late twentieth century as an up-tempo calypso for dancing, with lyrics more often about partying than social issues. The popular party tune "Hot Hot Hot," originally recorded by Montserrat's The Mighty Arrow and later covered by former New York Dolls lead singer Buster Pointdexter (David Johansen), is an example of soca. Calypso and soca bands use a variety of instrumentation, including a U.S.-style rhythm section, horns, steel drums, and Latin percussion. Many of Trinidad's most prominent calypso artists, including the Mighty Sparrow and Calypso Rose, migrated to New York City, which became home for more than half a million people of West Indian descent.

Steel Bands

Steel Bands are also unique to Trinidad, and like calypso, their development was closely connected to Carnival. The **steel drum** or "pan" first appeared in the 1930s, an outgrowth of a musical tradition called "tamboo bamboo" that emerged after the banning of drums in the 1880s, in which performers hit different lengths of bamboo together to create percussive sounds in a variety of pitches. During the 1930s, musicians started hitting metal oil drums with bamboo to make a louder sound, and they began to pay attention to the tones coming from the metal surfaces. By the 1940s, they were modifying oil drums and other metal containers to create flattened areas that could be tuned to specific pitches, thus giving birth to the modern steel drum.

Because the culture of early steel bands mimicked the violent traditions of *calinda*, the Trinidadian middle and upper classes at first felt threatened by the music, but the government embraced the style. The steel band is now a trademark of the island, and Trinidadians take pride in the development of the drums from found materials into an art form by the Afro-Trinidadian working class. By the 1950s, steel bands were active in many communities, and steel drums that could play complete chromatic scales came about in the 1960s. The 1970s saw inclusion of steel bands in the public school curriculum, as well as the formation of all-female groups. Today there are over a hundred steel bands in Trinidad, and during Carnival large steel band orchestras are formed with as many as 100 members, making them some of the world's largest musical ensembles. The repertoire encompasses calypso, Caribbean styles, classical music, and pop.

Internet Listening Exercise

Listen to the following samples of calypso and soca.

Harry Belafonte: "Jamaican Farewell"

The Mighty Sparrow: *16 Carnival Hits*

The Mighty Arrow: "Hot Hot Hot"

Buster Pointdexter: "Hot Hot Hot"

Internet Listening Exercise

Listen to the following samples of steel-band music.

Various Artists: *Steel Band Music of the Caribbean*

Andy Narell: *The Passage*

Chapter Summary

- The influence of Afro-Caribbean and Latin music fundamentally influenced the development of many American popular styles, as far back as ragtime and early jazz.

- Afro-Caribbean and Latin styles are diasporic: They developed through the flows of people and cultures among the United States, the Caribbean, and Latin America.

- The retention of African cultural and musical elements was critical to the development of Afro-Caribbean music, and Afro-Christian hybrid religions such as *Santería* played important roles in retaining and developing key African musical practices.

- Central to the development of Latin styles, Cuba gave birth to *son* (the "grandfather of salsa"), as well as mambo and other important styles.

- Latin rhythm instruments—blends of African, European, and Caribbean hybrids—greatly influenced the evolution of Afro-Caribbean musics.

- Early uses of Latin styles in American music treated them as exotic novelties. The first authentic Afro-Cuban recording popular in the United States was Don Azpiazu's "*El Manicero* (The Peanut Vendor)" in 1930. Immigration of Puerto Rican and Cuban musicians to New York fostered the further developments of Latin music in the United States.

- The 1940s marked important progress in the evolution of Latin jazz; the 1950s saw the heyday of the mambo; the 1960s witnessed bossa nova, boogaloo, Latin soul, and small-group Latin jazz; the 1970s gave birth to salsa; the 1980s contributed *salsa romántica* and merengue; and the 1990s witnessed the development of Latin pop.

- The impact of Latin and Afro-Caribbean styles grew steadily, culminating with the inauguration of the Latin Grammy Awards in 1999. The popularity of Latin pop also built markets for Spanish-language and bilingual recordings in the United States.

- Jamaican music played a key role in the evolution of American popular music over the three final decades of the twentieth century. Each successive Jamaican style—ska, rock steady, reggae, dub, and dancehall—had global impact. Jamaican sound systems and DJs were the precursors of rap.

- The rich multicultural texture of Trinidad produced three prominent Caribbean styles: calypso, soca, and steel bands.

Key Terms

Abakuá

barrio

bolero

bongo drums

boogaloo

bossa nova

cajones

calypso

Candomblé

Carnival

cencerro

chantwell

charanga

clave

claves

conga drum

conjunto

contradanza

cubop

dancehall

danzón

décima

diaspora

dub

guajira

guiro

habanera

Latin soul

Macumba

mambo

mento

merengue

montuno

música campesina

Nuyorican

pachanga

Palo

ragga

reggae

rock steady

rumba

salsa

salsa romántica

samba

Santería

ska

soca

son

sound system

steel drum

timbales

tres

trova

tumbao

Voudou

Yoruba

Study and Discussion Questions

1. What are diasporas, and how did they influence the development of Afro-Caribbean and Latin music?

2. Discuss the role of African retentions in Afro-Caribbean music. What are they and why are they important? What was the role of Afro-Christian hybrid religions such as *Santería*?

3. What are the instruments of Latin music and their cultural origins?

4. What is the *clave* rhythm and how does it function in Afro-Caribbean music?

5. What is *son*? Discuss the role of *son* in the evolution of Afro-Cuban styles.

6. Who were central figures in the evolution of Latin music in the United States during the 1920s and 1930s, and what were their most important contributions?

7. How did Latin jazz evolve, and what roles did Mario Bauzá, Machito, Dizzy Gillespie, and Chano Pozo play?

8. How did the mambo develop, and which musicians are associated with it?

9. How did Brazilian music influence American popular music?

10. What was the transitional role of boogaloo and Latin soul?

11. What is *salsa*? How did it develop?

12. What are the origins of reggae?

Notes

1. Interview with the authors.

2. John Storm Roberts, *The Latin Tinge: The Impact of Latin American Music on the United States* (Tivoli, NY: Original Music, 1985), 87.

3. Walter Aaron Clark, ed., *From Tejano to Tango: Latin American Popular Music* (New York: Routledge, 2002), 252–53.

4. John Storm Roberts, *Latin Jazz: The First of the Fusions, 1880s to Today* (New York: Schirmer, 1999), 46.

5. Roberts, *Latin Jazz,* 71.

6. Steven Loza, *Tito Puente and the Making of Latin Music* (Urbana: University of Illinois Press, 1999), 8.

7. Ibid., 8.

8. Ibid., 16.

9. Sue Steward, *Musica! Salsa, Rumba, Merengue, and More: The Rhythm of Latin America* (San Francisco: Chronicle Books, 1999), 60.

10. Juan Flores, "Cha-Cha with a Backbeat: Songs and Stories of Latin Boogaloo," in *Situating Salsa: Global Markets and Local Meaning in Latin Popular Music,* edited by L. Waxer (New York: Routledge, 2002), 78, 81.

11. Isabelle Leymarie, *Cuban Fire: The Story of Salsa and Latin Jazz* (London: Continuum, 2002), 220–21.

12. Eddie Palmieri profile, http://www.salsacrazy.com/salsaroots/ArtproEddie.htm.

13. Marisol Berríos-Miranda, "Is Salsa a Musical Genre?" in *Situating Salsa: Global Markets and Local Meaning in Latin Popular Music,* edited by L. Waxer (New York: Routledge, 2002), 29.

14. Chuy Varela, "All Hail the Queen," http://www.metroactive.com/papers/metro/09.19.02/celiacruz-0238.html.

15. Frances Aparicio, "La Lupe, La India, and Celia: Toward a Feminist Genealogy of Salsa Music," in *Situating Salsa: Global Markets and Local Meaning in Latin Popular Music,* edited by L. Waxer (New York: Routledge, 2002), 153.

16. Interview with the authors.

17. Interview with the authors.

1840 - 2000

1800s Popular European dances blend with traditional folk styles in Mexico, leading to new hybrids ♪
1848 End of Mexican War; Southwest annexed by U.S.

1861–1865 U.S. Civil War
1870s German, Czech, and Polish immigrants arrive in northern Mexico, bringing accordion and polka ♪

1885 Mexican Cavalry Band performs in New Orleans and influences the development of early jazz ♪
1898 Spanish-American War ends

1908 First mariachi recordings made in Mexico ♪
1910 Mexican Cavalry leads to increased Mexican immigration to U.S., creating the first barrios in Texas and California
1914–1918 World War I

1920s First Chicano recordings made in U.S., including *corridos, rancheras,* and *orquestas típicas* ♪
1929–1930s Great Depression; New Deal begins
1934 Mexico–U.S. border is formalized
1934 Lydia Mendoza makes first recording to become the first star of Mexican American music ♪

1940s Traditional *conjunto* style becomes firmly established in *Tejano* and *Norteño* music ♪
1940s Swing merges with *ranchera* and *orquesta típica,* and *orquesta tejana* is born ♪
1940s *Pachuco* movement in L.A. embraces the sounds of jump swing and Latin jazz ♪
1941–1945 U.S. in World War II
1943 Legal importation of Mexican workers to the U.S. is allowed
1943 Zoot suit riots in L.A.
1950s Birth of Chicano rock and roll ♪
1950s *Orquesta tejana* evolves into early *Tejano* music ♪
1954 School segregation outlawed; civil rights movement begins
1958 Conjunto Bernal records "*Mi Unico Camino,*" representing the zenith of the *conjunto* style ♪
1958 "La Bamba" recorded by Ritchie Valens, eventually becomes an anthem of Chicano rock ♪

1960s Chicano rock continues to evolve in Southern California ♪
1963 Civil rights march on Washington; John Kennedy assassinated
1964–1973 Vietnam War
1969 Santana plays Woodstock, signifying the birth of Latin rock ♪
1970s Chicano civil rights movement takes hold
1970s Chicano civil rights movement is reflected in the music of a new wave of Chicano Latin rock and R & B bands ♪
1970 Chicano Moratorium and ensuing riot become watershed events in Chicano activism
1976 Little Joe records Chicano anthem "*Las Nubes*" and Chicano activism begins to flavor *Tejano* music ♪

1982 First *Tejano* Music Awards held in San Antonio ♪
1987 Los Lobos cover of "La Bamba" becomes major hit ♪
1987 Seventies rock star Linda Ronstadt acknowledges her Chicano roots with the release of *Canciones de Mi Padre* ♪
1990s Major labels enter *Tejano* market; *banda* emerges in the U.S. as a new *Mexicano* pop style ♪
1992 Los Angeles riots/uprising following Rodney King trial
1995 *Tejano* music star Selena killed at the height of her career ♪
1999 First Latin Grammy Awards ♪

2001 9/11 terrorist attacks

1840	1860	1880	1900	1920	1940	1960	1980	2000

Chapter 9

Chicano and Mexican Popular Music in America

Although the Chicano/*Mexicano* population is the fastest-growing ethnicity in the country, the study of American popular music has seldom emphasized their music. The term **Chicano** is currently accepted by most Mexican Americans to mean people of Mexican descent born in the United States, while **Mexicano** refers to people born in Mexico. The terms also imply a particular cultural identity in which music plays a distinctive part.

Chicano/*Mexicano* recordings now account for two-thirds of the U.S. Latin music market. We can best understand the evolution of this music in terms of two regions: Texas and California. The earliest Chicano music emerged in Texas in the early twentieth century, and the region remains the center of *Tejano* and *Norteño* musical styles.[1] California was also central to the evolution of Chicano music, with the development of *pachuco* swing, Chicano doo-wop, R & B, and rock from the 1940s through the present. The continuing arrival of first-generation *Mexicanos* has added to the cultural mix, as witnessed by the popularity of mariachi, *banda*, and *narcocorrido* in the early 2000s. This chapter examines the development of Chicano musical traditions as well as the musical influences of first-generation Mexican immigrants—and their cross-border interplay.

HISTORICAL PERSPECTIVE

Most of the Southwest was part of Mexico until 1848, when the Mexican War concluded with U.S. annexation of the Southwest and most of California. Overnight, the national identity of over 80,000 Mexicans was forcibly transformed, as Chicano musician/historian David Stevens notes:

> We are made to feel like foreigners in our own land. We are not accepted by the white European culture in the United States and we are not accepted in Mexico because we live in the United States. In the States we are Mexicans and in Mexico we are *pochos* [Anglicized Mexicans].[2]

During Mexico's long history of colonization, musical styles were colored by Spanish, indigenous, African, and other European influences. French elements came into play by the mid-nineteenth century, and popular styles among the Mexican aristocracy expanded to include a variety of European classical music and

**Internet
Listening Exercise**

Listen to samples of the traditional Mexican *canción* style.

Linda Ronstadt: *Los Laureles*

dance styles. Musical preferences in Mexico coincided with social class, and as music moved from urban aristocracy to rural peasantry, indigenous and folk influences caused the gradual "Mexicanization" of European styles. Opera and the Italian *bel canto* singing style, for example, were incorporated into rural folk styles such as the **canción,** which dominated nineteenth-century Mexican popular music.

Musical instruments used in Mexico in the late nineteenth century reflected multiple influences. Spanish influences included violins, harps, flutes, oboes, and guitars. Guitars blended particularly well with indigenous Mexican styles, and several variations on the instrument developed, including the **vihuela,** a small, five-string instrument; the **guitarrón,** a large acoustic bass guitar; and the **bajo sexto,** a twelve-string guitar. Afro-Caribbean instruments, including the **marimba,** a wooden xylophone with resonating tubes below each wooden bar; maracas; and bongos also arrived in Mexico. The introduction of European symphony orchestra instrumentation and brass band traditions led many cities and towns to establish *bandas municipales* (municipal bands), and the Sousa-style band tradition blended with folkloric styles to create a popular wind band style called *banda* (discussed later).

European dances and rhythms such as the waltz, schottische, minuet, and mazurka, as well as the Cuban *contradanza habanera,* provided popular "salon music" for the Mexican middle class in the mid-1800s. The **huapango,** a folk dance rhythm of eastern Mexico, was also popular, and the arrival of German, Czech, and Polish immigrants in northern Mexico in the late nineteenth century introduced the accordion and the **polka,** a lively partner dance of Bohemian origin in duple meter. These subsequently became signature elements of *Tejano* and *Norteño* music.

In 1885, when the World Industrial and Cotton Centennial Exposition was held in New Orleans, the Mexican government sent the band of the Eighth Regiment Mexican Cavalry as its representative. The Mexican band was reportedly the highlight of the gathering, playing compositions featuring the polka, mazurka, habanera, and Mexican folkloric styles that had an impact on New Orleans musicians then experimenting with variations on Sousa-style band music. Within a year, several of the Mexican band's arrangements were published in the city and played by early jazz bands.

TEJANO AND *NORTEÑO* MUSIC TAKE ROOT

Texas was home to the earliest styles of Chicano music in the United States, many of which developed along the Texas-Mexico border. Most Chicano music made in Texas came to be called **Tejano,** while **Norteño** described music that straddled the border between Texas and Mexico; people often used the names interchangeably. The arrival of the accordion in Northern Mexico in the late nineteenth century signaled an important stylistic direction for *Norteño* and *Tejano* music, because Mexican musicians integrated it with European and Mexican styles. The result was **conjunto,** an accordion-based Chicano/*Mexicano* vernacular ensemble that played polkas, waltzes, and *rancheras* and became the first popular Mexican American ensemble style. Border culture and commerce were also developing, and migration of *Norteños* into Texas led to the development of song styles such as *corrido* and *ranchera.*

Some of the first recordings of Mexican music were actually done in Mexico as early as 1908, but not until after the success of "Crazy Blues" in 1920 did major labels try to expand the race record market to U.S. Spanish-speaking communities. The new performing and recording opportunities encouraged Chicano musicians to experiment with such styles as the early *orquestas típicas* and *corridos.* **Orquestas típicas** first appeared before the turn of the twentieth century on both sides of the border, playing variations on traditional Mexican dances. The instrumentation of the early ensembles combined brass, woodwinds, violins, and guitars.

Corridos were narrative ballads that told the story of heroic events or tragedies. They have been a popular music form on both sides of the border for over a hundred years. *Corridos* and European American folk ballads shared similarities in form and style: Both favored straightforward delivery and attention to detail, though *corridos* had more rhythmic variety, encompassing polkas, waltzes, and even marches. *Corridos* served as oral history, telling stories of outlaws, trail drives, politics, and heroism. They also voiced social commentary, addressing issues such as discrimination, immigration, and smuggling, with heroes who were often underdogs, in the Robin Hood tradition. *Corridos* were usually based on real events until the 1930s, when composers began to use imaginary characters in order to avoid offending historical figures.

Lydia Mendoza (1916–) was the first star of Mexican American music. Her songs represented the emotions and values of many levels of Mexican American society during the 1930s and 1940s. As historian/producer Chris Strachwitz

Internet Listening Exercise

Go to http://www.arhoolie.com and sample the following *corridos.*

Pedro Rocha and Lupe Martinez: "Gregorio Cortez" (1929) (from *Corridos y Tragedias de la Frontera*)

Various Artists: *"Orquestas Típicas" Pioneer Mexican Dance Orchestras (1926–38)*

© Chris Strachwitz, www.arhoolie.com

Legends of Chicano music. Left to right: Narciso Martínez, Lydia Mendoza, and Valerio Longoria.

CD LISTENING EXERCISE

CD 1/30

Listen to *"Mal Hombre"* by Lydia Mendoza. Even if you do not understand Spanish, does Mendoza's vocal style provide clues to the meaning of the lyrics? How would you describe her voice? Listen to the guitar accompaniment. What qualities made this song a hit in Mexican American communities throughout the Southwest in the thirties?

argues, "These songs and *corridos* constitute the literature of the people."[3] Mendoza was born in poverty to a family of musicians in Houston. In 1927 at the age of eleven, Mendoza began performing with her family. Their repertoire favored **rancheras**—traditional Mexican songs of love, hope, and loss performed in a variety of rhythmic styles. Like classic country and blues artists of the era, the Mendozas made their initial recordings in 1928 at a makeshift studio in a hotel room where they recorded twenty songs for the Okeh label. Mendoza's success as a solo artist began in earnest in 1934 with her hit song *"Mal Hombre"* ("Bad Man"), which showcased her clear and emotional singing style accompanied by twelve-string guitar. Mendoza recalled how she learned *"Mal Hombre"*:

> They used to print the lyrics of popular songs on gum wrappers there in Mexico. . . . I made a collection of many songs. . . . One time a variety show came from Mexico City. . . . When they announced "Mal Hombre" I became very excited . . . and I got out the paper, the gum wrapper. . . . That was how I learned "Mal Hombre."[4]

With the release of the recording and radio airplay, listeners throughout the Southwest heard Mendoza's music. Although still in its infancy, radio rapidly gained influence in Mexican American communities. During their seven-decade career, Lydia Mendoza, her sisters, and the rest of her family recorded close to 1,200 songs in a variety of styles—tangos, boleros, *corridos*, and *rancheras*—a rich legacy of border music.

THE ACCORDION AND THE BIRTH OF *CONJUNTO*

Having first appeared in northern Mexico around 1860 brought by central European immigrants, the **accordion** became the dominant musical symbol of *Tejano* musical culture around the middle of the twentieth century. The instrument was adopted because it was cheap, available, and a perfect fit for most social events, requiring little or no accompaniment. The *bajo sexto, tololoche* (string bass), and *tambora de rancho* (ranch drum) often accompanied the accordion, forming the basic *conjunto* instrumentation.

The *conjunto* style reached full flower in the 1930s, led by accordionist **Narciso Martínez** (1912–1992), often called the "father" of the genre. Martínez's accordion style focused on melody, with short, accented notes that yielded a bright, articulated texture. His first hit was a polka called *"La Chicharronera"* (1935), and polkas remained a staple of

CD LISTENING EXERCISE

CD 1/31

Listen to *"Muchachos Alegres,"* recorded by Narciso Martínez in 1946. Note how Martínez's accordion plays melody notes while the *bajo sexto* plays the bass line and the chords.

his repertoire. Dubbed *"El Huracán del Valle"* ("The Hurricane of the Valley") in the Chicano community, Martínez was marketed by his record label in Cajun country as "Louisiana Pete" and in Polish areas as "Polski Kwartet." Innovations in *conjunto* continued over the next few decades. Valerio Longoria (1924–2000) was one of the first to introduce vocals into the style in 1949, and their use rapidly became standard. He also added a drum set to provide more of a beat for dancing. Tony de la Rosa reworked the polka in the mid-1950s, offering up a staccato style reminiscent of Martínez with added western swing and country influences, and Conjunto Bernal took *conjunto* to its zenith with three-part vocal harmony and sometimes two accordions.

Internet Listening Exercise

Go to http://www.arhoolie.com, click on "Tejano," and listen to samples of the trio-style harmonies and modernized *conjunto* sound of Conjunto Bernal.

Conjunto Bernal: *Mi Único Camino*

WORLD WAR II

World War II dramatically impacted Chicano culture: It introduced a more cosmopolitan perspective into the community; a Chicano middle class developed in the larger cities of the Southwest; and participation in the war effort brought Chicanos into contact with people of many ethnicities. The swing and Latin jazz sounds of the 1940s affected Chicano/*Mexicano* musicians in different ways in Texas and Southern California. Ethnomusicologist Manuel Peña argues that urbanized Chicanos in Texas sought to distance themselves from the working-class *conjunto* and *corrido* styles of traditional Mexican culture by embracing the music of new, larger *orquesta tejana* ensembles.[5] Los Angeles, on the other hand, saw the development of *pachucos*—members of a rebellious Chicano youth culture drawn to swing, the new Latin music, and the hipster culture of the African American jazz world.

Orquesta Tejana and the Birth of *Tejano* Music

Orquesta tejana was an outgrowth of *orquesta típica* that borrowed from the swing, boogie, and foxtrot styles of American big bands, as well as the mambo, *rumba*, and cha cha of Latin jazz. Texan **Beto Villa** (1915–1986), the "father" of *orquesta tejana*, got his commercial break in 1946 when he developed his hybrid of *ranchera* and the more sophisticated *orquesta* instrumentation, creating a bicultural sound that appealed to an emerging Chicano middle class. Villa wanted to promote swing in the Mexican American market, where working-class Chicanos had derisively labeled it *jaitón* (high tone).

Flaco Jiménez with his button accordion, the signature instrument of *Tejano* music.

© Chris Strachwitz, www.arhoolie.com

Internet Listening Exercise

Go to http://www.arhoolie.com, click on "Tejano," and listen to the following samples.

Beto Villa: "Monterrey"

Isidro López: *"Mala Cara"* (from *15 Original Hits*)

Internet Listening Exercise

Listen to samples from the following CDs.

Roy Milton: *Roy Milton and His Solid Senders*

Various Artists: *Jump and Shout: R & B Allstars Vol. 3*

Don Tosti/Lalo Guerrero: *Pachuco Boogie*

As bandleader/composer Lalo Guerrero, a contemporary of Villa's, recalled, "We were all looking for the gold. . . . But Beto started it all. He was hot. God-damn he was hot. Anywhere in the Southwest—California, Arizona, Colorado—everywhere the jukeboxes were full of his records."[6]

One of the founders of modern *Tejano* music, **Isidro López** (1929–2004), focused more on *conjunto, ranchera,* and mariachi than Villa did. By incorporating the sound of mariachi into what was beginning to be called Tex-Mex music, he created a style called *Texachi.* He also began to work with accordions and, in later recordings, fused rock with his *orquesta* sound to pave the way for contemporary *Tejano* music. As he put it, "I was the first Chicano to do it, to record with mariachi. And I recorded with conjunto and of course with orquesta. But to me the conjunto and orquesta—they're equal."[7]

Los Angeles and the Emergence of *Pachuco* Culture

Immigration to Southern California during the early twentieth century significantly expanded the Mexican community in the Los Angeles area. While first-generation immigrants identified with Mexican culture and music, by the 1940s a U.S.-born generation was coming to terms with its social position in a cultural borderland. One response, the emergence of *pachuco* youth culture, symbolized youth resistance to assimilation. *Pachucos* generated a complex of new cultural symbols: They developed their own dialect, *Caló,* which was a blend of

Multicultural Note

Zoot Suit Riots, Then and Now

Chicano-Anglo relations came to a low point in Los Angeles in the 1940s. The death of a young Chicano (the Sleepy Lagoon murder) in 1942 caused hundreds of young Chicanos to be rounded up and put on trial, and the resulting media barrage branded anyone wearing a zoot suit a gang member. As historian Mauricio Mazón argues, "Zoot suiters transgressed the patriotic ideals of commitment, integrity, and loyalty with non-commitment, incoherence, and defiance. . . . They were seen as culturally and aesthetically un-American."[8]

Things came to a head in 1943 when a group of bored American sailors started attacking *pachuco* zoot suiters, igniting ten days of mayhem called the zoot suit riots. As *Time* magazine reported, "The police practice was to accompany the caravans of soldiers and sailors in police cars, watch the beatings, and jail the victims."[9]

The zoot suit riots became a symbolic event in Chicano history. Playwright/film maker Luis Valdez portrayed it in the play and 1981 film *Zoot Suit.* The riots were later appropriated during the 1990s neoswing revival in the hit song "Zoot Suit Riot" recorded by the Cherry Poppin' Daddies, which played on the party ambience of the zoot suit era while ignoring its cultural and political significance.

Spanish slang, English, Nahuatl (an indigenous Mexican language), and archaic Spanish words; they embraced African American culture and the hipster jazz scene; and the zoot suit became the garb of choice for young *pachuco* men— oversized suit, baggy pants worn tight around the ankles, stylish hat, and long watch chain. For music, *pachucos* favored a new style called jump blues (see Chapter 13) and the Latin jazz of Machito.

Although not well-known in the Anglo world, **Lalo Guerrero** (1916– 2005) was legendary in Chicano communities for his gruff vocal style, wry humor, and broad repertoire. Born in Tucson to Mexican immigrant parents, Guerrero grew up learning *rancheras* and other traditional Mexican music, but stars of the 1930s such as Al Jolson, Bing Crosby, and Rudy Vallee also influenced him. Because of existing patterns of bias, Guerrero could not cross over to perform for white audiences, so he performed in Spanish for Chicano audiences instead. During World War II, he incorporated Afro-Cuban styles as well as swing, and he became popular among zoot suiters in Los Angeles. Guerrero's repertoire from the period included the swing tune "Marijuana Boogie," the *guaracha* "Chucos Suaves," and the hybrid *"Vamos a Bailar,"* which shifted between swing and mambo. (Luis Valdez used the latter two in the score of *Zoot Suit.*) After the war, Guerrero settled in Los Angeles, had a hit in the mid-1950s with a parody of Disney's "The Ballad of Davey Crockett," and became a central musical figure in the Chicano civil rights movement of the 1960s.

Internet Listening Exercise

Listen to the following tune.

Cherry Poppin' Daddies: "Zoot Suit Riot"

Internet Listening Exercise

Listen to samples from the following CD.

Lalo Guerrero: *Vamos a Bailar— Otra Vez (Let's Dance—One More Time)*

CHICANO ROCK MAKES ITS MARK

Chicano musicians in Southern California followed a different muse than their Texas counterparts. Because these Chicanos often lived in the same communities as African Americans, black music significantly influenced them. This resulted in a distinct Chicano rock style, along with a fan base that still carries a torch for classic doo-wop and sweet soul ballads of the fifties and sixties. According to historians David Reyes and Tom Waldman,

> They [recordings of doo-wop and soul ballads] are romantic music for people who take romance very seriously. . . . The term "oldies" is almost a misnomer; the records are chronologically old, but they have a special meaning for each succeeding generation of Chicanos.[10]

The dissemination of early 1950s rock to the Mexican American community in Southern California was an interesting case of transcultural media flow, driven by a small group of mainly white DJs who sensed the pulse of their Chicano listeners, particularly their attraction to black music. One of the DJs, Art Laboe, is said to have coined the term *oldies but goodies,* and he was one of the first to take listeners' requests as dedications.

In 1958 a young Chicano guitarist from Pacoima, California, named **Ritchie Valens** (Ricardo Valenzuela, 1941–1959) cut his first record and changed the history of Chicano music. During his brief career, Valens recorded a handful of hits that became Mexican American anthems as well as rock classics, and his tragic death at seventeen in a plane crash while on tour with rockers Buddy

The Selvin Collection

Chicano rocker Ritchie Valens in a classic record publicity photo.

Holly and the Big Bopper sanctified him as a legend. Hundreds of artists covered Valens's biggest hits—"La Bamba" and the ballad "Donna." Based on a traditional Mexican *huapango*, "La Bamba" was one of the few U.S. rock hits performed in Spanish. Valens was a confident performer who put his aggressive guitar playing center stage. His repertoire featured a variety of song styles, from rock to country to early surf guitar, reflecting the musical flexibility often found in Chicano bands. According to David Reyes and Tom Waldman,

> Valens is the first and best example of the cultural cross currents that pervade Chicano Rock 'n'. Roll. He was open to everything. . . . This connects Valens to . . . Chicano rock and R & B performers who came after him, such as Thee Midniters and Los Lobos, who also took their music in many directions.[11]

CD LISTENING EXERCISE

CD 1/32

Listen to Ritchie Valens's original 1958 recording of *"La Bamba."* What elements made the song a hit? *"La Bamba"* and "Donna" were originally released as the B and A sides of the same 45 rpm single. When *"La Bamba"* hit big, producers reversed the labels. *"La Bamba"*/"Donna" turned out to be a rare double-hit single.

Although the untimely death of Ritchie Valens left a hole in Southern California Chicano rock, the scene was far from dead. Within a few years, bands such as Thee Midniters, who had a hit with "Whittier Boulevard," celebrating the lowrider culture of East Los Angeles, and Cannibal and the Headhunters, who had a hit with "Land of a Thousand Dances," achieved recognition for their "Eastside sound." David Reyes and Tom Waldman describe the sound: "Chicano rock 'n' roll employed a huge beat, clear-as-a-bell guitar lines—on ballads and

Multicultural Note

The Commodification of Ritchie Valens

After the release of the 1987 film *La Bamba,* which chronicled Ritchie Valens's life story, the marketing of the deceased artist became a growth industry. The Los Lobos cover version of the movie's title song became a national hit, Valens received a post-humous star on the Hollywood Walk of Fame, and his picture appeared on a com-memorative postage stamp. Valens and "La Bamba" became saleable commodities for anyone from politicians to beer companies marketing messages to Chicano/ *Mexicano* audiences.

up-tempo songs—and vocals that were often surprisingly, yet appealingly, un-derstated. There were no shouters in Chicano rock 'n' roll." [12]

Sixties Chicano rock was not confined to Southern California, and sev-eral Texas-based Chicano rock artists temporarily eclipsed *Tejano* styles. Sunny Ozuna made the national charts (as Sunny and the Sunglows) with his 1963 hit "Talk to Me" but later shifted back to a more traditional *Tejano* sound. Another Texas-based Chicano rock group, Sam the Sham and the Pharaohs, had two hits: "Wooly Bully" (1965) and Li'l Red Ridin' Hood" (1966). "Wooly Bully's" use of bilingual lyrics and its legendary count-off in Spanish *("Uno, dos, tres, cuatro . . .")* endeared the tune to Chicanos. Question Mark and the Mysterians were a great Chicano "one-hit wonder" band with the 1966 two-chord classic, "Ninety-Six Tears."

TEJANO AND CHICANO POP ARTISTS AFTER THE 1960s

The term *Tejano* is generally used today to describe a hybrid of *ranchera,* polka, *cumbia* (a simple two-beat Colombian rhythm popular for dancing), R & B, pop, and country. Over the years, the style has carried several other names as well: "Tex-Mex," "brown soul," *"La Onda Chicana"* ("The Chicano Wave"). From its inception, the popularity of *Tejano* music grew steadily, and by the early 1970s it entered what some called its first golden age as radio airplay increased and new record labels appeared. The instrumentation of *Tejano* bands came to in-clude accordion, *bajo sexto,* drum set, electric bass, and sometimes a horn sec-tion. New *Norteño* bands such as Los Tigres del Norte also entered the scene, and traditional players such as Tony de la Rosa updated their sounds and built new audiences.

The most important Tejano group to emerge in the era was Little Joe y La Familia. Texas-born **Little Joe Hernández** (1940–) became a professional musician at age seventeen and soon led his own group called Little Joe and the

Internet Listening Exercise

Listen to samples of the following songs that represent 1960s Chi-cano rock.

Cannibal and the Headhunters: "Land of a Thousand Dances"

Thee Midniters: "Whittier Boulevard"

Sunny Ozuna: "Talk to Me"

Sam the Sham and the Pharaohs: "Woolly Bully"

Question Mark and the Mysterians: "Ninety-Six Tears"

Latinaires. Hernández moved the band to California in the early 1970s, where he came under the spell of the blues, jazz, the Latin rock of Santana and Malo, and the horns of Tower of Power. Influenced by the Chicano civil rights movement, he renamed his band Little Joe y La Familia, expanded his instrumentation to include Latin percussion and horns, and looked to his Mexican roots for new material. In 1976 Hernández recorded the hit *"Las Nubes,"* a Mexican standard reshaped with a *ranchera* sound and driving horns. According to Ramiro Burr,

> "Las Nubes" is very much Like Bruce Springsteen's "Born in the U.S.A." Both have infectious sing-along choruses that soar over stark lyrics of reflection, despair, and disillusionment. . . . This song became arguably a national anthem for Tejano culture.[13]

www Internet Listening Exercise

Listen to samples of the mid-1970s Tejano sound of Little Joe y La Familia.

Little Joe y La Familia: *20 Grandes Éxitos*

Hernández returned to Texas in the late 1970s and frequently won *Tejano* Music Awards throughout the 1980s, as well as being the first *Tejano* act to win a Grammy.

Tejano music declined in the late 1970s when disco, punk rock, and MTV eclipsed it. To survive, many young Tejano acts moved to an arena-rock format, and the founding of two major *Tejano* music events—the *Tejano* Music Awards and San Antonio's *Tejano* Conjunto Festival—rekindled interest in *Tejano* styles. New artists such as La Mafia, La Sambra, Mazz, and Patsy Torres arose, often enhancing their appeal by adding rap and contemporary dance rhythms to their sound. *Conjunto*-style accordion virtuosos Flaco Jiménez, Mingo Saldivar, and Steve Jordan also saw an upturn in popularity. The national visibility of Chicano and *Tejano* music increased with the 1987 Los Lobos hit cover of "La Bamba" and pop singer Linda Ronstadt's return to her Mexican roots with the release of a mariachi album. As critic Ramiro Burr has put it, "All of a sudden it seemed to be cool for Latinos to bring their ethnicity out of the closet and put it on display—to admit they listened to Mexican, salsa, or Tejano music or ate beans and rice."[14]

Vocalist **Linda Ronstadt's** (1946–) Chicano roots remained hidden from the public for many years. An Arizona native with Mexican, German, English, and Dutch ancestry, Ronstadt first appeared on the L.A. scene in the mid-1960s with a folk-rock hit, and in the 1970s she became one of the most high-profile female stars of the rock world with a string of hit albums. In the 1980s, Ronstadt shifted her focus to operetta, jazz, and country, but she also surprised the public by returning to her Mexican roots with the release of *Canciones de Mi Padre* ("My Father's Songs," 1987). The Grammy-winning album featured Ronstadt backed by the world-famous Mariachi Vargas de Tecalitlán.

With her big voice and a sure feel for the American popular song, **Vikki Carr** (1941–) became one of the most successful Chicano performers in popular music. Born Florencia Bisenta de Casillas Martínez Cardona in El Paso, the artist eventually changed her stage name to Vikki Carr after successful stints in Las Vegas and Hawaii, beginning a four-decade career as a Grammy-winning mainstream pop entertainer. Major hits came in the 1960s with "It Must Be Him," "Can't Take My Eyes off of You," and "For Once in My Life." She began to record in Spanish in the early 1970s and subsequently appeared throughout Latin America and Europe, singing both in Spanish and in English.

Tejano music flourished in the early 1990s. Record companies that had previously ignored *Tejano* seemed willing to gamble on the style, and the crossover success of the Texas Tornados and the popularity of Selena added to the buildup. The **Texas Tornados** were the first band marketed as a *Tejano*/country crossover. Formed in 1989 with a superstar lineup—Flaco Jiménez on accordion, Freddy Fender on guitar, Augie Meyers on keyboards and *bajo sexto,* and Doug Sahm on guitar—the Tornados became known as "The Tex-Mex Grateful Dead" for their eclectic blend of rock, country, *Norteño,* oldies, and Tex-Mex originals. The group's first self-titled 1990 release, performed in English and Spanish, featured the Grammy-winning classic *conjunto* tune *"Soy de San Luis"* and extended their popularity beyond the Chicano/*Mexicano* community.

The rapid rise and tragic death of **Selena Quintanilla** (1971–1995) paralleled *Tejano's* most successful era. Selena was the most high-profile female performer in Chicano music history, whose charisma, provocative performance style, and vocal skills endeared her to *Tejano* fans. Though she grew up speaking English, Selena's father encouraged her to form a band with her brother and perform in Spanish. Selena and Los Dinos worked the *Tejano* circuit in the Southwest, specializing in a catchy *cumbia*-based sound popular among *Tejanos.* In 1994 the band released the album *Amor Prohibido,* which contained the hit "Bidi Bidi Bom Bom," and Selena's superstardom seemed assured. Sadly, in 1995 her emotionally disturbed fan club president murdered the artist. Within a month of her death, Selena had five CDs on the charts, and shortly thereafter her long-awaited English crossover album, *Dreaming of You,* was released. Selena's brother, A. B. Quintanilla III, stayed in the music business and continued to influence the direction of *Tejano* music by producing the Kumbia Kings and other young *Tejano* artists. According to sociologist Deborah Vargas, "Selena created a 'place' for her fans to come 'home' to. . . . Her music represented the unique social location of Texas-Mexicans."[15]

Internet Listening Exercise

Listen to samples of the following CDs.

Linda Ronstadt: *Canciones de Mi Padre, Linda Ronstadt's Greatest Hits, Volume I*

Vikki Carr: *Live at the Greek Theatre*

© Barbara Laing/Time & Life Pictures/ Getty Images

Selena was the biggest female star in the history of *Tejano* music.

CALIFORNIA CHICANO ROCK AFTER THE 1960s

The watershed Chicano civil rights movement of the late 1960s and early 1970s brought the term *Chicano* into use as an affirmation of identity. A major event that coalesced Chicano consciousness in Southern California was the Chicano Moratorium of 1970, an

antiwar demonstration in Los Angeles that turned into a police riot that killed three people. Beyond cultural pride, the movement emphasized farm worker rights, political power, educational opportunity, and legal rights. Chicanos were no longer a small minority confined to the Southwest; communities were growing throughout the country. In contrast with its earlier sounds, California Chicano rock took on a different tone in the late 1960s. New Spanish and indigenous band names reflecting Latino/Chicano identity came into use: Santana, Tierra, El Chicano, Azteca, Malo, Sapo, Yaqui, and Los Lobos del Este de Los Angeles. Sources of musical inspiration also broadened beyond classic rock and R & B to encompass acid rock, Afro-Caribbean, jazz, soul, funk, and Mexican folkloric styles.

Santana and San Francisco Latin Rock

A unique Latin rock sound emerged from the multicultural setting of San Francisco's Latino/bohemian Mission district in the late 1960s, when integration and cultural acceptance were the norm. Latino, African American, white, and Asian American musicians merged to build San Francisco Latin rock.

Carlos Santana (1947–) was the most influential rock musician of Latino origin in the United States. His appealing fusion of Afro-Caribbean percussion, the blues, and a signature crying electric guitar spanned five decades and outlasted numerous musical trends. Over the course of his career, Santana garnered many Grammys as well as a 1998 induction into the Rock 'n' Roll Hall of Fame. Born in Jalisco, Mexico, as the son of a mariachi violinist, Santana first played in his father's mariachi group. He discovered American rock and blues when the family moved to Tijuana. In the 1960s, when flower power and a new rock scene were blossoming, he migrated to San Francisco. One night in 1967 when he sat in on a jam session at the Fillmore Auditorium, Santana's playing so impressed rock impresario Bill Graham that he quickly booked Santana's band as the opening act for the Who. Graham also took over management of the Santana group and got them a slot at the Woodstock festival in 1969, where a searing performance of "Soul Sacrifice" provided one of the festival's highlights. Success at Woodstock led to other hits such as "Evil Ways," "Jingo," "Black Magic Woman," and Tito Puente's *"Oye Como Va."* Santana's sound was not distinctly Mexican. According to critic Rubén Guevara, "The muse that Carlos followed was the blues—all that note-bending on guitar plus the wave of percussion he took from *salsa.*" [16] Although the artist was a major force in rock throughout the 1970s, by the 1990s he had no record contract. Then he signed with Arista Records and released the multiple Grammy-winning *Supernatural* (2001), featur-

Latin rock legend Carlos Santana in the late 1960s.

ing younger stars such as Lauryn Hill, Rob Thomas, Everlast, and Wyclef Jean. According to rock critic James Sullivan, "Santana, the guitarist with the parabolic sustain, might well be the only classic rocker from his era to translate for the new millennium."[17]

In the wake of Santana's success, record labels descended on the San Francisco Bay Area. Hordes of multicultural barrio garage bands got a chance to record—many of them with large horn sections influenced by soul, jazz, Latin big bands, and horn groups such as Chicago and Blood, Sweat and Tears. One of the first Latin rock groups to follow Santana was Malo, formed in 1971. The band introduced horns to Latin rock and had a hit with *"Suavecito,"* which is still a staple of Chicano popular culture. The band's first album cover featured a memorable image of an Aztec warrior holding his sleeping princess. The most creative of the San Francisco Latin rock bands, Azteca, produced a powerhouse of musical talent, including musicians who later worked with Journey, Chick Corea, and Herbie Hancock. One of the band's most popular tunes was "Whatcha Gonna Do." Group cofounder Pete Escovedo went on to a successful career in Latin jazz as a percussionist and bandleader.

CD LISTENING EXERCISE

CD 1/33

Listen to *"Oye Como Va,"* a tune written by Tito Puente and recorded by Carlos Santana in 1970. Santana's Latin rock rhythm section and blazing guitar solo turned Puente's simple cha-cha into a Latin rock anthem. Millions of fans remained unaware of the simple translation of the title: "Hey, what's happening?" Next, go online and compare this to a sample of Tito Puente's original recording of *"Oye Como Va."*

Internet Listening Exercise

Listen to samples of CDs by the following San Francisco Latin rock groups.

Malo: *The Best of Malo*

Azteca: *Azteca*

L.A. Chicano Bands of the 1970s

Chicano bands of East Los Angeles in the early 1970s shifted from classic early 1960s rock to a sound that blended R & B and jazz with Latin percussion, Spanish song titles and lyrics, and Latin song forms such as cha-cha, bolero, *huapango,* and *son montuno.* Visual images also reflected Chicano identity, as in El Chicano's album *Revolución,* which employed images of Mexican revolutionary heroes Emiliano Zapata and Pancho Villa.

El Chicano, whose Latin rhythms, percussion, and Hammond B-3 organ sound resembled Santana's, had a 1970 hit with a midtempo instrumental cha-cha called *"Viva Tirado,"* originally written by jazz composer/bandleader Gerald Wilson. The popularity of the tune with multiple audiences produced some perplexing moments for the group. When they played at the Apollo Theater in Harlem, for example, the audience expected a black band; according to one group member, "They looked at us and said, 'What are they, Indians?'"[18] Tierra was another influential L.A. Chicano group formed in the early 1970s. Known for sweet soul vocal classics such as "Together" and "Gonna Find Her," the band was a favorite of the lowrider culture of Los Angeles.

The appeal of classic R & B and doo-wop has endured in Chicano communities, partly because many Chicano artists have been R & B and rock innovators. The lasting Chicano popularity of acts such as War, Tower of Power, and other old-school and classic oldies groups was further promoted through "cruising" compilation albums sold at car shows or flea markets and played on oldies radio shows. Car shows were centered around lowriders. A **lowrider** is a cus-

Internet Listening Exercise

Listen to samples of 1970s L.A. Chicano rock albums.

El Chicano: *Viva El Chicano! Their Very Best*

Tierra: *Tierra Greatest Hits*

tomized car or truck that has had the suspension system modified so that the car rides low to the ground. People who drive such vehicles and who are part of the surrounding car culture are also known as lowriders. Historian George Lipsitz describes the parallels between Chicano car and musical cultures:

> Just as Chicano car customizers "improved" on the mass-produced vehicles from Detroit, Chicano rock songs like "Whittier Boulevard" celebrated Mexican-American appropriations of automobiles as part of a community ritual.[19]

But lowriders were not the only Chicano fans of classic R & B music. According to ethnomusicologist Russell Rodriguez, Chicano/*Mexicano* musical tastes could be quite eclectic: "My neighbors blast out a range of repertoires—Mexican stations, the Crusaders, James Brown, War, Tower of Power, and Thee Midniters."[20]

One of the most popular and eclectic funk groups of the 1970s, **War** blended soul, Latin, jazz, blues, reggae, and rock to craft a laid-back, groove-oriented sound categorized by the music industry as Latin funk. Formed in 1969, the group originally served as backup band for rocker Eric Burdon, the former lead singer of the Animals. The collaboration yielded the hit "Spill the Wine" (1970). After splitting from Burdon, War had a series of hits throughout the 1970s: "All Day Music," "Slippin' into Darkness," "The Cisco Kid," "Low Rider," and "Why Can't We Be Friends." In recognition of its popularity in Chicano/Latino communities, the group released "Cinco de Mayo" and a Spanish-language version of "Low Rider," a tribute to Chicano car culture, in the 1980s.

Tower of Power was a ten-piece soul band specializing in funky, horn-driven tunes and silky, soulful ballads. The mostly white group emerged in the San Francisco area in the late 1960s with hits such as "Sparkling in the Sand," "You're Still a Young Man," "What Is Hip," and "So Very Hard to Go." The hybrid musical vision of a Chicano (cofounder Emilio Castillo) and a white (cofounder Stephen Kupka) produced a sound stemming from soul flavored by doo-wop. According to critic Rubén Guevara,

> Their roots were in James Brown and big production balladry, not Machito or Tito Puente. Their show-stopping epic ballad "Sparkling in the Sand" was really just elongated doo-wop. Two of their three Top 40 hits ("So Very Hard to Go" and "You're Still a Young Man") were soulful ballads very much in the Eastside (LA) tradition—Li'l Julian Herrera meets James Brown.[21]

L.A. Chicano Rock of the 1980s and Beyond

Chicano rock in East Los Angeles saw a new burst of musical activity at the beginning of the 1980s, influenced by the creative anarchy of punk and the rise of roots rock. Like sixties Chicano rock, punk was energetic and exciting, inspiring such popular Chicano rock groups as the Plugz, Cruzados, the Brat, Los Illegals, and Los Lobos. The groups often led a dual existence, playing one night for Chicano crowds in East Los Angeles, the next for white Hollywood rock crowds in West Los Angeles.

www Internet Listening Exercise

Listen to samples from the following CDs.

War: *The Very Best of War*

Tower of Power: *The Very Best of Tower of Power: The Warner Years*

Chicano rock band Los Lobos (left to right): Louis Perez, Steve Berlin, Cesar Rosas, Conrad Lozano, and David Hidalgo in 1990.

Mixing accordions and electric guitars, Mexican boleros and roots-rock tunes, **Los Lobos** set a new standard for Chicano rock, reflecting a biculturalism that appealed to both Chicano and mainstream audiences. According to historian George Lipsitz,

> [Los Lobos] juxtaposed multiple realities, blending Mexican folk music with Afro-American rhythm and blues, playing English language songs in a Mexican style for audiences filled with Spanish speakers, and answering requests for both Mexican and rock music with the same song—"La Bamba." [22]

Although initially influenced by rock, Los Lobos also shared an interest in traditional Mexican styles when the group came together in the early 1970s. Initially called "Los Lobos del Este de Los Angeles" ("The Wolves of East Los Angeles"), the band spent almost a decade developing its Mexican repertoire and building a following in the Chicano/*Mexicano* community. The arrival of punk drew them back to rock, and they were hired as the opening act for a U.S. tour of the Clash. By 1981 the transformation of Los Lobos to a rock band was complete. They signed with a major label, released successful albums, and won a Grammy. Los Lobos achieved national success with the soundtrack for *La Bamba* (1987), and the following year they released the Grammy-winning *La Pistola y el Corazón*, an all-Spanish compilation of folkloric music. Los Lobos was the first Chicano rock group to succeed commercially at presenting a conscious hybrid of musical cultures. Although respectful of their Mexican heritage, they remained unapologetic rockers.

 **Internet Listening Exercise**

Listen to samples from the following CD.

Los Lobos: *Just Another Band from East LA (Box Set)*

Internet Listening Exercise

Listen to samples from the following CDs.

Dr. Loco's Rockin' Jalapeño Band: *Movimiento Music*

Ozomatli: *Ozomatli*

Quetzal: *Sing the Real*

By the mid-1990s, other Chicano groups appeared, following a similar multicultural muse. These included Ozomatli, Quetzal, East LA Sabor Factory, Domingo Siete, Aztlan Underground, and, in the San Francisco area, Dr. Loco's Rockin' Jalapeño Band. Dr. Loco's often political and bilingual repertoire covered a variety of styles including *cumbia*, reggae, blues, *salsa*, Latin jazz, *Tejano*, doo-wop, R & B, and rock. Ozomatli was a twelve-piece politicized amalgam of hip-hop, salsa, ska, funk, merengue, South American folkloric, and jazz styles. Drawing on Latin-funk ideas from Malo, Azteca, and War, they combined a Chicano protest ethos, cranked-up ska, and cutting-edge hip-hop with lyrics in Spanish and English. Quetzal had an altogether different feel from Ozomatli. Founded in 1993, the group blended Mexican indigenous music with rock and Caribbean/Mexican influences, particularly *son jarocho*.

MEXICAN MUSIC IN THE UNITED STATES

First-generation immigrants from Mexico brought to the United States a love of popular Mexican music, and genres such as mariachi, *banda*, Mexican film music, and a contemporary *corrido* sound called *narcocorrido* became popular mainstays. The genres evolved in the context of cross-border diasporas, and though they had Mexican origins, they retained close ties to the United States in an ongoing cycle of cultural hybridization.

Mariachi

Mariachi is a traditional Mexican musical genre widely popular throughout the Chicano/*Mexicano* communities of the United States. It serves as one of Mexico's most important symbols worldwide. Although the term *mariachi* originally described Mexican folk musicians, modern mariachi also involves a distinct repertoire, instrumentation, and attire. Influences from three Mexican *son* styles merged to develop the genre: *son jalisciense,* which first appeared in Jalisco, a state on Mexico's central Pacific coast, and used violins, guitars, and harps; *son jarocho,* from Vera Cruz on the Mexican Gulf coast, which employed a rhythm typified by the folk song "La Bamba"; and *son huasteco* from southeast Mexico, which often employed the flute.

The first mariachi recordings were made in Jalisco just after the turn of the twentieth century, giving early evidence of a well-developed repertoire. Mariachi became politicized in the 1930s, when populist Mexican president Lázaro Cárdenas invited the famous Mariachi Vargas de Tecalitlán to tour Mexico with him to create a sense of national pride and common cultural tradition. Promoters consciously elevated mariachi, originally a working-class music, and brought it into the cultural mainstream. To upgrade the genre's image, the *calzón blanco* (white cotton peasant attire) traditionally worn by mariachi musicians was replaced by the more macho *traje de charro* (cowboy dress suit of sombrero, bolero jacket, and tight, silver-filigreed pants). Influences of jazz and Cuban music also added the trumpet to the mariachi lineup, and by the 1940s modern mariachi instrumentation had become standardized: violins, *guitarrón, vihuela,* guitar, trumpets, and sometimes a harp. People on both sides of the border can now hear mariachi ensembles of various sizes performing at weddings, parties, restaurants, and other venues.

One of the most popular and longest-lasting mariachi acts was Mariachi Vargas de Tecalitlán, which dated back to its founding in Jalisco in 1898. The undisputed king of mariachi/*ranchera* vocals, Vicente Fernandez, created the hit *"Volver, Volver"* (1976), which became an anthem in the mariachi/*ranchera* canon. Pepe Aguilar developed a pop-tinged mariachi sound with electric guitars and pop-rock rhythms that climbed the charts with *"Por Mujeres Como Tú"* (1998), while traditionalists decried what they considered a watered-down sound.

Interest in mariachi grew in Chicano/*Mexicano* communities over the last two decades of the twentieth century. As the Chicano rights movement of the 1960s encouraged development of Chicano studies programs at schools in the West, music educators and students formed mariachi ensembles as part of new, culturally infused music education curricula.

Banda

Another important Mexican genre is **banda.** Performed by a large ensemble of a dozen or more brass and woodwinds wrapped around the oom-pah of a tuba, the genre developed as a regional brass band style in small villages in western states such as Sinaloa on Mexico's Pacific coast. *Banda* instrumentation became standardized in the 1920s to include clarinet, trumpet, valve trombone, saxophone, tuba, snare drum, and bass drum. Sinaloan *bandas* were often called *tamboras* (bass drum) because the drum predominated in the ensemble sound. The famous Mexican cavalry band that traveled to New Orleans in 1885 was already incorporating Mexican folkloric music into its brass band repertoire, and the early *banda* repertoire likewise featured *corridos,* polkas, waltzes, and *rancheras.* Clear differences in status existed between the municipal or military brass bands of the cities and the less-respected *bandas* of the *pueblos* (rural villages). Local *fiestas* where *bandas* played were associated with alcohol, womanizing, and violence. Further, the government never transformed *banda* into national folkloric music, as they had done with mariachi.

Banda El Recodo was one of the oldest and most respected traditional Sinaloan *bandas.* Founded in 1938, the group still topped the Latin Regional Mexican charts at the end of the twentieth century and won the *banda* Latin Grammy in 2001. The original instrumental *banda* style remained unchanged until the 1980s, when musicians added vocals and saxophones and replaced tubas with bass guitars and synthesizers, thereby producing a variant called *technobanda.* This change intrigued Mexican and Mexican American youths, as reported in 1992: "The Mexican music with German roots has caught on big with young Latinos and the format has propelled [Spanish-language station] KLAX-FM to No. 1."[23] The group that led the U.S. *banda* explosion was the fourteen-piece *technobanda* **Banda Machos.** In the early 1990s, two of the group's albums re-

Internet Listening Exercise

Listen to samples of the following mariachi CDs.

Mariachi Vargas de Tecalitlán: *Colección Diamante*

Vicente Fernandez: *La Historia de un Idolo Vol. 1*

Pepe Aguilar: *Y Tenerte Otra Vez*

mained in the top twenty on *Billboard*'s Top Latin Albums/Regional Mexican chart for months, causing the magazine to dub 1993 "the *banda* year."

Part of the appeal of *banda* was the dance step called the **quebradita** (little break), in which the male partner bent his partner over backwards until her head brushed the floor. Another part of the appeal centered on the genre's celebration of cultural pride through the attire of cowboy hats, jeans, boots, and Western belts; some *banda* clubs even imposed a *vaquero* (cowboy) dress code. According to researcher Helena Simonett,

> As young people of Mexican descent became more sensitive to racial discrimination and exploitation, they began to take an increased interest in their own and their parents' and grandparents' heritage and traditions . . . to reaffirm and bolster their ethnic consciousness, and to express their cultural loyalty.[24]

Initially popular in Los Angeles, *banda* subsequently spread to Chicago and other Mexican communities in the United States. Ultimately, cross-border cultural flows caused the diasporic music to become accepted in Mexico. As one immigrant in Los Angeles put it, "I grew up with banda music. At that time, not very many people liked it. At least in Mexico, only the poor listen to that type of music. . . . Here in California, it cuts through the classes. Here it doesn't matter."[25]

Banda was also influenced by the popularity of *Norteño narcocorridos,* many of which *bandas* covered. An important figure in the *banda narcocorrido* movement was vocalist Chalino Sanchez, whose slurred, off-key voice blanketed Mexican Los Angeles in the early 1990s. An admirer of Pancho Villa, he dressed as a Mexican revolutionary and lived the *bandido*-hero myth, dying by kidnapping and assassination in 1992. By the early 2000s, *banda* was well established in Mexico, and top acts such as international dance music diva Thalia began to put out *banda*-flavored CDs. Some artists moved the music away from the synthesizer-driven *technobanda* sound; others, such as the California duo AKWID, fused *banda* with hip-hop.

Internet Listening Exercise

Listen to *banda* samples from the following CDs.

Various Artists: *Billboard Hot Latin Tracks: Best of Regional Mexican*

Banda Machos: *Banda Machos*

Banda El Recodo: *No Me Sé Rajar*

AKWID: *Proyecto AKWID*

Narcocorridos

The **narcocorrido** was a modern incarnation of the *corrido* that was popular in Mexico and the Chicano/*Mexicano* communities of the United States at the turn of the twenty-first century. Popular *Norteño* and *banda* artists performed *narcocorridos* as accordion-driven, *conjunto*-style polkas and waltzes. The roots of the style, traditional *corridos*, often focused on social topics such as border issues and smuggling. By the late 1930s, the *corrido* seemed to be in decline, but the style reemerged in the 1970s with a refreshed, high-energy musical flavor and drug trafficking as its theme.

The *Norteño* group **Los Tigres del Norte** (based in San Jose, California) became the most popular *narcocorrido* group as well as major superstars of Mexican music. The group's first *narcocorrido* hit, *"Contrabando y Traición"* ("Smuggling and Betrayal," 1972), told of a drug deal gone bad: A pair of drug runners named Camelia and Emilio had smuggled into the United States a load of marijuana hidden in the tires of their car. After the sale was completed, Emilio gave

Camelia her share of the profits and announced that he was leaving to visit his true love. Angered and jealous, Camelia killed him.

Sonaron siete balazos, Camelia a Emilio mataba,	Seven shots rang out, Camelia killed Emilio,
La policia solo halló una pistola tirada,	The police found only the discarded pistol.
Del dinero y de Camelia nunca más se supo nada.	Of the money and Camelia nothing more was ever known.

Although popular in Mexican communities in the United States, controversy surrounded *narcocorridos* in Mexico; some accused the style of glorifying drug trafficking and attempted to ban the genre from radio airplay. Nonetheless, commercial success continued unabated, and other popular *Norteño* groups and *bandas* began to play *narcocorridos,* including Grupo Exterminador, Ramón Ayala y los Bravos del Norte, and Los Alegres de Terán.

Internet Listening Exercise

Listen to Los Tigres del Norte's *norteño/narcocorrido* style.

Los Tigres del Norte: *16 Zarpazos*

THE SCENE IN THE EARLY 2000s

Latinos were the fastest growing population in the United States in the early 2000s, and people of Mexican heritage made up the largest Latino group in the country. According to the Recording Association of America, "Regional Mexican music"—encompassing *banda, Norteño, grupero,* and *Tejano*—dominated U.S. Latin music sales, outselling Latin pop two to one. Latin pop nonetheless

Multicultural Note

Narcocorridos *and Gangsta Rap*

Narcocorridos and gangsta rap reached the height of their popularity in the 1990s and the early 2000s, with several artists blending the two genres. Although they differed in their sound, groove, and cultural context, they shared a similar lyrical content. Some viewed gangsta rap as a reflection of urban realities for poor people of color, particularly African American youth, but critics decried its glorification of violence and misogyny. Fans of *narcocorrido* saw the genre as a vehicle for exploring issues of class oppression in Mexico, but detractors said that it exploited violence and drugs.

The folksy sound of *narcocorridos* performed in *conjunto/Norteño* style created a musical texture that contrasted with provocative lyric content. Hip-hop fans might well chuckle at the idea that anyone could be offended by the folksy *conjunto* sound of *narcocorrido*. Do the aggressive grooves of gangsta rap interact with the lyrical content of the style differently? How do radically different styles of music play similar roles in different cultures?

received the lion's share of the spotlight, particularly at the Grammys and Latin Grammys. In fact, Los Tigres del Norte and several other regional Mexican acts turned down their Latin Grammys in 2000, citing bias.

Whether awarded or not, multiple strands of Chicano/*Mexicano* musical developed in the United States in the early 2000s:

- Thalia, an international pop-techno diva and Mexican soap opera star, released dance albums, a *banda* remix album, and then a bilingual Latin pop album.

- A. B. Quintanilla III, the late Selena's brother, became a major voice in blending *cumbia* with hip-hop by producing a series of albums for the Kumbia Kings and other young *Tejano* artists.

- Jessie Morales, an L.A.-born Chicano hip-hop artist, issued an album heavy with *banda* and *Norteño* sounds and with covers of Snoop Dogg and Patsy Cline, followed by a *banda*/hip-hop tribute album for deceased *narcocorrido* pioneer Chalino Sanchez.

- Artists such as Grupo Limite, La Conquista, and El Gran Silencio popularized a new *Tejano* style called *grupero*, a pop-*Norteño* fusion that energized traditional *corridos* with upbeat dance rhythms and hip-hop attitude.

- *Son jarocho,* the folkloric music of Vera Cruz on Mexico's Caribbean coast, drew the attention of major California Chicano artists such as Los Lobos and Quetzal.

- Multiple hip-hop hybrids with various Mexican styles, exemplified by artists such as Ozomatli and AKWID, continued to develop.

- *Norteño, banda,* and mariachi maintained great appeal for first-generation immigrants and U.S.-born Mexican Americans, and *narcocorridos* gained mainstream acceptance.

- Chicano rockers such as Santana and Los Lobos displayed a timeless, broad-based appeal; a new genre called rock en Español, which translated the energy of punk into Spanish, showed potential to expand with bands such as Jaguares and Molotov; *Tejano* rockers Los Lonely Boys garnered a 2005 Grammy; and the Chicano love for classic R & B seemed everlasting.

Chicano/*Mexicano* music embodies a diasporic musical tradition expressing many themes: cultural pride, social commentary, warmth of family and community, love and loss, partying, and dancing. As U.S. demographics continue to shift, diverse artists of Mexican heritage will expand their audiences and new hybrids will continue to appear.

Chapter Summary

- The history of Chicano/*Mexicano* culture in the United States began with displacement in 1848; this and similar issues continued to affect subsequent generations.

- The music of Spain and Europe initially influenced the musical styles in Mexico, but the "Mexicanization" of various styles developed hybrid genres.

- The arrival of the accordion in Northern Mexico in the late nineteenth century influenced *Norteño* and *Tejano* music; the instrument became an important symbol of Tejano culture and contributed to the development of *conjunto*.

- Record companies turned to Spanish-speaking communities in the 1920s to record artists such as Lydia Mendoza. *Orquesta típica* and *corrido* were popular in the era.

- *Orquesta tejana* emerged in the 1940s and 1950s, borrowing from big bands, Latin jazz, and *orquesta típica*. Isidro López and Beto Villa were central to the development of the style, and it subsequently blended with rock to generate *Tejano* music.

- Further developments in Chicano music in the 1940s followed two regional paths: California and Texas. *Pachuco* youth culture in California fused jump blues and Latin dance styles.

- *Conjunto* reached its zenith in the 1950s with Conjunto Bernal. The roots of Chicano rock were also being planted in Southern California, where the first star of Chicano rock, Ritchie Valens, recorded "La Bamba." A multi-generational tradition of Chicano appreciation for old-school R & B was also nurtured by Los Angeles DJs of the era.

- A new generation of Chicano rock bands appeared in the early 1960s with groups such as Cannibal and the Headhunters, Thee Midniters, and Sam the Sham and the Pharaohs. The late 1960s saw a Chicano civil rights movement and new sense of cultural pride. Santana put Chicano rock in the national spotlight once again, and groups such as Malo, El Chicano, Azteca, and Tierra enjoyed brief popularity.

- The popularity of *Tejano* music slowly expanded, marked by the success of Little Joe y La Familia in 1976, the establishment of the *Tejano* Music Awards in 1982, major label recording contracts for *Tejano* artists in the 1990s, and the brief rise of Selena.

- Chicano rock further evolved in the 1980s and 1990s with the success of bands such as Los Lobos and Ozomatli.

- Mexican musical styles including mariachi, *Norteño*, and *banda* grew in popularity on both sides of the border, and mariachi was promoted as a symbol of cultural pride to be taught in schools throughout the Southwest.

Key Terms

accordion	*huapango*	*orquesta típica*
bajo sexto	lowrider	*pachuco*
banda	mariachi	polka
canción	marimba	*quebradita*
Chicano	*Mexicano*	*ranchera*
corrido	*narcocorrido*	*tambora de rancho*
cumbia	*Norteño*	*Tejano*
guitarrón	*orquesta tejana*	*vihuela*

Study and Discussion Questions

1. What historical circumstances influenced the development of Chicano culture and music?

2. Who was Lydia Mendoza and what role did she play in the history of Chicano music?

3. What is the background of the accordion in *Norteño/Tejano* music? What is *conjunto* music and what is the instrumentation of a typical *conjunto* band?

4. What is a *corrido* and what role does it play in Chicano cultural history? What place does the *narcocorrido* have in contemporary Mexican music?

5. How did the the *orquesta tejana* evolve, and what role did it play in the changing demographics of *Tejano* culture in the 1940s and 1950s?

6. What are *pachuco* culture, its historical importance, and the music that accompanied it?

7. How did radio affect the development of Chicano popular music traditions? What role did classic rock and R & B play in Chicano music?

8. How did *Tejano* music evolve? Who were some principal innovators?

9. How did the Chicano civil rights movement impact Chicano rock? Who were some important innovators in the style?

10. Which artists stand at the forefront of Chicano music today? Why is their music significant?

11. What Mexican styles have taken root in the United States and why? What are the differing cultural roles of mariachi and *banda?*

Notes

1. The term *Tejano* signifes a musical style as well as people of Mexican descent who live in Texas; *Norteño* also refers to both a musical style and the cultural traits of the Northern Mexico border areas.

2. Interview with the authors.

3. Chris Strachwitz and James Nicolopulos, eds., *Lydia Mendoza: A Family Autobiography* (Houston: Arte Público Press, 1993), p. vii.

4. Ibid., 12.

5. Manuel Peña, *The Texas-Mexican Conjunto: History of a Working-Class Music* (Austin: University of Texas Press, 1985), 8–9.

6. Manuel Peña, *The Mexican American Orquesta: Music, Culture, and the Dialectic of Conflict* (Austin: University of Texas Press, 1999), 148.

7. Ibid., 163.

8. Mauricio Mazón, *The Zoot-Suit Riots: The Psychology of Symbolic Annihilation* (Austin: University of Texas Press, 1984), 69.

9. Ibid., 69.

10. David Reyes and Tom Waldman, *Land of a Thousand Dances: Chicano Rock 'n Roll from Southern California* (Albuquerque: University of New Mexico Press, 1998), xix.

11. Ibid., 36–37.

12. Ibid., 62.

13. Ramino Burr, *The Billboard Guide to Tejano and Regional Mexican Music* (New York: Billboard Books, 1999), 26, 133.

14. Ibid., 31.

15. Deborah R. Vargas, "Bidi Bidi Bom Bom: Selena and Tejano Music in the Making of Tejas," In *Latino/a Popular Culture,* edited by Michelle Habell-Pallán and Mary Romero (New York: New York University Press, 2002), 122–23.

16. Rubén Guevara, "The View from the Sixth Street Bridge: The History of Chicano Rock," in *The First Rock and Roll Confidential Report,* edited by David Marsh et. al. (New York: Pantheon, 1985), 123.

17. James Sullivan, "Santana's Glorious Rebirth," *San Francisco Chronicle,* May 6, 2003, p. D3.

18. Reyes and Waldman, *Land of a Thousand Dances,* 120.

19. George Lipsitz, *Time Passages: Collective Memory and American Popular Culture* (Minneapolis: University of Minnesota Press, 1990), 147.

20. Interview with the authors.

21. Guevara, "View from the Sixth Street Bridge," 123.

22. Lipsitz, *Time Passages,* 149.

23. *Los Angeles Times,* quoted in Helena Simonett, *Banda: Mexican Musical Life across Borders* (Middletown, CT: Wesleyan University Press, 2001), 26.

24. Simonett, *Banda,* 78.

25. Ibid., 89.

1400 - 2000

13,000 B.C.E.–Present Thousands of Native cultures developed over 15,000 years

1492 Columbus lands in the West Indies

1500s Spanish conquest of Latin America
1500s Thousands of Native cultures decimated by Europeans

1607 First British community in North America, Jamestown, is settled
1619 First African slaves brought to America
1620 Pilgrims arrive at Plymouth Rock
1621 First Thanksgiving
1622 First Native retaliation for European encroachment on Native lands

1700s American colonies expand
1700s Encroachment on Native lands continues as most Native people in the U.S. are driven west
1744 Treaty of Lancaster creates Appalachian dividing line between Native and European Americans
1754–1763 French and Indian War
1776 Declaration of Independence and beginning of Revolutionary War

1803 Louisiana Purchase annexes vast western lands from France
1830–1840 Indian Removal Act and "Trail of Tears" force relocation of most Indians to reservations in Oklahoma territory
1840s–1880s Continuing forced removal and genocide
1848 End of Mexican War; Southwest annexed by U.S.
1849 California gold rush
1861–1865 Civil War
1876 Battle of Little Big Horn
1890 Massacre of Natives by U.S. troops at Wounded Knee
1898 Spanish American War

1914–1918 World War I
1929–1930s Great Depression; New Deal begins
1934 Prohibitions against Native American religious ceremonies and music are ended ♪
1941–1945 U.S. participates in World War II
1950–1953 Korean War
1951 First Native record company, Canyon Records, is formed ♪
1954 School segregation outlawed; civil rights movement begins
1963 Civil rights march on Washington; John Kennedy assassinated
1964–1973 Vietnam War
1970s Early crossover Native rock by XIT and Redbone ♪
1972 First Native American public radio station is founded on Navajo reservation ♪
1983 R. Carlos Nakai's first recording for Canyon Records ♪
1990s American economic high-tech "bubble"
1994 Music for the Native Americans recorded by Robbie Robertson, gaining exposure for contemporary Native American popular music ♪
1998 Native American Music Awards established ♪

2000 First Grammy award for Native American Music ♪
2001 9/11 terrorist attacks

1400	1500	1600	1700	1800	1900	2000

Chapter 10

Native American Popular Music

This chapter investigates Native American musical traditions and their contemporary manifestations. Although research on Native musical traditions has grown in recent years, scholars have paid the least attention to contemporary Native musical styles. Despite the significant contributions that Native Americans have made to America's popular music, many fans of rock, blues, and country music remain unaware of the Native American heritage of such legendary performers as Jimi Hendrix, Hank Williams, Charlie Patton, and Robbie Robertson. Public television and Native American radio have played pivotal roles in the development of contemporary Native American music, and the intertribal powwow movement also supported the reemergence of Native pride and consciousness throughout North America.

IN THIS CHAPTER

- Historical Context
- Musical Traditions of Native America
- Traditional Native American Instruments
- Powwow Traditions
- Contemporary Native American Music
- Contemporary Native Musicians
- The Sacred, the Secular, and the Future

Multicultural Note

Native American, Indian, Indigenous, or First Nations?

How to refer respectfully to the cultures that are native to North America remains an unresolved issue. The term *Indian* dates back to Columbus's mistaken assumption that he had reached India. In Canada, many Native cultures have openly embraced the terms *aboriginal* or **First Nations,** and **indigenous** is widely used internationally.

Tribal names in original languages often translate into English simply as "the people"; many tribes now identify themselves with terms from their own languages, such as the Navajo use of the term *Dineh*. The terms *Indian* and *Amerindian* are also in wide use, with many universities awarding degrees in American Indian Studies.

In the music industry, the Native American Music Awards were established as an annual celebration of contemporary Native music. This text follows the lead of that terminology. Native American artists are also identified by their tribal affiliation wherever possible.

HISTORICAL CONTEXT

Long before the arrival of the first Europeans, a diverse range of Native American cultures covered North America. Anthropologists believe that the first inhabitants arrived from northern Asia over 15,000 years ago, although many Native Americans believe that their ancestors originated in North America. Following the arrival of Christopher Columbus in 1492, European explorers and settlers exploited material wealth and land while decimating Native peoples through disease and **cultural genocide**—the systematic destruction of an entire way of life.

Succeeding centuries witnessed continued expansion of white settlement. In 1830 the Indian Removal Act banished virtually all Native cultures to lands west of the Mississippi River. The "Trail of Tears" of 1838, a forced eviction of thousands of Cherokee people from homelands in the Southeast, caused hundreds of deaths as the U.S. government forced people to walk 1,500 miles to reservations in Oklahoma. By the end of the nineteenth century, most Native peoples had been forced onto reservations, with their cultures destroyed, their treaties broken, and hundreds of thousands of their lives lost. The early twentieth century brought policies of forced assimilation: Children were forced to attend boarding schools and abandon their traditions and languages, the U.S. and Canadian governments banned many Native religious ceremonies, and the U.S. government forcibly relocated tens of thousands of rural Native Americans to cities. Today most Native Americans live in urban settings in the West. Cities with the largest Native American populations include New York and Los Angeles. In a positive upswing, the early 2000s saw a resurgence in the Native American population to over four million.

MUSICAL TRADITIONS OF NATIVE AMERICA

The preservation of musical traditions has posed a continuous challenge for Native Americans. From the beginning, European–Native American interaction often resulted in the destruction of music considered pagan by Europeans, and such losses were exacerbated by the deaths of elders or practitioners of sacred ceremonies. Further, non-Native scholars found the investigation of Native musical traditions difficult, because after centuries of exploitation, Native Americans were reluctant to share their culture with outsiders. In the late twentieth century, however, a new appreciation of Native American traditions emerged as part of a movement to preserve vernacular culture. For example, the creation of the Federal Cylinder Project by the Library of Congress's American Folklife Center in the late 1970s led to the restoration of recordings of Native American music made early in the century by field researchers such as Frances Densmore and Alice Cunningham Fletcher. The recordings enabled tribes to recreate traditional musics that had been lost, and they shed new light on musical traditions that permeated the daily lives of Native Americans.

Historically, six regions in North America denoted areas of distinct musical styles: the Plains, Southwest, Northwest Coast, Great Basin and Plateau, Eastern

Woodlands, and California. Within these styles, regional variations stemmed from tribal affiliation and clan. For centuries, song and dance served as central components of sacred and secular life. Most Native peoples traditionally believed that music was a gift of the creator—that music emanated from the universe. Further, in Native American historian Bryan Burton's words, "Individuals are allowed by the Creator to 'catch' a song from this source."[1] Songs were usually composed individually or collectively and transmitted orally, although some Native composers began to publish written music in the late twentieth century. Music was also closely tied to dance. Some songs could be performed only by specific tribe members, and many traditional songs were performed only by men. In the late twentieth century, however, some tribes began to include more women in singing. Important traditional functions of Native music included joining the natural with the supernatural, and the person with the creator. Native peoples also commonly used music to perform religious and healing ceremonies; to bring success in war, hunting, or agriculture; to praise worthy individuals; to tell stories; and to accompany work, games, courting, and other social events.

Most Native American singing features the use of **vocables**—lyrics made up of syllables that have no clear linguistic meaning but that are often considered sacred. Although Hollywood Westerns often misrepresented vocables as Indian stereotypes, Native Americans still regard their use as a respected tradition. Vocables differ greatly from the nonsense syllables of jazz scat singing: Once established for a specific song, they usually remain the same, and again they often have sacred implications. The origin of the practice remains uncertain.

CD LISTENING EXERCISE

CD 2/1

Listen to Ulali singing the song "Mother," recorded in 1994. This is an example of the use of vocables in a contemporary Native American song.

TRADITIONAL NATIVE AMERICAN INSTRUMENTS

Drums (membranophones) and percussion (idiophones) were the most commonly used instruments in traditional Native American music. The drums developed by different tribes included small hand drums, water drums, and large bass drums. The larger drums originated with the tribes of the Great Plains and later became focal points at intertribal powwows. Drums and percussion instruments were made of hollowed logs, branches, pottery, baskets, animal skins, and rawhide. One of the most common Native instruments found throughout North America, rattles were made from gourds, turtle shells, animal bones, horns, hide, or tree bark. Other percussion instruments included scrapers, bells, and rasps.

With the exception of the flute, traditional Native American music seldom used melodic instruments. Evidence exists of a few stringed instruments (chordophones), including the Apache violin or fiddle, a bowed instrument using one or two strings made of horsehair strung on the stalk of a century plant. Modern-day Yaqui and Tohono O'odam Indians of southern Arizona have also embraced

Internet Listening Exercise

Listen to samples of *waila* music.

Pima Express: "Crazy Spinning Chicken"

Desert Horizon: "San Pedro"

the stringed instruments of Mexican American border music and mariachi, including the *guitarrón* and the *vihuela,* to play a style of music called **waila** or **chicken scratch.**

Native flutes (aerophones) come in a variety of shapes, sizes, and styles. They are made of wood (especially cedar), cane, clay, or metal. Many Plains tribes have long-established flute traditions, and Southwest tribes may have had flute traditions that have become lost. Prominent contemporary flute players include R. Carlos Nakai (Navajo-Ute), Robert Mirabal (Taos Pueblo), John Rainer, Jr. (Taos Pueblo), and Joseph Fire Crow (Northern Cheyenne). The Plains-style flute became popular in the late twentieth century, its meditative sound having particular appeal for fans of new age music. Some Native American musicians found this amusing, because their music and culture were hardly new. Ancient rock art in the Southwest often depicted **Kokopelli** the flute player, a trickster deity whose playing restored balance in the universe.

POWWOW TRADITIONS

The **powwow** is an important tradition of contemporary Native America that presents traditional music, dance, food, arts, and fun with central themes of honor, respect, generosity, unity, and friendship. The origins of the modern powwow stem from the **grass dances** of the Northern Plains Indians. The dances originally provided an opportunity for warriors to reenact brave deeds, and in the late nineteenth century they represented one of the few types of dances not outlawed by the U.S. government. The commodification of Plains Indian culture through venues such as *Buffalo Bill's Wild West Show* also unintentionally preserved and disseminated grass dances. The adoption of these and other Plains traditions at modern powwows by other tribes came about because

Multicultural Note

Commodification, Appropriation, and Preservation

The *Wild West Show* exemplified the complexity of commodification and cultural appropriation. Buffalo Bill Cody was a legendary figure of the American west— a frontiersman and Indian fighter who led the battle that avenged the death of Custer. Later in the 1880s, Cody created the *Wild West Show,* a theatrical extravaganza that appropriated and commodified Native traditions and shaped "cowboy and Indian" stereotypes that persisted for over 100 years. Many components of the show were clearly fantasy, but some of the Native cultural performances retained substantial accuracy. Although the existence of the *Wild West Show* is offensive from a contemporary perspective, it paradoxically preserved and reinterpreted Native cultural forms that might otherwise have been lost.

many tribes east of the Mississippi River had lost much of their traditional music and dance. The 1934 removal of a federal ban on Native American music and religious celebrations opened the door for a reemergence of Native traditions and led to the birth of the modern intertribal powwow. At that time, tribes also hosted the events to bring tourist dollars into Indian communities. Modern powwows occur most weekends somewhere in the United States and Canada, in urban as well as rural areas.

Music at a modern intertribal powwow centers on a Plains Indian tradition known as the powwow drum—*drum* referring to both the instrument and the ensemble that accompanies the drumming. The instrument, which is the size of a large bass drum, is made from a wooden shell covered with cowhide or buffalo hide; performers play it with drum sticks that have padded heads. Most powwow drum groups include between six and eight musicians who perform a large repertoire of traditional and contemporary songs. Modern powwow music falls into northern and southern styles, although many of the same dances take place at powwows in both regions. Native peoples perform traditional dances such as the grass dance, men's fancy war dance, women's fancy shawl dance, jingle dance, hoop dance, and eagle dance, as well as intertribal social dances in which everyone is invited to participate.

Contemporary powwow drum groups include people from all walks of life, as demonstrated by the two groups profiled here: Yellow Wolf Drum, based in Victoria, British Columbia, and the Sweetwater Singers, based in San Francisco, California. Members of Yellow Wolf came mostly from an extended family of mixed tribal ancestry—part Nez Pierce and part Coast Salish. The Sweetwater Singers were from various tribal backgrounds including Mescalero Apache,

Courtesy of Glenn Appell

The Yellow Wolf Drum performs for the opening of a First Nations art gallery in Victoria, British Columbia (2002).

Cherokee, and Apelusa, as well as non-Natives. Yellow Wolf drummer/singer John Sampson, explained how his group was formed:

> I was at Mission Powwow on the mainland and I got inspired listening to a group. When I got back home I told my family that I wanted to start a singing group in memory of our mother . . . a Nez Pierce from Idaho. This type of singing was done by the men from our mother's tribe.[2]

The current powwow circuit in the northwestern United States and southwestern Canada features gatherings almost every weekend from April through October. According to Sampson,

> We perform because we like to share our culture to the non-Natives and it makes us feel good about ourselves. Whoever we perform for enjoys our singing and dancing . . . along with the songs and history of who we are. . . . Powwows have been going on for centuries, but no one noticed.[3]

The Sweetwater Singers formed in 1990 when a professor of American Indian Studies at San Francisco State University began the group as a "teaching drum." The group's purpose was to share drum traditions with urban Native American students and to teach non-Native students about drum traditions. Their goal was to "sing in the old way" by performing a repertoire of traditional Lakota drum songs in that language. Spokesperson Jacob Perea, a university dean, explained that members have included a lawyer, a music store owner, students, and Perea's son John-Carlos, who also leads his own contemporary Native American jazz group. Its focus on traditional songs made Sweetwater a favorite among elders, and the group performs for special ceremonies and celebrations as well as at schools and prisons. The group also performs at urban powwows, which are important cultural events for urban American Indians, many of whom have never lived on a reservation. An important facet of powwow performances is humor, as Perea noted:

> One of the best things about a powwow is the humor. Teaching, humor, and even bad jokes all take place around the drum. The dancing is beautiful, drumming is marvelous, but a good arena director or master of ceremonies is worth their weight in gold. They come across with jokes, pick up on little things, tease, et cetera.[4]

Powwow drum traditions have recently begun to include women as well as men. John Sampson's sister belonged to Yellow Wolf, the Sweetwater Singers included women, and "The Man Killers," a San Francisco–based, all-female powwow drum, also developed a strong following. When asked what the major lesson of a powwow drum was, Perea replied, "Sharing."[5]

CONTEMPORARY NATIVE AMERICAN MUSIC

Many innovators of American popular music shared a Native American heritage, including guitarist Jimi Hendrix, early blues legend Charley Patton, guitarist/songwriter Robbie Robertson, and singer-songwriters Rita Coolidge, Buffy

www Internet Listening Exercise

Listen to samples of powwow drum music, paying attention to the timbre of the Plains-style singing.

Black Lodge Singers: "Seasons," "Old Blackfeet Song"

Kicking Woman Singers: "Grand Entry"

High Noon: "Grass Dance"

Sainte-Marie, Hank Williams, Ray Price, Kitty Wells, and Crystal Gayle. Beginning in the late 1980s, Robertson, Saint-Marie, and Coolidge began to reexamine their Native roots, fostering the development of a new genre called *contemporary Native American music.*

Native American Radio

The development of Native American public radio in the late twentieth century was key to the emergence of contemporary Native music. Prior to 1972, Native-owned and -operated radio stations hardly existed, and most radio available to rural Native Americans came from commercial stations with little acknowledgment of Native cultures. In the early 1970s, the federal government established the public telecommunications facilities program, which spurred the growth of Native American radio. The first such station began in 1972 on the Navajo Reservation. At that time, however, broadcasters had only a small repertoire of contemporary Native American music available for airplay. According to Peggy Berryhill (Muscogee), founder of the Native Media Resource Center, the only successful native groups from the early 1970s were XIT and Redbone: "Without radio, no artist had a chance to have a hit."[6] This left fledgling Native stations with limited playlists dominated by traditional powwow music, which had little meaning for East Coast Indians, who did not have such traditions. Moreover, most of the music of Zuni and other Pueblo people of the Southwest was too sacred to be broadcast on the radio.

By the mid-1980s, the growing popularity of world music helped new contemporary Native artists gain exposure, and a few of them, including vocalist/songwriter Buffy Sainte-Marie and jazz saxophonist Jim Pepper, crossed over. Other Native artists to receive airplay included singer/songwriter Sharon Burch, poet/saxophonist Joy Harjo, flutist R. Carlos Nakai, and numerous powwow drums from the United States and Canada. The development of AIROS (American Indian Radio on Satellite) in the 1990s increased access, and new weekly shows were broadcast throughout North America. By the early 2000s, close to thirty Native public radio stations operated in the United States.

Contemporary Musical Styles

The first contemporary musical inroads came in the 1970s through artists such as Redbone, XIT, and A. Paul Ortega. Tom Bee, who later founded the SOAR (Sounds of America Recordings) label, led the rock band XIT. The group toured widely, recorded for Motown Records, and served as a role model for later Native rock musicians. By the mid-1980s, contemporary Native musicians had gained national visibility, and cedar flutist R. Carlos Nakai recorded a string of popular albums with Canyon Records. The movement expanded in the 1990s with Robbie Robertson's groundbreaking work with the Red Road Ensemble and the music of Ulali, Walela, Kashtin, Jim Wilson, and Douglas Spotted Eagle. By the early 2000s, a broad range of contemporary Native American popular music artists were playing folk, country, rock, new age, hip-hop, reggae, and R & B styles.

Native American cedar flute master R. Carlos Nakai.

The Native American Recording Industry and the Nammies

Native-owned record companies played a major role in preserving and disseminating Native American music. Currently, more than fifty such labels exist. Canyon Records, one of America's oldest independent record labels, started in 1951 with the mission of recording music that Native people wanted to hear, rather than ethnomusicological recordings aimed at scholars. The label's current catalogue includes over 400 recordings in a variety of styles, and its recordings have won numerous awards.

A milestone in the growth of contemporary Native American music was the establishment in 1998 of the annual Native American Music Awards ("Nammies") to honor the work of traditional and contemporary Native American musical artists. In addition to annual awards, Lifetime Achievement Awards were presented to artists such as Jimi Hendrix (1998), singer/songwriter Hank Williams (1999), saxophonist Jim Pepper (2000), and flutist R. Carlos Nakai (2001). After an intensive lobbying campaign, the National Academy of Recording Arts and Sciences also established a new Grammy category—"Best Native American Music Album"—in 2001.

CONTEMPORARY NATIVE MUSICIANS

Native American cedar flute player **R. Carlos Nakai** (1946–) was one of the most popular contemporary Native American musicians of the late twentieth century. Native flute traditions had been almost completely eradicated; however, Nakai's recordings of the 1980s played a central role in establishing a new contemporary Native flute genre. Nakai took a multicultural approach by incorporating the flute into diverse styles. He recorded more than twenty-five albums, including collaborations with jazz, rock, blues, folk, classical, and country artists, as well as musicians from Japan and Tibet. Radio producer Gregg McVickar described Nakai's music as "neo-classical, instrumental, soft, ethereal, transcendent . . . with spiritual overtones."[7] According to ethnomusicologist David McAllester,

> [Nakai] draws inspiration from mountains, valleys, canyons, wind, rains, sunsets, the scent of juniper, from wildlife, and from the earth itself. His music describes the Southwest particularly and has a vivid sense of his ancestors moving through this landscape."[8]

When critics questioned the authenticity of his eclectic approach, Nakai pointed out that Native American cultures had been adapting and blending with other cultures since the dawn of time. According to the artist, Native American music, like most music, is always changing:

> Many of the traditional ceremonial chants that you hear today are very much unlike the chants based on the wax recordings and wire recordings that emanated out of the Smithsonian over time and are performed in a very different manner today. One reason is because of the influence of cultural change and the influence of different philosophies and ways of looking at how we are today.[9]

In Nakai's opinion, the music of the United States is based on the involvement, interaction, and influence of all of our cultures. He also believes that all cultures share a similar underlying need to communicate through music: "There is no significant difference in the human community. They all have similarities of involvement, communication, and expression that we have to get out somehow."[10]

Guitarist/vocalist/songwriter **Robbie Robertson** (1944–) was one of the premier songwriters of the rock era of the late 1960s and early 1970s. Born in Toronto, Canada, the son of a Jewish father and Mohawk mother, Robertson listened to Native and country music as a child. At age fifteen he joined the backup band for rockabilly star Ronnie Hawkins. Robertson and the Hawks stayed with Hawkins un-

CD LISTENING EXERCISE

CD 2/2

Listen to an excerpt from the Second Movement from the *Two World Concerto* composed for Nakai by African American classical composer James De-Mars. Nakai is the first person to use the **cedar flute** with a symphony orchestra. Most cedar flutes are not tuned or designed to play each note at the same pitch as European classical instruments. This is the result of a different cultural value system regarding intonation. How is this piece an example of a cultural borderland in music?

til 1963, when they came to the attention of Bob Dylan. Dylan hired them as the supporting band for his 1965–1966 world tour, when he shocked the music world by going electric. Robertson and his bandmates renamed themselves "The Band" and became one of rock's seminal acts. They made a series of influential records, including *Music from Big Pink* (1968) and *The Band* (1969), which featured songs written by Robertson that examined American mythology and lore. After the breakup of The Band, Robertson pursued a successful career in the 1980s writing film scores. In 1994 he returned to his roots, teaming up with a coalition of contemporary Native American artists called the Red Road Ensemble to produce *Music for the Native Americans,* an album for a television

www **Internet Listening Exercise**

Listen to samples of songs from *Music for the Native Americans.*

Robbie Robertson: "Ghost Dance," "It Is a Good Day to Die"

Kashtin: *"Akua Tuta"*

Walela: "The Cherokee Morning Song"

documentary series. The album brought contemporary Native music to a mass audience for the first time.

Born on a Cree First Nations reservation in Canada, singer/songwriter **Buffy Sainte-Marie** (1941–) conveyed a strong sense of her heritage in her music. Sainte-Marie's earliest albums appeared at the height of the 1960s folk music boom, and over the next several decades artists such as Janis Joplin, Barbra Streisand, Elvis Presley, Neil Diamond, and Tracy Chapman recorded her work. One of her most popular songs, "Up where We Belong," was used as the theme of the film *Top Gun* in the 1980s.

Grammy-winner **Rita Coolidge** (1945–) began her career in 1970 singing with rock artists Joe Cocker, Eric Clapton, George Harrison, and Leon Russell. Her recording career produced dozens of albums, including the multiplatinum *Anytime . . . Anywhere.* In the 1990s, Coolidge joined her sister and daughter-in-law to form the vocal trio Walela (Cherokee for "hummingbird"). Touring internationally, the group gained prominence in the contemporary Native American music movement, and their 2002 release, *Walela,* was especially well received.

The vocal trio **Ulali** became known for their unique harmonies and powerful voices. Group members argued that their music reflected Native musical

Photo by Katherine Fogden, copyright 2000 Corn Beans & Squash Music

Contemporary vocal trio Ulali (left to right): Jennifer (Tuscarora), Soni (Mayan, Apache, Yaqui), and Pura Fé (Tuscarora).

themes that influenced the development of the blues and gospel through interactions between Native American and African cultures during the early days of slavery in the Southeast. The artists complemented their singing with hand drums, rattles, and stomps. Their work was featured on the soundtrack of the 1998 film *Smoke Signals*.

Another Native artist, **Joanne Shenandoah,** drew on her Iroquois heritage to create striking compositions that embellished traditional songs with contemporary folk instrumentation. She sang with a distinctive, passionate, and clear vocal style that led to a Grammy nomination.

One of the most versatile session guitarists of the 1960s and 1970s, **Jesse Ed Davis** (Kiowa), played on albums by John Lennon, Eric Clapton, Jackson Browne, and Taj Mahal. He also appeared in George Harrison's 1971 Concert for Bangla Desh benefit. In 1986 Davis collaborated on a landmark album with spoken-word artist John Trudell called *AKA Graffiti Man*, which Bob Dylan called "the best album of 1986." According to Trudell,

> With Jesse and me, we each came from our collective Indian experience, and had our individual experiences in the non-Indian world. We had both literally been to the last door of hell, opened it, and saw what was inside.[11]

The emergence of Native American hip-hop in the late twentieth century played an important role in Native youth culture, with a focus on human rights and self-respect. The Internet provided a key medium for connecting and publicizing the Native hip-hop community, which rarely received attention in the mainstream media. Prominent Native hip-hop artists included WithOut Rezervation, Litefoot, Trurez Crew, and Robert Bee. Many Native artists performed in a variety of other styles as well, including country artist Buddy Red Bow, hard rockers Indigenous, indie rocker Keith Secola, reggae band Native Roots, rock singer Arigon Starr, and singer-songwriter Sharon Burch.

THE SACRED, THE SECULAR, AND THE FUTURE

Native American music retained a distinction between the sacred and the secular, although many other U.S. music styles lost this distinction. Speaking of the continuing respect for the sacred power of music in Native American communities, radio producer Gregg McVickar told how a contemporary R & B artist who had recently discovered her own Native roots decided to record a sacred tribal song with a "kick-ass reggae backbeat."[12] After radio airplay, song keepers from the affected tribe protested this use of a sacred song for a secular purpose, and the song was eventually taken off the air. While we should not romanticize such an account, it does suggest a reverence for the spiritual nature

---

CD LISTENING EXERCISE

CD 2/1

Listen to "Mother," performed by Ulali. The song is an example of a Cree round dance that has been augmented with contemporary three-part harmony more commonly found in country music or rhythm and blues. The lyrics are vocables. Notice how the song modulates to a higher key on each successive verse. In Native American traditions, this is known as "raising the song." What effect does raising the song have on your listening experience?

Internet Listening Exercise

Listen to samples of female contemporary Native American popular music artists.

Walela: "Cherokee River"

Joanne Shenandoah: "Heartbeat"

Sharon Burch: "First Cry"

Buffy Sainte-Marie: "Now That the Buffalo's Gone"

Internet Listening Exercise

Listen to samples of the following contemporary Native artists.

John Trudell: "Bombs over Baghdad"

Indigenous: "C'Mon Suzie"

Buddy Red Bow: "Journey to the Spirit World"

WithOut Rezervation: "Are You Ready for W.O.R.?"

Sharon Burch: "First Cry"

of music that appears less in other American musical styles—with the possible exception of the Christian, gospel, and new age genres.

Despite centuries of cultural genocide, prospects for the development and growth of Native American cultures and expression seemed promising at the start of the twenty-first century. New Native musical styles emerged that reflect both past and present. As Gregg McVickar noted, "There is the sense that the Native population, after being practically decimated in the 1800s, is coming back really strong, and the culture is coming back, and there's this big up-curve that's happening. Now's the time."[13]

Chapter Summary

- Native American history stretches back over 15,000 years in North America, reflecting a diverse range of cultures. Contact with European settlers over a 500-year period largely decimated these cultures, however.

- Traditional Native American musics can be divided into six stylistic regions: the Plains, Southwest, Northwest Coast, Great Basin and Plateau, Eastern Woodlands, and California. Most Native cultures viewed music as a gift from the creator, and music addressed distinct sacred and secular purposes. Much Native music was tied to dance, and it was primarily transmitted orally.

- The use of vocables (syllables with no clear linguistic meaning) was common in the singing of many Native American cultures.

- Traditional Native American instruments included drums, rattles, stringed instruments, and the Plains-style flute, which became popular and crossed over into other genres.

- Powwows evolved into intertribal celebrations including music, dance, food, arts and crafts, and fun. Central themes were honor, respect, generosity, unity, and friendship. Musical groups known as powwow drums proliferated as a way of preserving and developing Native musical traditions.

- Many great American popular music artists shared a Native American heritage, including rocker Jimi Hendrix, country singer/songwriter Hank Williams, early blues legend Charley Patton, rock guitarist/songwriter Robbie Robertson, and folk singer/songwriter Buffy Sainte-Marie.

- The development of Native American public radio beginning in 1972 served as a catalyst for contemporary Native American music.

- A new genre called contemporary Native American music emerged in the late 1980s, as prominent Native rock and folk artists began to examine their heritage. By the early 2000s, the genre was flavored by folk, country, rock, new age, hip-hop, reggae, and R & B styles.

- The Native American music recording industry supported the emergence of contemporary Native American music with over fifty independent Native American record labels.

Key Terms

cedar flute	grass dance	vocables
chicken scratch	indigenous	*waila*
cultural genocide	*Kokopelli*	
First Nations	powwow	

Study and Discussion Questions

1. How did 500 years of repression affect the development of Native American musical traditions?

2. What instruments are commonly found in traditional Native American music?

3. What were some major functions of traditional Native American music?

4. What are the origins and contemporary functions of the intertribal powwow?

5. Can you identify several influential mainstream pop artists of Native heritage? Discuss the possible influences of this heritage on their music.

6. How did contemporary Native American music develop?

7. What role did the cedar flute play in building contemporary Native music?

8. What role did radio play in the development of an audience for contemporary Native music?

Notes

1. Bryan Burton, *Moving within the Circle: Contemporary Native American Music and Dance* (Danbury, CT: World Music Press, 1993), 22.

2. Interview with the authors.

3. Interview with the authors.

4. Interview with the authors.

5. Interview with the authors.

6. Interview with the authors.

7. Interview with the authors.

8. R. Carlos Nakai, James DeMars, and David P. McAllester, *The Art of the Native American Flute* (Phoenix, AZ: Canyon Records Productions, 1997), 113.

9. Interview with the authors.

10. Interview with the authors.

11. John Trudell website, http://www.johntrudell.com/.

12. Interview with the authors.

13. Interview with the authors.

1840 - 2000

1848 End of Mexican War; Southwest annexed by U.S.

1849 California gold rush; the first Chinese arrive in California to work in gold fields, beginning a 150-year pattern of Asian immigration

Mid-1800s Asian musicians perform within ethnic communities ♪

1861–1865 Civil War

1870 The Chinese population in U.S. reaches 63,000

1882 The Chinese Exclusion Act is passed, limiting further immigration by Chinese to the U.S.

1897 Hawaii is annexed by the U.S.

1898 Spanish-American War; Philippines becomes U.S. colony at conclusion of war

1900–1920 The Japanese American population grows

1902 The Philippine Constabulary forms a brass band, bringing a new American popular style to the Philippines

1914–1918 World War I

1920s–1930s Filipino immigration grows

1924 Immigration Act of 1924 cuts off Asian immigration

1929–1930s Great Depression; New Deal begins

1930s Hawaiian music is popularized in Hollywood films; steel guitar crosses over from Hawaiian to country music ♪

1941–1945 U.S. participates in World War II

1942 Over 120,000 Japanese Americans incarcerated

1942–1944 Nisei swing bands form in internment camps ♪

1946 The Philippines gain independence from the U.S.

1950–1953 Korean War

1950s *Flower Drum Song,* a Rodgers and Hammerstein musical set in a Chinese community, is popular on stage and film ♪

1954 School segregation outlawed; civil rights movement begins

1959 Cuban Revolution; Alaska and Hawaii become states

1961 President John Kennedy inaugurated; Peace Corps established

1963 Civil rights march on Washington; John Kennedy assassinated

1964–1973 Vietnam War

1965 New immigration law expands Asian immigration

1968–1970 The Asian American civil rights movement begins, fueling socially informed artistic developments ♪

1968 Martin Luther King and Robert Kennedy assassinated

1970s The "Hawaiian Renaissance" begins, fueling an indigenous rights movement and new musical creativity ♪

1972 Karaoke first appears in Japan ♪

1975 South Vietnamese government in Saigon falls; refugee migration begins

1979 U.S. establishes diplomatic relations with China

1990s American economic high-tech "bubble"

1992 Los Angeles riots/uprising following Rodney King trial

2000 Census shows Asians as rapidly growing, diverse population group

2001 9/11 terrorist attacks

2001 Founder of U.S. taiko drum movement receives National Endowment for the Arts award ♪

2002 Yo-Yo Ma's *Silk Road Project* presented nationally, a successful hybrid of Asian classical and folk styles ♪

2004 Jin becomes the first Asian hip-hop artist to record with a major label ♪

| 1840 | 1860 | 1880 | 1900 | 1920 | 1940 | 1960 | 1980 | 2000 |

Chapter 11

Asian and Pacific American Popular Musics

The contributions of Asian and Pacific Americans to American popular music have not always been widely visible, although their work in classical music has been somewhat more prominent.[1] Census figures show that Asians in the United States numbered over ten million in 2000, an increase of almost 50 percent from 1990, making them one of the fastest-growing populations in the country. As Asian American communities became established in the country, they drew on unique cultural traditions to create new popular music hybrids. We begin with an examination of the history of Asian immigration, followed by summaries of Chinese American, Japanese American, Filipino American, South Asian American, Vietnamese American, and Hawaiian contributions to American popular music.

ASIAN IMMIGRATION TO THE UNITED STATES

Asian immigration to the United States began over 150 years ago, so that by the start of the twenty-first century, Asian American communities had formed a complex array of hybrid cultures. The United States saw two major waves of Asian immigration: The first took place as approximately one million people of Asian origin entered the country between the California gold rush of 1849 and the Immigration Act of 1924; the second came after 1965, when the government eased discriminatory immigration restrictions.

The first Asians who came to the United States in substantial numbers were Chinese. By 1870 they numbered over 60,000, working in the gold fields, building major portions of the transcontinental railroad, and developing the infrastructure of the West. However, at the end of the nineteenth century, Congress passed a series of discriminatory laws to limit Chinese immigration. Consequently, other groups were imported up until 1924 to fill labor needs—Japanese, Koreans, Filipinos, Indians, and finally Mexicans. By the turn of the century, the Japanese American population had surpassed that of the Chinese. The Immigration Act of 1924 prevented most further Asian immigration, while still allowing the entrance of large numbers of European immigrants. Later, World War II precipitated a series of racially biased events when President Franklin

Roosevelt signed Executive Order 9066 in 1942, forcing the removal and detention of over 120,000 people of Japanese descent, two-thirds of whom were American citizens, to relocation camps in desolate locations.

The country's racialized immigration policy was redressed in 1965 when the Immigration and Nationality Reform Act set equitable annual quotas for every country in the world. The infusion of new arrivals transformed Asian immigrant communities around the country. South Asian immigration to the United States, which had experienced a modest first wave from 1907 to 1924, saw a much larger wave in the 1980s and 1990s. By 2000 the population had reached 1.7 million, concentrated mainly in California and New York.[2] In 1975, with the fall of Saigon and the end of the Vietnam War, large numbers of Southeast Asian refugees began to arrive in the United States. Initially dispersed throughout the country by government resettlement policies, they often regrouped through secondary migration in specific geographical locations to form vibrant communities.

Chinese American rapper Jin Auyeung, also known as Jin MC.

© Evan Agostini/Getty Images

CHINESE AMERICAN INFLUENCES

Chinese American communities reflected many differences, determined by dialect, region, area of origin, and socioeconomic class. A rapid increase in Chinese immigration in the last few decades of the twentieth century led to the expansion of Chinese-language mass media in the United States. Media developments in Hong Kong, Taiwan, and China also influenced this growth by disseminating Asian pop, Chinese film music, Western classical music, opera from different regions of China, and Chinese classical music.

Chinese classical music and opera groups had long histories in the Chinese communities of New York City, San Francisco, and Los Angeles; in 1852 a company of 120 performers presented in San Francisco one of the earliest Cantonese opera performances in the United States. Performing groups generally concentrated on one genre, such as Cantonese opera, Beijing opera, or Chinese classical music. They employed traditional Chinese instruments such as the *guzheng* (Chinese zither), *er hu* (two-string violin), *pipa* (lute), *yangquin* (dulcimer), *sheng* (bamboo mouth organ), and *dizi* (flute), as well as Chinese drums, gongs, bells, and cymbals.

More recently, many other forms of music also became popular in America's Chinese communities, including hip-hop, R & B, jazz, classical, and rock. An Asian American record label called AARising formed in 1990 to promote diverse pop music sounds performed by Chinese American and other Asian American artists. The success of the film *Crouching Tiger, Hidden Dragon* in 2001 brought the Oscar-winning soundtrack of Chinese composer Tan Dun to the mainstream. In addition, cellist Yo-Yo Ma's *Silk Road Project* in 2002 presented a successful hybrid of popular, classical, and folk styles of Eastern and Central Asia. Rock musician and performance artist Bertrand Wang performed in the New York area with his band, Yellow Peril, and New York–based Chinese American rapper Jin Auyeung set a milestone in popular music by becoming the first Asian American MC to release a hip-hop album on a major label when Virgin issued *The Rest Is History* in 2004. According to critic Jeff Chang,

> Jin does present something wholly new, not just in American but also global pop: an unapologetically working-class, second-generation kid flowing in Cantonese and New York–inflected Ebonics with the same fluency. He's no pricey Hong Kong import, no sexless high-kicking martial arts expert in yellowface.[3]

Pop musics from Hong Kong, Taiwan, China, and Japan also became popular in Chinese American communities, as did karaoke. Many Chinese Americans also participated in free jazz and pan-Asian musical activities, including pianist/composer Jon Jang, saxophonist/composer Fred Ho, and saxophonist/flutist Francis Wong. Trumpeter Robbie Kwock and pianist Murray Lowe were both respected players in straight-ahead and Latin jazz. Vocalist/pianist Magdalen Hsu-Li was active in free jazz circles and as an alternative singer/songwriter.

Internet Listening Exercise

Listen to samples of popular work by Chinese and Chinese American artists.

Various Artists: *Classical Chinese Folk Music*

Yo-Yo Ma/Silk Road Ensemble: *Silk Road Journeys—When Strangers Meet*

Magdalen Hsu-Li: *Evolution*

Jin MC: *The Rest Is History*

JAPANESE AMERICAN INFLUENCES

From the early part of the twentieth century, people in Japanese American communities showed an interest in Japanese traditional music as well as American popular music. In the 1930s, **nisei** (second-generation Japanese American) youths formed numerous swing dance bands, and some of these musicians took American dance music back to Japan. There they blended it with traditional Japanese folk songs to contribute to a new form of Japanese popular song called *kayokyoku,* which is still widely heard in Japan.

After the Pearl Harbor attack, the U.S. government brought over 120,000 people of Japanese descent, most of whom were American citizens, to **internment camps,** where they spent the rest of the war held against their will in guarded compounds. Swing bands swiftly sprang up in the camps as the music of choice. Formed by youthful nisei musicians, the bands at various camps took such creative names as the Jive Bombers (Manzanar Detention Camp), the Music Makers (Poston Detention Camp #1), or the Starlight Serenaders (Gila River Detention Camp). Despite the psychological impact of their incarceration, the nisei musicians expressed themselves and their multicultural identities through jazz. Percussionist Anthony Brown's Asian American Orchestra premiered and

Courtesy of George Yoshida

The Music Makers, a Japanese American dance band from the Poston Detention Camp (1943). Left to right: Frank Oshima, Tug Tamaru, George Yoshida, Paul Matsuda, and Yuki Miyamoto.

Internet Listening Exercise

Listen to the samples of work by Japanese American artists.

Anthony Brown's Asian American Orchestra: *Big Bands behind Barbed Wire*

Pat Suzuki: *The Very Best of Pat Suzuki*

Hiroshima: *Hiroshima*

Kitaro: *Best of Kitaro, Volume 2*

Akira Tana/Rufus Reid: *Back to Front*

Toshiko Akiyoshi: *Remembering Bud—Cleopatra's Dream*

Linkin Park: *Hybrid Theory*

performed a Grammy-nominated work for large ensemble called *Big Bands Behind Barbed Wire* in the early 2000s, which memorialized the music of the internment camps.

Several Japanese American female vocalists enjoyed successful postwar jazz or pop careers, including Ethel Azama and Pat Suzuki, the latter of whom starred in Rodgers and Hammerstein's musical *Flower Drum Song* in the late 1950s. Although stereotypical by today's standards, the musical used Asian artists rather than white actors with "Asian" makeup. Rewritten by playwright David Henry Hwang, the work opened again on Broadway in 2002 with an all-Asian cast featuring Filipina vocalist/actress Lea Salonga in a lead role.

Japanese American artists worked in diverse genres of American popular music in the latter part of the twentieth century. Beginning in the 1970s, June Kuramoto and the jazz group Hiroshima played a smooth style of jazz fusion with overtones of the **koto,** a classical Japanese stringed instrument. Japanese musicians such as Ryuichi Sakamoto and Kitaro also became popular in the 1970s and 1980s, marketed as new age artists. ***Taiko* drumming,** a traditional form of drum-based Japanese folk music, developed a following; in 2001 the National Endowment for the Arts honored Seiichi Tanaka, the founder of the U.S. *taiko* movement. Many Japanese Americans such as bassist/composer Mark Izu, pianist Glenn Horiuchi, and bassist Tatsuo Aoki were active in free jazz and pan-Asian musical activities, and Japanese American musicians involved in mainstream jazz included drummer Akira Tana, pianist Kei Akagi, guitarist

David Yamazaki, trumpeter John Worley, and bassist John Wiitala. Many native Japanese musicians also succeeded in jazz, including pianist/composer Toshiko Akiyoshi, trumpeter Terumasa Hino, saxophonist Sadao Watanabe, and trumpeter Shunzo Ono. In the alternative rock world, the multiplatinum, Grammy-winning, nu-metal group Linkin Park featured Mike Shinoda as MC/vocalist, keyboardist, and guitarist, making him one of the most prominent Asian Americans in American pop.

FILIPINO AMERICAN INFLUENCES

The indigenous traditions of the Philippines and its colonial history as a Spanish and U.S. colony shaped a hybrid musical and cultural heritage. Musical traditions in the Philippines ranged from traditional indigenous folk music and dance to orchestras, brass bands, pop, rock, R & B, and hip-hop. The great nineteenth-century Filipino patriot and national hero, José Rizal, authored numerous song lyrics in addition to his better-known work as a novelist and poet. Filipino folk music prior to the Spanish occupation included love songs, planting songs, work songs, war songs, and funeral songs, as well as the traditional indigenous drum-based music of Mindanao called **kulintang,** which showed a resurgence in the contemporary Filipino American community in the twentieth century. Spanish influences in the Philippines showed in dances such as the fandango, paso doble, tango, and habanera and in guitar string bands called *rondalla*. With American occupation at the end of the nineteenth century came a rich brass band tradition, resulting in the formation of the respected Philippine Constabulary Band in 1902. American colonialism later brought other popular American musical styles as well. For example, in the 1920s, early Filipino immigrant farm workers in the United States enjoyed American popular music, and when they had time off from their work in the fields, they went to dancehalls where bands such as the "Manila Serenaders," an eighteen-piece dance orchestra, played jazz and popular music.

Although a rich tradition of Filipino protest music had long expressed opposition to the country's long series of colonial occupiers, the country's music—often sung in English—did not always express a clear Filipino cultural identity. The **Pinoy** (slang for Filipino) song movement in the country during the 1970s and 1980s, a blend of rock, folk, and ballads sung in the Tagalog (Pilipino) language, represented a conscious attempt to create a Filipino national and popular culture and was promoted by

Contemporary Filipina vocalist/actress Lea Salonga.

© Jamie Painter Young/CORBIS

Internet Listening Exercise

Listen to samples of a range of music by Filipino and Filipino American artists.

Kulintang Ensemble: *Kulintang*

Freddie Aguilar: "Anak," "Pinoy"

Lea Salonga: "I Have Dreamed," "A Whole New World"

Bobby Enriquez: *The Wildman Returns*

Jocelyn Enriquez: "A Little Bit of Ecstasy"

Neal McCoy: *Neal McCoy Super Hits*

Susie Ibarra: *Flower after Flower*

CD LISTENING EXERCISE

CD 2/3

Listen to "Razor Blade Alcohol Slide" by DJ Q-Bert. How does the piece blend various sounds into a complex musical collage? Compare the sound of this with other DJ music you have heard. What stands out about DJ Q-Bert's work?

such artists as Freddie Aguilar. Nonetheless, American popular culture continued to influence Filipino music.

Many artists of Filipino origin succeeded in diverse genres of American popular music. Vocalist Lea Salonga starred on Broadway in *Miss Saigon, Les Misérables,* and a revival of *Flower Drum Song.* She also sang on several Disney film soundtracks *(Aladdin, Mulan, Lion King).* Country music superstar Neal McCoy, the Texas-born son of Irish and Filipino parents, had a *Billboard* top ten album of the year in 1995 and was named Country Music Entertainer of the Year in the late 1990s. Numerous Filipino American musicians became successful jazz artists. Pianist Bobby Enriquez—known as the "Madman from Mindanao"—was a well-regarded mainstream jazz player, as was Louis Armstrong's longtime drummer, Danny Barcelona. Pianists Flip Nuñez and Rudy Tenio were West Coast jazz players who served as role models for other Asian American musicians, and saxophonist/flutist Melecio Magdaluyo found success in the jazz, Latin, and pop music worlds. Percussionist Susie Ibarra made a name in the New York free jazz scene, and Latin percussionist Jimmy Biala excelled in salsa and avant garde jazz. Pop artists with strong careers in both the United States and the Philippines included dance pop vocalist Jocelyn Enriquez, female vocal group Pinay, and male hip-hop group Kai. Filipino Americans also helped lead the turntablism movement. **Turntablism** is a technique in which DJs use multiple turntables and various audio effects to blend snippets of sound from existing vinyl records to create new music. Three of the members of the first influential turntablist group, Invisbl Skratch Piklz—DJ Q-Bert (Richard Quitevis), DJ Apollo (Apollo Novicio), and Shortkut (Jon Cruz)—were Filipino Americans.

SOUTH ASIAN AMERICAN INFLUENCES

The South Asian diaspora grew largely out of the nineteenth-century British system of indenture, which sent contracted workers throughout the world from the region that now comprises India, Pakistan, and neighboring countries. Today, South Asians remain geographically dispersed but are linked through the cultural flow of mass media. By the mid-1990s, South Asian cultural elements had begun to enter U.S. pop culture as appropriations, including the *mehndi* hand designs using henna that were popularized by dance pop vocalist Madonna, as well as the elaborate *bindi* forehead ornaments worn by both Madonna and vocalist Gwen Stefani of No Doubt. In addition, two major forms of South Asian music—**Bollywood** (Bombay + Hollywood) film music and North Indian **bhangra** music—inspired many Western pop artists at the turn of the twenty-first century. A prominent example of this was "Beware of the Boys *(Mundian to Bach Ke)*" in 2003, a remix by rapper Jay-Z of a bhangra piece originally by Panjabi MC (Rajinder Rai). The primary sound of bhangra, the traditional form of Punjabi (North Indian) music, comes from the heavy, resounding beat of a double-barreled drum called the *dhol,* accompanied by smaller *tumbi* drums and Punjabi lyrics. According to Panjabi MC,

> It is a fusion of all different styles. Bhangra is like the Indian form of hip-hop because while it started brewing in the U.K., hip-hop started in New York. There are a lot of cultural references in both forms of music.[4]

As early as the 1970s, Beatle George Harrison and other Western artists incorporated Indian instruments and rhythms into their music. The market for such fusion grew because of a flourishing Western interest in world music and the crossover success of classical artists such as Indian sitarist Ravi Shankar and Pakistani vocalist Nusrat Fateh Ali Khan. Beginning in the late 1990s, Algerian-born, San Francisco–based turntablist DJ Cheb I Sabbah produced a series of cult classics that mixed classical and sacred South Asian music over dance beats. Other non-Asian rappers before Jay-Z also experimented with Indian music, including hip-hop producer Timbaland, who used samples of the classical Indian tabla and *tumbi* drums on Missy Elliot's 2001 hit "Get Ur Freak On," and several others. **Tabla** drums consist of a pair of tuned drums played with both hands. The 2004 Britney Spears tune "I'm a Slave for You" also lifted South Asian musical elements, as did the Hollywood film *The Guru.* Popular films such as *Bend It Like Beckham* and *Monsoon Wedding* promoted bhangra with appealing soundtracks. A musical called *Bombay Dreams* also arrived on Broadway in 2004, and nightclubs in New York, Los Angeles, and San Francisco for one night a month became "Bollywood discos" or held "bhangra nights."

Panjabi MC was not the only South Asian artist experimenting with dance music hybridization. Before him, a genre arose known as "Asian Underground" (also called "Asian Massive"), the work of a collective of British and American South Asian DJs and musicians in the mid-1990s. Talvin Singh, a classically trained tabla player, along with other artists such as DJ/tabla player Karsh Kale, popularized the fusion of classical Indian music with modern electronica. One popular club in San Francisco held a monthly *Dhamaal* ("ruckus") night that meshed Hindustani classical music on one floor and a modern fusion of traditional and electronic music and turntablism on another. The L.A.-based South Asian hip-hop group Karmacy rapped in Punjabi, Gujarati, and English.

Internet Listening Exercise

Listen to samples of a variety of South Asian musics and hybrids.

Ravi Shankar: *Full Circle—Carnegie Hall 2000*

Nusrat Fateh Ali Khan: *The Final Studio Recordings*

Panjabi MC: "Beware of the Boys (Mundian to Bach Ke)" and "Beware (Jay-Z remix)"

Missy Elliot: "Get Ur Freak On"

DJ Cheb I Sabbah: *Krishna Lila*

Karmacy: *The Movement*

Karsh Kale: *Liberation*

Various Artists: *Bend It Like Beckham* soundtrack

Various Artists: *Monsoon Wedding* soundtrack

VIETNAMESE AMERICAN INFLUENCES

With the fall of Saigon in 1975, the Vietnam War ended and a mass exodus began, resulting in the rapid growth of Vietnamese expatriate communities in the United States, France, Australia, Canada, and elsewhere. Ethnomusicologist Adelaida Reyes argues that the melancholic sense of loss of the refugee experience influenced the character of Vietnamese American popular music.[5] The production of much Vietnamese American music and other electronic media centered near Los Angeles in an area called "Little Saigon," concentrating a large number of Vietnam's best-known musicians in one place. Although numerous styles of Vietnamese music existed, two genres predominated in the United States: *tan nhac* (modern, Westernized music—by far the most popular) and *dan ca* (folk songs).

Tan nhac first emerged in Vietnam in 1938 as a result of French colonialism. It featured tango, cha-cha, bolero, and paso doble dance rhythms as well as Vietnamese scales and folk traditions, to which electric guitars and synthesizers were later added. The *tan nhac* played in the United States reflected multiple patterns: nostalgia for Vietnam, resistance and struggle for the reconquest of the country, descriptions of prisoners' lives in Vietnam, versions of music from Hong Kong and Taiwanese films with Vietnamese lyrics, and new pop music developed in Vietnam.

Among the best-known Vietnamese pop singers living outside of Vietnam were Khánh Ly, who performed worldwide for expatriate Vietnamese communities, as well as Huong Lan and Thanh Hà. After the thawing of U.S.-Vietnamese diplomatic relations in the 1990s, new artists from Vietnam such as Thanh Lam and Phuong Thanh also gained popularity. Several Vietnamese artists crossed over and established careers in other fields of popular music—jazz in particular. Jazz guitarist Nguyen Le, for example, developed his *Tales From Vietnam* project in 1996, a melding of jazz, Vietnamese traditional song, ancient instruments, and electronic sampling. Bassist Chris Minh Doky became sought after in contemporary jazz circles, playing with top artists such as saxophonist Michael Brecker, pianist Bill Evans, guitarist John Scofield, and vocalist Dianne Reeves. Numerous young Vietnamese American hip-hop artists also emerged, and Vietnam-based pop music increasingly integrated elements of R & B and hip-hop during the early 2000s.

**Internet
Listening Exercise**

Listen to samples of music of the Vietnamese diaspora.

Various Artists: *The Music of Vietnam*

Next, go to http://www.vn-style .com/Music/index.html and listen to samples by various Vietnamese pop artists.

Nguyen Le: *Tales from Vietnam*

Chris Minh Doky: *Minh*

Azn Pride: "Got Rice"

PAN-ASIAN MUSICAL TRENDS

Two musical trends cut across multiple Asian American cultures in the late twentieth century: karaoke and the Asian American jazz movement. Karaoke was a form of participatory musical entertainment practiced in clubs, restaurants, or homes, and the Asian American jazz movement was a hybrid of jazz and traditional Asian styles that became a new creative force in the jazz world.

Karaoke

The term **karaoke** was derived from *kara* (Japanese word meaning "empty") and *oke* (abbreviation of the Japanese pronunciation of the English word *orchestra*). The word came to mean either a place or a machine that allowed users to sing with prerecorded musical accompaniment. Karaoke first appeared in Japan in 1972, and the first eight-track tape karaoke machine came on the market in 1976, subsequently evolving into sophisticated digital systems for home and commercial use. Karaoke is popular worldwide—particularly in Asia—as well as in U.S. Asian American communities. This trend is significant for at least two reasons. First, it provides a unique form of social and community support for many Asian immigrants; they use it as a way to reinforce memories of the past and a sense of community through musical expression. Second, it enables the general public to perform, reclaiming mass media and making it their own through the insertion of their own cultural voices over a prerecorded background. According to ethnomusicologist Deborah Wong, "Karaoke takes the very notions of live and canned and messes them up, rendering them ambiguous."[6]

Asian American Jazz/Creative Music Movement

A political/cultural movement called **Asian American jazz/creative music** was initiated in the 1970s by Asian American musicians to promote an agenda of self-determination and artistic expression. The initiative grew out of the Asian American political movement of the late 1960s. According to pianist/composer Jon Jang, "It was a shedding of silence and an affirmation of identity."[7] Multidisciplinary, community-based Asian American arts groups appeared as a key element of the broader political movement, and artists from a wide variety of disciplines—including music—began for the first time to identify themselves as Asian Americans. They grounded their art in their developing ethnic and political consciousness. Influenced in part by the Association for the Advancement of Creative Music (AACM) in Chicago and the Black Artists' Group (BAG), their work centered on self reliance. According to Jang, "The philosophy was that this music was contributive and not competitive, and it was coming out of our community."[8] The first wave of the movement included baritone saxophonist Gerald Oshita, alto saxophonist Russell Baba, bassist Mark Izu, and pianist Paul Yamazaki.

The movement grew in strength in the 1980s. The Asian American Jazz Festival began in 1982, and in the same year Paul Yamada, Jon Jang, and Francis Wong founded Asian Improv Records as a nonprofit label to provide a venue for Asian American artists to produce their own records. The founding of Asian Improv aRts followed in 1987 as a nonprofit arts organization, supporting a newsletter, symposia, performances, and the record label. Jang also formed the Pan Asian Arkestra, which performed widely through the 1980s and early 1990s, and percussionist Anthony Brown formed the Asian American Orchestra, a large jazz ensemble, in 1998.

The work of Asian American artists associated with the Asian American jazz/creative music movement continues to evolve. While these musicians shy away from categorization, preferring to call their music "creative music," musicologist Deborah Wong has described it as "new music with a strong base in African American jazz."[9] By no means do they represent all Asian American jazz artists, yet they signify a conscious attempt to recast the traditional black–white racial dynamic of American jazz and popular music, in order to express a

Internet Listening Exercise

Listen to samples of contemporary Asian American creative music.

Jon Jang: *Self Portrait*

Fred Ho: *Once upon a Time in Chinese America*

Various Artists: *Sounds Like 1996 —Music by Asian American Artists*

Multicultural Note

Who Speaks for a Culture?

The use of the term *Asian American* to describe an arts movement could be mis-interpreted as a claim to represent all artists of that ethnicity, although that was not the intent of the artists who pioneered this movement. Who speaks on behalf of a cultural group?

U.S. culture tends to support an oversimplified view of identity. For example, when Dr. Martin Luther King, Jr., was alive, he was often identified in the public media as "the leader of Black America." After his passing, periodic media reports speculated on who "the new leader" would be. Cultural identity and representation are a good deal more complex than this. We all inhabit multiple identities, and respecting dif-ference without presuming that someone from a particular heritage "speaks for" all others of that heritage is an important goal.

unique Asian American musical voice. As trumpeter Robbie Kwock puts it, "They wanted to have something that they could call their own, and develop music around their political views." [10] The diverse musics now emerging from this movement have not achieved great commercial success—their performing venues are mostly colleges, cultural centers, festivals, and occasional nightclubs. The music, however, has had an impact on Asian American communities.

POPULAR MUSIC IN HAWAII

Hawaiian popular music evolved from a strong indigenous musical tradition. Although it was initially commodified by Hollywood and the music industry be-ginning in the 1920s and 1930s, Hawaiian music became far more than stereo-typed images of aloha shirts, ukuleles, and leis. The period from 1930 to 1960 was a "golden age" of Hawaiian music, characterized by big band interpretations of Hawaiian songs played in Waikiki ballrooms and performers such as the leg-endary Don Ho. The 1970s saw the emergence of the "Hawaiian Renaissance," an indigenous rights movement that contributed to the development of a vari-ety of local, roots-based musics. The last two decades of the twentieth century saw the development of the reggae-influenced Jawaiian style. Today an active Hawaiian entertainment and recording industry produces traditional Hawaiian music as well as a variety of contemporary Hawaiian popular styles. Hawaii also has its own version of the Grammy awards called the *Hoku* (Stars of Distinction) Awards.

Hawaiian Instruments and Instrumental Innovations

Music has long played an integral role in Hawaiian culture. Traditional Hawaiian music combined rich vocal harmonies with percussion, winds, and a bowed stringed instrument called the *ukeke*. Percussion included drums, gourds, sticks, rattles, and tubes; winds included nose flutes, whistles, and conch shells. There were several varieties of vocal music. One was called *oli*, a solo form of chant. Another more well-known form was the *mele hula*, a choral chant or song accompanied by dance, drama, and instrumental performance. From these a variety of **hulas** evolved that served a range of cultural purposes. Beginning with the Hawaiian Renaissance of the 1970s, a resurgence of native Hawaiian identity led to the preservation and development of integrated hula performance.

As Hawaiian music evolved in the twentieth century, several instrumental innovations emerged that interacted with other genres of American popular music and helped give Hawaiian music its unique flavor. The **ukulele** is a small, stringed instrument derived from the Portuguese *braguinha*, first introduced in 1879 by Portuguese sugar cane workers. The ukulele quickly grew popular among Hawaiians and became a central part of their music. **Slack key guitar** is a Hawaiian finger-picked guitar style with "slacked" (alternately tuned) strings that create unique intervals different from those usually used on the guitar. The style first developed when a Hawaiian king hired Spanish cowboys (*paniolos*) from California to come to Hawaii in the 1830s to help herd cattle. The cowboys brought the guitar with them and taught Spanish and Mexican guitar styles to the Hawaiians. Important Hawaiian slack key artists included Gabby Pahinui, Cyril Pahinui, and Keola Beamer.

Steel guitar, a style of guitar playing invented in Hawaii in the 1890s, involved the movement of a straight metal edge along the fingerboard of a guitar to produce a sliding sound. As we saw in Chapter 7, the style influenced early delta blues and was later electrified to become popular in country music starting in the 1940s. The steel guitar was invented in 1885 by Joseph Kehuku, who was widely popular in Hawaii, the United States, and Europe, touring, teaching, and popularizing the instrument. Sol Ho'opi'i, the "King of the Steel Guitar," brought the steel guitar to Hollywood in the 1930s when the film industry experienced a brief fad for things Hawaiian. By the 1940s, the instrument had evolved into its two modern configurations: the lap steel guitar and the pedal steel guitar. The former was preferred in Hawaiian music; the latter in country music. Both versions of the instrument, however, shared the unique sliding metallic sound that captured the attention of listeners and made it a signature sound of Hawaiian and country music.

Hawaiian Musical Styles

Hawaiian music falls into five broad, often overlapping categories. *Hula ku'i* refers to traditional indigenous Hawaiian language songs with a series of stanzas, generally intended for performance as hula. *Mele Hawai'i* were Hawaiian language songs modeled on alternating verse-chorus formats used in Hawaiian

© 1998 Mountain Apple Company Hawai'i/Big Boy Records. Album cover: IZ: The Man and His Music—In Concert. Artist: Israel "IZ" Kamakawiwo'ole.

CD LISTENING EXERCISE

CD 2/4

Listen to Israel Kamakawiwo'ole, also known as "IZ," performing "Hawai'i 78." This contemporary song reflects some of the sentiments of the Hawaiian native rights movement. The simple, almost chantlike melodic style accompanied by the ukulele reflects earlier traditional music. Iz was a member of the famed Makaha Sons and one of the musical leaders of the indigenous rights movement until his death in 1997.

Contemporary Hawaiian musician Israel (IZ) Kamakawiwo'ole.

Internet Listening Exercise

Listen to samples of various Hawaiian styles.

Jack De Mello: *Music of Hawai'i*

Don Ho: *Greatest Hits*

Gabby Pahinui: *Gabby*

Keola and Kapono Beamer: *Honolulu City Lights*

The Sunday Manoa: *Guava Jam*

Keali'i Reichel: *Kawaipunahele*

Israel Kamakawiwo'ole: *Facing Future*

Various Artists: *Island Warriors*

Christian hymns. *Hapa haole* (half-white) songs were tunes written in English about Hawaii, usually in 32-bar standard American popular song form, popular in tourist shows and movies in the mid-twentieth century. Traditional Hawaiian music experienced a resurgence beginning in the 1970s with the Hawaiian Renaissance. The same decade saw the growth of a fourth category, an "island contemporary sound," which integrated soft rock and Hawaiian traditional sounds, often blending Hawaiian and English. Finally, reggae hit the islands in the 1980s and 1990s, and a local interpretation known as **Jawaiian** music became popular, causing many formerly acoustic groups to add drums, electric guitar, and electric bass.

A poll in the early 2000s listed the following musicians as most influential on contemporary Hawaiian music: slack key guitarist Gabby Pahinui, traditional/contemporary vocal group the Brothers Cazimero, traditional/contemporary vocalist Keali'i Reichel, traditional/contemporary vocal group the Makaha Sons, and vocalist Israel Kamakawiwo'ole.

Chapter Summary

- Because Asian Americans comprise a range of distinct cultures, including Americans of Chinese, Japanese, Korean, Filipino, Southeast Asian, and South Asian origin, generalizing about such a diverse group is difficult.

Each culture has faced discrimination, yet many musical traditions have survived and blended to form new hybrids.

- The first Asian immigrants to the United States were Chinese, who arrived during the gold rush of the mid-nineteenth century. Traditional music and opera groups performed in the largest Chinese settlements, and many Chinese Americans later became active in jazz, pan-Asian music, and hip-hop.

- Although incarcerated during World War II, young Japanese Americans embraced the swing era and formed big bands. Contemporary jazz and pop music later saw a growing number of Japanese and Japanese American musicians rise to prominence. *Taiko* drumming and karaoke also grew popular.

- Filipino American music was a hybrid of indigenous, Spanish, and American influences. Numerous well-known jazz musicians emerged from the Filipino community, as did stars of Broadway, R & B, country, and the emerging art of DJ turntablism.

- South Asian American musics appeared mostly in Bollywood film scores and bhangra, a drum-driven North Indian folk dance rhythm that found its way into dance clubs and hip-hop samples.

- Vietnamese American communities favored a hybrid pop style called *tan nhac*, often flavored with nostalgia for Vietnam. Younger Vietnamese Americans also developed careers in jazz and hip-hop.

- The Asian American jazz/creative music movement was an important force in the affirmation of Asian American art and culture.

- Hawaiian music made significant contributions to important mainstream styles, such as blues and country music, through the development of the slack key and steel guitars. In the late twentieth century, the Hawaiian indigenous rights movement led to the development of multiple contemporary Hawaiian popular styles.

Key Terms

Asian American jazz/ creative music	*kulintang*
bhangra	nisei
Bollywood	*Pinoy*
dhol	slack key guitar
hula	tabla
internment camps	*taiko* drumming
Jawaiian	*tan nhac*
karaoke	*tumbi*
koto	turntablism
	ukulele

Study and Discussion Questions

1. How did U.S. immigration policies affect the development of Asian American communities and their music?

2. How and why did Japanese swing bands arise during World War II?

3. What various musical styles developed in Chinese American, Japanese American, Filipino American, South Asian American, and Vietnamese American communities?

4. What was karaoke, and what accounted for its popularity?

5. What was the significance of the Asian American jazz/creative music movement?

7. How did the Vietnamese American musical experience differ from that of some other Asian American communities?

8. What were some major Hawaiian musical instruments and stylistic innovations?

Notes

1. The term *Asian American*, by which we mean Americans of Chinese, Japanese, Korean, Filipino, Southeast Asian, or South Asian origin, developed out of the Asian American political movement beginning in the late 1960s. Although generalizing about such a diverse group is difficult, the term is widely used in communities and academia; thus, we use it here. The term *Asian and Pacific American*, implying descent from Asia or the Pacific islands, is also widely used and appears in this chapter when appropriate.

2. The term *South Asian* implies descent from the nations of India, Pakistan, Bangladesh, Sri Lanka, Afghanistan, Nepal, or Bhutan.

3. Jeff Chang, "Look at Me: Chinese American Rapper Jin Attacks Invisibility," *San Francisco Bay Guardian* 39 (No. 3, October 20–October 26, 2004), http://www.sfbg.com/39/03/art_music_jin.html.

4. "Panjabi MC: The Bhangra Crossover Master," http://www.vibe.com/modules.php?op=modload&name=News&file=article&sid=100.

5. Adelaida Reyes, *Songs of the Caged, Songs of the Free: Music and the Vietnamese Refugee Experience* (Philadelphia: Temple University Press, 1999).

6. Deborah Wong, "I Want the Microphone: Mass Mediation and Agency in Asian-American Popular Music," *TDR—The Drama Review—A Journal of Performance Studies* 38 (No. 3, 1993): 152–67.

7. Interview with the authors.

8. Interview with the authors.

9. Deborah Wong, "Just Being There: Making Asian American Space in the Recording Industry," in *Musics of Multicultural America: A Study of Twelve Musical Communities,* edited by Kip Lornell and Anne K. Rasmussen (New York: Schirmer, 1997), 301.

10. Interview with the authors.

1940 - 2000

Early 1940s The seeds of bebop are planted ♪
1941–1945 U.S. participates in World War II
1942 Record industry strike prevents the recording of early bebop ♪
1945 Classic bebop recordings by Charlie Parker and Dizzy Gillespie become models for the style ♪
1945 Swing ends its reign as the country's most popular music ♪
1945 52nd Street in New York becomes center of the jazz world ♪
1947 Dizzy Gillespie and Chano Pozo record groundbreaking Latin jazz ♪
1949 *Birth of the Cool* sessions led by trumpeter Miles Davis signal the birth of cool jazz ♪

1950–1953 Korean War
1951 Pianist Dave Brubeck forms his first quartet; West Coast cool is born ♪
1954 School segregation outlawed; civil rights movement begins
1954 Hard-bop trumpeter Clifford Brown records with drummer Max Roach ♪
1955 Drummer Art Blakey forms the Jazz Messengers with pianist Horace Silver ♪
1957 Miles Davis begins collaborations with arranger Gil Evans ♪
1959 Cuban Revolution; Alaska and Hawaii become states
1959 Legendary jazz albums *Kind of Blue* by Miles Davis, *Time Out* by Dave Brubeck, and *Giant Steps* by John Coltrane are recorded ♪

Early 1960s Miles Davis's classic quintet records major albums ♪
1960 Ornette Coleman releases *Free Jazz*, signaling the birth of the free jazz movement ♪
1963 Civil rights march on Washington; John Kennedy assassinated
1964–1973 Vietnam War
1964 John Coltrane records *A Love Supreme* ♪
Mid-1960s The British Invasion and acid rock sweep the nation ♪
1966 Cecil Taylor records *Unit Structures* ♪
1967 Funk, acid rock, and the counterculture begin to influence jazz ♪
1968 Martin Luther King and Robert Kennedy assassinated
1969 Miles Davis records *In a Silent Way* and *Bitches Brew*, signaling the birth of fusion ♪

1973 Herbie Hancock records pivotal fusion album *Headhunters* ♪
1975 Pat Metheny records his first album *Bright Size Life*, with Jaco Pastorius ♪
1977 Weather Report records the popular *Heavy Weather* ♪
1978 President Carter holds first annual White House jazz festival ♪
1979 Sony Walkman (personal listening device) is introduced ♪

1980 Miles Davis returns to the jazz world after five-year hiatus ♪
1983 Compact disc introduced to the general public ♪
1984 Wynton Marsalis wins Grammys in jazz and classical genres ♪
1987 Michael Brecker releases first self-titled album as leader ♪
1989 Miles Davis autobiography published ♪

1990s American economic high-tech "bubble"
1992 Los Angeles riots/uprising following Rodney King trial
1996 "Jazz at Lincoln Center" becomes a constituent member of Lincoln Center ♪

2001 9/11 terrorist attacks

| 1940 | 1950 | 1960 | 1970 | 1980 | 1990 | 2000 |

Chapter 12

From Bebop to Acid Jazz

From its birth, the development of jazz was driven by experimentation and a quest for musical growth. By the late 1940s, as the swing era drew to a close, jazz turned away from the popular mainstream to follow a more art-oriented direction. Bebop was the first in a series of new jazz styles, followed over the next three decades by cool, hard bop, funky/soul, modal, free, and jazz-rock fusion styles. Other styles that became prominent near the end of the twentieth century included Latin jazz, acid jazz, and a neoclassicism that returned to the roots of the genre. Jazz also received critical and academic respect in the 1990s as a highly evolved indigenous art form, one of the country's most significant contributions to twentieth-century art.

IN THIS CHAPTER

- Bebop and the Birth of Modern Jazz
- Post-Bop Styles of the 1950s
- Free Jazz
- Mainstream Jazz in the 1960s
- Bop and Post-Bop Vocal Jazz
- Fusion
- Contemporary Directions

BEBOP AND THE BIRTH OF MODERN JAZZ

Bebop was the first new style to emerge in the 1940s, signaling the beginning of the modern jazz era. According to historian Ted Gioia,

> The leading jazz modernists of the 1940s developed their own unique style, brash and unapologetic, in backrooms and after-hours clubs, at jam sessions and on the road with traveling bands. This music was not for commercial consumption. . . . Modern jazz was an underground movement.[1]

Bebop contributed ingredients that became essential constituents of most subsequent jazz genres.

What Was Bebop?

- Small ensembles predominated: rhythm section (bass, piano, and drums) fronted by horns.
- The jam session was the center of creativity and experimentation.
- The music focused on improvisation rather than dancing.
- Tunes were often performed at fast tempos, and virtuosity was a requisite for participation.

- Improvisation focused more on chord structure than on melody.
- Jazz harmonies became increasingly complex.

By the mid-1940s, formulaic white bands had come to dominate the commercial swing scene. Jazz was shifting from big bands to smaller ensembles, with the music's focus moving from dancing to listening. Some historians suggest that bebop innovators rejected swing because they could no longer express themselves musically in that context; others argue that bebop was more of a natural outgrowth of swing. When the bebop style emerged, listeners by no means universally embraced it, and many questioned its legitimacy. As swing bandleader Cab Calloway once told trumpeter Dizzy Gillespie after a solo, "Man, listen, will you please don't be playing all that Chinese music up there!"[2]

Alto saxophonist Charlie Parker and trumpeter Dizzy Gillespie played central roles in the development of bebop. **Charlie Parker's** (1920–1955) inventive improvisation, dazzling technique, unique timbre, and uncanny ability to deconstruct and reassemble melodies became the standard of excellence in jazz performance and improvisation. According to historian Gary Giddins, "Parker was the only musician after Armstrong to influence all of jazz and al-

© Frank Driggs Collection/ Getty Images

The architects of bebop: Charlie Parker and Dizzie Gillespie.

most every aspect of American music—its instrumentalists and singers, composers, and arrangers."[3]

The Kansas City–born artist began his career at age sixteen, playing in dance bands and influenced by saxophonists Lester Young and Chu Berry and pianist Art Tatum. He moved to New York in 1939 and played in jam sessions where the elements of bebop first coalesced. Parker returned to Kansas City in 1940, where he earned the nickname "Yardbird" and met future collaborator Dizzy Gillespie, who was touring with the Cab Calloway band.

South Carolina–born **John Birks "Dizzy" Gillespie** (1917–1993) started playing professionally with swing bands in his midteens, influenced by swing-era trumpet virtuoso Roy Eldridge. He moved to New York in 1937 and soon started to experiment with some of the same approaches to improvisation as Parker. According to Gillespie,

> The moment I heard Charlie Parker, I said there is my colleague. . . . I never heard anything like that before. . . . Charlie Parker and I were moving in the same direction too, but neither of us knew it.[4]

When Parker returned to New York in 1942, he joined some of the best players in jazz at a time when they were experimenting with bebop in competitive jam sessions. Because of a musician's strike, few recordings were made during the formative years of bebop. When the strike ended in 1945, Gillespie and Parker made a series of historic recordings, including Gillespie's "Groovin High" and "Salt Peanuts"; Parker's "Billie's Bounce," "Now's the Time," and "Koko"; and the duo's co-composed barn burner, "Shaw 'Nuff." Their collaboration was short-lived, however, because Parker was a chronic drug abuser, and Gillespie grew tired of his unreliability. After their split, Parker played with other bebop innovators such as trumpeter Miles Davis, drummer Max Roach, and pianist Bud Powell. Roach was known for making the drums an independent jazz voice, while Powell was known as an innovator of bebop-style **comping—** the playing of chords to accompany improvised solos. Parker unfortunately followed a downward spiral that led to an early death in 1955. Gillespie went on to pave the way for Latin jazz in the late 1940s, and he performed with small groups and big bands over the next forty years as a global ambassador of jazz.

Although **Thelonious Monk** (1920–1982) was one of the most inventive composers and pianists in jazz history, critics during bebop's formative years often dismissed his unorthodox piano technique. Monk's compositions encompassed angular melodies, unexpected chord progressions, and syncopated dissonance; over time they became a wellspring of inspiration for other musicians. The artist's behavior often matched his idiosyncratic music.

CD LISTENING EXERCISE

CD 2/5

Listen to "Shaw 'Nuff," recorded in 1945 by Dizzy Gillespie and Charlie Parker. The arrangement is symmetrical, beginning and ending with the same thematic material. The introduction is followed by a unison statement of the up-tempo melody played by perfectly balanced trumpet and alto sax. This is followed by blazing improvised solos by Parker, Gillespie, and Al Haig on piano. "Shaw 'Nuff" exhibits the technical prowess of bebop's founders at their peak.

**Internet
Listening Exercise**

Listen to samples of Thelonious Monk compositions.

Thelonious Monk: "Straight No Chaser," "Well You Needn't"

Ultimately, however, Monk was viewed as an influential voice in the development of modern jazz, and many of his compositions became jazz standards.

POST-BOP STYLES OF THE 1950s

The 1950s saw the emergence of a variety of post-bop jazz styles, including cool jazz, hard bop, funky or gospel jazz, and modal jazz. Although many jazz musicians were associated with the development of a specific style, most great players of the post-bop era crossed genres freely.

The Birth of the Cool

Cool jazz was a dramatic departure from bebop. Lighter, softer, and slower than bebop, it took jazz in a more reflective direction. The style's emphasis on understatement rather than technical prowess made it accessible for musicians who lacked the virtuosity of the bebop masters. Cool jazz was also the first major jazz style to which white musicians were generally credited with making important contributions. A series of 1949 recordings led by trumpeter Miles Davis entitled *Birth of the Cool* signaled the beginning of the new direction. As Davis recalled,

> Bird and Diz played this hip, real fast thing, and if you weren't a fast listener, you couldn't catch the humor or the feeling in their music. . . . "Birth of the Cool" was different because you could hear everything and hum it also.[5]

**Internet
Listening Exercise**

Listen to samples of cool jazz.

Miles Davis: "Boplicity"

Modern Jazz Quartet: "Django"

The sessions employed the unusual instrumentation of trumpet, trombone, alto and baritone saxophone, French horn, tuba, bass, drums, and piano. Many musicians on the recording became influential, including baritone saxophonist Gerry Mulligan, who also wrote most of the arrangements; alto saxophonist Lee Konitz, who subsequently became a leading figure of the cool movement; classical French horn player Gunther Schuller, later known for a blend of classical music and jazz called third-stream jazz; pianist John Lewis, whom the project inspired to form the Modern Jazz Quartet, the premier African American ensemble of the cool era; and innovative bebop drummers Max Roach and Kenny Clarke.

Miles Davis

Trumpeter **Miles Davis** (1926–1991) was the most influential jazz musician of the post-bop era. The St. Louis–born musician briefly attended New York's Julliard School of Music:

> I remember one day being in a music history class and a white woman was the teacher. She was up in front of the class saying that the reason black people played the blues was because they were poor and had to pick cotton. . . . My hand went up in a flash and I stood up and said, "I'm from East St. Louis and

my father is rich, he's a dentist and I play the blues. . . ." That's the kind of s———— that was happening at Julliard and after a while I got tired of it.[6]

Davis began his jazz career working with Charlie Parker, but he did not have the phenomenal technique of Gillespie and could not express himself fully in the technically demanding bebop style. The *Birth of the Cool* sessions served as a turning point that enabled him to begin shaping his own musical voice. Throughout his four-decade career, Davis embraced musical experimentation, showed a great ear for talent, and consistently surrounded himself with superb musicians. Listeners could instantly recognize the artist's dry trumpet tone, understated phrasing, and use of space. Davis recorded a series of successful small-group albums in the mid-1950s that refined his personal sound. He next collaborated with arranger Gil Evans on a series of large ensemble recordings, including *Miles Ahead,* an album of songs from Gershwin's *Porgy and Bess,* and *Sketches of Spain,* which showcased jazz arrangements of Spanish composer Joaquín Rodrigo's *Concierto de Aranjuez.*

In 1959 Davis led what may be the most popular jazz recording of all time, *Kind of Blue.* The album introduced **modal jazz,** a style of improvisation based on the exploration of one scale for an extended period of time. The work's all-star lineup included saxophonists Julian "Cannonball" Adderley and John Coltrane, pianists Bill Evans and Wynton Kelly, bassist Paul Chambers, and drummer Jimmy Cobb. Davis continued to record and perform in the early 1960s with a new generation of players that included pianist Herbie Hancock and saxophonist Wayne Shorter. By the late 1960s and early 1970s, Davis once again appeared at the forefront, this time as a pioneer of jazz-rock fusion (the blending of jazz and rock). In the 1980s he performed in a lighter, funk-jazz style, remaining an active and controversial figure until his death.

© Herb Snitzer/Time & Life Pictures/Getty Images

Trumpeter Miles Davis was the most important jazz innovator of the post-bop era.

CD LISTENING EXERCISE

CD 2/6

Listen to an excerpt of "So What" from the album *Kind of Blue.* The 32-measure form is based on two chords and is a classic example of modal jazz. Davis explained modal jazz: "When you play this way you can go on forever. You don't have to worry about changes and s———— like that. You can do more with the musical line. The challenge here is to see how inventive you can become melodically."[7] Listen to how the extended use of modal harmony allows the improvisers to explore different melodic possibilities.

Miles Davis's Contributions

Stylistic Innovator

The most influential jazz musician of the post-bop era, Davis stayed on the cutting edge, playing a major role in creating styles such as cool jazz, hard bop, modal jazz, and jazz-rock fusion.

Bandleader and Musical Mentor

He led what many consider the finest quintet in jazz history. Throughout his career, he surrounded himself with the finest musicians, most of whom later regarded their time spent with him as pivotal to their musical development.

Recorded Legacy

His discography is one of the most extensive in jazz, and he was the leader for the recording of *Kind of Blue* (1959), considered by many to be the single greatest album in jazz history.

Unique Trumpet Style

He was known for his recognizable trumpet tone and improvisational style, which made the spaces between the notes as important as the notes themselves.

West Coast Cool

Following the release of *Birth of the Cool* in the early 1950s, the cool sound spread through the jazz world. When baritone saxophonist **Gerry Mulligan** (1927–1996) formed a pianoless quartet with trumpeter Chet Baker (1929–1988) in Southern California, critics dubbed the sparse sound of the ensemble **West Coast cool.** Without the thicker harmonic texture contributed by the piano, the group's sound emphasized the bass and the counterpoint of two horns. Baker's chiseled good looks; laid-back demeanor; dry, Miles Davis–style trumpet tone; and appealing vocal style also popularized the music. Many musicians associated with West Coast cool were white.

Pianist **Dave Brubeck** (1920–) and alto saxophonist Paul Desmond (1924–1977) dominated West Coast cool in the mid- and late 1950s. Brubeck's classically flavored keyboard style and Desmond's dry tone on alto became synonymous with the sound of cool. When the cover of *Time* magazine featured Brubeck in 1954, the Dave Brubeck Quartet achieved national celebrity. The quartet shortly thereafter became one of the most popular groups in jazz history with the release of *Time Out* (1959), the first jazz album to sell over a million copies. Planned as an experiment in odd meter compositions in five, seven, and nine beats per measure, the album produced a surprise hit—"Take Five."

Internet Listening Exercise

Listen to samples of West Coast cool.

Dave Brubeck Quartet: "Take Five"

Gerry Mulligan: "Line for Lyons"

© Bettmann/ CORBIS

Pianist Dave Brubeck and alto saxophonist Paul Desmond helped define the sound of cool jazz in the 1950s.

 Multicultural Note

Cool Jazz and White Contributions to Jazz

Since the birth of jazz, debates have raged about the role of race in its development. Most scholars agree that jazz was primarily of African American origin, although historian Richard Sudhalter argues in his book *Lost Chords* that the contributions of white musicians to jazz have been underappreciated.

During the cool jazz era, however, many white musicians did seem to lead jazz innovation. Some argued that the relaxed nature of the cool style was a comfortable fit for white musicians. Miles Davis, on the other hand, saw it as simply another example of cultural appropriation:

> A lot of white musicians like Stan Getz, Chet Baker, and Dave Brubeck—who had been influenced by my records—were recording all over the place. Now they were calling the kind of music they were playing "cool jazz." ... Now I'm not saying these guys weren't good musicians ... but they didn't start nothing and they knew it.[8]

Some musicians in the black jazz community also embraced the cool style. The Modern Jazz Quartet (John Lewis, piano; Milt Jackson, vibraphone; Percy Heath, bass; and Connie Kay, drums) embodied urban sophistication with a polished style that critics often compared to classical chamber music.

Hard Bop and Funky Jazz

In the early 1950s, just as cool jazz was taking jazz in a laid-back direction, the aggressive side of bebop was also moving toward a style called **hard bop.** An assortment of young players—pianist Horace Silver; drummers Art Blakey and Elvin Jones; trumpeters Clifford Brown, Lee Morgan, and Freddie Hubbard; and saxophonists John Coltrane, Cannonball Adderley, and Sonny Rollins—developed the style. Hard bop reflected the renewed influence of the blues, and some musicians began to play a substyle called funky jazz or soul jazz. **Funky jazz** incorporated elements of R & B such as repeated prewritten patterns in the rhythm section along with gospel, soul, and blues inflections while retaining a major focus on improvisation.

What Was Hard Bop?

- It was a natural extension of bebop, using similar instrumentation and musical forms.

- It incorporated funky, R & B–based rhythms with extensive jazz improvisation.

- The civil rights and black pride movements of the early 1960s contributed a flavor of cultural pride, and elements of gospel and soul found their way into the style.

- It extended harmonic possibilities by adding modal harmony as a central component.

In helping to redefine jazz piano styles in the 1950s and 1960s, pianist **Horace Silver** (1928–) became one of the most popular jazz composers and performers of the post-bop era. He favored simple melodies, repeated rhythmic patterns, and Latin and gospel influences. Many of Silver's compositions remain popular as repertoire for beginning jazz players, and some of his recordings blurred the line between R & B and jazz. Hard-swinging drummer **Art Blakey** (1919–1990) led the Jazz Messengers, one of the most influential ensembles of the post-bop era. First formed in the mid-1950s as a collaboration with Horace Silver, Blakey's Jazz Messengers saw some of the best young talent in the jazz world rotate through the group for over thirty years. Because members were encouraged to write and arrange, the ensemble served as a living school for such artists as trumpeters Clifford Brown, Lee Morgan, Freddie Hubbard, and Wynton Marsalis; saxophonists Benny Golson, Jackie McLean, and Wayne Shorter; trombonist Curtis Fuller; pianists Bobby Timmons, George Cables, and Cedar Walton; and bassist Reggie Workman.

Clifford Brown (1930–1956) was a gifted trumpeter and composer whose beautiful tone and superb technique left his mark on jazz in a series of early-1950s recordings with drummer Max Roach. Composer/saxophonist Benny Golson wrote the jazz standard, "I Remember Clifford," at the time of Brown's untimely death to commemorate the artist's unfulfilled legacy. Trumpeter Lee

Internet Listening Exercise

Listen to samples of the hard bop sound of Horace Silver.

Horace Silver: "Song for My Father," "Sister Sadie"

Multicultural Note

Was It R & B or Jazz?

With the fading of the swing era in the mid-1940s, R & B became increasingly popular, and many jazz musicians worked in both styles. Most R & B was intended as dance music, requiring a steady beat as well as rhythmic, melodic, and harmonic repetition. By the 1950s, jazz had mostly become music for listening, with improvisation as its centerpiece and with few *set parts* (prewritten, repeated patterns) played by anyone. Horace Silver fashioned an appealing compromise of the two genres by writing compositions with set parts played in the rhythm section in a practice similar to R & B, while encouraging soloists to follow the jazz tradition of extended improvisation.

Morgan (1938–1972) was known for his soulful, bluesy phrasing, warm tone, and passionate melodic approach to improvisation. His recordings with the Jazz Messengers and as a leader contributed to the lineage of jazz trumpet styles. Freddie Hubbard (1938–), an artist with rich tone and complete technical mastery of the trumpet, started off with Art Blakey and the Jazz Messengers and rapidly developed his own hard-bop style as a leader. In the early 1970s, Hubbard played a central role in the development of fusion through a series of albums produced by Creed Taylor on the CTI label.

Tenor and soprano saxophonist **John Coltrane** (1926–1967) is considered by many to be the most influential saxophonist of the post-bop era. He began playing professionally in the late 1940s, but it was his work with Miles Davis and Thelonious Monk in the 1950s that first brought national attention. Much like Davis, Coltrane consistently pushed in new musical directions throughout his career—from the music of his first album as a leader, *Blue Train* (1957), until the end of his life. The artist practiced obsessively to explore all melodic and harmonic possibilities of a tune, and he proved equally masterful on tender ballads or up-tempo hard bop, as heard on his classic *Giant Steps* album. Coltrane scored a minor pop hit in 1960 with his modal rendition on soprano sax of Richard Rodgers's "My Favorite Things," from *The Sound of Music*. Coltrane's quest for musical freedom meshed well with the emergent free jazz ethic, which eschewed predefined form and structure, though many of his fans were disappointed that he seemed to be abandoning hard bop. Coltrane began to play with a speed and intensity that have often been described as "sheets of sound." While controversy swirled around the content of his impassioned live performances and forays into free jazz, he re-

Internet Listening Exercise

Listen to samples of hard-bop trumpeters.

Clifford Brown: "A Night in Tunisia"

Art Blakey and the Jazz Messengers (with Lee Morgan): "Moanin'"

Freddie Hubbard: "Red Clay"

CD LISTENING EXERCISE

CD 2/7

Listen to "My Favorite Things." How does Coltrane use the familiar melody as a central theme of his improvisation? His solo employs a modal approach that extensively explores one scale, but he also adds scales of his own choosing. Note the distinctive tone of the artist's soprano saxophone. How does he interact with the rest of the ensemble? Coltrane's band included drummer Elvin Jones, one of the most technically advanced drummers in jazz, and McCoy Tyner, one of the finest pianists in jazz.

corded *A Love Supreme* (1964), a harmonically grounded musical culmination of his work that he considered a spiritual gift to humanity.

The career of tenor saxophonist **Sonny Rollins** (1930–) spanned five decades. As one of the finest improvisers in jazz, he used simple melodies as thematic material to generate endless creative variations. Charlie Parker influenced Rollins's early hard-bop style, and Rollins worked with Miles Davis in the mid-1950s before branching out on his own. The artist's playing and composing often embraced the infectious sound of Trinidadian calypsos, as heard in his composition "St. Thomas," which became a jazz standard.

Many considered alto saxophonist **Julian "Cannonball" Adderley** (1928–1975) as Charlie Parker's successor. A master improviser fluent in hard bop, modal, and funky jazz, Adderley became best known for his work with Miles Davis on *Kind of Blue* as well as for funky jazz standards such as "Work Song" and "Mercy, Mercy, Mercy." According to historian Mark Gridley, "The effect of his tone was warm and glowing. He bent his huge tone with blue notes and wails, thereby creating an earthy, legato style that has been called 'blues drenched.'"[9]

FREE JAZZ

Jazz ventured into uncharted waters in the late 1950s and early 1960s as a new generation of musicians, inspired in part by the civil rights and black power movements, pushed the limits of jazz melody, harmony, and structure by experimenting with an approach called **free** or **avant-garde jazz.** Although most free jazz innovators—including alto saxophonist Ornette Coleman, bassist Charlie Haden, trumpeter Don Cherry, tenor saxophonist Albert Ayler, and pianist Cecil Taylor—were young players, established mainstream artists such as John Coltrane, Sonny Rollins, and Charles Mingus soon paid close attention. Though never a popular style, free jazz opened the door for the exploration of unstructured compositions and sonic noise by generations of rockers.

Alto saxophonist **Ornette Coleman** (1930–) and pianist **Cecil Taylor** (1929–) were early leaders of the movement. In the late 1950s, Coleman formed a quartet whose 1959 debut at the Five Spot club in New York proved to be a major cultural event. Everyone in the art world had an opinion about the new music—they either loved it or hated it. Bassist Charlie Haden described his experience playing with Coleman: "It was like being born again. . . . I was hearing music so much more deeply than I ever heard it before."[10] Classical composer and conductor Leonard Bernstein declared Coleman a genius, and John Coltrane began to sit in with the band whenever he could. Others had different responses. Swing-era trumpeter Roy Eldridge commented, "I listened to him drunk and I listened to him sober and I couldn't understand him either way."[11] In the opinion of historian Albert Murray, "This music was called free jazz but what is freer than jazz? . . . You can't embrace entropy, you can't embrace chaos."[12] Critics viewed Coleman's 1960 album *Free Jazz: A Collective Improvisation* as a benchmark of the free jazz idiom. The compositions generally began with a loosely played melody followed by extended free improvisation that abandoned most elements of form and structure.

Although many performers in the free jazz movement avoided using chordal instruments, the classically trained Cecil Taylor was the style's principal innovator on piano. According to historian Ted Gioia,

> A half-decade before free jazz became an established style, Taylor was already employing arch dissonances, fragmented single note lines, disjointed rhythms and the jackhammer piano attack that would characterize his mature work.[13]

Taylor's playing rarely employed swing, and he avoided preset chord progressions. His live album *Unit Structures* (1960) was often cited as his most important recording. After the 1960s, numerous mainstream jazz musicians incorporated elements of free jazz into their work, and a smaller number made it the centerpiece of their style.

Internet Listening Exercise

Listen to samples of classic free jazz work.

Ornette Coleman: "Free Jazz"

Cecil Taylor: "Unit Structures"

MAINSTREAM JAZZ IN THE 1960s

While the free jazz movement briefly took center stage in the early 1960s, other developments continued in mainstream jazz. The Miles Davis Quintet and Art Blakey's Jazz Messengers served as launching pads for artists such as pianist Herbie Hancock, saxophonist Wayne Shorter, bassist Charles Mingus, and pianist Bill Evans.

Wayne Shorter (1933–) first came to light performing and composing with the Jazz Messengers in the late 1950s and early 1960s. When he joined the Miles Davis Quintet in 1964, his unique tenor sound and compositional approach proved a good fit for the intuitive style of the group. Critics viewed many

Contemporary jazz masters (left to right): pianist Herbie Hancock, saxophonist Michael Brecker, and pianist Chick Corea (1988).

of Shorter's mid-1960s recordings as a leader, including *Speak No Evil* and *Ju Ju*, as masterpieces. In the 1970s, the artist cofounded the fusion group Weather Report, but in the early 2000s he resumed acoustic performances with a variety of players as well as his former partner, Herbie Hancock.

CD LISTENING EXERCISE

CD 2/8

Listen to an excerpt from Herbie Hancock's 1973 fusion version of his classic "Watermelon Man." Originally recorded in 1963, the funky jazz classic was one of the rare jazz tunes to receive radio airplay. Hancock updated his recording on the fusion album *Head Hunters*. In this version, Hancock has deconstructed the tune. It begins with a long rhythmic introduction followed by the bridge, which appears long before the original melody. How does the use of electronic instruments influence the song's texture? Notice the interplay of African percussion, funk-style bass, and funk-style drums.

Internet Listening Exercise

Listen to samples of 60s jazz masters.

Wayne Shorter: "Speak No Evil"

Charles Mingus: "Goodbye Parkpie Hat"

Bill Evans: (From *Kind of Blue*) "Blue in Green"

Herbie Hancock's (1940–) style was influenced by the funky, rhythmic playing of Horace Silver, the chord voicings and modal approach of Bill Evans, the harmonic textures of classical impressionists Maurice Ravel and Claude Debussy, and the jazz-inflected classical compositions of George Gershwin. While making his own acoustic jazz recordings, he participated in Miles Davis's important early fusion albums, *In a Silent Way* and *Bitches Brew*. Several of Hancock's tunes from the era, including "Maiden Voyage" and "Watermelon Man," became jazz standards. His first foray as a leader into the fusion arena was the funk-flavored *Head Hunters* (1973), which sold over a million copies and yielded the hit "Chameleon." A subsequent fusion album, *Future Shock,* produced the hit "Rockit." Hancock's *Gershwin's World* (1999) shredded jazz conventions by encompassing a range of styles with guest appearances by Stevie Wonder, Joni Mitchell, and opera singer Kathleen Battle.

Charles Mingus (1922–1979) left a legacy of respected original compositions and virtuoso bass performances, and some historians compared him favorably to Duke Ellington. He began his career working with many of the jazz masters of the 1940s, becoming a respected composer in the 1950s. Mingus's work encompassed funky jazz, New Orleans jazz, swing, bebop, free jazz, solo piano, small and large ensembles, film scores, and third stream. His best-known composition was "Goodbye Porkpie Hat," a tribute to saxophonist Lester Young.

Bill Evans (1929–1980) first garnered national attention in the late 1950s as a member of the Miles Davis group, particularly with his performance and arrangements on *Kind of Blue*. Evans's delicate touch, floating beat, and original chord voicings represented a fresh, influential approach to jazz piano. **Voicing** refers to the selection and ordering of notes that a performer uses to play a given chord. After Evans left Davis, he recorded a series of influential trio albums in the early 1960s.

BOP AND POST-BOP VOCAL JAZZ

Historians and musicians have often viewed vocal jazz as less significant than instrumental jazz. In recent years, however, many in the jazz field have challenged this perspective, arguing that vocal jazz has played a more substantial role in the evolution of jazz than was previously acknowledged. In the latter half of the twentieth century, several key artists pushed vocal innovations in fresh influential directions.

Sarah Vaughan (1924–1990) was one of a handful of singers to enter the jazz scene during the bebop era. Over a four-decade career, her repertoire encompassed bebop, swing, Latin, cool jazz, and hard bop. Vaughan's warm tone, flawless control, and multi-octave range made her one of the most versatile and expressive singers in jazz, and she often reworked melodies to enhance their meaning. Her piano work and knowledge of jazz harmony also won her the respect of the jazz community. Billy Eckstine's (1914–1993) rich baritone made him one of the first African American jazz singers to achieve broad popularity in the 1940s. At one time touted as the "black Sinatra," Eckstine had top-ten hits with "Cottage for Sale" and "Prisoner of Love." He also led one of the most creative big bands of the bebop era. Equally skilled in jazz and blues, Joe Williams (1918–1999) starred as the singer for the Count Basie Band in the mid-1950s. He was also known for his use of the blue yodel, a vocal technique originally attributed to country legend Jimmie Rodgers (see Chapter 7).

The principal jazz vocal stylists of the post-bop era included Carmen McRae (1920–1994) and Betty Carter (1929–1998). McRae's relaxed phrasing recalled Billie Holiday, while Carter's unusual phrasing and improvisational skills legitimized the voice as an integral part of the improvisational ensemble. The agile vocalist Eddie Jefferson (1918–1979) pioneered **vocalese,** a technique that uses recorded instrumental solos as the basis for vocal melodies that are often harmonized. The vocal trio of Jon Hendricks, David Lambert, and Annie Ross were major innovators of group vocal jazz in the 1950s and early 1960s. They used vocalese, scat singing, and mimicry of big band textures, and their work influenced later groups such as Manhattan Transfer and New York Voices.

Developments in vocal jazz continued in the last two decades of the twentieth century. Al Jarreau (1940–) moved seamlessly among pop, R & B, and mainstream jazz, scoring both pop and jazz hits with songs such as "We're in This Love Together" and "Blue Rondo a la Turk." Cassandra Wilson (1955–) and Bobby McFerrin (1950–) explored approaches that were sometimes experimental, other times commercial. McFerrin used his multi-octave range to fashion a varied repertoire, including the hit pop song "Don't Worry, Be Happy." While rooted in a vocal jazz improvisational style influenced by Betty Carter, Wilson explored multiple genres in jazz contexts, including the Robert Johnson blues tune, "Come on in My Kitchen." Diana Krall (1965–) and Norah Jones (1979–) both paired their piano skills

Internet Listening Exercise

Listen to samples of post-bop vocal jazz.

Sarah Vaughan: "My Funny Valentine"

Billy Eckstine: "Prisoner of Love"

Joe Williams: "All Right, Okay, You Win"

Carmen McRae and Betty Carter: "What's New"

Eddie Jefferson: "Moody's Mood"

Lambert, Hendricks, and Ross: "Twisted"

Jazz vocalist/pianist Diana Krall remains one of the most popular jazz performers of the early 2000s.

© Reuters/ CORBIS

with appealing vocal work to straddle the jazz and pop charts. Krall's understated, sultry vocal style, as heard in "When I Look in Your Eyes," and Jones's lyrical, jazz-inflected pop style, exemplified by "Come Away with Me," made them Grammy winners and major concert draws in the early 2000s. Group vocal jazz styles, as heard in the work of Manhattan Transfer, New York Voices, and Take Six, expanded to encompass pop, rock, soul, gospel, R & B, Latin, and world music.

FUSION

With the rock revolution of the late 1960s, important jazz venues began to shut their doors, major labels abandoned jazz to pursue rock, and jazz artists left the country to pursue playing opportunities abroad. Younger audiences increasingly chose the Beatles, Jimi Hendrix, or the politically oriented folk music of Bob Dylan over jazz. As a result, new hybrids of rock and jazz developed—some fueled by jazz players interested in rock and funk, others by rockers interested in jazz. When trumpeter Miles Davis crossed over to a new rock-inflected, amplified sound with his influential *Bitches Brew* album in 1970, the new style of **jazz-rock fusion** entered the jazz mainstream for about a decade, and graduates of Davis's experiment went on to succeed in 1970s fusion supergroups. Fusion was followed by a lighter, radio-friendly style called smooth jazz, which ultimately diminished the legitimacy of fusion in the minds of jazz purists.

Early Jazz-Rock Experiments

Early experiments in the hybridization of rock and jazz began in the late 1960s. Young rock players started to dabble in jazz, and young jazz musicians tried to find a musical voice in jazz that did not cut them off from the culture of their

 Music Industry Note

··

Jazz-Rock Fusion and the Invention of the Synthesizer

The texture of jazz-rock fusion came in part from electronic keyboard technology, which included the distinctive tone of the Fender Rhodes electric piano and the keyboard-controlled synthesizer. The latter instrument enabled musicians to fashion new timbres that had not existed before. Synthesizer technology advanced rapidly in the 1970s, beginning with monophonic instruments that sounded only one note at a time and advancing to polyphonic synthesis, which allowed the playing of multiple notes simultaneously. Digital synthesis subsequently paved the way for *sound sampling*, which enabled musicians to sample any sound in their environment and manipulate it in a musical piece. Major innovators of the synthesizer in jazz-rock fusion included Herbie Hancock, Joe Zawinul, and George Duke.

generation. Fusion guitarist Larry Coryell recalled his early motivations: "Everybody was dropping acid and the prevailing attitude was 'Let's do something different.' We were saying . . . 'We love Coltrane but we also love the Beatles. We love Miles but we also love the Rolling Stones.'"[14] Young New York jazz artists such as guitarist Coryell and vibist Gary Burton made a conscious effort to connect with a younger rock audience, growing their hair long and wearing hipper fashions. As Burton noted, "One reason why jazz isn't more popular with younger audiences is that it's hard for them to identify with forty-ish musicians in tailored suits. They could loosen up some."[15]

One of the most significant of the early fusion groups was Dreams, which featured trumpeter Randy Brecker, saxophonist Michael Brecker, drummer Billy Cobham, and guitarist John Abercrombie. Although the group was short-lived, its members went on to influential careers: Billy Cobham's explosive drumming was featured in John McLaughlin's Mahavishnu Orchestra and later on his own solo outings; the Brecker brothers succeeded with their own jazz-funk unit and later as individual players. The Breckers scored a top-forty hit with "Sneakin' up behind You" in 1975. Other more rock-flavored efforts also appeared. One of the most successful jazz-rock groups was Blood, Sweat, and Tears. The nine-piece group's 1969 Grammy-winning album produced three hits: "You've Made Me So Very Happy," "Spinning Wheel," and "And When I Die." Chicago was another jazz rock–inflected horn band. Emerging in 1970, the group was ultimately one of the top ten best-selling U.S. pop acts of all time, producing hits such as "25 or 6 to 4," "Does Anybody Really Know What Time It Is?" and the Grammy-winning "If You Leave Me Now."

Miles and His Disciples

In the late 1960s, Miles Davis was listening to Sly Stone and Jimi Hendrix, while his label pressured him to put out records that would match rock sales. In response, he created *In a Silent Way* (1969), an album with a deep electric groove. According to rock critic Lester Bangs, "This is the kind of album that gives you faith in the future of music. It's not rock and roll but it's nothing stereo-typed as jazz either. . . . It's part of a transcendental new music which flushes categories away."[16] A year later, Davis released the Grammy-winning *Bitches Brew* album, which pointed the way toward jazz-rock fusion and validated the new direction for many. With his trumpet channeled through a wah-wah pedal, Davis presided over a thick electronic ensemble. Record company promotion eschewed the term *jazz,* calling the work "a new direction in music," successfully pushing it into the top forty. Davis's subsequent engagements at Bill Graham's Fillmore East and Fillmore West—together with a rock-star wardrobe—signaled a new path.

Davis's sidemen subsequently struck out on their own to produce influential fusion work that dominated much of the 1970s. Drummer Tony Williams formed the group Lifetime with guitarist John McLaughlin and produced several albums. McLaughlin next teamed up with drummer Billy Cobham and keyboardist Jan Hammer to form the Mahavishnu Orchestra, creating its signature blistering tempos and unusual time signatures. Pianist Chick Corea formed

Internet Listening Exercise

Listen to samples of early jazz-rock fusion.

Larry Coryell: "Lady Coryell"

Brecker Brothers: "Sneakin' up behind You"

Blood, Sweat, and Tears: "You've Made Me So Very Happy"

Chicago: "25 or 6 to 4"

**Internet
Listening Exercise**

Listen to samples of fusion work by Miles Davis and his alumni.

Miles Davis: "Bitches Brew"

Herbie Hancock: "Chameleon"

Tony Williams Lifetime: "Emergency"

Chick Corea: "Spain"

Mahavishnu Orchestra: "Meeting of the Spirits"

Weather Report: "Birdland"

Return to Forever and released fusion standards such as "500 Miles High" and "Spain." Saxophonist Wayne Shorter and pianist Joe Zawinul joined with bassist Miroslav Vitous—and later bassist Jaco Pastorius—to form Weather Report, one of the most popular of the fusion supergroups. For fifteen years and in as many albums, the band's free-floating sound combined jazz, rock, funk, Latin, and world musics, including the hit "Birdland" that became a jazz standard.

Smooth Jazz

Fusion remained popular until the end of the 1970s, when a less aggressive form of amplified instrumental music called **smooth jazz** supplanted it. **The Crusaders** (formerly the Jazz Crusaders) were among the first to codify the groove-based, jazz-funk instrumental style of smooth jazz when they moved away from hard bop in the early 1970s to produce the funky instrumental hit, "Put It where You Want It." The sound of smooth jazz was also heard in movie scores and television show instrumental themes. By the mid-1970s, however, critics had begun to present the down side of smooth jazz. As critic Robert Palmer said at the time,

Multicultural Note

Why Did Kenny G Anger Jazz Purists?

Kenny G appealed to millions of smooth jazz fans with his focus on melody, emotion, and music that did not tax the listener. The mere mention of the artist's name to some jazz purists and musicians, however, could provoke an angry response. Criticism ranged from the artist's pitch problems (he was said to play flat), to his sideways embrochure, his lack of improvisational skill, and even his hair. Most angering to many was a 1999 release in which Kenny G electronically blended his sax playing over a classic Louis Armstrong track, "What a Wonderful World." Guitarist Pat Metheny's denunciation of the release was widely circulated over the Internet:

> Kenny G decided that it was appropriate for him to defile the music of the man who is probably the greatest jazz musician that has ever lived by spewing his … jive, pseudo bluesy, out-of-tune, noodling, wimped out … playing all over one of the great Louis's tracks.[18]

Was this anger over Kenny G's work justified?

Electric jazz/rock fusion music is a mutation that's beginning to show signs of adaptive strain. . . . Fusion bands have found that it's a good idea to . . . stick with fairly simple chord voicings. Otherwise the sound becomes muddy and overloaded. This means that the subtleties of jazz phrasing, the multi-layered textures of jazz drumming and the music's rich harmonic language are being abandoned.[17]

In the 1980s and 1990s, a successful smooth jazz radio format emerged that blended soft R & B with pop-jazz instrumentals. Guitarists such as Lee Ritenour, Larry Carlton, and Jeff Lorber became masters of smooth jazz, but the biggest-selling artist of the style was soprano saxophonist **Kenny G** (Kenny Gorelick, 1950–). A former member of Jeff Lorber's group, Kenny G debuted as a solo act in 1982 and became a star in 1986 with "Songbird." A subsequent release, *Breathless*, topped eight million copies in sales—an unheard-of feat in jazz circles, and the artist ultimately sold seventy million copies over a two-decade period.

Artists such as David Benoit, Eric Marenthal, Spryo Gyra, the Yellowjackets, and the Rippingtons also contributed to the smooth jazz tradition, often writing tunes to comply with rigid smooth jazz radio formats. One radio station manager clearly laid out the style's commercial imperative: "We are looking for bright tempos and melodies that are recognizable. . . . We want melodic strength that the casual listener or non-aficionado can pick up on."[19]

CONTEMPORARY DIRECTIONS

At the start of the twenty-first century, although no revolutionary new styles on the order of swing, bebop, or free jazz had appeared, new developments continued. A generation of jazz players who had grown up on hip-hop created acid jazz, Latin jazz became more prominent, the role of women expanded, and a neoclassical movement focused attention on the roots of jazz.

The Continuing Legacy of Instrumental Jazz

Following fusion's heyday in the 1970s, early fusion innovators such as Herbie Hancock, Chick Corea, Freddie Hubbard, Tony Williams, and Wayne Shorter returned to acoustic formats for some of their work while also performing cutting-edge mergers of jazz and contemporary amplified styles. In addition, a new generation of instrumental artists emerged whose playing reflected the expanded possibilities of a range of popular styles. Major saxophone innovators included Michael Brecker, Branford Marsalis, Joshua Redman, Kenny Garrett, and Joe Lovano. Brecker in particular served as a leader of his generation, with an intense contemporary style that traversed the boundaries of jazz harmony while never completely losing touch with his R & B roots. The most well known jazz personality at the turn of the century was trumpeter Wynton Marsalis.

 **Internet Listening Exercise**

Listen to samples of smooth jazz.

The Crusaders: "Put It where You Want It"

The Jeff Lorber Fusion: "Wizard Island"

Spryo Gyra: "Morning Dance"

The Yellowjackets: "Homecoming"

Kenny G: "What a Wonderful World"

Internet Listening Exercise

Listen to contemporary jazz musicians.

Pat Metheny: "Opening"

Nicolas Payton: "When the Saints Go Marching In"

Michael Brecker: "Delta City Blues," "El Niño"

Marcus Roberts: "Maple Leaf Rag"

Conrad Herwig: "Central Park West," "Grand Central"

Other major trumpet innovators included Terence Blanchard (who was also a respected film score composer), Nicholas Payton, Jon Faddis, Wallace Roney, and Roy Hargrove.

Although the guitar was the icon of rock instruments, not until the advent of fusion did the instrument become a prominent jazz voice. One influential guitarist, Pat Metheny, became known for his trademark electronic tone and repertoire of innovative compositions. Metheny also staunchly defended amplified jazz in the face of growing opposition to nonacoustic music among some in the jazz community. Contemporary trends in jazz piano were articulated by Keith Jarrett, Marcus Roberts, and Billy Childs, as well as veterans such as Herbie Hancock, Ahmad Jamal, Chick Corea, and Oscar Peterson. New possibilities for jazz trombone were explored by Steve Turre, Robin Eubanks, and Conrad Herwig. Leading bass players included John Patatucci, Dave Holland, and Christian McBride, and innovators on the drums included Dennis Chambers, Jeff "Tain" Watts, and Brian Blades.

In the 1990s, a substyle called **acid jazz** developed out of electronica, as DJs fashioned remixes of jazz recordings and hip-hop rhythm tracks. The hybrid provided some listeners with their first exposure to jazz, and young musicians followed up to develop a new sound that blended jazz improvisation with hip-hop grooves. One of the most successful early acid jazz recordings was Us3's "Cantaloop" in 1994, which merged samples of Herbie Hancock's original "Cantaloupe Island" with modern rap. Performers who explored acid jazz included saxophonist Branford Marsalis, guitarist Charlie Hunter, and the organ trio Medeski, Martin, and Wood.

Latin Jazz

Latin jazz gained new prominence in the jazz world beginning in the 1980s, and the music of Cuba played a significant role in that evolution. The Cuban group Irakere significantly influenced the style with its hybrid of hard-bop improvisation, Afro-Caribbean instruments and rhythms, and rock, funk, and classical music. The respected Cuban pianist Chucho Valdés founded the band in the mid-1970s with other early members, including alto saxophonist Paquito D'Rivera and trumpeter Arturo Sandoval. All three went on to careers as jazz superstars.

New music and musicians from Cuba also reinvigorated the Latin jazz scene in the United States, and mainstream jazz musicians increasingly turned to Latin music for inspiration. Prominent Latin musicians such as pianist Eddie Palmieri and percussionist Ray Barretto became recognized beyond the Latin dance scene for their contributions to jazz. Further, members of Palmieri's rotating multicultural ensemble, including saxophonist David Sanchez and trombonist Conrad Herwig, went on to lead important Latin jazz units of their own.

On the West Coast, Latin percussionist Poncho Sanchez, who began his career with vibraphonist Cal Tjader, took over the reins of Tjader's influential Latin unit after his death in 1982. Another West Coast Latin jazz innovator was Chicano percussionist Pete Escovedo, who surrounded himself with artists such as

Internet Listening Exercise

Listen to contemporary Latin jazz artists.

Eddie Palmieri: *Palmas*

Ira Kere: "Gira Gira," "Ilya," "Solo te Echaron Un Medio"

Pancho Sanchez: "Joseito," "Para Ti," "One Mint Julep"

Pete Escovedo: "Mis Amigos," "Ah Bailar Cha Cha Cha"

trombonist/composer Wayne Wallace and pianist/composer Rebeca Mauleón. Another figure in the growth of West Coast Latin jazz, percussionist/educator John Santos, created the San Francisco–based Machete Ensemble. Other players, such as the Brazilian trumpeter Claudio Roditi, fused Afro-Cuban traditions with a broader Latin American perspective.

New voices in Latin jazz piano included Panamanian Danilo Pérez, Dominican-born Michel Camilo, and Cuban-born Gonzalo Rubalcaba. Pérez performed with mainstream jazz legends such as Wayne Shorter while developing his own jazz hybrid of Central American and African folkloric traditions. Camilo garnered great respect in both Latin and straight-ahead jazz styles, and Rubalcaba, whom Dizzy Gillespie first brought to international attention, was a master of polyrhythms.

Women in Jazz in the 1990s and 2000s

Jazz was a male-dominated field for most of its history. According to historian Sherrie Tucker,

> While no inherent differences exist between men and women that would make the latter less suited for jazz musicianship, societal definitions of appropriate gender roles result in quite different expectations. . . . A woman who shows up for an audition or jam session with a tenor sax or trumpet in her gig bag is greeted with a special variety of raised eyebrows, curiosity and skepticism. Is she serious? Can she play?[20]

Beginning in the 1990s, a growing number of female jazz artists came into prominence. Among them were big band composer/arranger Maria Schneider, whose work with arranger Gil Evans and command of classical music and jazz fostered an original jazz compositional style. Drummer Terri Lyne Carrington, who worked with Wayne Shorter and Herbie Hancock, displayed a mastery of funk, fusion, and straight-ahead styles. With ten albums as a leader to her credit, soprano saxophonist Jane Ira Bloom gained international recognition as an important new voice. New York–based trumpeter Ingrid Jensen was one of the most sought-after players on the New York scene, and respected San Francisco bassist Ruth Davies performed and recorded with numerous major blues and jazz artists. Brazilian pianist/composer Eliane Elias, Azerbaijanian pianist/composer Amina Figarova, and San Francisco–based pianist/composer Jessica Williams all developed dedicated followings. Figarova, for example, stood out with her fusion of classical technique and hard-swinging contemporary jazz.

Neoclassicism and the Jazz Repertory Movement

Beginning in the 1980s, as jazz innovation diminished, some younger musicians —notably trumpeter Wynton Marsalis—concluded that contemporary jazz had lost its link with its historical roots in blues and swing. In an effort to re-examine the jazz legacy, such musicians gave birth to what is called **neoclassi-**

Internet Listening Exercise

Listen to contemporary women jazz musicians.

Jane Ira Bloom: "Chasing Paint," "Jackson Pollock"

Maria Schneider: "Harry Gliding," "Sea of Tranquility"

Amina Figarova: *Night Train*

Elaine Elias: "One Note Samba," "Black Orpheus"

Terri Lyne Carrington: "Jazz Is," "Witch Hunt"

Jessica Williams: "As Time Goes By," "All Alone"

**Internet
Listening Exercise**

Compare samples of the repertory
version of an Ellington piece with
the original.

Lincoln Center Jazz Orchestra:
"Rockabye River"

Duke Ellington: "Rockabye River"

cal jazz. As part of the return to these roots, leading arts organizations such as
Lincoln Center, Carnegie Hall, and the Smithsonian Institution formed **repertory jazz** ensembles. They focused on the early New Orleans jazz of early Louis
Armstrong and Jelly Roll Morton, the swing of Duke Ellington, and other classic jazz artists. Some in the jazz community criticized what they saw as the "mu-
seumization" of jazz, but others were thrilled to have the opportunity to hear
legendary works performed live.

A gifted jazz and classical trumpeter, **Wynton Marsalis** (1961–) served as
the most prominent artist associated with the neoclassical movement. A member of a musical New Orleans family, Marsalis gained early entrance to Julliard but then dropped out to begin a jazz career with Art Blakey and the Jazz
Messengers. After establishing his own voice in contemporary jazz, Marsalis
shifted to classic jazz. In 1991 he became director of the jazz division of Lincoln
Center, and in 1996 "Jazz at Lincoln Center" became a constituent member of
the influential fine arts institution. Marsalis used his new position to advocate
for jazz education and to speak out on jazz issues. His outspoken embrace of traditional jazz and rejection of jazz-rock fusion stirred controversy, though he
also revived interest in the music of Duke Ellington, Louis Armstrong, and
other legends of early jazz. Marsalis was the first jazz composer to win a Pulitzer
prize, which he received for his extended jazz oratorio, *Blood on the Fields*, in
1997. He also served as principal advisor to Ken Burns for the 2000 documentary series, *Jazz*.

Chapter Summary

- Modern jazz began with the birth of bebop: The underlying structure of
  bebop became the model for most styles of jazz that followed. Pivotal
  figures in the development of bebop included alto saxophonist Charlie
  Parker, trumpeter Dizzy Gillespie, and pianist Thelonious Monk.

- The seminal bebop years, 1945–1949, were followed by an expansion of
  jazz styles in the 1950s that yielded cool jazz, hard bop, funky or soul jazz,
  and modal jazz.

- Trumpeter Miles Davis contributed greatly to jazz evolution in the 1950s,
  1960s, and 1970s; some called him the most important innovator in jazz.
  Davis was central to the development of cool jazz, hard bop, modal jazz,
  and fusion. Other musical leaders of the 1950s included pianist Horace
  Silver, pianist Dave Brubeck, and drummer Art Blakey.

- The music of saxophonist John Coltrane straddled styles and decades, representing a pinnacle of jazz excellence. Coltrane's complete mastery of the
  saxophone as well as most jazz styles was probably unparalleled in jazz
  history.

- The early 1960s witnessed the flowering of free jazz, a controversial style that rejected preset song forms and chord structures. Saxophonist Ornette Coleman was a major leader of the movement.

- Vocal jazz, while often downplayed in jazz history, continued to evolve in the post-bop era with major contributions from a variety of artists.

- The influences of funk, R & B, and rock led to the development of jazz-rock fusion in the late 1960s and early 1970s. The style was controversial among jazz purists, who rejected the notion that electronically amplified music could be considered jazz. Fusion also formed the basis of smooth jazz.

- As jazz entered its second century, new developments included the hip-hop/jazz hybrid of acid jazz, growing prominence for Latin jazz, enhanced visibility of women, and renewed interest in classic jazz styles.

Key Terms

acid jazz
avant-garde jazz
bebop
comping
cool jazz
free jazz
funky jazz
hard bop
jazz-rock fusion

modal jazz
neoclassical jazz
post-bop
repertory jazz
smooth jazz
vocalese
voicing
West Coast cool

Study and Discussion Questions

1. What was modern jazz, and what musical developments during the bebop era gave birth to modern jazz?

2. What were the main musical ingredients of bebop? Who were central figures in its emergence, and what social conditions encouraged its development?

3. What was cool jazz? How did it differ from bebop? Who were central figures in the birth of the cool?

4. What were hard bop and funky jazz? Why were these styles closely connected, and who were central figures in their development?

5. Describe the free jazz movement. Who were some founding artists of the movement, and why was it controversial?

6. What musical and social events led to the emergence of jazz-rock fusion? Who were key figures in its development?

7. What is smooth jazz? Why do some jazz purists dismiss the style?

8. Why were female jazz musicians marginalized? Who were some major women jazz artists of the 1990s and 2000s?

9. How would you describe the recent trends of Latin jazz, acid jazz, and the neoclassical movement? Which of these do you believe is advancing jazz?

Notes

1. Ted Gioia, *The History of Jazz* (New York: Oxford University Press, 1997), 201.

2. Dizzy Gillespie and Al Fraser, *To Be or Not to Bop: Memoirs—Dizzy Gillespie* (New York: Doubleday, 1979), 111.

3. Gary Giddins, *Visions of Jazz: The First Century* (New York: Oxford University Press, 1998), 261.

4. Gillespie and Fraser, *To Be or Not to Bop*, 117.

5. Miles Davis and Quincy Troupe, *Miles: The Autobiography* (New York: Simon & Schuster, 1990), 119.

6. Ibid., 59.

7. Ibid., 225.

8. Ibid., 141, 156.

9. Mark Gridley, *Jazz Styles: History and Analysis*, 8th ed. (Englewood Cliffs, NJ: Prentice-Hall, 2003), 195.

10. "The Adventure," in *Jazz*, DVD, directed by Ken Burns (Washington, DC: Florentine Films, WETA, 2000).

11. Ibid.

12. Ibid.

13. Gioia, *History of Jazz*, 347.

14. Stuart Nicholson, *Jazz-Rock: A History* (New York: Schirmer, 1998), 29.

15. Ibid., 33.

16. *Rolling Stone*, December 1969, p. 33.

17. Joachim Berendt, *The Jazz Book: From Ragtime to Fusion and Beyond* (Brooklyn, NY: Lawrence Hill Books, 1992), 42.

18. "Pat Metheny on Kenny G," http://www.jazzoasis.com/methenyonkennyg
    .htm.

19. *Downbeat,* August 9, 1979, p. 23.

20. Sherrie Tucker, "Women in Jazz: History in the Key of Jazz,"
    http://www.pbs.org/jazz/time/time-women.htm.

1940 - 1960

1941–1945 U.S. participates in World War II

1945 Louis Jordan scores major R & B and pop hits ♪

1946 DJ Alan Freed first uses the term *rock and roll* on the air ♪

1947 Chess Records founded in Chicago; Atlantic Records founded in New York ♪

1948 Columbia introduces 33⅓ rpm LP album format ♪

1948 Wynonie Harris and Roy Brown record "Good Rockin' Tonight" ♪

1949 RCA introduces the 45 rpm single record format ♪

1949 *Billboard* establishes separate pop, country, and R & B charts ♪

1950–1953 Korean War

1950 McCarthy "Red Scare" Senate hearings

1950 Patti Page has #1 hit with "Tennessee Waltz"; Nat "King" Cole records "Mona Lisa"; Fats Domino has first R & B hit ♪

1950 *Your Hit Parade* radio show moves to TV ♪

1951 "Rocket 88"—the "first rock record"—is released ♪

1952 DJ Alan Freed hosts first rock and roll show in Cleveland ♪

1953 President Dwight Eisenhower inaugurated

1953 Bill Haley's "Crazy, Man, Crazy" is the first white rock hit ♪

1954 School segregation outlawed; civil rights movement begins

1954 Big Joe Turner records "Shake, Rattle, and Roll" ♪

1955 Elvis Presley, Little Richard, Bo Diddley, and Chuck Berry first make the pop charts; the film *Blackboard Jungle* is released ♪

1956 Soviet Union invades Hungary; Cold War is in full swing

1956 Elvis Presley breaks out with major hits and TV appearances ♪

1957 Dick Clark's *American Bandstand* premieres on national TV ♪

1958 First U.S. satellite launched

1958 Little Richard, Chuck Berry, Buddy Holly, and Everly Brothers have multiple hits; Elvis is drafted ♪

1959 Cuban Revolution; Alaska and Hawaii become states

1959 Plane crash kills Buddy Holly, Ritchie Valens, Big Bopper ♪

1960 Congress begins payola hearings; Sam Cooke scores multiple hits ♪

1940   1950   1960

Chapter 13

Early R & B and Rock: The Late 1940s and the 1950s

No musical development in the latter half of the twentieth century changed the American musical landscape more than the birth of rock. In a few short decades, the genre went from a nameless offshoot of R & B to the country's most powerful musical export, perhaps the most popular musical style in the world. A complex blend of blues, R & B, country, swing, and boogie woogie, rock offers the quintessential example of cultural hybridity. The main cultural force in the evolution of rock was African American music, and rock's development replicated a pattern of cultural appropriation of black musical styles in American popular music that had begun 100 years earlier with minstrelsy. Rock, however, developed into something different, as critic Robert Palmer argues,

> The music *became something else*—not just the same old r&b or white approximations of it, but a broader idiom, influenced not only by black originators but by new production styles, new players, and the new context of a potentially wider and more diverse audience.[1]

IN THIS CHAPTER

- The Culture of the Early 1950s
- The Birth of R & B
- West Coast R & B
- Doo-Wop
- Independent Labels and Black-Oriented Stations
- The White Teen Market for "Forbidden" Music
- Regional Origins of R & B and Rock
- Fifties Rock after Elvis
- "The Day the Music Died"

THE CULTURE OF THE EARLY 1950s

The social and political climate of the 1950s greatly influenced the birth of rock. The era witnessed unprecedented economic prosperity, the growth of suburbia, and a baby boom that created a new class of consumer: the white teenager. Cars were increasingly available, and new music listening technologies came on the scene. The 1950s were also shaped by the Cold War and the civil rights movement, which signaled a revolution in race relations.

The postwar era saw technological advances in radio, recording, and television. Radio had found its way into almost every home and car throughout the country. By the late 1950s, people widely used portable, Japanese-made transistor radios, which freed teenagers from adult supervision of programming choices. In 1948 two major record labels, RCA and Columbia, engaged in a "battle of the record speeds." Columbia championed the 12-inch 33⅓ rpm **LP record** for classical music and jazz, while RCA promoted its 7-inch **45 rpm record** for popular music. The 45 single took on a life of its own as manufacturers developed portable 45 rpm record players to market directly to teens.

Internet Listening Exercise

Listen to samples of songs from the early 1950s.

Perry Como: "Hoop Dee Doo"

Bing Crosby: "Dear Hearts and Gentle People"

Patti Page: "How Much Is That Doggie in the Window?"

Frankie Laine: "Cry of the Wild Goose"

Television also expanded exponentially. By 1955 nearly two-thirds of American households had them. According to historian Glenn Altschuler, "Television spread the gospel of prosperity, barely acknowledging the existence of poverty or conflict."[2] Popular music on national television during the early 1950s reflected the bland mix that prevailed on the pop charts. Musical variety shows hosted by stars of the swing era were popular, as were broader variety programs such as the *Steve Allen Show* and the *Ed Sullivan Show*. R & B and rock-oriented dance-party shows for teens started to appear in the mid-1950s, including Dick Clark's *American Bandstand*. Although some early rock acts filtered into national television programming in the early 1950s, not until Elvis Presley's eleven television appearances in 1956 did rock become firmly established in the medium.

By most standards, the mainstream pop music of the early 1950s was bland. As critic Robert Palmer pointedly notes, "It was somnolent and squeaky clean. . . . For the most part, fifties pop was treacle."[3] Popular white artists of the era included crooner Perry Como, ballad singer Frankie Laine, and vocalist Patti Page, whose big hit was "How Much Is That Doggie in the Window?" Beginning in 1949, *Billboard* magazine reorganized its hit-record charts to recognize three major categories of popular music: popular, country and western, and rhythm and blues. These largely separate musical worlds produced few crossovers, and the only African American artists featured on the pop chart for 1950 were mainstream-sounding crooners such as Nat "King" Cole and Billy Eckstine.

Within a few years, the situation had changed completely By 1956 black and white R & B and rock artists such as Fats Domino, Little Richard, Chuck Berry, the Platters, the Coasters, Ivory Joe Hunter, Elvis Presley, Bill Haley and His Comets, Carl Perkins, and Johnny Cash had filled the pop charts. Presley, for example, had four top-ten singles that year. The shift to rock had begun.

Cultural Changes Associated with Rock

- Youth culture was born and teens began to pursue a rebellious "politics of fun" while creating pop music trends by using their newfound spending power.

- Cars became an integral part of youth culture, and rock played an important role in the teen automotive experience.

- Radio stations reached out to the newly mobile young population, and DJs became a powerful force in disseminating rock and shaping popular culture.

- The singer-songwriter emerged, making the creation of songs no longer the sole province of publishing houses and composers.

- The "standard" form of American popular song shifted from the 32-bar structure used by Tin Pan Alley composers to the 12-bar blues structure. Harmonic and melodic simplicity became the rule, and direct emotion replaced subtlety and irony in lyrics.

- The electric guitar emerged as the instrumental icon of popular music.

- The downsizing of music playback technology began with 45 rpm records and transistor radios.

THE BIRTH OF R & B

Although no one can say exactly when rock was born or who recorded the first rock song, historians agree that R & B was rock's closest musical relative. R & B developed as a result of several factors, as critic Nelson George argues,

> The term originated in the 1940s as a description of a synthesis of black musical genres—gospel, big-band swing, blues—that, along with new technology, specifically the popularization of the electric bass, produced a propulsive, spirited brand of popular music. A decade later it would be called rock & roll to camouflage its black roots, and subsequently soul, disco, rap, and other offspring would rise from these roots.[4]

From Race Music to Early R & B

Recall that, beginning in 1920, producers called popular music recordings by African Americans *race records*, and the term remained in use until the late 1940s. *Billboard* magazine had just begun to chart the sale of race music in 1946 when record labels became uncomfortable with the term and started to use coded alternatives such as "ebony" or "sepia." In 1949 *Billboard* without comment redesignated the category as *rhythm and blues,* using a term coined by a young writer, Jerry Wexler (later an Atlantic Records producer).

Early rhythm and blues (R & B) was a hybrid that mainly served as dance music for the African American community. As R & B pioneer Louis Jordan said, "I wanted to play music on stage that made people forget what they did that day."[5] By the end of World War II, the swing era of the 1930s and 1940s had peaked; however, although the new bebop style was moving jazz away from its dance-based roots, some swing band elements lived on in R & B. An aggressive rhythmic style known as **jump blues,** which began in the 1930s with Count Basie's Kansas City–based, riff-style big band, served as the prototype for postwar R & B. The format was ideal for smaller postwar bands that featured simple, blues-based tunes, explosive improvised solos, and the spontaneity lacking in many swing bands of the time. According to historian Charlie Gillett,

> At a time when the contemporary white big bands of Glenn Miller, Les Brown, and the Dorsey Brothers . . . were tending to impose arrangements on their musicians, the black bands had opened up and let their musicians run free. The sound of a sax solo breaking loose from a series of driving riffs is one of the most exciting experiences of this century's music.[6]

African American bandleaders such as Cab Calloway, Lionel Hampton, Jimmy Lunceford, Lucky Millinder, and Louis Jordan created their own versions of jump blues.

 **Internet Listening Exercise**

Listen to samples of jump blues.

Count Basie: "One O'Clock Jump"

Cab Calloway: "Jumpin' Jive"

Jimmy Lunceford: "Tain't What You Do (It's the Way That Cha Do It)"

Sister Rosetta Tharp with Lucky Millinder and His Orchestra: "Shout, Sister, Shout!"

© Bettmann/ CORBIS

Influential R & B legend Louis Jordan at a recording session in 1954.

Known to many as "the father of rhythm and blues," alto saxophonist, singer, and band leader **Louis Jordan** (1908–1975) had a string of hits in the late 1940s that made him the first artist to chart in all three popular music categories simultaneously. According to historian Arnold Shaw,

> Jordan is the pivotal figure in the rise of R & B . . . because his fantastic success on disk, on the radio, in personal appearances, and on the screen fired the imagination of black artists and independent record producers. He demonstrated that, not only was there a market for black-oriented material and black-styled music, but it was a big market, white as well as black."[7]

Jordan's boogie-woogie-based jump blues and performance style directly influenced both white and black artists, including Bill Haley, Chuck Berry, B. B. King, and James Brown. He was also the unrecognized "grandfather" of rap, owing to his satirical, spoken-word commentaries on social topics that were set to a jump-swing groove. In addition, Jordan and his band, the Tympany Five, were one of the first acts to dress in wild costumes and perform elaborate, tightly rehearsed shows. This outrageous visual style enabled the artist to produce some of the first *soundies*, late-1940s film equivalents of music videos that people viewed through visual arcade jukeboxes.

The Arkansas-born Jordan began his career with the Rabbitfoot Minstrels, where he developed versatile entertainment skills. In the late 1930s, he joined the Chick Webb Orchestra, which also featured singer Ella Fitzgerald. As one of Webb's vocalists, Jordan started performing the novelty songs that became central to his repertoire. A **novelty song** is a humorous song, often with a nonsense theme, sometimes employing special sound effects. Shortly thereafter, Jordan moved to start his own band, and by the late 1940s he was a household name. His success partly stemmed from his association with Decca Records, one of the first major labels to dispense with the race record category, which promoted Jordan's recordings to both black and white audiences. The artist's string of hits included "Five Guys Named Moe" (1942); "G.I. Jive" (1943); "Caldonia" (1945); his roots-of-rap classic, "Beware" (1945); and "Saturday Night Fish Fry" (1947). By the early 1950s, his musical style was influencing R & B and early rock artists throughout the country. Although his music was central to the formation of rock, Jordan never crossed over to the new genre, and by the late 1950s he had disappeared from the limelight.

CD LISTENING EXERCISE

CD 2/9

This excerpt from "Saturday Night Fish Fry" (1947) by Louis Jordan demonstrates the artist's place as the most influential entertainer in early R & B. Listen for Jordan's use of humor and spoken-word performance style, the early use of the term *rockin',* and the swinging jump blues groove of the tune.

R & B Shouters, Criers, and Honkers

Historians often group early R & B performers into three categories: shouters, criers, or honkers. **Shouters** came out of the riff-based big band tradition, in which a jump-style band was fronted by high-energy, blues-based vocals that were very nearly shouted. Famous R & B shouters included Wynonie Harris, Big Joe Turner, Jimmy Witherspoon, Ruth Brown, Little Esther Phillips, and Willie Mae "Big Mama" Thornton. Although only a few shouters crossed over to rock, they did influence rock vocal styles. Ruth Brown's (1928–) sophisticated blues style scored hits with "Teardrops from My Eyes" (1951) and "Oh What a Dream" (1954). Big Joe Turner's (1911–1985) major hit "Shake, Rattle, and Roll" (1954) was covered with great success by Bill Haley and Elvis Presley. Although not a crossover success, Wynonie Harris (1915–1969) had an R & B hit with his 1948 recording of "Good Rockin' Tonight," later covered by Elvis Presley. Some historians identify "Good Rockin' Tonight" as the first rock and roll song. Despite their appeal, most R & B shouters were considered too adult in style, their lyrics too sexual, for the ears of white teenage rock fans.

Internet Listening Exercise

Listen to samples of R & B shouters.

Ruth Brown: "Oh What a Dream"

Big Joe Turner: "Shake, Rattle, and Roll"

Wynonie Harris: "Good Rockin' Tonight"

With close connections to black gospel music, the R & B **crier** tradition, which projected the image of one overcome by emotion, also greatly affected rock vocal styles. The crier tradition influenced a host of blues, R & B, and rock singers, including Elvis Presley, Little Richard, Jackie Wilson, James Brown, and B. B. King. Singer/songwriter **Roy Brown** (1925–1981) was a consummate blues crier. He composed and recorded the first version of "Good Rockin' Tonight" (1948), covered by Harris later that year, and released other crier-style tunes such as "Hard Luck Blues" (1950) and "Big Town" (1951). Other R & B criers included Amos Milburn and Little Willie John.

The sound of the **honker,** or a performer playing a screaming, honking tenor saxophone, provided another essential ingredient of R & B and early rock. According to historian Charlie Gillett,

Internet Listening Exercise

Listen to samples of R & B criers.

Roy Brown: "Good Rockin' Tonight"

Amos Milburn: "Trouble in Mind"

Little Willie John: "Talk to Me, Talk to Me"

**Internet
Listening Exercise**

Listen to samples of R & B honkers.

Bill Doggett: "Honky Tonk"

Earl Bostic: "Temptation"

Big Jay McNeely: "There Is Something on Your Mind"

King Curtis: "Night Train"

During the first period of rock 'n' roll, 1954 to 1956, its most distinctive "trademark" was a break two-thirds of the way through the record, in which a saxophone player produced a sound that was liable to tear the paper off the walls, a fast screech that emphasized almost every beat for several bars.[8]

The honking R & B sax style was embodied in the work of players such as Earl Bostic, Bill Doggett, Sam "the Man" Taylor, Big Jay McNeely, and King Curtis. Particularly prolific, Curtis recorded with the Drifters and many other R & B artists. Throughout much of the 1950s, one could hear the sound of a blazing sax solo on almost every rock record.

WEST COAST R & B

The West Coast played a major role in the evolution of R & B, according to R & B pioneer Johnny Otis,

> Now R & B started here in LA. Roy Milton was here, Joe Liggins was here, T-Bone Walker was here, Charles Brown was here, I was here, and others, too. By '48 or '49 it was set—we had an art form, though we didn't know it then.[9]

Industrial growth during World War II drew over two million African Americans to California from Texas, Arkansas, Oklahoma, and Louisiana, and the wartime social climate encouraged desegregation of public places. One important West Coast stylistic innovation was a new style of ballad-oriented, smooth blues singing associated with Nat "King" Cole and Charles Brown. Another was the heightened prominence of the electric guitar, pioneered by T-Bone Walker. He was the first R & B performer to use the sustained tone made possible by electric amplification to play the guitar like a horn. He was also the first to make the guitar a central theatrical focus of his act—playing behind his back, over his head, with his teeth, and between his legs—well before Chuck Berry's duck walk of the 1950s or Jimi Hendrix's psychedelic antics of the 1960s.

Band leaders **Johnny Otis** (1921–) and **Roy Milton** (1907–1983) made major contributions to the L.A. R & B scene. While most early innovators of R & B were African American, Otis was a white Greek American who identified strongly with the African American community. In the 1950s, he led one of R & B's most successful acts, the "Rhythm and Blues Caravan." Otis described the sound that he and others were developing:

> It surely wasn't a big band; it wasn't swing, it wasn't country blues. It was what was to become known as rhythm and blues, a hybrid form that became an art form in itself. It was the foundation of rock 'n' roll.[10]

Otis had his first hit with "Harlem Nocturne"(1946), and he made the shift to rock in the 1950s with such hits as "Willie and the Hand Jive" (1958). In addition to performing, he found success as a writer and producer who discovered and promoted major R & B artists including Jackie Wilson and Little Esther Phillips.

Roy Milton and the Solid Senders had one of the biggest R & B hits of the 1940s called "R.M. Blues." The million-selling jump blues was one of the first tunes to use a rock backbeat, and Milton's innovative drumming became central to the development of rock drum patterns. Other influential West Coast R & B artists included Ruth Brown, Ivory Joe Hunter, and Lowell Fulson. Charles Brown influenced Ivory Joe Hunter's early work, and Hunter later became one of the earliest black artists to cross over to the country charts.

Nat "King" Cole (1917–1965) was already an accomplished jazz pianist when he introduced his smooth vocal style in the mid-1940s. Although many West Coast nightclubs were beginning to integrate, upscale Hollywood clubs generally remained segregated because they had no interest in blues and R & B. Because the patrons of such clubs wanted to converse over a quiet musical background, Cole played lounge-style piano backed by smooth, warm vocals. A black singer who crooned like Bing Crosby was a novelty, and Cole's subdued baritone voice became an immediate hit. Ultimately, Cole's style stood so far removed from African American performance traditions that white audiences often found him more popular than black audiences did. His hits included "Straighten Up and Fly Right" (1944), "Get Your Kicks on Route Sixty Six" (1945), "The Christmas Song" (1947), "Mona Lisa" (1950), and "Unforgettable" (1952). The last song was posthumously rerecorded in 1991 as a duet by Cole's daughter Natalie.

Although Nat "King" Cole was never a blues singer, his vocal style significantly influenced the smooth, bluesy, ballad style of singer/songwriter/pianist **Charles Brown** (1922–1999). Brown in turn influenced a generation of R & B

Internet Listening Exercise

Listen to samples of early L.A. R & B artists.

Johnny Otis: "Willie and the Hand Jive"

Roy Milton: "R.M. Blues"

Ivory Joe Hunter: "I Almost Lost My Mind"

Multicultural Note

Nat "King" Cole—America's First African American TV Host

Nat "King" Cole's success with white audiences opened doors previously closed to black performers. For example, he became the first African American to host his own prime-time TV variety show from 1956 to 1957. The program initially had no sponsors, because advertisers feared that white southern audiences would boycott their products. When an executive from Max Factor suggested that "a Negro couldn't sell lipstick," Cole responded, "What do they think we use, chalk? Congo paint?" [11]

When no full-time sponsors ultimately appeared, producers took the show off the air. During the program's sixty-five-week run, however, many of the biggest stars in the music business—including Ella Fitzgerald, Tony Bennett, and Peggy Lee—appeared for far less than their normal salaries.

How have color lines changed in the entertainment business today? Are there any hip-hop artists hosting mainstream TV shows?

artists with his own emotion-laden, crooning blues style. According to vocalist/guitarist Bonnie Raitt,

> Charles was the master of the blues ballad. In the evolution from blues and jazz in the 30s and 40s to modern R & B and pop, Charles Brown's importance simply can't be overstated. . . . He introduced the nuances of great pop and jazz singing into the world of R & B. And you will hear his legacy in everyone from Ray Charles to Sam Cooke, to Marvin Gaye, to Babyface, to D'Angelo.[12]

The Texas-born Brown began his musical career in Los Angeles as pianist with Johnny Moore's Three Blazers, a group that fashioned its sound on Nat "King" Cole's trio. Brown's own melancholy, smooth blues sound flavored his first hit, "Driftin' Blues" (1946), which sold a million copies and knocked Louis Jordan out of first place. The lyrics to the song struck a raw nerve with soldiers, sailors, and migrant workers throughout the country who had been cut adrift by war:

> I'm driftin' and driftin' like a ship out on the sea
> I ain't got nobody in this world to care for me.

After Brown left the Blazers to record under his own name, he scored numerous hits throughout the 1940s. His holiday blues classic "Merry Christmas Baby" (1948) was covered by artists as diverse as Elvis Presley, Otis Redding, Lou Rawls, and Bruce Springsteen.

DOO-WOP

Doo-wop, or group vocal harmony grounded in black gospel and barbershop harmony, was a hallmark sound of the 1950s.

The Mills Brothers and the Ink Spots

We can trace the roots of the R & B vocal group tradition back to two legendary African American vocal groups—the Mills Brothers and the Ink Spots. The father of the original Mills Brothers, a barber in Ohio, belonged to a black barbershop quartet; the brothers first sang in front of their father's barbershop and in African American church choirs. The Mills Brothers' first hit, "Tiger Rag" (1931), was the first vocal-group recording to sell over a million copies. They generally started songs in a sweet ballad style, picking up the tempo in the second verse. They also developed a repertoire of vocal imitations of musical instruments that became a trademark. Other hits included "Paper Doll" (1942) and "Glow-Worm" (1952).

The Ink Spots began their career in the early 1930s singing fast jump tunes. Later in the decade they switched to a ballad style often interspersed with spoken dialogue. The group's main hits included "If I Didn't Care" (1939), "Java Jive" (1940), and "I'll Never Smile Again" (1940). The work of both the Mills Brothers and the Ink Spots was characterized by clear standard English diction

Internet Listening Exercise

Listen to samples of Nat "King" Cole and Charles Brown.

Nat "King" Cole: "Straighten Up and Fly Right," "Unforgettable"

Charles Brown: "Driftin' Blues," "Merry Christmas, Baby"

Internet Listening Exercise

Listen to samples of the Mills Brothers and the Ink Spots.

The Ink Spots: "If I Didn't Care"

The Mills Brothers: "Glow-Worm"

The Coasters (left to right): Cornel Gunther, Will "Dub" Jones, B Guy, Carl Gardner, and guitarist Adolphi Jacob.

Multicultural Note

The African American Origins of Barbershop Quartets

The contemporary image of a barbershop quartet is a group of white men dressed in turn-of-the-century outfits. The roots of the style, however, lay in African American barbershops of the late nineteenth century. Barbering was a low-status occupation performed by European immigrants or African Americans. In the black community, barbershops often served as hubs of social and musical activities, and the close harmonies and performance styles of the barbershop quartet style developed in this milieu.

The early recording industry contributed to the racial shift from black to white barbershop quartets by recording primarily white barbershop groups. Once barbershop became popular in the 1930s, it was promoted by an organization called the SPEBSQSA (Society for the Preservation of Barbershop Quartet Singing in America). The group, like many other male fraternal organizations before the civil rights era, admitted only white members. Over time, the shift of barbershop from a black to a white art form became complete.[13]

and songs with unprovocative, neutral content, which enabled them to cross over to white audiences.

Early Doo-Wop

Primarily an urban African American phenomenon, doo-wop was usually performed by young men and featured group harmony with traditional choir arrangements (tenor, baritone, bass), often with an added **falsetto** (high voice). Increasing numbers of gospel artists entered the record market in the 1940s, and gospel harmony fed the new doo-wop vocal style. The use of nonsense syllables on background parts was also standard, evolving from "doo-wahs" and "doo-wops" to more-complex articulations. Singers could start a doo-wop group with no instrumental accompaniment, and rehearsals could take place anywhere, anytime—in attics, in garages, or on street corners.

Doo-wop groups often took the colorful names of songbirds or cars: the Orioles, the Ravens, the Penguins, and the Flamingos, as well as the Impalas, the Fleetwoods, and the El Dorados. Popular early doo-wop groups included the Ravens, who scored hits with "Write Me a Letter" (1948) and "Rock Me All Night Long" (1952); the Orioles, a Baltimore group, who made the charts with "It's Too Soon to Know" (1949) and "Crying in the Chapel" (1953); and the Dominoes, who found success with the controversial "Sixty Minute Man" (1951), whose lyrics boasted of sexual prowess and provoked the ire of white conservatives. Two lead singers from the Dominoes, Clyde McPhatter and Jackie Wilson, went on to successful solo careers.

After leaving the Dominoes, McPhatter formed the Drifters. When McPhatter left to become a soloist, he was replaced by Ben E. King, who led the Drifters through a series of hits, including "There Goes My Baby" (1959), "This Magic Moment" (1960), and "Save the Last Dance for Me" (1960). Hank Ballard and the Midnighters scored with "Work with Me Annie" (1954), "Sexy Ways" (1954), and "Annie Had a Baby" (1954). The three songs together told a sad story of pleading, gratification, and the laws of cause and effect—three of doo-wop's central themes. There were numerous doo-wop "one-hit wonders," including the Chords, whose megahit was "Sh-Boom" (1954), and the Penguins, who produced "Earth Angel" (1955). The Crew Cuts, a white doo-wop group, released covers of black doo-wop hits which often charted higher than the originals.

Doo-Wop's Golden Age

Doo-wop entered its golden age in the late 1950s, as groups began to integrate advanced choreography and white doo-wop acts started to record original material. Frankie Lymon and the Teenagers, who later influenced Michael Jackson and other Motown artists, scored one of the biggest doo-wop hits of all time with "Why Do Fools Fall in Love?" in 1956. The Coasters and the Platters gained particular prominence in the late 1950s. The Coasters, who featured novelty songs with spoken words, had hits with "Yakety Yak" (1958), "Charlie Brown" (1959), and "Poison Ivy" (1959). The Platters, sometimes called "the new Ink

Spots," were the first black doo-wop group to reach number one on the pop charts with "The Great Pretender" (1955). Other hits included "Only You" (1955) and "Smoke Gets in Your Eyes" (1958).

While most doo-wop groups were male, some successful female and mixed-gender vocal groups gained popularity. The most prominent all-female group, the Chantels, charted with "He's Gone" (1957), "Maybe" (1958), and "Every Night (I Pray)" (1958). Many white vocal groups of the late 1950s were Italian American. Dion and the Belmonts, the most popular of the groups, had a million-seller with "Teenager in Love" (1959). The Four Lovers, after changing their name to the Four Seasons, became stars in the early 1960s with hits such as "Sherry" (1962) and "Walk Like a Man" (1962). Although the doo-wop era ended by 1960, it paved the way for the girl-group and Motown vocal ensemble sounds of the 1960s.

INDEPENDENT LABELS AND BLACK-ORIENTED STATIONS

In the 1940s, small, regionally based record labels began distributing the new sound of R & B. Although a few major R & B artists, such as Louis Jordan and Nat "King" Cole, recorded for large record companies, most others recorded on the new independent labels. One reason for this was a shift in how music was licensed and published in the era. The major labels, associated with ASCAP, geared their product for the mass white audience. BMI, on the other hand, was aggressively signing R & B and country songwriters. The new record labels also set their sights on the underserved, marginal markets. The independent labels were central to the development of R & B and early rock for two decades.

New radio stations—some with powerful transmitters that provided national coverage—also expanded the reach of R & B in the late 1940s. Located mainly in the South and West, the stations began to program for the African American market for the first time, simultaneously giving greater voice to the new sounds of R & B. The financial logic was clear, according to Nelson George:

> The sales staff of Memphis's powerful 50,000-watt WDIA weren't shy about the fact that they reached 1,237,686 Negroes (10 percent of all black Americans) and that Negroes constituted 40 percent of the Memphis market.[14]

In addition to R & B, the stations often also played blues, gospel, and jazz. Whites owned almost all the black-oriented stations, and their sound was defined by the personalities of their DJs, who were both white and black. Many black and white listeners—including a young Elvis Presley—received their early musical schooling from the R & B stations.

THE WHITE TEEN MARKET FOR "FORBIDDEN" MUSIC

In the early 1950s, white teens found themselves drawn in increasing numbers to the new, rhythmic sounds and adult—often sexual—lyrical content of R & B. As media commentator Jeff Greenfield recalls, "Brewed in the hidden

Internet Listening Exercise

Listen to samples of doo-wop.

The Orioles: "Crying in the Chapel"

The Dominoes: "Sixty Minute Man"

The Drifters: "There Goes My Baby"

Hank Ballard and the Midnighters: "Work with Me Annie"

The Chords: "Sh-Boom"

The Penguins: "Earth Angel"

Frankie Lymon and the Teenagers: "Why Do Fools Fall in Love?"

The Coasters: "Charlie Brown"

The Platters: "The Great Pretender"

corners of black American cities, its rhythms infected white Americans, seducing them. . . . Rock and roll was elemental, savage, dripping with sex; it was just as our parents feared."[15] As white teens began to frequent black clubs and to seek out R & B records at black record stores, the merchants took note and passed word on to radio DJs, who fed the growing teen interest. At WLAC in Nashville, Gene Nobles played jazz and early R & B in the early 1940s; in Los Angeles, Hunter Hancock played R & B on KFVD; and the legendary Alan Freed started out on WJW in Cleveland, subsequently moving to New York's WINS. One of the few early black DJs was Nat Williams on WDIA in Memphis. According to one young white listener, "It didn't make any difference what color they were, it just made me feel good."[16]

An influential DJ and the first rock concert producer, **Alan Freed** (1922–1965) opened the door to white acceptance of black music by refusing to play white cover versions of R & B originals. He was also among the first to use the term *rock and roll* to describe R & B, although its earliest referent was sex, as

Multicultural Note

Conservative Reactions to Rock and Roll

The more attractive R & B became to white youths, the more controversy it engendered. Rock and roll shows often featured black artists and attracted racially mixed audiences, so adult fear of new forms of adolescent rebellion was coupled with none-too-subtle racism. Some white southern conservative groups painted rock as a plot by the NAACP to corrupt white youth. One city eliminated rock from municipal swimming pool jukeboxes because the beat attracted "undesirable elements" who practiced "spastic gyrations" in abbreviated bathing suits. The *New York Times* quoted a psychiatrist who branded rock as "a cannibalistic and tribalistic" form of music.[17]

The popular music industry establishment grew alarmed not so much at the spectacle of teen rebellion as at threats to the bottom line. Established pop artists of the late 1940s and early 1950s, as well as the major record labels and ASCAP, grew defensive. Vocalist Frank Sinatra, who himself had caused swooning bobbysoxers to riot at his performances a decade earlier, announced his verdict on rock:

> It smells phony and false. It is sung, played, and written for the most part by cretinous goons, and by means of its almost imbecilic reiteration and sly, lewd, in plain fact dirty, lyrics it manages to be the martial music of every side-burned delinquent on the face of the earth.[18]

By the end of the decade, the major players in the music business had begun a more careful strategy of co-optation, recognizing that rock would be a lasting musical style.

singer/songwriter Roy Brown recounted, "Now, 'Good Rockin' Tonight,' you know what that means. I had my mind on this girl in the bedroom, I'm not going to lie to you. Listen, man, I wrote them kind of songs. I was a dirty cat."[19] Freed started working in radio in the early 1940s, playing records by Louis Jordan and other jump-blues artists. He began to call himself the "Moondog," and his show evolved into *The Moondog Rhythm and Blues House Party*. He soon branched out into concert promotion, producing history's first rock concert, "The Moondog Coronation Ball," at a Cleveland hockey arena in 1952. The overpromoted event turned into a riot because of lack of security and overcrowding, and the resulting media coverage was memorable:

> There were some 20,000 rabid blues fans. . . . Males were wearing their hats inside a public space, guzzling liquor without restraint from pocket flasks, and, here and there, actually shooting themselves with narcotics in the midst of a crowd![20]

Freed also launched the first sold-out national rock tour in 1953 with an all-star R & B revue headlined by the Dominoes and the Drifters.

Freed moved to WINS in New York in 1954 and took the station to the top. According to singer/songwriter Paul Simon, "New York was a pool of sounds, but only one station was playing rock and roll, the station Alan Freed was on."[21] Freed's decline began in 1958 when violence erupted at one of his concerts and resulted in legal charges. He was also indicted and convicted for accepting

MICHAEL OCHS ARCHIVES.COM

Bill Haley and His Comets in a 1957 publicity shot for the film *Don't Knock the Rock*.

payola (bribes to push certain records) from record companies. His contributions to early rock later became the subject of the popular 1978 film *American Hot Wax.*

Bill Haley (1925–1981) was the first white artist to successfully adapt the R & B style for a mass pop audience. With his band, the Comets, Haley fused elements of country, western swing, jump blues, and early R & B to produce some of the first rock hits. His "Crazy, Man, Crazy" (1953) was the first rock song to make the pop charts. Featured in *The Blackboard Jungle,* which was the first rock-and-roll movie, "Rock around the Clock" (1954) topped the pop charts and eventually sold 22.5 million copies. Rock music had never before been used as the soundtrack to a movie, and the film showcased rock as an emblem of teen rebellion. Both the song and the movie signaled the arrival of a new musical era.

Haley started out playing western swing and country music in the 1940s. He also learned a great deal from Louis Jordan, with whom he shared producer Milt Gabler at Decca Records. Gabler here describes his studio work with Haley's band:

> We'd begin with Jordan's shuffle rhythm . . . and we'd build on it. I'd sing Jordan riffs to the group that would be picked up by the electric guitars and tenor sax. They got a sound that had the drive of The Tympany Five and the color of country and western.[22]

Haley's voice was unmistakably white, but he drew his rhythm from black music. Haley's recording career began in 1951 with a cover version of Jackie Brenston's "Rocket 88." He experimented with his band's name, changing it from the Four Aces of Western Swing to the Saddlemen and finally to Bill Haley and His Comets. In 1954 he released "Rock around the Clock" as well as "Shake, Rattle, and Roll," a sanitized cover of Joe Turner's earlier R & B hit. Haley's popularity declined in the late 1950s, when younger rockers such as Little Richard and Elvis came across as both more attractive and more dangerous. Although listeners associated Haley's early music with teen rebellion, he was far from a rebel:

> A lot of people blamed juvenile delinquency on us, hot rods, drinking, everything. But rock got the kids off the streets and around the jukeboxes. They said it was a bad influence. Well, we always kept our lyrics clean and we never did any protest songs.[23]

According to rock critic Chet Flippo,

> Haley was as unlikely a rock 'n' roll star as you could find anywhere. He was too old and overweight, even at the start, and didn't have the right moves, but he did have the right songs at the right time. Haley was a country-and-western singer and bandleader who accidentally became a rock 'n' roll pioneer.[24]

CD LISTENING EXERCISE

CD 2/10

"Rock around the Clock" (1956), composed and recorded by Bill Haley and His Comets, is a 12-bar blues. Listen carefully for the intermittent and tentatively played backbeat on the snare drum. In the early days of rock, the backbeat had not yet become the standard rhythmic device it is in dance music today. The song also features an electric guitar rather than a saxophone solo, another defining ingredient in the shift from R & B to rock and roll. Are there country influences in Haley's vocal style?

REGIONAL ORIGINS OF R & B AND ROCK

As R & B and rock developed, performers and producers generated distinctive hybrids reflecting regional musical styles. Three regions were particularly important: New Orleans, Chicago, and Memphis.

New Orleans

Known as the birthplace of jazz, New Orleans also influenced the evolution of R & B and rock. Although none of the major independent record labels headquartered there, the city hosted an active recording scene. The distinctive, piano-based sound of New Orleans R & B showed in the music of artists such as Fats Domino and Lloyd Price. Many influential early New Orleans rock records were recorded in a tiny studio built and staffed by a white producer named Cosimo Matassa. These recordings, which were sold to Los Angeles–based independent labels, made stars out of artists such as Fats Domino and Little Richard.

Fats Domino (1928–) was one of the most successful rock artists of the 1950s, second only to Elvis Presley. Selling more than sixty-five million records, Domino made the transition from R & B to rock with pleasant, upbeat songs and an engaging piano style. White audiences found him less frantic and threatening than many of his contemporaries, according to critics Grace Lichtenstein and Laura Dankner:

> Neither dynamic nor demented nor dangerous onstage . . . he was instead a pudgy little guy with a great smile beaming out beyond the keyboard who won his audience over with a catchy rolling bass line, not swiveling hips. . . . His songs had hooks that grabbed hold of listeners in an instant and wouldn't let them sit still.[25]

Listeners could instantly recognize Domino's sound. His piano style was classic boogie woogie, influenced by pianists such as Professor Longhair and Amos Milburn, and his voice was uniquely his own. Domino cowrote most of his hits with bandleader Dave Bartholomew, who helped produce Domino's characteristic New Orleans sound. The artist broke into the pop market in 1955 with "Ain't That a Shame." White teen idol Pat Boone quickly covered the tune and drove it to the top of the charts. Domino subsequently appeared in several early rock and roll movies and recorded such rock standards as "Blueberry Hill" (1956), "I'm in Love Again" (1956), "Blue Monday" (1957), and "I'm Walkin'" (1957). Other early rock artists—including Elvis Presley, Chuck Berry, Jerry Lee Lewis, and Little Richard—also covered many of his songs. Unlike the many black artists who were exploited by record companies, Domino had a contract that paid royalties to him as songwriter based on sales of records, rather than a single flat fee for a song. He was also one of the first black artists on national television in the 1950s, and he toured widely in Alan Freed's rock and roll package shows.

Little Richard (Richard Penniman, 1932–) was the first self-styled "King of Rock and Roll." His raucous stage performance, pounding piano, wild falsetto, high pompadour, outrageous makeup, flashy dress, and gleeful sexuality

Internet Listening Exercise

Listen to samples of New Orleans piano-based R & B.

Professor Longhair: *Big Easy Strut: The Essential Professor Longhair*

Fats Domino: *The Fats Domino Jukebox*

Lloyd Price: *Lloyd Price—20th Century Masters, The Millennium Collection*

Recording Early Rock

Early rock records were generally made in small studios with primitive equipment—a far cry from today's multitrack, digital facilities. At Cosimo Matassa's studio in New Orleans, producer Dave Bartholomew had only one microphone for the whole band. Little Richard's producer, Bumps Blackwell, recorded in the same studio:

> The studio was just a back room in a furniture store.... There'd be a grand piano just as you came in the door. I'd have the grand's lid up with a mike in the keys.... Earl Palmer's drums were out the door, where I had one mike as well. The bassman would be way over the other side of the studio.... If it didn't sound right I'd just keep moving the mikes around.... It might take me forty-five minutes, an hour, to get that balance within the room, but once those guys hit a groove you could go on all night.[26]

Historians Colin Escott and Martin Hawkins describe a similar situation at Sam Phillips's Sun Records studio in Memphis, where Elvis Presley and many other early blues and rock artists were first recorded:

> It was a small storefront property at 706 Union Avenue.... By 1954 he had two recorders: one console model and another mounted on a rack behind his head for the tape delay echo, or "slapback" for which Sun became famous. By "bouncing" the signal from one machine to another, with a split-second lag between the two, he created his characteristic echo effect.... Phillips recorded his most important music with that configuration.[27]

MICHAEL OCHS ARCHIVES.COM

Little Richard and his band the Upsetters perform in the 1957 film *Mister Rock and Roll*.

personified the wildness and danger of rock for white audiences. Richard's songs were up-tempo, all-out raves: he was one of rock's first composers with his 1956 hit "Tutti Frutti." His boisterous stage act influenced everyone from Jerry Lee Lewis and James Brown to the Beatles, Mick Jagger, and Jimi Hendrix. Richard's use of costumes and makeup, far in advance of David Bowie, Boy George, Queen, and Prince, also made him the first androgynous rock star, with his thinly veiled homosexuality predating that of other rock artists by decades. Producer Bumps Blackwell recalled his first impression of the artist: "There's this cat in this loud shirt, with hair waved up six inches above his head. He was talking wild, thinking up stuff just to be different, you know? I could tell he was a mega-personality."[28]

CD LISTENING EXERCISE

CD 2/11

"Tutti Frutti" (1956), recorded by Little Richard, is a classic 12-bar blues. Benign nonsense lyrics replaced the original "offensive" lyrics. How does Richard's over-the-top vocal delivery energize the tune? Notice how Richard's piano-based rhythm section aggressively drives the song. Notice also the boogie woogie flavor of the piano, and how the sax solo reflects a classic R & B honking style. How does the use of rhythm breaks add energy?

The Georgia-born artist began his career singing gospel, playing piano in church, and traveling with medicine and minstrel shows. A successful demo tape led Richard to New Orleans to record with producer Bumps Blackwell and the same band that backed Fats Domino. The first recordings sounded inhibited, but over a lunch break Richard started to play a throwaway tune called "Tutti Frutti," which turned into a hit:

I'd been singing "Tutti Frutti" for years, but it never struck me as a song you'd *record.* . . . Sure, it used to crack the crowds up when I sang it in the clubs, with those risqué lyrics: Tutti Frutti, good booty / If it don't fit, don't force it / You can grease it, make it easy. But I never thought it would be a fit, even with the lyrics cleaned up.[29]

The tune's whooping vocals and wild piano-banging set a tone for Richard's future hits. Sold to white and black audiences—ultimately over three million copies—it had a widespread impact, quickly covered by white artists Pat Boone and Elvis Presley. Richard followed up with "Long Tall Sally" (1956), "Rip It Up" (1956), and "Ready Teddy" (1956), all of which white artists covered multiple times. Richard toured behind his hits with his fine and aptly named band, the Upsetters. When he left the group to work as a solo act, a young vocalist named James Brown replaced him, then another named Otis Redding did. Richard's hits continued into 1958 with "Lucille," "Keep a Knockin'," and "Good Golly Miss Molly," but by that time he had decided to leave secular music for the Christian ministry. Richard periodically returned to rock in the 1960s and 1970s, touring Europe with the Beatles and the Rolling Stones. Of the numerous "kings" of rock, Little Richard may have actually deserved the title.

Chicago

Extensive migration of African Americans from the deep South made Chicago a center of important developments in jazz and blues for the first half of the twentieth century. The Chicago blues sound, especially the work of Muddy Waters, helped build the early musical vocabularies of many sixties groups such as the Rolling Stones, who took their name from a Muddy Waters tune. In addition, the city gave rise to Chuck Berry and Bo Diddley, who both recorded with the independent Chess/Checker Records, Chicago's seminal blues/R & B label.

Chess Records' founders, brothers Leonard and Phil Chez, were Polish Jews who migrated to the United States in the late 1940s and westernized their names to Chess. They founded Aristocrat Records in 1947, changing the name to Chess two years later. Chicago blues quickly became their specialty, and Muddy Waters, with his synthesis of rural and electric urban blues, became their star. Other Chess artists included Howlin' Wolf, John Lee Hooker, and Sonny Boy Williamson. By the mid-1950s, Chess had entered the world of rock with doo-wop recordings by the Moonglows and the Flamingos, but the work of Chuck Berry and Bo Diddley is what put Chicago and Chess records at the center of rock history.

With the possible exception of Little Richard, no other artist deserved the title "architect of rock" more than **Chuck Berry** (1926–) did. According to historian Charlie Gillett,

> If importance in popular music were measured in terms of imaginativeness, creativeness, wit, the ability to translate a variety of experiences and feelings into musical form, and long term influence and reputation, Chuck Berry would be described as the major figure of rock 'n' roll.[30]

Berry was rock's first electric guitar hero and one of early rock's most prolific songwriters. He was also one of the first to understand that rock was music for teenagers, the new consumer class. Berry crafted songs specifically for teens, shaping them around blazing, T-Bone Walker–style guitar solos. His music also influenced a generation of rock artists including the Beatles, Bob Dylan, and the Rolling Stones. Berry's recording career began with "Maybelline" (1955), followed by "Roll over Beethoven" (1956), "School Day" (1957), "Rock and Roll Music" (1957), "Sweet Little Sixteen" (1958), and "Johnny B. Goode" (1958).

Berry's early musical influences included R & B and country styles; he greatly admired Louis Jordan, T-Bone Walker, and Charles Brown. Berry first auditioned for Chess with the country-flavored tune "Ida Red," and after some reworking (and retitling as "Maybelline"), the tune became a hit. The artist's clear enunciation and vocal style also made his recordings sound ethnically ambiguous—that is, he was a black performer who sounded "white." In addition, Berry used stage antics pioneered by T-Bone Walker, notably his patented duck walk, in which he slid across the stage, crouched with one leg in front of the other, with the guitar perched precariously in front of him.

By the end of the 1950s, Berry had become one of the most successful black entertainers of all time. In 1960, however, in a racially motivated prosecution, he was arrested and imprisoned for two years on trumped-up morals charges. The artist returned to make records in the 1960s and 1970s, including "Nadine" (1964) and "No Particular Place to Go" (1964), and he toured with the Beatles and the Rolling Stones. According to historian John Collis,

Berry's effect on rock and roll was greater than any other individual. Whereas Elvis caused a revolutionary change in pop music with a voice and an image, Berry was the complete article, a writer and musician with the imagination to show that rock could venture into previously uncharted territory.[31]

Within a few weeks of Chuck Berry's first recording for Chess Records, **Bo Diddley** (1928–), one of early rock's most idiosyncratic performers, walked a few blocks from his house into the Chess Records studio and asked, "Man, y'all make records in here?"[32] His audition tape, "Bo Diddley," became one of the influential songs of early rock. The rhythmic foundation of the song, similar to the three-two clave of Afro-Caribbean music, became

CD LISTENING EXERCISE

CD 2/12

"Roll over Beethoven" (1956), composed and recorded by Chuck Berry, is another early rock tune set to a 12-bar blues. Berry's ability to craft lyrics that spoke directly to teenagers gave his music great appeal. The T-Bone Walker–inspired guitar solo that starts the song was mimicked on numerous subsequent recordings by other artists, including the Beach Boys in "Surfin' USA." For many listeners, Berry's use of standard English masked his ethnicity.

known as the "Bo Diddley beat" and was adopted by numerous rock performers. The idiosyncratic artist's unusual band included a maraca player and a female electric guitarist, both rarities in the male world of 1950s rock. Diddley also played an assortment of bizarre guitars, many of which he built himself. Subsequent hits included "I'm a Man" (1955) and "Who Do You Love" (1956).

Internet Listening Exercise

Listen to samples of Bo Diddley's music.

Bo Diddley: *20th Century Masters—Bo Diddley's Greatest Hits, The Millennium Collection*

Memphis

Memphis played a central role in the development of jazz, blues, R & B, and rock throughout the twentieth century. Situated on the Mississippi River in western Tennessee, near the border of Mississippi and Arkansas, the city straddled the route between New Orleans and Chicago; its location in part made it a magnet for aspiring musicians from throughout the region. Beginning in the late 1940s, Memphis also developed as a recording center, and many influential artists of the postwar period got their start there.

Rock mythology would not be complete without the story of Memphis-based producer Sam Phillips and his Sun Records label. Best remembered as the man who "discovered" and first recorded Elvis Presley, **Sam Phillips** (1923–2003) also helped develop and popularize rockabilly music, and he was the first to record many influential blues artists. Phillips had an intuition for talent: In an eight-year period he recorded B. B. King, Howlin' Wolf, Ike Turner, Rufus Thomas, Elvis Presley, Johnny Cash, Jerry Lee Lewis, Carl Perkins, Charlie Rich, and Roy Orbison. Like other independent labels of the era, Sun Records pioneered rock and challenged the dominance of the major record labels. Phillips heard blues, spirituals, and country music while growing up in Depression-era Alabama. While working as a DJ in Memphis, he realized that there were few facilities to record the wealth of black talent in the area: "Beale Street convinced me that with the talent coming out of the Delta, especially, I really wanted to try to do something with that talent because I was very close to it all of my life."[33]

Phillips opened up his recording studio in 1950 with a straightforward business slogan: "We Record Anything—Anywhere—Anytime." At first he recorded local artists such as B. B. King and Howlin' Wolf and then sold or leased the masters to independent record labels. Phillips's recordings featured tape echo, distortion, and skillful use of room acoustics to create a big sound with unusually small groups of musicians. He hit the jackpot in 1951 with the number-one R & B hit "Rocket 88" by Jackie Brenston; many call it the first rock and roll record because of its booming boogie rhythm driven by distorted guitar. During the drive to Memphis for the recording session, the guitar amplifier fell off the top of the band's car, breaking the speaker cone. According to Sam Phillips, "We had no way of getting it fixed . . . so we started playing around with the damn thing. I stuffed a little paper in there and it sounded good. It sounded like a saxophone." This accident thus gave birth to fuzztone guitar. According to historian Robert Palmer, "From then on, when Phillips was recording a blues combo, he let the guitarist wail." [34]

Phillips established his own label, Sun Records, in 1952, and the next year he scored his first major R & B hits with Little Junior Parker's "Mystery Train" (later covered by Elvis Presley) and Rufus Thomas's "Bear Cat." Despite Sun's R & B hits, Phillips concluded that the demographic base for his product was too narrow. To solve this problem, he decided to branch out and record white artists. As his secretary, Marion Keisker, recalled, "Over and over, I remember Sam saying, 'If I could find a white man who had the Negro sound and the Negro feel, I could make a billion dollars.' " [35] With Elvis Presley, Phillips found that sound; after Presley, he pursued it repeatedly with a series of artists whom he tried to fit into his newfound rockabilly mold— Carl Perkins, Johnny Cash, Jerry Lee Lewis, Roy Orbison, and Charlie Rich. The "Sun sound" that Phillips achieved—"long on feel and short on contrivance"—is still a recording industry catchphrase. [36] Many of the artists he recorded established or redefined the musical genres in which they worked, and for many of them the recordings they did with Phillips may have been their best work.

Elvis Presley (1935–1977) stood as the first enduring national star of rock and roll and the biggest single attraction in the history of popular music. During his twenty-one-year career, he had sixty-seven top-twenty hits, thirty-eight top-twenty albums, and sold over a billion records worldwide. The first artist to effectively combine all the essential ingredients of rock—R & B, blues, country, and gospel —Presley became the first white performer of the 1950s to harness the passion and sexuality of R & B for a mass audience. With the swivel of his hips and the curl of his lip, Presley enhanced rock's aura of teenage rebellion. According to critic Dave Marsh,

MICHAEL OCHS ARCHIVES.COM

Elvis Presley outraged fans with his swiveling hips on the Milton Berle television show in 1956. On his next television appearance, Presley was shown only from the waist up.

"Among the countless clichés Elvis embodied, 'living legend' is the most perfectly realized. There is no 'real' Elvis. That man, whoever he may have been, disappeared long ago into the mists of legend." [37]

Presley was born in Tupelo, Mississippi. His early musical influences came from church and the radio, where he heard blues, country, pop, and black gospel. Presley identified the Pentecostal church as his primary source of musical training:

> When I was four or five, all I looked forward to was Sundays, when we all could go to church. This was the only singing training I ever had. . . . Rock and roll is basically just gospel music, or gospel music mixed with rhythm and blues. [38]

In his early teens, Presley moved with his family to Memphis, where he grew long hair and sideburns, shopped for flashy clothing on Beale Street, entered talent shows, and participated in all-night gospel sings. His taste in blues and R & B had begun to sharpen: "I dug the real low-down Mississippi singers, mostly Big Bill Broonzy and Big Boy Crudup, although they would scold me at home for listening to them. 'Sinful music,' the townsfolk of Memphis said it was." [39]

In 1953 Presley stopped in at Sam Phillips's Memphis Recording Service to make a recording for his mother. When he sang a couple of ballads by the Ink Spots, he sufficiently impressed Marion Keisker, who was handling the studio that day, to make a backup tape of the performances to share later with her boss. Phillips eventually called Presley back to record, backed by guitarist Scotty Moore and bassist Bill Black, and after many false starts they stumbled on the new style that Phillips had in mind. Presley was on a break fooling around

Multicultural Note

Elvis, Race, and Cultural Appropriation

Presley's new black–white hybrid sound had to be marketed skillfully in a time of racial segregation. Once Presley and his band had recorded Crudup's "That's All Right," they joked nervously that such race-mixing might get them run out of town. When the "black" sound of Presley's initial recordings first hit the airwaves, confusion arose about his racial identity. Promoters quickly hustled Presley onto the air to announce that he had graduated from a white high school.

Even so, white conservatives remained angered by his use of black dance, performance, and dress styles. Racial segregation was still the norm in many parts of the United States, and the appropriation of black styles by whites was seen as suspect. How have times changed? Does the appropriation of black styles by white pop artists such as Eminem or Britney Spears still cause white outrage? What about black outrage over such appropriations?

with blues singer Arthur "Big Boy" Crudup's "That's All Right" when Phillips's excited shouts from the control booth signaled that they finally had what he wanted. Phillips quickly arranged for a local DJ to play the tune on his show and it became a regional hit—once it was made clear that Presley was white.

Presley began to tour the South with his band, and he had regional hits with his follow-up Sun recordings. In 1955 he signed with manager "Colonel" Tom Parker, a former carnival barker, who had big plans for the young rocker. One of Parker's first moves was to shop around for another record company. Why Sam Phillips sold Presley's contract to RCA for $35,000—even though it was an impressive sum at the time—will always remain a mystery. At the RCA studios in Nashville, producers changed the artist's sound by adding vocal group harmonies, drums, heavily electrified guitars, and orchestral arrangements. According to historian Charlie Gillett, "Presley's voice became more theatrical and self-conscious as he sought to contrive excitement and emotion which he had seemed to achieve on his Sun records without any evident forethought." [40] Many purists argue that Presley's Sun sessions represent the height of his artistic accomplishment and that the haphazard way RCA handled his subsequent releases bore witness to his role as a commodity and little else.

Presley broke out onto the national scene in 1956—appearing on major television shows, topping the charts with "Heartbreak Hotel," and signing a three-movie deal. Follow-up hits included "Don't Be Cruel," "Hound Dog," "Love Me Tender," and "All Shook Up," and his first films, *Love Me Tender* and *Jailhouse Rock,* were also smashes. It all ended in 1958 as Presley was drafted into the U.S. Army and took a two-year enforced musical hiatus. When he returned to the civilian world in 1960, he devoted most of his energy to making movies. Although his undistinguished films (*GI Blues, Blue Hawaii, Viva Las Vegas*, and others) and their soundtrack albums made money, they reflected little of the artistic vision and excitement of his initial work with Sun Records. Under the guidance of manager Tom Parker, Presley engaged primarily in turning a profit. As researcher George Plasketes argues, "To a younger generation who did not grow up listening to Elvis or experiencing his liberating impact on American culture, he represents nothing more than a registered trademark." [41] With the arrival of the Beatles and Bob Dylan in the mid-1960s, Presley had already faded as a major force. He briefly rebounded in 1968 with a comeback television special and made some new recordings that did well on the charts, but then he moved into a new phase as a Las Vegas and arena performer, becoming a cultural cliché. Dressed in outlandish jumpsuits, oversized aviator sunglasses, bangles, and sequins, he approached self-parody. Presley's shows became overblown affairs crafted to appeal to the adulation of aging fans. According to critic Harry Sumrall, "The man who had virtually created the image of the rock and roll star also became the symbol of the flabby, out-of-control rock star burnout." [42]

Presley increasingly retreated into seclusion at Graceland, his Memphis mansion, and a lifestyle of overindulgence led to his death by heart failure in 1977. Critic Greil Marcus reflects on the role Presley still plays as a complex cultural symbol, reflecting many conflicting views:

Elvis Presley is a supreme figure on American life, one whose presence, no matter how banal or unpredictable, brooks no real comparisons. . . . Elvis has emerged as a great artist, a great rocker, a great purveyor of schlock, a great heart throb, a great bore, a great symbol of potency, a great ham, a great nice person, and, yes, a great American.[43]

However one views Presley—as god or disappointment—his impact remains clear: His appearance forever transformed the face of American popular music.

Sam Phillips's success with Elvis Presley encouraged Phillips to replicate it with other young southerners who had comparable styles and materials. He switched almost completely from black singers to white artists, whom he tried to cast in his rockabilly mold: Carl Perkins, Johnny Cash, Jerry Lee Lewis, Roy Orbison, and Charlie Rich.

Carl Perkins (1932–1998) established rockabilly with his smash hit "Blue Suede Shoes" (1956) and launched Sun Records into national prominence. The song was the first rockabilly record to sell a million copies and one of the first three-way crossover hits (on the pop, country and western, and R & B charts). Perkins also served as one of rock's first singer-songwriters and an early rock presence on national television. After an auto accident, Perkins remained on the scene primarily as a second-tier country artist, often performing as a sideman with Johnny Cash.

Topped only by Little Richard for flamboyance, **Jerry Lee Lewis** (1935–) was one of the most outrageous figures of fifties rock. With three top-ten hits in the 1950s ("Whole Lotta Shakin' Goin' On," "Great Balls of Fire," and "Breathless"), he became the premier white piano and vocal stylist of early rock. According to one critic, "Lewis didn't sing his songs as much as he ravaged them."[44] Lewis's career took a dive in the late 1950s, when the press revealed that he had married his thirteen-year-old second cousin. Despite an erratic life, Lewis continued to tour as a country artist and enjoyed periodic country hits from the 1960s through the 1980s.

Texan **Roy Orbison** (1936–1988) started out as a Sun rockabilly artist but found greater fame after leaving Sun, with ballads that showcased a quavering tenor voice and twanging guitar ("Only the Lonely" [1960], "Crying" [1961], and "Oh, Pretty Woman" [1964]). Dressed in black, with sunglasses and slicked-back hair, Orbison became "the Caruso of rock and roll," according to one critic.[45] Popular in Great Britain as well as the United States, Orbison toured with the Beatles and served as a bridge between rock's first golden age and the British invasion of the 1960s. Such rockers as Bruce Springsteen, Elvis Costello, and Bonnie Raitt later recognized Orbison as a seminal influence.

FIFTIES ROCK AFTER ELVIS

Numerous rock and R & B artists appeared between Elvis Presley's explosion on the national scene in 1956 and the end of the decade. Some added new levels of emotional complexity to rock, others were manufactured as "teen idols," and

Internet Listening Exercise

Listen to samples of Elvis Presley's early sessions at Sun Records.

Elvis Presley: "That's All Right," "Blue Moon of Kentucky," "Good Rockin' Tonight," "Mystery Train"

Then listen to samples of Presley tunes recorded later on RCA.

Elvis Presley: "Hound Dog," "Don't Be Cruel," "Love Me Tender," "Can't Help Falling in Love," "Viva Las Vegas"

Internet Listening Exercise

Listen to samples of other Sun artists.

Carl Perkins: "Blue Suede Shoes"

Jerry Lee Lewis: "Great Balls of Fire"

Roy Orbison: "Oh, Pretty Woman"

still others applied the power of black gospel music to secular pop styles, as African American crossover artists.

The Second Wave

A second wave of rock artists appeared around 1957, bringing heightened emotional complexity to rock through well-crafted tunes, emotional lyrics, and soaring vocals. Most of them wrote much of their material, played their own instruments, and took a hand in record production. Though less explosive and bluesy than their immediate predecessors, these artists broadened the palette of rock.

Texas-born singer/songwriter **Buddy Holly** (1939–1959) created songs that combined country sweetness with a rock edge. Though he blended the backbeat of black R & B with country and pop material around the same time that Sam Phillips and Elvis Presley did, Holly's sound differed from the rockabilly of Sun Records. With horn-rimmed glasses and a shy demeanor, Holly contrasted with the flamboyant styles of Little Richard and Elvis Presley. His well-crafted songs stood the test of time; his band, the Crickets, established the classic rock-band instrumental lineup (lead and rhythm guitar, electric bass, and drums). Holly's major hits included "That'll Be the Day" (1957—later covered by Linda Ronstadt), "Peggy Sue" (1957), "Not Fade Away" (1957—later covered by the Rolling Stones), and "It's So Easy" (1958). Holly moved to New York in late 1958 to explore an orchestral sound, only to have his career cut short in the 1959 plane crash that also killed rockers Ritchie Valens and the Big Bopper.

The **Everly Brothers** (Don Everly, 1937– ; Phil Everly, 1939–) were a popular vocal duo of the 1950s whose tight country harmonies influenced a generation of rockers including the Beatles, the Hollies, the Beach Boys, the Byrds, Simon and Garfunkel, and the Eagles. From 1957 through 1962, the Everlys hit the top ten of the singles chart twelve times and sold more than thirty-five million records. Major hits included "Bye Bye Love" (1957), "Wake up Little Susie" (1957), All I Have to Do Is Dream" (1958), "'Til I Kissed You" (1959), and "Cathy's Clown" (1960). Displaced in the early 1960s by British invasion groups, many of whom they had inspired, the Everlys broke up in the 1970s but reunited in the 1980s to release "On the Wings of a Nightingale," written for them by an admiring Paul McCartney. The duo continued to tour nationally in the early 2000s, appearing as part of a Simon and Garfunkel reunion tour.

Other important second-wave rock artists peaked in the late 1950s. Ritchie Valens (1941–1959) became the first Chicano rock star. Early rockabilly vocalist/guitarist Eddie Cochran (1938–1960) performed the widely covered "Summertime Blues" (1958) and influenced a generation of British rockers prior to his 1960 death in a car crash in Britain. Gene Vincent (1935–1971) was a leather-clad, rockabilly bad boy whose "Be-Bop-a-Lula" (1956) was every bit as dangerous as Elvis, but when U.S. popularity eluded him, he withdrew to England to become a British rock icon. Ricky Nelson (1940–1985), the son of television's "Ozzie and Harriet," gained popularity in the late 1950s and early

Internet Listening Exercise

Listen to samples of Buddy Holly's music.

Buddy Holly: *Greatest Hits*

Internet Listening Exercise

Listen to samples of the Everly Brothers and those they influenced.

Everly Brothers: *20th Century Masters: The Millennium Collection —The Everly Brothers*

Simon and Garfunkel: "Bye Bye Love"

1960s through heavy media exposure with a blend of ballads, rockabilly, and pop. He also became a country rock pioneer with his Stone Canyon Band in the 1970s, and was followed into the rock business in the 1990s by his sons who formed the group Nelson. Duane Eddy (1938–), rock's best-selling instrumentalist, put the "twang" in rock-and-roll guitar by playing the instrument's bass strings, thereby influencing generations of rockers including John Fogerty, George Harrison, Bruce Springsteen, and Chris Isaak with tunes such as his 1958 hit, "Rebel Rouser."

Teen Idols

The pop charts of the late 1950s also filled with **teen idols**—wholesome and attractive young performers, largely the products of record companies, who were sculpted to appeal to perceived youth taste. Their sound often had more in common with the last gasps of the bland Tin Pan Alley sound of the early 1950s than with R & B and rock. Further, the more conservative elements of the entertainment industry and social establishment probably felt more comfortable with the idols, who were clean-cut, malleable, and white. The manufacturing of face and image over content and ability that characterized the teen idol era has occurred repeatedly in American popular music ever since.

The first and most commercially successful teen idol of the 1950s was **Pat Boone** (1934–), a wholesome young crooner whose first hits were sanitized versions of R & B hits by Little Richard ("Tutti Frutti," "Long Tall Sally") and Fats Domino ("Ain't That a Shame"). He ultimately had thirty-eight top-forty hits. As one critic points out, "Boone began as a safe alternative to Elvis, and is still a safe alternative to just about everything."[46]

Another teen idol, **Paul Anka** (1941–), composed and performed hits such as "Diana" and "Put Your Head on My Shoulder." These mainstream ballads with mild rock trimmings exemplified the teen idol style at its most operatic. Anka ultimately sold over 100 million records, became a nightclub and cabaret performer, and composed over 400 songs, including Frank Sinatra's "My Way" and the "Tonight Show Theme."

Several Philadelphia-based teen idols of the late 1950s—Bobby Rydell, Frankie Avalon, and Fabian among them—were launched into national success through appearances on the television show *American Bandstand,* hosted by Dick Clark, who sometimes held financial interests in the singers' record companies. Like the white boy-bands of the 1990s, these artists were promoted more for their appearance than their vocal abilities, and many of them moved into movies and television. Avalon, for example, soon teamed up with fellow teen idol and former Mouseketeer Annette Funicello in such films as *Beach Party* (1963) and *Beach Blanket Bingo* (1965).

Internet Listening Exercise

Listen to samples of second-wave rock artists of the late 1950s.

Eddie Cochran: "Summertime Blues"

Gene Vincent: "Be-Bop-a-Lula"

Ricky Nelson: "Hello Mary Lou," "Garden Party"

Duane Eddy: "Rebel Rouser"

Internet Listening Exercise

Listen to samples of the music of late-1950s teen idols.

Pat Boone: "Love Letters in the Sand"

Paul Anka: "Diana"

Bobby Rydell: "Wild One"

Frankie Avalon: "Venus"

Fabian: "Tiger"

MICHAEL OCHS ARCHIVES.COM

Smooth and soulful crooner Sam Cooke.

Black Crossover Artists of the Late 1950s

By the late 1950s, black and white pop music had become resegregated for the most part, and the rock-and-roll package tours that formerly featured many black artists had become primarily white. Nonetheless, important black artists continued to cross over, bringing the sounds of black gospel and vocal group music into the rock mainstream and laying the basis for soul music.

Sam Cooke (1931–1964), one of the most popular and influential black singers of the late 1950s, successfully blended gospel and pop. With his clear, sensual tenor voice, Cooke pioneered what would later be called soul music. He was also one of the first black artists to write his own songs and control his recording career by establishing a record label and music publishing company. Cooke's vocal influence would appear in the work of artists as diverse as Otis Redding, Rod Stewart, and Al Green. The son of a Chicago minister, Cooke began his career in black gospel music; by 1950 he was lead singer of the Soul Stirrers, one of the most influential gospel quartets of the era. In 1956 he crossed over to secular music and scored hits with "You Send Me," "Chain Gang," "Twistin' the Night Away," "Cupid," and "Having a Party." According to critic Robert Palmer, "Sam Cooke was drop-dead, supper-club cool at watering holes like the Copa; for r&r/r&b gigs . . . the jacket, tie, and cuff links came off and the sexy soul man took charge."[47] Cooke launched his own record label and music publishing house in 1961, but his promising career was brought to a premature end by gunfire in 1964.

One of the premier black vocalists of the late 1950s and early 1960s, **Jackie Wilson** (1934–1984) effortlessly combined the raw style of James Brown with the polished, gospel-pop of Sam Cooke. Later emulated by Michael Jackson, his stage moves were legendary, and his ringing vocal style ranged from up-tempo rock to ballads. As Robert Palmer put it, "Jackie Wilson squeezed every drop of emotion out of his ballads and punctuated his up-tempo vocal gymnastics with faultless splits, spins, and knee-drops."[48] After his discovery in 1951 by Johnny Otis, the Detroit native joined the Dominoes. He went solo in 1956 to score hits such as "Lonely Teardrops" (1958), "Baby Workout" (1963), and "(Your Love Keeps Lifting Me) Higher and Higher" (1966). Wilson's career was eventually eclipsed by soul music in the 1960s.

Vocalist/keyboardist **Ray Charles** (1930–2004) brought together the energy of black gospel music, the secular lyrics of the blues and country, and the sophistication of big band jazz in a hybrid that became enormously popular with both black and white audiences in the late 1950s and early 1960s.

MICHAEL OCHS ARCHIVES.COM

Ray Charles performing with the Raylettes, backed by his big band in the 1966 movie *Blues for Lovers*.

Charles's throaty, gospel-based vocal style influenced virtually all of the soul singers of the 1960s, as well as many English rockers, including Mick Jagger, Eric Burdon, and Joe Cocker. Charles introduced the electric piano to the rock and jazz world with his first major pop hit, "What'd I Say" (1959), a tune that embodied the classic call and response of the African American church. The song was later covered by Elvis Presley, Jerry Lee Lewis, and Bobby Darin. Charles was also the first black artist to score hits in the country field, and he was well regarded in the jazz world.

Charles started his career in the early 1950s as a crooner in the blues style of Nat "King" Cole and Charles Brown, but he began infusing secular songs with gospel sounds in the mid-1950s with tunes such as "I Got a Woman" (1955) and "Hallelujah, I Love Her So." He followed "What'd I Say" with a Tin Pan Alley ballad ("Georgia on My Mind"), as well as up-tempo R & B hits ("Hit the Road Jack" and "Unchain My Heart"). In the early 1960s, he formed his own record and music-publishing companies and released a series of crossover country ballad smashes that included "I Can't Stop Loving You" and "Your Cheatin' Heart." Charles continued to record throughout the rest of the twentieth century, retaining control over most of his music, and he was the subject of the Oscar-winning 2004 film *Ray*.

 **Internet Listening Exercise**

Listen to samples of the work of Sam Cooke, Jackie Wilson, and Ray Charles.

Sam Cooke: "You Send Me," "Having a Party"

Jackie Wilson: "Lonely Teardrops"

Ray Charles: "What'd I Say," "Georgia on My Mind"

"THE DAY THE MUSIC DIED"

The end of the 1950s brought a confluence of events that changed the character of rock: Numerous artists were lost through death, conscription, imprisonment, ostracism, or religious conversion, According to singer/songwriter Don McLean in his 1969 song "American Pie," the 1959 plane crash that killed Buddy Holly, Ritchie Valens, and the Big Bopper signified "the day the music died." Holly and Valens were important new singer/songwriters who were taking the music in fresh new directions at the time of their deaths. In many ways, rock also lost its premier icon, Elvis Presley, at the height of his popularity when he was drafted into the U.S. Army in 1958. Presley was never the same, argues critic Robert Palmer:

> The Elvis Presley who returned from his U.S. Army tour of duty was no longer the sneering, ducktailed "hillbilly cat," decked out in Beale Street's gaudiest pimpwear. The new Elvis celebrated his return to civilian life by donning a tux and singing a television duet with . . . Frank Sinatra?[49]

Other losses to the rock world mounted: Little Richard entered the seminary in 1957, Chuck Berry was imprisoned on a morals charge in 1959, Jerry Lee Lewis was ostracized for marrying his thirteen-year-old second cousin in 1958, and promoter Alan Freed was indicted and convicted of payola.

Rock seemed under attack from many sides: Major record labels and music publishers wanted to regain their dominance, clergy and local politicians decried the music on moral grounds, and Congress began to probe payola. Tin Pan Alley business leaders saw their control over the music business being threatened, and rock served as a convenient target for their wrath. ASCAP, which had dominated prerock songwriting and publishing, was also threatened by BMI, which represented many rock, R & B, and country songwriters. Congressional hearings into payola took place in 1959 and 1960 at the urging of ASCAP, which sent stars such as Frank Sinatra in to demonize the new rock music business.

Although "cleanup" of the rock-and-roll business supposedly followed, the primary effect was the reconcentration of power in the hands of traditional music business centers at the expense of the independent labels and DJs. Radio stations reigned in DJs and instituted program directors and playlists to homogenize what had been a freewheeling domain. This resulted in the sanitized pop-rock sound of teen idols. Some historians refer to the events of the late 1950s as the "death" of rock and roll, but that is an overstatement. Just over the horizon lay soul music, girl groups, surf music, and the British invasion, as well as new producers, songwriters, and performers. By 1960, rock was here to stay, and the power centers of the music business had moved to take control of a genre they had earlier dismissed.

Chapter Summary

- Rock may be the most popular music in the world today. Its emergence co-incided with the appearance of a youth culture, for which rock served as a primary voice. Rooted in African American R & B and jazz, the new hybrid grew to become more than the sum of its parts.

- The 1950s were a time of rapid cultural change in the United States, reflected by the growth of white suburbia and Cold War anxiety. New technologies such as radio and television, as well as economic prosperity, supported the development of the new teen consumer class. Simultaneously, white teens were discovering new R & B music that was developing in black communities.

- R & B was a blend of African American styles: jazz, big band swing, gospel, blues, and boogie woogie. By the late 1940s, it had replaced swing as popular dance music, although only a few black musicians, such as Louis Jordan, crossed the color line. Small independent record labels emerged to accommodate the growing demand for black dance music, and in 1948 *Billboard* established the new category of "rhythm and blues."

- Early vocal groups such as the Ink Spots and the Mills Brothers were forebears of doo-wop, a new vocal style born in urban African American communities. The style centered on harmony singing and required no instruments. Groups such as the Coasters, the Platters, and the Drifters developed styles that white musicians embraced and that became central to 1950s rock. The style also paved the way for the following decade's girls groups and soul vocal ensemble sound.

- When the growth of R & B-oriented radio stations made black music accessible to white teenagers, a racist backlash followed. The vitality of the music was difficult to quash, however, as Little Richard, Fats Domino, and Bill Haley and other artists founded the music DJ Alan Freed baptized as "rock and roll."

- Three major urban areas—New Orleans, Chicago, and Memphis—served as important spawning grounds for early rock styles. New Orleans, the birthplace of jazz, was the source of the piano-based roots rock sound of Little Richard and Fats Domino. Chicago's amplified urban blues gave birth to the music of early rockers Chuck Berry and Bo Diddley. Memphis and Sun Records produced a rockabilly hybrid of blues, gospel, and country music, as well as rock's first megastar, Elvis Presley.

- A second wave of late-1950s rock innovators included Buddy Holly, the Everly Brothers, Ritchie Valens, Roy Orbison, Jerry Lee Lewis, and Carl Perkins. The late 1950s also set the stage for the birth of sixties soul music with the work of Sam Cooke, Jackie Wilson, and Ray Charles.

- Rock and roll presented a threat to the music establishment, which responded with the introduction of white teen idols. As the 1950s came to a close, rock seemed to be imploding on its own with the deaths, jailings, and religious conversions of major players, as well as congressional investigations. But this was only the end of rock's first chapter.

Key Terms

crier
doo-wop
falsetto
45 rpm record
honker
jump blues

LP record
novelty song
payola
shouter
teen idol

Study and Discussion Questions

1. What was mainstream pop like in the early 1950s before rock?

2. What significant economic, cultural, political, and technological changes in the 1950s interacted with the development of rock?

3. In what ways is rock an offshoot of R & B? In what ways is it something completely different?

4. Who were some shouters, criers, and honkers, and how did they contribute to the development of R & B and rock?

5. How did R & B innovators such as Louis Jordan and T-Bone Walker contribute to the development of rock?

6. What role did West Coast artists play in developing early rock and R & B?

7. What part did independent record labels, R & B radio stations, and DJs play in developing early R & B and rock?

8. What was the importance of the following regions and artists associated with them: New Orleans, Chicago, and Memphis?

9. What was Bill Haley's contribution to rock?

10. Why was Elvis Presley significant? What might have happened if he and Sam Phillips had not gotten together to develop their county-blues hybrid?

11. Who were some of the rock artists of the late 1950s who followed Elvis?

12. What happened to rock by the end of the 1950s? Why do some commentators argue that rock "died" at this point?

Notes

1. Robert Palmer, *Rock and Roll: An Unruly History* (New York: Harmony Books, 1995), 33.

2. Glenn C. Altschuler, *All Shook Up: How Rock 'n' Roll Changed America (Pivotal Moments in American History)* (New York: Oxford University Press, 2003), 10.

3. Palmer, *Rock and Roll*, 16.

4. Nelson George, *The Death of Rhythm and Blues* (New York: Penguin Books, 1998), x.

5. John Chilton, *Let the Good Times Roll: The Story of Louis Jordan and His Music* (Ann Arbor: University of Michigan Press, 1994), 122.

6. Charlie Gillett, *The Sound of the City: The Rise of Rock and Roll* (New York: Da Capo Press, 1996), 127.

7. Arnold Shaw, *Honkers and Shouters: The Golden Age of Rhythm and Blues* (New York: Macmillan, 1978), 64.

8. Gillett, *Sound of the City*, 132.

9. Shaw, *Honkers and Shouters*, 175.

10. Ibid., 161.

11. Gary Giddins, *Visions of Jazz: The First Century* (New York: Oxford University Press, 1998), 405.

12. Liner notes to *A Life in the Blues: Charles Brown*, Rounder Records ROUN2074, 2003.

13. Gage Averill, *Four Parts, No Waiting: The Social History of American Barbershop Harmony* (New York: Oxford University Press, 2003).

14. George, *Death of Rhythm and Blues*, 40–41.

15. Altschuler, *All Shook Up*, 8.

16. Ibid., 18.

17. Ibid., 26.

18. Palmer, *Rock and Roll*, 135–36.

19. Ibid., 15.

20. Nick Talevski, *The Unofficial Encyclopedia of the Rock and Roll Hall of Fame* (Westport, CT: Greenwood Press, 1998), 10.

21. Ibid., 14.

22. Shaw, *Honkers and Shouters,* 64.

23. Chet Flippo, *Everybody Was Kung-Fu Dancing: Chronicles of the Lionized and the Notorious* (New York: St. Martin's Press, 1991), 89.

24. Ibid., 87.

25. Grace Lichtenstein and Laura Dankner, "Fats," in *Rock and Roll Is Here to Stay,* edited by W. McKeen (New York: Norton, 2000), 93.

26. Charles White, *The Life and Times of Little Richard: The Quasar of Rock* (New York: Harmony Books, 1984), 48.

27. Colin Escott and Martin Hawkins, *Good Rockin' Tonight: Sun Records and the Birth of Rock 'n' Roll* (New York: St. Martin's Press, 1992), 17–18.

28. White, *Life and Times of Little Richard,* 47.

29. Ibid., 55.

30. Gillett, *Sound of the City,* 80.

31. John Collis, *The Story of Chess Records* (New York: Bloomsbury, 1998), 130.

32. Ibid., 115.

33. "Sam Phillips: The Sound and Legacy of Sun Records," November 28, 2001, http://www.npr.org/programs/morning/features/2001/nov/ phillips/011128.sam.phillips.html, accessed on May 9, 2005.

34. Palmer, *Rock and Roll,* 202.

35. Peter Guralnick, *Lost Highway: Journeys and Arrivals of American Musicians* (Boston: Godine, 1979), 125.

36. Escott and Hawkins, *Good Rockin' Tonight,* ii.

37. Dave Marsh, *Elvis* (New York: Thunder's Mouth Press, 1992), xiii.

38. Ibid., 9.

39. Gillett, *Sound of the City,* 28.

40. Ibid., 29.

41. George M. Plasketes, "Taking Care of Business: The Commercialization of Rock Music," in *America's Musical Pulse: Popular Music in Twentieth-Century Society,* edited by K. Bindas (Westport, CT: Greenwood Press, 1992), 149.

42. Harry Sumrall, *Pioneers of Rock and Roll: 100 Artists Who Changed the Face of Rock* [Billboard Hitmakers' Series] (New York: Billboard Books, 1994), 212.

43. Greil Marcus, *Mystery Train: Images of America in Rock 'n' Roll Music,* 4th ed. (New York: Penguin Books, 1997), 120–21.

44. Sumrall, *Pioneers of Rock and Roll,* 166.

45. Ibid., 197.

46. Richie Unterberger, http://www.allmusic.com.

47. Palmer, *Rock and Roll,* 143.

48. Ibid., 145.

49. Ibid., 144.

1870 - 1970

1870s The Fisk Jubilee Singers introduce the U.S. and Europe to spirituals ♪

1898 Spanish American War

1914–1918 World War I
1919–1933 Prohibition

1920 Nineteenth Amendment gives women right to vote
1929–1930s Great Depression; New Deal begins

1930s Thomas Dorsey pioneers new gospel music forms ♪

1941–1945 U.S. participates in World War II
1947 Gospel legend Mahalia Jackson records her biggest hit, "Move on up a Little Higher" ♪

1950–1953 Korean War
1954 School segregation outlawed; civil rights movement begins
1955–1961 Songwriters Jerry Leiber and Mike Stoller write and produce a string of hit songs, including "Stand by Me" ♪
1959 Cuban Revolution; Alaska and Hawaii become states
1959 Ray Charles releases the gospel-soul classic "What'd I Say" ♪

1960 Sam Cooke scores multiple hits ♪
1960 Chubby Checker creates a new dance craze with the Twist ♪
1960–1965 The Brill Building becomes the Tin Pan Alley of rock ♪
1961–1965 The Beach Boys score multiple hits to popularize surf music ♪
1961 Ben E. King records "Spanish Harlem" and "Stand by Me" ♪
1962 Supreme Court bans school prayer; first black student enters University of Mississippi
1963 Civil rights march on Washington; John Kennedy assassinated
1963 Mahalia Jackson performs at Martin Luther King's "I Have a Dream" national civil rights rally in Washington, D.C. ♪
1964–1973 Vietnam War
1964 Phil Spector's "wall of sound" production, "You've Lost That Lovin' Feelin'" by the Righteous Brothers, hits number one ♪
1965 Watts riots
1965 James Brown lays groundwork for funk with the groove-based "Papa's Got a Brand New Bag" ♪
1965 Wilson Picket records "Midnight Hour" in Memphis at Stax Records ♪
1966 Supreme Court rules on *Miranda* case; Vietnam War protests begin
1966 Motown is in its prime with hits by the Temptations and the Supremes ♪
1967 Urban riots in Detroit; "Summer of Love" in San Francisco
1967 Aretha Franklin breaks out with "Do Right Woman" ♪
1967 Otis Redding dies in a plane crash ♪
1968 Martin Luther King and Robert Kennedy assassinated

1970 Antiwar protesters killed at Kent State University in Ohio ♪

| 1870 | 1890 | 1910 | 1920 | 1930 | 1940 | 1950 | 1960 | 1970 |

Chapter 14

Girl Groups, Surf Music, Gospel, and Soul

The 1960s witnessed immense change in American popular music. Several completely new genres emerged in this short period—possibly the most prolific decade in twentieth-century popular music. The 1960s dawned with an aura of hope as a young president rose to power and a range of new civil rights for minorities seemed within the nation's grasp. Perhaps more than at any other time in the country's history, popular music at this time embodied the politics of identity and cultural revolution. An impressive array of artists emerged, whose work remains known and loved worldwide. The early part of the decade began as a transition from the music of the 1950s to the 1960s, embodied in girl groups, surf music, gospel, and soul.

IN THIS CHAPTER

- Producers, a New Tin Pan Alley, and Girl Groups
- Surf Music
- Gospel Music
- Soul Music

PRODUCERS, A NEW TIN PAN ALLEY, AND GIRL GROUPS

By the late 1950s and early 1960s, much of rock and R & B was being crafted by a new breed of producer/songwriters who advanced the work of record production to an art form. They ultimately gained control of many aspects of record production, from songwriting and artist selection to studio production and marketing.

Leiber and Stoller

In the 1950s and 1960s, **Jerry Leiber** (1933–) and **Mike Stoller** (1933–) wrote an impressive string of hit R & B and rock songs, arranged and produced numerous recordings by seminal artists, and advanced the music with a new kind of wit and musical sophistication. According to Robert Palmer,

> Beneath the surface of teen-oriented lyrics, the songs often bristled with social satire and political irony. Long before Dylan and the Beatles, Leiber and Stoller were making rock and roll records with the most sophisticated and self-conscious artistry.[1]

They were also the first to introduce strings and other varied instrumentation on R & B records.

Internet Listening Exercise

Listen to samples of tunes written or produced by Leiber and Stoller.

The Coasters: "Riot in Cell Block #9"

Willie Mae "Big Mama" Thornton: "Hound Dog"

Wilbert Harrison: "Kansas City"

The Coasters: "Yakety Yak"

The Drifters: "There Goes My Baby"

Ben E. King: "Stand by Me"

The Dixie Cups: "Chapel of Love"

Internet Listening Exercise

Listen to samples of tunes written by Brill Building songwriters.

Gerry Goffin/Carole King: "The Loco-Motion" (Little Eva)

Barry Mann/Cynthia Weil: "You've Lost That Lovin' Feelin'" (Righteous Brothers)

Howard Greenfield/Neil Sedaka: "Breaking up Is Hard to Do" (Neil Sedaka)

Jeff Barry/Ellen Greenwich: "Chapel of Love" (The Crystals)

Doc Pomus/Mort Shuman: "Save the Last Dance for Me" (The Drifters)

The pair met in Los Angeles in 1950. Leiber was the lyricist; the classically trained Stoller wrote the music. Early on, they formed an alliance with R & B promoter Johnny Otis to produce the legendary "Hound Dog" (1953) by Willie Mae "Big Mama" Thornton, which was later covered by Elvis Presley.

Leiber and Stoller moved to New York in 1957 to work with Atlantic Records. There they developed a style of telling stories in songs using humorous lyrics, such as these hits by the Coasters: "Yakety Yak" (1958), "Charlie Brown" (1959), and "Poison Ivy" (1959). Hits with other artists included Wilbert Harrison ("Kansas City," 1959), the Drifters ("There Goes My Baby," 1959; "Save the Last Dance for Me," 1960; "On Broadway," 1963), and Ben E. King, former lead singer of the Drifters ("Stand by Me," 1961; "Spanish Harlem," 1961). The pair also wrote songs for Elvis Presley's 1957 film *Jailhouse Rock*. In the mid-1960s, Leiber and Stoller also wrote hits for girl groups such as the Dixie Cups ("Chapel of Love," 1964) and the tough-girl Shangri-Las ("Leader of the Pack," 1964). They continued through the early 1970s to produce artists that included jazz vocalist Peggy Lee ("Is That All There Is," 1969), and *Smokey Joe's Café*, a show featuring their work, opened on Broadway in the 1990s.

The Brill Building

As rock's popularity grew steadily throughout the 1950s, producers eventually began to recognize teen tastes. At first baffled by rock, the music industry now sought to manipulate it by returning to the traditional Tin Pan Alley production model. Numerous song publishing firms set up shop in and around the **Brill Building,** located at 1619 Broadway in New York City, and gathered together some of New York's best young songwriters, many of whom worked in teams: Carole King and Gerry Goffin, Barry Mann and Cynthia Weil, Neil Sedaka and Howard Greenfield, Barry and Ellie Greenwich, Doc Pomus and Mort Shuman, Burt Bacharach and Hal David, Bobby Darin, and Neil Diamond. Songwriter/musician Al Kooper described the Brill Building environment:

> Every morning . . . I'd come to work and I'd go into this cubicle that had a little upright piano and fake white cork bricks on the wall . . . and a door that locked from the outside. And every day from ten to six we'd go in there and pretend that we were thirteen-year-old girls and write these songs. That was the gig.[2]

Brill Building songwriters brought the professionalism of the Tin Pan Alley tradition to rock songwriting, while demonstrating genuine interest in teenagers—their values, emotional needs, and language. Rather than sheet music, the songwriters used audiotaped "demos" to market new songs. Some demos were good enough to be released as records, and writers such as Carole King, Neil Sedaka, Bobby Darin, and Neil Diamond went on to successful recording careers. Although the Brill Building era did not last long, at its height it fueled the girl groups, teen idols, and the top-forty charts of the early 1960s.

Girl Groups

From 1958 through 1965, hundreds of songs by **girl groups** with names like the Chantels, the Shirelles, the Crystals, the Marvelettes, the Ronettes, and the Shangri-Las filled the airwaves. According to songwriter Gerry Goffin, "In the sixties, God was a young black girl who could sing. That was the dominant sound."[3] The girl-group sound was sweet and melodramatic, mixing hooks and doo-wop harmonies. The groups were usually trios or quartets fronted by a lead singer, and many became one-hit wonders. The girl-group sound influenced 1960s pop from Motown to the Beatles, who covered such girl-group tunes as "Please Mr. Postman" (the Marvelettes) and "Baby It's You" (the Shirelles). Brill Building songwriters composed most of the girl-group songs. Group members were predominantly young black women who never played instruments and were seldom identified as individuals in marketing publicity.

CD LISTENING EXERCISE

CD 2/13

Listen to "Will You Love Me Tomorrow," performed by the Shirelles and composed by Carole King and Gerry Goffin. In a recent interview, Carole King explained that this classic girl-group record from 1960 comments on the ultimate taboo of teen love: "If we make love tonight will you respect me in the morning?" The lyrics also reflect the genius of Brill Building song writers, who managed to capture essential elements of the teen experience in the early 1960s. How does the apparent young age of the performers affect the believability of the message?

One of the first popular girl groups was the teenage Chantels, whose hit "Maybe" (1958) did well on both the pop and R & B charts. The Shirelles, one of the most enduring groups of the genre, scored hits with "Dedicated to the One I Love" (1959), "Will You Love Me Tomorrow" (1960), "Mama Said" (1961), and "Baby It's You" (1962). Unusually frank in their subject matter, the Shirelles often directly addressed "the boy" in their songs, acting as surrogates for their young female listeners. In an interview, Carole King explained that "Will You Love Me Tomorrow" comments on the ultimate taboo of teen love: "Should we 'do it' or not? Will you still respect me in the morning?"[4]

Multicultural Note

Girl Groups and Gender Roles

Created at a time when the nuclear family and marriage served as the paradigm of normalcy for girls and women, girl-group songs documented the sexual mores of the early 1960s. Lyrics of many of the songs focused on "the boy" as fantasy object because, according to researcher Patricia Juliana Smith, "Teenage girls ... possessed little more than fantasy and emotionality, two of the few entities that were theirs and theirs alone."[5] Many feminist scholars now view girl-group music as a way of documenting changes in female consciousness and social conditions at a time when gender roles and relations were beginning to shift.

MICHAEL OCHS ARCHIVES.COM

The Ronettes (left to right): Estelle Bennet, Ronnie Bennet, and Nedra Talley in the early 1960s.

www Internet Listening Exercise

Listen to samples of girl-group tunes.

The Chantels: "Maybe"

The Crystals: "He's a Rebel"

The Ronettes: "Be My Baby"

The Shangri-Las: "Leader of the Pack"

Several influential girl groups were associated with producer Phil Spector (discussed in the next section). The first to work with him, the Crystals, produced such hits as "He's a Rebel" (1962) and "Da Doo Ron Ron" (1963). Spector's classic mid-1960s girl group was the Ronettes, whose towering black beehive hairdos and dark eye makeup made them the first group to have a public relations identity and a major male audience because of their smoldering, "bad-girl" sexuality. Their major hits included "Be My Baby" (1963) and "Baby I Love You" (1963). The Shangri-Las were one of the last girl groups. The group's producer injected innovative touches, such as the sounds of crashing waves and revving motorcycles into songs about dead bikers, teenage runaways, and doomed love affairs, into their songs. According to researcher Patricia Juliana Smith, the Shangri-Las

> specialized in . . . spoken bits of conversation between group members interpolated into the song itself—against a backdrop of gothic terror displaced onto a contemporary urban, working-class setting with an ample dose of soap opera sensationalism.[6]

Memorable Shangri-la hits included "Leader of the Pack" (1964) and "I Can Never Go Home Anymore" (1965).

Phil Spector and the "Wall of Sound"

Phil Spector (1940–), probably the most influential producer in the history of rock, became best known for his **wall of sound** production technique. He achieved this without stereo or multitrack recording by packing the studio with musicians, running prior recordings through the studio sound system to fill out the sound, and using echo chambers. Spector also used some of the best songwriters of the day, as well as the best L.A. studio musicians, whom he called his "wrecking crew." He brought sophistication and complexity to record production, scoring hits from 1962 through 1966 for the Crystals, Darlene Love, the Ronettes, and the Righteous Brothers.

The Bronx-born Spector came to Los Angeles as a teenager, where he produced his first hit, "To Know Him Is to Love Him" (1958), at age eighteen. He then moved back to New York to work as an understudy for Leiber and Stoller, and there he coauthored Ben E. King's solo debut, "Spanish Harlem" (1960), as well as other hits. During the early 1960s, back in Los Angeles, he fully realized his "wall of sound" with a series of girl-group hits including the Crystals' "He's a Rebel" (1962) and "Then He Kissed Me" (1963) and the Ronettes' "Be My Baby" (1963) and "Baby I Love You" (1964). Spector's career reached its high point with the release of the blue-eyed soul-flavored Righteous Brothers' tune "You've Lost That Lovin' Feelin'," which reached number one in 1964. He followed with "Unchained Melody" (1965) and "Ebb Tide" (1966), also by the duo.

Spector's self-inflicted downfall came in 1966 when his production of "River Deep, Mountain High" by Ike and Tina Turner, a costly and monumental pop symphony, fared only moderately well on the charts. Chagrined by what he perceived as a failure, Spector became a recluse, emerging only occasionally to work with artists such as John Lennon ("Instant Karma"), the Beatles *(Let It Be),* and George Harrison *(All Things Must Pass).* Critic Mary Elizabeth Williams summarizes Spector's contributions:

> He was the man who gave the "American Bandstand" generation a darker and more sexual edge, the prodigy who inspired everyone from the Beach Boys to the Rolling Stones to Bruce Springsteen. He was the first punk, the visionary who fused the pathos of jazz with the vitality of rock 'n' roll.[7]

Other Early 1960s Artists and Dance Crazes

Other significant rock and R & B artists achieved popularity in the early 1960s. Some reflected the influence of the Brill Building sound, others had links to prior genres such as doo-wop or jazz, and still others pushed the envelope to pioneer new genres.

Numerous white rock artists emerged in the early 1960s, many from Italian neighborhoods in the New York–New Jersey–Philadelphia region. They played what one critic called "Italo-American rock," much of it fueled by the Brill Building. Among them were Dion and the Belmonts, a teen idol/doo-wop vocal group whose hits included "A Teenager in Love" (1959), "Runaround Sue" (1961), and "The Wanderer" (1962). The Four Seasons, featuring the falsetto of lead singer Frankie Valli, crossed over to black audiences with "blue-eyed soul" hits such as "Sherry" (1962), "Big Girls Don't Cry" (1962), and "Walk Like a Man" (1963). The Young Rascals, also blue-eyed soul specialists, scored later in the 1960s with "Good Lovin'" (1966), "Groovin'" (1967), and "A Beautiful Morning" (1968).

The most eclectic of the Italo-American rockers was Bobby Darin (1936–1973). A Brill Building songwriter and Sinatra admirer, Darin explored multiple genres throughout his career with hits such as "Splish Splash" (teen idol rock, 1958), "Mack the Knife" (musical theater, 1959), "Beyond the Sea" (big band jazz, 1960), and "If I Were a Carpenter" (folk rock, 1966). Actor Kevin Spacey directed and starred in a film of Darin's life called *Beyond the Sea* in 2004. Neil Diamond (1941–), another Brill Building songwriter, gradually assumed a Vegas-style lounge act veneer with "Cherry Cherry" (1966), "Holly Holy" (1969), "Sweet Caroline" (1969), and "He Ain't Heavy . . . He's My Brother" (1970). Jay and the Americans, a white doo-wop throwback produced by Leiber and Stoller, had pseudo-operatic hits with "Come a Little Bit Closer" (1964), "Cara, Mia" (1965), and "This Magic Moment" (1969).

The early 1960s probably saw more new dances in a short span of time than almost any other era in American popular music did. It seemed as if every week

Internet Listening Exercise

Listen to samples from the Phil Spector album *Back to Mono* [box set].

Teddy Bears: "To Know Him Is to Love Him"

Darlene Love: "(Today I Met) The Boy I'm Gonna Marry"

The Crystals: "Da Doo Ron Ron"

The Ronettes: "Be My Baby"

The Righteous Brothers: "You've Lost That Lovin' Feelin'"

Ike and Tina Turner: "River Deep, Mountain High"

Internet Listening Exercise

Listen to samples of white Italo-American and other East Coast rockers of the early 1960s.

Dion and the Belmonts: "The Wanderer"

The Four Seasons: "Big Girls Don't Cry"

The Young Rascals: "Good Lovin'"

Bobby Darin: "Mack the Knife," "If I Were a Carpenter"

Neil Diamond: "Cherry Cherry"

Jay and the Americans: "Come a Little Bit Closer"

brought a new dance, with an intriguing name and a hit song to promote it. One reason for this was the rise of nationally broadcast television shows such as *American Bandstand,* which required visuals of attractive teens showcasing their latest moves. Dances that came and went in the early 1960s included the Twist, the Hucklebuck, the Stroll, the Watusi, the Limbo, the Loco-Motion, the Fly, the Pony, the Mashed Potatoes, the Monkey, the Swim, the Jerk, and the Hitchhike. Popularized by Chubby Checker in a 1960 recording, the Twist maintained the longest shelf life of any of the dances of the era and inspired follow-ups such as the Isley Brothers' "Twist and Shout" (1962), later covered by the Beatles. Much simpler than earlier teen dances of the 1950s, the Twist crossed over to the adult nightclub world.

SURF MUSIC

A West Coast phenomenon of the early 1960s, **surf music** enjoyed two incarnations: instrumental and vocal. Although surfing had been introduced to California from Hawaii at the turn of the twentieth century, not until 1959 did the sport receive national attention thanks to the movie *Gidget,* the tale of a girl in love with two surfers. Naïve and mythic, surf music romanticized a white male teen culture of hot rods, surfing, and "honeys." It featured twangy, trebly guitars, Chuck Berry–style guitar licks, falsetto male vocal harmonies, throbbing tom toms, and topical lyrics of car and surf culture. For a brief time in the early 1960s, according to historian Timothy White,

> At Capitol, Dot, Liberty, Decca, Columbia, Tower, RCA, Warner Brothers, Mercury, and dozens of smaller labels there was a feeding frenzy afoot for anything that smelled of sea air, surf wax, and West Coast fuel exhaust.[8]

Surf music helped create the myth of the good life in Southern California and fueled the fantasies of young listeners at great distances, reaching as far as Europe and Japan. The genre lasted briefly as a national craze until the British Invasion hit in 1964.

Instrumental Surf Music

Instrumental surf music first became popular around 1960, when artists such as the Ventures, the Surfaris, the Chantays, and Dick Dale and His Del-Tones broke out. Flavored by reverb-drenched guitar and rolling instrumentals designed to sound like crashing waves, the music was harmonically simple, while exploring new sonic territories. Except for the Ventures, who had a long run of popularity in Japan to sustain them, most instrumental surf artists were one-hit—or "no-hit"—wonders. Yet instrumental surf music showed its staying power with tunes such as the Ventures' "Walk—Don't Run," the Surfaris' "Wipeout," and Dick Dale and His Del-Tones' "Miserlou." Further, surf rock's influence appeared later in the music of Blondie, the Go-Go's, and U-2's lead guitarist, the Edge. The style made a splash again when Dick Dale's tune "Miserlou" was used on the soundtrack of *Pulp Fiction* (1994).

Multicultural Note

The Arabic Roots of Surf Guitar

Dick Dale was born as Richard Monsour to a Lebanese father and Polish mother. Attracted to the hypnotic, minor-key Middle-Eastern melodies of his father's homeland—as well as Eastern European scales—he incorporated them into his guitar playing. Dale was among the first in any genre of American popular music to use these cultural sources.

Dale also picked single notes on his guitar in a rapid staccato fashion, particularly on songs such as the Greek-origin "Miserlou," in a style he had heard an uncle use on the *oud* (an Arabic ancestor of the guitar). The breakneck speed of Dale's picking technique remained unrivaled until it entered the repertoires of metal virtuosos such as Eddie Van Halen.

Critic Robert Palmer described Dale's style as "fast, twangy, and metallic, with long-lined Middle Eastern melodies slithering along atop shimmering Spanish-inflected chording, punctuated by slamming slides up the neck."[9]

The originator of the surf guitar style, **Dick Dale** (1937–) was the fieriest, most technically gifted musician the genre produced. Once called the "father of heavy metal," Dale worked closely with the California-based Fender company to push the limits of electric amplification technology. He helped develop new equipment to produce thick, clearly defined tones at high volumes, and he pioneered the use of portable reverb effects, creating a signature sonic texture. An avid surfer, Dale sought ways to mimic the surging sounds of the ocean on his guitar. The exciting instrumental sound performed at surfer "stomps" in beach-front auditoriums by Dick Dale and His Del-Tones built a fan base, who helped Dale's "Let's Go Trippin'" (1961) and "Miserlou" (1962) become hits.

The Ventures were the most prominent exponents of an early 1960s instrumental guitar ensemble style often lumped with surf music. Unlike Dale, the Ventures created no startling new sound; they consolidated what other musicians had done before them, producing a clean, rhythmic, lyrical sound. The Seattle-based group had hits with "Walk—Don't Run" (1960), "Slaughter on Tenth Avenue" (1964), and "Hawaii Five-O" (1969).

Vocal Surf Music

Two groups wrote the history of vocal surf music: Jan and Dean and the Beach Boys. Although Jan and Dean achieved mass popularity first, the Beach Boys, propelled by the songwriting/producing genius of Brian Wilson, eclipsed them over time.

Jan Berry (1941–) and **Dean Torrence** (1940–) charted thirteen top-thirty singles and sold over ten million records worldwide from the late 1950s

Internet Listening Exercise

Listen to samples of instrumental surf music.

Dick Dale: "Miserlou"

The Surfaris: "Wipeout"

The Chantays: "Pipeline"

The Ventures: "Walk—Don't Run"

Internet Listening Exercise

Listen to samples of vocal surf music by Jan and Dean.

Jan and Dean: "Surf City," "Dead Man's Curve"

MICHAEL OCHS ARCHIVES.COM

The Beach Boys from the cover of the single "Surfin' USA" (left to right): Brian Wilson, Mike Love, Dennis Wilson, Carl Wilson, and David Marks (Al Jardine had temporarily left the group).

**Internet
Listening Exercise**

Listen to songs by the Beach Boys.

Beach Boys: "Surfin' U.S.A.,"
"Good Vibrations"

to the mid-1960s. Initially a doo-wop act, Jan and Dean became surf music converts after sharing the same bill with the nascent Beach Boys in 1962. With the writing assistance of Beach Boy Brian Wilson, they scored a number-one hit with "Surf City" (1963), followed by "Dead Man's Curve" (1964) and "Little Old Lady from Pasadena" (1964). Although not rock innovators, Jan and Dean did host the influential concert film *The T.A.M.I. Show* in 1964, which showcased James Brown, the Rolling Stones, Marvin Gaye, the Beach Boys, the Supremes, and the Miracles. Jan Berry also influenced Brian Wilson, introducing him to L.A. studio musicians and production techniques.

The essence of sixties surf music, the **Beach Boys** defined the California myth of surfers, hot rods, sun, beaches, and girls. Led by songwriter/producer Brian Wilson (1942–), the group wrote their own material at a time when most rock artists sang tunes provided by professional songwriters. By the mid-1960s, Wilson's increasingly sophisticated productions employed a wide range of instrumentation, styles, and sound effects rivaled only by the Beatles and their producer, George Martin. The Beach Boys were also the only American rock group who challenged the popularity of the Beatles. Made up of three brothers and a neighborhood friend, the group originated in a coastal suburb of Los Angeles, spurred by Wilson's fascination with the jazz-inflected harmonies of such white 1950s vocal groups as the Four Freshmen. Wilson also admired Phil Spector's "wall of sound" production techniques.

Early Beach Boys hits included "Surfin' Safari" (1962)—virtually a remake of Chuck Berry's "Sweet Little Sixteen"—"Surfin' U.S.A." (1963)," "Fun, Fun, Fun" (1964), and "I Get Around" (1964). The group went on tour in 1964, recording the first live rock album to top the charts. After suffering a nervous breakdown, Wilson quit touring and went back to the studio to produce the acclaimed "California Girls" (1965), which showcased elaborate production techniques, and the *Pet Sounds* album, which was said to influence the Beatles' *Sgt. Pepper*. Dismayed by the album's lack of commercial success, Brian returned to the studio and worked obsessively for six more months to produce "Good Vibrations" (1966), widely regarded as his crowning achievement. As he continued work on the next album, *SMILE*, Wilson's mental state declined, his drug use accelerated, and he ultimately destroyed many of the album's tracks. The Beach Boys—minus Wilson—continued to tour, eventually becoming reduced to the oldies circuit. Wilson made a comeback with a Grammy-winning reconstruction of *SMILE* in 2004.

GOSPEL MUSIC

African American **gospel music** came into its own in the mid-twentieth century, spinning off artists who contributed major innovations affecting soul, R & B, and rock. Gospel music was important both for its enormous influence on popular music styles and for its independent status as a unique, indigenous American musical genre. As historian Clarence Boyer put it, "Gospel music mends the broken heart, raises the bowed-down head, and gives hope to the weary traveler." [10]

Spirituals and Early Gospel

The earliest Christian religious music developed by African Americans in the eighteenth and nineteenth centuries took the form of *spirituals*, which were used to construct community, provide hope for a better life, offer metaphors of liberation, and preserve African cultural memory. Their development resulted from an exchange of musical styles between whites and blacks. Originally relying on Protestant hymns by English composers, the African American church began to develop its own music by publishing its first hymnal in 1801. Further significant innovation took place at camp meetings, which formed a part of the Second Awakening revival movement of the early nineteenth century. Outside the confines of a formal church setting, traditional African melodic concepts blended easily with the simple hymn melodies to energize and transform the music. In the 1870s, the **Fisk Jubilee Singers,** a group from all black Fisk University in Nashville, first introduced spirituals to the world. They began touring the country in 1871, presenting concerts devoted exclusively to African American religious music. These concerts provided one of the first opportunities for mainstream audiences to hear serious African American music, as opposed to minstrel songs.

The latter part of the nineteenth century witnessed the development of a new style called **gospel.** While spirituals were born in rural camp meetings,

 **Internet Listening Exercise**

Listen to music by the Fisk Jubilee Singers.

Fisk Jubilee Singers: "Ezekiel Saw De Wheel," "Down by the Riverside," "Nobody Knows the Trouble I See"

gospel evolved in urban settings. Early gospel songwriters blended spirituals with popular Tin Pan Alley styles and instrumentation. The new genre began to take off in the early twentieth century, particularly in the churches of the holiness, sanctified, and Pentecostal sects. Many of these groups employed African traditions as well as contemporary popular music styles and instruments, though at first the mainstream African American denominations disapproved of the energy and rhythmic abandon of the new style.

Spirituals and Gospel Music Compared

Spirituals	*Gospel*
Instruments	**Instruments**
No instrumental accompaniment —all a cappella.	Piano, organ, rhythm section, horns, and guitar were integral to performance.
Lyrics	**Lyrics**
Focus on Biblical events and figures, staying close to Biblical text.	Coverage of wide-ranging topics such as conversion, salvation, and spirituality.
Rhythm	**Rhythm**
Less rhythmic intensity than gospel.	Rhythmic intensity marked by syncopation and percussive instrumental rhythms.
Song Forms	**Song Forms**
One or two strains repeated again and again.	Songs with verses and refrains, structured like popular music.
Melodies	**Melodies**
Infrequent use of bent tones.	Use of bent tones—flatted thirds and sevenths—similar to blues.
Improvisation	**Improvisation**
Improvisation was limited.	Extensive use of improvisation encouraged.

Note: Adapted from Eileen Southern, *The Music of Black Americans: A History,* 3rd ed. (New York: Norton, 1997), 459–60.

The first important gospel hymn writer, Philadelphian Charles Tindley (1851–1933), published a popular collection of his music in 1916, and in 1921 the largest black church denomination embraced the style by publishing a song collection called *Gospel Pearls.* Chicago became the center for the development of the genre in the 1920s, and much of that development came from pianist/composer **Thomas A. Dorsey** (1899–1993), the "father of gospel music." Born in Georgia to a religious family, Dorsey took a detour at a young age to work with some of the greatest blues artists of the era, including singer "Ma" Rainey. Known as "Georgia Tom" in the blues world, he teamed with Chicago blues great Tampa Red to produce such earthy blues hits as "It's Tight Like That" (1928). Dorsey also began to write gospel songs while he was still an active blues pianist and writer. As he put it, "If I could get into the gospel songs the feeling and the pathos and the moans and the blues, that [would get] me over."[11] During the Depression, Dorsey moved into the gospel field exclusively and began to innovate rapidly, bringing to bear his experience from the pop music world. He organized the first female vocal gospel quartet in history, established the world's first gospel choruses in Atlanta and Chicago, set up a national gospel choral organization, and formed his own gospel music publishing house. Ultimately Dorsey composed close to a thousand gospel songs, including the beloved "Precious Lord, Take My Hand" (translated into over fifty languages) and "There'll Be Peace in the Valley."

Internet Listening Exercise

Listen to songs written by Thomas A. Dorsey.

Thomas A Dorsey (with P. H. Harris): "Peace in the Valley"

Merle Haggard: "Precious Lord, Take My Hand"

Gospel Forms Take Hold

By the end of the 1930s, gospel was an established commercial genre, with professional gospel performers touring the church-concert circuit. Gospel was also presented in for-profit venues, and Thomas Dorsey pioneered gospel competitions, calling them "battles of song" and charging an admission fee. The competitions manifested the African American musical tradition of the "cutting contest," in which musicians competed to best one another, and the events became important in the gospel world. Independent record companies also recognized gospel as a profitable commodity, and many of the same labels that marketed race records also kept major rosters of gospel artists. In 1938 **"Sister" Rosetta Tharp** (1921–1973) took gospel into a secular setting for the first time: She performed with bandleader Cab Calloway in a show at the Cotton Club in New York, accompanying herself on guitar. The legendary "Spirituals to Swing" concert at Carnegie Hall, a retrospective of African American musical heritage, also featured gospel that year.

By the mid-twentieth century, three distinct categories of gospel performance had arisen: soloists, gospel quartets, and gospel choruses. Important soloists included Mahalia Jackson, Clara Ward, Alex Bradford, Shirley Caesar, and James Cleveland. Several of these performers also led their own vocal ensembles, and Caesar and Cleveland were ordained pastors. Gospel vocal styles, including vocal turns and embellishments called **melismas,** influenced soul, R & B, and eventually most U.S. pop vocal styles.

MICHAEL OCHS ARCHIVES.COM

Legendary gospel singer Mahalia Jackson.

CD LISTENING EXERCISE

CD 2/14

Listen to Mahalia Jackson's recording of "Nobody Knows the Trouble I've Seen" (1963). How does Jackson's powerful and passionate delivery interact with the lyrics of this gospel standard? Notice Jackson's use of vocal turns and embellishments, known as melismas, which have become standard in pop music today. What contemporary vocalists can you identify who make frequent use of this essential element of gospel vocal styles?

Mahalia Jackson (1911–1972) was probably more responsible than any other performer for bringing gospel to the attention of the mainstream audience. Jackson began recording regularly in 1946, and she had her best-known hit, "Move on up a Little Higher," in 1947. She toured extensively in the United States and abroad and had her own weekly network radio show beginning in 1954. Other appearances included the *Ed Sullivan Show*, the Newport Jazz Festival, and the 1961 inauguration of President John Kennedy. In her most moving performance, Jackson sang just before Martin Luther King, Jr., delivered his famous "I Have a Dream Speech" at the civil rights march on Washington in 1963. Jazz critic Marshall Stearns once described audience reaction to a 1959 Jackson performance:

> Gentle old ladies on all sides start to "flip" like popcorn over a hot stove. Directly in front, an angular woman springs to her feet, raises her arms rigidly on high, and dances down the aisle shouting, "Sweet Jesus!" A white-clad nurse, one of thirty in attendance, does her best to quiet her. This is religious possession, as old as Africa itself.[12]

Dubbed the "crown prince of gospel," **James Cleveland** (1931–1991) was a hallmark vocal performer and one of the most gifted composers of his generation, influencing many artists, including Billy Preston and Aretha Franklin. Starting off as a gospel quartet member, he founded the first of several groups in 1959 and became a leading gospel figure in the 1960s. Major recordings included *The Love of God* and *Peace, Be Still*. Cleveland also became an ordained minister and founded an influential church in Los Angeles.

Gospel vocal quartets also influenced American popular music heavily, and many artists in the soul and R & B world got their start in such groups. The style shaped 1950s doo-wop, the subsequent R & B vocal group stylings of groups such as the Temptations, the O'Jays, and Boyz II Men, as well as the white boy-bands of the 1990s such as *Nsync. The quartets, which were usually male, sang a cappella with barbershop harmony, and they added percussive effects by snapping their fingers and slapping their thighs in the African American tradition of patting juba. The quartets generally fell into two distinct styles: "sweet" gospel—characterized by close harmony, precise attacks and releases, and understated rhythm—and "hard" gospel, characterized by emotive singing, preaching delivery, physical gestures, and strong rhythms. Major sweet gospel groups included the Dixie Hummingbirds, the Soul Stirrers, and the Swan Silvertones. Well-known hard gospel groups included the Blind Boys of Alabama, the Five Blind Boys of Mississippi, and the Mighty Clouds of Joy. Popular R & B or soul figures with roots in gospel quartets included Sam Cooke (the Soul Stirrers), Johnnie Taylor (the Soul Stirrers), Bobby Womack (the Womack Brothers), Lou Rawls (the Pilgrim Travelers), Wilson Pickett (the Violinaires), and the Isley Brothers.

Internet Listening Exercise

Listen to samples of gospel and gospel-influenced vocal artists.

James Cleveland: "Peace, Be Still," "Thank You Jesus I'm Satisfied"

Shirley Caeser: "He's Working It Out for You"

Beyoncé: "Dangerously in Love 2"

An influential gospel keyboard accompaniment style rooted in ragtime, barrelhouse, and Protestant hymns became established in the middle part of the twentieth century, further adding to the characteristic gospel sound. By the 1960s, the keyboard style was fully developed and had begun to permeate American popular music. The approach featured heavy chords played at the center of the keyboard, rolling bass, and punctuated riffs in the upper register. Gospel pianists also improvised in a call and response format, filling open spaces in songs or sermons. Major gospel keyboard stylists included Arizona Dranes, Clara Ward, James Cleveland, Jessy Dixon, and Alex Bradford. The "queen of soul," Aretha Franklin, was also a fine gospel pianist, frequently accompanying herself in gospel and soul performances.

Skillful gospel keyboardists frequently integrated both piano and organ. The Hammond B-3 organ, first introduced to gospel in 1939, brought percussive effects and reverberating crescendos into the church. R & B and jazz performers eventually adopted the organ after its introduction through gospel music. Important gospel organ innovators included Alfred Bolden and Billy Preston, who also worked with the Beatles and had his own pop recordings in the 1970s.

Contemporary Gospel Directions

By the 1960s, gospel had become big business; major artists filled large venues, performance fees rose exponentially, and hits such as "O Happy Day" (1969),

Internet Listening Exercise

Listen to samples of music by gospel quartets.

The Dixie Hummingbirds: "Trouble in My Way"

The Soul Stirrers: "That's Heaven to Me"

The Blind Boys of Alabama: "Living on Mother's Prayer"

The Mighty Clouds of Joy: "Mighty High"

Next, listen to samples of music by popular artists influenced by gospel quartet styles.

Temptations: "Just My Imagination"

O'Jays: "Love Train"

Boyz II Men: "It's So Hard to Say Goodbye to Yesterday"

*Nsync: "I Want You Back"

Multicultural Note

The Cultural Borderland between R & B and Gospel

Despite the common origins of R & B and gospel music in African and African American musical cultures, the two are separate genres. From the first emergence of the blues, many Christians—black and white—called the blues "the devil's music." Leaving gospel for secular music, as well as integrating secular music into gospel performances, was controversial. Many artists who crossed over to the secular side—including Little Richard, Al Green, and Solomon Burke—subsequently returned to gospel.

The work of contemporary artists CeCe Winans and Kirk Franklin offered interesting case studies of pop-gospel boundaries. Winans created controversy in the early 1990s by collaborating with brother BeBe on a pop-influenced album called *Different Lifestyles,* which topped the R & B charts and scored two number-one hits. In subsequent years, however, she began working her way back to a more traditional gospel sound. Kirk Franklin burst onto the gospel and R & B scene in 1996 with a controversial gold album called *Whatcha Lookin' 4,* which incorporated hip-hop elements for the first time. In subsequent work, however, he more closely aligned himself with core gospel traditions by collaborating with gospel icon Shirley Caesar. What do these experiences tell us about the complexities of making art in cultural borderlands?

Internet Listening Exercise

Listen to samples of songs by gospel keyboard artists.

Arizona Dranes: *Complete Recorded Works, 1926–29*

Clara Ward: "How I Got Over"

Jessy Dixon: "Nothing but the Blood"

Billy Preston: "Just a Closer Walk with Thee," "Nothing from Nothing"

Next, listen to samples by rock artists influenced by gospel keyboard styles.

Leon Russell: "Roll away the Stone"

Elton John: "Border Song"

The Band (pianist Richard Manuel, organist Garth Hudson): "Tears of Rage"

Santana (organist Gregg Rolie): *"Oye Como Va"*

Internet Listening Exercise

Listen to samples of contemporary gospel.

Edwin Hawkins: "Oh Happy Day"

BeBe and CeCe Winans: "Addictive Love"

Kirk Franklin: *The Rebirth of Kirk Franklin*

recorded by Edwin Hawkins with a gospel chorus, and the funky gospel/soul tune "I'll Take You There" (1972) by the Staples Singers received major airplay. Musical changes accelerated in the 1990s as younger performers began to explore blending secular genres with gospel. Artists such as the Winans, Take 6, and Kirk Franklin explored pop-gospel boundaries and created fusions of gospel with R & B, hip-hop, and jazz. Traditionalists such as Shirley Caesar, however, remained dedicated to the core of gospel tradition. Both types of artists sought to carry on the legacy of Thomas A. Dorsey, who was himself the first pop-gospel crossover artist.

SOUL MUSIC

When rock was developing in the 1950s, the term *R & B* seemed sufficient to describe the new blues-based music being produced by black and white artists. Rock, however, had started to differentiate from R & B by the end of the decade, so that by the early 1960s most black-oriented music had come to be known as **soul music.** The soul sound was a hybrid of gospel styles and secular music, as vocalist Cissy Houston recalled,

> You started to hear gospel in black popular music in the mid-fifties because that's what was going on in black life. Everybody was getting crazy that R&B was making it big, crossing over for whites and all. But gospel stations were just as exciting to listen to. Gospel was making folks jump in a big, big way.[13]

From the late 1950s through the early 1960s, artists increasingly used gospel vocal styles as a source of excitement and intense emotion. By the mid-1960s, the soul style became fully realized, with musical arrangements consciously constructed to complement the sound.

While Ray Charles, Sam Cooke, and Jackie Wilson had laid the groundwork of soul in the late 1950s, other important black artists also contributed to the style's early development. **Ben E. King** (1938–), formerly the lead singer of the Drifters, made R & B sophisticated and accessible to mainstream pop audiences with his smooth baritone voice and clear enunciation. King's hits, "Spanish Harlem" (1961), "Stand by Me" (1961), and "Don't Play That Song (You Lied)" (1962), were forerunners of the Motown sound.

Admired for her gritty, precise, and penetrating voice, **Dinah Washington** (1924–1963) felt equally at home in R & B, jazz, and pop, and she influenced many subsequent R & B and jazz artists, including Nancy Wilson and Esther Phillips. Although already a major R & B star in the late 1940s and 1950s, Washington crossed over to the pop charts with "What a Diff'rence a Day Makes" (1959), "Baby (You've Got What It Takes)" (1960), and "This Bitter Earth" (1960).

Ike (1931–) **and Tina Turner** (1939–) first came on the R & B and pop scene in the late 1950s. Prior to forming the Ike and Tina Turner Revue, Turner was an influential artist and producer on the Memphis R & B scene who had led the backup band on the original rock classic, "Rocket 88" (1951). The Turners, who had one of the most potent live R & B acts before a publicized breakup in the mid-1970s, generated the hits "A Fool in Love" (1960) and "River Deep—Mountain High" (1966). After some restyling in response to pop trends of the late 1960s, they had crossover hits with covers of the Beatles' "Come Together" (1970), Sly Stone's "I Want to Take You Higher" (1970), and Creedence Clearwater's "Proud Mary" (1971). When Tina Turner split from her increasingly abusive husband, she recast herself as a mainstream rocker in the 1980s with hits such as "What's Love Got to Do with It" (1984) and "Private Dancer" (1985). A film, also called *What's Love Got to Do with It* (1999), was later made of Tina Turner's life.

The **Impressions** and leader/songwriter **Curtis Mayfield** (1942–1999) exemplified the rich late doo-wop/early soul scene of Chicago in the 1960s. The Impressions launched the careers of soul legend Jerry Butler as well as Curtis Mayfield. Sweet harmonies, Mayfield's guitar, occasional Latin rhythms, and the evolving use of civil rights themes marked the Impressions' style. Hits included "For Your Precious Love" (1958), "Gypsy Woman" (1961), "Keep on Pushing" (1964), "Amen" (1964), and "People Get Ready" (1965). After Mayfield left the group in the early 1970s, he scored again with the soundtrack to the blaxploitation film *Superfly* (1972) and other well-received projects.

Internet Listening Exercise

Listen to samples of early 1960s R & B.

Ben E. King: "Stand by Me"

Dinah Washington: "What a Diff'rence a Day Makes"

Ike and Tina Turner: "Proud Mary"

The Impressions: "Gypsy Woman"

How Did Rock and Soul Differ?

Rock	Soul
Roots and Sources	**Roots and Sources**
A mix of roots in jazz, R & B, Chicago blues, rockabilly, country, and folk music.	Early roots in the African American ring shout; contemporary roots in gospel, R & B, and other blues styles.
Lyrical Content	**Lyrical Content**
Lyrics focused on teenage concerns, shifting to encompass social issues in the 1960s.	A self-consciously black idiom; civil rights themes appeared, along with issues of love and passion.
Vocalization	**Vocalization**
Hybrid of blues, country, and folk.	Vocals were often delivered with emotional power derived from gospel, including vocal embellishments (melismas).
Rhythm	**Rhythm**
Insistent driving beat with a focus on even eighth notes.	Rhythms on up-tempo tunes emphasized the groove with interlocked polyrhythms of the electric bass and drums; tendency toward swing.

The godfather of soul, James Brown, in 1968.

Quintessential Soul Artists

Two artists stood out in the development of soul: James Brown and Aretha Franklin. Though they came from different backgrounds and produced divergent sounds, both embodied the essence of the music.

James Brown (1928–) was like a cat with at least nine lives. Despite repeated brushes with the law, the "Hardest Working Man in Show Business" excelled for most of his seven decades as a performer, dancer, composer, bandleader, businessman, and musical visionary. Critic Robert Palmer describes Brown in performance:

> His band locks into a chopping rhythm riff and Brown strides purposefully from the wings. . . . His head jerks to the beat, his hips shimmy, and suddenly he's snaking across the stage on one foot, his other leg windmilling along with his long, limber arms, he does a split, erupts into a pirouette, whirls like a dervish, and ends up at the microphone just in time to shriek "bayba-a-a-ay." [14]

The artist embodied the soul explosion, and then pioneered funk—an entire new style—almost single-handedly. Brown continued to tour into the 2000s with his twenty-piece funk band of two drummers, two bassists, three guitarists, several horn players, and numerous singers and dancers. Having learned gospel while imprisoned as a youth, the Georgia-born artist formed a band called the Famous Flames after his release. Brown's first hit, "Please, Please, Please" (1956), remained a signature tune throughout his career. He followed up with "Think" (1960) and "Night Train" (1962). With a tightly rehearsed and choreographed show polished to perfection, he played to sellout audiences in African American communities across the country in the early 1960s, and his 1963 recording *Live at the Apollo* firmly established him as a major artist.

Brown made music history with the release of the seminal "Papa's Got a Brand New Bag" in 1965. Here, Brown threw away traditional song structure to focus on the groove—the entire song was an extended vamp, with few chord changes and little melody. The song also featured a new guitar sound made by choking the guitar neck and strumming percussively to produce a sound Brown called "chank." A highly syncopated and percussive bass grounded the tune with a powerful pulse, and the drums locked in tightly with the bass. Brown realized that he had found something powerful:

> I had discovered that my strength was not in the horns, it was in the rhythm. I was hearing everything, even the guitars, like they were drums. . . . Later on they said it was the beginning of funk. I just thought of it as where my music was going. [15]

Brown followed up with "Cold Sweat" (1967). According to Atlantic Records producer Jerry Wexler, "'Cold Sweat' deeply affected the musicians I knew. It just freaked them out. For a time, no one could get a handle on what to do next."[16] By 1968 Brown had shifted to civil rights themes with "Say It Loud I'm Black and I'm Proud," and he was credited with helping quell riots after the assassination of Martin Luther King, Jr. He continued to make cutting-edge dance music into the 1970s with a funky rhythm section that included bassist Bootsie Collins: "Mother Popcorn" (1969), "Get Up (I Feel Like Being a) Sex Machine" (1970), "Super Bad" (1971), and "The Payback" (1974). Along the way he shifted record labels in a deal that gave him creative control and allowed him to bring his past catalog of recordings to the new label.

Despite recurring legal problems, Brown continued to tour and record into the 2000s, periodically surfacing in films, hip-hop samples, and other facets of popular culture. He pioneered two major musical genres—soul and funk—and his single-minded artistic vision and riveting performance style made him a legend. Brown's accomplishments as an American popular music innovator placed him alongside giants such as Louis Armstrong, Duke Ellington, and the Beatles in pop music history.

James Brown's Contributions

Funk Innovation

He pioneered funk by emphasizing polyrhythms and extended grooves.

Performance Style

His performance style influenced performers ranging from Mick Jagger to Sly Stone

Album Format

His 1963 album, *Live at the Apollo,* was one of the best live pop albums in history and was the first LP album bought in volume by African Americans.

Black Pride and Self-Determination

He was one of the first African American musical artists to champion black pride and political consciousness in the late 1960s. He was also one of the first black artists to achieve independence from his record company in terms of production and packaging.

Hip-Hop Influence

He influenced hip-hop, whose artists mimicked his vocal talking-singing style and sampled his powerful rhythm tracks.

Aretha Franklin (1942–) was the most exciting and influential female soul singer of the 1960s. Her gospel roots ran deep: While still a teenager, she began her performing career touring with the gospel troupe of her father, the Reverend C. L. Franklin. According to Franklin, "The best, the greatest gospel singers passed through our house in Detroit. Sometimes they stayed with us. James Cleveland lived with us for a time, and it was James who taught me to play the piano by ear." [17] Vocalists Mahalia Jackson and Clara Ward were also frequent visitors, and they served as mentors to the young Franklin.

When Franklin signed with Columbia Records in 1960, the label toned down her powerful voice, banished her soulful gospel piano playing, and cast her as a jazzy, Tin Pan Alley–style vocalist. It was not a good match: After nine albums, all Columbia had to show was a minor Franklin hit with the Al Jolson standard, "Rock-A-Bye Your Baby with a Dixie Melody." The young vocalist became confused and depressed, but once Columbia released her in 1966, Atlantic Records immediately signed her. Within a year, Franklin had become the most successful singer in the nation. Her 1967 recordings "I Never Loved a Man (the Way I Love You)" and "Do Right Woman—Do Right Man" were immediate hits, and the album that contained them, *Lady Soul,* also produced the soul classics "Dr. Feelgood" and "Respect." Franklin's version of "Respect," written by Otis Redding, made the tune a feminist anthem and turned the girl-group sound on its head with strong vocals and a powerful female gospel trio for backup. Saxophonist King Curtis described how Franklin made songs her own: "When Aretha records a tune she kills a copyright. Because once she's worked out the way to do it. . . . it's damn sure you're not going to be able to improve on how she's done it, her way." [18] Franklin also recorded "(You Make Me Feel Like) A Natural Woman," "Chain of Fools," and "Think" in the same period. Producer Jerry Wexler describes her musicianship:

> I needed Aretha to finish "Do Right"—in a hurry. . . . She came to the studio . . . and made a miracle. She overdubbed two discrete keyboard parts, first playing piano, then organ; she and her sisters hemstitched the seamless background harmonies; and when she added her glorious lead vocal, the result was perfection.[19]

Ultimately, Franklin scored ten major hits in an eighteen-month span between early 1967 and late 1968, as well as a steady stream of hits for the next five years. She was probably the first soul artist to conceive of her albums as whole, thematically unified pieces of work, and they were huge sellers. Her choice of material could also be interesting and eclectic, encompassing originals and gospel, blues, pop,

An early publicity shot of the queen of soul, Aretha Franklin.

and rock covers of the Beatles ("Eleanor Rigby"), the Band ("The Weight"), Simon and Garfunkel ("Bridge over Troubled Water"), Stephen Stills ("Love the One You're With"), Elton John ("Border Song"), Sam Cooke ("You Send Me"), and Ben E. King ("Spanish Harlem"). Franklin's commercial and artistic success continued into the early 1970s, when she produced two of her most respected and earthiest albums: *Live at Fillmore West,* which expanded her popularity with a young white audience and reflected Fillmore impresario Bill Graham's philosophy of blending styles in the acts he booked, and *Amazing Grace,* a double album, recorded with James Cleveland and the Southern California Community Choir, that reconnected her to her gospel roots.

CD LISTENING EXERCISE

CD 2/16

Listen to Aretha Franklin's recording of "(You Make Me Feel Like) A Natural Woman," composed by Brill Building songwriters Carole King and Gerry Goffin. Does Franklin's background in gospel music show in her performance? What is the meter of the song? How does her vocal performance on the bridge affect the emotional energy and drive of the arrangement? Is Franklin's performance style appropriate to the message of the lyrics?

During her years of preeminence, 1967–1970, Aretha Franklin found more success than virtually any other black pop artist had. She achieved phenomenal record sales, critical praise, and massive support from both black and white audiences. Having completed the transition from gospel to soul, Franklin symbolized the essence of the new genre. According to producer Jerry Wexler,

> "Genius" is the word. Clearly Aretha was continuing what Ray Charles had begun—the secularization of gospel, turning church rhythms, church patterns, and especially church feelings into personalized love songs.[20]

Motown: Northern Soul

Motown in its mid-1960s musical heyday knew no peers in African American popular music: It was the most successful record label and publishing house in the history of soul. At a time when most independent record labels had died out, Motown marketed a mass-produced pop sound that was drenched in black tradition, and Motown hits of the 1960s revolutionized American popular music. Much of the label's success came about because of the company's founder, Berry Gordy, Jr. A former boxer and record-store owner, he synthesized the musical lessons of the previous decade, taking ideas from the Brill Building, independent labels, doo-wop stylists, and girl groups. For more than a decade, Gordy and his talented artists, songwriters, arrangers, and musicians embodied the company's slogan: "The Sound of Young America." According to vocalist/songwriter Smokey Robinson,

> Berry wanted to make crossover music. Crossover at that time meant that white people would buy your records. Berry's concept in starting Motown was to make music with a funky beat and great stories that would crossover, that would *not* be blues. And that's what we did.[21]

Gordy started his musical career in the 1950s as a songwriter in Detroit looking to capitalize on the developing R & B scene. Early hits that he produced included Marv Johnson's "You've Got What It Takes" (1960) and Barrett

A classic record publicity photo of Smokey Robinson (third from left) and the Miracles from the mid-1960s.

Strong's classic "Money (That's What I Want)" (1960). These successes enabled Gordy to form the Tamla label in 1960, and he immediately scored a hit with "Shop Around" written by Smokey Robinson, who was then a member of the Miracles vocal group. Gordy brought him into the company's management, and Robinson proved to be a superb songwriter responsible for an impressive range of Motown hits over the years. Singer-songwriter Bob Dylan once described Robinson as "one of America's greatest poets." [22]

Gordy's studio, literally a converted bungalow, teemed with aspiring artists, including Marvin Gaye, Mary Wells, and the Marvelettes. Gordy expanded his stable of writer-producers by forming the prolific team of Lamont Dozier and Brian and Eddie Holland. Starting with "Heat Wave" (1963) by Martha and the Vandellas, the team systematized Gordy's production techniques and amassed eighteen top-twenty hits in three years. The signature sound of Holland-Dozier-Holland—and Motown—reached its pinnacle in hits such as the Four Tops' "Reach Out, I'll Be There" (1966) and the Supremes' "You Can't Hurry Love" (1966). Motown's sound also owed much to the label's house band, the Funk Brothers, which featured bassist James Jamerson. According to historian Robert Palmer,

> Everyone at Motown . . . agreed that James Jamerson . . . was the band's real linchpin, its most consistently creative player. The other musicians might be given specific figures to play; Jamerson, given a chord sheet for the song and perhaps a run-through with voice and piano, created his own parts, and in the process became the most influential bassist of the 60s. [23]

Characteristics of the Motown Sound

- Use of gospel vocal styles in a pop context.
- Simple lyrical content and stories that could easily cross over to white pop audiences.
- Adaptation of vocal group harmony styles from doo-wop and girl groups.
- Extended repetition of memorable musical hooks.
- Strong, coherent musical backup by experienced jazz musicians from the label's house band, the Funk Brothers.
- Bassist James Jamerson's lyrical, moving bass lines.
- Percussion highlighted in a "hot" mix with loud cymbals, booming bass, hand claps, and tambourine.
- Use of melodic horn and string parts to provide a smooth, uptown veneer.

Motown was not just about the sound—it was also about Gordy's goal of breaking into the mainstream market. To do this, he admitted that he adopted an assembly-line approach: "I worked on the Ford assembly line, and I thought, 'Why can't we do that with the creative process?' You know, the writing, the producing, the artist development." [24] He turned Motown into a "finishing school" with classes in choreography, music theory, and social graces. He fostered competition among the producers and songwriters as well, much as had been done in the Brill Building, pressuring writers to produce the next hit for the Temptations or the Supremes. Rifts appeared in the Motown family near the end of the 1960s as producers and artists jumped ship over monetary and creative disputes. Major artists such as Marvin Gaye and Stevie Wonder also negotiated new contracts that gave them artistic control, and Motown moved its headquarters from Detroit to Los Angeles. The old Motown system dissolved, acts drifted away, and Gordy sold his company to MCA in 1988. Jerry Wexler of Atlantic Records sums up Gordy's accomplishments:

> Berry Gordy and Motown found something that we [at Atlantic Records] didn't or couldn't do. . . . He went with his version of black music directly to the white teenage buyer. Motown has left its impact on people in a way that no other music has done. [25]

Throughout its heyday, Motown was blessed with a talented roster of artists. Although Berry Gordy dictated the direction of the sound, and the producers and the house band provided material and instrumental backup, the individual vocalists ultimately conveyed the Motown image, producing an impressive array of hits during the 1960s.

Marvin Gaye (1939–1984) served as one of soul music's most charismatic and enigmatic figures, as well as one of its most important stylists. With a career spanning the history of R & B, from 1950s doo-wop to 1980s dance music,

Internet Listening Exercise

Listen to samples of early Motown hits.

Marv Johnson: "You've Got What It Takes"

Barrett Strong: "Money (That's What I Want)"

The Marvelettes: "Please Mr. Postman"

Smokey Robinson and the Miracles: "Shop Around"

Next, listen to samples of Motown songs produced by Holland-Dozier-Holland.

Martha and the Vandellas: "Dancing in the Streets"

Temptations: "Reach Out, I'll Be There"

Supremes: "You Can't Hurry Love"

Gaye embodied the Motown sound with some of the most enduring hits of the 1960s and then broadened the boundaries of soul in the 1970s with an intensely personal and political form of expression. The gospel-trained artist scored hits throughout the 1960s such as "Pride and Joy" (1963)," "How Sweet It Is to Be Loved by You" (1965), "Ain't That Peculiar" (1965), and "I Heard It through the Grapevine" (1968). He also joined vocalist Tammi Terrell for such hits as "Ain't No Mountain High Enough" (1967) and "Ain't Nothing Like the Real Thing" (1968). Gaye demanded and received an unprecedented level of artistic control for his 1971 *What's Going On* album—a bold musical experiment filled with social commentary and prophetic language. The best-selling album Motown had ever released, it compared favorably with the Beatles' *Sgt. Pepper,* yielding hits such as "What's Going On," "Mercy, Mercy Me (The Ecology)," and "Inner City Blues (Make Me Wanna Holler)." Gaye subsequently cut loose with a sensual masterpiece, *Let's Get It On* (1973), and later followed the same vein with "Got to Give It Up " (1977) and "Sexual Healing" (1982).

Motown's most successful female group, the **Supremes,** scored ten major hits between 1964 and 1967, briefly rivaling the Beatles. With their sophisticated though sometimes formulaic sound, they embodied Berry Gordy's dream of crossover success. Early hits included "Where Did Our Love Go?" (1964), "Baby Love" (1964), "Stop! In the Name of Love" (1965), and "I Hear a Symphony" (1965). They toured Europe in 1965 and achieved Gordy's goal of performing in top U.S. nightclubs such as New York's Copa Cabana. As the group's lead singer, **Diana Ross** (1944–), started to receive top billing, the hits kept coming: "You Keep Me Hangin' On" (1966), "Love Child" (1968), and "Someday We'll Be Together" (1969). When Ross left the Supremes in 1970 to pursue a solo career, Gordy shifted focus to promote her as a multimedia star. Ross had several hit songs ("Ain't No Mountain High Enough," 1970; "Touch Me in the Morning," 1973; "Do You Know Where You're Going To," 1975), acted in three films, and performed on Broadway. Ross's star began to fade in the late 1980s, however, and as critic Diane Cardwell puts it,

> Today she is something of a camp artifact, an icon of fabulous bitchiness and Vegas glitz rather than the serious recording artist and vibrant performer she once was. . . . It is a universal irony of icons: to freeze in the very image they create.[26]

The Temptations were Motown's most popular and longest-lasting male vocal group. The quintet featured two lead singers and precise onstage dance routines. Despite personnel changes, they maintained a consistent sound, and they were one of few Motown acts to remain viable into the 1970s. The group originally came together in the late 1950s, signing with Berry Gordy in 1960. In 1964 they achieved the first in a series of thirty-seven top-ten hits with "The Way You Do the Things You Do," followed up with "My Girl" (1965), "Get Ready" (1966), and "Ain't Too Proud to Beg" (1966). Around 1967 producer Norman Whitfield took over the Temptations and began to experiment with Sly Stone–style funk flavorings and socially conscious lyrics to produce hits such as "Cloud Nine" (1969), "Ball of Confusion" (1970), and "Papa Was a Rolling Stone" (1972), while still producing a sweet vocal sound in tunes such as "Just My Imagination" (1971). According to critics Joe McEwen and Jim Miller, "The

Temptations quite simply stood as the finest vocal group in Sixties soul: they could outdress, outdance and outsing any competition in sight." [27]

Atlantic, Stax, and Muscle Shoals: Southern Soul

Soul music produced in the South, sometimes called the **southern groove,** differed from the Motown sound: It was hard-edged, more gospel-based, and less arranged. It also appealed more often to black than to white audiences. Historian Charlie Gillett describes the making of the southern groove:

> Session men . . . instead of playing written arrangements which represented a producer's concept,
> evolved their own "head arrangements," jam session "grooves" which were gradually rationalized to accommodate verse structures of songs.[28]

CD LISTENING EXERCISE

CD 2/17

Listen to "My Girl" (1965), composed by Smokey Robinson and performed by the Temptations. Recorded during the studio's most successful period, this classic example of the Motown sound was one of the most well crafted songs of the era. Good pop songs require memorable musical hooks, and "My Girl" has an impressive variety of them. Although recorded over forty years ago, most listeners still instantly recognize the song. What makes "My Girl" a classic?

The development of the sound involved a web of relationships among Atlantic Records in New York, Stax Records in Memphis, and a pair of studios in Muscle Shoals, Alabama. Atlantic had the marketing muscle and many of the most popular artists under contract, while Stax and Muscle Shoals had the studio musicians to produce the musical texture. Great performances by artists such as Otis Redding, Wilson Pickett, Solomon Burke, Aretha Franklin, Joe Tex, Carla Thomas, Sam and Dave, Percy Sledge, and Booker T and the MGs were produced through the set of shifting alliances. The studio musicians who crafted the black-oriented southern groove were a racially mixed group; the band at Stax in Memphis was fully integrated, while the groups in Muscle Shoals were almost all white.

Atlantic Records, founded in New York in 1947, was one of the original independent labels of the 1950s that give birth to R & B. It was also the most successful of the independents, surviving multiple takeover attempts by major record labels and expanding throughout the 1960s. Led by Ahmet Ertegun and Jerry Wexler, Atlantic employed a hands-on approach with great R & B artists of the 1950s such as Ruth Brown, Big Joe Turner, the Coasters, Clyde McPhatter, and Ray Charles. In the 1960s, the label shifted to southern soul, bringing out classic work by Otis Redding, Wilson Pickett, Sam and Dave, Aretha Franklin, and Solomon Burke, as well as groundbreaking rock records by Buffalo Springfield, Led Zeppelin, and Crosby, Stills, and Nash.

The southern soul sound coalesced for Atlantic in the mid-1960s with singer **Wilson Pickett** (1941–), a hard gospel shouter, whom the label recorded backed by the band at Stax Records in Memphis. According to producer Jerry Wexler,

> I called Jim Stewart in Memphis and said, "Would you let me bring an artist down there, cut him in the studio with your band?" He said, sure. So I took Wilson down there, and opened up that southern thing for us.[29]

White-owned but black-oriented, Stax Records began operating in 1959, out of an old theater building in the African American section of Memphis. A record shop in the front of the theater was used to test new records. According to the label's owner, Jim Stewart,

> Now what we were doing was called the Stax sound or the Memphis sound. It wasn't Chicago, and it wasn't New York, and it sure wasn't Detroit. It was a southern sound, a below-the-Bible-Belt sound. It was righteous and nasty.[30]

The label's early hits by Rufus and Carla Thomas—"'Cause I Love You" (1960) and "Gee Whiz" (1961) by Carla Thomas—piqued Atlantic's interest in developing a national distribution agreement with the label. By 1965 Stax had produced a series of hits (distributed on ATCO, Atlantic's second label) by Otis Redding, one of the greatest southern soul singers. The Stax rhythm section (Booker T and the MGs) sounded to Wexler like just the right fit for Pickett. When the artist walked into the Stax studio, he immediately sat down with guitarist Steve Cropper to produce "In the Midnight Hour" (1965), one of the biggest soul hits of all time. As Cropper recalled,

> Somebody came up and says, "Hey, write a tune for Wilson." . . . I grabbed the only album of his I could find . . . and at the end of each fade-out he'd say, "Yeah, wait for the midnight hour, baby." . . . I thought that would be a heck of an idea for a tune, and when he came in I presented it to him, and he said . . . "I've got this little rhythm thing I've been working on for a good while." There was really nothing to it.[31]

The classic Stax sound dated from that session. Eddie Floyd's "Knock on Wood" (1966) and Sam and Dave's "Hold on I'm Coming" (1966) and "Soul Man" (1967) all had a similar feeling to "In the Midnight Hour."

Although the Atlantic-Stax collaboration succeeded, business disagreements cut it short, and Atlantic looked further south to Alabama for the gritty, soulful southern flavor. Stax continued to produce hits for several more years, as well as a successful live concert film called *Wattstax* (1972). Major Stax artists included Carla and Rufus Thomas, Booker T and the MGs, the Bar-Kays, the Staples Singers, Albert King, Little Milton, Johnnie Taylor, the Dramatics, the Emotions, and Isaac Hayes. The Stax sound was resurrected in 1980 in the film *The Blues Brothers*, which featured tunes by Stax artists and members of the original Stax rhythm section.

Atlantic's search for an alternative to Stax led in 1965 to a small studio near Muscle Shoals, Alabama, called Fame Records, which had already scored soul hits with vocalist Joe Tex ("Hold What You've Got," "One Monkey Don't Stop No Show"). Almost all the Muscle Shoals musicians were white, producing a consistent sound hard to distinguish from the Memphis Stax sound. According to Charlie Gillett,

> On slow numbers, Muscle Shoals arrangements tended to be more "churchy," with piano or organ conjuring images of heads bowed in humble dedication. . . . On fast ones, [producer] Rick Hall's trademark was to have a particular riff on guitar repeated throughout a song.[32]

Internet Listening Exercise

Listen to samples of the Stax/ Atlantic southern groove.

Wilson Pickett: "In the Midnight Hour"

Eddie Floyd: "Knock on Wood"

Sam and Dave: "Hold on I'm Coming," "Soul Man"

Internet Listening Exercise

Listen to samples of the Stax sound.

Carla Thomas: "Gee Whiz"

Booker T and the MGs: "Green Onions"

The Bar-Kays: "Soul Finger"

Staples Singers: "I'll Take You There"

Johnnie Taylor: "Who's Making Love"

The Dramatics: "Whatcha See Is Whatcha Get"

Early in 1966, Wexler took Wilson Pickett to record in Muscle Shoals, producing "Land of 1000 Dances," "Mustang Sally," and "Funky Broadway." Another Muscle Shoals artist, vocalist Percy Sledge, had a hit around the same time with "When a Man Loves a Woman." Wexler also brought the newly signed Aretha Franklin to Muscle Shoals in 1967 for her first Atlantic recording session, producing Franklin's breakout hits—"I Never Loved a Man (the Way I Loved You)" and "Do Right Woman—Do Right Man." Wexler later transported key members of the Muscle Shoals band to New York to record on other Franklin records such as "Respect," "(You Make Me Feel Like) A Natural Woman," and "Chain of Fools."

The black–white musical collaborations that produced southern soul continued through 1968, until the assassination of Martin Luther King, Jr., in Memphis. Although soul and R & B were already changing because of James Brown and Sly Stone's funk innovations, King's murder pushed soul toward a more rigorously black sound and message. As Muscle Shoals producer Rick Hall recalls,

> Pickett was here in Muscle Shoals when Dr. King was shot in Memphis. The whole mood and atmosphere in the studio suddenly changed, and in fact we called off the session, out of respect to Dr. King. . . . But there was a change from that night on.[33]

The two studios in the Muscle Shoals area shifted to backing up white country and rock artists for the next decade, including the Osmonds, Paul Anka, Jerry Reed, Alabama, Joe Cocker, Leon Russell, Paul Simon, Rod Stewart, and Bob Seger.

Internet Listening Exercise

Listen to samples of tunes recorded at Muscle Shoals.

Joe Tex: "One Monkey Don't Stop No Show"

Wilson Pickett: "Land of 1000 Dances"

Percy Sledge: "When a Man Loves a Woman"

Aretha Franklin: "I Never Loved a Man (The Way I Loved You)"

Multicultural Note

Racial Politics and the Production of Soul Music

Northern soul music was dominated by Motown, a black-owned firm with black performers, black producers, and mostly black musicians. Although the label served as a pioneering example of black capitalism, its goal ("The Sound of Young America") was to avoid the blues and aim for the white market. Motown's Berry Gordy also played on his black identity when marketing his artists to black radio stations. When Motown hit it big, however, Gordy stopped using black booking agencies and shifted to white industry giants such as the William Morris agency.

Much grittier than Motown, southern soul targeted the black market. Yet the white-owned Atlantic and Stax labels dominated the style. The artists were black, the producers were black and white, the musicians in Memphis were black and white, and the musicians in Alabama were all white. What do these examples tell us about the complex interplay of race, economic power, appropriation, and identity in American culture and music?

Soul legend Otis Redding.

MICHAEL OCHS ARCHIVES.COM

Internet
Listening Exercise

Listen to samples of songs by Otis Redding.

Otis Redding: "Respect," "(Sittin' on) The Dock of the Bay"

Otis Redding (1941–1967) was the greatest of the 1960s southern soul men. He broadened the appeal of soul to white audiences with a raw, spontaneous style that sharply contrasted with Motown. According to Robert Palmer,

> He combined a pleading vulnerability (mostly on ballads) with an aggressively rhythmic, highly improvisational up-tempo style, interpolating "gotta-gotta-gottas" and "nah-nah-nahs" so freely that his creations frequently eclipsed the song's original melody and lyrics.[34]

Redding wrote or cowrote most of his own songs, and some became hits for other artists (such as "Respect" for Aretha Franklin and "Sweet Soul Music" for Arthur Conley). When Redding brought soul music to new crossover heights at the 1967 Monterey Pop Festival, he did so by sticking to his roots: Macon, Georgia, by way of Memphis. His early work reflected Little Richard, but by the time of his first Stax hit ("These Arms of Mine," 1963), Redding's style had fully formed. He toured regularly, usually backed by one of Stax's two bands, Booker T and the MGs or the Bar-Kays, and became popular in Europe. In 1965 he broke through in the United States with "I've Been Loving You Too Long (to Stop Now)" and "Respect," followed up in the next two years with "I Can't Turn You Loose," "Try a Little Tenderness," and a cover of the Rolling Stones' "Satisfaction." Appearing as the only soul act at the Monterey Pop Festival in 1967, Redding drew legions of new white fans with his incendiary stage performance. Sadly, he passed away in 1967 at age twenty-six in a plane crash, and the posthumous release of his chart-topping "(Sittin' on) The Dock of the Bay" gave further evidence of his talent.

Chapter Summary

- The early 1960s brought an impressive scope of innovation in rock and soul music. Multiple overlapping, new genres emerged in the decade.

- The 1960s began with the rise of a new breed of record producers/songwriters who made record production into an art form. In Los Angeles, the team of Mike Leiber and Jerry Stoller, along with "wall of sound" producer Phil Spector, played prominent roles in the new production style. In New York's Brill Building, rock, pop, and soul songwriters such as Carole King and Gerry Goffin, Barry Mann and Cynthia Weil, Neil Sedaka and Howard Greenfield, Bobby Darin, and Neil Diamond ushered in a brief new era of contemporary popular songwriting in the tradition of Tin Pan Alley.

- The early 1960s also saw the rise of the girl groups, including the Chantels, Shirelles, Crystals, Marvelettes, and Ronettes. The sweet and melodramatic girl-group sound mixed hooks and doo-wop harmonies. The groups were usually trios or quartets fronted by a lead singer, and many were one-hit wonders.

- Early 1960s white rock artists included the Four Seasons, Dion and the Belmonts, Bobby Darin, and Neil Diamond. A plethora of new dance styles also appeared, including the Twist, Hucklebuck, Stroll, Watusi, Limbo, Loco-Motion, Fly, Pony, Mashed Potatoes, Monkey, Swim, Jerk, and Hitchhike.

- Guitarist Dick Dale led the emergence of surf music, which was brought into the national spotlight by the Beach Boys, with their close harmonies and mythic California images of cars, girls, and surf.

- African American gospel music came into its own in the mid-twentieth century, establishing a unique, indigenous American genre and spinning off numerous artists who contributed important innovations to R & B, soul, and rock.

- R & B began to evolve into soul, featuring such artists as Ray Charles, Sam Cooke, Jackie Wilson, Ben E. King, Dinah Washington, Ike and Tina Turner, and Curtis Mayfield and the Impressions.

- Soul came into full flower in the mid-1960s, embodied by artists such as James Brown and Aretha Franklin. Motown produced a northern version of soul with such artists as the Supremes, the Temptations, Smokey Robinson, and Marvin Gaye. A grittier style of southern soul emanated from Atlantic, Stax, and Muscle Shoals to flavor the work of artists such as Wilson Pickett and Otis Redding.

Key Terms

Brill Building	melismas	surf music
girl groups	soul music	wall of sound
gospel music	southern groove	

Study and Discussion Questions

1. Why were the 1960s a prolific era in the history of American popular music? What social, political, and commercial issues served as catalysts for the explosion of musical styles?

2. Discuss the contributions of the L.A.-based producer/songwriters and the New York–based Brill Building songwriters to early 1960s pop music. Who were important figures in this movement toward professionalism in rock and roll and R & B?

3. Who were the girl groups of the 1960s, and what was their significance?

4. What was surf music? Who were some of its major artists? What was its cultural significance?

5. What were the origins and development of African American gospel music? What are some examples of its influences on R & B and rock?

6. Discuss the evolution of soul music. What were the principal styles that emerged? What were Motown's accomplishments, and who were some major artists?

7. What was the southern groove? How was it produced, and who were some of its major artists?

Notes

1. Robert Palmer, *Rock and Roll: An Unruly History* (New York: Harmony Books, 1995), 33.

2. Ibid., 35.

3. Ibid.

4. "Episode 2: In the Groove," in *Rock and Roll,* video recording, produced by David Espar and Hugh Thomson (South Burlington, VT: WGBH, 1995).

5. Patricia Juliana Smith, "Ask Any Girl," in *Reading Rock and Roll: Authenticity, Appropriation, and Aesthetics,* edited by Anthony DeCurtis, Kevin Dettmar, and William Richey (New York: Columbia University Press, 1999), 94.

6. Smith, "Ask Any Girl," 110.

7. Mary Elizabeth Williams, "Brilliant Careers: Top of the Pops: How Phil Spector Invented Teen Lust and Torment," http://www.salon.com/bc/1998/11/cov_10bc.html, accessed May 8, 2005.

8. Timothy White, *The Nearest Faraway Place: Brian Wilson, the Beach Boys, and the Southern California Experience* (New York: Holt, 1994), 194.

9. Palmer, *Rock and Roll,* 41.

10. Clarence Boyer, *How Sweet the Sound: The Golden Age of Gospel* (Washington, DC: Elliot & Clark, 1995), 259.

11. Eileen Southern, *The Music of Black Americans: A History,* 3rd ed. (New York: Norton, 1997), 460–61.

12. Boyer, *How Sweet the Sound,* 189.

13. Gerri Hirshey, *Nowhere to Run: The Story of Soul Music* (New York: Times Books, 1984), 26.

14. Robert Palmer, "James Brown," in *Rolling Stone Illustrated History of Rock and Roll,* edited by Jim Miller (New York: Random House, 1980), 136.

15. James Brown and Bruce Tucker, *James Brown: The Godfather of Soul* (New York: Thunder's Mouth Press, 1997), 158.

16. Palmer, *Rock and Roll,* 245.

17. Hirshey, *Nowhere to Run*, 231.

18. Charlie Gillett, *Making Tracks: Atlantic Records and the Growth of a Multi-Billion Dollar Industry* (New York: Dutton, 1974), 211.

19. Jerry Wexler with David Ritz, "The Queen of Soul," in *Rock and Roll Is Here to Stay: An Anthology,* edited by William McKeen (New York: Norton, 2000), 510.

20. Ibid., 506.

21. Hirshey, *Nowhere to Run,* 133.

22. Ibid., 137.

23. Palmer, *Rock and Roll,* 87–88.

24. Ibid., 86.

25. Ibid., 89.

26. Diane Cardwell, "Diana Ross," in *Trouble Girls: The Rolling Stone Book of Women in Rock,* edited by Barbara O'Dair (New York: Random House, 1997), 122.

27. Joe McEwen and Jim Miller, "Motown," in *Rolling Stone Illustrated History of Rock and Roll,* edited by Jim Miller (New York: Random House, 1980), 243.

28. Gillett, *Making Tracks,* 172.

29. Ibid., 185.

30. Hershey, *Nowhere to Run,* 294.

31. Gillett, *Making Tracks,* 194.

32. Ibid., 201.

33. Palmer, *Rock and Roll,* 96.

34. Ibid., 93.

1750 - 1970

1765 Thomas Percy publishes a major collection of British folk music that establishes the first folk music canon ♪

1776 Declaration of Independence and beginning of Revolutionary War

1880s Frances James Childs publishes the Child ballad collections, further codifying the British folk canon ♪

1803 Louisiana Purchase annexes vast western lands from France

1861–1865 Civil War

1898 Spanish American War

Early 1900s British song collector Cecil Sharp proves that British folk music exists in rural America, and he furthers the myth of folk purity ♪

1910 John Lomax publishes his collection of cowboy songs ♪

1914–1918 World War I

1929–1930s Great Depression; New Deal begins

1940s John and Allen Lomax become America's foremost song collectors and promote the career of songster Leadbelly ♪

1940 Woody Guthrie meets Pete Seeger, forming the backbone of the American political folk song movement ♪

1941–1945 U.S. participates in World War II

1950s Skiffle music lays the groundwork for the British "beat" sound ♪

1950 McCarthy "Red Scare" Senate hearings

1950 The Weavers score unlikely pop hits with "Goodnight Irene" and "On Top of Old Smoky" ♪

1954 School segregation outlawed; civil rights movement begins

1956 Harry Belafonte popularizes the calypso with the release of "Jamaica Farewell" ♪

1958 The Kingston Trio moves folk into the mainstream with their hit "Tom Dooley" ♪

1960–1964 Folk music explodes on college campuses ♪

1961 President John Kennedy inaugurated; Peace Corps established

1963 Civil rights march on Washington; John Kennedy assassinated

1963 Bob Dylan releases his early LP masterpiece *The Freewheelin' Bob Dylan,* which includes "Blowin' in the Wind" ♪

1964–1973 Vietnam War

1964 Beatles and Rolling Stones spearhead the British Invasion ♪

1965 Watts riots

1965 Dylan goes electric at the Newport Folk Festival ♪

1965 The Byrds' version of "Mr. Tambourine Man" sets the standard for folk rock ♪

1965 First "acid tests" in San Francisco set the stage for the psychedelic explosion

1966 Jimi Hendrix forms the Jimi Hendrix Experience in London

1966 Supreme Court rules on *Miranda* case; Vietnam War protests begin

1966 Sly Stone becomes first African American rocker to sign with a major label ♪

1967 Urban riots in Detroit; "Summer of Love" in San Francisco

1967 Beatles release *Sgt. Pepper;* Monterey Pop Festival; Hendrix records classic LPs ♪

1968 Martin Luther King and Robert Kennedy assassinated

1968 Eric Clapton and Cream release "Sunshine of Your Love" ♪

1969 Woodstock music festival ♪

1969 President Nixon sworn in; largest antiwar rally in history held

1970 Jimi Hendrix and Janis Joplin die of drug overdoses ♪

1700	1800	1900	1940	1950	1960

Chapter 15

Folk-Rock, the British Invasion, and Psychedelia

In the latter half of the 1960s, the United States saw war, assassinations, protests, drugs, and the birth of a counterculture that dreamed of a revolution of peace and love. Music reflected the values and struggles of the period and remains a vivid soundtrack of the era. Much of the music that the performers of the 1960s gave us has stood the test of time to become "classic rock." The kaleidoscope of musical innovations that swirled out of the period included folk-rock, the British Invasion, and psychedelic rock.

IN THIS CHAPTER

- The Folk Music Revival and the Birth of Folk-Rock
- The British Invasion
- The Birth of a Counterculture
- The L.A. Rock Scene in the Late 1960s
- Woodstock, Altamont, and the End of an Era

THE FOLK MUSIC REVIVAL AND THE BIRTH OF FOLK-ROCK

In the late 1950s and early 1960s, a significant contribution to the evolution of rock emanated from an unlikely source—folk music. The period was marked by a **folk revival** that reflected a growing interest in European folk music, rural blues, spirituals and gospel, mountain and country music, cowboy music, and other vernacular styles from around the world. Historian Norm Cohen characterized the revival as "the 'discovery' by sophisticated, culture-conscious urban artists, of traditional, generally American folk music, and its presentation by those artists to audiences of similar social background."[1]

Roots of American Folk Music

At the root of the folk music movement was the practice of **song collecting,** which actually originated in eighteenth-century England with British poet Thomas Percy (1729–1811). Percy claimed to have discovered a collection of old song manuscripts that had been discarded, and when he published his own extensively edited version of the collection in 1765, he initiated a continuing debate among successive generations of folk music aficionados over conceptions of purity and authenticity. A century later, Francis James Child (1825–1896) and Cecil Sharp (1859–1924) codified their versions of British and American folk music. Child's five-volume work, *The English and Scottish Popular Ballads,* became the definitive source of early folk balladry. He argued that no European folk ballad tradition had survived in the United States, though he was later

335

proven wrong by twentieth-century song collectors who found many of the ballads in the Child collection still being performed in the vernacular and folk repertoire of American musicians in New England, Appalachia, and rural areas of the Southeast. Folk revivalists of the 1960s such as Joan Baez and Judy Collins recorded ballads from the influential Child collection, and Simon and Garfunkel had a hit with a variant of a Child ballad called "Scarborough Fair" (1968).

Cecil Sharp was a British composer and teacher who collected hundreds of folk songs in the Appalachian mountains to produce *English Folk Songs from the Southern Appalachians* (1917). He believed that U.S. mountain people lived in the sort of isolated conditions that constituted a kind of cultural purity linked to an idealized time in Britain's past. This generated a fantasy of folk purity that many folk revivalists of the 1950s and 1960s would replicate. The work of Child and Sharp resulted in the canonization of British, Scottish, Irish, and other music of European origins as the "true" American folk music. According to historian Benjamin Filene, "The most significant effect of the myth of the white ballad singer was to help block African American folk music from gaining a central place in the canon of America's musical heritage." [2]

John Lomax (1867–1948) and his son **Alan** (1915–2003) were two of the twentieth century's most important song collectors and advocates for vernacular musics. A Harvard-educated Texan, John Lomax started collecting cowboy and western songs in the early twentieth century, and his *Cowboy Songs and Other Frontier Ballads* (1910), which introduced such tunes as "Home on the Range," contributed greatly to the American folk canon. The first commercial recordings of country, African American, and Mexican American musical styles in the 1920s also expanded the conception of American folk music beyond the Child/ Sharp model, encouraging the Lomaxes and other collectors to seek out additional folk music. The father-and-son team worked tirelessly throughout the

Multicultural Note

What Is Folk Music?

One of the challenges of the folk revival was to define **folk music.** Historian Norm Cohen offered this definition: "Folk music is a song that survives without the necessity of commercial media. There is no requirement of antiquity, anonymity, variability, or simplicity, though all of those attributes certainly are signs that a song has survived without commercial media." [3]

During the revival, folk music was also defined as acoustic music performed in the style of folk songs that dated back 50 years or more. In addition, many folk adherents promoted images of folk music as rural, simple, honest, pure, and admirable; pop music, on the other hand, was often characterized as urban, crass, dishonest, and polluted. What issues do such distinctions raise?

1930s to collect and promote the music and performers they found, in the process furthering the myth of the "true" folk singer. The Lomaxes also produced a landmark collection of American folk music entitled *American Ballads and Folksongs*. Alan Lomax subsequently worked for the Library of Congress as head of the Archive of American Song, collaborating with such legendary folk, jazz, and blues musicians as Woody Guthrie, Pete Seeger, Leadbelly, Jelly Roll Morton, and Muddy Waters. He later collected folk music of all styles from many parts of the world and produced an influential television series on American folk culture entitled *American Patchwork,* as well as an award-winning book, *The Land where Blues Began*, in the 1990s.

Leadbelly (Huddie Ledbetter, 1889–1949) was a twentieth-century version of an African American songster. He performed folk songs, blues, cowboy and country music, popular songs, and dance tunes. His songs "Goodnight Irene" and "Rock Island Line" became twentieth-century folk music standards. The Lomaxes, who first encountered Leadbelly in the Louisiana State Penitentiary serving a life sentence for murder, viewed him as an ideal figure to challenge the Child/Sharp canon. After the Lomaxes secured his release from prison, Leadbelly spent the rest of his career working for the Lomaxes—sometimes as a performer, other times as their chauffeur. The Lomaxes packaged Leadbelly as an authentic folk hero untainted by commercialism, encouraging him to perform in prison garb or farmer's overalls to convey authenticity. A resulting *New York Herald Tribune* headline for one of the artist's appearances proclaimed, "Sweet Singer of the Swamplands Here to Do a Few Songs Between Homicides." [4] Leadbelly's work ultimately became a staple of the folk revival. He was also honored in a 1990 tribute album, *A Shared Vision: A Tribute to Woody Guthrie and Leadbelly*, which featured his songs performed by Little Richard, Brian Wilson, and Willie Nelson, and in 1993 Kurt Cobain and Nirvana performed a Leadbelly tune for an *MTV Unplugged* album.

 **Internet Listening Exercise**

Visit http://www.rounder.com, go to the Alan Lomax collection, and listen to samples of Leadbelly's songs.

Leadbelly: "Rock Island Line," "Goodnight Irene," "Midnight Special"

MICHAEL OCHS ARCHIVES.COM

The Almanac Singers popularized the folk-song sing-along or "hootenanny." Left to right, front row: Woody Guthrie, Bess Lomax (Alan's sister), and Pete Seeger.

Woody Guthrie, Pete Seeger, and the Political Song Movement

The two most prominent white American folk musicians of the twentieth century were Woody Guthrie and Pete Seeger. The two came from contrasting class backgrounds: Guthrie grew up in a working-class family in Oklahoma, where his father played guitar and banjo in cowboy bands and his mother sang British ballads and folk songs; Seeger's father was a respected musicologist and experimental classical composer, and his mother was a classical violinist.

Woody Guthrie (1912–1967) was one of the most colorful figures in twentieth-century American music, best known for composing the folk anthem "This Land Is Your Land." According to author John Steinbeck,

> He sings the songs of a people, and I suspect that he is, in a way, the people. Harsh voiced and nasal, his guitar hanging like a tire iron on a rusty rim, there is nothing sweet about Woody, and there is nothing sweet about the songs he sings. But there is something more important for those who will listen. There is the will of the people to endure and fight against oppression. I think we call this the American spirit.[5]

Guthrie's early years were a real-life version of Steinbeck's Depression-era tale, *The Grapes of Wrath*. Family tragedies left Guthrie on his own at age sixteen. The infamous dust storms of 1935 forced him, along with thousands of other dust bowl refugees known as "Okies," to head west to California. When he arrived there and experienced antimigrant discrimination firsthand, Guthrie developed a lifelong commitment to social justice. This period of his life inspired some of the artist's most famous compositions, later recorded as the *Dust Bowl Ballads*.

When the artist moved to New York in 1939, he connected with a small community of progressive urban folk revivalists that included Alan Lomax, Pete Seeger, and Leadbelly. Lomax saw Guthrie as a white, working-class troubadour, and he recorded a series of interviews and performances with him for the Library of Congress. Guthrie lived a vagabond lifestyle, traveling to Oregon, where he composed "Roll on Columbia." In the early 1950s he began to suffer from degenerative health problems, which plagued him until his death in 1967. His legacy was kept alive by Pete Seeger, Guthrie's son Arlo, Bob Dylan, Bruce Springsteen, Ani DeFranco, and many others.

Pete Seeger's (1919–) repertoire of folk songs in large part comprises the contemporary canon of American folk music, and his compositions, such as "The Hammer Song" and "Where Have All the Flowers Gone," are folk standards. Seeger became fascinated with folk music as a young man when his parents were working with Alan and John Lomax. He briefly attended Harvard but dropped out to work as Alan Lomax's assistant at the Archive of American Folk Song in the Library of Congress, where he also took up the five-string banjo and learned many of the songs being archived. When Seeger met Woody Guthrie in 1940 at a migrant worker benefit concert, the two began a series of musical collaborations. Alan Lomax once described this meeting as the beginning of modern American folk music. In 1940 Seeger was a founding member of the **Almanac Singers,** a short-lived, New York–based political folk song ensemble. The group popularized the term **hootenanny** to describe large gatherings of folk

Internet Listening Exercise

Listen to samples of songs by Woody Guthrie.

Woody Guthrie: "This Land Is Your Land," "Worried Man Blues"

Next, go to http://www.rounder.com and listen to samples of selections by Woody Guthrie in the Library of Congress recordings in the Alan Lomax Collection.

musicians, broke new ground by using traditional folk tunes to address contemporary social topics, performed on easy-to-play instruments, and employed simple arrangements and harmonies that could be sung by untrained singers. In 1946, after returning from wartime military duty, Seeger cowrote "The Hammer Song" ("If I Had a Hammer"), one of the most popular songs in the American folk repertoire.

In 1948 Seeger joined forces with Lee Hays, Ronnie Gilbert, and Fred Hillerman to form the **Weavers,** a group that performed a broad range of American and international folk songs. The group had major hits in 1950 with Leadbelly's "Goodnight Irene" and an Israeli folk song, "Tzena Tzena." Though the record industry did not know how to classify the Weavers, they scored again the following year with "On Top of Old Smoky" and "Across the Wide Missouri." Because of their progressive politics, the Weavers fell victim to the Red Scare of the early 1950s, and by 1953 they had disbanded. The group later performed at periodic reunions, and a 1980 documentary called *Wasn't That a Time?* presented their history.

CD LISTENING EXERCISE

CD 1/16

Listen to Pete Seeger playing the classic "Oh! Susanna" by Stephen Foster. Notice Seeger's use of the five-string banjo as accompaniment. The artist's energetic and open singing style encouraged audience participation, and Seeger's singalong performances were legendary.

Internet Listening Exercise

Listen to samples of tunes written and performed by Pete Seeger and by the Weavers.

Pete Seeger: *If I Had a Hammer: Songs of Hope and Struggle*

The Weavers: *Best of the Decca Years: The Weavers* (MCA Records)

The Folk Revival Gets Under Way

New folk music strands and new performers began to enter the spotlight in the mid-1950s as the folk revival got under way. Harry Belafonte, a New York actor and folk singer with Caribbean roots, saw major success with a series of albums featuring *calypso,* a lively, syncopated song style with roots in Trinidad and Jamaica. His recordings of the "Banana Boat Song" and "Jamaica Farewell" sold in the millions. Although Elvis swept away many U.S. teens in 1956, a growing folk scene on college campuses offered an alternative to rock. To capitalize on the trend, three clean-cut business majors in California started a singing group in 1957 called the Kingston Trio. They began their career with a series of successful folk club engagements, which resulted in a record contract and their first hit, "Tom Dooley" (1958). According to historian Norm Cohen,

> They were business administration students from elite colleges who sported neat crew cuts and button-down Ivy League sport shirts. They demonstrated overnight that one need not be a political leftist or a counterculture rebel to sing folk songs.[6]

The door thus opened for new pop-style folk singers to record commercial, polished versions of traditional folk songs. One popular folk revival group called the New Lost City Ramblers introduced old-time country and string band music of the 1920s and 1930s to the folk revival, reanimating a connection of folk styles with traditional country and bluegrass music.

The new interest in folk music caused numerous colleges to mount folk festivals, which soon became the center of the folk music world. At the festivals, the "old guard" of political folk song—Pete Seeger, Alan Lomax, and others—

© AP/Wide World Photos

Bob Dylan performs at the Concert for Bangla Desh in 1971 (George Harrison to Dylan's left).

**Internet
Listening Exercise**

Listen to samples of calypso, folk revival, and protest music.

Harry Belafonte: "Jamaica Farewell"

Kingston Trio: "Tom Dooley"

Pete Seeger: "Which Side Are You On?"

would mix with roots-music legends such as the Carter Family, Bill Monroe, and Sonny Terry and Brownie McGee, as well as younger folk performers such as Arlo Guthrie, Joan Baez, and Bob Dylan. Because the renewed political activism of the civil rights movement in the early 1960s coincided with the progressive sentiments of many folk artists, folk-based protest music became a central component at marches and rallies. Traditional folk songs such as "We Shall Not Be Moved" and American labor movement songs such as "Which Side Are You On" were recast as civil rights songs and often performed with one of the original anthems of the civil rights movement, "We Shall Overcome."

Dylan and His Disciples

Few figures in the history of rock or folk music have been as influential, controversial, or enigmatic as **Bob Dylan** (Robert Zimmerman, 1941–). During the course of his forty-year career, people have alternately adored and despised Dylan, who all the while continued to deeply influence two generations of musicians. In 1961, twenty-year-old Robert Zimmerman moved from his home in Minnesota to New York with a guitar, a bag full of original folk songs, a new name (Bob Dylan—after poet Dylan Thomas), and a fictionalized life story. Like most teenagers of his era, Zimmerman had been a huge fan of 1950s rock, but while in college he became fascinated with Woody Guthrie. According to historian James Miller,

Dylan almost obsessively identified with Guthrie. He would listen to Guthrie's famous Dust Bowl Ballads endlessly, mastering his Oklahoma twang, mimicking his artless, almost deadpan vocal style, admitting to one Minneapolis friend that he was "building a character."[7]

Once in New York, Dylan visited Woody Guthrie and began to perform in Greenwich Village folk clubs. Producer John Hammond signed Dylan to his first recording contract, and the artist's second album, *The Freewheelin' Bob Dylan* (1963), set his career on fire with such tunes as "Masters of War," "A Hard Rain's A-Gonna Fall," "Don't Think Twice, It's Alright," and "Blowin' in the Wind."

In 1963 the civil rights movement and the folk revival reached their peak. In the folk world, Dylan was being anointed as a new troubadour; the annual Newport Folk Festival, a central event of the folk world, ended its 1963 session with Pete Seeger joining hands with Dylan; Peter, Paul and Mary; Joan Baez; and the African American gospel group the Freedom Singers to sing "We Shall Overcome."

Dylan's songs enabled the trio of **Peter, Paul and Mary** to become one of the most popular folk groups of the 1960s. The group had a hit with Dylan's "Blowin' in the Wind" and "Don't Think Twice, It's Alright." Other hits for the group included Pete Seeger's "If I Had a Hammer" and a children's song called "Puff, the Magic Dragon."

Joan Baez (1941–) became one of the most promising young stars of the folk world after her initial appearance at Newport in 1959. Baez had an appealing combination of talent, passion for folk music, and commitment to social causes. She also became a regular companion of Dylan, and from 1963 to 1965, she toured and performed with Dylan and recorded his songs. Baez generated many successful albums during the folk revival, and her ringing voice came to be closely associated with numerous protest and folk anthems.

By 1964 Dylan had begun a personal and musical transformation, using complex imagery and moving away from themes of social protest toward introspection. Many view the 1965 Newport Folk Festival as the beginning of the end of the folk revival, with Dylan as the one who put the first nail in the coffin. The most anticipated performer at the festival, the artist took the stage with an electric band and performed a truncated set of two amplified songs, leading the band with electric guitar in hand. As the audience booed loudly, folk godfathers Pete Seeger and Alan Lomax had to be physically restrained from pulling the plug backstage. Dylan abruptly left the stage, and only after much pleading did he return to do one final acoustic number, "It's All Over Now Baby Blue." For the next few years, folk fans who viewed his move to rock as a sellout treated Dylan as a pariah. Nonetheless, the cultural explosion created by the arrival of the Beatles continued to rekindle Dylan's early interest in rock. The artist's next two recordings, *Highway 61 Revisited* (1965) and *Blonde on Blonde* (1966), served as rock milestones. "Like a Rolling Stone" pushed the envelope of rock songwriting to a new level. Dylan also began to use a new group of backup rock musicians, soon known as the Band.

His interest in both rock and folk thus opened the door to a new genre, **folk-rock.** Once described by David Crosby as "folk [chord] changes with a rock and roll beat,"[8] folk-rock was characterized by folk-style vocal performances backed by amplified acoustic guitars, electric bass, and drums.

Internet Listening Exercise

Listen to samples of songs by Peter, Paul and Mary, Joan Baez, and Bob Dylan.

Peter, Paul and Mary: "Don't Think Twice, It's Alright" (Bob Dylan), "This Land Is Your Land" (Woody Guthrie), "Puff, the Magic Dragon," "If I Had a Hammer" (Pete Seeger)

Joan Baez: "We Shall Overcome," "Diamonds and Rust"

Bob Dylan: "Like a Rolling Stone," "Lay, Lady, Lay," "Gotta Serve Somebody"

**Internet
Listening Exercise**

Listen to samples of the band on
The Band

While Dylan was recuperating from a sobering 1966 motorcycle accident in Woodstock, New York, he spent several months jamming, making home recordings, and exploring his folk, blues, rock, and country roots. The results were later released as the *Basement Tapes*. He also began to take a mellower musical direction on his *John Wesley Harding* album (1969). During this time, the Band also released their own seminal rock albums: *Music from Big Pink* (1968) and *The Band* (1969), becoming one of rock's most respected roots-oriented acts of the late 1960s and early 1970s.

Toward the end of the 1960s, Dylan began a confusing musical odyssey. His first stop was Nashville, where he recorded the country-flavored *Nashville Skyline* (1969), which scored hits with "Lay, Lady, Lay" and "Girl from the North Country," a duet with Johnny Cash. He ended the 1970s with the announcement that he had become a born-again Christian, and a 1979 song reflecting his new faith called "Gotta Serve Somebody" garnered him his first Grammy. In 1992 Columbia Records held a concert honoring the thirtieth anniversary of Dylan's first record release, and he followed up with the release of his first folk-oriented record in thirty years, the Grammy-winning *World Gone Wrong* (1994). Although Dylan's musical choices and changing personas often perplexed the public, he stood out as one of America's greatest songwriters and innovators who pioneered multiple genres and influenced myriad artists.

Bob Dylan's Contributions

Folk-Rock Innovations

Since the early 1960s, he has served as one of the most influential artists in rock and folk. He was also the central figure in the creation of folk-rock.

Songwriting

As one of the finest songwriters in rock history, he played a central role in establishing the singer-songwriter tradition in rock. His lyrics are one of the most closely scrutinized bodies of work in pop music history.

Range of Styles

He performed in broad range of musical styles, including traditional folk, folk-rock, rock, and country. By recording in Nashville, Dylan helped to reconnect rock and country.

Other Influential Folk-Rock Innovators

Deeply influenced by Dylan's blend of folk and rock, the L.A.-based **Byrds** in turn shaped the sound of subsequent artists such as the Eagles, Tom Petty, R.E.M., and Fleetwood Mac. Formed in 1964, the Byrds were hailed by some as Los Angeles's answer to the British Invasion. Bandleader/guitarist Roger McGuinn worked with vocalist David Crosby to craft the band's close harmonies and jangly twelve-string guitar sound. At Dylan's suggestion, they recorded his "Mr. Tambourine Man" (1965), a hit that solidified the folk-rock style, and they scored again with "Turn, Turn, Turn" (1966), a melody by Pete Seeger set to lyrics from the Bible. The group subsequently went psychedelic with "Eight Miles High" (1966), a song influenced by LSD and jazz saxophonist John Coltrane. By 1968 many group members had moved on to other projects, but the remaining Byrds, joined by country devotee Gram Parsons, recorded one last influential album called *Sweetheart of the Rodeo* (1968). The work's country rock hybrid laid the groundwork for the sounds of the Eagles as well as contemporary country music of the 1990s and 2000s.

CD LISTENING EXERCISE

CD 2/18

Listen to Bob Dylan's "Blowin' in the Wind" (1963). The piece is one of the most well known folk songs of the twentieth century and a defining example of Dylan's early folk style. Listen carefully to the lyrics. Why did some folk musicians of the early sixties view Dylan as their new "messiah"?

Simon and Garfunkel (Paul Simon, 1941–) (Art Garfunkel, 1941–) became one of the most successful folk-rock acts of the mid-1960s with an appealing, close-harmony vocal style influenced by the Everly Brothers, along with intellectual, socially conscious lyrics. The duo recorded their first album, *Wednesday Morning, 3 A.M.* (1964), in an acoustic 1960s folk style but saw little success. Without the duo's knowledge, their producer, who also produced Dylan, later remixed one of the album's cuts, "The Sound of Silence," adding electric guitar, bass, and drums to produce a major folk-rock hit. Simon and Garfunkel's subsequent albums, *Sounds of Silence* and *Parsley, Sage, Rosemary, and Thyme* (1966), followed the new folk-rock style and fared much better. The artists next recorded the successful soundtrack to the 1968 movie *The Graduate*, featuring their hit song "Mrs. Robinson," followed by *Bookends* (1968) and their fourth and final album, *Bridge over Troubled Water* (1970). Although the Grammy-winning record brought them huge success, the duo parted ways.

Paul Simon continued with a successful solo career, crafting songs that exploited a wide variety of musical styles. He drew extensively from African and Latin American sources, and he stood at the forefront of the blending of world music and pop. His popular *Graceland* album (1987), recorded in South Africa, featured the vocal group Ladysmith Black Mambazo. While doing the album, Simon made a controversial move by breaking an international boycott against travel to South Africa. His explanation that his interests were musical and not political did not persuade those who viewed his work with world musicians as a form of cultural appropriation. Major hits for Simon as a solo act included "Mother and Child Reunion" (1972), "Me and Julio Down by the School Yard" (1972), "Loves Me Like a Rock" (1973), "Still Crazy after All These Years" (1975), and "Graceland" (1986).

Internet Listening Exercise

Listen to samples of the Byrds, Simon and Garfunkel, and Paul Simon.

The Byrds: "Mr. Tambourine Man," "Hickory Wind," "Eight Miles High"

Simon and Garfunkel: "The Sound of Silence," "Bridge over Troubled Water"

Paul Simon: "Mother and Child Reunion," "Graceland"

THE BRITISH INVASION

Within ten years of the birth of rock, American popular music experienced its second revolution with the arrival of the Beatles in 1964. A host of other British groups followed: the Rolling Stones, the Animals, the Who, the Kinks, the

Hollies, and others. Deeply influenced by classic American blues, R & B, and rock, these groups filtered the sounds through the British cultural experience and reintroduced them to American teens. The new bands, their sound, and the changes they wrought were called the **British Invasion.**

Origins of Early 1960s British Rock

The British Invasion stemmed from several decades of British interest in American roots music. In the early 1950s, a young Scottish musician named **Lonnie Donegan** (1931–2002) began recording American folk songs accompanied by guitar, bass, and washboard. Two of the tunes—"Rock Island Line" and "John Henry"—became hits in Britain and made the top ten in the United States in 1956. Donegan's music came to be called **skiffle**—drawn from an early African American term for rent-party music. The most consistent hitmaker in Britain from 1956 to 1959, Donegan drew indiscriminately from the entire folk heritage of the United States, particularly the repertoires of Leadbelly and Woody Guthrie. According to Charlie Gillett,

> Donegan performed their songs with a quick dance beat, in a high, nasal, fake American voice. Despite being almost completely derivative in his material and style, he was much better at what he did than were any of the British contemporary rock 'n' roll singers at representing American rock 'n' roll.[9]

As Donegan's audiences discovered the original sources of his music, they began buying albums by artists such as Big Bill Broonzy, Leadbelly, and Woody Guthrie. One of Donegan's most important accomplishments was that he inspired countless British teens to take up the guitar to play skiffle. A Liverpool skiffle band called the Quarrymen became the Beatles; they cited Donegan's "Rock Island Line" (1956) as one of the most influential records of their youth. Many other British rock musicians, such as Van Morrison and Queen's guitarist Brian May, also saw Donegan as a primary influence. According to May, "He really was at the very cornerstone of English blues and rock. He really was the first guy to bring the blues to England. I think he's probably the principal reason I picked up a guitar."[10]

British interest in the blues was also fueled by a London musician named **Alexis Korner** (1928–1984), who admired blues artists such as Howlin' Wolf and Muddy Waters. Korner formed a blues band that influenced numerous British 1960s rockers, so that by 1963, rhythm and blues had become the dominant style in London clubs. The sounds of mid-1950s U.S. rockers such as Bill Haley, Elvis Presley, Little Richard, and Buddy Holly were also well known to teen fans in the United Kingdom, many of whom styled themselves as "teddy boys" and sported black leather jackets and Elvis hairstyles.

Two distinct styles of British rock ultimately emerged: "beat" music from the Liverpool and Manchester areas, and rhythm and blues from London. *Beat music,* shortened from "Merseybeat" and named for the river that ran through Liverpool, was a pop music made by local bands in the Liverpool area, many of whom were former skiffle groups. The Beatles became by far the most successful of the beat groups, but others included Cliff Richard, the Searchers, Gerry

Internet Listening Exercise

Listen to samples of British skiffle and early blues.

Lonnie Donegan: "Rock Island Line," "John Henry"

Alexis Korner: "I Got My Mojo Workin'," "Spoonful"

and the Pacemakers, Herman's Hermits, Freddie and the Dreamers, and the Hollies. The Merseybeat groups exuded a cheerful, accessible pop sound and a well-scrubbed, nonthreatening "mod" look.

The rhythm and blues acts—or blues revivalists—came mostly from London and included John Mayall's Bluesbreakers, the Rolling Stones, the Yardbirds, the Animals, the Kinks, and the Who. These bands, according to Charlie Gillett, "exuded a more defiant spirit, expressed in snarling vocals, raucous guitars, and baleful glares at photographers" than did the beat groups.[11] The Beatles—particularly the sweeter, pop-oriented work of Paul McCartney—embodied the skiffle-Merseybeat strand, while the Rolling Stones exemplified the rhythm and blues strand of early 1960s British rock.

The Beatles

The Beatles (John Lennon, 1940–1980; Paul McCartney, 1942– ; George Harrison, 1943–2001; Ringo Starr, 1940–) were the most important rock group in history. From their arrival on U.S. shores in early 1964 until their breakup in 1970, the group took rock in important new directions. According to critic Greil Marcus,

> The Beatles combined the harmonic range and implicit equality of the Fifties vocal group (the Dell-Vikings, say) with the flash of a rockabilly band (the Crickets or Gene Vincent's Blue Caps) with the aggressive and unique personalities of the classic rock stars (Elvis, Little Richard) with the homey this-could-be-you manner of later rock stars (Everly Brothers, Buddy Holly, Eddie Cochrane) with the

Internet Listening Exercise

Listen to samples of Merseybeat artists.

Cliff Richard and the Shadows: "Move It"

The Searchers: "Sugar and Spice"

Gerry and the Pacemakers: "Ferry 'cross the Mersey"

Freddie and the Dreamers: "I'm Telling You Now"

Now, listen to samples of British R & B artists.

John Mayall's Bluesbreakers: "Parchman Farm"

The Yardbirds: "For Your Love"

The Animals: "House of the Rising Sun"

The Kinks: "You Really Got Me"

The Who: "My Generation"

Multicultural Note

Indiscriminate Appropriation Equals a Rock Revolution

Beginning in the 1920s, British musicians appropriated numerous African American styles such as New Orleans jazz, swing, and boogie woogie. By the 1940s and 1950s, a movement developed in the United Kingdom that paralleled the U.S. folk revival and sought out "authentic" American roots artists. The late 1950s in Britain witnessed the appearance of *skiffle*, a crazy quilt of anything vaguely folksy, bluesy, or rootsy, as well as a blues revival. Finally, an interest in classic 1950s rock put the frosting on the cake that led to the British Invasion bands.

The Beatles led the mid-1960s assault of British rock acts on U.S. markets, presenting a "new" sound. In fact, as all of the British Invasion artists pointed out, they were recycling classic American styles and genres, albeit filtered through a British adolescent male lens. Why did the British Invasion acts sound "new" to the ears of U.S. teens, if the artists were primarily appropriating and recycling U.S. musical styles? What changes can happen during the process of cultural appropriation and reinterpretation?

The Beatles performing on the *Ed Sullivan Show* in 1964.

**Internet
Listening Exercise**

Listen to samples of tunes by the Beatles and the R & B artists they covered. If you have trouble finding Beatles tunes on the Internet, try purchasing albums or borrowing them from friends or the library.

Chuck Berry/The Beatles: "Roll over Beethoven"

The Isley Brothers/The Beatles: "Twist and Shout"

The Marvelettes/The Beatles: "Please Mister Postman"

endlessly inventive songwriting touch of the Brill Building, and delivered it all with the grace of the Miracles, the physicality of "Louie Louie," and the absurd enthusiasm of Gary "U.S." Bonds.[12]

The story of the Beatles began in 1957 when John Lennon, who was playing with a rock-skiffle group, met Paul McCartney in Liverpool. They began to write songs together and appeared as a duo until in 1958 they added fifteen-year-old guitarist George Harrison. They named themselves "the Beatles," with a spelling that emphasized the word *beat*—as in Merseybeat. From 1960 to 1961, the band played in the seaport dives of Hamburg and Liverpool, honing their style. By 1962 they had settled on Ringo Starr on drums and hooked up with manager Brian Epstein, who wangled them a record contract. Once in the studio, the group began a long-term association with producer George Martin, a classically trained oboist and composer later known as the "fifth Beatle," who was won over by their originality. Early Beatles albums featured combinations of originals with covers of U.S. R & B hits such as "Twist and Shout" (Isley Brothers), "Roll over Beethoven" (Chuck Berry), "Baby It's You" (the Shirelles), "You've Really Got a Hold on Me" and "Money" (Smokey Robinson and the Miracles), "Long Tall Sally" (Little Richard), and "Please Mister Postman" (the Marvelettes).

The Beatles' 1963 release "Please Please Me" hit number one in Britain, followed by "Twist and Shout," the band's showstopper that featured Lennon literally screaming at the top of his lungs. This began the growth of a pop explosion known as "Beatlemania." Late in 1963, the band released "She Loves You," the best-selling British record of the 1960s, and they captivated a growing audience by shaking their mop-tops and crying "Wooo" in a self-conscious imitation of Little Richard. Teen hysteria mushroomed as teens mobbed the group's hotel and followed their limousine in packs. At first the Beatles did not catch on in the United States, but within a year Beatlemania hit the country full force. Following the release of their first U.S. smash, "I Want to Hold Your Hand," the Beatles came to the United States in 1964, not long after Kennedy's assassination. Capitol Records mounted a crash publicity campaign, and the group's historic performance on the *Ed Sullivan Show* became a national cultural event seen by 73 million people, then the largest audience in the history of television.

A seemingly unending series of releases poured out of the Beatles from 1964 to 1966, as did two movies—*A Hard Day's Night* and *Help!* During one week in 1964, they had the top five records in the country, and in 1965 they achieved six number-one LPs. The band improved rapidly as musicians Lennon and McCartney grew as songwriters. In 1966 they released the breakthrough *Rubber*

Soul album. Inspired by Bob Dylan and the folk-rock sound blossoming in the States, the musical texture of the Beatles' sound in *Rubber Soul* differed greatly from their previous work. Tunes ranged from acoustic pieces such as "Yesterday" and "You've Got to Hide Your Love Away," to the sitar of "Norwegian Wood," to the fuzztone guitar of "Think for Yourself," to the French cabaret style of "Michelle," to the yearning introspection of "In My Life." According to Paul McCartney, when he saw Bob Dylan after the release of *Rubber Soul,* Dylan said, "Oh, I get it. You don't want to be cute anymore."[13]

The Beatles went on their last tour and ended public performances in 1966, arguing that their most recent music had become almost impossible to reproduce on stage and that they were seldom heard over screaming crowds. Spurred by the new psychedelic sounds of their pop competitors Bob Dylan *(Blonde on Blonde),* the Beach Boys *(Pet Sounds),* and the Byrds *(Fifth Dimension),* the Beatles went back into the studio and produced *Sgt. Pepper's Lonely Hearts Club Band* (1967). It featured experimental recording techniques, diverse song styles, and hallucinogenic images. The album's release was a monumental event, and its sound blanketed the world. As critic Langdon Winner recalled,

> I happened to be driving across the country on Interstate 80. In each city where I stopped for gas or food—Laramie, Ogallala, Moline, South Bend—the melodies wafted in from some far-off transistor radio or portable hi-fi. It was the most amazing thing I've ever heard. For a brief while the irreparably fragmented consciousness of the West was unified, at least in the minds of the young.[14]

Shortly after the release of *Sgt. Pepper,* the Beatles' manager Brian Epstein died, and the group began a slow slide to their 1970 breakup. They briefly dallied with an Indian guru and put out a poorly received film called *Magical Mystery Tour.* They also took control of their own recordings and business affairs by forming AppleCorps, and in 1968 they released a two-disc *White Album* (actually entitled *The Beatles),* which featured solo vocals and divergent musical visions from the band's two lead songwriters—harder rock tunes for Lennon and softer melodies for McCartney. The Beatles released the well-regarded *Abbey Road* in 1969, but by 1970 the breakup was a fait accompli. Lennon explained his rationale for leaving the band: "My life with the Beatles had become a trap. A tape loop. . . . I started the band. I disbanded it. It's as simple as that."[15]

Contributions of the Beatles

- They exerted a sweeping influence on U.S. and global youth culture, inspiring many teens to begin playing music for themselves.
- They revitalized rock with a fresh, clean sound in contrast to the overproduced U.S. rock of the early 1960s.
- They established rock music as a valid art form.
- They blended multiple genres of U.S. and British popular music: R & B, girl groups, rockabilly, folk, and skiffle.

- *Sgt. Pepper* set a new standard for the concept album and album cover design.

- Together with Bob Dylan and others, they solidified the singer-songwriter tradition in rock.

- By writing songs of a personal, philosophical, and political nature, they brought a lyrical sophistication to rock.

- Their songs had engaging melodies and harmonies that went beyond three-chord, blues-based harmonic progressions.

- They introduced a wide array of song styles (love songs, ballads, novelty songs, folk, country, R & B) into the rock format.

- They codified the self-contained rock band format (lead guitar, rhythm guitar, electric bass, drums) earlier pioneered by Buddy Holly's Crickets.

- Their use of sophisticated arrangements and studio production techniques in rock broke new ground.

- They introduced novel instruments into rock, including the Indian sitar.

Adapted in part from Brock Helander, *The Rockin' 60s* (New York: Schirmer, 1999).

The Rolling Stones

The **Rolling Stones** initially served as symbols of the English R & B movement, which challenged the Merseybeat sound of the Beatles in 1963. Promoters marketed the band as a kind of dark and dangerous anti-Beatles with the question "Would you want your daughter to go out with a Rolling Stone?"[16] Initially one of the finest British interpreters of American R & B, the Stones developed into one of the most popular rock and roll bands of the 1960s and 1970s and sustained their popularity into the 2000s as the world's longest-lived rock band. Although contemporary teens may wonder at their continuing appeal, the Stones in their prime conveyed a dark, seductive edge.

In the 1960s, playing their version of Chicago electric blues and Mick Jagger's flamboyant stage presence, the group cultivated an arrogant and dangerous image that made them one of the most identifiable British Invasion groups and the only serious competition to the Beatles. Journalist Stanley Booth described his first visual impression of the Stones' lead singer, Mick Jagger (1943–), and guitarist Keith Richards (1943–) in 1969:

> The Stones Gang: Wanted Dead or Alive, though only Mick Jagger, standing like a model, his knife-blade ass thrust to one side, was currently awaiting trial. Beside him was Keith Richards, who was even thinner and looked not like a model but an insane advertisement for a dangerous carefree Death—black ragged hair, dead-green skin, a cougar tooth hanging from his right earlobe, his lips snarled back from the marijuana cigarette between his rotting fangs, his gums blue.[17]

Jagger and Richards developed into a powerful songwriting team that produced such classic hits as "(I Can't Get No) Satisfaction" (1965), "Ruby Tuesday"

© Hulton-Deutsch Collection/CORBIS

The Rolling Stones—the "bad boys" of the British Invasion (left to right): Brian Jones, Mick Jagger, Keith Richards, Charlie Watts, and Bill Wyman.

(1967), "Jumpin' Jack Flash" (1968), "Honky Tonk Woman" (1969), and "Brown Sugar" (1971). Guitarists Brian Jones (1942–1969) and Keith Richards provided lean, interlocking rhythm guitars, while the strong yet subtly swinging rhythm section of bassist Bill Wyman (1936–) and drummer Charlie Watts (1941–) anchored the band. Though they experimented briefly with psychedelia in the mid-1960s and disco in the 1970s, the Stones focused primarily on realizing their vision as a blues-soaked hard-rock quintet. They also often toured with their blues idols, including Howlin' Wolf and Chuck Berry.

Despite their self-conscious bad-boy posturing, the Stones demonstrated a dedication to their art—initially the blues, later the hard-rock mainstream. They continued to record and perform into the 2000s: Few other bands have enjoyed such a broad fan base or staying power. It is difficult to hear the groups that followed them without detecting some influence, whether musical or aesthetic. According to critic Robert Christgau,

> They lived the life of art, their art got better all the time, and as it got better, remarkably enough, it reached more people. But although their art survives, its heroic quality does not; the Stones betray all the flaws of the counterculture they half-wittingly and -willingly symbolized. Their sex was too often sexist, their expanded consciousness too often a sordid escape; their rebellion was rooted in impulse to the exclusion of all habits of sacrifice, and their relationship to fame had little to do with the responsibilities of leadership, or allegiance.[18]

 **Internet Listening Exercise**

Listen to samples of songs by the Rolling Stones. Then listen to samples of classic blues and rock artists, and compare them with the sound of the Stones.

Rolling Stones: "(I Can't Get No) Satisfaction," "Ruby Tuesday," "Honky Tonk Woman"

Howlin' Wolf: "Back Door Man," "Wang Dang Doodle"

Bo Diddley: "Bo Diddley"

Muddy Waters: "Got My Mojo Working," "I'm Your Hoochie Coochie Man" (on CD)

Other British Artists from the 1960s

After the successes of the Beatles and the Rolling Stones in the 1960s, artists from the British Commonwealth (England, Ireland, and Australia) commonly made the U.S. pop charts. While many of these artists had a strong affinity for the blues, others displayed more eclectic influences.

Taking Robert Johnson as his mythic role model, **Eric Clapton** (1945–) was one of the first "guitar heroes" and a fervent British blues revivalist. Clapton had his first major gig with the Yardbirds in the early 1960s, but when they turned psychedelic, he left them to join John Mayall's Bluesbreakers. The resulting *Bluesbreakers with Eric Clapton* (1966) was one of the best British blues albums of the era. The following year he teamed up with bassist Jack Bruce and drummer Ginger Baker to form Cream, one of the first rock **power trios**—a group consisting of electric guitar, electric bass, and drums. This instrumentation was later common in heavy metal and hard rock. With hits such as "Sunshine of Your Love" (1968), "White Room" (1968), and Robert Johnson's "Crossroads" (1969), the band produced a deafening sound that laid the foundation for much subsequent blues-rock and hard rock of the 1960s and 1970s. After Cream broke up, Clapton scored two 1970 hits of his own with "After Midnight" and "Layla," as well as two subsequent hits later in the decade: "I Shot the Sheriff" (1974) and "Lay Down Sally" (1978). Clapton appeared in the early 1990s on MTV's *Unplugged,* a performance that produced a Grammy-winning album, and he remained active through the 2000s.

Another legendary British blues-rock band, the **Who,** featured ringing power chords and explosive beats that made them one of the most influential groups of their era. As the godfathers of punk, they established a violent, anarchic rock performance style with smashed guitars and blown-up drum sets that succeeding generations would embellish. The sight of guitarist Pete Townshend leaping into the air with his guitar and spinning his right hand in exaggerated windmills became a classic rock image. Major hits included "My Generation" (1967), "I Can See for Miles" (1967), "I'm Free" (1969), "Pinball Wizard" (1969), and "Summertime Blues" (1970). One of the group's signal achievements was its production of the first rock opera, *Tommy* (1970), written by Townshend. The opera was performed several times with orchestral backing, produced as a film in 1975, and mounted on Broadway in 1993.

Irish soul man **Van Morrison** (1945–) created a distinctive fusion of R & B, jazz, blues, and Celtic folk music, winning a cult audience that followed him throughout his career. Morrison started with skiffle and scored hits in 1965 with "Gloria" and "Here Comes the Night." He moved to Los Angeles in 1967 to go solo as a singer-songwriter, crafting a floating, folk/jazz/soul sound heard in hits such as "Brown-Eyed Girl" (1967), "Domino" (1971), and "Moondance" (1977).

Joe Cocker (1944–) parlayed a Ray Charles–flavored vocal style and an eccentric stage presence into a string of hits such as "With a Little Help from My Friends" (1968), "She Came in through the Bathroom Window" (1970), "The Letter" (1970), and "You Are So Beautiful" (1975). Cocker remained in demand in the 1980s and 1990s as a vocalist for film scores, producing hits such as the ballad "Up Where You Belong" (1982) from the film *An Officer and a Gentleman.*

The **Hollies** were a popular Merseybeat-flavored British invasion band with a Beatle-esque sound. Named after Buddy Holly, the group had more hit singles in Britain than any band but the Beatles. Although less popular in the United States, they did score with "Bus Stop" (1966), "Stop, Stop, Stop" (1967), and "Carrie-Anne" (1967). Graham Nash, a founding member of the band, left in 1968 and subsequently cofounded the folk-rock supergroup Crosby, Stills, and Nash.

Many other British rock/pop artists performed in an eclectic range of styles in the wake of the Beatles and the Stones: Donovan, a psychedelic folkie, who had a string of hits such as "Mellow Yellow" (1966) and "Sunshine Superman" (1966); Tom Jones, a Welsh soul man with Vegas flair, whose hits included "It's Not Unusual" (1965) and "What's New Pussycat" (1965); Dusty Springfield, Britain's best white soul vocalist, who had hits with "You Don't Have to Say You Love Me" (1966) and "Son-of-a-Preacher Man" (1969); Petula Clark, whose hit "Downtown" (1965) made her Britain's most commercially successful female singer; the Moody Blues, an orchestral-rock group who produced LPs *(Days of Future Passed)* and occasional hits such as "Nights in White Satin (1972); and Procol Harum, a group built around blues-rock and classical themes that produced hits such as "A Whiter Shade of Pale" (1967) and "Conquistador" (1972).

The British Invasion established a permanent space in the U.S. pop market for British Commonwealth artists, and subsequent acts such as the Bee Gees, Elton John, David Bowie, Pink Floyd, the Sex Pistols, the Clash, the Police, and U2 continued to find fertile ground in the New World. Rock had become the lingua franca of the English-speaking world, and many artists became increasingly transnational.

THE BIRTH OF A COUNTERCULTURE

The United States went through a difficult period of social turmoil in the mid-1960s. The Vietnam War and the struggle for civil rights influenced many young people to dream of a "revolution" that would move American culture in the direction of peace, love, and harmony, and this message became intertwined with the music of the era. To add to the mix, the Beatles imported new styles of long hair and outrageous clothing from London, an uninhibited attitude toward sexuality began to develop, and in some parts of the United States a back-to-the-earth movement took shape as young people opted out of "the system." This amorphous composite of alternative ideologies and lifestyles was known at the time as the *counterculture.*

Psychedelic Music

A particularly flamboyant strand of the 1960s **counterculture** developed in San Francisco, flavored by a new style of psychedelic rock music and the hippie countercultural movement. **Psychedelic music,** or **acid rock,** drew its inspiration from the experience of taking mind-altering drugs, with characteristic

Internet Listening Exercise

Listen to samples of work by British rock artists who emerged in the 1960s.

Eric Clapton: "Sunshine of Your Love," "Layla"

The Who: "My Generation," "Pinball Wizard"

Van Morrison: "Gloria," "Moondance"

Joe Cocker: "With a Little Help from My Friends"

The Hollies: "Bus Stop"

Internet Listening Exercise

Listen to samples of songs by British pop artists of the 1960s.

Donovan: "Mellow Yellow"

Tom Jones: "It's Not Unusual"

Dusty Springfield: "You Don't Have to Say You Love Me"

Petula Clark: "Downtown"

Procol Harum: "A Whiter Shade of Pale"

The Moody Blues: "Nights in White Satin"

features including modal melodies, lengthy instrumental solos, esoteric lyrics, and special electronic effects. Though the same social unrest experienced by the rest of the country fueled the counterculture, it took on flavor when a new mind-altering hallucinogenic drug called **LSD** (lysergic acid diethylamide), or acid, was added to the mix. The drug was said to create heightened awareness, make time stand still, bring the world alive with new colors and images, and imbue the simplest things with profound meaning; the term *psychedelic* came into use to describe the experience. However, with LSD the desired euphoria could turn into a lengthy nightmare, and impure doses could lead to psychosis. Nonetheless, LSD and marijuana became the movement's drugs of choice, and one of the results of the massive chemical experiment was the development of psychedelic music.

In 1965 author Ken Kesey teamed up in San Francisco with a band of friends known as the "Merry Pranksters" to stage LSD happenings called "acid tests." The music for these events was supplied by a ragged, R & B-inspired band called the Grateful Dead. For the price of a dollar, one could receive a dose of acid and admission to a house decorated and wired for a psychedelic multimedia experience. The Grateful Dead provided the music, and the events lasted the length of a typical acid trip—eight to twelve hours. According to Ken Kesey,

> Americans invented the blues: This is what we have got to be proud of. It ain't the nuclear stuff, it's not putting the man on the moon, it's the blues. And when the blues ran up against psychedelics, rock and roll really took off.[19]

With music as its central feature, the psychedelic scene expanded in San Francisco over the next few years. Hundreds of new rock bands formed, including the Grateful Dead, Jefferson Airplane, Janis Joplin with Big Brother and the Holding Company, Santana, Country Joe and the Fish, and Sly and the Family Stone. Huge dance parties took place at venues such as the Avalon Ballroom and the Fillmore Auditorium, and audiences flocked to the experimental, psychedelic sounds. The music was illuminated by light shows that transformed performance spaces, removing the barrier between performer and audience. Accompanying the music was a crazy Day-Glo world of posters, art, clothing, and underground comics.

The Psychedelic–Acid Rock Sound

- Music rooted in blues folk, rock, and country, with heavy amplification
- Guitar as solo instrument of choice, with effects including the following:

   Distortion: The electronic alteration of a musical tone to produce an intentionally unclear or fuzzy timbre

   Feedback: A squealing electronic effect achieved by placing a microphone or guitar pickup directly in front of the speaker through which it is being amplified

   Fuzz-tone: An electric guitar effect that sounds exactly as the name implies (see *distortion*)

Sustain: The extension of the duration of a musical tone through electronic amplification

Wah-wah: An effects pedal that modulates the timbre of an amplified tone to create a "wah"-like sound

- Loosely structured vocal harmonies
- Light shows accompanying live performances
- Loose song structures and lengthy, rock-style improvisation

The psychedelic scene burst into the national spotlight in 1967 when a massive "Human Be-In" took place in San Francisco's Golden Gate Park. The hippie gathering featured music, poetry, and food. The national media blanketed the event, broadcasting images of willowy flower children and hirsute, blissed-out revolutionaries. By the time of the "Summer of Love" that year, young people from throughout the country, drawn by Scott Mackenzie's song, "San Francisco (Be Sure to Wear Flowers in Your Hair)," had flocked to San Francisco's Haight/Ashbury neighborhood to tune in, turn on, and drop out. Within a year, however, the myth had devolved into a dead end, and the Haight was overrun with homeless, unemployed, often drug-addicted youth living on the streets.

In late 1967, L.A. rock producer Lou Adler and his partner John Phillips of the Mamas and the Papas vocal group staged their own commercialized version of a San Francisco hippie gathering in the picturesque coastal town of Monterey. The three-day Monterey Pop Festival brought together an eclectic group of artists: Indian sitar virtuoso Ravi Shankar, soul singer Otis Redding, South African trumpeter Hugh Masakela, the Byrds, the Who, Simon and Garfunkel,

Multicultural Note

Drugs and Music

Throughout history, drugs and music have had a symbiotic relationship: for example, both have played essential roles in the religious rituals of many cultures. In U.S. pop music before the 1960s, many legendary musicians were associated with drug use, though few credited drugs as the source of their creativity. Alto saxophonist Charlie Parker, for example, was addicted to heroin, but no one suggested that it contributed to his genius.

On the other hand, many artists consciously identified LSD as a source of creativity during the psychedelic era. Psychedelic rock innovators spoke of the sense of timelessness that the drug created. Many of the textures still used in contemporary rock —feedback, fuzztone, and wah-wah—stem from the LSD-inspired sounds of the late 1960s. Even at the height of psychedelia, however, there was a thin line between creative moments and meandering.

Buffalo Springfield, the Mamas and the Papas, Jefferson Airplane, Janis Joplin, the Grateful Dead, the Paul Butterfield Blues Band, and Jimi Hendrix. This watershed event attracted 50,000 participants, as well as top record industry executives anxious to cash in on the new music. According to critic Joel Selvin,

> The performers came to make their statements, not their careers. Nevertheless, many powerful people in the music industry experienced the new music for the first time in Monterey. . . . The festival managed to simultaneously sum up and accelerate the dramatic changes sweeping through pop music. . . . Never again would rock music be the charmingly uncorrupted force it was at Monterey.[20]

Bands of the San Francisco Psychedelic Era

The **Grateful Dead** served as the standard-bearers for psychedelic music for more than thirty years. According to guitarist Jerry Garcia,

> For some people, taking LSD and going to a Dead show functions like a rite of passage. Each person deals with the experience individually. . . . But when people come together, this singular experience is ritualized. I think the Grateful Dead serves a desire for a meaningful ritual, but it's a ritual without dogma.[21]

The Dead were a mix of trained and amateur musicians. Although their earliest acid test performances were ragged, they soon developed an improvisational style that fit the psychedelic mindset. The band lived communally in San Francisco's Haight/Ashbury, performing free outdoor concerts regularly, and their music remained much the same for three decades—a mix of country, folk, and rock with extended, rock-based improvisations. The Dead built their reputation on live performance, and by the early 1970s their mammoth, custom P.A. systems set the standard for high-quality rock amplification. Though they found only limited commercial success with recordings, their legions of fans, known as Deadheads, traveled thousands of miles to hear the band perform for entire tours of twenty or thirty shows. As critic Blair Jackson once observed,

> Deadheads flock to Grateful Dead concerts like cripples to Lourdes. . . . A Dead concert is a symbiosis on a grand scale. . . .Together, the Dead and their fans form a peculiarly amorphous organism that is completely unlike anything that lives or breathes in this world.[22]

Internet Listening Exercise

Listen to samples of songs by the Grateful Dead.

Grateful Dead: "Uncle John's Band," "Truckin'," "Casey Jones"

But there was another view of the Dead, as historian Jack McDonough reports: "In the face of all this homage let it be acknowledged that there are plenty of people who think the Dead the most consummately boring band in the world."[23] The band's seminal albums were *Working Man's Dead* (1971), *American Beauty* (1971), and *Live Dead* (1970), featuring songs such as "Uncle John's Band," "Casey Jones," "Truckin'," "Ripple," and "Dark Star." The group appeared at the Monterey Pop Festival in 1967, Woodstock in 1969, and the Watkins Glens Festival in 1973 before a crowd of over 600,000.

No one represented the passion, fantasy, and tragedy of the psychedelic era better than **Janis Joplin** (1943–1970), the first female superstar of rock. Joplin's meteoric rise and tragic, drug-induced death typified the ecstasy and overindulgence of rock stardom. She was a white blues singer with a harsh, emotionally intense vocal style so raw that it actually damaged her vocal cords. The Texas-born Joplin left home at age seventeen and moved to San Francisco, where she hooked up with Big Brother and the Holding Company, quickly becoming the popular band's main attraction. At the Monterey Pop Festival, Joplin put on the show of her life with an incendiary performance that thrust her and the band into the national spotlight. A subsequent hit album, *Cheap Thrills* (1968), presented searing Joplin renditions of "Summertime," "Piece of My Heart," and "Ball and Chain." Within a year, Joplin left Big Brother, toured extensively, and appeared on national television. As her popularity grew, so did her drug use. Her work on the album *Pearl* (1971) appeared promising, but she died of a drug overdose shortly before its completion. The posthumously released album produced a number-one hit with "Me and Bobby McGee."

Formed in 1965, **Jefferson Airplane** became the first San Francisco band to achieve national visibility, as well as popularity on the psychedelic dance scene with songs of drugs, politics, and love. The band's sound reflected an eclectic mix of rock, folk, and blues performed in an improvisational style that generally struck a fine balance between song structure and psychedelic flexibility. Originally formed by vocalist Marty Balin (1942–) and guitarist Paul Kanter

© AP/Wide World Photos

Jefferson Airplane from the cover of the album *Surrealistic Pillow*.

**Internet
Listening Exercise**

Listen to samples of songs by Janis Joplin, Jefferson Airplane, and Jefferson Starship.

Janis Joplin: "Piece of My Heart," "Ball and Chain," "Me and Bobby McGee"

Jefferson Airplane (Starship): "White Rabbit," "We Can Be Together," "We Built This City"

**Internet
Listening Exercise**

Listen to samples of songs by Creedence Clearwater Revival.

Creedence Clearwater Revival: "Proud Mary," "Born on the Bayou," "Bad Moon Rising"

(1942–), the Airplane's biggest impact on the rock world came with their second album, *Surrealistic Pillow* (1967), which featured singer Grace Slick (1939–) on "White Rabbit" and "Somebody to Love." Slick was a powerful vocalist whose voice blended well with Balin's, and their dual vocal style defined the band's sound. Over the next few years, the Airplane's material became increasingly controversial, culminating with *Volunteers* (1969), which reflected the increasingly radical sentiments of the counterculture in the chorus of the song, "We Can Be Together": "Up against the wall, motherf——." By 1970 the band had begun a series of seemingly unending personnel shifts and name changes (Jefferson Starship), though a brief reunion produced "Miracles" (1975), one of their biggest hits. Over the years the band moved away from politically infused psychedelia to a middle-of-the-road pop sound, exemplified by their mid-1980s hit, "We Built This City."

San Francisco Bay Area–based **Creedence Clearwater Revival** dominated top-forty radio for two years during the late 1960s while remaining popular with the counterculture—no easy feat. At its peak, the group produced rock standards such as "Proud Mary" (1969), "Bad Moon Rising" (1969), and "Born on the Bayou" (1969), all written and sung by bandleader John Fogerty (1945–). Creedence was not a psychedelic band; instead, they featured a distinctive rockabilly hard-rock sound flavored by vocalist Fogerty's southern drawl. After Fogerty left the group in 1972, he released several solo recordings.

Hendrix and Sly: Black Psychedelia

Jimi Hendrix (1942–1970), possibly the greatest guitarist in the history of rock, became one of the genre's dominant icons. Hendrix revolutionized the electric guitar in rock, and many components of his style are virtually required repertoire for rock guitarists. His dynamic stage performances also served as prototypes for the pop extravaganzas standard in the music industry today. Although the artist's entire output of studio recordings included only three releases over a two-year period—*Are You Experienced?* (1967), *Axis: Bold as Love* (1968), and *Electric Ladyland* (1968)—much of his work still sounds fresh. According to critic David Fricke,

> The combination of that creative drive with his stunning technique, sonic imagination, and ingenious, painterly exploitation of effects like wah-wah, feedback, distortion and sheer earthquaking volume transformed rock and roll—and its primary instrument, the electric guitar—forever. Hendrix left an indelible, fiercely individual mark on popular music, accelerating rock's already dynamic rate of change in the late Sixties with his revolutionary synthesis of guitar violence, improvisational nerve, spacey melodic reveries and a confessional intensity born of the blues.[24]

Hendrix was steeped in the guitar traditions of two generations of African American performers. He grew up in Seattle listening to Robert Johnson, Muddy Waters, T-Bone Walker, Charlie Christian, B. B. King, and Chuck Berry. Unlike most of his less-experienced psychedelic contemporaries, the artist honed his guitar skills through extensive work on the R & B circuit as a sideman with artists such as Jackie Wilson, Sam Cooke, Wilson Pickett, Little Richard, and the Isley Brothers.

Hendrix was performing in New York in 1966 when a member of the Animals heard him and convinced him to move to London, where the artist assembled his prototype power trio. He broke the mold for British fans who expected an African American musician to fit stereotypes of electric Chicago blues or classic soul; instead, they found themselves confronted with a completely original psychedelic style. The Beatles, the Rolling Stones, the Who, and Eric Clapton were some of the artist's most avid fans; Clapton wrote his classic "Sunshine of Your Love" as a tribute to Hendrix after hearing a live show.

Hendrix burst onto the U.S. rock scene in 1967 with an incendiary performance at the Monterey Pop Festival, where once again he confounded white expectations by appearing dressed in modish ruffles and splashy colors and by playing psychedelic music at an outrageous volume with a British band. Hendrix let out all the stops: He played the guitar behind his back and with his teeth like T-Bone Walker; he thrust the instrument provocatively between his legs like Chuck Berry, while playing intricate lead and rhythm guitar simultaneously like Robert Johnson;

Jimi Hendrix at the Woodstock Rock Festival.

and he drenched the audience in the psychedelic effects of the wah-wah pedal, controlled distortion, and screeching feedback. As the set reached its climax, Hendrix burned his legacy into the annals of live performance when he knelt before his guitar, doused it with lighter fluid, lit it on fire, and fanned the flames like a possessed snake charmer. As the guitar burned, Hendrix picked it up by the neck and smashed it to pieces while feedback still issued from the instrument.

Within days Hendrix was a sensation. His first album, *Are You Experienced?* was released in the United States, and songs such as "Purple Haze" and "Foxey Lady" received wide airplay. He rapidly became one of rock's most popular acts, touring and recording at a blistering pace. In summer 1969, Hendrix appeared at Woodstock and delivered a riveting psychedelic performance of "The Star Spangled Banner" that became etched in the memory of a generation. He next assembled an African American rock/funk trio, the Band of Gypsys; recorded a live album at the Fillmore East on New Year's Eve, 1969; and branched out to jam with jazz musicians such as Miles Davis. However, just when Hendrix's music seemed to be entering a new creative phase, he died of an apparent drug overdose in 1970. Hendrix had created a repertoire that ranged from sensitive ballads to blistering rock—all infused with the blues and a transcendent psy-

Internet Listening Exercise

Listen to samples of Jimi Hendrix's music.

Jimi Hendrix: "Foxey Lady," "Purple Haze," "Manic Depression," "Red House," "The Star Spangled Banner"

© Allan Koss/The Image Works

chedelic quality. According to critic Greil Marcus: "Every hard-rock and heavy-metal band from Anthrax to ZZ Top owes great debts of inspiration and often direct influence to the Jimi Hendrix experience."[25]

Sly Stone (Sylvester Stewart, 1944–) developed a soul-rock synthesis in the late 1960s that, together with James Brown's innovations, formed the basis of funk. By harnessing many of the disparate musical and social trends of the late 1960s, Stone created a hybrid of soul, rock, R & B, and psychedelia that broke down musical and cultural boundaries. Rock critic Greil Marcus describes the appeal of Sly and his band, the Family Stone:

> There was an enormous freedom to the band's sound. It was complex, because freedom is complex; wild and anarchic. . . . And it was all celebration, all affirmation, a music of endless humor and delight, like a fantasy of freedom.[26]

Stone dominated pop music from 1968 to 1970, appeared at Woodstock, and offered a new direction for soul and rock after the death of Otis Redding and the growing disillusions of the white counterculture when it became evident that there was a downside to flower power. The San Francisco–based band was rock's first fully integrated group—black and white, male and female—and its sound stemmed from the black music of Stax and James Brown as well as the open spirit of acid rock. Before Stone, few black groups had delved into political and social commentary; after him, it became a tradition. The band's sound combined Stone's gospel-tinged vocals and organ, jazzy horns, and soul-rock guitar, as well as bassist Larry Graham's innovative slap-style bass lines, which hypnotized dancers and inspired an entire generation of bass players. According to historian Rickey Vincent,

> For mainstream America the ambassador of funk was . . . Sly Stone. His outlandish appearance, infectious smile, throaty soul-singing voice, and hyperactive rock music turned America on at a time when the nation was searching for identity.[27]

Originally a DJ and record producer, Stone recruited a six-piece band in 1966 that could play the latest rock with the energy of soul and gospel singers. The band signed with Columbia in 1966, making Stone the first black rock star packaged by a major corporate label. The 1968 album *Dance to the Music* was a major success, with a crossover hit single of the same name. The next album, *Stand!* (1969), produced hits such as "I Wanna Take You Higher" and "Stand!" More hits followed: "Hot Fun in the Summertime" (1969) and "Thank You (Falettin Me Be Mice Elf Agin)" (1970), seen by some as the first funk masterpiece. By late 1970, Stone was performing erratically and went into seclusion, but he returned in 1971 with a challenging, politicized album, *There's a Riot Going On,* which confounded fans who were expecting more party music. The album's one hit, "Family Affair," pioneered the use of the electronic drum machine in pop music.

Sly Stone had a wide impact on black music. His innovative funk led to new arrangements for Motown's Temptations and the Jackson 5. Jazz pianist Herbie Hancock began to play Sly-influenced funk on his *Headhunters* album. Finally, other funk bands appeared in the early 1970s following Stone's dance funk for-

The multicultural innovators of early funk, Sly and the Family Stone, in 1968. (Sly is standing second from the left.)

mula—Kool and the Gang; Earth, Wind, and Fire; War; K. C. and the Sunshine Band; the Commodores; and the Ohio Players. Rickey Vincent summarizes Stone's influence as follows:

> He was the catalyst for a culture of musical and social unity not known before or since. . . . The Godfather broke the door open, but Sly let everyone in. The standard by which togetherness is measured is Sylvester Stewart's richest gift to music.[28]

Bill Graham and the Expansion of Rock Promotion

Promoter **Bill Graham** (1931–1991) was central to the commercial development of the late-1960s rock scene. His innovative approach to presenting rock in large-scale venues became an industry standard. An orphaned refugee from postwar Eastern Europe,

CD LISTENING EXERCISE

CD 2/19

Listen to Sly and the Family Stone's recording of "Thank You (Falettin Me Be Mice Elf Agin)" (1970). The song was number one on both the pop and R & B charts at the same time, and many critics have identified it as the first funk tune. Listen to the popping bass, funky rhythm guitar, syncopated drumming, and unison ensemble vocals—all key funk ingredients. What made this a popular dance tune?

Graham was a street-smart survivor who came to the West Coast in the late 1950s hoping to be an actor. Instead, he took a job as business manager for the San Francisco Mime Troupe, a political theater group, where he came up with the idea of staging a benefit rock concert as a fund-raiser. The concert's enormous success put Graham on the road to producing ever larger, ever more-profitable rock events. Graham's bare-knuckled survivor instincts also cut a wide swath through the laid-back San Francisco rock scene, according to journalist Joel Selvin:

> He made a lot of lip service to things he didn't really live up to. . . . It was always in the interest of trying to catch an extra nickel for himself. . . . He studied very hard and he could bluff it, but he had no aesthetic judgment. . . . He equated the sale of tickets with the quality of the act.[29]

Graham opened San Francisco's Fillmore Auditorium (later moved to Fillmore West) in 1966, following up with a sister venue called Fillmore East in New York. For three years he controlled the two most important rock venues in the nation. In 1971, however, Graham closed down both theaters, seeing greater profit in promoting large-scale stadium rock shows. Bill Graham Presents subsequently became the world's most powerful rock concert production company. Graham also saw himself as a manager and developer of talent, and he briefly managed Jefferson Airplane and Carlos Santana. Further, he made a point of booking white rock bands with major black music innovators. One of the concerts he was most proud of was a 1971 Fillmore West show featuring Aretha Franklin, Tower of Power, King Curtis, and Ray Charles:

> [It was] one of the genuine orgasms of my life. For the first time in my life I was able to do something I've always dreamed of, to have a fifty-fifty audience, black and white, like each other for a night. And at the end of the night Ray and Aretha are hand in hand, King Curtis is playing and I look out into the audience . . . you can't buy that. That's why I'm in this business.[30]

THE L.A. ROCK SCENE IN THE LATE 1960s

Around the same time that the psychedelic rock scene was developing in San Francisco in the late 1960s, Los Angeles was witnessing a new, eclectic pop scene in the aftermath of surf music. The styles that emerged ranged from Beatles imitators, to middle-of-the-road pop, to innovative hybrids of folk, rock, and country.

Several Beatle-esque, L.A.-based rock groups sprang up: Gary Lewis and the Playboys (1965–1966), a band led by the son of comedian Jerry Lewis, which had hits such as "This Diamond Ring," "Count Me In," and "She's Just My Style"; Paul Revere and the Raiders (1966–1969), who sported American colonial costumes and mimicked British Invasion groups with hits such as "It's Just Like Me," "Kicks," and "Hungry"; and the Monkees (1966–1968), a corporate construction who starred on their own wholesome television show and produced a series of chart-topping pop hits such as "I'm a Believer," "Last Train to Clarksville," and "Pleasant Valley Sunday."

Sonny and Cher were a middle-of-the-road pop duo with modest folk-rock roots. Sonny Bono (1935–1998) was an apprentice to producer Phil Spector when he met the teenage, big-voiced Cher (Cherilyn Sarkisian, 1946–). The pair signed with Atlantic records and had a series of hits from 1965 to 1967 that included the Dylan-penned "All I Really Want to Do," "I Got You Babe," and "The Beat Goes On." They starred in a hit television show in the early 1970s, and Cher later pursued a solo career which produced sporadic dance pop hits.

Another L.A. group, the **Mamas and the Papas,** plied the folk-rock genre. The vocal quartet featured lustrous vocal harmonies backed up by some of the finest studio musicians in Los Angeles. Their first album, *If You Can Believe Your Eyes and Ears* (1966), topped the American charts in a rare challenge to the Beatles with hits such as "California Dreamin'" and "Monday, Monday." Bandleader John Phillips also coproduced the Monterey Pop Festival and wrote "San Francisco (Be Sure to Wear Some Flowers in Your Hair)," the song that drew thousands of young Americans to San Francisco in the 1967 "Summer of Love."

Buffalo Springfield was a short-lived but highly influential band which, together with the Byrds, pioneered folk-rock in Los Angeles from 1966 to 1968. The group combined electric instrumentation and drums with incisive songwriting and intricate vocal harmonies, at times expanding beyond their folk-rock base into hard rock and psychedelia. Buffalo Springfield featured three excellent singer-songwriter-guitarists—Neil Young (1945–), Steven Stills (1945–), and Richie Furay (1944–). Major hits included "For What It's Worth," "Rock and Roll Woman," and "Broken Arrow." Interpersonal tensions and creative battles caused Young to leave for a solo career, though he would later reunite periodically with Stephen Stills. Other band members went on to form high-profile groups such as Little Feat, and Loggins and Messina.

Crosby, Stills, and Nash (and sometimes **Young**) stood as the quintessential close-harmony, acoustic, singer-songwriter supergroup of the late 1960s. Formed from the Byrds (David Crosby, 1941–), Buffalo Springfield (Stephen Stills, 1945–), and the Hollies (Graham Nash, 1942–), the band was periodically joined by Neil Young (1945–), who contributed a harder-edged rock flavor. For years, other groups would emulate the artists' unmistakable sound. The band performed at Woodstock, and they were among the first rock artists to adopt political and environmental causes. Their debut album, *Crosby, Stills, and Nash* (1969), featured tunes such as "Marrakesh Express," "Suite: Judy Blue Eyes," "Helplessly Hoping," and "Wooden Ships." After Neil Young joined, they produced *Déjà Vu* (1970), which featured songs such as "Woodstock," "Teach Your Children," and "Our House." The band split in 1970 but released a final live album that included "Cowgirl in the Sand," "Southern Man," "Ohio," and "Love the One You're With."

A different sort of L.A. band, the **Doors,** showed little connection to the warmth of folk-rock. Their approach was anchored in the nihilism, surreal poetry, and sexuality of lead singer Jim Morrison (1943–1971), as well as the jazz-influenced keyboard work of Ray Manzarek. Over their brief career from 1967 to 1971, the Doors explored the dark side of life, years before heavy metal or punk. The band's debut album, *Light My Fire* (1967), became a massive hit that blended blues, classical music, Eastern music, and pop into dark but beguiling

Internet Listening Exercise

Listen to samples of late-1960s L.A. pop.

Gary Lewis and the Playboys: "This Diamond Ring"

Paul Revere and the Raiders: "Just Like Me"

The Monkees: "I'm a Believer"

Sonny and Cher: "I Got You Babe"

Internet Listening Exercise

Listen to samples of late 1960s L.A. rock.

The Mamas and the Papas: "California Dreamin'"

Buffalo Springfield: "For What It's Worth"

Crosby, Stills, and Nash: "Suite: Judy Blue Eyes"

The Doors: "Light My Fire"

melodies. The album was also one of the first popularized through the new alternative medium of FM radio, and it stayed on the charts for two years. Other memorable songs produced by the group included "People Are Strange," "Hello I Love You," "Riders on the Storm," and "L.A. Woman."

WOODSTOCK, ALTAMONT, AND THE END OF AN ERA

The decade of the 1960s did not go "quietly into the night." As the volatile period came to a close, the Woodstock and Altamont music festivals of 1969 symbolized the contradictions of the age. Woodstock, which could have been a disaster, signified much that was good about the 1960s; Altamont revealed a darker side.

The Woodstock rock festival was a three-day rock marathon, held in summer 1969, which featured most of the great bands of the decade. Promoted as "three days of music and peace," the event was modeled on the Monterey Pop Festival. A ticket for the whole weekend cost 18 dollars, and promoters sold 50,000 tickets in advance. When close to 400,000 people showed up, the organizers abandoned ticket sales and announced that the concert was free. Supplies of food and water ran short, portable toilets overflowed, rain created a giant mud pit, and hundreds were treated for bad reactions to LSD—but the music played on. For three days, the youth counterculture had somehow actualized its philosophy of peace and love. For many, Woodstock represented the musical and social culmination of the counterculture, and a popular film of the event cemented its mythic status.

A second free concert in 1969 held at Altamont Speedway in California provided a different story. Hastily organized by the Rolling Stones' management to serve as the backdrop for a concert film, the event started out on the wrong foot when the Hells Angels motorcycle gang was hired to do security for the concert and they were paid in beer. Like Woodstock, the event was overcrowded with rowdy concertgoers, though in this case they were enclosed in a much smaller space. When the Angels assaulted concertgoers with pool cues in a misguided attempt at crowd control, they injured hundreds of people; one person was stabbed to death, possibly by the Angels. Jefferson Airplane refused to play after lead singer Marty Balin was knocked out. By the time the Stones came on to perform, the situation was uncontrollable. The film of the event, *Gimme Shelter,* offered a grim reminder that the myth of peace and love of the 1960s could sometimes be little more than naïve hype.

As the 1960s came to a close, it seemed to many young people who had bought into the counterculture myth that things were falling apart: the Beatles were on the verge of breaking up, rock was being usurped by reassertion of corporate control, the Vietnam War was escalating, Richard Nixon was President, and the ideals of the civil rights movement and the youth counterculture also seemed to have been co-opted.

Chapter Summary

- The scope of innovation in rock during the latter part of the 1960s was impressive. Multiple overlapping genres developed, many of which were later codified as "classic rock."

- A folk revival got under way in the 1950s, advanced by urban intellectuals and embodied by the music of Woody Guthrie, Pete Seeger, the Weavers, Leadbelly, and the thousands of songs collected by John and Alan Lomax.

- By the mid-1960s, folk-rock emerged, led by Bob Dylan, who was influenced by Woody Guthrie. Other folk-rock innovators included the Byrds and Simon and Garfunkel.

- The British Invasion, led by the Beatles and the Rolling Stones, changed rock music forever in the mid-1960s. The Beatles went on to become the most popular band in the history of rock.

- The origins of psychedelic rock could be traced to the San Francisco counterculture and the use of LSD to generate the new music of the Grateful Dead, Jefferson Airplane, Janis Joplin, Jimi Hendrix, and Sly and the Family Stone.

- In the late 1960s, Los Angeles saw the emergence of the folk-rock sounds of Buffalo Springfield and Crosby, Stills, and Nash (and Young), as well as the darker, apocalyptic visions of Jim Morrison and the Doors.

- Some saw the Woodstock festival in 1969 as the musical and social culmination of the counterculture era. Others viewed it as the tipping point in the commercialization of rock.

Key Terms

acid rock	folk-rock	psychedelic music
British Invasion	folk revival	skiffle
counterculture	fuzz-tone	song collecting
distortion	hootenanny	sustain
feedback	LSD	wah-wah
folk music	power trio	

Study and Discussion Questions

1. What social, political, and commercial forces served as catalysts for the explosion of musical styles in the 1960s?

2. How did American folk music evolve in the twentieth century, and what were the sociopolitical implications of its codification? What precipitated the folk revival of the early 1960s, and who were some key innovators?

3. Which artists most influenced the emergence of folk-rock music? Discuss Bob Dylan's importance as a songwriter and lyricist.

4. What were the building blocks of the British Invasion? How did the Invasion impact American popular music? Why are the Beatles called the greatest rock band of all time?

5. What was acid rock? What were its roots and how did it become a central style of rock and roll? Who were the prominent groups of the genre, and what later styles of music did they influence?

6. Why were Jimi Hendrix and Sly Stone important to American popular music?

7. What innovations in popular music occurred in Los Angeles in the late 1960s?

8. Which rock musicians from the 1960s do you think are the most important? What music from the 1960s still appeals to you? Why?

Notes

1. Norm Cohen, *Folk Song America: A 20th Century Revival* (Washington, DC: Smithsonian Institution Press, 1991), 4.

2. Benjamin Filene, *Romancing the Folk: Public Memory and American Roots Music* (Chapel Hill: University of North Carolina Press, 2000), 27.

3. Cohen, *Folk Song America*, 5.

4. Filene, *Romancing the Folk*, 62.

5. John Steinbeck, quoted in Joe Klein, *Woody Guthrie: A Life* (New York: Knopf, 1980), 160.

6. Cohen, *Folk Song America*, 46.

7. James Miller, *Flowers in the Dustbin: The Rise of Rock and Roll, 1947–1977* (New York: Simon & Schuster, 1999), 220.

8. "Shakespeares in the Alley," Episode 3 of *Rock and Roll*, VHS (Boston, WGBH: 1995).

9. Charlie Gillett, *The Sound of the City: The Rise of Rock and Roll* (New York: Da Capo Press, 1996), 259.

10. "'Skiffle King' Donegan Died," BBC News, http://news.bbc.co.uk/1/hi/entertainment/music/2400229.stm, accessed May 12, 2005.

11. Gillett, *Sound of the City*, 267.

12. Greil Marcus, "The Beatles," in *The Rolling Stone Illustrated History of Rock and Roll*, 3rd ed., edited by Anthony DeCurtis and James Henke (New York: Random House, 1992), 217.

13. Miller, *Flowers in the Dustbin*, 231.

14. Marcus, "The Beatles," 216–17.

15. John Lennon, "The Ballad of John and Yoko," in *Rock and Roll Is Here to Stay*, edited by William McKeen (New York: Norton, 2000), 314–15.

16. Robert Palmer, *Rock and Roll: An Unruly History* (New York: Harmony Books, 1995), 118.

17. Stanley Booth, *Dance with the Devil: The Rolling Stones and Their Times* (New York: Random House, 1984), 9–10.

18. Robert Christgau, "The Rolling Stones," in *The Rolling Stone Illustrated History of Rock and Roll*, 3rd ed., edited by Anthony DeCurtis and James Henke (New York: Random House, 1992), 246–47.

19. Palmer, *Rock and Roll*, 157.

20. Joel Selvin, *Monterey Pop* (San Francisco: Chronicle Books, 1992), 5.

21. Palmer, *Rock and Roll*, 161.

22. Jack McDonough, *San Francisco Rock: The Illustrated History of San Francisco Rock Music* (San Francisco: Chronicle Books, 1985), 135.

23. Ibid.

24. David Fricke, *Rolling Stone*, No. 623, February 6, 1992, p. 45.

25. Ibid., 46.

26. Greil Marcus, *Mystery Train: Images of America in Rock 'n' Roll Music*, 4th ed. (New York: Penguin Books, 1997), 70.

27. Rickey Vincent, *Funk: The Music, the People, and the Rhythm of the One* (New York: St. Martin's Press, 1996), 89.

28. Ibid., 99.

29. Interview by the authors.

30. McDonough, *San Francisco Rock*, 41.

1970 - 2000

1970s The synthesizer becomes a major force in music ♪

1970–1976 Soul is dominated by Stevie Wonder, Al Green, Roberta Flack, Donny Hathaway, and the Isley Brothers ♪

1970–1973 Philly soul smooths out the sound of R & B, leads to disco ♪

1971 Massive antiwar demonstrations

1971 Blaxploitation films such as *Shaft* and *Superfly* become a venue for new R & B styles ♪

1973–1976 Funk artists Kool and the Gang; Earth, Wind, and Fire; Ohio Players; and Chaka Khan achieve national recognition ♪

1974 President Nixon resigns over Watergate

1974 Disco appears and begins a five-year run at the top of pop ♪

1975 The German synthesizer group Kraftwerk introduces electronica with the release of "Autobahn" ♪

1977 Disco climaxes with the Bee Gees and the popular film *Saturday Night Fever* ♪

1979 Sony Walkman introduces age of personal listening devices ♪

1979 Sugar Hill Gang's "Rapper's Delight" becomes the first rap record on a major label ♪

1981 AIDS epidemic first recognized

1981 MTV is born as an all-white rock TV network ♪

1982 Michael Jackson's *Thriller* breaks the MTV color barrier ♪

1983 The CD is introduced and changes the record industry ♪

1983 Run-D.M.C.'s first hit; rap goes mainstream ♪

1984 Prince achieves stardom with the film *Purple Rain* ♪

1984 Madonna releases *Material Girl* to begin twenty years of stardom ♪

1985 Whitney Houston scores her first hits and attains diva status ♪

1987 Public Enemy sets the standard for "conscious" rap ♪

1988 NWA releases *Straight Outta Compton;* gangsta rap is born ♪

1988 R & B evolves with the new sound of New Jack Swing ♪

1989 Berlin Wall falls; Cold War fades

1989 MTV begins to program rap regularly with *Yo! MTV Raps* ♪

1990s American economic high-tech "bubble"

1990s New R & B divas and next-generation girl groups appear ♪

1990s Women rappers become major players ♪

1991 First Persian Gulf War

1992 Los Angeles riots/uprising following Rodney King trial

1993 Snoop Dogg's first album enters the charts at number one, and gangsta rap dominates the rap world ♪

Mid-1990s The white boy-band phenomenon ♪

1995 Rapper Tupac Shakur hits the charts, dies within a year ♪

1996 Internet and MP3 transform music commerce ♪

1999 President Clinton impeached

2000 Destiny's Child launch new diva Beyoncé Knowles ♪

2001 9/11 terrorist attacks

2003 *American Idol* TV show creates a new marketing format ♪

1970   **1980**   **1990**   **2000**

Chapter 16

R & B and Its Descendants after the 1960s

During the last three decades of the twentieth century, American pop music became dominant around the globe. In R & B, soul faded, but a modernized, smoother R & B style developed. A style called funk also emerged, whose rhythm tracks and bass lines were sampled heavily in the 1980s to build hip-hop, the most significant development in American popular music in the late twentieth century. Hip-hop, in turn, yielded scratching and turntablism in the 1990s and 2000s. In the mid-1970s, dance music exploded with the advent of disco, which influenced electronica in the 1990s and 2000s. By the 1980s and 1990s, new technologies of music production and distribution—including digitization, sampling, portable music devices, music videos, and the Internet—had revolutionized modalities of music production and dissemination, and record companies consolidated into a small number of media conglomerates.

IN THIS CHAPTER

- Technological Changes
- R & B from the 1970s to the Millennium
- Disco
- Dance Pop
- Hip-Hop
- Turntablism and Scratching
- Electronica

TECHNOLOGICAL CHANGES

New technologies radically influenced American popular music in the final three decades of the twentieth century. The invention of the polyphonic analog synthesizer in the 1970s, followed by the digital synthesizer with its sound sampling capabilities in the 1980s, influenced music almost as much as the musicians themselves did. **Sampling** technology enabled artists to digitally copy almost any sound and seamlessly blend it into their music. The advent of smaller music playback hardware—the Walkman cassette player in the 1970s and 1980s, portable CD player in the 1980s and 1990s, and MP3 player in the 2000s—increased the availability of music. Low-priced digital recording and editing hardware and software further revolutionized popular music in the 1990s, so that almost anyone could produce a recording with a modest investment. The growth of the Internet in the 1990s created another vital access point for music. Online file sharing and digital music files gained momentum from the creation of the **MP3** electronic file format, which decreased the memory required to store and transmit musical files. Music industry profits plummeted, so that in the early 2000s, the online distribution of music was a mixture of record industry lawsuits and promising commercial distribution efforts.

The Evolution of Popular Music as a Commodity

The advent of Internet file sharing in the late 1990s initiated an important debate over the equitable dissemination of popular music. Record labels claimed that the illegal downloading of music files represented the biggest threat the music industry had ever faced. In fact, the entire history of popular music has seen an evolving series of technological innovations that periodically raise issues of ownership and control, beginning with the first sheet music. Music formats have shifted numerous times over 150 years of American popular music, as the following summary shows.

Prehistory–1850: Live Performance

Live performance was the only practical medium for disseminating popular music.

1865–1920s: Sheet Music

Improvements in the printing press enabled sheet music to dominate the commercial dissemination of popular music.

1877–1920s: Sound Recording

Edison's invention of the tinfoil cylinder phonograph, followed by Berliner's development of the gramophone, radically changed the dissemination of music.

1920s–1940s: Radio

The invention of the radio presented the first challenge to the fledgling recording industry.

1940s–1950s: Format Wars

In 1949 the invention of the 33⅓ rpm LP record challenged the 78 rpm records that had dominated the industry since the 1920s. By the mid-1950s, the proliferation of independent labels had encouraged the majors to create a new 45 rpm format. The "45" became the format of choice for top-forty music and jukeboxes.

1960s–1970s: Cassette Tapes

The invention of the cassette tape in 1963 loomed as a new industry threat, because people could now tape previously recorded music for their own use. In 1979 Sony introduced the Walkman, giving birth to the age of personal listening.

1982: Compact Discs

The invention of the digitally recorded compact disc—the CD—revolutionized the record industry again, but it also contributed to new fears of piracy, because people could copy digitally recorded music without significant loss of fidelity.

1990s: File Sharing

The development of new electronic audio file formats such as MP3, as well as transmission protocols over the Internet, enabled digitally recorded music to be compressed into easily transmitted files, and illegal **file sharing** became a threat to record industry control. In 2003 Apple introduced its iTunes site and software, which allowed customers to legally download music for just under a dollar a song, and several other companies followed suit.

R & B FROM THE 1970s TO THE MILLENNIUM

Although R & B went through several name changes between 1970 and 2000, it continued to serve as the bedrock for much of American popular music. Just as R & B had been the source of rock in the 1950s, it provided the basis for the new funk, disco, and hip-hop styles of the 1970s and 1980s. R & B also inspired the new dance pop genre and, through disco, the evolution of electronica. If the television show *American Idol* was any gauge, classic R & B had become the "default" style of American popular music by the early 2000s.

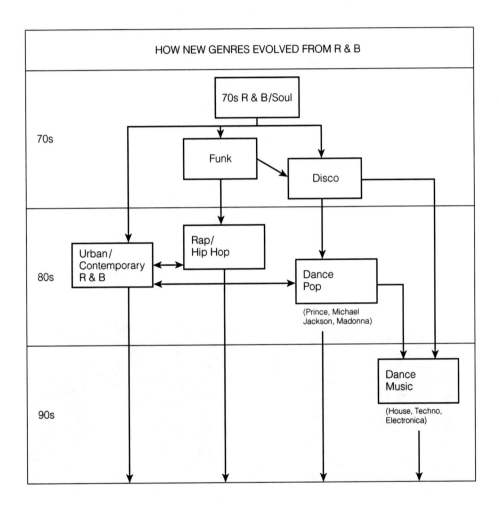

R & B in the 1970s

In the 1970s, R & B saw the decline of soul and the rise of two styles—*funk,* a hard-core, black-oriented, groove-based dance music, and a smoother, heavily produced crossover soul style that ultimately fed into disco. Black-themed films with R & B soundtracks also became a Hollywood staple. Much of 1970s R & B was dominated by the genius of Stevie Wonder, who integrated Motown, jazz, funk, and Tin Pan Alley influences to form a distinctive amalgam that influenced generations of R & B artists.

Internet Listening Exercise

Listen to samples of Al Green's vocal work.

Al Green: "Tired of Being Alone," "Let's Stay Together," "Call Me"

Now, listen to samples of tunes popularized by other artists, which Al Green covered.

Al Green: "Funny How Time Slips Away" (Willie Nelson), "How Can You Mend a Broken Heart" (Bee Gees), "Unchained Melody" (Righteous Brothers)

Al Green (1946–) was the first great soul singer of the 1970s and the last southern soul man. Green blended elements of gospel with the influences of Sam Cooke and Otis Redding. Critic Robert Christgau describes the artist's signature vocal work: "Soft-edged, almost indolent phrasing, full of audacious slurs, with his startling falsetto adding an intensity that was suffering soul and sweet pop at the same time."[1] Tight and quietly funky, the rhythm section that backed Green featured shuffle-style drums that counterpointed with simple, melodic horn and string lines. When the artist reached the peak of his popularity in the mid-1970s, personal excesses caused him to return to his gospel roots. Hits included "Tired of Being Alone" (1971), "Let's Stay Together" (1972), and "Call Me" (1973).

The most influential and acclaimed black musician of the early 1970s, **Stevie Wonder** (1950–) remained an integral part of American popular music for over four decades:

> His skills at writing sinuous melodies and gen   uplifting harmonies, and his cheerful yet determined eclecticism—from funk to   ads, bossa nova to quasi-show tunes—have made Mr. Wonder a one-man Tin Pan Alley through two decades of rock.[2]

Wonder, who came up through the Motown system, became best known for his classic albums of the early 1970s: *Music of My Mind, Talking Book, Innervisions, Fulfillingness' First Finale,* and *Songs in the Key of Life.* Hits from the period included "Superwoman" (1972), "Superstition" (1972), "You Are the Sunshine of My Life" (1973), and "Living for the City" (1973). Wonder ushered in an era in which R & B albums became cohesive artistic statements. He also pioneered the

The Selvin Collection

R & B legend Stevie Wonder in the early 1970s.

use of synthesizers in R & B and introduced the funky sound of the *clavinet*, an electronic keyboard with a distinctive organlike tone. The artist's vocal approach, with its shifting timbres and melismatic swoops and dives, influenced a generation of R & B singers, including Brian McKnight, D'Angelo, R. Kelly, and Usher. Wonder earned seventeen Grammys as well as an Oscar, and his record sales ranked alongside those of the Beatles and Elvis Presley.

A smooth style called **Philadelphia soul** also flavored early 1970s R & B. The style was orchestrated with strings and horns; supported by a relaxed, steady groove; flavored by the innovative textures of the marimba, vibes, or sitarlike electric guitar; and fronted by gospel-tinged vocals. As critic Jim Miller notes, Philly soul owed much to the work of a team of key producer/songwriters:

> Architects of a new style in dance music, Top 40 hitmakers of a proven caliber, creative artists in a cutthroat field—[Kenny] Gamble, [Leon] Huff, and Thom Bell are to the Seventies what Holland-Dozier-Holland and Smokey Robinson were to the Sixties: the preeminent soul producers of the decade.[3]

Also like Motown, the Philly soul groove came from a veteran group of studio musicians, in this case called MFSB (Mother Father Sister Brother). The streamlined pulse of MFSB in tunes such as "Love Train" (O'Jays, 1973), "TSOP (The Sound of Philadelphia)" (MFSB, 1974), and "Bad Luck" (Harold Melvin and the Blue Notes, 1975) shaped the subsequent disco style of the 1970s. Major artists of the Philly soul era included the Stylistics, the O'Jays, the Spinners, Harold Melvin and the Blue Notes, and the last group's lead vocalist, Teddy Pendergrass.

Seventies R & B featured prominently in the **blaxploitation movies** of the early part of the decade. With funky soundtracks, stylish clothes, and flashy cars, the black-themed action films capitalized on a mass public fascination with African American style. The first such film, *Sweet Sweetback's Baadasss Song* (1970), directed by Melvin Van Peebles, set the standard for the new genre. The most influential blaxploitation films were *Shaft* (1971) and *Superfly* (1972). *Shaft,* the story of a black private eye in Harlem, featured an Oscar- and Grammy-winning soundtrack by Isaac Hayes. *Superfly,* a film about drug dealing, was distinguished by Curtis Mayfield's powerful soundtrack. Blaxploitation soundtracks proliferated, influencing the sound of R & B. According to critic Nelson George,

> Longer, more orchestrated, more introspective—some black albums had the continuity and cohesion of soundtracks even when they weren't. Latin percussion . . . suddenly became rhythmic requirements, adding a new layer of polyrhythmic fire to the grooves. Minor chords, frowned on during the soul years, began appearing.[4]

The film *Jackie Brown* (1997) served as director Quentin Tarantino's homage to blaxploitation films.

Funk

Funk, a dance-tempo R & B style that emphasized complex, syncopated, rhythmic interplay, developed out of R & B in the early 1970s. Originating from an

Internet Listening Exercise

Listen to samples of songs by an R & B master.

Stevie Wonder: "You Are the Sunshine of My Life," "Superstition," "Living for the City"

Internet Listening Exercise

Listen to samples of Philadelphia soul.

Harold Melvin and the Blue Notes: "Wake up Everybody," "If You Don't Know Me by Now"

O'Jays: "For the Love of Money," "I Love Music"

Stylistics: "Betcha by Golly, Wow"

Spinners: "Could It Be I'm Falling in Love"

Internet Listening Exercise

Listen to samples of music from blaxploitation film soundtracks of the 1970s.

Isaac Hayes: "Shaft"

Curtis Mayfield: "Superfly"

Marvin Gaye: "Trouble Man"

Bobby Womack: "Across 110th Street"

African American slang term for "stink," funk was the rawest, most African form of R & B up to that time.

The Ingredients of Funk

Groove

The syncopated, polyphonic, dance-oriented groove created by interlocking parts played by each instrument in the ensemble is the critical element of funk.

Bass

The bass drives the music—thumping or popping. The bass line is often the most memorable part of a funk tune, as well as the dimension most often sampled in succeeding decades by hip-hop artists. The bass often emphasizes the first beat of the measure, known as playing "on the one."

Guitar and Keyboards

The bass line is complemented by an interlocking web of short, scratchy guitar rhythm chords—in a style called "chanking," sometimes run through a wah-wah pedal. Electronic keyboards can fulfill similar roles, interlocking with guitar parts. When soloing, funk guitarists often employ Hendrix-style fuzz-tone.

Drums

Drumming is clean, sparse, and highly syncopated while continuing to emphasize the backbeat.

Horns

Usually a combination of trumpet, saxophone, and trombone, the horn section provides call and response with vocals as well as punchy, percussive accents.

Vocals

Vocals follow one of three styles: (1) the gruff and gospel-influenced style of James Brown, (2) falsetto, or (3) the sardonic, nasal style pioneered by Sly Stone. Unison chant-style vocals are also common, as well as spoken-word and rhyming (pre-rap).

Funk was not confined to the classic verse/chorus song structure; using the same concept that rappers would soon employ, funk artists took what had been the break or extended jam section of an R & B tune and stretched it into an entire song. True to its African roots, funk also allowed for more freedom and improvisation once the groove was established. Though seldom at the top of the charts, funk ultimately shaped disco, jazz-rock fusion, and hip-hop. The tunes most often cited as the origins of funk are James Brown's "Papa's Got a Brand New Bag" (1965) and Sly Stone's "Thank You (Falettin Me Be Mice Elf Agin)" (1970). James Brown took the key step of placing rhythmic emphasis "on the one" (the downbeat), turning R & B's traditional emphasis on the backbeat on its head. Brown's bassist from the early 1970s, Bootsy Collins, continued the rhythmic style in George Clinton's groups. Sly Stone's band furthered the development of funk by adding a rock-influenced fuzz-tone guitar, slap-style bass, chant-style choral vocals, and the synthesized drum machine. Major funk acts of the 1970s included Kool and the Gang; Earth, Wind, and Fire; the Ohio Players; Rufus and Chaka Khan; and the Commodores.

CD LISTENING EXERCISE

Listen to "Mother Popcorn" by James Brown (CD 2/15) and "Thank You (Falettin Me Be Mice Elf Agin)" by Sly and the Family Stone (CD 2/19). Both are recognized as funk classics. What core elements of funk can you identify in each tune? How do the tunes differ?

The most commercially successful funk band of the mid-1970s, **Earth, Wind, and Fire** incorporated jazz, soul, gospel, pop, rock, and African music. The group could harmonize like a Motown quartet, work a groove like James Brown, and improvise like a jazz fusion group. Major hits included "Reasons" (1975), "Shining Star" (1975), "Got to Get You into My Life" (1978), and "September" (1979). Earth, Wind, and Fire was one of the most popular bands in the world during the late 1970s. According to historian Ricky Vincent,

> Earth, Wind, and Fire . . . [wore] brightly colored skin-tight suits, platform shoes, ridiculous lapels, streamers, bellbottoms, and thousands of sequins. . . . Wall-to-wall splash, sprints, slides, screams, sweat, and soul, Earth, Wind, and Fire was a soul christening.[5]

George Clinton (1941–) was a visionary, theatrically inclined artist who took funk to a new level in the early 1980s. With two large funk aggregations, Parliament and Funkadelic, Clinton delivered freewheeling performances that disseminated an eclectic mythology of space-age cartoon images about motherships, star wars, and atomic dogs—all driven by a band clad in silver jumpsuits, diapers, and rainbow wigs. Critic Arthur Kempton described the visual impact of Clinton's shows:

> A "mothership" . . . descend[ed] thunderously from the eaves of cavernous public spaces. . . . Clinton, the ringmaster who wore long "fright" wigs, tall boots, and outlandish sci-fi raiment, would make his entrances riding in a "polyester pimpmobile." . . . A half-decade before MTV, Clinton had conceived of aural videos.[6]

Clinton had more lasting influence on subsequent developments in black music—hip-hop in particular—than did any other musician of his era. He introduced the electronic "clap" sound, synthesizer-bass (bass track played by a keyboard), and elaborately layered horn and vocal lines. Major hits included "Tear the Roof off the Sucker (Give up the Funk)" (1976), "One Nation under a Groove" (1978), and "Atomic Dog" (1983).

 **Internet Listening Exercise**

Listen to samples of two decades of funk.

Charles Wright: "Express Yourself"

Kool and the Gang: "Funky Stuff"

Earth, Wind, and Fire: "Shining Star"

Ohio Players: "Skin Tight"

Rufus and Chaka Khan: "Tell Me Something Good"

Commodores: "Brick House"

George Clinton: "Tear the Roof off the Sucker (Give up the Funk)"

1980s R & B: Quiet Storm, Divas, and Drum Machines

While R & B spun off new genres in the 1980s such as hip-hop, it also maintained a core style that emphasized melody. Much of the R & B of the decade received airplay on radio stations that broadcast in formats variously called "urban contemporary," "retronuevo," or "quiet storm." A far cry from the gritty soul of the 1960s, 1980s R & B showcased a new generation of vocalists who aimed at crossing over with a smooth, upscale sound. The sound also drove away some in the hip-hop generation, as Public Enemy's Chuck D proclaimed in a rap tune: "When the quiet storm comes on I fall asleep."[7] The advent of hip-hop, however, also revitalized up-tempo, dance-oriented R & B to generate the beat-happy, rap-infused New Jack Swing style, so that throughout the decade, sampling and synthesizers ruled.

Major female vocalists in the 1980s included the ultimate R & B diva Whitney Houston, the jazz-inflected Anita Baker, and the smoothly sensual Sade. **Whitney Houston** (1963–) had a powerful voice and vocal technique that dominated the charts from 1985 to the mid-1990s. Trained as a gospel singer, Houston's best-selling debut album in 1985 produced multiple hits: "You Give Good Love," "Saving All My Love for You," and "The Greatest Love of All." After another successful album in 1987, Houston turned her talents to soundtrack albums for films in which she appeared, such as *The Bodyguard* (1992) and *Waiting to Exhale* (1995). The artist's recording of the Dolly Parton–penned "I Will Always Love You" for *The Bodyguard* was the one of the biggest-selling singles in pop music history. According to critic Gerri Hirshey,

> Whitney had the genes, the pipes, the looks, the connections and the iron will that have since sustained her through countless trials-by-tabloid. . . . The truth is, any time she chooses, Whitney Houston can sing the bejesus out of the Yellow Pages. It is the mark—and prerogative—of the true diva to do exactly as she pleases.[8]

Important male R & B vocalists of the decade included the smooth crossover crooner/songwriter Lionel Richie, soulful ballad virtuoso Luther Vandross, and other smooth soul men such as Jeffrey Osborne, Peabo Bryson, and Frankie Beverly and his band Maze. **Lionel Richie** (1949–) got his first break with the funky Commodores, but once he developed his songwriting in the late 1970s, he detoured from funk to smooth crossover ballads. In critic Nelson George's account, "Richie's voice, oozing with country melancholy, projected lyrics as sentimental and courtly as roses on the first date. . . . Richie's early funk voice was just a facade. He wanted to be Kenny Rogers."[9] Hits included "Endless Love" (1981), "Truly" (1982), and "All Night Long" (1983). **Luther Vandross** (1951–2005) was one of the most gifted vocalists of his era, as well as a successful producer. Major hits included "Bad Boy/Having a Party" (1982), Burt Bacharach's "A House Is Not a Home" (1982), "Here and Now" (1989), and "Endless Love" (1994).

By the late 1980s, R & B producers began to integrate a more street-oriented feel into R & B vocal music to create a style called **New Jack Swing.** Pioneered by producer Teddy Riley and Prince alumni Jimmy Jam and Terry Lewis, the

Internet Listening Exercise

Listen to samples of songs by Whitney Houston, Anita Baker, and Sade.

Whitney Houston: "Saving All My Love for You," "I Will Always Love You"

Anita Baker: "Caught up in the Rapture"

Sade: "Smooth Operator"

Internet Listening Exercise

Listen to samples of male vocalists of the 1980s.

Lionel Richie: "Endless Love"

Luther Vandross: "A House Is Not a Home"

male-dominated sound employed snippets of rap, synthesized drum and bass lines, and multipart doo-wop harmony. As historian Rickey Vincent observes, "The 'New Jack Swing' sound mixed hip-hop beats with soulful melodies to bring bite-sized portions of funk for a new generation to digest."[10] Major New Jack artists included Bobby Brown, Keith Sweat, Bell Biv Devoe, Tony Toni Tone, and Boyz II Men. **Boyz II Men,** who called their group vocal harmony style "hip-hop doo-wop," released their first album *Cooleyhighharmony* (1991) to yield hits such as "Motownphilly" and "It's So Hard to Say Goodbye to Yesterday." Recognizing that their greatest appeal lay in their lush four-part harmonies, the group abandoned up-tempo New Jack Swing in favor of ballads, subsequently scoring with "End of the Road" (1992) and "I'll Make Love to You" (1994). The New Jack style went on to influence dance pop of the 1990s and early 2000s.

The 1990s: Urban/Contemporary and Neo-Soul

R & B displayed several substyles in the 1990s, and while the urban contemporary sound was still common, a new, street-flavored vocal approach called hip-hop soul appeared. A fresh crop of R & B divas also hit the airwaves, and doo-wop–styled close harmony returned in some female and male vocal groups. The next generation of soulful male ballad crooners, some sweetly emotive, others down and dirty, also entered the scene. In addition, a new sound that prized rootsy, soulful authenticity called neo-soul emerged.

The R & B diva pipeline seemed inexhaustible in the 1990s, with sounds ranging from the smooth flavor of Toni Braxton to the hip-hop street sass of Mary J. Blige. Other young divas such as Brandy, Monica, Aaliyah, and Beyoncé struck a stylistic middle ground. The designer-attired queen of hip-hop soul, **Mary J. Blige** (1971–), evoked a blend of sophistication and street. Blige began her career as the protégé of producer Sean "Puffy" Combs with the debut album *What's the 411?* (1992), and her powerful mix of modern R & B and edgy hip-hop impressed listeners. Often compared favorably to Chaka Khan or Aretha Franklin, Blige brought new textures and flavors to R & B. As critic Gerri Hirshey observes, "Having lived the kind of gritty urban life Mariah Carey would hire rappers to describe, Blige turned inward, began writing her own material, and re-emerged as a smart, sad-eyed survivor."[11] Major hits included "Real Love" (1992), a cover of Chaka Khan's "Sweet Thing" (1993), and "Not Gon' Cry" (1996).

The 1990s also saw the rise of several female R & B vocal groups who packed vocal power, gospel harmonies, and sexy, in-your-face delivery, including En Vogue, SWV, TLC, and Destiny's Child. One of the most popular female R & B groups of the late 1990s and early 2000s, Destiny's Child produced major hits with "Say My Name" (2000), "Survivor" (2001), and "Soldier" (2004). Lead singer/songwriter Beyoncé Knowles also went solo to score with *Dangerously in Love* (2003).

Not to be outdone by female vocal groups, Blackstreet carried the torch for male vocal group harmony. Founded by New Jack Swing pioneer Teddy Riley,

Internet Listening Exercise

Listen to samples of New Jack Swing.

Bobby Brown: "Don't Be Cruel"

Bell Biv Devoe: "Do Me"

Tony Toni Tone: "Feels Good"

Boyz II Men: "Motownphilly," "I'll Make Love to You"

Internet Listening Exercise

Listen to samples of songs from the "diva pipeline" of the 1990s.

Mary J. Blige: "Real Love," "Not Gon' Cry"

Destiny's Child perform at the thirtieth anniversary of the *Soul Train* television show in 2001 (left to right): Kelly Rowland, Beyoncé Knowles, and Michelle Williams.

the group merged soulful vocal harmonies with catchy, bass-heavy, hip-hop beats, and they incorporated appearances by hip-hop artists as well. Major hits included "Before I Let You Go" (1994) and "No Diggity" (1996).

A raft of new male crooners—many flavored by hip-hop—gained prominence in the 1990s and early 2000s. These vocalists, including Babyface, R. Kelly, and Usher, recast the soulful, romantic male R & B voice. R. Kelly remained popular throughout the decade with multiplatinum releases such as the carnally flavored "Bump 'n' Grind," "You Remind Me of Somethin'" (1995), and the Grammy-winning "I Believe I Can Fly" (1996) from the film *Space Jam*. Usher started out in R & B in the late 1990s as a teen pop star, but he moved to the sultry adult side with his third album, *8701*, in 2001. In 2004 he released *Confessions*, which contained the chart-topping hit single, "Yeah!"

A new R & B substyle called **neo-soul** emerged in the late 1990s in the work of artists who consciously paid homage to the "old-school" soul of the 1960s and 1970s. Neo-soul had a sweet, retro tone as well as a social conscience, and many of the style's artists also wrote and performed their own material, resuscitating the singer-songwriter tradition in R & B. The work of Lauryn Hill, first with the Fugees and later on her own in 1998, greatly influenced the neo-soul scene, as did the appearance of Erykah Badu in 1997. Other female neo-soul artists included Macy Gray, Jill Scott, India.Arie, and Alicia Keys. Male artists in the style included D'Angelo, Maxwell, and Raphael Saadiq. The Fugees, comprised of rappers Pras and Wyclef Jean and vocalist Lauryn Hill (1975–), blended rap, soul, reggae, and R & B in their Grammy-winning 1996 album *The Score*, which

Internet Listening Exercise

Listen to samples of R & B vocal groups of the 1990s.

Destiny's Child/Beyoncé: "Survivor"

Blackstreet: "No Diggity"

Internet Listening Exercise

Listen to samples of smooth male R & B vocalists of the 1990s.

Babyface: "When Can I See You Again?"

R. Kelly: "I Believe I Can Fly"

Usher: "Yeah!"

Internet Listening Exercise

Listen to samples of music by neo-soul artists.

Fugees/Lauryn Hill: "Killing Me Softly with His Song"

Erykah Badu: "On and On"

D'Angelo: "Brown Sugar"

Alicia Keys: "If I Ain't Got You"

included new arrangements of Roberta Flack's "Killing Me Softly with His Song" and Bob Marley's "No Woman No Cry." Hill followed in 1998 with her smash solo album, *The Miseducation of Lauryn Hill.* Alicia Keys (1981–) debuted with the Grammy-winning album *Songs in A Minor,* which produced "Fallin'" (2001), to follow in 2003 with *The Diary of Alicia Keys,* which yielded "You Don't Know My Name" and "I Ain't Got You."

DISCO

In the 1970s, a new genre of popular dance music began to evolve out of R & B. Initially taking the form of disco, it subsequently morphed into dance pop and electronica in the 1980s and 1990s. **Disco** was a formulaic, R & B-based commercial sound accompanied by a hedonistic party scene that cut a wide swath through top-forty music. The *discotheque,* a stylish dance club with flashy decor and recorded dance music, originated in France in the early 1960s, where club owners hired DJs to save money on live bands. As the trend spread to the United States, it was first adopted in the gay, black, and Latino communities of New York and other major cities. Rooted in funk and R & B, disco music featured rhythm tracks with nonstop bass lines and repetitive drumming varying so little that DJs could spin records continuously without breaking the groove. As critic Nelson George observes, "At least the Philly disco records sounded like they were made by humans. Soon, Eurodisco invaded America. . . . It was a music with a metronomelike beat . . . almost inflectionless vocals, and metallic sexuality."[12]

Disco first hit the airwaves in 1974 with two soundalike tunes—"Rock the Boat" by the Hues Corporation and "Rock Your Baby" by George McCrae. Another popular disco group, KC and the Sunshine Band, also scored with "Get Down Tonight" and "(Shake, Shake, Shake) Shake Your Booty." "The Hustle" (1975) by Van McCoy, accompanied by a dance of the same name, provided another influential disco hit. Barry White (1944–2003) crafted a sexy, soulful sound by blending lush orchestration, funky grooves, and his own half-sung, half-spoken baritone delivery. White and his group, the Love Unlimited Orchestra, scored a string of early 1970s hits with "Can't Get Enough of Your Love, Baby," "Never Gonna Give You Up," and "Love's Theme." Donna Summer (1948–) was the reigning diva of the disco era. Her first hit, "Love to Love You Baby" (1975), was a seventeen-minute ode to lovemaking. She followed up with the Grammy-winning "Last Dance" (1978) and "Hot Stuff" (1979). Vocalist Gloria Gaynor (1949–) contributed the Grammy-winning "I Will Survive" (1975), one of the last anthems of the disco era.

The disco era reached its zenith with the release of the film *Saturday Night Fever* (1977). The movie, which starred actor John Travolta as a disco king, produced the most successful soundtrack album of all time. It featured music by numerous R & B artists, as well as a string of new songs by British pop veterans the Bee Gees including "Stayin' Alive," "Night Fever," and "How Deep Is Your Love." Disco went into decline by the late 1970s, but the Village People—a theatrical, gay, disco vocal group—scored two major hits to close out the era with "Macho Man" (1978) and "YMCA" (1979).

Internet Listening Exercise

Listen to samples of disco.

George McCrae: "Rock Your Baby"

KC and the Sunshine Band: "Get Down Tonight"

Van McCoy: "The Hustle"

Barry White: "Can't Get Enough"

Gloria Gaynor: "I Will Survive"

Donna Summer: "Last Dance"

Bee Gees: "Stayin' Alive"

Village People: "YMCA"

DANCE POP

The disco era drew to a close at the end of the 1970s, in part because of the progression of pop styles, in part because of the rise of a new era of social conservatism and the nascent HIV/AIDS epidemic. Nonetheless, the demand for dance music persisted, and the next wave of danceable pop emerged in the early 1980s in the music of Michael and Janet Jackson, Prince, and Madonna.

The Birth of MTV

The growth of dance pop gained momentum from MTV (Music Television), a late-1970s brainchild of the new cable television industry. When cable was first established, many of its networks focused on single themes such as movies, news, or weather—and, in this case, music. Founded in 1981 by Warner Communications and American Express, MTV at first consisted of three-minute video clips of musical groups signed to Warner. Programming mimicked radio formats, with **VJs** (video DJs) introducing the latest releases. A new record-marketing process was thus established; hit songs would now also require hit videos. For its first few years, MTV was an all-white medium; the network's editorial policy stated that it was a rock network whose market was white suburban youth. Ultimately, however, the dance pop sound of the early 1980s—led by Michael Jackson's *Thriller* (1982)—broke through MTV's color barrier.

The Jackson 5 in an early seventies publicity shot. (Michael is second from the right.)

The Jackson Family

As the self-proclaimed "King of Pop," **Michael Jackson** (1958–) was one of the most successful performers in American pop music history, as well as one its most perplexing personalities. Jackson began his career as a child singing lead for the successful family vocal act, the Jackson 5, scoring hits that included "I Want You Back," "ABC," and "I'll Be There." The entire Jackson family received a congressional citation for "contributions to American youth" in 1972. When Michael Jackson released his first major solo album, *Off the Wall* (1979), he achieved a record-setting four top-ten hits: "Don't Stop Till You Get Enough," "Rock with You," "Off the Wall," and "She's Out of My Life." His next album, *Thriller* (1982), sold more copies than any other record in pop music history, over 50 million copies worldwide. A collaboration with legendary producer Quincy Jones, the album yielded an unprecedented seven top-ten singles, including "Thriller," "Billie Jean," and "Beat It," which featured a blazing guitar solo by metalist Eddie Van Halen. The album's music was flavored by Jackson's signature vocals, funky synthesized bass lines, interwoven keyboard and guitar parts, and well-arranged, R & B–style horns. Producer L. A. Reid describes the sound of another song from that album, "Billie Jean":

> Everything in that song was catchy and every instrument was playing a different hook. You could separate it into twelve different musical pieces and I think you'd have twelve different hits. Every day I look for that kind of song.[13]

Through the rest of the 1980s, Jackson's support for social causes and continuing musical success enhanced his reputation. During the 1990s, however, the artist's star began to tarnish. Charges of inappropriate behavior, coupled with his own increasingly surreal appearance, incurred negative media attention, and mixed reviews of his music cast shadows on his career.

Michael Jackson's sister, **Janet Jackson** (1966–), followed her brother in the 1980s to her own pop stardom. Though she did not have the musical talents of her brother, Janet produced a string of hit records that relied on New Jack Swing and dance-oriented videos. A decade later, dance pop divas such as Britney Spears and Christina Aguilera would replicate the artist's formula. Jackson followed her successful breakout album, *Control* (1986), with the popular *Rhythm Nation 1814* (1989). Her work in the 1990s and early 2000s featured material with increasingly sexual overtones.

Prince and Madonna

The work of **Prince** (1958–) played a central role in the advancement of dance pop. Widely recognized as one of the most talented musicians of his generation, he demonstrated his versatility by singing and playing all the instruments on many of his records. Beginning in the late 1970s, Prince recorded more than twenty albums with a unique blend of funk, rock, and R & B. He also followed a tortuous path mapped by a lengthy battle with the record industry as well as his own quirks. Prince emerged from Minneapolis, Minnesota, releasing a series of albums that displayed a penchant for erotic songwriting, most apparent

Internet Listening Exercise

Listen to samples of music by the Jackson family.

Jackson 5: "ABC"

Michael Jackson: "Billie Jean," "Beat It"

Janet Jackson: "Nasty," "Miss You So Much"

Prince "embraces" his guitar in this 1981 performance.

© CORBIS

Internet Listening Exercise

Listen to samples of songs by Prince.

Prince: "When Doves Cry," "1999," "Purple Rain," "Red Corvette." ("When Doves Cry" was a radical musical departure from earlier dance pop songs because there was no bass part.)

on his third album, *Dirty Mind* (1980). Interest in the artist's work grew steadily, fostered by the release of *Controversy* (1981) and *1999* (1982). When the hit single and video of "Little Red Corvette" (1983) provided the artist's MTV breakthrough, he joined Michael Jackson to become one of the first African American artists to achieve significant airplay on MTV. Next, Prince's Grammy- and Oscar-winning autobiographical film, *Purple Rain,* yielded hits with "When Doves Cry," "Let's Go Crazy," and "Purple Rain." The artist's career entered a strange period of decline in 1993 when he changed his name to an unpronounceable symbol as part of a multiyear battle with his record label. The end of the dispute at the turn of the millennium, however, saw the reinvigoration of his career.

Madonna (Madonna Louise Ciccone, 1958–) transformed her image and style with a skill and frequency that kept her at the forefront of popular culture for over two decades. With entertainment industry acumen, a feminist image of self-determination, multiple "personalities," and the ability to stir controversy, Madonna became an enduring pop music icon. Raised in Michigan, the artist made her first forays into pop music at the end of the disco era in New York and scored her first record deal in 1982. Madonna's timing was perfect for achieving extensive MTV exposure, and she stirred early controversy with an interracial love scene in a video. With modest vocal skills but great production values, the artist carefully synchronized her music with her evolving looks, which included a Marilyn Monroe-esque "Material Girl," a prim Evita Perón, and a provocative haute couture dominatrix. Madonna scored a string of dance pop hits beginning with *Madonna* (1983), followed by the controversial *Like a Virgin* (1984), which yielded the hit title song as well as "Material Girl." New controversy sprang from the release of "Papa Don't Preach" (1990), which encouraged single women to keep their babies, and "Like a Prayer" (1990), which the Vatican censured. When Madonna set up her own production company in 1992, she cemented her position as one of the most successful business women in pop music history. In 1995 she played the lead role in the film version of Andrew Lloyd Webber's Broadway musical *Evita*.

Other Dance Pop Divas

Grammy-winning pop superstar Mariah Carey (1970–) burst onto the scene in the early 1990s with a five-octave range and a soulful voice to power the sales

Multicultural Note

James Brown and Tina Turner—Dance Pop Role Models

When Michael and Janet Jackson, Prince, and Madonna set the tone for contemporary dance pop performance, they owed a debt to their predecessors, James Brown and Tina Turner, who themselves had built on decades of black performance traditions. Brown and Turner were two of the most dynamic performers in the history of popular music, and their onstage acrobatics were emulated by many, but mastered by few.

Tina Turner set the female benchmark for high-energy pop singing and dancing, and although many contemporary dance pop stars such as Janet Jackson and Britney Spears rely on prerecorded vocal tracks to sing and dance simultaneously, Turner had no need of such support. And while Prince and Michael Jackson amazed fans with their intricate dance steps and choreography, most of it had been done before by James Brown. Brown was the master of high-energy live performance and one of the greatest dancers in pop music history. Channeling the prior collective history of African American stage performance of such legendary performers as Bill "Bojangles" Robinson, Cab Calloway, and Louis Jordan, Brown laid the groundwork for most great R & B dancers who followed in his footsteps.

of over 140 million records. Carey's music was a mix of pop ballads and up-tempo dance pop rooted in soul and gospel music with a touch of funk. Hits included "Emotions" (1991), "Hero" (1993), "Fantasy" (1995), and a collaboration with Boyz II Men, "One Sweet Day" (1995). Although most of her hits were ballads, Canadian-born superstar Celine Dion (1968–) became a ubiquitous presence in the dance pop music world in the early 1990s. With a powerful, clear voice, Dion scored multiple hits and sold more than 100 million records worldwide. She became best known for her performance of the theme from the film *Titanic* (1997): "My Heart Will Go On." Former Mouseketeers Britney Spears (1981–) and Christina Aguilera (1980–) emerged on the dance pop scene as major teen stars in the late 1990s. Both singers initially portrayed a contradictory appeal of innocence and sexuality that drew public attention, and they were marketed in a fashion similar to the marketing of the teen idols of the 1950s. While Aguilera's vocal power matched her celebrity status, Spear's singing ability was viewed more skeptically by some. Spears scored her biggest hit with "Baby One More Time" (1999); Aguilera did so with "Genie in a Bottle" (1999).

Internet Listening Exercise

Listen to samples of music by dance pop divas.

Madonna: "Material Girl," "Like a Prayer," "Papa Don't Preach"

Mariah Carey: "Fantasy," "One Sweet Day"

Celine Dion: "My Heart Will Go On"

Britney Spears: "Baby One More Time"

Christina Aguilera: "Genie in a Bottle"

© Neal Preston/CORBIS

Tina Turner "steppin' out" sometime in the 1980s.

© CORBIS

Madonna in one of her many guises (1986).

Multicultural Note

Madonna—Role Model or Sex Object?

Building on the women's movement of the early 1970s, women in pop music in the 1980s contributed to new, independent female role models in Western popular culture. Few female figures in popular culture became more visible in this realm than Madonna. Singer Liz Phair once described Madonna's influence on her: "In high school ... the only videos I cared about were Madonna's. ... It made me feel sexy, like a woman, to emulate her. She was cool and independent; she had muscles and boobs."[14]

Phair's comments raise a central issue about Madonna's influences. Is she a model of feminist independence, a sex object who plays to sexist stereotypes, or a bit of both? Madonna further complicated matters with allusions to lesbianism, bisexuality, and sadomasochism.

Multicultural Note

Boy Bands, Cultural Appropriation, and Race

In an interesting twist of race and power, the white boy-band phenomenon of the 1990s was actually initiated in the late 1980s by Maurice Starr, an African American producer. Starr had been a force behind the successful early-1980s African American vocal group, New Edition; following the demise of that group, Starr sought to replicate and even surpass their success with a group of young white vocalists. He did this with New Kids on the Block, and the white boy-band phenomenon was born.

Ultimately, the greatest profits from the boy bands still went to white producers and artists—particularly the Orlando, Florida-based teen pop mastermind Lou Pearlman, who managed *Nsync, the Backstreet Boys, and O-Town. But in a complex racial role reversal, it is a black producer who invented the first white boy-bands.

Boy Bands

In the mid-1990s, a new wave of young white male vocal groups called *boy bands* hit the dance pop market. Among the best known were New Kids on the Block, the Backstreet Boys, *Nsync, and 98 Degrees, all of whom were carefully molded by producers to appeal to young female audiences as the teen idols of the late 1950s had done. The boy bands produced sterile renderings of soul, contemporary doo-wop, and New Jack Swing, specializing in dance pop, ballads, and hip-hop choreography.

The first white boy band, New Kids on the Block, enjoyed a string of hits in the late 1980s, topped by "Hangin' Tough." The Back Street Boys and *Nsync followed up as the genre's most successful acts of the 1990s. Both groups emerged from Orlando, Florida, and used close connections to the Disney Corporation to implement successful marketing strategies. By the early 2000s, the boy-band phase had drawn to a close, with only *Nsync's lead singer, Justin Timberlake, able to transition to a solo career.

Internet Listening Exercise

Listen to samples of white dance pop vocal groups of the 1990s.

Backstreet Boys: "I Want It That Way"

*Nsync: "Tearin' up My Heart"

HIP-HOP

The appearance of hip-hop, especially its subgenre rap, was the single most important development in late-twentieth-century American popular music. According to historian Tricia Rose, at its most basic, "rap music is a form of rhymed storytelling accompanied by highly rhythmic, electronically based music. . . . Rap music is a black cultural expression that prioritizes black voices from the margins of urban America."[15] At its start, rap represented a new musical genre, although it had direct African and African American musical roots. Many critics argue that it has now taken its place as one of four major black musical forms:

the blues, jazz, rhythm and blues, and rap. Equally importantly, rap and its accompanying hip-hop culture expressed a voice of rebellion, something that had been absent from most popular music for decades. Through the new genre, people in the poorest urban communities of the country crafted a new cultural product that came to pervade American popular music and popular culture—from clothing styles to music to language.

The Innovations and Influences of Hip-Hop

- It was a new genre in American popular music, taking its place with the blues, jazz, and R & B.
- Over two decades, it became the most influential American popular music style.
- It served as the basis for a new global youth cultural identity.
- Rich African and African American cultural and musical traditions provided its source.
- It evolved from the country's poorest communities to produce a valued and profitable art form.
- It served as a new voice of rebellion against cultural domination.
- The use of sampling became popularized through hip-hop.
- Interest in poetry and spoken-word expression increased because of hip-hop.
- The subgenre of turntablism came from it.

The Cultural Roots of Rap

Rap and hip-hop reflected African and African American cultural traditions interacting with contemporary technologies and social conditions. As we have seen, traditional African societies highly valued oral traditions, saw oration as a sophisticated form of expression, and treated the *griot* as a respected member of society. The capacity to command oral language—seen in ministers, politicians, poets, and other artists—remains an important dimension of African American culture. Other black oral traditions such as call and response, use of double meanings, jive talk developed by jazz hipsters such as Cab Calloway, Louis Jordan's early spoken-word R & B hits, and "playing the dozens" (competitive word games) all became sources for the language of rap and hip-hop.

Predecessors to rap came in the 1960s and 1970s in the work of the Last Poets, whose performance pieces, such as "Niggers Are Scared of Revolution" and "White Man's Got a God Complex," were chanted over African percussion. Poet-singer Gil Scott Heron's (1949–) work also influenced rap and bridged the gap between African American oral and musical traditions. His classic "The Revolution Will Not Be Televised" combined poetry, song, social commentary, and the everyday language of black communities. Rap also owed much to the funk of James Brown and George Clinton, as well as the earthy raps of singer Millie Jackson.

Immigration patterns from the Caribbean to New York added many things to the rap mix: the massive sound systems of Jamaican music, the toasting of Jamaican DJs, the recitations of Jamaican dub poets, and the macho boasting and social criticism of Trinidadian calypsonians. Afro-Cuban music also contributed a focus on *breaks*—the rhythmic break-downs common in salsa—as well as break dancing. According to rap innovator Afrika Bambaataa,

CD LISTENING EXERCISE

CD 2/9

Listen again to "Saturday Night Fish Fry" by R & B artist Louis Jordan. Notice his use of spoken words over a rhythmic background. Jordan was performing a version of early rap fifty years before the genre rose to dominance.

> Break music is that certain part of the record that you just be waiting for to come up and when that certain part comes, that percussion part with all those drums, congas, it makes you dance real wild. . . . That break is so short in the record, you get mad, because the break was not long enough for you to really get down to do your thing.[16]

These multicultural traditions coalesced in the South Bronx in the 1970s to form rap.

Internet Listening Exercise

Listen to samples of artists who were predecessors to rap.

Cab Calloway: "Minnie the Moocher"

The Last Poets: "Niggers Are Scared of Revolution"

Gil Scott-Heron: "The Revolution Will Not Be Televised"

James Brown: "Say It Loud (I'm Black and I'm Proud)"

Millie Jackson: "The Rap"

Old-School Rap

The earliest manifestations of hip-hop culture—which included rap music, break dancing, graffiti, and street fashions—appeared in the mid-1970s in the work of two influential DJs: DJ Hollywood and DJ Cool Herc. These artists attracted the attention of black and Latino youths who were unmoved by disco. Rather than being generated through commercial studio recordings, early hip-hop was a live art form performed by New York City DJs for dancers and audiences in parks and clubs. The absence of recordings precluded radio airplay, although taped mixes of hip-hop performances began to make the rounds, sold on street corners and played on boom boxes.

DJ Hollywood (1954–) stood at the top of the rap hierarchy in the Bronx of the late 1970s. According to entrepreneur Russell Simmons, "In the days before hip-hop records were being made, Hollywood expanded the market in New York for MC-ing and break beats. . . . Of all the party rockers, Hollywood was the best entertainer."[17]

Another rap innovator, Jamaican immigrant **Kool Herc** (1955–), brought the Jamaican toasting and sound system culture to New York, spinning short sections of records and talking over them. He also played records on two turntables at the same time; with the aid of a sound mixer he faded in and out between records, sometimes mixing passages from one song into another. The artist often set up his massive speakers (called "Herculords") and turntables outside a housing project or a park. According to historian Robert Palmer,

> His dances attracted homegrown aspirants who begged for a chance to "get on the mike" and "rock the house," and an athletic new breed of "break" dancers who cut jerky, robot-like movements in with more fluid steps,

then flipped over and stood on their heads, spinning and whiplashing to the rhythms.[18]

A third pivotal force in the early days of rap was former gang member and DJ Africa Bambaataa, who organized the Zulu Nation to channel the anger of African American and Puerto Rican youths into music, dance, and graffiti art.

Grandmaster Flash (1958–), an electronics student by day, was early rap's technical genius who paved the way for record sampling:

> I was in the experimentation phase of trying to lock the beat together. I had to be able to hear the other turntable before I mixed it over. . . . I'm saying to myself, wow, how can I take these records and blend them on time, keep this music going without missing a beat.[19]

The wiring of twin turntables to a mixer allowed a performer to "scratch" the sound of two different records while rapping into a mike. Following Flash's invention of sampling, DJs began to tap into huge catalogs of records and other sounds. Sampling became hip-hop's link with history and tradition, according to Africa Bambaataa,

> Myself, I used to play the weirdest stuff at a party. . . . I'd throw on the Pink Panther theme for everybody who thought they was cool, and then I would play "Honky Tonk Woman" by the Stones and just keep that beat going. I'd play something from metal rock records like Grand Funk Railroad. . . . I'd throw on "Sergeant Pepper's Lonely Hearts Club Band"—just the drum part. . . . I'd throw on the Monkees.[20]

A consistent nomenclature developed. **Rap** was the term used to describe the spoken-word art of chanting rhymes over rhythmic accompaniment often made up of sampled sounds or scratched records. **Hip-hop** described the urban youth culture of music, dance, dress, speech, and art that was associated with— and included—rap music. Two distinct performance functions also emerged: the MC and the DJ. The **MC** worked the crowd at the front of the stage, performing raps and rhymes, mixing elements of slang, personal experience, and humor. MCs had to be authoritative, and "dissing" the competition became a cornerstone of early rap. The **DJ** (sometimes two DJs) worked the turntables to create musical collages and percussive scratching effects. They also employed techniques created by Grandmaster Flash such as *cutting* (moving between tracks exactly on the beat), *back-spinning* (manually turning records to repeat brief samples of sound), and phasing (manipulating turntable speeds).

At first, rap and hip-hop did not offer much competition to established performers and recording artists, but in 1979 one of disco's last hits, Chic's "Good Times," was sampled for its rhythm track to make rap's first commercial hit—"Rapper's Delight"

CD LISTENING EXERCISE

CD 2/20

Listen to an excerpt from "Rapper's Delight" (1979) by the Sugar Hill Gang. Heard through a contemporary ear, the rapping in "Rapper's Delight" sounds simplistic in its verbal flow, rhyme schemes, and rhythms. Notice how each spoken line is divided into predictable rhythms that fit within the ¼ meter of the tune. Contemporary MCs now rap across bar lines in less predictable ways by playing with the beat and sometimes ignoring the meter of the tune, creating complex spoken-word styles. Has the lyric content of rap changed as well?

(1979) by the Sugar Hill Gang. The song featured staccato wordplay and verbal dexterity layered over funk rhythms.

Grandmaster Flash and the Furious Five quickly followed with their own "Superrappin'" (1979), establishing a group sound in which different rappers alternated, taking a verse and infusing it with their own style. Flash next released "The Message" (1982), a piece demonstrating that hip-hop could be a vehicle of social commentary as well as dissing and boasting. **Kurtis Blow** (1959–) was one of rap's first solo performers on a major white-owned label (Mercury). Blow was managed by Russell Simmons, who soon became an entrepreneurial magnate of hip-hop music and culture. Blow struck a macho posture, in both lyrical content and attire, featuring a bare chest and heavy gold chains. Not to be up-staged, **Africa Bambaataa** (1960–) released his first major commercial record, "Planet Rock," in 1982. Sampling from German techno-rock group Kraftwerk and using a drum machine, Bambaataa gave birth to a sound he called electro-funk—combining the synthesized beats of disco and the sound-system bass of early Jamaican dancehall styles. Bambaataa also incorporated the new industrial sound that was influencing rock and heavy metal. "Planet Rock" paved the way for the introduction of funk, techno, and drum synthesizers into rap.

As rap developed, approaches to describing and differentiating the sounds of the genre also evolved. By the early 2000s, musicologists were devising aesthetic systems to classify the sounds of rap.

Internet Listening Exercise

Listen to samples of old-school rap.

Grandmaster Flash and the Furious Five: "The Message"

Kurtis Blow: "The Breaks"

Africa Bambaataa: "Planet Rock"

Emerging Aesthetic Categories of Rap

Flow

The term **flow** describes the rhythmic delivery of the spoken-word performance of the MC. Flow involves the increasingly complex rhythmic styles of the MC, timbre of the voice, as well as the quality of the rhymes. It is the flow of rap that has evolved most significantly over the life of the genre from old-school to contemporary styles.

Musical Style

The musical tracks that accompany the spoken word of the rap have become increasingly sophisticated. Common techniques include the use of sampling, accompanied by layering and loops of samples. Original bass and drum parts—usually synthesized—are also frequently used, often employing sophisticated polyrhythms.

Content of Lyrics

Lyrical content gets the most attention in critical media commentaries, yet content varies considerably. There are many sexual, misogynistic, and violent lyrics, but there are also political commentaries as well as classic exhortations to party.

Note: Adapted from Adam Krims, *Rap Music and the Poetics of Identity* (New York: Cambridge University Press, 2000), and Tricia Rose, *Black Noise: Rap Music and Black Culture in Contemporary America* (Hanover, NH: Wesleyan University Press, 1994).

Rap Legends Run-D.M.C. in 1988 (left to right): Run, Jam Master Jay, and D.M.C.

East Coast Rap

East Coast rap dominated much of the genre's first decade. The East Coast style gravitated toward aggressive beats and sample collages, and MCs prided themselves on their dexterity in crafting complex lyrics. By the late 1980s, East Coast rap had become a music intended as much for listening as for dancing, and the style started to gain respect as an art form. Although West Coast rap and southern rap became major forces in the 1990s, the East Coast continued as an important influence.

Rap's first superstars, **Run-D.M.C.,** catapulted the genre into the crossover mainstream. With spare beats and excursions into heavy metal, the trio were tougher and more menacing than their predecessors. Emerging from a middle-class section of Queens, Run-D.M.C. performed in street clothes such as black fedoras, unlaced Adidas sneakers, sweat suits, and warm-up jackets. The artists released their first single, "It's Like That"/"Sucker M.C.'s," in 1983, a hit that sounded like no other rap at the time—stripped down and spare, with hard beats, powerful vocals, and two MCs overlapping to finish each other's lines. Follow-up hits included "Hard Times"/"Jam Master Jay" (1983) and "Rock Box" (1984). Run-D.M.C.'s career peaked in 1986 with the album *Raising Hell,* which scored hip-hop's first MTV hit, "Walk This Way," performed with aging hard-rockers Aerosmith. When *Raising Hell* became rap's first platinum album, it elicited the first widespread coverage of hip-hop culture by the mainstream media. The group's use of the power of hard rock also pioneered the subsequent metal-rap hybrids that flavored much of the mainstream rock of the 1990s and early 2000s.

L. L. Cool J (James Todd Smith, 1968–) began his career with "I Can't Live without My Radio" (1986), which embodied the importance of music to African American youth. L. L. also developed an alternate "lover's rap" style epitomized by "I Need Love" (1987). His follow-up 1989 album, *Walking with a Panther,* featured an image of the artist with three black women, a bottle of champagne, a cell phone, and a panther on a thick gold chain. When criticized by more politicized rappers," L. L. responded with the Grammy-winning "Mama Said Knock You Out" (1990).

By the late 1980s, some were accusing popular rappers such as Run-D.M.C. and L. L. Cool J of having lost touch with the streets, and new groups such as Public Enemy, KRS-One, and XCLAN, which had political messages, stepped in. **Public Enemy,** the brainchild of a college student named Chuck D (Carlton Ridenhour, 1960–), became the most influential and controversial rap group of the late 1980s and, for many, the definitive rap group of all time. From their 1987 release, *Yo! Bum Rush the Show,* to their 1994 recording, *Muse Sick-N Our Mess Age,* Public Enemy set the standard for political—or "conscious"—rap. According to Chuck D,

> Everybody in rap at that time was talking about gold chains and being stupid, and . . . I wanted to find a new direction. . . . What always gave rap a leg up on other music was the anger in it, but the anger was always directed at other rappers. . . . When we came along, we decided to direct our anger at something real.[21]

As hip-hop's leading public intellectual, Chuck D pointed to the spiritual and physical maladies of urban America. In a much-quoted statement, he called rap "the black CNN."

Musically, Public Enemy was just as revolutionary. Their production team, called the Bomb Squad, crafted a dense sound with unrecognizable samples, piercing sirens, and relentless beats. The group's second album, *It Takes a Nation of Millions to Hold Us Back* (1988), served as their most influential and innovative work. Major singles included "Bring the Noise" (1988), "Fight the Power" (1989 —done for Spike Lee's film *Do the Right Thing*), and "911 Is a Joke" (1990). Other socially conscious rappers included A Tribe Called Quest and De La Soul in the early 1990s, followed by Mos Def in the mid-1990s.

The most successful hip-hop entrepreneur and producer of the mid-1990s, **Sean Combs** (Puff Daddy or P. Diddy, 1970–) crafted appealing, groove-based party jams that often relied on rhythm tracks of familiar tunes. The Howard University graduate started his career producing hits for Mary J. Blige and Heavy D and the Boyz, and by 1993 he had his own firm, signing Craig Mack and multiplatinum artist Notorious B.I.G. Both soon found success—Mack with "Flava in Ya Ear" (1994) and B.I.G. with "Big Poppa" (1995). Combs also signed R & B vocalist Faith Evans, and he produced numerous artists for other labels. Acting out a mythical battle between East Coast and West Coast rap, Combs soon became embroiled in a set of tragic events. After he and B.I.G. began feud-

Internet Listening Exercise

Listen to samples of early East Coast rap.

Run-D.M.C.: "It's Like That"/"Sucker M.C.'s," "Walk This Way,"

L. L. Cool J: "I Can't Live without My Radio," "I Need Love"

Internet Listening Exercise

Listen to samples of conscious rap.

Public Enemy: "Bring the Noise," "Fight the Power," "911 Is a Joke"

A Tribe Called Quest: "Check the Rhime"

Mos Def: "Black Star"

**Internet
Listening Exercise**

Listen to samples of work produced or performed by Sean Combs.

Mary J. Blige: "You Remind Me"

Craig Mack: "Flava in Ya Ear"

Notorious B.I.G.: "Big Poppa"

Puff Daddy: "I'll Be Missing You," "It's All about the Benjamins"

**Internet
Listening Exercise**

Listen to samples of work by leading female rappers.

Queen Latifah: "Ladies First," "U.N.I.T.Y."

Missy Elliott: "Get Ur Freak On," "Work It"

**Internet
Listening Exercise**

Listen to samples of tunes by Jay-Z.

Jay Z: "Ain't No Nigga/Dead Presidents," "Big Pimpin," "'03 Bonnie and Clyde"

ing with rapper 2Pac and Suge Knight, the head of L.A.'s Death Row Records, 2Pac was shot in 1996, and B.I.G. was shot in 1997. Combs subsequently issued his first solo album, the Grammy-winning *No Way Out* (1997), featuring a B.I.G. tribute called "I'll Be Missing You," as well as other songs of sorrow and anger. Subsequent misadventures diminished the artist's output in the late 1990s, but by the early 2000s he was starring in a Broadway revival of the classic African American drama by Lorraine Hansberry, *Raisin in the Sun*.

Although rap began as a male-dominated genre, some major female artists emerged, notably Salt-N-Pepa, MC Lyte, Queen Latifah, Lil' Kim, Foxy Brown, Eve, and Missy Elliott. **Queen Latifah** (Dana Owens, 1970–) was the first female rapper to become a major star. While in college, the New Jersey–born artist became influenced by the Afrocentric hip-hop philosophy of Afrika Bambaataa. Her first album, *All Hail the Queen* (1989), which contained the influential single "Ladies First," offered a mix of conscious hip-hop, reggae, and R & B. According to critic Gerri Hirshey, "The Queen has said that she is not so much about pan-feminism as about 'getting mine.' . . . 'Ladies First' . . . is the ultimate answer to James Brown's 'It's a Man's Man's Man's World,'"[22] Latifah was also the first female rapper to branch out into other media, appearing in numerous films.

Missy "Misdemeanor" Elliott (Melissa Elliott, 1971–) was the reigning female rapper of the early 2000s. Before breaking into rap, she worked as a writer, arranger, and producer in the 1990s, contributing to over twenty hit songs for divas such as Aaliyah, Whitney Houston, and Mariah Carey. Elliott established herself with her debut album, *Supa Dupa Fly*, in 1997, and she also became known for her stylish and eccentric videos. Hits included "She's a Bitch" (1999), the Grammy-winning "Get Ur Freak On" (1999), and "Work It" (2002).

Jay-Z (Shawn Carter, 1970–) dominated the New York rap scene in the late 1990s and early 2000s. Though catchy enough to become pop hits, his songs were sufficiently witty and detailed to maintain his hip-hop reputation. According to journalist Harry Allen, "Jay Z has great density. He writes very compact code. His lyrics do more per word than most artists'."[23] The artist's debut album, *Reasonable Doubt* (1996), showcased a hard-core gangsta flavor, but subsequent albums, such as *In My Lifetime* (1997), shifted to a more accessible pop-rap style. By the release of *Blueprint* (2001), the artist had secured his position at the top of the heap in New York rap. Hits included "Ain't No Nigga/Dead Presidents" (1996), "Big Pimpin" (2000), and "'03 Bonnie and Clyde" (2003). Jay-Z also experimented with interesting hybrids, including rapping over the Beatles' *White Album* and rapping over an Indian bhangra record.

West Coast Rap

The West Coast—mainly Los Angeles and Oakland—dominated hip-hop for much of the 1990s with **gangsta rap,** a toughened sound with gritty, street-level subject matter that reclaimed rap's primary function as party music. N.W.A., the L.A.-based group that introduced gangsta rap, also introduced important artists such as Ice Cube and Dr. Dre. Dre drove the West Coast sound of the 1990s, discovering Snoop Dog; developing a slow, rolling signature sound called G-funk; and shaping the sound of Death Row Records. Other important L.A. artists in the gangsta style were Ice-T, 2Pac, and Coolio; northward in Oakland, rapper Too Short produced a variant that extolled the pimp life. Additional artists active in the West included Oakland's pop rapper MC Hammer and funk-flavored Digital Underground, as well as Los Angeles' alternative jazz-rappers Pharcyde, Latino rappers Cypress Hill and Kid Frost, and Seattle's Sir Mix-A-Lot.

N.W.A. (Niggaz With Attitude) first appeared in Los Angeles in the late 1980s, capitalizing on the sonic breakthroughs of Public Enemy, while largely ignoring their social message. During its brief life, the group celebrated the violence and hedonism of the thug life in blunt language. The group's most influential record, *Straight Outta Compton* (1988), established gangsta rap and the West Coast sound with harsh raps written by MC Ice Cube (1969–) and innovative production by Dr. Dre (1965–). *Straight Outta Compton* gained a national audience with neither radio nor MTV support. The group also caught the attention of the FBI, who issued the group's record label a warning regarding the single "F———— tha Police." N.W.A. did not last long. Ice Cube was the first to leave in 1989, to score several successful solo albums as well as a lucrative film career. Dre went on to form Death Row Records with the unsavory Suge Knight. There, Dre produced his first solo album, *The Chronic* (1992), which established him as hip-hop's premier producer of the mid-1990s. His signature *G-funk* sound involved George Clinton–influenced synthesized bass, deep, rolling grooves, with whiny treble synthesizers on top. Together with Snoop Dog and 2Pac, Dre made Death Row the dominant hip-hop label of the early 1990s. Dre subsequently left Death Row, formed his own label, and did strong production work with Snoop Dogg, Eminem (whom he discovered), and the vocal group Blackstreet.

Ice-T (Tracy Morrow, 1959–) contributed to the founding of the L.A. gangsta rap sound. The New Jersey–born artist grew up in South Central Los Angeles and gained a national audience with *Rhyme Pays* (1987) and *O.G.: Original Gangster* (1991). He was criticized in the media—and gained career-enhancing exposure—for his 1992 song, "Cop Killer" (1992). Ice-T was also active in films and television.

Snoop Dogg (Calvin Broadus, 1972–) embodied 1990s gangsta rap. Discovered by Dr. Dre, Snoop grew famous for his slow, drawled rhyming. Dre's singles "Nuthin' but a 'G' Thang" and "Dre Day" prominently featured Snoop, and they became crossover hits in 1993. Snoop's hit solo album, *Doggystyle* (1993) yielded the hits "What's My Name" and "Gin and Juice." He subsequently scored several high-profile movie roles, and by the turn of the century, Snoop's albums were secondary to his clownish yet subversive media personality.

2Pac (Tupac Shakur, 1971–1996) was a definitive rapper of the 1990s, a compelling film presence, and an iconic hip-hop martyr with a taste for the

CD LISTENING EXERCISE

CD 2/21

Listen to L.A. based Chicano rap group Cypress Hill's 1993 hit "Insane in the Brain." Cypress Hill helped move gangsta rap performance beyond the confines of the African American community. The "in your face" style of gangsta rap dominated rap music in the 1990s. What is the musical appeal of this recording? Does their use of harsh language have the same shock value today that it might have had in the early 1990s?

Multicultural Note

Gangsta Rap, Violence, and Responsibility

The lyrics of gangsta rap engendered controversy from the style's inception. While some criticized the style for its misogyny and glorification of violence, others defended it as a reflection of inner-city life. Because record industry executives were usually more concerned with the bottom line than with social and political implications, the criticism directed at gangsta rap actually created the opportunity for multilevel marketing by media conglomerates. Further, because the parent companies of media giants such as AOL/Time Warner also owned most major record companies, a *Time* magazine cover story on the evils of gangsta rap could enrage one population segment while encouraging the sale of millions of records to another. Was gangsta rap a source of cultural empowerment for inner-city African Americans, an expression of violence and misogyny, a form of corporate manipulation, or some of each?

Internet Listening Exercise

Listen to samples of gangsta rap.

Ice Cube: "Once upon a Time in the Projects"

Dr. Dre: "The Chronic," "Dre Day"

Ice-T: "O.G. Original Gangster," "Cop Killer"

Snoop Dogg: "Nuthin' but a 'G' Thang," "Gin and Juice"

2Pac: "Dear Mama/Old School," "California Love"

N.W.A.: "Straight Outta Compton"

thug life. The New York–born artist followed his successful debut album, *2Pacalypse Now* (1992), with a strong acting performance in the film *Juice*. His 1995 album, *Me Against the World,* entered the charts at number one, followed by *All Eyez on Me* (1996), which produced "California Love." 2Pac enjoyed further successful acting roles, but the real gangsta world soon intervened, as his feud with rival Notorious B.I.G. ended with 2Pac's death in a drive-by shooting in 1996. Major hits by 2Pac included "Brenda's Got a Baby" (1992), "Keep Ya Head Up" (1994), and "Dear Mama/Old School" (1995).

Southern Rap

Southern rap, centered in Atlanta, Miami, and New Orleans, emerged in the 1990s as a fertile scene distinct from the East Coast and West Coast styles. Its earliest example appeared in the late 1980s with the work of Miami-based 2 Live Crew; Atlanta–produced artists such as Arrested Development, OutKast, Goodie Mob, and Ludacris; and New Orleans–produced Master P and his No Limit posse and Mystikal.

2 Live Crew popularized the booming, hard-driving sound of Miami bass music and a dance-oriented rap style with explicit chants and up-tempo grooves known as "booty rap." Group leader Luther Campbell and his crew ignited controversy with the graphic sexual content of their 1989 album, *As Nasty as They Wanna Be.* The album's hit single, "Me So Horny," climbed into the top forty despite nonexistent airplay.

OutKast—Andre Benjamin (Andre 3000, 1975–) and Antwan Patton (Big Boi, 1975–)—brought to rap an understanding of the roots of funk and soul, a command of rap flow and rhyme, and solid musical production skills. Starting out as rivals, the eclectic rappers teamed up and released their first hit single,

"Player's Ball," in 1994, followed by their debut album, *Southernplayalisticadillac-muzik*. With its easy funk groove, lyrics that reflected everyday life, and sample-free production, the record went platinum. OutKast's subsequent hit albums included *ATLiens* (1996) in which they imagined themselves as comic-book extraterrestrials; *Aquemini* (1998), featuring the single "Rosa Parks"; and *Stankonia* (2000), which included the hits "Ms. Jackson" and "So Fresh, So Clean." The stage was set for the 2003 release of the Grammy-winning *Speakerboxxx/The Love Below*, which produced multiple hits including "Hey Ya," "The Way You Move" (a collaboration with Earth, Wind, and Fire), and "Roses."

Ludacris (Chris Bridges, 1978–), who started out as a DJ in Atlanta, released the hit single, "What's Your Fantasy" (2000), followed by the album *Incognegro*. Supported by producers such as Timbaland and the Neptunes, the artist's *Word of Mouf* (2001) album yielded the hits "Area Codes" and "Saturday Ooh Ooh." Ludacris's rapid flow and comedic wit took center stage on his 2003 album, *Chicken-N-Beer*, which featured the hit "Stand Up." According to critic Touré, "Ludacris is one of the most liquid MCs in the game today. He varies his flows with such dexterity and has so much musicality in his tones that his mouth truly seems like an instrument."[24]

 **Internet Listening Exercise**

Listen to samples of southern rap.

2 Live Crew: "Me So Horny"

OutKast: "Hey Ya"

Ludacris: "Stand Up"

Multicultural Rap

Although predominantly an African American style, rap has had many other influences. As the genre expanded, Latino artists made contributions, as did white artists. Global developments in rap included French rapper MC Solaar as well as hybrids blending rap and Indian bhangra music. Rap and hip-hop culture came to reach around the globe, from Poland to Peru, Jamaica to Japan.

Latino artists made Spanish bilingual rap records as early as 1981, and U.S. Latino rap acts included Kid Frost, Cypress Hill, Mellow Man Ace, and Gerardo. The L.A.-based Kid Frost expanded rap's vocabulary by celebrating his Chicano heritage. His debut album, *Hispanic Causing Panic*, and his single "La Raza" (1990) became an anthem for Chicano hip-hop fans. In 1995 he shortened his name to Frost and recorded several more albums with a G-funk-influenced L.A. gangsta sound. L.A.-based Chicano rappers Cypress Hill were the first Latino hip-hop superstars. The group's slow, rolling bass-and-drum loops mirrored G-funk. The group's self-titled debut album in 1992 scored with "How I Could Just Kill a Man" and "The Phuncky Feel One," and *Black Sunday* (1993) produced the crossover hit "Insane in the Brain." Subsequent albums integrated rock, reggae, and rap.

White rappers also made names for themselves—some respected, some not. Major white rappers included the Beastie Boys, Vanilla Ice, Eminem, Kid Rock, and Everlast. The **Beastie Boys** were the first white artists to make hip-hop their main focus. By the time they recorded their 1984 single, "Rock Hard," they were deeply into rap, and their first album, *Licensed to Ill* (1986), mixed metal and rap. Their second album, *Paul's Boutique* (1989), prefigured much of the genre-bending eclecticism that would follow in 1990s rock, and they refined their approach with 1992's *Check Your Head*. Major singles included "(You Gotta) Fight for Your Right (to Party!)" (1987), "Hey Ladies" (1987), "Get It

Internet Listening Exercise

Listen to samples of Latino rappers.

Kid Frost: "La Raza"

Mellow Man Ace: "Mentirosa"

Various Latino Rappers; *Latin Lingo* (Rhino records)

Together" (1994), and "Intergalactic" (1998). As critic Neva Chonin observes, "No other hip-hop crew or rock band combines politics and surreal goofing so seamlessly." [25]

Eminem (Marshall Mathers, 1972–) became one of the top rappers of the early 2000s. A protégé of Dr. Dre, the artist emerged in 1999 with biting verbal skills, venting his displeasure on myriad topics. Originally from Detroit, Eminem worked to win over underground hip-hop audiences by battling other MCs in hard-core rap clubs. A tape of his music came to the attention of influential producer Dr. Dre, who was surprised to learn that Eminem was white, and Dre began to work with him. Major albums included *Slim Shady LP* (1999), *Marshall Mathers LP* (2000), and *The Eminem Show* (2002). Hit singles included "My Name Is" (1999), "The Real Slim Shady" (2000), and "The Way I Am" (2000). Eminem also helped discover and produce influential hard-core East Coast rapper 50 Cent, who topped the charts in the early 2000s.

TURNTABLISM AND SCRATCHING

The term *Turntablism* came about to describe a new style of music making developed by hip-hop DJs. It was coined to distinguish DJ techniques such as scratching and beat juggling from simple mixing. According to San Francisco–based DJ Pone, **scratching** "comes from the simple motion of moving a record back and forth to cue the record. Scratching has two primary components: moving a record back and forth, and turning the sound of the turntable off and on." [26]

Beat juggling occurs when DJs bounce back and forth between two grooves. A *turntablist* is a DJ who has mastered the live performance art of creating new sounds and grooves using two or more turntables. The blended recordings create a new composition that often leaves the original source of the music unrecognizable.

Because turntablism and scratching were closely tied to the development of hip-hop, rap, and acid-jazz, DJs became part of the standard instrumentation of many hip-hop and rock acts. One of the first recorded works of turntablism was Grandmaster Flash's "The Adventures of Grandmaster Flash on the Wheels of Steel" (1981). DJ Grandmixer DST's scratching on Herbie Hancock's hit fusion tune "Rockit" (1983) provides another early example. DJ Jazzy Jeff's turntablist work with Will Smith, when the latter was known as the Fresh Prince, on *He's the DJ, I'm the Rapper* (1987) also exemplified the early development of the style. Turntablism gained respect in the mid-1990s as scratch DJs moved from beat juggling and live remixing to the composition of original music

CD LISTENING EXERCISE

CD 2/3

Listen to "Razor Blade Alcohol Slide" by DJ Q-Bert. Turntablism turned the art of scratching into a new form of electronic composing. DJ Q-Bert created an entirely new musical composition that might be described as a sound collage. How does Q-Bert's work compare with that of a traditional DJ? Do you think that turntablism will ever make it into the top forty?

via turntables. DJ Q-Bert's recording of "Razor Blade Alcohol Slide" from the album *Wave Twisters* (1996) stood as a strong example of pure turntablism.

ELECTRONICA

Beginning in the 1980s, dance music became the musical home for a host of electronically generated musical styles now referred to as **electronica.** Many critics suggest that the German group Kraftwerk initiated the electronica movement, which subsequently evolved into such subgenres as house, techno, trance, jungle, drum 'n' bass, trip-hop, breakbeat, and newer hybrids including acid house and ambient-house. Early electronica first became popular in the disco and postdisco club scenes of Great Britain and Western Europe before migrating to the United States. Electronica further evolved in the late 1980s and 1990s in Britain as the soundtrack for **raves**—all-night parties held in fields, farms, or warehouses. DJs played acid house, trance, and other styles of electronica including techno until dawn, and a new drug called Ecstasy often fueled the dancing. The rave culture spread to the United States in the 1990s, but it never achieved the same degree of popularity as it had in Europe.

The Evolving Styles of Electronica

Multiple genres of electronica developed over two decades. Codification of the principal styles of electronica saw continuous flux, subjecting it to a variety of interpretations.

House music emerged in Chicago in the early 1980s as a postdisco underground dance style that was initially popular in black and gay clubs. The term *house* came from "The Warehouse"—the name of the club where the style originated. The disco-influenced style was propelled by an insistent ¾ beat and deep bass, overlaid with Latin soul, synth-pop, reggae, rap, or jazz. Early hits in-

Music Industry Note

The Development of MIDI

The evolution of electronically generated dance music depended largely on the development of the personal computer and the interface between computers and synthesizers known as musical instrument digital interface—*MIDI*. The interface created new options in music that included digital recording and mixing, as well as the creation of pure electronic music. MIDI allowed computers, electronic musical instruments, synthesizers, and other forms of digital processing to be synchronized. This enabled musicians to create new, electronically generated music in real time.

cluded "On and On" by Jesse Saunders, "Jack Your Body" by Steve "Silk" Hurley, and "Move Your Body—The House Music Anthem" by Marshall Jefferson. By the late 1980s, the style had spread to Detroit, New York, and London, and it appeared in the work of popular artists such as Madonna. As the house style spread, an offshoot called **acid house** became the first popular music of the rave scene. "Where's Your Child" by Bam Bam exemplified acid house. In the United States, the popularity of house peaked in the 1990s, but it remained popular in Europe into the early 2000s.

Techno emerged from the Detroit house music scene of the mid-1980s. Techno innovator Derrick May credited Kraftwerk's influence, describing the style as "Sounding like George Clinton and Kraftwerk stuck in an elevator with only a sequencer to keep them company."[27] A completely electronic style, techno remained primarily an underground phenomenon until the early 1990s. "The Bells" by Jeff Mill, "Innovator" by Derrick May, and "Faces and Phases" by Kevin Saunderson embodied the style.

Trance music focused on brief, repeated synthesizer lines looped (repeated) over and over with minimal variations and occasional "ear candy"—synthesized musical effects—layered on top of a trance-inducing basic rhythm track. In the late 1990s and early 2000s, trance became one of the most popular electronic dance styles worldwide. Recorded examples of trance included "An Accident in Paradise" by Sven Vath and "Sandstorm" by Darude.

The terms *breakbeat* and *trip-hop* first appeared in the English press in the early 1990s to describe a new style of electronica that emulated jazz, funk, and soul-inflected, hip-hop grooves. With rhythmic roots in funk, **breakbeat** emphasized syncopation and clearly defined percussion, with a heavy backbeat on beats two and four. Rhythmic breaks also occurred, in which all musical elements were suddenly suspended, creating a kind of "musical hiccup." "Take California" by the Propeller Heads was an example of breakbeat. **Trip-hop** was usually wordless, and it reflected a more ambient, psychedelic quality than did traditional hip-hop. One of the first styles of electronica to reach the musical mainstream, trip-hop remained popular into the early 2000s. Examples of trip-hop could be found on the albums *Nine Deadly Venoms* by Depth Charge and *Massive Attack* by Blue Lines.

Drum 'n' bass and *jungle* were closely related styles that critics often compared to American hip-hop. Both styles relied on electronic drums and deep bass played at frenetic tempos to create high-energy music. **Drum 'n' bass** was also blended with jazz, reggae, dub, calypso, and trip-hop to create new sounds. **Jungle** was an electronica style with British origins that featured the use of a deep resonant bass for the melody. Examples of drum 'n' bass include "Warhead" by DJ Krust and "Inner-City Life" by Goldie.

One of the most experimental components of electronica, **ambient** music had a formlessness that sometimes caused people to call it "space music." The lack of steady tempo and definable melody made limitless variations possible. Almost any sound could be mixed with another to create ambient music, and most electronica styles incorporated some ambient-infused derivatives. Brian Eno became one of the best-known proponents of the style.

Internet Listening Exercise

Listen to samples of different styles of electronica.

House Music: Steve "Silk" Hurley, "Jack Your Body"

Acid House: Bam Bam, "Where's Your Child"

Techno: Kevin Saunderson, "Bassline"

Trance: Darude, "Sandstorm"

Trip-Hop: Blue Lines, "Blue Lines"

Drum 'n' Bass: DJ Krust, "Warhead"

Ambient: Brian Eno, *Music for Airports*

Major Electronica Artists

Kraftwerk was the best-known group in the electronica genre, as well as the band most often cited as its progenitor. According to historian Simon Reynolds,

> Kraftwerk invented the pristine, posthuman pop phuture we now inhabit. The story of techno begins not in the early 80s Detroit, as is so often claimed, but in the early 70s Düsseldorf, where Kraftwerk built their Klingklang sound factory and churned out pioneering synth-and-drum-machine tracks like "Autobahn," "Trans-Europe Express," and "The Man-Machine." [28]

The group first appeared in 1970 with a minimalist, rhythmic, electronically generated sound that subsequently became a worldwide model for electronica. The group's first hit was the title song from the album *Autobahn* (1975), featuring the distinctive sound of the early Moog synthesizer. The group followed up with a string of albums that included *Trans-Europe Express* (1977), *The Man Machine* (1978), and *Computer World* (1981). Kraftwerk also developed a following in the African American hip-hop community, and Afrika Bambaataa borrowed directly from two Kraftwerk songs—"Trans-Europe Express" and "The Numbers"—for his 1982 hit, "Planet Rock." Derrick May, one of the founders of techno, also credited Kraftwerk as a direct influence. Kraftwerk toured and recorded into the early 2000s, performing on a bare stage with laptop computers, while a computer-controlled light show was projected behind them.

Moby was one of the few individual artists in the field of electronica to achieve major commercial success. His ability to mix techno-style grooves into a song-oriented format made his music accessible. The artist's self-titled album included his first major hit, "Go" (1992), and it was credited with bringing rave music into the commercial mainstream. Moby briefly moved away from electronica toward alternative rock in the mid-1990s, but he redeemed himself in the eyes of techno fans with the release of *Play* (1999). The album provided an eclectic mix of sounds crafted into a collage of seductive new dance grooves and melodies that sold over ten million copies.

Over the last thirty-five years, the musical descendants of R & B have become influential components of American popular music and culture. As of the early 2000s, complex blends of R & B, hip-hop, dance pop, and electronica continue to evolve, redefining the shape of American popular music.

Internet Listening Exercise

Listen to samples of well-known electronica artists.

Kraftwerk: "Autobahn"

Moby: "Go"

Chapter Summary

- Technological changes dominated the development of American popular music in the last three decades of the twentieth century. Major innovations included synthesizers, personal computers, personal listening devices, CDs, music television, digital recording/editing hardware and software, and Internet file sharing in the MP3 format.

- Seventies R & B was flavored in part by funk, in part by the 1970s soul of Stevie Wonder and Al Green, and in part by the smooth grooves of Philadelphia ("Philly") soul.

- The disco era dominated the popular music of the mid-1970s. Artists such as Donna Summer, Barry White, and the Bee Gees became household names as the era climaxed with the film *Saturday Night Fever* in 1977.

- The development of music television in 1981 changed the way music was disseminated and promoted. This coincided with the emergence of a new generation of dance pop music exemplified by superstars such as Michael Jackson, Madonna, and Prince.

- The R & B of the 1980s and 1990s was dominated by the smooth urban contemporary sound, New Jack Swing, neo-soul, and multiple generations of divas and vocal groups.

- The release of "Rappers Delight" in 1979 signaled the beginning of the hip-hop era. Rap and the hip-hop culture that surrounded it evolved into a variety of styles and subcultures including East Coast, West Coast, and southern rap. Rap also influenced a variety of other styles including rock, electronica, and R & B.

- Electronica developed from disco-era music styles and the invention of the synthesizer. Subsequently, electronically generated music played a dominant role in dance music for three decades. This led to the evolution of the role of the DJ from record spinner to musician and composer, an evolution that also resulted from the development of scratching and turntablism.

Key Terms

acid house	flow	rap
ambient	gangsta rap	raves
beat juggling	hip-hop	sampling
blaxploitation movies	house music	scratching
breakbeat	jungle	techno
disco	MC	trance
DJ	MP3	trip-hop
drum 'n' bass	neo-soul	VJ
electronica	New Jack Swing	
file sharing	Philadelphia soul	

Study and Discussion Questions

1. How did the technological developments of the last three decades of the twentieth century affect popular music in America and the world? In your opinion, which developments had the most significant impact?

2. What is funk? What were its musical origins? What role did funk play in 1970s music and in subsequent genres?

3. Why was Stevie Wonder considered one of the greatest artists of the 1970s? What contributions to the development of R & B did he make ?

4. What were the key features of the disco era? Who were the biggest stars, and what led to the era's demise?

5. How did MTV affect the marketing and distribution of music?

6. How did Michael Jackson become one of the biggest stars in pop music history? What musical elements pushed Jackson to the top, and what was his role in breaking MTV's color barrier?

7. What role did Madonna play in the evolving image of women in popular culture? How did she maintain her star status for more than twenty years?

8. What are the roots of rap? Trace the evolution of contemporary rap from old-school styles to the early 2000s. Who were the major artists and how did the music evolve?

9. Was gangsta rap a voice of the inner city, an example of corporate manipulation and internalized racism, or a combination of these elements?

10. What is electronica? What were its primary styles, and how did it impact dance pop music during the last two decades of the twentieth century? What is turntablism?

Notes

1. Robert Christgau, "Al Green," in *Rolling Stone Illustrated History of Rock and Roll*, edited by Jim Miller (New York: Random House/Rolling Stone Press, 1980), 361.

2. "Past Honorees: Stevie Wonder," The Kennedy Center Honors, 1999, http://www.kennedy-center.org/programs/specialevents/honors/history/honoree/wonder.html, accessed May 12, 2005.

3. Jim Miller, "The Sound of Philadelphia," in *Rolling Stone Illustrated History of Rock and Roll*, edited by Jim Miller (New York: Random House/Rolling Stone Press, 1980), 373.

4. Nelson George, *The Death of Rhythm and Blues* (New York: Penguin Books, 1998), 124.

5. Rickey Vincent, *Funk: The Music, the People, and the Rhythm of the One* (New York: St. Martin's, 1996), 187–88.

6. Arthur Kempton, *Boogaloo: The Quintessence of American Popular Music* (New York: Pantheon, 2003), 402.

7. Alan Light, "Rap and Soul: From the Eighties Onward," in *Rolling Stone Illustrated History of Rock and Roll,* 3rd ed., edited by Anthony DeCurtis and James Henke (New York: Random House, 1992), 684.

8. Gerri Hirshey, *We Gotta Get Out of This Place: The True, Tough Story of Women in Rock* (New York: Atlantic Monthly Press, 2001), 149–50.

9. Nelson George, *Buppies, B-Boys, BAPs and BoHos: Notes on Post-Soul Black Culture* (Cambridge, MA: Da Capo Press, 2001), 201.

10. Vincent, *Funk,* 305.

11. Hirshey, *We Gotta Get Out of This Place,* 175.

12. George, *Death of Rhythm and Blues,* 154.

13. *Rolling Stone Magazine,* April 15, 2004, 124.

14. Hirshey, *We Gotta Get Out of This Place,* 128.

15. Tricia Rose, *Black Noise: Rap Music and Black Culture in Contemporary America* (Hanover, NH: Wesleyan University Press, 1994), 2.

16. Robert Farris Thompson, "Hip-Hop 101," in *Droppin' Science: Critical Essays on Rap Music and Hip-Hop Culture,* edited by William Eric Perkins (Philadelphia: Temple University Press, 1996), 215.

17. Russell Simmons with Nelson George, *Life and Def: Sex, Drugs, Money, and God* (New York: Crown, 2001), 36–37.

18. Robert Palmer, *Rock and Roll: An Unruly History* (New York: Harmony Books, 1995), 281.

19. William Eric Perkins, ed., *Droppin' Science: Critical Essays on Rap Music and Hip-Hop Culture* (Philadelphia: Temple University Press, 1996), 7.

20. Ibid., 8.

21. Ibid., 21.

22. Hirshey, *We Gotta Get Out of This Place,* 148.

23. Quoted in Touré, "Superstardom Is Boring: Jay-Z Quits (Again)," *New York Times,* November 16, 2003, p. 23.

24. Touré, "Ludacris CD Review," http://www.rollingstone.com/reviews/cd/review. asp?aid=2047638&cf=78466, accessed May 14, 2005.

25. Neva Chonin, "Beasties Keep Rocking the Mike at BFD," June 14, 2004, http://sfgate.com/cgi-bin/article.cgi?file=/chronicle/archive/2004/06/14/DDGBF74FLE1.DTL, accessed May 14, 2005.

26. Interview with the authors.

27. Simon Reynolds, *Generation Ecstasy: Into the World of Techno and Rave Culture* (New York: Little, Brown, 1999), 14.

28. Ibid., 15.

1970 - 2000

1970 Led Zeppelin and Black Sabbath pave the way for heavy metal ♪
1970 The Carpenters hit number one with "Close to You" ♪
1971 Massive antiwar demonstrations
1971 Carole King releases *Tapestry* ♪
1971 Deaths of Jim Morrison (the Doors) and Duane Allman (Allman Brothers Band) ♪
1973 Led Zeppelin breaks box-office touring records: Stadium rock is born ♪
1973 Pink Floyd releases *Dark Side of the Moon,* which stays in the top 200 albums for 14 years ♪
1974 President Nixon resigns over Watergate
1974 Punk takes off; the Ramones become house band at CBGB's; Patti Smith releases first record ♪
1974 Joni Mitchell goes electric with *Court and Spark* ♪
1975 Bruce Springsteen hits the charts with "Born to Run" ♪
1976 Elton John has three number-one hits in one year ♪
1976 The Eagles' first greatest hits album becomes the biggest-selling domestic album in history ♪
1977 Fleetwood Mac releases *Rumours* ♪
1977 Elvis Presley dies ♪
1977 The Clash record their first album ♪
1978 Metalists Van Halen release their first album ♪

1980s Rock splinters into new genres—new wave, post punk, and synth-pop; heavy metal subgenres appear ♪
1981 AIDS epidemic first recognized
1981 MTV is born ♪
1982 Compact disc is invented and recorded music goes digital ♪
1983 David Bowie's "Let's Dance" hits number one with Stevie Ray Vaughan on guitar ♪
1983 Metallica blends metal with punk on *Kill 'em All* ♪
1984 Bruce Springsteen releases his biggest hit, *Born in the USA* ♪
1986 First annual inductions into the Rock and Roll Hall of Fame ♪
1987 Paul Simon releases *Graceland* recorded with South African musicians ♪
1987 U2 hits number one with *The Joshua Tree* ♪
1989 Berlin Wall falls; Cold War fades

1990s American economic high-tech "bubble"
1990s Alternative styles start to emerge, blending punk, metal, singer-songwriter, funk, and rap into new hybrids ♪
1990s The Internet age and digital online file sharing grow steadily into the early 2000s ♪
1991 First Persian Gulf War
1991 Grunge sound breaks through with Nirvana's *Nevermind* ♪
1992 Los Angeles riots/uprising following Rodney King trial
1992 Second-generation singer-songwriters Annie Lennox and Tori Amos release their first albums ♪
1992 Seattle becomes ground zero for grunge ♪
1994 Nirvana's Kurt Cobain dies; Green Day and Weezer debut ♪
1995 Alanis Morrisette's "Jagged Little Pill" breaks sales records for a solo artist; Neil Young and Pearl Jam collaborate ♪

2000s Classic rock 1960s bands mount repeated reunion tours ♪
2001 9/11 terrorist attacks

1970   **1980**   **1990**   **2000**

Chapter 17

Rock after the 1960s

Rock music continued to develop over the final three decades of the twentieth century. The high-energy acid rock of the 1960s led to hard rock, which branched into arena rock and heavy metal by the end of the decade. The 1970s followed with an explosion of a large palette of rock styles: southern and country rock emerged, blending country influences with hard rock and blues roots; the singer-songwriter tradition initiated earlier by Bob Dylan and the Beatles expanded; art rock—an eclectic blend of rock, classical music, jazz and other styles—developed; and soft rock emerged to offer an easy-listening alternative. To fill the void created by soft rock and to rebel against disco, the punk movement emerged in the late 1970s, returning rock to a harder-edged sound. Punk was followed in the 1980s by new wave, synth pop, and post-punk. The 1980s also saw the beginning of a fascination with world music. In the 1990s, rock styles that had come of age in the 1960s and 1970s blended to form many new hybrids; by the turn of the century, rock artists had hybridized genres as diverse as punk, heavy metal, hip-hop, funk, blues, psychedelic rock, and garage rock to produce an alternative rock sound that became the new mainstream.

IN THIS CHAPTER

- Hard Rock Branches Out
- Arena Rock
- Heavy Metal
- Southern Rock and Country Rock
- Art Rock
- Singer-Songwriters
- Soft Rock
- World Music
- Punk and Its Descendants
- Hybrid Styles of the 1990s and Early 2000s

HARD ROCK BRANCHES OUT

The aggressive, high-volume rock of the late 1960s laid the groundwork for **hard rock** and **heavy metal.** Both styles subsequently diversified into an array of substyles: hard rock branched into mainstream arena rock, southern rock, and art rock; heavy metal morphed into thrash metal, funk metal, and nu metal. Two defining musical ingredients of early hard rock were the power trio ensemble and guitar-bass unison riffs. The *power trio,* originally a British concept embodied by the Jimi Hendrix Experience and Cream, stripped the rock band to its core: drums, bass, and lead guitar. The *unison-riff style* was comprised of riffs played repeatedly in unison by the bass and guitar to create a hypnotic effect. While hard rock and heavy metal share many musical traits, most fans and critics acknowledge some distinctions between the two styles.

Differences Between Hard Rock and Heavy Metal

Hard Rock	*Heavy Metal*
• Diverse range of additional musical styles including rock ballads and "unplugged" (acoustic) material	• Lead vocal styles rooted in high-pitched, aggressive singing/shouting
• Complex song forms with varying degrees of harmonic sophistication	• Limited harmonic choices
• Wide assortment of lead vocal styles	• Heavy reliance on blues roots
• Diverse instrumentation, including synthesizer and keyboards	• Standard power trio instumentation, often with guitar or keyboard added
• Broad range of song subjects	• Dark song subjects such as fear, loneliness, death, social decay, and the occult
• Fans across a wide demographic spectrum	• Fans often predominantly young white men

 **Internet Listening Exercise**

Listen to two seminal hard-rock power trios playing in the guitar-bass unison riff style.

Jimi Hendrix Experience: "Manic Depression"

Cream: "Sunshine of Your Love"

Led Zeppelin is often cited as the godfather of hard rock and heavy metal. Guitarist Jimmy Page's Hendrix-influenced playing and vocalist Robert Plant's high-pitched, screamed delivery defined the British group's aggressive, high-volume style. Led Zeppelin's theatricality in live performance became a hallmark, as one fan recalled,

> They flailed around like dervishes, making so much sound the air was heavy with metal. Two hours after the lights went out, as the band sauntered offstage, the audience was a delirious, raving, parched mass crawling through the rock and roll desert thirsting for an encore.[1]

Zeppelin's music reflected the electric Chicago blues, as well as Celtic folk music, mythology, and the occult. One of the band's most popular songs, "Stairway to Heaven," featured an elaborate arrangement that moved from acoustic folk instrumentation to a full-blown, heavy metal finale. Other tunes such as "Whole Lotta Love" (1970) and "Dazed and Confused" (1969) still receive frequent airplay. Led Zeppelin formed in England in 1968 and toured frequently in the United States during the early 1970s, performing in stadiums and laying the foundation for arena rock. The group's theatrics created a spectacle, generating enough musical energy to satisfy an audience of 15,000—well before the invention of giant projection television screens. By 1973 they had broken the Beatles' box-office records, and by 1975 Zeppelin had become the most popular rock band in the world.

The late 1960s produced other influential hard rock groups, including Steppenwolf and Deep Purple. Formed in Los Angeles in 1967, Steppenwolf was

Hard-rock legends Led Zeppelin performing in the mid-1970s (left to right): Robert Plant, John Paul Jones, and Jimmy Page.

known primarily for the hit "Born to Be Wild" (1968). The song appeared on the soundtrack of the counterculture film *Easy Rider,* and its lyrics contained the prescient term *heavy metal thunder.* Deep Purple, formed in Britain in 1968, performed up through the 1990s. The group's sound started out as a blend of rock and classical keyboard styles, but by the early 1970s it had shifted to the hard-rock sound heard in "Smoke on the Water" (1973).

ARENA ROCK

Led Zeppelin's stadium-show success encouraged other bands with hard-rock roots to take a similar path, even though a successful arena rock concert required sales of over 10,000 tickets. The sound of **arena rock** was thus born, characterized by highly amplified music, songs that often made use of rock clichés and hooks, and exaggerated stage performance techniques, in order to be seen and heard in large sports arenas or venues of similar size.

One of the most successful and long-lived hard-rock bands of the era, **Aerosmith** formed in 1970 and remained active into the early 2000s. Fronted by Steve Tyler, a Mick Jagger lookalike, Aerosmith produced its first hit song, "Dream On" (1975); this became the model for the **power ballad,** which featured high-energy vocals and driving rhythms played at a slow tempo. They followed with "Walk This Way" (1976), went into decline, and later staged

Internet Listening Exercise

Listen to samples of early hard rock.

Led Zeppelin: "Whole Lotta Love," "Dazed and Confused," "Stairway to Heaven"

Deep Purple: "Smoke on the Water"

CD LISTENING EXERCISE

CD 2/22

As you listen to "Born to Be Wild" (1968) by Steppenwolf, pay attention to each instrument in the band. How do the parts interact to create the foundations of hard rock? How would you describe the vocal style? What is the guitar's tone? Does the title, repeated in the chorus, work as an effective hook?

a comeback in the 1980s with the help of MTV. Their collaboration with Run-D.M.C. on "Walk This Way" (1986) was the first successful blend of rap and hard rock.

The Doobie Brothers started as a mellow Northern California bar band in 1970, ultimately becoming a soul-inflected arena-rock act. The band's best-known work occurred with Michael McDonald as lead vocalist in the mid-1970s. Major hits included "Listen to the Music" (1972), "What a Fool Believes" (1978), and "Minute by Minute" (1979). McDonald subsequently left the band for a successful solo career. In the mid-1970s, Boston found arena-rock success with one of the fastest-selling debut albums in rock history. The band was assembled by guitarist and MIT-trained mechanical engineer Tom Scholz, who produced most of their first records in an early home studio. Hits included "More Than a Feeling" (1976), "Don't Look Back" (1978), and "Amanda" (1986).

Journey was a high-profile, San Francisco–based group formed in 1973 by alumni of the Santana band. The group scored its biggest hits with the release of *Infinity* (1978) and *Escape* (1981), which included the hit single "Who's Crying Now." With their youthful good looks, the group benefited from the advent of MTV and continued to release successful albums through the 1980s. New York–based Foreigner's unique blend of keyboard-driven heavy metal with a pop-oriented sound achieved a mainstream success rarely garnered by harder-edged metal bands. Their debut album, *Foreigner* (1977), yielded the hits "Cold as Ice" and "Feels Like the First Time." They followed it with *Double Vision* (1978), which yielded the single "Hot Blooded." Another major hard-rock act, Bon Jovi, gained popularity in the 1980s. Founded by New Jersey–based guitarist John Bongiovi in 1983, the band's record company "de-ethnicized" the artist's Italian surname to "Bon Jovi." For their second album, *Slippery When Wet* (1986), the band test-marketed potential album tracks to New York–area teens, resulting in massive sales. The album yielded hits with "You Give Love a Bad Name" and "Livin' on a Prayer," and MTV featured the band heavily.

HEAVY METAL

With consistent ingredients and simplicity of form, heavy metal and its descendants offered one of the clearest evolutionary timelines in rock. The genre was also home to a devoted, predominantly youthful, white male fan base that developed into its own subculture over a period of thirty years. The British band **Black Sabbath** emerged in 1970 as the progenitor of the heavy metal style: "Mixing equal parts bone-crushing volume, catatonic tempos, and ominous pronouncements of doom and gloom delivered in [lead singer] Ozzy Osbourne's keening voice, Black Sabbath was the heavy metal king of the 70s." [2] The group's message of social decay, death, and darkness, infused with allusions to Satanism and the occult, came to typify heavy metal. As historian Robert Palmer observes, "Black Sabbath, borrowing their name from a lurid mid-1960s horror film, link the hoodoo traditions of the blues to a B-movie version of European occultism and take blues-based rock one step beyond—into heavy metal." [3] Though panned by critics and receiving almost no airplay, Sabbath's second album, *Paranoid* (1971), sold over four million copies. A darkly gothic poem printed on the

www **Internet Listening Exercise**

Listen to samples of arena-rock bands of the 1970s and 1980s.

Aerosmith: "Walk This Way"

Doobie Brothers: "Listen to the Music," "Minute by Minute"

Boston: "More than a Feeling"

Journey: "Who's Crying Now"

Foreigner: "Hot Blooded"

Bon Jovi: "Livin' on a Prayer"

band's first album, set inside an inverted crucifix, summed up what one critic called the band's "cheesy, comic-book demonology":[4]

> Still falls the rain, the veils of darkness shroud the
> blackened trees, which contorted by some unseen violence,
> shed their tired leaves, and bend their boughs toward a
> grey earth of severed bird wings. Among the grasses,
> poppies bleed before a gesticulating death, and young
> rabbits, born dead in traps, stand motionless, as though
> guarding the silence that surrounds and threatens to
> engulf all those who would listen.[5]

Numerous bands in Britain and the United States jumped on the heavy metal bandwagon in the 1970s and early 1980s, including a host of British groups that were called the "new wave" of British heavy metal: Judas Priest, Def Leppard, Iron Maiden, Motörhead, and AC/DC. In the United States, theatrical artists such as Kiss and Alice Cooper laid the groundwork for subsequent U.S. metal bands Van Halen, Mötley Crüe, and Twisted Sister to emerge out of the L.A. rock scene in the 1970s. Many of the groups came to be called "hair bands," for their long-hair styles.

By the late 1970s, when elements of punk began to enter the metal reper-toire, "faster and louder" became the new mantra. One of the first metal bands to incorporate punk was the British group Motörhead. The U.S. group Metal-lica pushed the style further, playing a central role in creating a new subgenre called *power metal* and eventually moving into **thrash metal.** According to his-torian Ian Christe, "While power metal was heavy metal on steroids, thrash metal's repeated fluttering notes lifted effortlessly into flight. This music was

Multicultural Note

Exploring the Culture of Heavy Metal

The culture of heavy metal is an interesting hybrid. Its musicians and fans are pre-dominantly young, white working-class men. Over the years, heavy metal perfor-mance regalia has included long hair, tight leather clothing, makeup, outsized jew-elry, and stage sets that look as if Edgar Allen Poe and Adolf Hitler had collaborated in their design. Song themes often center on mayhem and destruction, and many groups also affect umlauts (¨) in their names, possibly to project a fantasized Germanic/Aryan identity. Some have embraced neo-Nazi imagery.

Many researchers have argued that heavy metal symbols signify youthful alien-ation, in the same way that punk does. Some claim that young white working-class men have used heavy metal to express feelings of frustration. Researchers have also argued that androgynous performance images of men in tight leather pants who have long, carefully coiffed hair and makeup, as well as violent themes of dark-ness, death, and hostility, may signify a quest for identity. What is the lasting appeal of heavy metal culture?

in motion, an intricate flood of enormous sound."[6] Other thrash metal bands included Anthrax, Slayer, and Death Angel. From there the style hybridized in the 1990s, producing funk metal and nu metal.

Several bands emerged as heavy metal took off in the 1970s and 1980s. Van Halen was one of the most popular American metal bands of the 1970s. Guitarist Eddie Van Halen developed several new electric guitar techniques that made innovative use of the instrument's neck and fretboard. The band emerged out of the Los Angeles club scene with a debut album, *Van Halen* (1978), which sold over six million copies. The act received significant MTV airplay in the early 1980s, and Eddie Van Halen's guitar solo on Michael Jackson's "Beat It" (1983) helped make the song a hit. Formed in Los Angeles in the mid-1980s, Mötley Crüe's live shows featured elaborate sets, fireworks, and female dancers. With its members' high-profile L.A. lifestyles, the band benefited from constant media exposure. Hit albums included the multiplatinum *Girls, Girls, Girls* (1987), *Dr. Feelgood* (1989), and *Decade of Decadence – '81 – '91* (1991). Although other British metalists such as Judas Priest and Iron Maiden sold millions of albums in the 1980s, Def Leppard was the most successful British metal band of the decade. Sometimes called a "pop-metal" act because of its clean, well-produced sound, Def Leppard's good looks meshed with the explosion of 1980s metal on MTV; in the words of one magazine, the group was "the heavy metal band you can bring home to mother."[7] The group scored its first major hit with *Pyromania* (1982), followed by *Hysteria* (1987), which yielded the hits "Pour Some Sugar on Me" and "Love Bites."

Metallica, one of the most innovative and influential American metal bands of the 1980s and 1990s, formed in Los Angeles in 1981. Ignoring the look and sound of reigning hair bands, the group instead ingested the energy of punk to craft the intense, sophisticated sound that came to be called thrash metal. Metallica's work featured complex song structures and lyrics dealing with personal and political issues. The act debuted with *Kill 'em All* (1984), but not until the release of *Metallica* (1991) did they chart at number one. Their success continued into the next decade.

Internet Listening Exercise

Listen to samples of influential heavy metal bands.

Black Sabbath: "Paranoid," "Iron Man"

Van Halen: "And the Cradle Will Rock," "Oh, Pretty Woman"

Mötley Crüe: "Smokin' in the Boys Room," "Home Sweet Home"

Def Leppard: "Rock of Ages," "Pour Some Sugar on Me"

Metallica: "No Remorse," "Until It Sleeps"

SOUTHERN ROCK AND COUNTRY ROCK

Southern rock—and its close cousin, country rock—appeared in the late 1960s and early 1970s. Southern rock was bluesy and aggressive, while country rock projected a more relaxed feel. Both styles contributed to the contemporary country music of the 1990s.

Southern Rock

Southern rock blended blues, R & B, country, and gospel with the aggressive feel of hard rock, drawing from the blues-rock of the late 1960s as well as honky-tonk and the Bakersfield sound to create a distinctive fusion. During the early 1970s, southern rock stood at the cutting edge of American hard rock.

Southern-rock innovators the Allman Brothers Band in an early publicity photo.

Pivotal to the emergence of southern rock, the **Allman Brothers** elaborated on the improvisational tendencies and loudness of Cream and the Grateful Dead, while staying closer to rock's blues and country roots. The group coalesced with a self-titled album in 1969, featuring intricately harmonized, dueling lead guitar work and two drummers. They broke through nationally with their third recording, *Live at the Fillmore East* (1971), and later scored with "Ramblin' Man" (1973) off the popular *Brothers and Sisters* album (1973). The band's original songwriting style and infectious jam-based approach served later as a model for the jam bands of the 1990s and early 2000s.

Other southern-rock bands emerged as well. The Charlie Daniels band began in the 1970s as a rock group but maintained a loyal following for over thirty years as it shifted from rock to country. Modeled on the Allman Brothers, the group's biggest hit was "The Devil Went down to Georgia," off the album *Million Mile Reflections* (1979). The hardest-rocking band to follow in the tradition of the Allman Brothers was Lynyrd Skynyrd, who tried to "one-up" the Allmans by using a three-lead-guitar lineup. Formed in Florida in the late 1960s, the group produced "Freebird" (1973) and the southern-rock anthem "Sweet Home Alabama" (1974). Texas-based ZZ Top's first blues-based, boogie recordings appeared in the early 1970s, but not until the early 1980s did the band's unique look of foot-long beards, snap-brim hats, and Ray-Bans make them camp icons on MTV.

Country Rock

Featuring a relaxed blend of country vocal harmonies, pedal steel guitar, and dobro with rock guitar, *country rock* emerged out of the L.A. rock scene to dominate mainstream rock briefly in the 1970s. The roots of the style lay in late-1960s folk-rock acts such as Buffalo Springfield and the Byrds, as well as Bob Dylan's country-infused work on *Nashville Skyline*. The Byrds' release of *Sweetheart of the Rodeo* (1968), done with Gram Parsons of the Flying Burrito Brothers, anticipated the country-rock sound. Artists such as the Eagles, Poco, and Linda Ronstadt came to define the style.

Gram Parsons and his band, the Flying Burrito Brothers, were the late-1960s godfathers of country rock. The Georgia-born Parsons had the radical notion of blending the then-conservative flavor of country with the laid-back, long-haired L.A. rock sound. Other group members of the Burritos included Chris Hillman and Michael Clarke of the Byrds, and future Eagles member Bernie Leadon. Poco, formed in 1968, was another early, L.A.-based country-rock group. Founding members included Richie Furay and Jim Messina of Buffalo Springfield and future Eagle Randy Meisner.

The **Eagles** stood as the unchallenged superstars of country rock, ultimately producing two of the best-selling domestic rock records of all time. When the group first joined forces in 1971, as Linda Ronstadt's studio band, they developed a successful musical formula, performing a well-defined blend of simple melodies, rich country harmonies, and laid-back rhythms. After signing as the Eagles, they produced a string of hits including "Take It Easy" (1972), "Peaceful Easy Feeling" (1972), "Desperado" (1973), "Life in the Fast Lane" (1976), and "Hotel California" (1976). *The Eagles' Greatest Hits* album surpassed Michael Jackson's *Thriller* in the early 2000s to become the biggest-selling pop record in the United States.

ART ROCK

The term **art rock** (also called *progressive rock*) began to appear in the 1970s to describe artists who drew on a wide range of musical styles, including rock, classical, folk, electronic, and jazz. Many historians point to the influence of the Beatles' *Sgt. Pepper* album (1967), with its complex layers of multiple musical styles, as being pivotal to the development of art rock. Although considered by some to be "bombastic and pretentious,"[8] the **Moody Blues** were one of the earliest pop groups to attempt a classical-rock fusion. The group started out as an R & B act, but by 1967 they were recording and performing with a full symphony orchestra. The string-infused "Nights in White Satin" (1967) became their biggest success, followed by *Days of Future Passed* (1968).

Genesis, formed in 1966, also contributed greatly to art rock. The group's first vocalist, Peter Gabriel, performed in a theatrical style with elaborate costumes, and the band practiced a kind of early performance art that built a cult following. When Genesis replaced Gabriel with drummer/vocalist Phil Collins in 1974, the group took on a more mainstream pop flavor, and both the band and vocalist Collins, who had his own successful career as a producer and solo

Internet Listening Exercise

Listen to samples of southern country rock.

Charlie Daniels Band: "The Devil Went down to Georgia"

Lynyrd Skynyrd: "Free Bird," "Sweet Home Alabama"

The Flying Burrito Brothers: "Sin City"

Poco: "Pickin' up the Pieces"

The Eagles: "Take It Easy," "Desperado," "Hotel California"

Allman Brothers: "Ramblin' Man"

Art-rock legends Pink Floyd (left to right): Roger Waters, Nick Mason, Syd Barret, and Richard Wright.

artist, became two of rock's most popular acts in the mid-1980s. After his departure from Genesis in 1974, Peter Gabriel (1950–) performed as a successful solo act for three decades. His biggest commercial success came with *So* (1986), which included the funky hit "Sledgehammer."

Pink Floyd was probably the most prominent art-rock band. Formed in 1965, the group performed a psychedelic blend of rock, blues, electronic effects, folk, country, and classical. They also experimented with extended compositional forms and were one of the first British acts to incorporate light shows into live performances. With *Dark Side of the Moon* (1973), Pink Floyd hit its commercial stride, producing an album that remained on the *Billboard* Top 200 for more than fourteen years, longer than any other album in history. "The themes were unremittingly bleak—alienation, paranoia, schizophrenia—and the music was at once sterile and doomy." [9] *The Wall* (1979), another dark and apocalyptic work, cemented Pink Floyd's position as a pop legend and yielded the number-one hit, "Another Brick in the Wall." This dark perspective resonated with succeeding generations of alienated youth for almost four decades. On *Dark Side of the Moon,* songs were joined together by means of foreboding bits of taped dialogue, and the surprise hit, "Money," made use of a tape loop of cash register drawers opening and closing.

David Bowie (1947–) constructed a forty-year career that featured a bewildering array of changes in persona and musical style. According to critic Jon Pareles,

One of rock's most astute conceptualists since the 1960's, he has toyed with the possibilities of his star persona, turned concerts into theater and fashion spectacles, and periodically recharged his songs with punk, electronics and dance rhythms.[10]

The British artist began his career in 1966 as a singer-songwriter, but by 1970 he had begun his transformation into a performance artist with the release of "Space Oddity." Influenced by New York pop artist Andy Warhol and the music of the Velvet Underground, Bowie created his theatrical alter ego, Ziggy Stardust, in 1972 by adorning himself with futuristic clothing and theatrical makeup. Bowie embraced several more stylistic shifts, including Philly soul, post-punk, and dance pop.

American singer/composer/guitarist **Frank Zappa** (1940–1993) was one of rock's most prolific artists and composers, ranging from doo-wop to satirical rock to full-blown symphonic works influenced by twentieth-century art music composers such as Igor Stravinsky, Edgard Varese, and Karlheinz Stockhausen. For much of his career, Zappa led the Mothers of Invention, a group formed in 1964, whose work sardonically questioned contemporary culture. Major albums included *Freak Out* (1966), *We're Only in It for the Money* (1967), *Cruising with Ruben and the Jets* (1968), and *Over-Nite Sensation* (1973). In the 1970s and 1980s, Zappa branched out to develop film scores and to record solo work, as well as to collaborate with jazz and classical musicians.

SINGER-SONGWRITERS

Over the latter half of the twentieth century, singers who wrote and performed their own songs—**singer-songwriters**—became prominent in American popular music. The phenomenon ran counter to the Tin Pan Alley practices that prevailed during the first half of the century, when professional songwriters provided the material for performers. Tin Pan Alley had started to lose its grip by the early 1950s, and by the 1960s Bob Dylan was spearheading a more introspective, autobiographical, and political song style.

Singer-Songwriters of the 1970s and 1980s

Joni Mitchell (1943–), an adventurous and respected singer-songwriter, first entered the New York scene in 1968 as a confessional folksinger, producing work that ultimately covered a range of styles. She ultimately came to influence artists as diverse as Prince, Madonna, Herbie Hancock, Robert Plant, Donna Summer, Tori Amos, and Courtney Love. According to vocalist/composer Elvis Costello,

> The people that have been overtly influenced by her, with the possible exception of Prince, are nowhere near as good as she is. Her range is much greater. . . . It's not just that she has no rivals among female singer-songwriters. She has very few peers among any songwriters.[11]

The artist scored her first hits as a songwriter in the late 1960s when Judy Collins recorded "Both Sides Now" and Tom Rush released "The Circle Game."

Internet Listening Exercise

Listen to samples of art rock.

The Moody Blues: "Nights in White Satin"

Peter Gabriel: "Don't Give Up," "Sky Blue"

Pink Floyd: "Money," "Another Brick in the Wall"

David Bowie: "Space Oddity," "Let's Dance"

Frank Zappa: "I'm the Slime"

Mitchell's first platinum album, *Ladies of the Canyon* (1970), produced a hit with "Big Yellow Taxi," which Janet Jackson sampled thirty years later. Although critics considered Mitchell's autobiographical *Blue* (1971) one of her finest albums, her first experiments with fusing folk, rock, and jazz on the album *Court and Spark* (1974) are what pushed her into the popular mainstream with the hit song "Help Me." Mitchell also became known for collaborations with prominent jazz musicians in the 1970s, and her 1994 album *Turbulent Indigo* was both a critical success and a Grammy winner.

A contemporary of Joni Mitchell, **James Taylor** (1948–) furthered the singer-songwriter tradition with introspective songs that blended folk, rock, jazz, acoustic guitar, and an understated tenor voice. Throughout his career, Taylor balanced standards such as Stephen Foster's "Oh! Susannah" and Carole King's "You've Got a Friend" with his own material. The artist's *Sweet Baby James* (1970) album produced hits with the title song as well as "Fire and Rain" and "Country Road."

Legendary singer-songwriter Joni Mitchell in 1989.

© Neal Preston/CORBIS

As one of the great Brill Building songwriters, **Carole King** (1942–) had already established her reputation in rock history with such 1960s hits as "Will You Still Love Me Tomorrow" and "Loco-Motion" before she started a solo career. King's album *Tapestry* (1971) went platinum, producing the hits "So Far Away" and "It's Too Late." Two other artists also had hits with songs from the album: James Taylor with "You've Got a Friend" and Aretha Franklin with "(You Make Me Feel Like) A Natural Woman."

British pianist/vocalist **Elton John** (1947–) shared a gift for melody and a charismatic stage presence that made him one the biggest singer-songwriter stars in rock. Billy Joel describes John's musical approach as follows:

> Elton brought back fantastic piano-based rock. Elton knows what his instrument is capable of. The piano is a percussion instrument like a drum. . . . You bang and strike a piano. . . . Elton knows exactly how to do that—he always had that rhythmic, very African, syncopated style that comes from being well versed in gospel and good old R&B.[12]

In live performance, John became known for his outrageous stage antics and wild costumes. He was also one of the earliest rock performers to acknowledge his bisexuality openly. John released his first album, which contained the hit "Your Song," in 1970. He followed this with a succession of early-1970s hits including "Rocket Man," "Goodbye Yellow Brick Road," and "Don't Let the Sun Go Down on Me." John also collaborated on the Grammy-winning music for the 1994 Disney film *The Lion King*.

Bruce Springsteen's (1949–) plainspoken style and high-energy live shows made him one of the biggest stars of rock in the 1980s. Given his repertoire of songs about the lives of real people, many viewed Springsteen as the working-class voice of rock, The artist's post-9/11 album, *The Rising* (2002), was also viewed as one of the strongest pop music statements on the event. According to Jackson Browne,

> In many ways Bruce Springsteen is the embodiment of rock and roll. Combining strains of Appalachian music, rockabilly, blues and R & B, his work epitomizes rock's deepest values: desire, the need for freedom and the search to find yourself.[13]

 Internet Listening Exercise

Listen to the music of classic singer-songwriters.

Joni Mitchell: "Big Yellow Taxi," "Help Me"

James Taylor: "Fire and Rain," "You've Got a Friend"

Carole King: "So Far Away," "Natural Woman"

Elton John: "Your Song," "Goodbye Yellow Brick Road"

Bruce Springsteen: "Born to Run," "Born in the USA"

Neil Young: "Heart of Gold," "Cinnamon Girl"

Springsteen first rose to prominence in the 1970s, and he scored a hit with "Born to Run" in 1975. Springsteen's landmark album, *Born in the USA* (1984), catapulted him permanently into the national spotlight. By the 1990s, Springsteen had scaled back his sound to the point where his album *The Ghost of Tom Joad* (1995) won a Grammy for Best Contemporary Folk Album.

Singer-songwriter **Neil Young's** (1945–) quavering tenor voice flavored an eclectic repertoire of acoustic folk ballads, mellow country rock, high-energy garage rock, and horn-based R & B. In the 1990s, some post-punk musicians even proclaimed him the godfather of grunge. As critic Don McCleese observes, "Young has served as an inspiration for his contemporaries and younger musicians alike . . . to blast away without diminishing one's artistry, to grow old without growing soft."[14] The Canadian-born artist had his first major gig with the late-1960s folk-rock act Buffalo Springfield, and he subsequently joined Crosby, Stills, Nash, and Young, contributing the hit song "Helpless" (1970). At the same time, he established his own long-running group called Crazy Horse, with whom he recorded *After the Gold Rush* (1970) and *Harvest* (1972), as well as his biggest hit, the country rock–flavored "Heart of Gold."

Multicultural Note

Artistic Growth versus Commercial Success

Some popular music performers have experimented and grown artistically, only to disappoint their original fans. Such was the case with Joni Mitchell and Neil Young. Beginning in the 1960s, as many singer-songwriters grew unwilling to accept the demands of commercial conformity, they evolved in new directions, often leaving fans to wonder what had happened to the "old" versions of their favorite artists. In one particularly perplexing challenge to artistic growth, Neil Young was sued by his own record label for recording "unrepresentative albums"—in other words, for "not sounding like Neil Young."

Have you ever attended a concert where your favorite performer has disappointed you by neglecting your favorite song or by performing in an unfamiliar new style? On the other hand, how will musicians grow as artists if they do not receive support in their experiments with the new and unfamiliar?

Recent Female Singer-Songwriters

Beginning in the 1980s, a new generation of female singer-songwriters with a primarily acoustic, folk-based flavor attained national prominence. Suzanne Vega (1959–) and Tracy Chapman (1964–) surprised the music business in the late 1980s with the success of their "uncommercial" releases. Vega's quiet folk-pop sound and literate lyrics laid the groundwork for what became the trademark sound of Lilith Fair, an annual musical tour featuring a new generation of female pop artists. Vega first scored with "Luka" (1987), a song about an abused child. Chapman succeeded with her Grammy-winning folk-style debut album, *Tracy Chapman* (1988), which yielded "Fast Car."

k.d. lang (1961–) and Melissa Etheridge (1961–) became heroes to gay and lesbian communities when they both publicly came out in the early 1990s. The Canadian-born lang established herself as a country-pop star with a smooth voice and a campy approach to country fare in two Grammy-winning albums: *Shadowland* (1988) and *Absolute Torch and Twang* (1989). Etheridge's earthier approach succeeded with the hit album *Yes I Am,* which featured the Grammy-winning song "Come to my Window" (1994). Annie Lennox (1954–) first came to light in the 1980s as the stylish, crew-cut lead singer of the British synth-pop group the Eurythmics. In the 1990s she embarked on a solo career the produced the well-received *Diva* (1992) and *Bare* (2003).

Virtuoso pianist Tori Amos's (1963–) intimate, confessional style exemplified the dominant theme that attracted many fans to the great female singer-songwriters of the era. She wrote about issues facing young women—including her own rape—in the song "Me and a Gun" from her debut album, *Little Earthquakes* (1992). In *Boys for Pele* (1996), she further challenged pop conventions by blending multiple styles and song structures. Recent releases have included *Scarlet's Walk* (2002) and *The Beekeeper* (2005). Canadian-born Alanis Morissette (1974–) became a major star in the mid-1990s with her cathartic, angst-ridden alternative rock. Her Grammy-winning *Jagged Little Pill* (1995) was the largest-selling album by a solo female artist in history, yielding "You Oughta Know," "Ironic," and "Hand in My Pocket." Morissette won further Grammys for "Uninvited" (1998). Ani DiFranco (1970–) built a following with a series of successful releases in the 1990s featuring an eclectic punk-funk-folk style. DiFranco became a thorn in the side of the music industry when she refused to sign with a major label and instead founded her own, amassing sales of over two million. Well-regarded DiFranco albums included *Out of Range* (1994), *Not a Pretty Girl* (1995), and *So Much Shouting, So Much Laughter* (2002).

 **Internet Listening Exercise**

Listen to samples of recent female singer-songwriters.

Suzanne Vega: "Luka"

Tracy Chapman: "Fast Car"

k.d. lang: "Constant Craving"

Melissa Etheridge: "Come to My Window"

Annie Lenox: "Walking on Broken Glass"

Tori Amos: "Sort of a Fairytale"

Alanis Morissette: "You Oughta Know"

Ani DiFranco: "Not a Pretty Girl"

SOFT ROCK

Soft rock—also referred to as *lite rock, mellow rock,* or *adult contemporary*—was a smooth, melodic style popular from the 1960s through the 1980s that met the casual listener's need for a pleasant, undemanding listening experience. The soft-rock sound typically consisted of slow-tempo, melodic songs with vocal harmonies performed over simple rhythmic grooves.

The L.A.-based songwriting team of **Burt Bacharach** (1928–) and **Hal David** (1921–) retained a bit of the flavor of Tin Pan Alley while scoring a series of definitive soft-rock hits in the 1960s with songs performed by Dionne Warwick (1940–), including "Walk on By," "Do You Know the Way to San Jose," and "This Girl's in Love with You." Warwick's soulful yet sparse vocal style endowed Bacharach's deceptively simple melodies with an appealing presence.

The **Tijuana Brass** was an instrumental soft-rock group led by trumpeter and future record-industry mogul Herb Alpert (1935–). The band scored a string of hits, including "The Lonely Bull" (1962) and "A Taste of Honey" (1965), with an Americanized pop mariachi sound that blended two trumpets playing Spanish-inflected melodies in a smooth, Bacharach style over a soft-rock rhythm section. The group's success led to the formation of A&M records, which went on to become the country's largest independent record label.

The Grammy-winning **Carpenters,** the sibling duo of Karen (1950–1983) and Richard (1946–) Carpenter, dominated soft rock in the 1970s. Karen's compelling alto voice and Richard's lush arrangements maintained the duo's place at the top of the charts until Karen's death from anorexia in 1983. According to critic Sue Cummings, "Karen may have been revered in her musicians' world as a great naïve genius, but her voice sounded worldly to an eight-year-old. . . . She was like a knowledgeable big sister intoning the esoteric mysteries of romance." [15] Hits included Bacharach's "Close to You" (1970) and "We've Only Just Begun" (1970), the Oscar-winning "For All We Know" (1971), "Rainy Days and Mondays" (1971), and "Superstar" (1971). Although scorned by rock purists, the Carpenters' wholesome, polished sound struck an appealing chord with many listeners. Karen Carpenter's work was reevaluated in a positive light in later years by such artists as Madonna, k.d. lang, Chrissie Hynde, and Sheryl Crow.

First formed in 1967 as part of the second wave of British Invasion bands, **Fleetwood Mac** was a perennially popular group that performed in a melodic pop-rock style, with a clean, accessible sound reminiscent of the arranging styles of the Beatles and the Beach Boys. The group hit its stride in the mid-1970s with the success of a self-titled album that yielded "Landslide" (1975), later covered by the Dixie Chicks in 2002. Turmoil and multiple permutations in romantic relationships among group members served as the source of material for the group's next record, the Grammy-winning *Rumours* (1977), which yielded "Go Your Own Way," "Dreams," and "Don't Stop."

WORLD MUSIC

The 1980s saw the importation, hybridization, and appropriation of traditional and pop music styles from around the globe into U.S. and British pop music. The term *world music* came to refer to folk or traditional musics from around the world, while *world beat* referred to those flavored by U.S. and British pop or rock. The market for the styles grew as *Billboard* and the Grammys recognized a world music genre; in 1991 the world music market share equaled the combined sales of classical music and jazz.

Internet Listening Exercise

Listen to samples of 1960s and 1970s soft rock.

Dionne Warwick: "Walk on By," "Do You Know the Way to San Jose," "This Girl's in Love with You"

Tijuana Brass: "The Lonely Bull," "Taste of Honey"

The Carpenters: "Close to You," "We've Only Just Begun," "Superstar"

Internet Listening Exercise

Listen to samples of songs by Fleetwood Mac, then compare Fleetwood Mac's "Landslide" with the later version by the Dixie Chicks.

Fleetwood Mac: "Go Your Own Way," "Dreams," "Don't Stop"

Dixie Chicks: "Landslide"

Factors Contributing to the Growth of World Music

- The rapid growth of global communication networks fostered a growing awareness of musics from around the world.

- New recording technologies made music more accessible and transportable.

- Globalization and the new world music category created multiple new markets for the record industry.

- Postcolonial transitions in Latin America, Africa, and Asia led to increased immigration from former colonies to the metropolitan centers of colonial powers—Paris, for example, became the capital of Afro-pop.

- The worldwide popularity of reggae and jazz encouraged global musical hybridization.

- American and British musicians such as Paul Simon, Peter Gabriel, David Byrne, Ry Cooder, and Sting hybridized and appropriated a range of world music styles into their work.

Globalized, transnational influences flowed in many directions. Historical precedents also existed: International artists had been drawn to American popular styles since the birth of sound recording, while international musics had also been infused into American popular music dating back to the Latin tinge in early New Orleans jazz. In the 1960s, the Beatles presaged the 1980s world beat phenomenon when they introduced rock fans to traditional Indian music through sitar virtuoso Ravi Shankar. The availability of the cassette tape in the 1960s also proved critical to the development of contemporary world music, making possible the rapid recording and dissemination of music almost anywhere. Many African-derived American and Caribbean styles such as jazz, rumba, R & B, funk, and blues ultimately went full circle to become ingredients for multiple Afro-pop styles, which in turn found their way back to the United States and United Kingdom as world beat. Musicologist Richard Waterman describes this circular transmission pattern as "reverse diffusion."[16]

Critics pointed out that the construction of world music as a genre raised issues of power and Eurocentrism, arguing that world music was simply an exotic way of describing "anything-not-from-here" with "here" meaning the United States or Western Europe.[17] Critic Timothy Taylor suggests that the development of the world music category was primarily a corporate marketing strategy:

It illustrates the kinds of drives that create markets and niches. . . . In one gesture the old but not quite gone "international" label . . . is supplanted by a trendier, less musty, less your-grandparents'-music category that encompasses everything from field recordings made by ethnomusicologists to the latest in pop and rock from outside Europe and North America.[18]

Although some African musicians became quite popular, western European and North American musicians—often working in tandem with world musicians—sold the most records. As one record company manager said, "If it isn't Celtic or the Gypsy Kings, it's very hard to get on the *Billboard* World Music chart." [19]

Further, in the 1980s, American and European pop artists often experimented with globalized musical hybrids. At times such efforts were criticized as instances of cultural appropriation. Paul Simon, for example, sowed controversy when he broke the anti-apartheid boycott against South Africa to record with the traditional vocal group Ladysmith Black Mambazo for his hit album *Graceland* (1986). Nonetheless, Ladysmith's career benefited from the experience. String virtuoso Ry Cooder had multiple successes in his world music collaborations with African as well as Cuban musicians, notably the Buena Vista Social Club. Singer-songwriter Sting also dabbled in world pop to score a hit with "Desert Rose" (2000), which featured Algerian *rai* singer Cheb Mami. *Rai* is a hybrid Algerian music style that uses rough-edged vocals sung in Arabic and fuses it with rock, funk, reggae, drum machines, and echo chambers. Besides starting his own world music record label, Peter Gabriel incorporated world music influences into some of his rock compositions. David Byrne, the eclectic leader of Talking Heads, became increasingly committed to world music during the 1980s and, like Gabriel, formed his own world music label in 1988. Despite the problematic power issues that the development and production of world music raised, styles such as Arabic music and *rai* from the Middle East, *highlife, ju-ju, soukous,* and township jive from Africa, Latin American folk and pop music, and Central, South, and East Asian musics all found interested audiences in the United States and Europe.

PUNK AND ITS DESCENDANTS

In response to the excesses of disco, arena rock, and art rock, **punk rock** developed in the 1970s. It was rebellious and intentionally outrageous in its cacophonous musical assault on the senses, lyrics of outrage, and extremes of appearance; it was calculated to challenge orthodoxy as well as to elicit a strong response. Punk music returned rock to its basics—three chords and a simple melody—but it did so by being louder, faster, and more abrasive than prior rock styles. Punk challenged the pretensions of 1970s pop and rock by suggesting that anybody could get up on a stage and play loud, distorted, angry rock and roll. Punk grew into a distinct genre in New York in the 1970s and then migrated to Britain. Subsequent styles spawned by the genre included new wave, postpunk, and the alternative-rock movements of the 1990s and early 2000s.

Proto-Punk

The earliest **proto-punk** groups or punk precursors were raw-sounding mid-1960s garage bands such as the Kingsmen, the Standells, and Question Mark and the Mysterians. As one artist put it, "Garage music means just that—garage

—as in inept, crummy, loose, primitive fun." [20] They were followed by the more artistically ambitious Doors, Velvet Underground, Iggy and the Stooges, and MC5. When these latter groups hit the spotlight, according to historian Robert Palmer, many listeners found them "decadent, crude, dark, negative, abrasive, nihilistic, and incompetent; 'The only thing this will replace,' predicted Cher when the Velvets first visited Los Angeles, 'is suicide.'" [21]

Although never commercially successful, the **Velvet Underground** had an extraordinary influence on punk. The group's raw sound and singer Lou Reed's (1942–) lyrics contributed a level of poetic sophistication and social realism to rock. According to one punk artist, "I think it started with the Velvets, the whole thing, in about 1965. No one was writing about real experiences—the Velvets did." [22] In the midst of the flower power movement of the 1960s, the Velvet Underground were deliberately subversive; dressed in black, they sang about sadomasochism and drugs, and they made painful use of feedback and amplifier noise. When the band toured the United States, they inspired the Doors in Los Angeles, as well as Iggy Pop and the Stooges and MC5 in Detroit. Major releases included *The Velvet Underground and Nico* (1967), which contained "I'm Waiting for the Man"; *White Light/White Heat* (1967); and *Loaded* (1970), which contained "Sweet Jane," one of vocalist Reed's best-known songs. Reed subsequently pursued a solo career, and in one of his best-known works, "Walk on the Wild Side," he saluted the misfits, male hustlers, and transvestites of New York.

Iggy Pop (1947–) and his band the **Stooges** played sexually charged and aggressive music. Pop formed the band in 1967 in the Detroit area, inspired by Lou Reed and the Doors' Jim Morrison. According to the artist,

> What our band did was basically make a big noise and create some movement with that noise. . . . A lot of it was based on the attitude of juvenile delinquency and general mental grievance that I'd gotten from these dropouts I was hanging around with, mixed in with the sort of music that I like: hard r&b, hard rock and roll, and the exciting elements of jazz, 'cause I was starting to listen to John Coltrane. . . . And then an added element was . . . like the drill presses at the Ford plant. . . . I thought, "Those are sounds that even we could master." [23]

One of rock's most exciting performers, Pop invented stage diving and worked himself into such a frenzy that he was often bleeding by the end of the night. Major releases included *Iggy and the Stooges* (1969), *Funhouse* (1970), and *Raw Power* (1973).

The **New York Dolls,** whose members sometimes were said to resemble a cross-dressing street gang, contributed to a new form of hard rock that presaged both punk rock and heavy metal. Building on the sound of the Rolling Stones, the androgyny of Mick Jagger, girl-group pop, glam rock, and the anarchic noise of Iggy and the Stooges, the Dolls influenced a generation of musicians in New York and London. Although the Dolls self-destructed quickly, the group's two albums, *The New York Dolls* (1973) and *Too Much Too Soon* (1974), numbered among the most popular cult records in rock history.

 **Internet Listening Exercise**

Listen to samples of proto-punk.

Velvet Underground and Lou Reed: "Sweet Jane," "Walk on the Wild Side"

Iggy Pop and the Stooges: "I Wanna Be Your Dog," "Raw Power"

New York Dolls: "Personality Crisis," "Looking for a Kiss"

New York Punk

Punk began to take hold in New York in 1974. At that time, a group called **Television** inaugurated a bar in the Bowery as an underground rock venue. Called CBGB's, it was a dive with great acoustics and a willingness to hire raw, unsigned bands. Heavily influenced by Velvet Underground, Television was a guitar-based band featuring challenging lyrics and sonic excursions that explored the ringing harmonics of the electric guitar. The early work of Television on their first album, *Marquee Moon* (1977), clearly forecast the jangly guitar sounds of 1980s post-punk bands such as U2 and R.E.M. The group may also have inaugurated the punk look, as Robert Palmer describes it: "Spiky, cropped hair, torn T-shirts and jeans that might well be held together with safety pins, and a glazed, 'pretty vacant' mien that spelled either 'youth apocalypse' or 'heroin.'"[24]

Rarely found in the limelight of commercial success, punk innovator **Patti Smith** (1946–) was seen by many as one of rock's finest poets—in the same mold as Bob Dylan. A regular at CBGB's, she was one of the first of the artists who played there to land a record deal. Her first recording, the 1974 single "Hey Joe," backed with "Piss Factory," is often cited as the first punk record. Although Smith only recorded sporadically, her rebellious poetry made her an icon in the punk and post-punk scene. Smith's most popular album, *Easter* (1978), had a modest hit with the Springsteen-penned "Because the Night."

Debuting at CBGB's about six months after Television, the **Ramones** were probably the first true punk rock band. Dressed in torn blue jeans and leather jackets in homage to 1950s rockers, the Ramones turned the conventions of 1970s rock inside out. Vocalist Joey Ramone described the band's sound as "sick bubblegum music."[25] Songs by the Ramones were short, simple, and fast—often with dark lyrics and depressing titles, blending early rock, girl-group pop, and surf rock. The Ramones toured constantly beginning in 1976, and when they played in London they jumpstarted the British punk movement. According to Johnny Ramone, "Everywhere we went, we met kids that said they were starting a band that week, and some of them turned out to be the Damned, the Clash."[26]

Blondie was the most commercially successful group to emerge out of the New York punk movement. With a passion for the Brill Building/girl-group sound, and fronted by a striking blonde singer named Debbie Harry (1945–), the band combined punk with a clean, sparse, and catchy sound featuring synthesizers and electronic keyboards that anticipated new wave. Harry's voice had a detached flavor, exemplified in the disco-inflected "Heart of Glass" (1978). Other tunes such as "The Tide Is High" explored reggae, later influencing the work of bands such as No Doubt.

Talking Heads drew on funk, African music, and *minimalism* (an artistic aesthetic stressing simplicity) to craft original and danceable music. Formed by a quartet of art school graduates and fronted by quirky vocalist/songwriter David Byrne (1952–), the band first played at CBGB's in 1975. Well-known tunes included "Psycho Killer" (1978), Al Green's "Take Me to the River" (1978), and "Burning Down the House" (1983). Multiple albums and individual members' projects followed, with *Speaking in Tongues* (1983) becoming their most

Internet Listening Exercise

Listen to samples of New York punk bands.

Television: "Marquee Moon," "See No Evil"

Patti Smith: "Hey Joe," "Because of Night"

Ramones: "Blitzkrieg Bop," "Beat on the Brat"

Blondie: "Heart of Glass," "The Tide Is High"

Talking Heads: "Psycho Killer," "Take Me to the River"

popular album. A well-regarded film called *Stop Making Sense* documented one of their tours, and the film's soundtrack album spent two years on the pop charts.

British Punk

British punk was born in 1976. As part of the movement, a generation of unemployed youths became the base for a punk subculture that ran its own clubs, formed its own record labels, and designed its own clothes, giving birth to punk's "do it yourself" (D.I.Y.) ethic. Tours by the Ramones got things started, and former New York Dolls manager Malcolm McLaren pushed the movement along by forming the Sex Pistols. Though their career was short-lived, the **Sex Pistols** revolutionized the idea of what rock could be. For a short time, some saw the band's disturbing image, lyrical violence, and anti-establishment attitude as an actual threat to the British government and monarchy. The Sex Pistols' cacophonous wall of sound and front man Johnny Rotten's disrespect for authority galvanized a legion of disenfranchised working-class British youth. Historian Robert Palmer describes the artist: "There stood Johnny Rotten in his 'I Hate Pink Floyd' T-shirt, with a sneer that was a dental disaster, eclectic musical tastes, zero musical experience, and a 'singing' voice that would make Bob Dylan sound mellifluous." [27] The publicity generated by the band's caustic first single, "Anarchy in the U.K." (1976), caused their record label to drop them, and their next record, "God Save the Queen" (1976), further outraged public sensibilities. The band toured the United States in 1978 but self-destructed after

Punk icons Sid Vicious and Johnny Rotten of the Sex Pistols performing during their 1978 U.S. debut.

CD LISTENING EXERCISE

CD 2/23

Listen to "White Riot" (1977) by The Clash. This is a classic example of late-1970s British punk, flavored with political undertones. The high-energy, up-tempo, guitar-driven song lasts only two minutes, and the simple politicized lyrics work well with the catchy groove: "White riot—I wanna riot / White riot—a riot of my own / White riot—I wanna riot / White riot—a riot of my own."

fourteen days. As Rotten asked the audience at the Sex Pistols' final show in San Francisco, "Ever get the feeling you've been cheated?"[28]

The Clash took the anger of the Sex Pistols and other British punk rockers and fashioned it into a more lasting political and aesthetic agenda. The musically adventurous band also branched out to encompass reggae, funk, and rap. The Clash performed their first concert in 1976 on the same bill with the Sex Pistols. Early albums such as *The Clash* (1977), featuring the hit "White Riot," and *Give 'em Enough Rope* (1978) did well in Britain. Not until the release of their double album, *London Calling* (1979), did they do well in the United States. Subsequent albums included the three-disc *Sandinista!* (1980) and *Combat Rock* (1982), which garnered a U.S. hit with "Rock the Casbah."

New Wave and Synth Pop

Not long after it appeared on the public's radar screen, punk splintered into multiple subgenres in the 1980s: new wave, which was pop-oriented; post-punk, which was more experimental and artier than punk; and a hard-core punk style, which maintained the initial punk aesthetic. While retaining the vigor and irreverence of punk, **new wave** added a fascination with electronics, style, and art, and its emergence coincided with the development of MTV. The early 1980s, as the British pop music bible *Melody Maker* magazine describes it, was the era of "the guitar versus the synthesizer."[29]

Elvis Costello (1954–) emerged from London's pub-rock scene in the mid-1970s with a sound that could not have differed more from the prevailing punk sounds of the era, featuring retro-flavored rock and ballads rooted in R & B, soul, old-time rock and roll, and even lounge music. With literate and complex lyrics, Costello's songwriting was always his greatest asset. Beginning with his first album, *My Aim Is True* (1977), Costello blended rock, country, Tin Pan Alley, reggae, and other genres. Costello released a series of well-regarded albums that yielded "From a Whisper to a Scream" (1981), "Everyday I Write the Book" (1983), "Veronica" (1989), and "The Other Side of Summer" (1991).

Formed in the late 1970s, the **Pretenders** and singer/songwriter Chrissie Hynde (1951–) bridged the gaps between punk, new wave, and top forty. Hynde was an appealing singer with a clear, intelligent sound, as well as a fine songwriter who refashioned the traditionally male lead singer role. The Pretenders featured a jangly guitar sound and a tight rhythmic feel. Their chart-topping, self-titled debut album in 1980 put them on the map, and over the years they had hits with "Brass in Pocket" (1980), "Message of Love" (1981), and "My Baby" (1987). As rock critic Neva Chonin says, "The Pretenders might have had their heyday in the '80s, but their music, so imbued with rock tradition, transcends eras."[30]

The reggae-influenced minimalist pop sound of the British trio the **Police** made them one of the most popular groups of the late 1970s and early 1980s. The trio had become global superstars by the time they disbanded in the mid-1980s. They crafted music with a rhythmic elasticity that could be hypnotic (as in "Tea in the Sahara," 1983), methodical (as in "Every Breath You Take," 1983), or driving (as in "Message in a Bottle," 1979). Bassist Sting subsequently parlayed his experience with the Police into a successful solo career, serving up a smooth, multicultural blend of jazz-inflected light rock to adult contemporary audiences. Critic Joel Selvin describes the artist's later work: "His musical integrity is unimpeachable, even if he tends toward the pedantic, and he cloaks his earnest entreaties in agreeably exotic musical atmospheres."[31]

The 1980s brought the dawning age of the synthesizer in rock. **Synth pop,** a spare, synthesizer-based dance pop sound, was its first embodiment. At the start of the decade, several groups, including Berlin, Gary Numan, Depeche Mode, Human League, and the Eurythmics, began to adapt the electronic innovations of the influential German band Kraftwerk to make music with a sterile, vaguely menacing, almost disembodied sound. As the style continued to evolve, it was reshaped by the bleach-blond MTV darlings Duran Duran, who grafted synthesized hooks onto a dance beat and produced appealing videos set in tropical landscapes.

Post-Punk

A style called **post-punk** developed in the 1980s. While still adhering to the D.I.Y. punk ethic, the style evolved in part as a reaction to the nihilism of punk. Post-punk artists often showed more artistic self-consciousness than the earlier pop-oriented new wave groups such as Duran Duran or the Police did. The post-punk sound of the mid-1980s took varying forms: avant-garde noise, jangling guitars, anthemic stadium rock, or roots rock.

Formed in 1979, the Minneapolis-based **Hüsker Dü** wrapped angst, abandon, and well-crafted pop songs into a furious guitar squall, contributing to the template for indie rock and grunge. Critics viewed the group's 1984 double album *Zen Arcade* as a classic, and 1985's *New Day Rising* was equally well regarded, as were *Candy Apple Grey (1986)* and *Warehouse: Songs and Stories* (1987). Rock critic David Fricke once described Hüsker Dü as

> a breathtaking canvas of rainbow slam pop and lyric liberation that eclipses nearly everything else in Eighties post punk rock, here or abroad, and an embarrassment to superstar acts that strut down from the mountaintop with their stone tablets every two or three years.[32]

Other groups would follow. Formed in New York City in 1981, **Sonic Youth** had its roots in abrasive, experimental music. According to critic Dave Thompson,

> A battered combination of punk, hardcore, no wave, pure noise, and feedback, Sonic Youth built their career by pushing every musical boundary beyond its

Internet Listening Exercise

Listen to samples of new wave.

Elvis Costello: "From a Whisper to a Scream," "Every Day I Write the Book"

Chrissie Hynde and the Pretenders: "Brass in Pocket," "Message of Love"

The Police: "Message in a Bottle," "Every Breath You Take"

Internet Listening Exercise

Listen to samples of synth pop.

Kraftwerk: "Autobahn"

Gary Numan: "Cars," "Are Friends Electric?"

Depeche Mode: "Everything Counts," "People Are People"

Human League: "Don't You Want Me," "(Keep Feeling) Fascination"

Eurythmics: "Sweet Dreams Are Made of This," "Here Comes the Rain Again"

Duran Duran: "Rio," "Hungry Like the Wolf"

CD LISTENING EXERCISE

CD 2/24

Listen to an excerpt from "Teenage Riot" (1988) by Sonic Youth, a seminal post-punk/alternative rock group of the 1980s and 1990s. This recording demonstrates more of a melodic style than earlier work by the band, which often focused on white noise. What musical elements do you hear that may have influenced alternative rock bands of the early 2000s?

Internet Listening Exercise

Listen to samples of 1980s post-punk music.

Hüsker Dü: "Never Talking to You Again," "New Day Rising"

R.E.M.: "Radio Free Europe," "Losing My Religion," "What's the Frequency, Kenneth?"

U2: "Sunday Bloody Sunday," "I Still Haven't Found What I'm Looking For," "Beautiful Day"

Dire Straits: "Sultans of Swing," "Money for Nothing"

breaking point to a place where new sound erupted, widening the definition of what alternative sound could become.[33]

Bad Moon Rising was the group's first album to secure a widespread release in both the United States and Britain, featuring "I'm Insane" and "Death Valley '69." In 1990 Sonic Youth signed with Geffen Records, building their reputation as godfathers of alternative rock with *Goo, Dirty,* and *A Thousand Leaves.* Group members also played a key role in the subsequent signing of Nirvana to Geffen Records, and they were pivotal to the formation of Courtney Love's band, Hole.

Combining ringing guitar hooks with mumbled, cryptic lyrics and a D.I.Y. aesthetic, **R.E.M.** marked the point when post-punk turned into alternative rock. Their first single, "Radio Free Europe" (1981), brought guitar-based rock back into the mainstream. Formed in Georgia in 1980, R.E.M. achieved a growing cult status for their folksy, "jangle-pop" sound. According to historian Robert Palmer, "Together with Tom Petty and the Heartbreakers, the Athens, Georgia–based R.E.M. revived the jangly 12-string guitar textures and folksy finger picking of the mid-sixties Byrds for audiences too young to remember the original."[34] By the early 1990s, R.E.M. was popular worldwide, acknowledged as a forerunner of the thriving alternative-rock movement; by the end of the decade, it was an institution. Important singles included "Orange Crush" (1988), "Losing My Religion" (1991), and "What's the Frequency, Kenneth?" (1994).

Through a combination of zealous righteousness and post-punk experimentalism, the Irish rock band **U2** became one of the most popular groups of the 1980s. Known for a sweeping sound and grandiose statements about politics and religion, U2 were rock crusaders in an era of synthesized pop and heavy metal. As lead singer Bono puts it, "It would be wrong for me to say, 'Yes, we can change the world with a song.' But every time I try writing, that's where I'm at. I'm not stupid. I'm aware of the futility of rock & roll music, but I'm also aware of its power."[35] U2's ever-shifting sound featured everything from jangly post-punk to country, techno, and hip-hop. Guitarist Dave "The Edge" Evans contributed to the group's signature sonic landscapes with his ringing, heavily processed guitar work, and lead vocalist Bono had a knack for grand gestures that played well in large arenas. By 1987 U2 had attained superstardom with the release of *The Joshua Tree.* Important singles included "Sunday Bloody Sunday" (1983), "I Still Haven't Found What I'm Looking For" (1987), "With or Without You" (1987), "Discotheque" (1997), and "Beautiful Day" (2000).

Fronted by guitarist/vocalist Mark Knopfler (1949–), the British act **Dire Straits** played with a laid-back, blues-rock style laced with country, jazz, and progressive rock. Although the group appeared in the post-punk era, they owed little to punk; rather, the roots revivalism of British pub rock fueled the band. Dire Straits' rootsy music was offset by Knopfler's introspective lyrics and Dylanesque delivery. The band's sixth album, *Brothers in Arms,* became an international blockbuster. Major hits included "Sultans of Swing" (1979), "Money for Nothing" (1985), and "So Far Away" (1985).

The mid-1980s also saw brief stirrings of a social conscience on the part of rock artists. Numerous benefit recordings and large-scale charity rock megaconcerts were organized, as major pop stars realized that they could use their power for social good. The godfather of charity rock was actually Beatle George Harrison, who sponsored and hosted his "Concert for Bangla Desh" in 1971 to help raise money to fight famine in Bangladesh. A series of benefit concerts including "Band Aid," "U.S.A. for Africa," "Live Aid," and "Farm Aid" were held in the mid-1980s, each serving a different worthy cause. Benefit recordings were also produced, the most famous being "We Are the World" (1985).

HYBRID STYLES OF THE 1990s AND EARLY 2000s

From the 1990s through the early 2000s, a new generation of artists created collages of punk, metal, hip-hop, funk, and singer-songwriter styles, crafting a new, guitar-driven hybrid called **alternative rock.** For most of the 1980s, the style was heard mainly on college campuses, in small clubs, and on small independent labels—and so it was also called *indie rock.* Alternative rock intertwined multiple prior strands of American pop music for a young audience who had little concern for prior genre boundaries. If rock in the 1980s was a duel of guitar versus synthesizer, then by the 1990s the guitar—the louder and more distorted the better—had clearly won.

Publicity photo from the "We Are the World" benefit (clockwise from left): Willie Nelson, Lionel Richie, Tina Turner, Bruce Springsteen, Michael Jackson, Cyndi Lauper, and Bob Dylan (center).

© Harry Benson

The alternative sound had its roots in punk and post-punk. A subgenre of alternative rock that developed in the late 1980s was called *industrial rock,* but the true hallmark of alternative rock was the *punk-metal* hybrid, which framed walls of raw noise into tight pop song structures, cementing the blueprint for alternative rock. One of the era's biggest bands was Seattle-based Nirvana, who embodied the *grunge* blend of punk, metal, and singer-songwriter styles. The Seattle area also saw the emergence of the feminist punk *riot grrrl* sound. Other acts, many from California, developed a *nu-metal* hybrid of metal and hip-hop, while others pumped out a related *funk-metal* hybrid. Still others were associated with *lo-fi,* an artsy amalgam that fluctuated from simple pop and rock songs to free-form song structures to pure noise and arty experimentalism. Britain also continued as an active source of innovation with the Beatles/

Stones-influenced sound of *Britpop*, and a *punk-pop* sound retained an active underground scene in many parts of the country. *Jam bands*, a folksy, blues-based style featuring extended jams, also developed, and a style called *emo* emerged as well, combining the thoughtfulness of folk with the D.I.Y. ethic of punk. By the early 2000s, a new take on American *garage rock* had reappeared, emphasizing three-minute songs and retro influences such as the blues and 1960s rock.

Despite the diversity of sounds and approaches of rock in the 1990s, the music industry employed the imperfect blanket designation of "alternative" to describe them for over a decade. Radio stations scrambled to develop new formats, floating terms such as *rock of the nineties* or *modern rock* to package the music for a younger audience, and the influential annual Lollapalooza rock tour offered a new generation of teens their own mini-Woodstock. The new sound presumably served as an alternative—but to what? In part it was an alternative to the existing mainstream of top-forty radio and MTV—the 1980s-flavored playlists that did not speak to the next teen generation. It also presented an alternative to the macho posturing of hair metal bands, while still reveling in the power of metal. Some critics argued that the alternative rock of the 1990s offered nothing new—that it simply recycled prior genres. Nonetheless, the era gave birth to a series of genre-bending hybrids of styles that had been previously thought of as discrete. Art takes its own path in each generation, and rock at the turn of the twenty-first century was a hybridized field of rich reinvention.

Antecedents of Alternative Rock

One precursor of alternative rock was **industrial rock.** Pioneered by Cleveland's **Nine Inch Nails,** the industrial sound was characterized by a tinny guitar roar and white noise. Fronted by vocalist Trent Reznor, the act scored with *Pretty Hate Machine* (1989) and *The Downward Spiral* (1994). Some likened Reznor's self-absorbed, dark sexuality in performance to that of the Doors' Jim Morrison.

The most influential sound in alternative rock was **punk-metal,** embodied in the work of bands such as Jane's Addition or the Pixies. **Jane's Addiction's** debut album, *Nothing's Shocking* (1988), blended metal, punk, folk, and jazz rhythms into a fresh, challenging sound, and *Ritual De Lo Habitual* (1990), the band's breakthrough, produced the singles "Been Caught Stealing," "Stop," and "Three Days." The group's lead singer, Perry Farrell, also founded Lollapalooza, the alternative-rock extravaganza, in 1991. Lollapalooza proved that eclectic and daring lineups could succeed commercially, promoted alternative culture, and made indie music mainstream in the 1990s. According to critic Jim DeRogatis,

> At its best in the early '90s, Lollapalooza represented a generation celebrating its individuality. However illusory, for one day, the outcasts took over. Musically, politically and socially, the traveling daylong alternative music festival was like the revenge of the nerds.[36]

 **Internet Listening Exercise**

Listen to samples of early alternative rock.

Nine Inch Nails: "Something I Can Never Have," "Head Like a Hole"

Jane's Addiction: "Mountain Song," "Been Caught Stealing"

Grunge

By marrying punk to the power of metal and the emotional possibilities of the singer-songwriter style, **grunge** artists of the 1990s took the underground into the mainstream. Centered predominantly in the Seattle area, the first wave of grunge bands—Green River, Mudhoney, and Soundgarden—were heavier than the second wave, which started with Nirvana. Though artists derived the guitar sound of grunge from early-1970s metal, the music's aesthetic and lyrical content proved more complex, and Nirvana was more melodic than their predecessors. After Nirvana crossed over to the mainstream, grunge lost many of its independent and punk connections and became the dominant hard-rock style of the 1990s. Similar bands included Pearl Jam, Alice in Chains, Smashing Pumpkins, and Creed.

During its brief existence, **Nirvana** turned youth culture inside out and dragged alternative rock onto center stage. Lead singer-songwriter Kurt Cobain (1967–1994) and his band mates could play hard and croon softly, tempering aggression with vulnerability. Nirvana's sound appealed to a broad-ranging youth audience with songs such as the hallmark "Smells Like Teen Spirit." The group's breakthrough second album, *Nevermind* (1991), reshaped the rock world, knocked Michael Jackson from the top of the charts, and signaled an end to the 1980s. By the time its follow-up, *In Utero,* appeared in September 1993, Nirvana's look and sound defined its generation.

Riot Grrrl

Riot grrrl was a feminist punk movement that developed out of early-1990s indie rock. The genre blended personal expression with political activism, presenting lyrics that addressed gender-related issues and were framed by punk-styled blasts of noise. Riot grrrl artists opposed alternative rock's corporate crossover success; the label that released many records in the style was called "Kill Rock Stars." The leading band of the riot grrrl movement was Bikini Kill, and the trio Sleater-Kinney emerged from the scene to become well-known indie stars, featuring songs with consummate instrumental skill and appealing hooks.

Funk Metal and Nu Metal

Beginning in the mid-1980s, a cluster of new bands in the Los Angeles area began to play a musical hybrid called **funk metal,** which drew on the hard-driving guitar riffs of heavy metal and the intricate, popping bass lines and syncopated rhythms of funk. The style was pioneered by the **Red Hot Chili Peppers** beginning in 1983. The group featured L.A. punk roots, a love for funk master George Clinton, and an explosive stage show. Hits included *Mother's Milk* (1989); *Blood Sugar Sex Magik* (1991), which yielded "Give It Away" and "Under the Bridge"; and *Californication* (1999). Other groups, including Faith No More and Fishbone, also took up funk metal.

By the mid-1990s, young rock artists had gone a few steps further, to blend rap, sampling, DJs, drum machines, and other new techniques with guitar-

Internet Listening Exercise

Listen to samples by grunge artists.

Nirvana: "Smells Like Teen Spirit," "Lithium," "Heart Shaped Box"

Pearl Jam: "Alive," "Even Flow," "Not for You"

Soundgarden: "Jesus Christ Pose," "Black Hole Sun"

Smashing Pumpkins: "Cherub Rock," "Disarm," "Bullet with Butterfly Wings"

Creed: "My Own Prison," "Torn," "What's This Life For"

Internet Listening Exercise

Listen to samples of riot grrrl music.

Bikini Kill: "Rebel Girl," "Feels Blind"

Sleater-Kinney: "Call the Doctor," "I Wanna Be Your Joey Ramone,"

driven metal to produce **nu metal** (also called *alt metal* or *rap metal*). Earlier successful fusions of rap and metal had included Run-D.M.C.'s collaboration with Aerosmith on "Walk This Way" (1986) and the Beastie Boys' *Licensed to Ill* (1986) album. Acts such as the Deftones, Korn, and Rage Against the Machine were nu metal's earliest innovators, followed by others including Incubus, Limp Bizkit, and Linkin Park. Popularization of the nu metal style came about with increased MTV exposure, and by the late 1990s nu metal had become a mainstream rock sound.

The Deftones were one of the first nu metal groups to alternate sinewy guitars, heavy metal crunch, and screamed vocals with more subdued music and eerie whispered vocals. The Sacramento-based group, which started out as a metal band, showed continuous willingness to experiment with their music.

The L.A.-based quartet Rage Against the Machine put out an innovative combination of progressive political rhetoric, hip-hop, and metal. The band's streetwise grooves and anti-establishment positions made them youth folk heroes with singles such as "Killing in the Name" (1992), "Bullet in the Head" (1992), and "Bulls on Parade" (1996). The Florida-based Limp Bizkit, one of the leading rock acts of 2000, combined metal, hip-hop break beats, and a humorous white-trash image. As critic Neva Chonin put it, Limp Bizkit was "Rage Against the Machine's rap-metal gone bad. The beginning of the end of the world as we know it and a return to all the dread 'M' words in the rock lexicon: macho, misogynistic, mediocre, moronic."[37] The Grammy-winning Linkin Park appeared in the early 2000s to give the nu metal hybrid a second wind, blending old-school hip-hop, classic rock, and electronic influences. Finally, Incubus rose to become one of the most popular nu metal bands of the early 2000s, setting themselves apart from the crowded field. According to critic Jim DeRogatis,

> Along with the Deftones and 311, the San Fernando Valley, Calif. quintet Incubus stands as one of the few shining examples of what nu-metal/rap-rock could (and should) be, in stark contrast to the likes of Limp Bizkit, Linkin Park and their ilk.[38]

Lo-Fi

During the late 1980s and early 1990s, lo fidelity—**lo-fi**—became a distinct genre, fluctuating from simple pop and rock songs, to free-form song structures, to electronica, pure noise, and arty experimentalism. By 1992, groups such as **Pavement** had become popular cult acts with willfully noisy, chaotic recordings. According to critic Joe Hagan,

> Ironic references were de rigueur and the half-hearted try was the badge of the so-called slacker generation. . . . An amalgam of garage rock, smart-alecky lyrics and haunting pop melodies, Pavement's music at its best was about transcending the banalities of suburbia through art. The band was a graduate school version of Nirvana.[39]

One of the most inventive and eclectic lo-fi figures was Grammy-winner **Beck.** The artist offered a host of contrasts, from the funk of *Midnite Vultures*

Internet Listening Exercise

Listen to samples of funk metal and nu metal.

Red Hot Chili Peppers: "Give It Away," "Californication"

Deftones: "My Own Summer (Shove It)," "Be Quiet and Drive Far Away"

Rage Against the Machine: "Killing in the Name," "Bulls on Parade"

Limp Bizkit: "Nookie," "My Way"

Linkin Park: "Crawling," "Somewhere I Belong"

Incubus: "Drive," "Wish You Were Here"

(1999), to the skewed, abstract humor of *Mellow Gold* (1994) and *Odelay* (1996), to the ruminative acoustics of *Mutations* (1998) and *Sea Change* (2002). Beginning with his 1994 hit "Loser, " many journalists saw Beck as the voice of the 1990s "slacker" generation. But there was more to his music, as critic Gerald Marzorati suggests:

> Beck's approach to music evinces a comprehension of bricolage and the impossibility of esthetic originality in a post-modern moment of information overload. . . . He's figured out that it's OK to be sincere and ironic about something worth caring about.[40]

Britpop

Ever since the Beatles, a long-running British tradition of tuneful, guitar-driven pop bands had continued. The term **Britpop** refers to a generation of 1990s British bands who embraced the melodic pop-rock tradition more than ever before.

Oasis broke out in 1994 by adopting the street-tough image of the Stones, blending it with Beatlesque melodies and hooks, song structures like those of the Kinks, and the guitar roar and sneer of punk. Oasis had several successful records—*Definitely Maybe* (1994), *(What's the Story) Morning Glory?* (1996), and *Be Here Now* (1997)—before their popularity began to subside. The group Blur was another early leader of Britpop, revitalizing guitar pop in Britain. The group reinvented themselves in the late 1990s by incorporating indie rock and lo-fi influences to achieve American success. Influential releases included *Parklife* (1994), *The Great Escape* (1995), and *Blur* (1999). Rounding out the first wave of Britpop, Radiohead was a 1990s success story influenced by Pink Floyd and U2. They first came to prominence with the single "Creep" (1993), which featured a pounding three-guitar arena rock attack and piercing feedback. With the Grammy-winning *OK Computer* (1997), according to critic Gerald Marzorati,

> Radiohead confronted the looming end of album-based, guitar-saturated, lyric-dense rock by counterintuitively releasing "OK Computer," a 70's-redolent concept album stuffed with grandly contoured melodies, rigorous guitar patternings, odd time signatures, melancholy minor chords and atonal changes. . . . [A] painstakingly wrought . . . beautiful concept album.[41]

The second-wave Britpop quartet Coldplay found the middle ground between accessibility and complex musicianship. In doing so, they produced the Grammy-winning debut album *Parachutes* (2000) and hit single "Yellow." They followed with a second Grammy winner, *A Rush of Blood to the Head* (2002).

Punk-Pop and Emo

Punk-pop was a post-grunge strand of alternative rock that combined pop melodies and chord changes with speedy punk tempos and loud guitars. Green Day and Weezer were the first bands to popularize the sound in the early 1990s, and many followed their stylistic blueprint. The style **emo** (short for *emotive*,

Internet Listening Exercise

Listen to samples of lo-fi.

Pavement: "Here," "Grounded"

Beck: "Loser," "Where It's At," "Sexx Laws"

Internet Listening Exercise

Listen to samples of Britpop.

Oasis: "Live Forever," "Wonderwall"

Blur: "There's No Other Way," "Song 2"

Radiohead: "Creep," "Fake Plastic Trees," "Karma Police"

Coldplay: "Yellow," "In My Place"

© Kim Kulish/CORBIS

Green Day poses to promote their 2004 release "American Idiot" (left to right): Mike Dirnt, Billy Joe Armstrong, and Tre Cool.

also called *emocore*) was an arty outgrowth of hard-core punk with lyrics that were often intimate confessionals. It played an important role in underground rock by the late 1990s. Important emo figures included Fugazi, Jimmy Eat World, and Dashboard Confessional.

With snappy, three-chord songs powered by driving rhythms and straight-ahead vocals, **Green Day** set the standard for punk-pop and resurrected the catchy, three-minute pop song. Based in Berkeley, California, the band moved from an active local punk scene to national prominence, bringing the sound of late-1970s punk to a new generation with *Dookie*, their 1994 major-label debut. Green Day's Grammy-winning rock opera *American Idiot* (2004) renewed their status as a leader.

L.A.-based quartet **Weezer** straddled the territory between pop-punk and emo. Fronted by songwriter Rivers Cuomo, who cultivated an ironic, nerdish cartoon image, the band's debut album, *Weezer* (*Blue Album*, 1994), sold 1.5 million copies in the United States. Subsequent albums *Pinkerton* (1996) and *Maladroit* (2002) did as well. As critic Stephen Dalton puts it, "The band . . . proved itself effortlessly adept at inspiring euphoric stage-diving hysteria with its anthemic, highly melodic bubblegum grunge."[42]

Jam Bands

The **jam band** style appeared in the early 1990s, influenced by the aesthetics of the Grateful Dead and the Allman Brothers. This folksy, blues-based style was characterized by extended jams that borrowed a variety of elements—everything from classic rock and bluegrass to soul jazz and world beat. The earliest jam bands such as Blues Traveler, Hootie and the Blowfish, and the Spin Doctors were primarily rock oriented, but as the decade progressed, the more eclectic approaches of Phish and the Dave Matthews Band appeared.

Phish stood out among other jam bands for their musical eclecticism, technical abilities, and underground popularity. Like the Grateful Dead, they sold more tickets than records. As critic Jon Pareles observes,

> The whole Phish template—making every performance different, allowing audiences to make and trade concert recordings, archiving and tabulating its collective works, letting every fan feel like an initiate rather than a consumer, never acting like rock stars—came from the Dead, as did a significant part of its musical approach.[43]

The **Dave Matthews Band,** formed by South African vocalist/guitarist Dave Matthews in Virginia in the early 1990s, presented a pop-oriented version of the Grateful Dead crossed with the world beat explorations of Paul Simon and Sting. As critic Neva Chonin describes the group: "An introspective, frequently dark singer-songwriter matched with a crack team of musicians, he and his group have gained a reputation for being the jam world's version of a fraternity house band."[44]

Garage-Rock Revival Bands

A new generation of **garage-rock** revival bands appeared in the early 2000s, emphasizing three-minute songs and retro influences from the blues and 1960s rock. Artists playing in the style included the Vines, the Hives, the Strokes, the White Stripes, and the Yeah Yeah Yeahs.

Influenced by the proto-punk sound of Iggy Pop and the Stooges and the Velvet Underground, the Strokes were a New York–based quintet that produced aggressively simple, well-crafted pop songs about love and partying. With the look of studiously disheveled fashion models, the band took MTV and the charts by storm in the early 2000s with *Is This It* (2001) and *Room on Fire* (2003). The White Stripes were a Detroit-based, minimalist blues-rock duo formed in 1997. Singer/songwriter/guitarist Jack White morphed between the folk blues of Blind Willie McTell, the 1960s garage pop of the Kinks, and the show tunes of Cole Porter to produce hits such as *The White Stripes* (1999) and the Grammy-winning *Elephant* (2003). White also collaborated with country legend Loretta Lynn to produce her Grammy-winning comeback album, *Van Lear Rose* (2005).

As we move into the twenty-first century, American popular music continues to reinvent itself. The cultural mix of the country is always in flux, changing the mix of what makes our music "American." In a continuous evolution, the digital age of global communication invites the instantaneous exploration of new sounds and styles as music from around the world continues to influence —and be influenced by—American popular music.

Internet Listening Exercise

Listen to samples of jam bands.

Phish: "Tweezer," "Down with Disease"

Dave Matthews Band: "What Would You Say?" "Everday"

Internet Listening Exercise

Listen to samples of garage-rock revival bands.

The Strokes: "Is This It," "Hard to Explain"

The White Stripes: "Hotel Yorba," "Seven Nation Army"

Chapter Summary

- The evolution of rock from the 1970s to the early 2000s saw the creation of multiple new genres. While some genres were completely original, others at the end of the century were hybrids of styles previously developed during rock's first two decades.

- The roots of hard rock and heavy metal go back to the music of pivotal classic rock artists such as Jimi Hendrix, Cream, and Led Zeppelin.

- The growing popularity of rock led to expanded corporate control of rock promotion and the use of larger performance venues, giving birth to arena rock.

- The culture of heavy metal stemmed from the godfather of the genre, Black Sabbath. Heavy metal became one of rock's most consistent styles.

- The development of country rock and southern rock in the 1970s subsequently influenced commercial country music of the 1980s and beyond. *The Eagles' Greatest Hits 1971–1975* is still the largest-selling pop record in the United States.

- The singer-songwriter tradition that began in the 1970s went in multiple stylistic directions. The 1980s and 1990s welcomed a new generation of powerful female voices to the tradition.

- Art rock, which began in the 1970s, blended rock with classical music and other influences to build a diehard constituency.

- The 1970s saw the soft-rock sounds of the Carpenters and others, who were heavily influenced by the late-1960s work of Burt Bacharach and Dionne Warwick. Fleetwood Mac subsequently perfected an appealing blend of country, pop, rock, and blues to become one of the most popular bands of the late 1970s.

- Worldwide musical influences on American popular music gained strength in the 1980s in the new genre of world music. The style, which sold as much as classical music and jazz combined, served as both a musical opportunity and a new form of corporate marketing.

- The emergence of punk in the 1970s laid the groundwork for many of rock's most important innovations over the next three decades. Early punk innovators, including the Ramones, the Sex Pistols, and the Clash, returned to the raw roots of rock with simple arrangements, short songs, hard-edged sounds, and a message of rebellion.

- The new wave sound of the late 1970s and early 1980s mixed punk aspirations with pop sensibilities to create a marketable pop sound.

- Electronically driven synth pop of the 1980s spawned by the German group Kraftwerk was embodied in the synth-based music of artists such as Gary Numan, Depeche Mode, Human League, and the Eurythmics.

- In the 1990s, numerous hybrid alternative styles of rock appeared that blended punk, metal, rap, funk, classic rock, garage, and other styles. The new hybrid styles, which came to dominate mainstream rock, included grunge, riot grrrl, funk metal, nu metal, lo-fi, Britpop, punk-pop, emo, jam bands, and garage rock.

Key Terms

alternative rock	heavy metal	punk rock
arena rock	industrial rock	punk-metal
art rock	jam band	punk-pop
Britpop	lo-fi	riot grrrl
emo	new wave	singer-songwriter
funk metal	nu metal	soft rock
garage rock	post-punk	southern rock
grunge	power ballad	synth pop
hard rock	proto-punk	thrash metal

Study and Discussion Questions

1. How did the evolution of rock in the early 1970s draw on the music of the 1960s? What were the major styles and bands to emerge in this era? Which styles and artists had the longest-lasting impact on rock?

2. Discuss the emergence and evolution of heavy metal music and culture. Who were the major players, and why did the culture of heavy metal remain so consistent and clearly defined?

3. How did the singer-songwriter tradition evolve over three decades from its inception in the 1970s? Discuss dominant figures and their musical contributions.

4. Discuss the meaning of the term *art rock*. Could one argue that all rock is art? Why or why not?

5. Who were the central artists of soft rock? Why was the style so popular in the 1970s? Is there an equivalent music style today?

6. How has music from around the world affected U.S. music throughout its history? What was the world music phenomenon of the 1980s? Why did some critics see the world music concept as Eurocentric?

7. What were the origins of punk? Discuss the central themes of the style. Why was it influential after so many years? Who were the major punk artists, and what contributions did they make?

8. How did new wave differ from punk? Who were the primary artists of new wave?

9. What were the various styles of alternative rock of the late 1980s and 1990s? What characterized each? Why was the term *alternative* used?

Notes

1. Pamela Des Barres, "Every Inch of My Love," in *Rock and Roll Is Here to Stay: An Anthology*, edited by William McKeen (New York: Norton, 2000), 300.

2. Patricia Romanowski, and Holly George-Warren, eds., *The New Rolling Stone Encyclopedia of Rock and Roll*, 3rd ed. (New York: Fireside, 2001), 81.

3. Robert Palmer, *Rock and Roll: An Unruly History* (New York: Harmony Books, 1995), 125.

4. Ibid., 126.

5. Ian Christe, *Sound of the Beast: The Complete Headbanging History of Heavy Metal* (New York: HarperCollins, 2003), 4.

6. Ibid., 137.

7. Romanowski and George-Warren, *New Rolling Stone Encyclopedia*, 247.

8. Ibid., 665.

9. Ibid., 761.

10. Jon Pareles, "David Bowie, 21st Century Entrepreneur," *New York Times*, June 9, 2002, sec. 2, p. 1.

11. Bill Flanagan, "Lady of the Canyon," *Vanity Fair*, June 1997, p. 38.

12. Billy Joel, "Elton John," *Rolling Stone*, April 15, 2004, p. 140.

13. Jackson Browne, "Bruce Springsteen," *Rolling Stone*, April 15, 2004, p. 102.

14. Don McCleese, "Neil Young," in *The Rolling Stone Illustrated History of Rock and Roll*, 3rd ed., edited by Anthony DeCurtis and James Henke (New York: Random House, 1992), 331.

15. Sue Cummings," Karen Carpenter," in *Trouble Girls: The Rolling Stone Book of Women in Rock*, edited by Barbara O'Dair (New York: Random House, 1997), 241.

16. Ben Ratliff, "Playing Catch with All Kinds of Styles," *New York Times*, November 3, 2002, sec. 2, p. 15.

17. Daisann McLane, "The Global Beat," in *The Rolling Stone Illustrated History of Rock and Roll*, 3rd ed., edited by Anthony DeCurtis and James Henke (New York: Random House, 1992), 633.

18. Timothy D. Taylor, *Global Pop: World Music, World Markets* (New York: Routledge, 1997), 3.

19. Ibid., 9.

20. Robot Hull, "The Original Punks: The Greatest Garage Recordings of the Twentieth Century," in *Rolling Stone's Alt-Rock-a-Rama*, edited by Scott Schinder et al. (New York: Delta, 1996), 62.

21. Palmer, *Rock and Roll*, 177.

22. Legs McNeill, in *Punk: The Definitive Record of a Revolution*, edited by Stephen Colegrave and Chris Sullivan (New York: Thunder's Mouth Press, 2001), 32.

23. Palmer, *Rock and Roll*, 176.

24. Palmer, *Rock and Roll*, 272.

25. Ibid., 271.

26. Ibid., 273–74.

27. Ibid., 273.

28. Ibid., 278.

29. Nick Johnstone, *Melody Maker History of 20th Century Popular Music* (London: Bloomsbury, 1999), 124.

30. Neva Chonin, "Pretenders Are Still the Real Thing: Hynde's Band Stirs Sold-Out Warfield with Tough, Timeless Rock," http://www.sfgate.com, March 3, 2003; accessed May 16, 2005.

31. Joel Selvin, "Sting, Where Is Thy Sting: Pretty Boy Can't Cut Loose," http://www.sfgate.com, February 20, 2004; accessed May 16, 2005.

32. David Fricke, "CD Review: *Warehouse: Songs and Stories,*" http://www.rollingstone.com/reviews/, March 26, 1987; accessed May 16, 2005.

33. Dave Thompson, *Alternative Rock* (San Francisco: Miller Freeman, 2000), 643.

34. Palmer, *Rock and Roll,* 285–86.

35. *Rolling Stone's Alt-Rock-a-Rama,* edited by Scott Schinder et al. (New York: Delta, 1996), 138.

36. Jim DeRogatis, "Alternative Fest: Frats Outnumber Freaks," http://www.jimdero.com/News2003/July14Lolla.htm, July 14, 2003; accessed May 16, 2005.

37. Neva Chonin, "Limp Bizkit and Eminem Revel in Teen Angst at Friday's Cow Palace Show," http://www.sfgate.com, December 31, 1999; accessed May 16, 2005.

38. Jim DeRogatis, "Album Review: Incubus: *A Crown Left of the Murder,*" http://www.jimdero.com/News2004/FEB22Albums.htm, February 22, 2004; accessed May 16, 2005.

39. Joe Hagan, "A Thinking Slacker's Rock Hero, Slightly Aged," *New York Times,* March 25, 2001, Arts, p. 33.

40. Gerald Marzorati, "Beck's Fugue," *New York Times Magazine,* March 23, 1997, p. 32.

41. Gerald Marzorati, "The Post-Rock Band," *New York Times Magazine,* October 1, 2000, p. 44.

42. Stephen Dalton, "The Glory That Is Geek," *Times of London,* August 24, 1996, p. 17.

43. Jon Pareles, "True to Form, Phish Disbands on Its Own Maverick Terms," *New York Times,* May 27, 2004, sec. E, p. 1.

44. Neva Chonin, "Mathews' Mellow Set Punctuated by Must-Boogies," *San Francisco Chronicle,* August 4, 2003, p. D1.

Abakuá A hybrid religion that developed in Cuba, combining elements of Roman Catholicism and African religious traditions.

accordion A handheld keyboard or button-operated wind instrument in which the wind is forced past metal reeds by means of a hand-operated bellows; this instrument became the dominant musical symbol of *Tejano* culture.

acid house Style of electronica that was an offshoot of house music and was the first popular music of the rave scene.

acid jazz Jazz substyle that developed in the 1990s out of electronica, as DJs fashioned remixes of jazz recordings and hip-hop rhythm tracks blended with improvisation.

acid rock Music inspired by the experience of mind-altering drugs and characterized by modal melodies, lengthy instrumental solos, esoteric lyrics, and special electronic effects. Synonymous with *psychedelic music.*

aerophones Wind instruments that produce sound by the vibration of air.

alt-country Country movement that developed in reaction to mainstream country's pursuit of pop styles and that represented an eclectic mix of traditional country, post-punk, and other influences.

alternative rock Guitar-driven style that developed in the 1990s, with roots in punk and post-punk and characterized by hybrids of punk, metal, hip-hop, funk, and singer-songwriter styles. Mainly produced by small, independent record companies. Synonymous with *indie rock.*

ambient Experimental, atmospheric electronica style designed to relax the listener with soothing sounds sampled from the environment or electronically generated, with no steady tempo and no definable melody.

ambiguous mode A type of music in which one cannot tell whether the key is major or minor.

anti-Semitism Hostility toward or discrimination against Jewish people.

arena rock Rock concert taking place in front of a crowd of 10,000 or more; characterized by highly amplified music, songs that often make use of rock clichés and hooks, and exaggerated stage performance techniques, in order to be seen and heard in large sports arenas or venues of similar size.

arranger One who writes individual parts for the instruments in a given ensemble, transforming often simple compositions into dramatic ensemble statements.

art rock Also called *progressive rock,* an eclectic blend of rock, classical music, jazz, and other styles that first developed in the late 1960s.

ASCAP The American Society of Composers, Authors and Publishers, founded in 1914, to help ensure copyright protection for musical compositions.

Asian American jazz/creative music A political/cultural movement initiated in the 1970s by Asian American musicians to promote an agenda of self-determination and artistic expression.

avant-garde jazz Usually synonymous with *free jazz,* a jazz style that pushed the limits of melody, harmony, and structure with inspiration that was sometimes associated with the civil rights and black power movements.

backbeat A sharp attack on beats two and four of a ¼ measure.

bajo sexto A large twelve-string guitar of Mexican origin used in *conjunto* bands.

ballad opera A form of musical theater popular in the eighteenth century that used spoken English dialogue and songs and lampooned society; one precursor of musical comedy.

banda Mexican popular music genre performed by a large ensemble of a dozen or more brass and woodwinds centered on the tuba; developed as a regional brass band style in small villages in western Mexican states.

barrio A Spanish-speaking neighborhood.

beat The underlying pulse of a rhythm.

beat juggling DJ technique of bouncing back and forth between two grooves.

bebop Jazz genre of the 1940s that featured small ensembles, jam sessions, improvisation, fast tempos, virtuosity, complex chord structures, and innovative harmonies; served as the basis for modern jazz.

bel canto ("beautiful singing") An Italian style of operatic singing that originated in eighteenth-century opera and that emphasizes mastery of vocal technique to produce a beautiful, clear sound throughout the vocal range. The style was also used in parlor songs and boleros.

bhangra Traditional form of Punjabi (North Indian) music, featuring the heavy, resounding beat of the *dhol*, accompanied by smaller *tumbi* drums and Punjabi lyrics; hybridized in hip-hop, electronica, and dance club music in the early 2000s.

big band A large jazz ensemble that developed in the 1930s and featured three to five trumpets, two to five trombones, three to five saxophones, and a standard rhythm section.

blackface A makeup style associated with minstrelsy in which the face is darkened with burnt cork and exaggerated facial features such as large lips and big eyes are drawn.

blaxploitation movies Black-themed action films of the early 1970s that capitalized on a mass public fascination with African American inner-city stereotypes and style.

blue notes Flatted third, fifth, and seventh notes of a major scale.

blue yodel A yodeling style blended with blue notes that was developed by Jimmie Rodgers in the 1920s. A *yodel* is a wordless vocal sound created in the back of the throat that rapidly alternates between two pitches

bluegrass Acoustic country music style that combines fiddle, banjo, mandolin, guitar, Dobro, and acoustic bass and vocally often involves either a high lonesome style or gospel-inspired harmonizations integrated with driving, syncopated banjo picking and a steady four-beat feel.

blues scale An African American creation, closely related to the minor pentatonic scale, that uses six notes (including the flatted third, flatted fifth, and flatted seventh of a major scale) to reach an octave; also called a hexatonic (six-tone) scale.

bolero A hybrid Latin style that started in the 1920s and combined European *bel canto* singing with slow romantic lyrics and music.

Bollywood Bombay + Hollywood, referring to South Asian films and the music and dance associated with them.

bongo drums Two small hand drums attached together with a piece of wood, one drum usually slightly larger than the other and pitched lower, played with the fingers and hands.

boogaloo A funky dance style from the sixties that integrated soul, rock, and English lyrics into Latin music.

boogie woogie An influential post-stride piano style that flourished in the 1930s and 1940s and became a central component of R & B and early rock and roll.

borderland The transitional space between cultures where people do not belong fully to one culture or another, or where they identify with multiple cultures; borderlands are often the source of important cultural innovations.

bossa nova Jazz-based, smooth Brazilian music style in which an acoustic nylon string guitar plays simple, hypnotic rhythms to accompany songs of unexpected harmonic complexity; popular in the United States in the sixties.

brass band A wind band with brass and percussion instruments only.

breakbeat Style of electronica emulating jazz, funk, and soul-inflected hip-hop grooves and emphasizing syncopation and clearly defined percussion, with a heavy backbeat on beats two and four.

bridge A transitional passage that connects two musical passages of greater importance.

Brill Building Located at 1619 Broadway in New York City, the place where the music industry briefly dominated rock in the early 1960s by returning to the traditional Tin Pan Alley songwriting model.

British Invasion U.S. rock revolution beginning in 1964 with the arrival of the Beatles and followed by other British bands.

Britpop Music played by a generation of 1990s–2000s British bands who embraced the melodic pop-rock tradition of the Beatles and the Rolling Stones.

broadside ballad Eighteenth-century British style of music with witty, often ribald, topical verses that uses everyday vocabulary.

burlesque Theater style, related to vaudeville, that contains a unifying thematic element, comedy with sexual themes, and female dancers.

cajones Drums common in Afro-Caribbean music, made of simple wooden boxes and first developed by African slaves from shipping crates and played with bare hands or *palitos* (sticks).

call and response A musical statement by a singer or instrumentalist followed by a response from other vocalists or instruments.

calypso Trinidadian music style stemming from creole songs, neo-African styles, British ballads, and *calinda*; today performed to a syncopated rhythm with a two-beat feel and lyrical content peppered with sexual innuendo and humor.

camp meeting A large, multiday, outdoor religious celebration attended by both blacks and whites; part of the Second Awakening, an evangelical movement of the early nineteenth century.

canción Mexican song style that emerged in the nineteenth century.

Candomblé A hybrid religion that developed in Brazil, combining elements of Roman Catholicism and African religious traditions.

canon The body of knowledge that is said to be central to a discipline.

Carnival Afro-Caribbean or Latin American event with outdoor celebrations and parades lasting for days.

cedar flute Native American wind instrument often pitched differently from European classical instruments.

cencerro Cowbell with the clapper removed, played with a wooden stick; used in Latin music.

chantwell Singer of a *calinda,* the musical accompaniment to a nineteenth-century stick-fighting ritual in Trinidad; the chantwell sang songs that praised one fighter while suggestively insulting the other.

charanga Ensemble that developed in the 1920s in Cuba to play *danzón* and that included wooden flute, violins, piano, string bass, guiro, and timbales.

Chicano An American of Mexican descent.

chicken scratch Modern-day Native American music from southern Arizona that employs the stringed instruments of Mexican American border music and mariachi. Synonymous with *waila.*

chord A combination of three or more notes sounded or played simultaneously.

chord substitution An approach to jazz playing that involves the adding and changing of chords in the performance of standard pop tunes.

chordophones Instruments that produce sound by means of a vibrating string.

chorus A lyric statement following the verse that is often repeated periodically throughout the song, usually containing the same lyrics and melody.

classic blues Early style of blues, primarily associated with female vocalists, that had a sophisticated, urban flavor and jazz accompaniment.

clave A group of syncopated rhythmic patterns that functions as an underlying unifier, connecting the polyrhythms of Afro-Cuban music.

claves Latin percussion instrument: a pair of wooden sticks played by resting one stick on the fingertips of a cupped hand that acts as a resonator, while tapping with the other stick.

collective improvisation A jazz practice derived from African music in which several musicians improvise at once.

commodification Process by which noncommercial goods or services such as a song, a story, a picture, or an artist are turned into marketable commodities.

comping Chord playing to accompany improvised solos in jazz.

concept albums Recorded works with a unifying artistic theme.

concept musical A type of musical, pioneered by Stephen Sondheim, that focuses on a single theme, often without a linear narrative or definitive resolution, and uses small casts with minimal sets.

conga drum A barrel-shaped drum that developed in Cuba and was based on African drums; it is played with hands and fingers and is made from strips of hardwood or fiberglass.

Congo Square Established in 1817, an outdoor gathering place in New Orleans that served as an active center of African music and dance until the late nineteenth century.

conjunto (1) Cuban *son* ensemble with an additional trumpet, a piano, and conga drums. See Chapter 8. (2) An accordion-based Chicano/*Mexicano* vernacular ensemble usually consisting of accordion, *bajo sexto,* acoustic bass, and drums that plays polkas, waltzes, and *rancheras.* See Chapter 9.

contradanza Spanish contradance: a formal group dance of the nineteenth century similar to the Virginia reel, using a caller to direct participants.

cool jazz Jazz style of the 1950s, characterized by understatement and laid-back rhythm.

coon song Popular style in the late nineteenth century that featured offensive racial stereotypes, strong rhythms, syncopation, and quick tempos that demanded a robust delivery.

corrido Narrative Mexican ballad that tells the story of a heroic event or tragedy.

counterculture A cultural group whose values differ from those of the dominant culture. The term is most commonly used to refer to the rebellious youth culture of the 1960s.

counterpoint The combination of two or more independent melodies into a single harmonic texture in which each melody retains its linear character.

country rock A hybrid of country and rock music that features a relaxed rhythmic feel and country-style vocal harmonies, blending country instrumentation (often including pedal steel guitar or Dobro) with hard-rock-style electric guitar and a rock rhythm section.

Creole New Orleans mixed-race social class originating in the 1700s and 1800s.

crier Early R & B vocalist who projected the image of being overcome by emotion.

crooning A smooth personal vocal style enabled by the invention of the microphone.

crossover Occurs when a song or musician associated with one style achieves popularity in two or more genres.

cubop Latin jazz style from the late forties and credited to Dizzy Gillespie, which blended Latin rhythms and *Abakuá* chants with swing and bebop.

cultural appropriation Process by which members of one cultural group take cultural elements from another cultural group, reshape them, and claim them as their own.

cultural genocide The systematic destruction of an entire way of life.

culture The changing pattern of human knowledge, belief, and behavior learned and transmitted through generations.

cumbia A simple two-beat Colombian rhythm popular for dancing; employed in a range of Latin musical styles.

cutting contest A competition in which rival musicians challenge one another's prowess.

dancehall Jamaican music featuring digital beats and worldly, often raw lyrics.

danzón Cuban dance rhythm played by a *charanga* ensemble or other small group.

décima Traditional Spanish ten-line verse form.

Delta or rural blues Form of the blues originating with northwestern Mississippi sharecroppers; influenced by church hymns and field hollers and characterized by an AAB lyric structure and flexible rhythm structures; often performed solo with guitar accompaniment.

dhol North Indian double-barreled drum.

diaspora The scattering of people far from their homelands, which leads to transmission of cultural and economic resources among countries when immigrants stay connected to their homelands.

disco A formulaic, R & B–based commercial sound accompanied by a hedonistic party scene, popular in the mid 1970s and early 1980s.

distortion The electronic alteration of a musical tone to produce an intentionally unclear or fuzzy timbre.

DJ A person who plays recorded music on the radio and for social functions; also, a performer who works the turntables to create musical collages and percussive scratching effects.

Dobro An acoustic steel guitar.

dominant culture A culture that is more powerful than others within a society.

doo-wop Group vocal harmony grounded in black gospel and barbershop harmony; a hallmark sound of the 1950s.

drum 'n' bass Style of electronica characterized by electronic drums and deep bass played at frenetic tempos to create high-energy music blended with jazz, reggae, dub, calypso, and trip-hop.

dub Mixed-down versions of tunes stripped to their instrumental basics to allow Jamaican DJs to toast (speak) over them in dancehall settings.

dulcimer Stringed instrument with a gentle melodic sound.

electric blues Form of the blues using amplified, sometimes distorted instrumental sounds of the guitar and harmonica in an ensemble setting.

electronica Describing several electronically generated musical styles that developed in the 1980s from dance music.

emo Short for *emotive* (also called *emocore*), an arty outgrowth of punk in the early 2000s with lyrics that were often intimate confessionals.

Ethiopian delineators Performers in minstrel shows who speak and sing in poor imitations of Black English dialect.

Ethiopian dialect A stereotyped imitation of African American speech used in minstrel shows.

ethnic musical Musical that takes place in a cultural setting exotic to the U.S. cultural mainstream.

ethnic novelty song Song that portrays members of ethnic groups in humorous but demeaning ways.

Eurocentrism The dominant view of Western culture that privileges European-derived cultural forms and generally reflects white, upper-middle-class, heterosexual male perspectives.

falsetto A method of voice production used by male singers to sing notes higher than their normal range.

feedback A squealing electronic effect achieved by placing a microphone or guitar pickup directly in front of the speaker through which it is being amplified.

field holler African-derived music sung or chanted by individual workers in rhythm with their work.

file sharing The act of making files on one computer accessible to others in a network; sharing music in this way became prevalent in the 1990s because of the evolution of the Internet and the MP3 audio file format.

First Nations The indigenous cultures of North America; term that replaces the erroneous term *Indian* used by Columbus.

flow The rhythmic delivery of the spoken-word performance of an MC in rap music.

folk music Vernacular music that originates with the ordinary people of a given culture. Folk music is usually acoustic music that survives without the reinforcement of commercial media.

folk revival In the 1950s and 1960s, U.S. interest in European folk music, rural blues, spirituals and gospel, mountain and country music, cowboy music, and other vernacular styles from around the world.

folk-rock A blend of rock and folk music characterized by folk-style vocal performances backed by amplified acoustic guitars, electric bass, and drums.

form The organizational structure of a musical composition.

45 rpm record Seven-inch-diameter record format primarily used for recording pop, R & B, rock, and country singles, first promoted in 1948 by RCA.

free jazz Synonymous with *avant-garde jazz,* jazz that dispenses with traditional definitions of form, melody, harmony, and rhythm.

front line Featured musicians in a jazz ensemble who usually stand in front during live performance—in New Orleans jazz, typically cornet or trumpet, trombone, and clarinet.

funk A highly syncopated style of pop music.

funk metal Musical hybrid that draws on the hard-driving guitar riffs of heavy metal and the intricate, popping bass lines and syncopated rhythms of funk.

funky jazz Jazz style that incorporates elements of R & B such as repeated prewritten patterns in the rhythm section along with gospel, soul, and blues inflections while retaining a major focus on improvisation. Also called *soul jazz.*

fusion See *jazz-rock fusion.*

fuzz-tone An electric guitar effect that sounds exactly as the name implies (see *distortion*).

gangsta rap A tough rap sound with gritty, street-level subject matter.

garage rock Rock genre of the early 2000s emphasizing three-minute songs and retro influences such as the blues and 1960s rock; also referring to a simple, raw form of rock and roll created by several American bands in the mid-1960s.

girl groups Groups of female performers producing a sweet and melodramatic sound that mixes hooks and doo-wop harmonies. Girl groups of the 1960s were usually trios or quartets fronted by a lead singer.

gospel music African American religious genre characterized by instrumentation of soloist, choir, piano, organ, rhythm section, horns, and guitar; lyrics covering a wide rang of spiritual topics; rhythmic intensity; structure akin to popular music; bent tones; and improvisation.

gramophone A device invented in 1887 that recorded sounds on a disc etched by the vibrations of a stylus.

Grand Ole Opry Country music's most famous performance venue in Nashville and for many years a radio program that featured string bands, traditional singers, gospel quartets, and banjo players, supported by colorful announcers, comedians, and ad-libbing costumed musicians.

grass dance Traditional Native American dance commonly performed at powwows in which the brave deeds of warriors are symbolically reenacted.

griot A West African tribal storyteller, tribal historian, and entertainer.

groove An African-derived rhythmic feature constructed by playing several highly rhythmic parts simultaneously, creating a momentary feeling of resolution when multiple parts arrive on the same beat.

groove-based tune Music that relies on repeated, open-ended structures and rhythmic themes rather than on a chorus/verse form.

grunge A 1990s blend of punk, metal, and singer-songwriter styles.

guajira A Cuban *música campesina* folk song style with gentle melodies and rural lyrical themes accompanied by guitar or *tres* and simple percussion.

guiro A serrated cylinder made of gourds, metal, wood, or fiberglass that is scraped and struck with a stick in a variety of rhythmic patterns.

guitarrón A large acoustic bass guitar.

habanera Havana contradance involving the addition of a syncopated beat to the traditional *contradanza;* also, the rhythm associated with the dance.

hard bop Jazz style that evolved from bebop and is characterized by a variety of musical elements that may include funky, R & B–based rhythms with extensive jazz improvisation, elements of gospel and soul, and modal harmony.

hard rock Rock style rooted in the power trio ensemble and guitar-bass unison riffs. Hard rock evolved into a diverse range of additional musical styles that included complex song forms with varying degrees of harmonic sophistication, a wide assortment of lead vocal styles, diverse instrumentation, and a broad range of song subjects.

harmony (1) Two or more musical notes produced or sounded at the same time, (2) the underlying chord structure of a song or piece of music, or (3) the study of the overall musical structure within a composition, genre, or style.

head arrangements Riff-based tunes that can be played by ensembles of all sizes without sheet music and that serve as the musical structure for improvisation.

heavy metal Rock style characterized by lead vocal styles rooted in high-pitched, aggressive singing/shouting; limited harmonic choices; heavy reliance on blues roots; and dark song subjects.

heterogeneous sound ideal An aesthetic perspective, characteristic of African music, that values the complex interplay of diverse musical textures.

high lonesome style Vocal bluegrass style characterized by a clear, dry, high-pitched tone.

hillbilly   Early term for country and western music, now considered offensive.

hip-hop   The urban youth culture of music, dance, dress, speech, and art that is associated with—and includes—rap music.

homophonic   Describing a harmonic texture created by a melody performed with simple harmonic accompaniment.

honker   Early R & B performer who played a screaming, honking tenor saxophone.

honky-tonk   (1) A loud, earthy, country music style, flavored with pedal steel guitar and lyrics about love (both lost and found) and partying, that developed in the late 1940s. (2) Depression-era bar in the South, usually built on the outskirts of town, with a large dance floor, jukebox, and live music.

hook   A catchy melody, rhythm, or lyric in a song that stays with the listener.

hootenanny   Large gathering of folk musicians.

house music   Disco-influenced style of electronica that emerged in Chicago in the early 1980s and was propelled by an insistent ¼ beat and deep bass, overlaid with Latin soul, synth-pop, reggae, rap, or jazz.

huapango   A folk dance rhythm of eastern Mexico.

hula   Hawaiian choral chant or song accompanied by dance, drama, and instrumental performance.

hybridity   The blending of different cultures or cultural forms such as music, language, or art.

idiophones   Percussion instruments made of materials such as wood, ceramic, or metal that have their own unique sound.

improvisation   The spontaneous creation of musical ideas; music that is composed on the spot.

indie rock   See *alternative rock*.

indigenous   Native to a particular place.

industrial rock   Precursor of alternative rock, characterized by a tinny guitar roar and white noise.

instrumentation   The group of instruments used in a performance.

internment camps   Compounds holding prisoners, including camps used in the United States in World War II to incarcerate Japanese Americans.

interpolation   In musical theater, the addition of a new, unrelated song to an existing show.

interval   The relationship or distance between two musical pitches or notes.

jam band   A folksy, blues-based rock style featuring extended jams, which appeared in the early 1990s and was influenced by the aesthetics of the Grateful Dead and the Allman Brothers.

jam session   Gathering of musicians to play together and match skills with one another.

Jawaiian   Reggae-influenced Hawaiian music.

jazz lineage   The historic contributions of jazz innovators and the styles they created.

jazz-rock fusion   The blending of jazz with various components of rock, funk, and electronic amplification.

jazz standard   A composition that is a widely accepted part of the repertoire of most jazz musicians.

Jim Crow   Minstrel character: a disabled African American stable hand who moves with a shuffle.

juke joint   A rudimentary nightclub or bar, usually located in an old building outside of town.

jump blues   Aggressive rhythmic R & B style, evolving out of black big bands of the 1930s and 1940s, that featured simple riffs, blues-based tunes, explosive improvised solos, and spontaneity.

jungle   Style of electronica, originally from Britain, featuring the use of a deep resonant bass for the melody.

jungle music   A colloquial expression used to describe the sound of Duke Ellington's band in the early 1930s and characterized by a mix of growling muted brass, unusual blends of saxophone and clarinet lines, and driving rhythms.

karaoke   A place or a machine that allows users to sing with prerecorded musical accompaniment.

keyed bugle   Invented in 1810, instrument that fostered the formation of all-brass ensembles that could play outdoors or in other settings inhospitable to chamber music.

Kokopelli   Native American trickster deity whose flute playing is said to restore balance in the universe.

koto   A classical Japanese stringed instrument.

kulintang   Traditional indigenous drum-based music of Mindanao (Philippines).

Latin soul   Style that integrates soul, rock, and English lyrics into Latin music.

Latin tinge   The influences of Afro-Caribbean musical traditions on jazz.

lining out   A traditional Scottish music instruction technique in which a leader sings one line at a time to the congregation, who repeat the newly learned material in a call and response format.

lo-fi   An artsy amalgam from the 1990s that fluctuated from simple pop and rock songs to free-form song structures to pure noise and arty experimentalism.

lowrider   A customized car or truck that has had the suspension system modified so that the car rides low to the ground. People who drive such vehicles and who are part of the surrounding car culture are also known as lowriders.

LP record The 12-inch 33⅓ rpm record format first promoted in 1948 by Columbia Records that enabled the recording of up to 45 minutes of music on two sides of a vinyl disc and offered the possibility of grouping songs thematically; initially used for classical and jazz recordings, it became used for pop recordings in the late 1950s and early 1960s.

LSD A mind-altering hallucinogenic drug (lysergic acid diethylamide), also known as *acid.*

lyrics The words or vocal sounds included in a musical composition.

Macumba A hybrid religion that developed in Brazil, combining elements of Roman Catholicism and African religious traditions.

mambo A 1950s music and dance craze with Cuban origins, centered on a highly syncopated bass line *(tumbao)* and piano rhythm *(montuno).*

mandolin A small guitar-shaped instrument, played like a guitar, with a fretted neck and four paired strings that are tuned like a violin, which makes it easy for fiddlers to learn as a second instrument.

mariachi Traditional Mexican musical genre, influenced by three Mexican *son* styles and played by an ensemble consisting of violins, *guitarrón, vihuela,* guitar, trumpets, and sometimes a harp.

marimba A wooden xylophone with resonating tubes below each wooden bar.

MC Performer who works the crowd at the front of the stage and performs raps and rhymes, mixing elements of slang, personal experience, and humor.

measure A consistent grouping of beats in time.

melismas Vocal turns and embellishments, originating in gospel music and spreading to R & B and other genres.

melody A song or tune; a succession of musical notes or pitches that seem to have a relation to one another and that express a musical thought.

membranophones Drums.

mento Jamaican folk music style that predated and influenced reggae, was influenced by migration, and was made up of *rumba*, tango, and samba layered over the African music of *Jonkanoo* celebrations.

merengue National music and dance of the Dominican Republic; has a hypnotic, up-tempo, two-beat feel.

meter The way beats are grouped, or number of beats per measure.

Mexicano A person from Mexico.

microtone A note that falls between two notes on the Western chromatic twelve-note scale.

minstrelsy The first indigenous American theatrical and popular music genre, popular in the 1800s; a variety show based on crude stereotypes of African Americans.

modal jazz A style of improvisation based on the exploration of one scale for an extended period of time.

monophonic Describing a musical texture created by a single unaccompanied melody.

montuno A syncopated, repeated piano vamp in *son,* salsa, and other Afro-Cuban styles.

motor rhythm A constant beat played at a consistent tempo.

MP3 Electronic file format developed in the 1990s that decreased the memory required to store and transmit musical files.

música campesina The country music of Cuba, including *guajira* and *trova.*

musicianer An African American slave who played music professionally.

narcocorrido Accordion-driven, *conjunto*-style polka or waltz popular in Mexico and the Chicano/*Mexicano* communities of the United States at the turn of the twenty-first century, with lyrics often centering on drug running.

Nashville sound Country music style that evolved in the fifties involving electric instruments and polished arrangements, targeting an adult audience, and employing strings, horns, choral backgrounds, smooth tempos, and reverb (echo).

neoclassical jazz A movement beginning in the 1980s in which jazz performers reexamined the historical roots of jazz and played the music of early jazz artists.

neo-soul R & B substyle that emerged in the late 1990s, characterized by a sweet, retro tone as well as a social conscience.

New Jack Swing A highly rhythmic, rap-infused R & B style of the 1980s that employed snippets of rap, synthesized drum and bass lines, and multipart doo-wop harmony.

new wave Punk subgenre of the 1980s centered on pop and featuring a fascination with synthesizers, electronics, style, and art.

nisei Second-generation Japanese American.

Norteño Music that straddles the border between Texas and Mexico and that maintains cultural traits of the Northern Mexico border areas. See also *Tejano.*

novelty song A humorous song, often with a nonsense theme, sometimes employing special sound effects.

nu metal Hybrid of rap, sampling, DJs, drum machines, and other new techniques with guitar-driven heavy metal; popularized in the late 1990s.

Nuyorican Person of Puerto Rican descent born in New York

off-Broadway A theatrical venue for the production of low-budget, small scale, or experimental works.

old-time music Early Appalachian folk music, which formed the basis of bluegrass.

opera Words set to music in a dramatic presentation involving characters and plot.

operetta European style of musical theater blending plot, music, lyrics, dance, and an integrated story line.

orquesta tejana Chicano music of the forties and fifties that integrated Mexican styles with the swing, boogie, and foxtrot styles of American big bands, and the mambo, *rumba*, and cha-cha of Latin jazz.

orquesta típica Chicano ensemble that combined brass, woodwinds, violins, and guitars.

Outlaw Country music sound originating in a loose network of musicians in the 1970s who favored a return to relaxed and simple arrangements, to counter the production-heavy flavor of the Nashville sound.

pachanga A hybridized form developed out of *charanga* in which two horns often replace the flute and violins of *charanga*.

pachuco A rebellious Chicano youth culture that formed in Southern California during the 1940s.

Palo A hybrid religion that developed in Cuba, combining elements of Roman Catholicism and African religious traditions.

parlor songs Sentimental ballads that speak of life, home, hearth, and family; prevalent in nineteenth-century American popular music.

patting juba African American–derived body drumming—striking the knees, shoulders, or other body parts with the hands to produce a rhythmic sound.

payola Bribes given by record companies to radio stations to promote certain records.

pentatonic scale Five-note scale.

Philadelphia soul Smooth R & B style of the early 1970s, orchestrated with strings and horns. Supported by a relaxed, steady groove, it shaped the sound of disco. Also known as *Philly soul*.

phonograph Invented by Thomas Edison in 1877, the first device capable of reproducing sound.

pickup Device made by wrapping a coil of wire around a magnet and placing it under metal guitar strings, thereby creating an electric signal that can be amplified and heard through a speaker.

Pinoy Slang for *Filipino*; song movement in the Philippines during the 1970s and 1980s that was a blend of rock, folk, and ballads sung in the Tagalog language.

plantation songs Nineteenth-century songs that portrayed nostalgia for the preindustrial tranquility of plantation life. In some cases, African Americans were portrayed in a sympathetic and humanistic light.

player piano The first mechanism for recording and reproducing music with good fidelity; operated by means of small holes, punched onto a roll of paper, that trigger a pneumatic lifter to strike the appropriate key on a specially manufactured piano.

pleasure gardens Private parks, originating in England, featuring arbors, fruit trees, mineral springs, tea gardens, fireworks, and music; inspired nineteenth-century composers to write love songs that formed the basis of parlor songs.

pogrom Eastern European and Russian genocide campaigns against Jews in the late nineteenth and early twentieth centuries

polka Lively partner dance of Bohemian origin in duple meter usually danced with a basic pattern of hop-step-close-step.

polyphonic Describing a musical texture that contains different melodies and rhythms that interlock.

popular culture The mass cultural forms of everyday life.

post-bop An era beginning in the 1950s characterized by a variety of jazz styles, including cool jazz, hard bop, funky or gospel jazz, and modal jazz.

post-punk Style that developed in the 1980s, in part as a reaction to the nihilism of punk, that took the form of avant-garde noise, jangling guitars, anthemic stadium rock, or roots rock.

power ballad Rock song featuring high-energy vocals and driving rhythms played at a slow tempo.

power trio A group consisting of electric guitar, electric bass, and drums. This instrumentation is common in heavy metal and hard rock.

powwow An important tradition of contemporary Native America that presents traditional music, dance, food, arts, and fun with central themes of honor, respect, generosity, unity, and friendship.

progressive rock See *art rock*.

proto-punk Describing raw-sounding garage bands of the 1960s that served as a precursor to punk.

psychedelic music Music inspired by the experience of mind-altering drugs and characterized by modal melodies, lengthy instrumental solos, esoteric lyrics, and special electronic effects. Synonymous with *acid rock*.

punk-metal The most influential sound in alternative rock, a hybrid form that developed in the late 1980s and that frames walls of raw noise into tight pop song structures.

punk-pop A post-grunge strand of alternative rock that combines pop melodies and chord changes with speedy punk tempos and loud guitars.

punk rock Genre that developed in the 1970s, characterized by a cacophonous sound, lyrics of outrage, and extremes of appearance. At the time, it returned rock to its basics—three chords and a simple melody—but in a way that was louder, faster, and more abrasive than prior rock styles.

quadruple meter (⁴⁄₄) A rhythmic pattern composed of recurring groups of four evenly spaced beats.

quebradita "Little break" *banda* dance step in which the male partner bends his partner over backward until her head brushes the floor.

ragga Digitized Jamaican dancehall music.

ragtime A piano-based music mixing complex syncopated rhythms with traditional European musical forms.

ranchera Traditional Mexican songs of love, hope, and loss performed in a variety of rhythmic styles in meters of two, three, or four.

rap The influential African American musical genre that first emerged in the late 1970s, in which rhyming, spoken-word lyrics are chanted to rhythmic accompaniment often made up of sampled sounds or scratched records.

raves All-night parties held in fields, farms, or warehouses and featuring electronica.

reggae Jamaican music combining the old-time shuffle feel of mento, the beat of rock steady, an electric guitar playing a steady off-beat rhythm, and a heavy bass underpinning; often has religious or political themes.

repertory jazz Re-creation of music from the early years of jazz, played in order to preserve and understand the rich heritage of jazz.

revue Broadway show similar to burlesque that includes music, comedy, dance, simple plots, and female dancers.

rhythm The arrangement of time in music, consisting of beat, tempo, measure, and meter.

rhythm section The chord-playing, bass, and percussion instruments of popular music, with standard instrumentation usually consisting of drum set, acoustic or electric bass, guitar, and piano or keyboard.

riff A short musical phrase, often repeated throughout a popular music composition.

ring shout An African-derived shuffling circular dance of chanting and hand clapping that often transports participants into an ecstatic trance.

riot grrrl A feminist punk movement that developed out of early-1990s indie rock; the genre is a blend of personal expression and political activism, with lyrics that address gender-related issues and are framed by punk-styled blasts of noise.

ritard To slow down gradually in a piece of music.

rock steady A transitional Jamaican style between ska and reggae that is slower than ska with more emphasis on vocals and a more dominant electric bass and that has an electric guitar playing a steady off-beat rhythm.

rockabilly A blend of country and R & B that first emerged in the early 1950s.

rubato To play music in a relaxed rhythm.

rumba Oldest African-derived secular style in Cuba, developing as a blend of Congolese traditions and Spanish flamenco in the late nineteenth century and performed by dancers accompanied by Afro-Cuban percussion, lead singer, and a chorus. The absence of a chord-making instrument gives *rumba* a distinctively African sound.

rural blues See *Delta or rural blues.*

sacred Having a religious or spiritual function or connection.

salsa A hybrid style of dance music that developed in the sixties from the Cuban *son,* it emphasizes Afro-Cuban rhythms and incorporates a variety of dance styles.

salsa romántica Style developed in the mid-1980s as a blend of romantic ballads and bolero-style vocals backed by salsa dance rhythms.

samba Afro-Brazilian music that emerged prior to 1920 in Rio de Janeiro as a part of Carnival.

sampling The art of digitally reproducing sounds and blending them into music.

Santería A hybrid religion that developed in Cuba, combining elements of Roman Catholicism and African religious traditions.

scat singing The use of improvised nonsense syllables in vocal jazz improvisation.

scratching The rapid movement of a vinyl record back and forth while it is playing on a turntable, creating a distinctive grating sound that is characteristic of hip-hop (including rap).

second line Mourners and celebrants who accompanied New Orleans wind bands at parades and funerals; also describes a syncopated beat of contemporary New Orleans jazz and R & B.

secular Not connected to religious concerns; worldly.

shape note Early American music notation system that gives each note in the scale a different shape—triangles, squares, circles, or diamonds—enabling nonliterate singers to perform complex multipart choral arrangements.

shouter Early R & B performer in a jump-style band who produced high-energy, blues-based vocals that were very nearly shouted.

singer-songwriter Singer who writes and performs his or her own songs.

singing cowboy Concept pioneered by Jimmie Rodgers that began the association of western images with country music.

ska Jamaica-born mixture of American and Caribbean music that has an unexpected emphasis on the off beat that lends a galloping, forward-leaning feel.

skiffle Music pioneered by British musician Lonnie Donnegan in the 1950s that was an indiscriminate blend of

American folk and blues styles. Most British Invasion artists were influenced by skiffle.

slack key guitar A Hawaiian finger-picked guitar style with "slacked" (alternately tuned) strings that create unique intervals different from those usually used on the guitar.

smooth jazz A groove-based, jazz, funk, and R & B–based instrumental style of jazz with a lighter sound than fusion.

soca Music that emerged in the late twentieth century in Trinidad as an up-tempo calypso for dancing, with lyrics more often about partying than social issues.

soft rock Smooth, melodic style popular from the 1960s through the 1980s that consists of slow-tempo, melodic songs with vocal harmonies, performed over simple rhythmic grooves.

son Latin music style that developed in rural Cuba in the late nineteenth century from a blend of European and Afro-Cuban elements; early instrumentation included guitar or *tres*, claves, and maracas; recognized as the progenitor of salsa.

song collecting Practice of gathering music manuscripts and samples of songs, particularly of folk music, begun by British poet Thomas Percy in the nineteenth century.

song plugger A person hired by Tin Pan Alley publishers to put sheet music into the hands of successful vaudeville performers in the early twentieth century.

songster An itinerant black musician of the nineteenth and twentieth centuries who played music with European and African sources that included comic songs, social songs, ballads, minstrel songs, and the blues.

sonority The overall tonal texture of a musical composition or performance.

soul music An African American musical style of the 1960s with roots in gospel, R & B, and blues; themes of civil rights, love, and passion; vocals delivered with emotional power; and groove-based rhythms.

sound system A portable disco, originating in Jamaica and consisting of up to thirty speakers, a turntable, and a DJ; essential to the early development of rap in New York in the late 1970s.

southern groove Soul music with a harder edge, more gospel influences, and fewer formal arrangements than the Motown sound.

southern rock A blending of blues, R & B, country, and gospel with the aggressive feel of hard rock, drawing from the blues-rock of the late 1960s as well as honky-tonk and the Bakersfield sound to create a distinctive fusion.

spiritual Nineteenth-century African American religious vocal genre focusing on Biblical events and figures and blending traditional African melodic concepts with European hymn melodies; used to construct community,

provide hope for a better life, offer metaphors of liberation, and preserve African cultural memory.

steel drum Trinidadian percussion instrument made from metal oil drums.

steel guitar Stringed instrument with a sliding sound that originated in Hawaii and became popular on the U.S. mainland in the early twentieth century.

stride piano Style of piano playing in which the left hand plays a bass note on the first and third of every four beats and a basic chord on the second and fourth beats and the right hand plays melody.

subordinate culture A culture that lacks access to power and is therefore less powerful than the dominant culture in a multicultural society.

surf music Genre from the early 1960s that features twangy, trebly guitars; Chuck Berry–style guitar licks; falsetto male vocal harmonies; throbbing tom toms; and topical lyrics of car and surf culture.

sustain The extension of the duration of a musical tone, often created through electronic amplification.

sweet band Big band music that features catchy melodies and riffs with easily identifiable hooks and that downplays improvisation in favor of a smooth, well-blended saxophone section that meshes with a warm brass sound.

swing (1) African-derived triplet-based rhythmic feel often encountered in jazz, blues, and R & B. A typical swing rhythm can be approximated by taking a series of even beats, then lengthening the first and shortening the second beat to create a sequence of pairs of long and short notes. (2) A period in jazz history, usually dated from the early 1930s through 1945, dominated by big bands playing in the swing style.

syncopation Accenting the weak or unexpected part of the beat.

synth pop A spare, synthesizer-based dance pop sound of the 1980s.

tabla Classical instrument from India made up of two small tuned hand drums played with both hands.

taiko **drumming** A traditional form of drum-based Japanese folk music that became adopted in the United States in the late twentieth century.

tan nhac Vietnamese pop music that blends Vietnamese scales and folk traditions with Western dance rhythms and amplified instruments.

techno Style of completely electronic music that emerged in Detroit in the mid-1980s.

teen idol Attractive young performer, largely the product of record companies, sculpted to appeal to perceived youth taste and used to promote record sales.

Tejano Chicano music made in Texas, as well as people of Mexican descent who live in Texas. See also *Norteño*.

tempo The speed of the beat in a piece of music.

texture The overall timbre created by a variety of instruments or voices producing musical sounds in a performance.

32-bar form A musical form consisting of two melodically identical eight-measure verses, followed by an eight-measure bridge, followed by a final eight-measure verse that may contain new lyrics or a restatement of an earlier verse, common in Tin Pan Alley–era songs and jazz.

thrash metal Late 1970s heavy metal subgenre with elements of punk; basis for funk metal and nu metal.

timbales A pair of metal drums similar to the modern snare drum, but without the snare; used predominantly in Afro-Cuban music.

Tin Pan Alley Center of the music publishing industry from the beginning of the twentieth century through about 1950.

TOBA Theater Owners Booking Association; owned by whites, a performing circuit of the 1920s in which many African Americans performed blues and vaudeville under difficult working conditions.

tone A quality of music that has four main components: pitch, timbre, duration, and dynamics.

trance Style of electronica with brief, repeated synthesizer lines looped over and over.

trap drum set A set of percussion instruments including the bass drum, tom tom, snare drum, and cymbals.

tres A small Cuban six-string guitar with three pairs of identically tuned strings, providing greater volume and resonance than single strings.

trip-hop Style of electronica, usually wordless, emulating jazz, funk, and soul-inflected hip-hop grooves and emphasizing a more ambient, psychedelic quality than traditional hip-hop.

triple meter (¾) A rhythmic pattern composed of recurring groups of three evenly spaced beats.

trova Style of Cuban *música campesina* that developed in the mid-nineteenth century and often blended current political issues with narratives of everyday life.

tumbao A syncopated Afro-Cuban rhythmic pattern played on the bass on the upbeat of beat two and on the downbeat of beat four in ¼ time.

tumbi North Indian drum.

turntablism A technique in which DJs use multiple turntables and various audio effects to blend snippets of sound from existing vinyl records to create new music.

12-bar blues A musical form written in three phrases of four measures each; the form can be repeated many times without the use of a chorus.

ukulele A small, four-string Hawaiian instrument derived from the Portuguese *braguinha*.

urban blues Form of the blues that developed in the 1930s, characterized by the coordinated use of guitar, piano, and sometimes a full rhythm section in an ensemble setting, playing a consistent, often up-tempo rhythm.

vaudeville An outgrowth of minstrelsy, a variety show featuring songs, dances, and comedy sketches with minimal plots.

vernacular music Folk or traditional music played in communities as a part of everyday life.

verse A lyric statement that tells a story, with each verse of a song presenting new information to the listener while following a similar melodic structure.

vibrato Light and rapid variations in pitch.

vihuela A small, five-string Mexican instrument.

VJ Video DJ.

vocables Lyrics made up of syllables that have no clear linguistic meaning but are often considered sacred; characteristic of Native American music.

vocalese A jazz singing technique that uses recorded instrumental solos as the basis for vocal melodies, which often are then harmonized.

voicing The selection and ordering of notes that a performer uses to play a given chord.

Voudou A hybrid religion that developed in Haiti, combining elements of Roman Catholicism and African religious traditions.

wah-wah An electronic effects pedal used with an electric guitar, keyboard, or other amplified instruments that modulates the timbre of an amplified tone to create a "wah"-like sound.

waila Modern-day Native American musical genre that employs the stringed instruments of Mexican American border music and mariachi. Synonymous with *chicken scratch*.

wall of sound Production technique, developed by Phil Spector in the early 1960s, achieved by packing the studio with musicians, running prior recordings through the studio sound system to fill out the sound, and using echo chambers.

waltz A musical style written in triple meter; popular at the end of the nineteenth century.

wax cylinder Medium on which sound recordings were made at the end of the nineteenth century.

West Coast cool Jazz style of the 1950s characterized by a smooth, laid-back, and sparse sound and often associated with white players.

western swing A 1930s hybrid of southern string bands, swing, Tin Pan Alley, and the African American, Cajun, Tex-Mex, German, Bohemian, and cowboy cultures of the Southwest, exemplified by the music of Bob Wills and the Texas Playboys.

wind band An ensemble with instrumentation usually consisting of brass, woodwind, and percussion instruments.

work song African-derived music sung by workers in rhythm with their work; often a call and response in which a lead singer acting as foreman sings a lyric to direct the work, then workers answer and perform the required task.

Yoruba A dominant West African culture and state prior to the mid-eighteenth century that included areas of Nigeria and parts of Benin and Togo. The Yoruba remain the largest ethnic group in Nigeria today.

Zip Coon Minstrel character: an African American "city slicker" who makes imperfect attempts to imitate white city folk.

CD Tracks

CPSIA information can be obtained
at www.ICGtesting.com
Printed in the USA
FFOW04n0120130717
37691FF

9 780155 0622